LIFE

AND CAMPAIGNS

OF

LIEUT.-GEN. THOMAS J. JACKSON,

(STONEWALL JACKSON.)

BY

PROF. R. L. DABNEY, D.D.,

OF THE UNION THEOLOGICAL SEMINARY, VIRGINIA.

ILLUSTRATED WITH STEEL PORTRAIT AND ELEVEN DIAGRAMS.

(RIGHT OF TRANSLATION RESERVED BY THE AUTHOR)

Harrisonburg, Virginia
SPRINKLE PUBLICATIONS
1983

ISBN 1-59442-051-3
Sprinkle Publications
P. O. Box 1094
Harrisonburg, Virginia 22801

SCRYMGEOUR, WHITCOMB & Co.,
Stereotypers,
15 WATER STREET. BOSTON.

To the Widows and Orphans

OF THE

SOUTHERN SOLDIERS WHO FELL IN THE CAUSE FOR WHICH

JACKSON GAVE HIS LIFE,

This Biography is Dedicated with profound Respect and Sympathy,

BY THE AUTHOR.

PREFACE.

THE cause for which General Jackson fought and died, has been overthrown. But it is believed that this fact has not diminished the affectionate reverence for his memory, and interest in his exploits, felt by those who labored with him in that cause. On the contrary, they regard the events which have occurred since his lamented death, as farther evidences of his genius and prowess. Although he who undertakes to write the history of an acknowledged failure usually has a hopeless and discouraging topic, yet the lustre of Jackson's exploits and character is too bright to be dimmed, even by disaster: and his is universally admitted, by his friends and foes, to be a name so spotless that it shines independent of the cause with which he was connected.

My chief motive for supplying this customary exordium to my book, is the wish to answer the natural question in the reader's mind, what right I suppose myself to have, to claim qualification for the task I have assumed. My answer is, that it has been entrusted to me by the widow and family of General Jackson, supported by the urgency of his successor in command, Lieutenant-General Ewell, of his venerable pastor, and of many other friends, in, and out of the army. One advantage for my work, I may claim, which brings far more of responsibility than of credit to me, in the possession of the fullest collection of materials. The correspondence of General Jackson with his family, his pastor, and his most prominent friends in public life, has been in my hands, together with copies of all the important official papers on file in the War Department of the late Confederate Government. I have had the advantage of the fullest illustrations of the battle-fields and the

theatre of war where General Jackson acted, from the topographical department of the same government, and from careful personal
inspection: It was also my privilege to enjoy his friendship, although
not under his orders, during the campaign of Manassa's, in 1861; and
to serve next his person, as chief of his Staff, during the memorable
campaigns of the Valley and the Chickahominy, in 1862. So that I
had personal knowledge of the events on which the structure of his
military fame was first reared.

My prime object has been to portray and vindicate his Christian
character, that his countrymen may possess it as a precious example,
and may honor that God in it, whom he so delighted to honor. It is
for this purpose that the attempt was made so carefully to explain and
defend his action, as citizen and soldier, in recent events. Next, it
was desired to unfold his military genius, as displayed in his campaigns. The prominent characteristic of General Jackson was his
scrupulous truthfulness. This Life has been written under the
profound impression, that no quality could be so appropriate as this,
in the narrative which seeks to commemorate his noble character.
Hence, the most laborious pains have been taken to verify every fact,
and to give the story in its sober accuracy, and with impartial justice
to all. I am well aware that perfection is not the privilege of man, in
any of his works; and hence I must be prepared to be convinced, by
the criticisms of others, that I have not been wholly successful in this
aim. But I trust I have been so far successful, as to receive credit for
right intentions. And especially would I declare, that in relating the
share borne by General Jackson's comrades and subordinates in his
campaigns, I have been actuated by a cordial and friendly desire to do
justice to all. If I shall seem to any to have done less than this, it
will be my misfortune, and not my intention.

If my story presents the hero without any of those *bizarre* traits,
which the popular fancy loves to find in its especial favorites, it is
hoped that the picture will be, for this reason, more symmetrical,
and if not so startling, more pleasing to every cultivated mind.
The reader may at least have the satisfaction of knowing that it
is the correct picture, save that no pencil can do justice to his

devoted patriotism, his diligence, his courage, and the sanctity of his morals.

The reader will note a certain polemic tone in the discussions which attend the narrative; and while strict truthfulness has been studied, candid expression has been given to the feelings natural to a participant in the recent struggle. The explanation is, in part, this: that the whole work was written before the termination of the contest; the first portion, containing all the controversial matter, was published in Great Britain more than a year ago, and has been circulated in that country and this; and the remainder of the biography was in process of publication when the Confederate armies surrendered. The *animus* of my book will not appear strange to any one who remembers, that when it was published, my fellow-citizens were universally engaged in a strenuous war against the United States, and I was myself in the military commission of the Confederate States. The question may be asked, Does not the termination of that contest by the complete submission of the South, point out the propriety of modifying the tone of the work? After a careful consideration of this question, I have been constrained to believe, that it was best to leave my original work substantially untouched. As has been stated, the first eight chapters, containing all that is most controversial, had been irrevocably given to the public, many months before the end of the war. To attempt to recall and suppress it now, would appear rather a foolish scrupulosity than sound wisdom. Nor would this course be consistent with the interests of literature. It has been often said, that cotemporaries cannot write impartial histories of their own times, because of their too lively sympathy with the passions which agitate the actors. It is more certainly true, that if cotemporaries do not write, with such partiality or impartiality as they may, it will be impossible for any other historian in posterity, to write a truthful narrative. None but eye-witnesses and actors can contribute the facts, which are to be the materials of future history. And their facts are esteemed by the philosophic and judicial compiler of the subsequent age, as scarcely more important than their *animus*. He wishes to know, not only what men did, but how they felt, — how the events transpiring

affected them, — from what impulses and views they acted. While
he does not blindly adopt the passions of either party, it is these
which enable him to reproduce the very complexion and color of the
times he describes. Hence, it is for the interests of historic truth that
those who describe cotemporary events, should give candid expression
to the emotions of their times.

It may also be asked: Does not the duty of promoting mutual forbearance, and the restoration of good feeling between the sections
lately at war, require the suppression of controverted opinions, and of
accusations, which, however true, can now be urged with no good
result? In answering this objection, I shall candidly acknowledge
myself utterly sceptical, both by temperament and conviction, of that
deceitful and glozing philosophy, by which it is dictated. There is no
true and solid basis for public well-being, but rectitude. The truth,
manfully spoken, can never be unwholesome. If the complaints of
the conquered section are just, then they ought to be stated and discussed, until a stable foundation for peace, good government, good
feeling, and prosperity, is laid in just and magnanimous treatment.
If those complaints are unjust, still it is best that they be candidly
stated, respectfully listened to, and calmly discussed, as long as they
are sincerely entertained in the hearts of the sufferers : for only in this
way can they be eradicated. It is to me simply incredible, that a
people so shrewd and practical as those of the United States, should
expect us to have discarded, through the logic of the sword merely,
the convictions of a lifetime; or that they could be deceived by us,
should we be base enough to assert it of ourselves. They know that the
people of the South were conquered, and not convinced; and that the
authority of the United States was accepted by us from necessity, and
not from preference. Should they hear the Southern people now dis-
claiming and reprobating the principles which are unfolded in my
book as the animating principles of General Jackson, they must inevitably remember, that this Southern people, three years ago, was
unanimously applauding and inciting him in acting them out : so that
it would be self-evident to our conquerors, that we were either traitor-
ously false to our darling hero, then ; or are equally false to them,

now. The people of the United States have too much shrewdness
ever to suppose, that the sons of the Revolutionary sires who, as their
comrades, assisted in winning liberty from the British Lion, and who
have recently given new proofs of their undegenerate manhood, are
spaniels, to be made affectionate by stripes. The people of the South
went to war, because they sincerely believed (what their political
fathers had taught them, with one voice, for two generations) that the
doctrine of State-sovereignty for which they fought, was absolutely
essential as the bulwark of the liberties of the people. They have
been convinced by main force, that they are unable to save that doctrine. The only way to make them truly loyal again to the government of the United States, is to convince them by just treatment,
that they went to war under a misapprehension, and that their liberties may still be securely and fully enjoyed under a consolidated
government. It would be only a useless and degrading concealment,
for the people of the South to profess a suppression of the honest convictions upon which they have lately acted, either at the dictate of
deceit on their part, or of persecution on the part of their conquerors.
For these reasons, it has appeared to me every way most manly and
beneficial, to leave this explication and defence of General Jackson's
resistance to the Federal Government, as it was written during the
progress of the conflict. Its suppression would conceal nothing, and
deceive nobody: its publication will give to subsequent generations a
lively picture of the temper of the times.

But I am ready to add, with equal candor, that when I thus declare
boldly the principles upon which the Virginians of 1861 acted, I do
not intend to be understood as retracting that acquiescence in the
result of the arbitrament of the sword, and that submission promised
by me in common with almost the whole South. I have voluntarily
sworn to obey the government of the United States, as at present
established and expounded to us by force of arms. That oath it is my
purpose to keep. The Federal agent who administered it to me
taught me expressly that its obligation was of this extent, and no
more: that it did not bind me to think or say the principles on which

I had acted were erroneous; but to abstain, in future, from the asser
tion of them by force of arms.

It only remains to add a few words in explanation of the illustrations which accompany the text. It is earnestly recommended to the
attentive reader, that he shall connect his perusal of the descriptive
parts of the narrative with a careful study of the map of Virginia.
This is so accessible to all Americans, that it was thought superfluous
to burden this work with the expense of its insertion. A simple
diagram is inserted, to facilitate the comprehension of each of the
more important battles. These plates have been carefully prepared,
from actual inspections and surveys, made by Confederate engineers;
but they are simplified by leaving out all except the most essential
lines and features. The intelligent reader, even though not a military
man, will readily apprehend, that the representation of the positions
of brigades and divisions of troops in action, by lines upon a diagram,
can only be approximately correct. The lines of ink are, of course,
stationary; the lines of troops in action are never long so. The
relative position assigned to two divisions on the diagram may be a
correct representation of their relation on the field of actual strife, for
a fleeting moment only; a minute more may have changed it. The
diagram must, perforce, either contain both of two divisions at once,
which in fact only occupied the field successively; or it must suggest
a still graver error, by the total omission of one of them. But if
these obvious considerations are borne in mind, and the illustrations
are studied in connection with the narrative, they will convey no
mistake, and will be found to represent, with general correctness, the
positions and movements of the Confederate troops.

ROBERT L. DABNEY.

Union Theological Seminary,
    Va., April 1, 1866.

CONTENTS.

CONTENTS.

CHAPTER X.

LIFE OF

LIEUT.-GEN. THOMAS J. JACKSON.

CHAPTER I.

PARENTAGE, AND EARLY YEARS.

THE family from which General Jackson came, was founded in Western Virginia by John Jackson, an emigrant from London. His stock was Scotch-Irish; and it is most probable that John Jackson himself was removed by his parents from the north of Ireland to London, in his second year. Nearly fifty years after he left England, his son, Colonel George Jackson, while a member of the Congress of the United States, formed a friendship with the celebrated Andrew Jackson of Tennessee, afterwards the victor of New Orleans, and President; and the two traced their ancestry up to the same parish near Londonderry. Although no more intimate relationship could be established between the families, such a tie is rendered probable by their marked resemblance in energy and courage, as illustrated not only in the career of the two great commanders who have made the name immortal, but of other members of their houses. John Jackson was brought up in London, and became a reputable and prosperous tradesman. He determined to transfer his rising fortunes to the British colonies in America, and crossed the seas in 1748, landing first in the plantations of Lord Baltimore. In Calvert County, Maryland, he married Elizabeth Cummins, a young woman also from London, of excellent character and respectable education. The young couple, after the common fashion of American emigrants, proceeded at once to seek for new and cheaper lands on which to establish their household gods, and made their first home on the south branch of the Potomac River, at the place now known as Moorefields, the county seat of Hardy County. But after residing for a time in this lovely valley, John Jackson, with his young family, crossed the main Alleghany ridge into Northwestern Virginia, where lands yet wider allured his enterprising spirit. He fixed his home on the Buchanan River, in what was first Randolph, but is now Upshur County, at a place long known as Jackson's Fort, now occupied by the little village of Buchanan. Here he spent his active life, and reared his family.

He is said to have been a spare, diminutive man, of plain mind, quiet but determined character, sound judgment, and excellent morals. His wife was a woman of masculine stature; and her understanding and energies corresponded to the vigor of her bodily frame. When the young couple emigrated to the Northwest, the Indians were still contesting the occupancy of its teeming valleys with the white men. The colonists were compelled to provide for their security by building stockade-forts, into which they retreated with their families and cattle at every alarm of a savage incursion. It is the tradition that, in more than one of these sieges, Elizabeth Cummins proved herself, though a woman, to have "the stomach and mettle of a man," and rendered valuable service by aiding and inspiriting the resistance of the defenders. In her industry and enterprise was realized King Lemuel's description of the ways of the virtuous woman: "She considereth a field, and buyeth it; with the fruit of her hands she planteth a vineyard." Several patents are still in existence, conveying to her, in her own name, lands which were afterwards the valuable possessions of her posterity. They have usually claimed that the characteristics of their race were largely inherited from her; that it was her sterling integrity, vigorous intellect, and directness of purpose which gave them their type.

The picturesque country, which now became the home ot tne Jacksons, descends gradually from the watershed of the Appalachian range to the Ohio river, but is filled with ridges parallel to the main crest, of which the nearest are also lofty mountains, while the more western subside into bold and fertile hills. The grander heights were covered with magnificent forests of spruce and fir, intermingled with tangled thickets of laurel: but as the traveller approached the Ohio, and the mountains sank into swelling highlands, he found the ridges fertile, almost beyond belief; the slopes, clothed to their tops with giant groves of oak and chestnut, poplar, linden, beech, and sugar-maple; the hills, separated by placid streams flowing through smooth valleys and meadows, and their sides everywhere filled with beds of the richest coal. The waters which refresh this goodly land flow northward, and compose the Monongahela, which contributes its streams at Pittsburg, in Pennsylvania, to form the Ohio in union with those of the Alleghany. The mingled currents then turn southward, and form the western border of Northern Virginia, separating it from the territory of Ohio. As all highlands usually decline in elevation with the enlargement of their watercourses, the northern part of this district, embraced within the boundaries of Pennsylvania, is less rugged than the southern. Settlements, therefore, naturally proceeded from the smoother regions of Western Pennsylvania, into the hills of Northwestern Virginia; and thus it came to pass that, in the latter district, the northern counties were at first the more cultivated, and the southern bore to them the relation of frontiers. The emigrants found that they had not descended very far from the loftier ranges of the Alleghany and Cheat mountains before they left behind them the rigors of their Alpine climate. Wherever the valleys were cleared of their woods, they clothed themselves with the richest sward, and teemed with corn, wheat, the vine, the peach, and all the products of Eastern Virginia. But this fertile region could only be reached from the east by a few rude highways, almost impracticable for carriages, which wound their way among and over the ridges of a wide labyrinth of mountains.

Hither the patriarch of the Jacksons removed before the war of the American Revolution. In that struggle, he and his elder sons bore their part as soldiers; and at its close, they returned to their rural pursuits. With the practical sagacity for which the Scotch-Irish emigrant is always noted, he and his wife bent their energies to founding fortunes for their children, by acquiring the most valuable lands of the country, while they were unoccupied and cheap. In this aim they were successful, and their numerous children were all endowed with farms, which now make their holders wealthy. After a long and active life, they removed to the house of Colonel George Jackson, their eldest son, at Clarksburg, the county seat of Harrison County, now a village of note on the southern branch of the great Baltimore and Ohio Railroad, and about forty miles from the Pennsylvanian border. The death of the old man, in this quiet retreat, is thus recorded by one of the most distinguished of his descendants, John G. Jackson, of Clarksburg, Judge of the Court of the United States for the Western District of Virginia. He writes to Mrs. Madison, whose sister he had married, in

1801:—"Death, on the 25th of September, put a period to the existence of my aged grandfather, John Jackson, in the eighty-sixth year of his age. The long life of this good man was spent in those noble and virtuous pursuits, which endear men to their acquaintance, and make their decease sincerely regretted by all the good and virtuous. He was a native of England, and migrated hither in the year 1748. He took an active part in the revolutionary war in favor of Independence, and, upon the establishment of it, returned to his farming, which he laboriously pursued until the marriage of his younger son, when he was prevailed upon by my father to come and reside near him; there he lived for several years with his wife, enjoying all his mental faculties, and great corporeal strength, until a few days before his death. I saw him breathe his last in the arms of my aged grandmother, and can truly add, that to live and die as he did would be the excess of happiness.

"He left a valuable real-estate at the entire disposal of the widow, with the concurrence of all the natural heirs, as his liberality had been amply experienced by them all in his lifetime."

Elizabeth, his wife, survived him until 1825, beloved and respected by all who knew her, and reached the extreme age of *one hundred and five* years. Hers were *stamina*, both of the physical and moral constitution, fitting her to rear a race that were men indeed. The reader will be detained a moment, to note the names and characters of her children, in order that the springs of General Jackson's nature may be the better illustrated, and also that his widely scattered kindred may be enabled to ascertain their relationship to this world-famous hero. The eldest son was George Jackson, who lived at Clarksburg, the seat of justice for Harrison County, and was a prominent and influential man in the settlement of Northwestern Virginia. Having taken part with his father in the Revolution-

ary War, he became a colonel in the forces which, at the close
of the great struggle, expelled the Indians finally from his
district. He was one of the first delegates from Harrison
County in the General Assembly of Virginia, was a member for
that county in the State Convention by which Virginia accepted
the Federal Constitution, and was first delegate from his district
to the first Congress of the United States which sat under it.
After his father's death, he removed to Zanesville, Ohio, where
his life was ended. The second son was Edward, the grandfather of General Jackson, who, after several removals, fixed
his home on the west fork of the Monongahela, four miles north
of Weston, the present chief town of Lewis County. He was
a man of a spare and athletic frame, energetic character, and
good understanding, beloved and respected by his acquaintances.
Filling for a long time the place of surveyor for the great
county of Randolph, he acquired much valuable land, and left to
each one of his fifteen children a respectable patrimony. He,
with his father and elder brother, was actively engaged in the
Revolutionary and Indian wars.

The third son was Samuel Jackson, who emigrated to Indiana,
and left a numerous family near the town of Terre Haute.
The fourth and fifth sons, John and Henry, lived near the place
of their birth on Buchanan river; but of their many children,
several found their way to the extreme West. Each of these
five sons of John Jackson was twice married, and left a numerous progeny. There were also three daughters, who married
residents of the country, and left descendants bearing the name
of Davis, Brake, and Regar.

Talent and capacity were not limited to this second generation. The sons of George Jackson deserve especially to be
noted among the men of the third generation. Of these, the
eldest was John G. Jackson, a lawyer of great distinction at

Clarksburg. He succeeded his father in Congress, married first Miss Payne, the sister of the accomplished lady who married Mr. Madison, President of the United States; and then, the only daughter of Mr. Meigs, Governor of Ohio, afterwards Post-master-General; who was appointed first Federal Judge for the district of West Virginia. This office he filled with distinction until his death about the year 1825. He was a learned lawyer, a man of great energy and enterprise, and sought to develop the resources of his country by the building of iron furnaces and forges, mills, woollen factories, and salt-works. These endeavors absorbed large sums of money, and at his death left his princely estate heavily embarrassed. The other sons of this family 'were Edward, a respectable physician; William L., a lawyer, and father of a relative and cotemporary of General Jackson; Colonel William L. Jackson, late Lieutenant-Governor of the State, and then Judge of the Superior Court; and George Washington, long a citizen of Ohio, and now an honorable exile, by reason of political persecution, for his fidelity to his native land. It was his son, Colonel Alfred Jackson, who, after serv-ing on the staff of the General, received a mortal wound in the battle of Cedar Run, and now lies near him, in the graveyard of Lexington.

The character which the founders impressed upon their house will now be understood. From their forethought and virtues, it became the most noted, wealthy, and influential in their country. They usually possessed the best lands and most numerous slaves, occupied the posts of influence and power which were in the gift of their .fellow-citizens, and sent some member of their family to the General Assembly of their State, or the Congress at Washington. They were marked by strong and character-istic physiognomies, close family attachments, determination and industry in their undertakings, and a restless love of adven

ture. Their race is now scattered from Virginia to Oregon.
More than one of them has been led, by his love of roving, to
the most secluded recesses of the Rocky Mountains, as explorers
and hunters. All of them were energetic and skilful to acquire
wealth, but not all of them were able to retain it. Many of
the second and third generations were noted for a passion for
litigation — prompted not so much by avarice as by the love of
intellectual excitement, and by a temper intolerant of supposed
injustice; and almost the whole race were utterly incapable of
resisting the fascination of machinery. Every Jackson owned
a mill or factory of some sort — many of them more than one, —
where they delighted to exercise the ingenuity and resources of
the self-taught mechanic. In a country like theirs, of sparse
population, and more devoted to the rearing of cattle than of
grain, it may easily be conceived that these toys ministered
more to their possessors' pleasure than to their wealth. Colonel
Edward Jackson, the grandfather of General Jackson, was, as
has been said, the second son of his parents. His second
marriage brought him nine sons and daughters. His first wife,
by birth a Hadden, bore three sons, George, David and Jonathan, and three daughters, of whom one married a gentleman
named White, and two, respectable farmers of German extrac-
tion, named Brake.

Jonathan Jackson, the father of the subject of this work,
adopted the profession of law, having pursued his preparatory
studies in the family, and under the guidance of his distinguished
cousin, Judge Jackson of Clarksburg. His patronage induced
him to go to that place — the last seat of his forefather's residence — to prosecute his calling. About the same time he
married Julia Neale, the daughter of an intelligent merchant
in the village of Parkersburg, in Wood County, on the Ohio
river. The fruits of this marriage were four children, of whom

the eldest was named Warren, the second Elizabeth, the third Thomas Jonathan, and the fourth Laura. Thomas was born in Clarksburg, January 21, 1824. The early death of his parents and dispersion of the little family, obliterated the record of the exact date, so that General Jackson himself was unable to fix it with certainty. Of these children none now live save the youngest, who survives as a worthy matron in Randolph County.

Jonathan Jackson, the General's father, is said to have been, what was unusual in his race, a man of short stature; his face was ruddy, pleasing, and intelligent; his temper genial and affectionate, and susceptible of the warmest and most generous attachments. He was a man of strong, distinct understanding, and held a respectable rank as a lawyer. While he displayed little of the popular eloquence of the advocate, his knowledge and judgment made him a valued counsellor, and his chief distinction was as a Chancery lawyer. His patrimony was adequate to all reasonable wants; the lands which he inherited from his father are now so valuable as to confer independence on their present owners. But a temper too social and facile betrayed him into some of the prevalent dissipations of the country; incautious engagements embarrassed him with the debts of his friends; and high play assisted to swallow up his estate. He at length became dependent wholly upon his professional labors, which yielded his family only a moderate support, while he owned no real estate but the house in which he lived. Not very long after the birth of his fourth child, and when Thomas was three years old, his daughter Elizabeth was seized with a malignant fever. He watched her sick-bed until her death, with a tender assiduity which, combined with his grief at the bereavement, and perhaps with his business troubles, prostrated his strength; and within a fortnight after his daughter

2

he sunk, by the same disease, into a premature grave. This unexpected end was all that was needed to complete the ruin of his affairs. Out of their wreck absolutely nothing seems to have been saved for his widow and babes. The Masonic Order, of which Jonathan Jackson was an officer, gave to the widow a little cottage of a single room. In this dwelling she applied herself to the task of earning a living for herself and children, by her needle and the labors of a little school.

She is represented as a lady of graceful and commanding presence, spare, and above the ordinary height of females, of a comely and engaging countenance. Her mind was cultivated and intelligent; and it is probable that much of the talent of her children was inherited through her. Her constitution had pulmonary tendencies, which were evidently entailed on her distinguished son. Her mind was sprightly, and her temperament mercurial, at one time rising to gaiety under the stimulus of social enjoyment, and at another sinking to despondency under the pressure of her troubles. But her character was crowned with unaffected piety. While her parentage and education would have inclined her to the Presbyterian persuasion, the difficulty of reaching their ministrations caused her to become a member of the Wesleyan or Methodist communion. General Jackson always spoke of her with tender affection, and traced his first sacred impressions to her lessons. When a daughter was born to him a few months before his own death, he caused her to be baptized with his mother's name, Julia Neale. In the year 1830, Mrs. Jackson, whose youth and beauty still fitted her to please, married Mr. Woodson, a lawyer of Cumberland County, Virginia, whom the rising importance of the Northwest had attracted, along with many other Eastern Virginians, to that country. He was a sort of decayed gentleman, much Mrs. Jackson's senior, — a widower, without pro-

perty, but of fair character, and of a popular, social turn.
The marriage was distasteful to Mrs. Jackson's relatives. They
threatened, as a sort of penalty for it, to take the maintenance
and education of the children out of the widow's hands, and
offered, as an inducement on the opposite side, liberal pecuniary
aid if she would continue to bear her first husband's name. But
love, as usual, was omnipotent. Upon her marriage to Mr. Woodson, his scanty resources compelled her to accept the protection
of her former husband's kindred for her children, which she had
at first declined as an infliction. The second husband's professional success was limited, and he very soon accepted from his
friend, Judge Duncan, who had also intermarried with the Jackson family, the office of Clerk of the Court in the county of Fayette, which lies on the New River, west of Greenbrier. After one
year of married life, Mrs. Woodson's constitution sank upon giving
birth to a son; two months after, she died, on the 4th of December, 1831; and her remains await their resurrection not far
from the famous Hawk's Nest of New River. Her husband
announced her death to her friends in these words:—"No Christian on earth, no matter what evidence he might have had of a
happy hereafter, could have died with more fortitude. Perfectly in her senses, calm and deliberate, she met her fate
without a murmur or a struggle. Death for her had no sting;
the grave could claim no victory. I have known few women
of equal, none of superior merit." The infant, thus early
bereaved of her care, lived to man's estate, and died of pulmonary disease, doubtless inherited from his mother, in the
State of Missouri. Thomas, then seven years old, with his
brother and sister, had been sent for to visit his mother in
her sickness, and he remained to witness her death. To his
Christian friends he stated, long afterwards, that the wholesome
impression of her dying instructions and prayers, and of her

triumph over the grave, had never been erased from his heart. In his manhood, he delighted to think of her as the impersona-tion of sweetness, grace, and beauty; and he could never relate, without tenderness, the events of his departure from his uncle's house, when she had him mounted behind the last of his father's slaves, "good old Uncle Robinson," and recalled him so anx-iously, to give the last touch to the arrangements for his com-fort. She had no other legacy to leave him than her prayers; but these availed to shield him through all the untoward inci-dents of his orphanage and his eventful life; and they were answered by the most glorious endowments of grace and virtue which the heart of a dying parent could crave for a child, — a cheering instance of God's faithfulness to his people and their seed.

The orphans thus thrown upon the wide world, received shelter at first from their father's sisters, Mrs. White—for whom Thomas always cherished a tender gratitude — and Mrs. Brake. His home was with the latter, about four miles from Clarks-burg. He was then a pretty and engaging child, with rosy and almost feminine cheeks, waving brown hair, and large pensive blue eyes. It was said of him that, in the waywardness and levity which are usually seen at his age, he never was a child. The little fellow had a manly innate courtesy, and strange, quiet thoughtfulness, united with a determination beyond his years, which drew wonder and love from his relatives. An incident, which is most fully authenticated, occurring when he was but eight years old, shows that nature made him, from the first, of another mould from that of common men. He appeared one day at the house of his father's cousin, Judge John G. Jackson, in Clarksburg, and addressing Mrs. Jackson by the title of aunt, which he usually gave her, asked her to give him dinner. While he was eating it, he remarked, in a very quiet tone, "Uncle Brake and I don't agree; I have quit him, and shall not go back any more." His kind hostess remonstrated against this purpose as a childish whim. He listened most respectfully to all her reasoning, but returned to the same resolute declaration, — "No; Uncle Brake and I can't agree; I have quit, and shall not go back any more." It would seem that the husband of his aunt, though an honest, was an exacting man, and had made the mistake of attempting to govern the orphan through force, instead of through his understanding and conscience. And the singular child, having concluded that his stay under his authority would never be congenial, had calmly determined, with the same inexorable will which he displayed in after years, to end the connexion at once. From Judge Jackson's he went to a favorite cousin's, lately married and living in her own house, and asked leave of her to spend the night. In the course of the evening he announced his purpose of leaving his home, and, after listening respectfully to her remonstrances likewise, returned resolutely to his old formula: "No; Uncle Brake and I don't agree; I have quit there; I shall not go back any more." Accordingly, the next morning, he set out from Clarksburg alone, and travelled on foot to the former home of his grandfather, in Lewis County, about eighteen miles distant, then belonging to Cummins Jackson, the half-brother of his father. There he was kindly received, and, in the affectionate protection of his uncle and of two maiden aunts, afterwards Mrs. Carpenter and Mrs. Hall, then residing with him, found the home he wanted. It was the more attractive to him that his elder brother, Warren, was now sharing the same refuge. This remarkable man deserves our notice, not only for his paternal kindness to the orphan, but for the influence which he exerted, and for that which, contrary to all human calculation, he failed to exert upon him. He was

then approaching middle life, a bachelor, of lofty stature and
most athletic frame, and full of all the rugged energy of his
race. The native powers of his mind, although not cultivated
by a liberal education, were so strong, that some of his acquaintances have declared him to be, in their opinion, the ablest man
they ever knew. His will was as strong as his understanding,
and his passions were vehement and enduring. As a friend, he
was steadfast, and generous, without stint; and, though forbearing and slow to take offence, as an enemy he was equally bitter
and unforgiving. Such was his liberality, that his poorer neighbors and dependants adored him.   He never had political
aspirations for himself, but his unbounded influence usually gave
the honors of his country to the person whom he favored.
Yet his business morals, save when he was bound by his own
voluntary promises, which he always sacredly fulfilled, were
accounted unscrupulous; and he was so passionately fond of
litigation, that his legal controversies consumed a large part
of the income of a liberal estate and the earnings of his own
giant industry.   He owned a valuable farm and mills, and was
one of the largest slaveholders in the county of Lewis. His
occupations were agriculture, and the preparation of lumber
and flour, diversified with the hardy sports of a forest country.   In this plain but plentiful home, Thomas lived until
he became a cadet of West Point, with one noted interval,
which shall be related. He received all the privileges of
a son of the family. The relation existing between him and
his uncle was, from the first, remarkable. He treated the little
boy more as a companion than as a child, soothing for him all
the ruggedness of his nature, imparting to him his plans and
thoughts as though to an equal and counsellor, making him his
delighted pupil in all the rural arts in which he was himself an
unrivalled adept, and always rather requesting than demanding

nis compliance with the discipline of his household. The child was thus stimulated in the work of his own self-government from a very early period, and left to an independence of action more suited for a man. But he did not disappoint his uncle's confidence. His peculiar method with the boy may perhaps be accounted for in part by the singular temperament of the race — passionately attached to the idea of independence; in part by the relaxation of parental restraints, which usually prevails in new countries; and partly by the profound sagacity of the guardian, who saw at a glance the noble nature with which he had to deal. He showed his affection, also, by earnestly seeking for Thomas, as well as for his elder brother, the best education he could place within their reach. He required of them a regular attendance upon the country school of the neighborhood, which Thomas was prompt to render; but Warren chafed under its restraints. He was now a hardy lad of fourteen years old, and, Jackson-like, began to feel his self-reliance, and to find the bread of dependence irksome. His discontent was probably increased by the consciousness that his little brother was more the favorite than himself. He therefore demanded that he should be allowed to seek his own fortunes, and choose his own home. His uncle, characteristically, gave him leave to please himself; and he departed, after a few months' residence. But he also induced Thomas, partly by his affection for him, and partly by the assumption of the authority of a senior, to go with him. They resorted at first to the house of Mr. Neale, a maternal uncle, a most respectable man, living on the Ohio river, at that island which has been made famous by the name and misfortunes of Blennerhasset, and the eloquence of Mr. Wirt. This relative also received them with cordial kindness. But Warren found that his love dictated the same policy which the affection of Cummins Jackson had prompted, requiring them to pursue their studies diligently at school. He soon wearied again of the restraint, and, taking his little brother, the next spring he went down the Ohio river, and disappeared from the knowledge of his friends for a time. In the fall of the year they returned, by the charity of some steamboat-master, travel-soiled, ragged, and emaciated by the ague. Their story was — that they had floated down to the junction of the Ohio with the Father of Waters, seeking adventures and a livelihood, until at length they contracted to cut firewood for the furnaces of the steamers, on one of the lonely islands of the Mississippi, near the southwestern corner of Kentucky. Here the two children had spent the summer alone, living in a temporary cabin, earning their bread by this rough labor, amidst the dreary forests of cotton-wood, and encircled by the turbid river; until their sufferings from the ague compelled them to seek a way homewards. How strange a world this for the fair and pensive child of nine summers! But such was the sturdiness of his nature, that he seemed scarcely to feel either its incongruity or its hardship. On their return to their native region, Thomas declared that he should go back permanently to the protection of his uncle Cummins Jackson, because he had experienced his kindness and loved his home. But Warren seemed still to feel some repugnance, and preferred to seek a refuge with one of his father's sisters, living near the old home of the family, on Bu-chanan river, Mrs. Isaac Brake. Here he was kindly received. The comforts of Thomas's home soon repaired the ravages of the ague in his body; but in Warren the disease had taken so fatal a hold that it could not be exorcised; it passed into a phase of pulmonary decline, and after a few years of lingering sickness, which seemed to be sanctified to the production of thorough gentleness and piety, it carried him to his grave in his nineteenth year. None of the little family now remained save

Thomas, sheltered under the stalwart but kindly arms of his uncle, and the girl Laura, who received her nurture from her mother's relatives in Wood County. Although they henceforth never occupied the same home, and could not meet very often, he always cherished for this sister the warmest affection. The first pocket-money he ever earned for himself, he expended wholly in buying her a dress of silk. It has been stated that Thomas always received from Cummins Jackson the liberal treatment of a son. Thenceforward his opportunities for education were just such as they would have been, had he been the heir of such a citizen. Classical academies were unknown in the country; and the sons of the most respectable persons, with the exception of a few who were sent Eastward for an education, were content with the plain studies of a country school. But the practical success and usefulness of many of the sons of the soil, besides General Jackson, have given proof that book-learning is by no means the only instrument of an efficient education. He seems to have been at all times eager for self-improvement. A worthy man, Mr. Robert P. Ray, then taught an English school at Cummins Jackson's mills, where Thomas, in company with the sons of the surrounding landholders, received the usual plain education of the country. Out of that school came several others who have not only been respectable citizens of their district, but have risen to influence as legislators or professional men. Thomas showed no quickness of aptitude for any of his studies, except arithmetic; in this he always outstripped his schoolmates, seemingly without effort. In all other branches his acquisitions were only made by patient labor. If he professed to be prepared for a recitation, all might be certain that he was thoroughly prepared; from the first, the intense honesty of his nature, and the sober judgment with which

3

he preferred the substance to the name of an acquisition, were singular. Nothing could induce him to leave a lesson behind him unmastered. If he had not been able to finish a previous one at the same time with his class-mates, he would continue to study it while they proceeded to the next, and when called on for his share of the succeeding recitation, he would flatly declare that he knew nothing about it, that he had not yet had time to begin it, and that all his time had been occupied upon the other. Thus he was, not seldom, nominally behind his class; but whatever he once gained was his forever; and his knowledge, though limited, was perfect as far as it went. His temperament at this time was cheerful, amiable, and generous; and his demeanor instinctively courteous. His truthfulness was at all times proverbial. To an intimate friend he once said, that so far as he remembered he had never violated the exact truth in his life, save once. This instance was one which many would justify, and most would palliate; but he himself condemned it. While lieutenant of artillery in the Mexican War, his company were ordered to proceed by a narrow path through a dense thicket of "chapparal," which was believed to be infested with guerillas. Jackson himself saw the leaves of the shrubs riddled with fresh bullet-holes; and the men were so intimidated by the dread of the unseen foe, that when the head of the column approached the dangerous spot it recoiled, and in spite of the expostulations of the officers, refused to advance. At length the young lieutenant went alone, far before his men, and waving his sword shouted to them: You see there is no danger; forward!" Yet, as he confessed, he knew at the moment that he was in extreme peril. At school he was also noted for a strong sense of justice, which made him as respectful towards the rights of others as tenacious of his own. As long as he was fairly treated by his playmates, his temper was perfectly gentle and complying; but if he believed himself wronged, his resistance was inexorable. In his occasional combats with his fellows, while superior strength might sometimes overpower him, it could never force him to acknowledge defeat. The victor might cuff him until he desisted from sheer weariness, but Thomas was still unsubdued, and ready to renew the fight whenever his antagonist dared to assail him. He was withal never moping nor surly, but always ready for the merry romp or play. He was not peculiarly swift of foot, but he usually led his playmates in jumping and climbing. When the school was divided into two companies for a game of bat and ball, or prisoners'-base, he was always captain of one, and his side was sure to win.

In all Western Virginia, the owners of land and their sons were accustomed to labor on their farms with their own hands, more than any population of equal wealth and comfort in America. This was the consequence partly, of the industrious habits which the Presbyterian Scotch and Irish, the ruling caste in those regions, brought from their native lands; partly of the comparative scarcity of labor, both slave and hired; and partly, of the absence of the abundant means of literary and professional cultivation, which an older society offers to the wealthy. Even in the households of slaveholders, like Cummins Jackson, who in that country were few, the males, when not at school, were regularly occupied in rural labors, except in that large allowance of time reserved for country sports. The reader will thus understand that Thomas, although in no sense reduced by his orphanage to a condition beneath that of the youths around him, was occupied, like his uncle, in the works of the farm and mills. Here he was always resolute and efficient. One of his most frequent tasks seems to have been, to transport from the woods the huge stems of the poplars and oaks, to be converted by the saw-mill into lumber. He became thus a famous driver of oxen. If any tree was to be moved from ground of unusual difficulty, or if it was more gigantic than the rest, the party of laborers was put under his command, and the work was sure to be effected. In this manner his life was passed from nine to sixteen years of age, between the labors of the school and of the farm. He was then, like his father, of short stature, but compact and muscular. He was capable of fatigue, and of indomitable physical endurance. His bearing was unpretending, but manly and courteous. But his constitution, even then, gave signs of infirmity. An obscure disease of the stomach and other organs of nutrition had seized upon him, harassing him with chronic irritations or prostrations of the nerves, sleepless nights, and lassitude. A year or two later, notwithstanding the means used to re-establish his constitution, these symptoms assumed the more ominous form of a slight paralysis. The latter, however, wore away after a time; and, about his second year at West Point his system seemed to escape a part of its burdens; he grew rapidly to a tall stature, and thus, instead of remaining short, like his father, he was conformed to the usual standard of his race. But the other affection clave to him, like a Nemesis, during his whole youth and the war with Mexico, and never relaxed its hold until after he came to Lexington as Professor in the Military Institute, when he subdued it by means of the waters of the alum springs of Rockbridge, in connection with his admirable temperance. His habits of uncomplaining endurance, and his modest reluctance to every display savoring of egotism, concealed the larger part of these sufferings. It should be remembered, in order that we may appreciate his capacity and energy, that his arduous studies at the military academy, and his brilliant services in Mexico, were performed by him while hag-ridden from time to time by this wretched tormentor.

The post of Constable in the northern half of Lewis County became about this time vacant. His friends procured the appointment for him, for two reasons : one was, that the life on horseback, it was hoped, might remove his disease and give him a firm constitution; the other was, that the little salary of the place might enable him to realize his ardent desire for a liberal education. So general was the favor borne him, and the desire to forward his aspirations for advancement, that the Court winked at the irregularity of appointing a minor to this office, accepting the suretyship of his uncle as a sufficient guarantee. We now see the manly youth, with his account-book and bag of bills and executions, traversing on horseback the hills of Lewis, a county then so large that the major parts of five counties have since been carved out of it. To readers who are not Virginians, a word of explanation may be needed concerning the office of Constable in our State. The Justices of the Peace, besides the County Courts which they hold jointly, are authorized to decide singly, in their own neighborhood, upon controversies for property or money, where the sum in dispute does not exceed twenty dollars. Of this little court, the Constable is the executive officer, serving its warrants, summoning its witnesses, and carrying into effect its decisions. The Justice, as conservator of the peace, may also issue his warrant for the arrest and examination of any person suspected of crime, however grave; and in this preliminary stage of proceedings, the Constable is his agent. This officer is also charged with the regulating of certain misdemeanors, and with the enforcement on slaves and free negroes of the police regulations peculiar to their condition. He is, in a word, a sort of minor sheriff.

The countrymen of young Jackson testified that he filled this office with industry and fidelity. In everything he was scrupulously exact; his engagements were uniformly kept; and the little claims intrusted to him for collection were always safe. While never cruel in the exercise of the powers of his place, he strictly enforced upon others a punctual compliance with their promises. In these duties his nerve was sometimes tried; but he always carried his point. One instance may be related, as illustrating his courage and resource. About two miles from the little village of Weston, the county seat of Lewis, there lived a man, who, under a garb of great religiousness, concealed an unscrupulous character. Jackson held an execution against his property for a little claim of ten dollars, which the creditor had more than once urged him to collect. After indulging the debtor for a time, and advising him rather to earn or borrow the sum than suffer the sale of some article of his property, he exacted from him a firm promise that, on a certain day, he would meet him in Weston, and, without further trouble, pay him the debt. He then told the creditor that, on the evening of that day, his money would be ready for him. At the appointed day, Jackson was in Weston, but no debtor appeared; and when the creditor came to receive his claim, he redeemed his punctuality by paying it out of his own purse. He then quietly remained in the village until the next morning, when, as he expected, the delinquent appeared in the street with a very good horse. It seems that there was, in their rude community, a sort of *lex non scripta*, established by usage, and more sacredly observed, perhaps, than many of the statutes of the Commonwealth, forbidding that any person should be taken by force, on any plea, from the back of his horse, and justifying the most extreme resistance to such a disgrace. Selecting a time, therefore, when his debtor was dismounted, Jackson went up and taxed him with his breach of promise, reminded him of his long endurance of these deceptions, and was proceeding to seize the horse to satisfy his execution. The other party, who had no idea of ever paying his debts, resisted, and a furious fight began in the street. During the engagement, he availed himself of a momentary advantage, and remounted his horse. Here, now, was a dilemma for the young representative of the law. On the one hand, his adversary seemed safely enthroned in that position which the sacred custom of the vicinage pronounced unassailable. But, on the other hand, it was not in his nature to accept defeat where his conscience told him he was in the right. Clinging to the horse's bridle, he looked around, and perceived at some distance the low-browed door of a friend's stable standing open. To this he forced the horse, amidst a shower of unregarded cuffs from his enemy, who found himself, by these ludicrous tactics, placed between the alternatives of being struck off by the lintel of the door, or else sliding from the saddle and relinquishing the horse. He prudently adopted the latter, and Jackson secured the prize triumphantly in the stable, while yet he respected, at least in the letter, the common law of the neighborhood.

But these occupations proved more favorable to the health of his body than of his character. They necessarily separated him much from home influences, and brought him acquainted with the worst people of his vicinage. Nor could his home influences be considered very auspicious. His aunts, before this period, had married, and the establishment of his uncle was that of a bachelor. Cummins Jackson, though temperate and energetic, was himself utterly devoid of Christianity, of a violent and unscrupulous character, and much given to assume, in its ruder phase, the character of a sporting gentleman. He kept race-horses, made up country race-matches, and employed his nephew as his favorite rider, whenever he expected a close contest. It was the gossip of all the country-side, that if a horse had any winning qualities in him, they would inevitably come out when young Tom Jackson rode him in the race. Moreover, the general morals of the community were loose, and irregularities too often found most countenance from those of highest station. The Christianity of the region was not influential; ministers were few, and deficient in intelligence and weight, being chiefly the most uncultivated members of the Baptist communion, or of the itinerant fraternity of the Methodists. If the citizens saw anything of Episcopacy or Presbyterianism, it was only from the transient visits and sermons of ministers from a distance. The state of religious opinion was just what the observing man would expect from such influences. The profession of Christianity was chiefly confined to the more ignorant classes; and among them Church discipline and Christian morals were relaxed. Men of the ruling houses, like the Jacksons, were too often found to be corrupted by the power and wealth, with which the teeming fertility of their new country was rewarding their talents. Minds such as theirs, self-educated by the activity and competition of their bustling times, were too vigorous to acknowledge the intellectual sway of a class of ministers who dispensed, for sermons, their crude notions of experimental piety, in barbarous English. There were few cultivated minds to represent the authority of the gospel. Consequently, most of the men of position were openly neglectful of Christianity, and some were infidels.

No one will wonder, then, that as young Jackson approached manhood, his conduct became somewhat irregular. He was, as he himself declared, an ardent frequenter of races, of "house-raisings," and of country-dances. But still his industry remained; his truthfulness and honesty continued untarnished; and the substantial foundations of integrity were never undermined in his nature. His irregularities were never more than temporary foibles, and they yielded to the wholesome influences of the first two years' discipline at the military academy, and to the encouragement of better prospects and gratified aspirations. During the first year's course, the "demerits" incurred show some remains of his wilder habits; but even then his comrades found in him nothing low or vile. And thenceforward he appeared at home, during vacations, perfectly exemplary in his demeanor, and at the school, regular, laborious, truthful, scorning everything base; modest, yet self-reliant; and although inexperienced in some of the forms of society, ever full of intrinsic dignity and courtesy.

It is manifest that his nature was intensely ambitious and aspiring. He thirsted eagerly for knowledge, and for well-earned distinction. He knew himself to be a depressed scion of a noble and influential stock; and while he felt no morbid shame at his poverty, he longed to reinstate himself in the foremost ranks of the kindred, from which orphanage and destitution had thrust him down. This was the ruling desire, the purpose of his early manhood, and it gives us the key to many of the singularities of his character; to his hunger for self-improvement; to his punctilious observance, from a boy, of the essentials of a gentlemanly bearing, even where he was ignorant of its conventionalities; to the uniform assertion of his self-respect. The wonder is, that the circumstances which surrounded him did not make him, simply, another Cummins Jackson. The generous kindness of this uncle, the force of his example, the similarity of the two in the strength and ardor of their natures, and the impress of a will so energetic and commanding, would seem naturally to tend to that result. But the nephew appears to have imbibed all the good traits of the uncle, and to have escaped the bad. How shall the formation of such a character, in such a state of society, be explained? Was it not due to that noble constitution of his nature, that reverence for the true and the right, that manly courage which the Creator impressed upon it, for his own ulterior ends, coupled with the purifying force of a Christian mother's teachings and prayers?

Of this uncle General Jackson always spoke with grateful affection; as he was evidently his favorite nephew. Cummins Jackson displayed his restless love of adventure by going, when he was forty-nine years old, to seek gold in California. He was also impelled in part by disgust at the persecutions of some of his neighbors, with whom his feuds had become perfectly inveterate. His ample farm and competency could not detain him; he crossed the plains with a well-equipped company of gold-hunters, of whom he was recognized as the chief, in 1849, and died the autumn of that year in the wilds of the mining region. Had he made a will, it is believed that General Jackson would have been a chief heir; but death disappointed such generous purposes if he had them; and his estate is destined to be divided among almost a hundred nephews and nieces.

It will be best here to anticipate so much as will be necessary, to complete the history of young Jackson's official life in Lewis. The law requires the county court to take bond and security of every constable to the amount of not less than two thousand dollars, for the faithful transaction of all the business committed to him. When a creditor places any claim in the hands of such an officer for collection, he usually exacts a receipt from him acknowledging the trust undertaken, and the amount and nature of the demand. The officer thus incurs a responsibility from which he must absolve himself, either by collecting and paying over to him the amount of the claim, or by making every lawful effort to do so, and showing that it was impracticable, by reason either of the insolvency or evasion of the creditor. When the hope of an immediate appointment, as cadet of the Military Academy, was suggested, young Jackson's abiding desire for a liberal education forbade his hesitating for any smaller concerns. He instantly resigned his place. It chanced that this was a season of stringency in the currency of the region, and his uncle found himself unable at the time to raise ready money for his outfit. By his advice, Thomas sold such claims for cash as could be thus disposed of, and transferred the remainder of his papers and business to him for adjustment. It would appear that even these prompt means failed to realize enough for his expenses. One can readily conceive that a boy of eighteen, with all his punctuality, would not be a thoroughly methodical accountant. So, when the settlements with suitors were made, in the absence of that personal recollection on which he largely relied, the more greedy succeeded in making him their seeming debtor for more than he had left in his uncle's hands. The consequence was, that a few suits were brought against the latter, as his security, for the payment of sums thus claimed. He, indeed, probably regarded this as rather good luck than ill, as it gave him additional occasion to exercise his restless mind in his beloved work of litigation; and his generosity to Thomas made him cheerfully pay the deficit. On the return of Thomas from West Point, he looked thoroughly into these transactions, and demanded a more accurate settlement of his accounts. To one claimant, for whom he had collected a variety of small sums at different times, thus making a somewhat intricate series of transactions, he said that this party ought to be able to remember the receipt of various payments on account, for which the written evidence was now lost; and that when the recollection was distinct and undeniable, he should insist on having credit. He required his antagonist to go over the whole account on this plan. When he sought to avoid allowing payments, which Jackson well knew had been made, by saying "he had no recollection of them," the latter would reply, "Yea, but you must recollect them;" and, by his firm countenance and reference to attendant circumstances, would constrain his unwilling party to make the just admissions. In this way he forced him to allow in Court sundry abatements of his claim. Finally, all the sums for which, as constable, he was bound to any one, were fully paid either by him or his uncle.

CHAPTER II.

THE CADET.

In 1841, the Hon. Samuel Hays was elected delegate, from the district to which Lewis County belonged, to the Congress of the United States. During his term, the place of cadet in the military academy at West Point became vacant. This famous school was founded and sustained by the Federal Government, and contained as many pupils as there were Congressional districts. These were treated as soldiers in garrison from the time they entered, and not only instructed and drilled, but fed, clothed, and paid by the public. The appointments were made by the Secretary of War, upon the nomination of the member of Congress, representing the district from which the application came. It may be easily comprehended that his recommendation was usually potential. As the scientific education given was thorough, and nearly the whole expense was borne by the Government, the place was much sought by the sons of the most prominent citizens. Mr. Hays, upon consultation with judicious friends, had given the nomination to a fatherless youth, of sprightly mind and good habits, whom his neighbors desired to help upward in the world. He had been appointed, had gone to West Point, and upon observing the condition of the cadets from without, had concluded that the restraints and military discipline of the place would be too irksome for his tastes. He therefore left the village with-

out reporting to the authorities of the school, and returned
home to resign his appointment. This occurred in the summer
of 1842. The self-indulgence of this youth, and the contrasted
energy and hardihood of Jackson, bore fruits which may well
be pondered by every young man. The former was consigned,
by the rejection of the providential occasion for self-improvement, to a decent mediocrity, from which his name has never
been sounded by the voice of fame. The latter, by his manly
decision, made of the same opportunity " a tide, which, taken
at the flood, led on to fortune." There was then living in the
village of Weston a German smith, one of those neighborly,
ingenious, gossiping men, who are as busy in discussing
their neighbors' affairs as in repairing their implements of
labor. Just at the time when the young man who has
been mentioned returned to the country, relinquishing his
West Point nomination, it so chanced that Cummins Jackson
had occasion to go to this smith, for the repair of some of the
machinery of his mill. The good man said to him, informing
him of the indiscretion of his young neighbor, " Here now
is a chance for Tom Jackson, as he is so anxious for an
education." The uncle replied that, on his return home that
evening, he would mention it to Thomas, and recommend him
to seek the appointment. When he did so, the young man
caught eagerly at it; and the result was that the next morning
he went to Weston, and applied to his influential friends for
their support in an application to the Honorable Mr. Hays, then
in Washington. All had known his industry, his integrity, and
his honorable aspirations. All sympathized warmly with him
in the latter. Nearly every prominent person connected with
the courts of the place concurred in his testimonial. To one
gentleman, a lawyer of influence, and a connection of his family,
he resorted for a more confidential letter. This person asked

him if he did not fear that his present education was too scanty to enable him to enter the military academy, or to sustain himself there. His countenance sank with mortification for a moment, then raising his head, he said, with a look of determination, " I know that I shall have the application necessary to succeed; I hope that I have the capacity; at least I am determined to try, and I wish you to help me to do this." The letter was written, with a hearty commendation of his claims to Mr. Hays, and a full description of his courageous spirit. These letters were despatched to Washington; and, meantime, Thomas applied himself diligently to reviewing his studies for entrance into the academy, under the gratuitous teaching of a lawyer of Weston, Mr. (afterwards Judge) Edmiston. In due time a reply came from Mr. Hays, promising to use his influence in his favor. Some one then suggested, that as the session at West Point had commenced, and as it was always safest to give personal attention to one's own interests, it might be best for him to go immediately to Washington, instead of waiting for the result of the application, and be ready to proceed at once, if successful, to his destination. Thomas declared his preference for this course, and departed without a day's delay. Borrowing a pair of saddle-horses and a servant from a friend, he hastened to Clarksburg, to meet the stage-coach which plied thence to Winchester and Washington. His garments were homespun, and his whole wardrobe was contained in a pair of leathern saddle-bags. When he reached Clarksburg the stage had passed by, but he pursued it, and at its next stopping-place overtook it, and proceeded to Washington city. Presenting himself thus before the Honorable Mr. Hays, he was kindly received; and his patron proposed that he, should go at once, with the stains of his travel upon him, to the office of the War Minister to procure his appointment. He presented him to that minister as a mountain youth, who, with a limited education, had an honorable desire of improvement. The Secretary was so much pleased with the directness and manliness of his replies, that he ordered his warrant to be made out on the spot. When Mr. Hays proposed to take him to his lodgings, for a few days, that he might see the sights of the metropolis, he declined, saying that as the studies of the academy were in progress, it was best for him to be in his place there, and that he should be content with a general view from the top of the dome of the Capitol. Having looked upon this panorama for a while he descended, and declared himself ready for West Point. Mr. Hays wrote to the authorities there, asking them, at the suggestion of some friend, to make the utmost allowance practicable in the preliminary examination for his defective scholarship, and in favor of his good character. And Jackson stated to his friends that this indulgence was very kindly extended to him, and that without it, he would scarcely have been able to stand the test. He entered West Point, July, 1842, being then eighteen years old. He had not attained his full stature, but was muscular in his frame, and of a fresh, ruddy countenance. His demeanor was somewhat constrained, but, by reason of its native dignity, always pleasing. The fourth-class men at this school were called by their comrades *plebes*, were subjected in many respects to restraints peculiar to their rank, were made to perform the menial duties of sweeping the barrack-grounds, and such-like, under the inspection of their more advanced fellow-students, and were severely drilled in their military exercises. It was thus the authorities proposed to form a soldierly subordination and hardihood. The infliction of practical jokes upon new-comers has always been carried to extremity in this school. The professors themselves seemed to connive at it as a useful discipline of the temper; and, by a

fixed usage of the cadets, he who grew restive under the tor-
ment only subjected himself to tenfold sufferings. Resistance
was vain. The third-class man, lately among the *plebes*, sought
his revenge from the body of new-comers below him, and from
victim became tormentor, with all the zest and ingenuity of a
practitioner just graduated in the art of teasing. When they
saw the country youth arrive, with his saddle-bags, in his homespun garments, they promised themselves rich sport with him;
but they speedily learned their mistake. Such was his courage,
his good temper, and the shrewdness and *savoir-faire*, acquired
during his diversified life in the country, that they were quickly
glad to leave him for more easy subjects.

It would be obviously unfair to judge his capacity by his
earlier acquisitions at West Point. His literary preparation
was defective. Although his rural occupations had given a
valuable cultivation of his powers, he lacked the facility of
taking in knowledge, which arises from practice; nor was his
apprehension naturally quick. He once stated to a friend that
he "studied very hard for what he got at West Point." The
acquisition of knowledge with him was slow, but what he once
comprehended he never lost. Entering, with such preparation,
a large and distinguished class, he held at first a low grade.
Generals M'Clellan, Foster, Reno, Stoneman, Couch, and
Gibbon, of the Federal army; and Generals A. P. Hill, Pickett
Maury, D. R. Jones, W. D. Smith, and Wilcox, of the Confederate army, were among his class-mates. From the first, he
labored hard. The same thoroughness and honesty which had
appeared in the schoolboy, were now more clearly manifested.
If he could not master the portion of the text-book assigned for
the day, he would not pass over it to the next lesson, but continued to work upon it until it was understood. Thus it happened that, not seldom, when called to the black-board, he

5

would reply that he 'had not yet reached the lesson of the day, but was employed upon the previous one. There was then no alternative but to mark him as unprepared. A distinguished student of the class next above him, now Major-General Whiting, rendered him valuable private aid, while all applauded his sturdy effort. But at the examinations which closed his first half-year's novitiate, the line which separated the incompetents, and condemned them to an immediate discharge, was drawn a very little below him. Nowise disheartened by this, but thankful that he had saved his distance, he redoubled his exertions. At the end of his first year, in a class of seventy-two, he stood 45th in mathematics, 70th in French, had 15 demerit marks for misconduct, and was fifty-first in general merit. In the next class, the studies were more extended and abstruse; but the examination at the end of his second year showed him 18th in mathematics, 52d in French, 68th in drawing, and 55th in engineering studies; while he had incurred 26 demerits, and ranked 30th in general merit.

In the second class, he proceeded from pure mathematics to chemistry and natural philosophy. His course was still more decidedly improved, and placed him at the end of the year in natural philosophy, 11th; in chemistry, 25th; in drawing, 59th; with no demerit for the year, and in general merit, 20th. In the studies of the final year, he was 12th in engineering, 5th in ethics, 11th in artillery, 21st in infantry-tactics, and 11th in mineralogy and geology. His demerit marks were seven, but, as he assured his friends, he might have wholly escaped these by laying the delinquencies charged to him upon comrades to whom they rightly belonged. He preferred to bear the undeserved blame, rather than break silence against them. His general standing as a graduate was 17th, notwithstanding the less successful years at the beginning, which were taken into the account. An examination of these records will show a steady progress; and, if the deficient preparation of his beginning be considered, there is evidence of a scholastic ability and acquirement very little below the highest. But scholastic ability is not the real test of a great mind. It also appears that he was usually least successful in a study when it was novel. In the science of military engineering, for instance, his first year's study placed him only 55th, but his last year 12th. He seems never to have become an adept in drawing; indeed nature had not gifted him with much of that manual dexterity, which is here more essential than even taste and correctness of eye. His greatest success was in ethics, where his grade was 5th — a correct prognostic of that transcendent ability in statesmanship and moral reasoning, which every great commander must possess. His teachers and comrades judged his mind sound and strong, but not quick. It was a frequent remark among the latter, that if the course were two years longer than it was, Jackson would assuredly graduate at the head of his class.

His manners, when he appeared at West Point, have been already described. When he returned upon furlough to his friends, they noted a great and progressive change in his person. The second year he grew, as it were by a leap, to the height of six feet. His bearing, though still deficient in ease, was punctiliously courteous and dignified. He was scrupulously neat in all his appointments, and, in his handsome cadet uniform, made a most soldierly appearance. At the military academy he was not morose, but reserved almost to shyness: fond of animated conversation and of the collision of intellect, when alone with one or two of his few intimates, but in a larger circle, a silent interested listener. The society there was usually stratified very distinctly, according to the classes. The fourth-class men, under the humble title of *plebes*, were the fags of all above them. At each stage of his advancement the cadet gained new privileges, which made him look down, like a superior mortal, on the younger. Hence the intimacies of the students were confined to their own classes, save where some more aspiring youth, by reason of distinguished scholarship or social advantages, sought the society of those above him. But Jackson, in selecting his few friends, disregarded all these bonds of caste, and most frequently chose them from the classes below him. His favorite recreation was walking; and almost every afternoon he might be seen, with a single companion, striding rapidly over the picturesque hills, or sitting upon one of the headlands which overhang the waters of the Hudson. In these confidential walks, his favorite topics were the graver subjects of moral reasoning, mental science, ethics, politics. He had enjoyed no collegiate training in these studies, the instruction in them at the military academy was limited, and his favorite associate in these discussions was a graduate of one of the Colleges which made this branch of science prominent. Yet, although his knowledge of the speculations of metaphysicians was limited, his friend found his notions always original, and usually correct, and his reasonings so ingenious and forcible, that he was never an easy antagonist to overcome. One of the most pleasing and noteworthy traits of his nature was his tenderness to the distressed. A case of sickness or bereavement, among the younger cadets especially, awakened all his sympathies; and he would devote himself to their help with a zeal so womanly, as to evoke the gibes of coarser natures. Perhaps, his profound impressions of the infirmity of his own frame quickened these sensibilities. He seemed to be under a habitual fear of some chronic and fatal disease, and began even then that rigid observance of such

laws of health as he apprehended to be suitable to him. One
of these rules was, never to bend his body in studying, lest the
compression of some of the important organs within should
increase their tendency to disease. Hence he sat always
bolt upright; his chair might as well have been without a
back.

It does not appear that Jackson was under the influence of
vital Christianity at West Point. Speculatively, he was a
believer; outwardly, he was observant of the decencies of
religion, and his morals were pure; but the sacred impression
of his mother's piety and teachings was as yet dormant. The
most authentic disclosure of his moral nature at that time is a
code of behavior which he compiled for himself, and carefully
engrossed in a blank book (in a large, correct, formal hand-
writing, that surprisingly contrasts with the indistinct, cursive
style of later years) under the title of "Maxims." These seem
to have been in part selected from books of that character, and
in part adopted from his own experience. They relate to
morals, manners, dress, the choice of friends, and the aims of
life. The standard of principle is simply that of a high secular
virtue, with such reference to religious responsibilities as every
thoughtful and reverent nature prompts. But they show already
that devotion to the sentiment of duty which his after-life manifested so grandly; and they reveal the loftiest aims. It is plain
that he habitually nourished the honorable ambition to make
himself the very greatest of which his nature was capable; and
that the limits which he assigned to this possibility were far
removed. Beneath his modest reserve and silence, so contrasted
with all the tricks of egotism, there burned the steady but
intense purpose, to place his character and his name high upon
the scale of true merit. Perhaps the most characteristic of

these maxims is the following, written in a conspicuous place:—

" YOU MAY BE WHATEVER YOU RESOLVE TO BE."

We shall see that this was, to him, a most practical dogma. His temper was recognized at West Point to be inflexible, without being petulant or aggressive. The only personal diffi- culty which he ever had with a fellow-student illustrates this trait; and the contrasted destiny of the two antagonists may well impress on every young man, the dreadfulness of base and relaxed principles, and the value of integrity. The cadet who was Jackson's sole enemy, resembled him in capacity and the conditions of his career. He was an orphan, from the far West, of rural training, of sound mind, and energetic and forci- ble character, capable of strenuous exertion, poor, and eager to advance himself. His early education had been neglected. Like Jackson he incurred the sportive malice of the students on his arrival at the Academy, by his appearance of rusticity and inexperience, and he defended himself with so much cour- age and good sense, and made such progress in his studies that all were at first inclined in his favor. There appeared no reason why he and Jackson might not run parallel courses of honor and usefulness. But, in his second year, he disclosed a laxity of principle, told less than the truth in order to evade " demerits," and contracted degrading associations in the neigh- boring village. Jackson was one of the first to perceive his lack of principle. One day his musket, which was always scrupulously clean, was replaced by one in most slovenly order. He called the attention of his captain (himself a senior cadet) to this loss, and described to him his private mark by which he identified his gun. That evening at the inspection of arms, it was found in the hands of the student who has been described, and when taxed with purloining it, the latter endeavored to shield himself by falsehood. Jackson had been indignant that he should commit such an act from mere indolence, but now his anger was unbounded. He declared that such a nuisance should not continue a member of the Academy, and demanded that he should be tried by a court-martial, upon his information, and expelled. It was only by means of the most persevering remonstrances of his comrades, and of the professors, that he could be induced to waive his right of pursuing the charge. The event proved that his estimate was more correct than that of his seniors. It was not long before his opponent was under arrest for disgraceful conduct, violated his parole, and was expelled on that account, a short time before he would have graduated. He resorted to the new State of Texas, and professed for a time to engage in the study of law. Not prospering in this, he embarked for California, endeavored to swindle the master of the ship out of his fare, and was summarily thrust ashore at Mazatlan, on the western coast of Mexico, without money or friends. There he wandered into the mountains, and attached himself to a roving tribe of the Tuscon Indians, among whom his skill in savage warfare, robbery, and murder, raised him to a sort of chieftainship, and the possession of half-a-dozen tawny wives. The last intelligence which reached the civilized world concerning him was, that he and his subjects had quarrelled concerning the murder of a poor pedlar, whom he had slain for his wares; and his miserable band, less savage than himself, had expelled him from their society. Jackson, meantime, has filled two hemispheres with his fame for every quality which is great and good.

The latter graduated at West Point, June 30th, 1846, being then twenty-two years old; and, according to custom, received the brevet rank of second lieutenant of artillery. The Mexican War was then in progress, and General Winfield Scott was proceeding to take supreme command. The young lieutenant was ordered to report immediately for duty with the 1st Regiment of Artillery; and proceeded through Pennsylvania, down the Ohio and Mississippi rivers to New Orleans, which was the rendezvous of the forces designed to reinforce the army in Mexico.

CHAPTER III.

IN MEXICO.

THE war of the United States against Mexico, beginning with the battles of Palo Alto and Resaca de la Palma in Western Texas, had rolled its waves, under General Zachary Taylor, up the Rio Grande, and into the province of New Leon. Monterey was occupied after a sanguinary victory, and the advanced forces had proceeded as far as Saltillo. But it was apparent, at the end of 1846, that successes on this line of operations would never bring peace, because 'it could only lead the arms of the United States aside from the heart of their enemy's strength. To reach the capital, a circuitous inland march would have been necessary; while the overpowering navy of the Union, if once Vera Cruz were occupied, would enable them to base upon the sea-coast a direct and short line of advance, by the great National Road. General Winfield Scott, who had been sent out as commander-in-chief of the whole forces, was therefore allowed to carry out his plan for organizing a powerful land and naval force against Vera Cruz, early in the year 1847. Most of the regular regiments were withdrawn from the command of General Taylor, and concentrated, during the month of February, at the seaport of Tampico, about two hundred and thirty miles north of Vera Cruz, where General Scott was also assembling his reinforcements. Young Jackson's company of heavy artillery formed a part of the

6

latter. On the 24th of February, the commanding general
commenced the assembling of his forces at Lobos Island, a convenient intermediate point, offering a roadstead for his numerous
ships unmolested by his enemies, a little north of Vera Cruz.
On the 9th of March, 13,500 land forces were disembarked in
one day from the fleet, upon the open beach near the city, without a single casualty. Young Jackson often referred to this as
a spectacle more grand and animating than man is often permitted to witness. The brilliant array proceeded to the land
under a cloudless sky, and in perfect order, in the innumerable
boats of the squadron, with colors displayed, martial music,
and the enthusiastic shouts of the soldiers, and by sunset the
whole force was paraded on shore, in order of battle. The
garrison of about four thousand partially organized troops were
in no condition to obstruct their advance.   On March 13th, the
city was formally invested, and on the 29th it capitulated, with
all the garrison, after a heavy bombardment. In this service
Jackson, who had on March 3d received the commission of
second-lieutenant, bore his part, but no occasion for special
distinction occurred. Meantime President Santa Anna, whose
activity and genius deserved greater success than he was fated
to achieve, assembled a force of about twenty thousand men in
the province of San Luis Potosi, between the three points of
Saltillo, Vera Cruz, and the capital, proposing from this central
position to strike his assailants in succession. His first attack
was upon General Taylor, who had been left at the first place
of the three, with a little more than five thousand men, of whom
nearly all were volunteers levied since the beginning of the
war. The result was the battle of Buena Vista, in which, on
the 23d of February, that small force inflicted a bloody repulse
upon the Mexicans.

Santa Anna, having failed in this well-conceived attempt,

reorganized and recruited his forces, to resist the advance of the Americans (now masters of Vera Cruz) on the capital. General Scott having set out for the interior on April 12th, he prepared himself for battle on the strong position of Cerro Gordo, a few miles east of Jalapa, crowning a line of precipitous hills with barricades and field-works ranging along, and commanding the great highway. After a reconnoissance effected by Captain Robert E. Lee of the Engineers (in which Lieut.-Col. Joseph E. Johnston of the cavalry received a severe wound), General Scott determined to adopt a plan of assault suggested by the former officer. This was to threaten the whole front of the enemy, but to direct the main attack against a hill at the western extremity of his position; because this post, if once seized by the Americans, commanded the only line of retreat for the discomfited Mexicans, as completely as, they supposed, their position commanded the great road. This vital attack was confided to the veteran division of Twiggs, powerfully supported by artillery, the whole being brought in front of the place to be assailed by an exceedingly rough and circuitous route, planned by Lee. The attack was made April 18th, and was completely successful. The Mexican army almost ceased to exist. It lost all its ordnance and several thousand prisoners; and the victory opened to Scott the town of Jalapa, the powerful fortress of Perote, and the city of La Puebla, within eighty-five miles of the capital.

It was in this assault that Captain John Bankhead Magruder, commanding a light field-battery, won brilliant distinction. But in such operations heavy artillery could only play a secondary part. The place of second-lieutenant in Magruder's battery was then to be filled, and most young officers shrank from it, because the commander was considered as an exacting disciplinarian, and the service of that arm was full of hardship and exposure to danger. But the latter reason was the very one which commended it to Jackson. He applied for, and quickly obtained, a transfer to it; and this change marks the beginning of his career of distinction. The old artillery, cumbersome in moving and slow in working, was usually posted at some permanent point, and must needs remain there for the day. If the tide of battle flowed towards it, it might render important service; if away from it, it was condemned to inactivity, and a partial disaster could compel its surrender. But the rapid manœuvring of the light artillery in action was then a new feature in American warfare. Its brilliant results at Palo Alto, at Resaca de la Palma, at Buena Vista, had delighted General Taylor, and electrified the country. Jackson foresaw that this arm of warfare was henceforth destined to be used in every battle, and to be always thrust forward to the post of danger and of honor. To a soul thirsting, like his, for distinction, this was motive enough for preferring it. And he said that, determined as he was to do his whole duty, and to consecrate himself wholly to his functions as a soldier, he had no fears of being unable to satisfy the rigidity of its captain. In this he was not disappointed; he speedily became one of his favorite officers.

General Scott, after remaining at La Puebla to rearrange and recruit his force, moved upon the city of Mexico with about eleven thousand men, August 7, 1847. President Santa Anna, meantime, had collected another powerful army, with abundant munitions of war, and had created every practicable obstacle to the approach of the city by the direct road. When the invader reached the mountain ridge of El Peñon, which assists to enclose the great basin in the centre of which the city stands, he found it so well fortified, that it was manifest the attempt to force his way through its defiles, would cost him a large part of his army. Here the ingenuity of his engineers again came to his aid. They showed him that by turning to the left, a way might be opened, practicable for artillery, by virtue of toil and hardihood, across a country scored with rugged volcanic ravines, to the southwest side of the city. This rendered the laborious defences of the Mexicans useless. By August 19, this arduous march was effected, and the head-quarters of the army were advanced to the village of San Augustin, about eight miles to the southwest of the city. No serious opposition was encountered, because the Mexican generals had supposed that the impracticable ground would be a sufficient defence of their flank.

But Santa Anna hastened to repair his omission, and again placed himself between the Americans and his capital, in a line of defences, which, if less elaborate than those in its front, was still formidable. Before San Augustin was the village of San Antonio, which he entrenched and occupied; at a considerable distance to the west of it he crowned an insulated hill at Contreras, with a strong detachment of infantry and artillery, and, in the rear of this post, he placed his heaviest force at the little village of Cherubusco, which he had also strengthened with field-works. A force at least three times as large as the American, with a hundred cannon, thus awaited their attack in position of their own selecting. But Santa Anna had committed the fatal blunder of choosing the two points which were the keys of his whole front, San Antonio and Contreras, so far apart, that they could not efficiently support each other. After heavy skirmishing on the 19th of August, General Scott turned the hill of Contreras by a night march, and at dawn, on the 20th, assailed it from the rear, either capturing or dispersing its five thousand defenders in a combat of a few minutes' duration, and seizing all their cannon. The Mexican force at San Antonio now found their communications violently threatened, and could only save themselves by a hasty retreat upon Cheru-

busco, pressed by an active enemy. He advanced immediately
to the attack of this last position; and as may be easily imagined, found its defenders assembled there in so confused a
manner, as to be ill prepared for a firm resistance. After
a sanguinary conflict of several hours, the village and entrenchments were carried, and the enemy retired nearer the city. To
Magruder's battery was assigned an important post in front of
the enemy's works, at the distance of nine hundred yards. Before long, his first lieutenant, Mr. Johnstone, was killed, and
Jackson thus became next in command to the captain, and took
charge of a section, or half of the battery; which he so handled,
as to win from Magruder, the following commendation in his
report: — "In a few moments, Lieutenant Jackson, commanding
the second section of the battery, who had opened fire upon the
enemy's works from a position on the right, hearing our fire
still further in front, advanced in handsome style, and being
assigned by me to the post so gallantly filled by Lieutenant
Johnstone, kept up the fire with great briskness and effect.
His conduct was equally conspicuous during the whole day, and
I cannot too highly commend him to the Major-General's favorable consideration."

In reward for his gallantry this day, he was honored with the
brevet rank of captain of artillery; and his actual rank in the
company was henceforth that of first lieutenant. On the 8th
of September, a fierce combat was fought at a point still nearer
the city, called Molino del Rey, in which the Americans were
again victorious. In this affair, Jackson had no other part than
to protect the flank of the force engaged, from the insults of
the Mexican cavalry, which he accomplished by a few well-
directed shots.

One more obstacle remained between the victors and
their prize; but this was the most formidable of all. The

Castle of Chapultepec, at first perhaps a monastery, was built upon an insulated and lofty hill overlooking the plain which extended up to the gates of the city, and commanding both the causeways by which the Americans aimed to approach them. The level country about the base of the mount was covered in part with corn, and in part with groves, and intersected with deep ditches, formed by the farmers for drainage and irrigation, impassable for artillery, and nearly so for infantry. As a previous examination of these was made impossible by swarms of sharpshooters, they only disclosed themselves to the advancing columns, when they arrived upon their brinks, shrouded as they were by the luxuriant grain, or by hedges of the thorny cactus. The castle was manned with a garrison, and around its base the remains of the Mexican army was posted in entrenchments, with batteries of cannon prepared to sweep every road which approached. The Americans, cut off at the time from their distant ships, found that the urgent want of supplies, which the city alone could furnish them by its surrender, compelled them to seek the reduction of this fort by some more speedy means than a regular siege. It was determined to storm it by several detachments, directed against its different sides, on the morning of September 13th. Major-General Pillow, to whom Magruder's battery was assigned, was directed to attack its west side, while Worth, the most skilful of Scott's lieutenants, was to march by a circuit beyond Pillow, and assail the north. Magruder was ordered by his general to divide his battery, and send one section forward, under Jackson, towards the northwest angle, while he assailed another part. Two regiments of infantry, under Colonel Tronsdale, accompanied the former section. The columns of attack advanced to the charge; the artillery, at every practicable point, striving to aid their approach by pouring a storm of shot upon the Mexican batteries. When the detachment, which Magruder supported with the section under his immediate command, had advanced so near the enemy that his fire was dangerous to his own friends, he proceeded to the front to join Jackson. The latter had been pushed forward by Colonel Tronsdale, under whose immediate orders the plan of the battle placed him, until he found himself unexpectedly in the presence of a strong battery of the enemy, at so short a range, that, in a few moments, the larger portion of his horses was killed, and his men either struck down, or driven from their guns by a storm of grape-shot; while about seventy of the infantry were holding a precarious tenure of their ground in his rear. Worth was just completing his detour, and bringing his veterans into connection with this party, when perceiving the desperate position of Jackson's guns, he sent him word to retire. He replied that it was now more dangerous to withdraw his pieces than to hold his position; and that if they would send him fifty veterans, he would rather attempt the capture of the battery which had so crippled his. Magruder then dashed forward, losing his horse by a fatal shot as he approached him, and found that he had lifted a single gun across a deep ditch by hand to a position where it could be served with effect; and this he was rapidly loading and firing, with the sole assistance of a sergeant; while the remainder of his men were either killed, wounded, or crouching in the ditch. Another piece was speedily brought over, and in a few moments, the enemy was driven from his battery by the rapid and unerring fire of Jackson and Magruder.

By this time the storming parties had pierced the castle on two sides, and the Mexicans were in full retreat upon the city. Orders had been given to the artillery that when this juncture arrived, they must pursue rapidly and scatter the disordered columns of the retreating foe. The horses of Jackson's guns

were nearly all slaughtered; those of his caissons, being farther
in the rear, had partially escaped. To disengage the dead animals from their harness and replace them with the others
would have consumed many minutes. The eager spirit of Jackson suggested the attachment of his guns to the limbers of his
ammunition-boxes instead of their own, and the leaving of the
remaining caissons on the ground. Thus, in an instant, his section was thundering after the discomfited Mexicans towards the
gates of the city. The next morning, September 14th, two of
those gates on the southwestern side were forced, the American
army entered, and after some partial combats with the riflemen
in the houses and upon the roofs, quelled all opposition and
took possession of the capital.

Jackson had displayed qualities which could not fail to draw
the eyes of his commanders upon him. The outline which has
been given of his share in the battles, is sustained by the following passages from the official reports of the Commander-in-
Chief, Generals Pillow and Worth, and his own captain. The
first says: —

"To the north, and at the base of the mound (Chapultepec),
inaccessible on that side, the 11th Infantry, under Lieut.-Colonel
Herbert, and the 14th under Colonel Tronsdale, and Captain
Magruder's field-battery, 1st Artillery (one section advanced
under Lieutenant Jackson), all of Pillow's division, had at the
same time some spirited affairs against superior numbers, driving the enemy from a battery in the road, and capturing a gun.
In these, the officers and corps named gained merited praise.
Having turned the forest on the west, and arriving opposite to
the north centre of Chapultepec, Worth came up with the
troops in the road under Colonel Tronsdale, and aided, by a
flank movement of a part of Garland's brigade, in taking the

7

one-gun breastwork, then under fire of Lieutenant Jackson's
section of Magruder's battery."

General Pillow says: —

" Colonel Tronsdale's command, consisting of the 11th and
14th Regiments of Infantry, and Magruder's field-battery, engaged a battery and large force in the road, immediately on the
west of Chapultepec. The advanced section of the battery,
under command of the brave Lieutenant Jackson, was dreadfully cut up, and almost disabled. Though the command of
Colonel Tronsdale sustained a severe loss, still he drove the
enemy from his battery, and turned his guns upon his retreating
forces. Captain Magruder's battery, one section of which was
served with great gallantry by himself, and the other by his
brave Lieutenant Jackson, in the face of a galling fire from the
enemy's position, did invaluable service preparatory to the
general assault."

General Worth, though commanding a different division of
troops, gives the following tribute: —

" After advancing some four hundred yards, we came to a
battery which had been assailed by a portion of Magruder's
field-guns, particularly the section under the gallant Jackson,
who, although he had lost most of his horses and many of his
men, continued chivalrously at his post, combating with noble
courage."

And Magruder thus recommends him for promotion: —

" I beg leave to call the attention of the Major-General commanding the division to the conduct of Lieutenant Jackson of
the 1st Artillery. If devotion, industry, talent, and gallantry
are the highest qualities of a soldier, then is he entitled to the
distinction which their possession confers. I have been ably
seconded in all the operations of the battery by him; and upon
this occasion, when circumstances placed him in command for a

short time of an independent section, he proved himself eminently worthy of it."

It is a singular coincidence, that this report of Captain Magruder was addressed immediately to one who has since had
disastrous occasion to verify its correctness. It was received
by Captain Joe Hooker, then acting as adjutant to General
Pillow, afterwards a Major-General in the Federal army, and
Commander at Chancellorsville.

For his conduct in the battle of Chapultepec, Jackson
received the brevet rank of Major. To this he had risen,
purely by the force of his merit, within seven months, from
the insignificant position of brevet second lieutenant. No
other officer in the whole army in Mexico was promoted so
often for meritorious conduct, or made so great a stride in
rank. If the conduct which has been detailed be examined, it
will be found to contain every evidence of bravery, thirst for
distinction, coolness, and military talent. We see the young
Lieutenant, the moment the fall of his immediate superior
placed him in command of a detachment at Churubusco, awaiting no orders, but guided by the sound of his Captain's guns
on his left, emulously pressing forward towards the enemy. At
Chapultepec he is assigned to the post of honor and danger,
and advances with alacrity. When Colonel Tronsdale, to
whom he owed merely a momentary subordination, thrust him
into a position almost desperate, and he was well-nigh deserted
by his men, he refused to retire without orders. Comprehending all the advantages and perils of his situation at once, he
proposed rather to exercise the further audacity of storming
the battery before him, than to attempt a disastrous retreat
exposed to its fire. And when the arrival of reinforcements
relieved him of his danger, he displayed his ready resource in
pursuing the defeated foe, where any other officer would have

felt fully justified, in busying himself only with carrying the shattered remains of his command to the rear.

Many years after, when his pupils were asking him the details of the scene, he modestly described it; and one of them exclaimed in astonishment, "Major, why did you not run, when your command was thus disabled?" He answered with a quiet smile, "I was not ordered to do so. If I had been ordered to run, I should have done so. But I was directed to hold my position, and I had no right to abandon it." He confessed also to an intimate friend, that the order of Major-General Pillow, separating his section, for the day, from his Captain, had excited his abiding gratitude; so that, while the regular officers were rather inclined to depreciate that general as an unprofessional soldier, he loved him because he gave him an opportunity to win distinction. His friends asked him if he felt no trepidation when so many were falling around him. He replied, no; the only anxiety of which he was conscious in any of these engagements, was a fear, lest he should not meet danger enough to make his conduct under it as conspicuous as he desired; and as the fire grew hotter, he rejoiced in it as his coveted opportunity. He also declared to those who were surmising the effect of the dangers of battle upon their spirits, that to him it was always exalting, and that he was conscious of a more perfect command of all his faculties, and of their more clear and rapid action, when under fire than at any other time. This, it will be remembered, was a distinguishing feature in the character of Napoleon's celebrated lieutenant, Marshal Ney. The Emperor was wont to say of him, that he was worth little as a general, saw nothing, and could do nothing, till he was enveloped in fire and smoke. Then he was all energy, sagacity, genius.

After the quiet occupation of the city, Major Jackson became a part of the garrison, and resided there, in a state of pleasant military leisure, until the diplomatists had matured a peace, and the American army was withdrawn. This season of rest continued several months. He was one of those who were quartered in the national palace, so that he used pleasantly to say, that no one had come nearer than himself to realizing the inflated predictions of the demagogues of the day in the United States, that "their soldiers should lodge in the halls of the Montezumas." His duties were light, and easily despatched in the early forenoon; the climate was delicious; every object around him was full of grandeur or interest to his active mind; and the cultivated hospitality of the Castilians was alluring. It is well known how easily the luxurious society of a capital can forget national prejudices and humiliations, at the call of social enjoyment, and learn to consider the accomplished and courteous professional soldier as no longer an enemy. Many Mexicans, moreover, regarded the invading army rather in the light of deliverers from a disorderly and oppressive government, than of intruders and oppressors. Immediately after the occupation of the city, therefore, the places of amusement were re-opened, and frequented by a mingled crowd of Americans and Mexicans, the ladies walked the streets in crowds, and the young officers began to cultivate the acquaintance of the most distinguished families.

To qualify himself for enjoying this society more freely, Jackson, with a young comrade, addressed himself to the study of the Spanish language. His active mind was, besides, incapable of absolute repose, and he wished to improve his leisure by acquiring knowledge. He was ignorant of Latin, which is not taught at West Point, and the only grammar of Spanish he could find was written in that ancient tongue. Yet he bought it, and nothing daunted, set himself to learn the paradigms of the language from it; and by the help of reading and constant conversation with the people, became in a few months a good Spanish scholar. It was an amusing trait of his character that he appeared afterwards proud of this accomplishment, and fond of exercising it, so far as his modest nature could be said to make any manifestation of pride. He ever took pleasure in testifying to the cultivation, hospitality, and flowing courtesy of the Spanish gentry in Mexico; and, like Napier, among their kindred in their mother-country, acknowledged the fascination of their accomplished manners, and their noble and sonorous tongue, and the indescribable grace and beauty of their women. Having formed the acquaintance of some educated ecclesiastics of the Romish Church (probably of the order of Canons), he went, by their invitation, to reside with them. He found their bachelor abode the perfection of luxurious comfort. Upon awaking in the morning, the servants brought him, before he arose from bed, a light repast, consisting of a few diminutive spiced cakes, and a single cup of that delicious chocolate which is found only in Spanish houses. He then dressed, went out, and attended to the drill of his company. Later in the morning, when the sun began to display his power, he returned to a breakfast of coffee, fruits, and game. The greater part of the day was then spent in study or visiting; and it closed with a dinner in which Parisian art vied with the tropical fruits native to the climate in conferring enjoyment. One family especially among his Spanish acquaintances extended to him a hospitality for which he was always grateful, and it possessed the attraction of several charming daughters. He confessed, years after, that he found it advisable to discontinue his visits there; and when asked the reason, said with a blush, that he found the fascination of some of the female charms which he met there was likely to become too strong for his prudence, unless he escaped them in good time. He declared that if the people of the city had been equal to their beautiful climate, in integrity and character, Mexico would have been the most alluring home for him in the world. But while his taste felt the charms of the Spanish grace and lofty courtesy, his sturdy English sense and pure honor taught him the incompatibility of a hollow and corrupt state of morals, and a debasing religion, with all his radical principles; and so he firmly withdrew himself, before his self-respect was tarnished.

But we have now reached the most important era in Jackson's life; the beginning of a vital change in his religious character. All the information which can now be gathered, points to the devout Colonel Frank Taylor, commanding his regiment of artillery, as his first official spiritual guide. This good man was accustomed to labor as a father for the religious welfare of his young officers; and Jackson's manly nature seems to have awakened his especial interest. During the campaign of the summer, his instruction and prayers had produced so much effect as to awaken an abiding anxiety and spirit of inquiry in Jackson's mind. He acknowledged his former practical neglect of this transcendent subject, and deplored the vagueness of his religious knowledge. It seems to have been almost a law of his nature even before it was sanctified, that, with him, to be convinced in his understanding of a duty was to set straightway about its performance. He resolved to make the Bible his study, and with a characteristic independence of mind, to take nothing, as to his own religious duties, from prejudice, or from the claims of the various denominations into which he saw the religious world divided. His attitude towards all creeds and sects was at this time singularly unbiassed. His parentage cannot be said to have belonged to any party in religion; his youth had been passed in a household where

Christianity was practically unknown; and his later education was obtained among a great company of young men, assembled from every church, under the slender instructions of an army chaplain. His own religious knowledge was at this time extremely scanty. Resolved to examine for himself and decide conscientiously, he concluded that there was now a rare opportunity to inform himself concerning one church at least, the Popish, from a high and authentic source. He was surrounded by educated Papists; and he determined to hear the very best they could say in commendation of their system. He therefore sought the acquaintance of the Archbishop of Mexico, introduced, probably, by his monastic friends, and had a number of interviews, in which that prelate entered at large into an explanation of the Romish system. Jackson always declared that he believed him a sincere and honest advocate of that Church, and that he found him not only affable, but able and learned. He also said that the system, as expounded by intelligent Romanists, was by no means so gross or so obnoxious to common sense as is represented by the mass of decided Protestants. The truth is (and herein is the subtlety of that form of error), the statements of doctrines are so artfully drawn up by the well-trained doctor of the Romish Church, that they may bear always two phases of meaning; the one more decided and gross, the other more akin to the evangelical truth. When, for instance, Rome requires her teachers to say that, in the sinner's justification, the "meritorious cause" is the righteousness of Jesus Christ, while the "formal cause" is the personal holiness inwrought by the grace of the gospel in the Christian's soul; the words in the hands of a Jansenist, may be made almost to mean that precious truth which every evangelical Christian, in every church, embraces in substance, that our acceptance before God is only in the merits of the Redeemer; while, in the hands of a self-righteous Jesuit, they will teach essentially a Pharisaic dependence on our own observances. So the doctrine of pen ance and absolution, in the instruction of the former, will be made to mean little more than that the minister of God's church is commissioned to publish therein His mercy to the truly peni tent soul; while, in the teachings of the latter, it will encourage the ignorant to believe, with a gross literality, that the priest, and the priest alone, can forgive sins. Doubtless, in the case of Jackson, the skilful polemic saw that his mind was too clear and strong to be hoodwinked by the darker phase of these dogmas. But with all the casuist's plausibility, he failed to commend Popery to his convictions. The inquirer departed unsatisfied, clearly convinced that the system of the Bible and that of Rome were irreconcilable, and that the true religion of Jesus Christ was to be sought by him elsewhere.

These studies seem to have left Jackson's mind for a long time in a singular state. His progress towards the full light was extremely gradual. He was henceforward conscientious, and more than ever punctilious about the purity of his life; he never remitted his interest in the great question of his own sal vation; yet, for more than two years after, he still remained in suspense. He apparently had no clear persuasion of his own acceptance before God, and no settled conviction as to the branch of the Church which he should select as his own.

His residence in Mexico, however, was not long protracted. On March 5, 1848, an armistice was concluded for two months between General Scott and the Mexican authorities; and on May 26th, a treaty of peace was finally ratified. The military occupation of the city and territory was therefore terminated as speedily as possible; and on the 12th of June, the last of the United States' forces left the capital to return home. Major Jackson's command was sent to Fort Hamilton, a post situated

8

upon Long Island, seven miles below New York city, and commanding the approach to its harbor, known as the Narrows.
Here we must follow his quiet career for a time through the
monotonous life of a garrison, diversified by occasional resorts
to the society of a great city.

CHAPTER IV.

LIFE IN LEXINGTON.

THE narrative of Major Jackson's introduction into the military academy of the commonwealth of Virginia at Lexington, is naturally preceded by a relation of the few incidents of his residence at Fort Hamilton. His life here was uneventful, save in his spiritual progress. The duties of the garrison fell lightly upon him; his rank as an officer of artillery entitled him to keep a horse, and thus indulge his passion for equestrian exercise; and the society of the post, enlivened by the presence of the superior officers' families, was attractive. Best of all, his Christian friend and father, Colonel Taylor, was residing near him, and continued to extend to him his pious advice. To him he ever after looked up, as one of the chief instruments of God in bringing him to a saving knowledge of the truth. Another spiritual guide now presented himself, in the chaplain of the garrison, the Rev. Mr. Parks. This gifted man was also an *alumnus* of the military academy at West Point, and a distinguished scholar. His religious zeal had led him to forsake the life of a soldier for that of a minister of the gospel in the Methodist Episcopal Church. In this communion he rose to distinction as a pulpit orator, and professor in their college, Randolph Macon, in Virginia. But his ecclesiastical views having undergone a change, he took orders in the Episcopal Church; and, as a clergyman of that communion, had, at one time, a post at West Point, and, at another, at Fort Hamilton. His ardent nature found much that was congenial in Jackson's. Under his ministry, the latter arrived at a comfortable hope of salvation, insomuch that ·he felt it his duty and privilege to apply for baptism, which he had never received. His conscientious inquiries into the claims of the different denominations of Christians were still continued, without, however, bringing him to any final conclusion. Popery he had examined, and rejected as anti-scriptural. Episcopacy he admitted to be an evangelical system; but some of its features he was unwilling to accept as of scriptural authority. This state of mind he explicitly avowed in asking for baptism at her door, stating that he should consider himself, if he obtained that privilege, not a member of the Episcopal denomination, but of the catholic body of Christ; and that, if ever his conscience and judgment were satisfied as to the most scriptural form of the Church, he should feel himself perfectly free to join it, whether it should be that or some other. But as his separation from civil life, and the society of other Christians, deprived him of the means of comparing and judging at that time, he felt that it was his duty, meanwhile, to assume, in the appointed rite, the name and service of the Redeemer, who, he hoped, had saved him. On this understanding, the Rev. Mr. Parks baptized him, and admitted him to his first communion.

After a residence of about two years at Fort Hamilton, Major Jackson was transferred to Fort Meade, near Tampa Bay, on the west coast of Florida. It is probable that the feebleness of his health, by no means invigorated by the fatigues and exposures of Mexico, was one motive of this change of residence. His abode at this post seems to have been as uneventful as it was short, for he rarely made any allusion to it. On the 27th of March, 1851, he was elected Professor of Natural and Experimental Philosophy and Artillery Tactics in the Military Academy of Virginia. This school, founded about twelve years before, upon the model of the one at West Point, had grown nearly to the distinction of its prototype, and was now attended by several hundred young men from Virginia and other Southern States. It is placed near the village of Lexington, in the county of Rockbridge, one of the most fertile and picturesque districts in the great valley of Virginia. Its castellated buildings, grandly situated on a commanding yet grassy eminence, overlook the country for many miles, and, on the east, confront the Blue Ridge Mountains, which form the boundary of the district on that side. The salubrity of the climate, and the intelligence of the society, graced also by the faculty of Washington College, have always made Lexington an attractive residence. The prosperity and growth of the Military Institute calling for another instructor in this department, the eyes of its governors were directed to Major Jackson, by his high character, scholarship, and brilliant career in Mexico. Other names were submitted by the Faculty of West Point, among which may be mentioned those of General George B. M'Clellan, General Reno, and General Rosecranz of the present Federal armies, and the distinguished General G. W. Smith of the Confederate army. But the high testimonials given to Major Jackson, and his birth as a Virginian, secured the preference of the visitors, who elected him by a unanimous vote. The fortunate issue of their selection illustrates the wisdom of that rule so often violated by the people of the South, to their own injury and reproach, to give the preference, in all appointments of trust, to citizens " to the manor born." The salary offered him was the modest sum of twelve hundred dollars, with commutation for quarters.

Jackson was no lover of garrison life, and accepted this

place promptly. He afterwards explained to an intimate friend, that while campaigning was extremely congenial to his tastes, the life of a military post in times of peace was just as repulsive; that he perceived the officers of the army usually neglected self-improvement, and rusted, in trivial amusements, at these fortresses; and that, on the recurrence of a war, the man who had turned, with a good military reputation, into the pursuits of a semi-civilian, and who thus vigorously prosecuted his mental improvement, might expect even more promotion in the army than those who had remained in the dull tread-mill of the garrison. But he declared that he knew war to be his true vocation, that his constant aim in life would ever be the career of the soldier, that he only accepted a scholastic occupation during peace, and that he was mainly induced to this by the military character of the school, and by the opportunities which, as professor of the art of the artillerist, he would enjoy of continuing his practical acquaintance with his chosen calling. He therefore repaired to the Military Institute in July, 1851; and in this honorable retirement spent nearly ten years.

The department of instruction committed to him, embraced the theory and practice of gunnery, and the sciences of mechanics, optics, and astronomy. These were taught in part by experiment, and in part by the application of mathematical analysis. To determine the theories of light and of motion, and the doctrines of astronomy, he employed the most abstruse and refined applications of geometry, and of the calculus of fluxions. The cadet was introduced from the simpler studies of pure mathematics to this arduous course, and, consequently, it was generally feared and disliked by him. Indeed, it may well be questioned, whether the minds of most youths have sufficient maturity, at the age when they usually complete their second year in the military school, to grapple with these discussions successfully. The major part of the classes were, probably, overcome by the demands made upon their powers of abstraction and logic, and floundered along, in the rear of their instructor, catching only occasional glimpses of the recondite truth. Major Jackson had never been a teacher, nor had the bustle of the life into which he plunged, at his first step from West Point, left him much opportunity to review these abstruse studies. When asked by a friend (after his success had long been assured) whether he had not been diffident of himself in undertaking so untried and arduous a course of instruction, he replied, "No; he expected to be able to study sufficiently in advance of his class; for *one could always do what he willed to accomplish.*"

His career as a professor was respectable, but never popular. None doubted the strength of his mind, nor his thorough scholarship, nor his conscientious industry, nor his justice and impartiality. But, while all his better students were accustomed to assert his thorough competency, discontent with his labors was not infrequent, both among his pupils and the *alumni* of the school. To all the better intellects of his class he communicated accurate scholarship, and the thoroughness of his mental drill was most useful. But the laggards lagged very far in the rear, and he was unsuccessful in bringing them up. This resulted, as has been already intimated, in part from the difficult nature of his department; but in part also from the constitution of Jackson's mind. He lacked some of the peculiar tact of the eminent teacher; and this was precisely because of the greatness of his endowments as a soldier and commander. The perceptions of his mind were so vigorous and distinct, and seized so exclusively on the main points of consideration, that all conclusions were with him perfectly defined. Hence there was, to him, but one formula of words which gave an exact expression to his thought. If one complained that his comprehension was imperfect, and asked for another statement, Jackson had no answer to make save to repeat his first formula. Now, to the leader, whose function it is to give orders to be obeyed, this trait is invaluable. In the teacher, whose work is to assist the comprehension of weaker minds, it is a defect. The very force and clearness with which Jackson's mind moved along from its premises to its conclusions, made it improbable that it would travel any second path, less plain than the one first perceived by his strong intuition. Hence, he lacked versatility and powers of elucidation. His intolerance of laziness, also, concurred to make the youth of defective comprehension dissatisfied with his teachings. But in the art of examining, one most essential to the efficiency of the teacher, he was eminent. His questions were always fair, always well chosen to eviscerate the subject, and always put in words carefully selected—words absolutely perspicuous, and true to the thought he aimed to propound, without the use of one superfluous phrase. If the pupil said he did not comprehend the point of the inquiry, Jackson was sure to repeat precisely the same words, with yet more deliberation. He held that when the form of the question was already perspicuous, an inability to comprehend it was, in fact, evidence of an inability to answer it. It may easily be conceived that this method was not likely to be peculiarly pleasing to an indolent youth, who, coming half prepared to his recitation, desired to extract a hint to assist his own ignorance, in the shape of a "leading question" from the teacher.

Another cause which detracted from Jackson's success as a teacher of the natural sciences, was the lack of practical skill in performing physical experiments. As has been remarked, he was not gifted with much of the minute manual dexterity which goes to the making of a skilful artisan or musician; nor had his mind that "mechanical turn" which Sir Walter Scott declared to be, in his opinion, the usual index of a little trumpery understanding. His experiments were not brilliant, and sometimes they resulted in ludicrous blunders, at which he laughed as heartily as any of the lads of his class.

One of the most painful consequences of his ill health was a weakness of the eyes, which rendered reading by any artificial light injurious, and threatened total blindness. This infirmity was not usually revealed by any visible inflammation, but rather affected the nerves of vision. He made it a conscientious duty, as well as found it a necessity, to forego all reading after nightfall, except the short portion of the Scriptures with which he invariably closed the day. But as the hours of daylight were necessarily much occupied with the duties of the class-room, the drill, and the Faculty, this deprivation of the quiet hours of night, which most scholars find so precious, was a serious difficulty, and imposed on him a peculiar method of study. During that part of the day which remained after his morning recitation, he carefully read over the text of the subjects which he wished to study for the next day, fixing the outlines of the discussion in his retentive memory. After devoting the remainder of his afternoon to domestic or social duties, he took his frugal supper, and proceeded to complete the studies of the morning without lamp, book or diagram, either pacing the floor of his chamber, or quietly seated with his face to the wall. In this mental review, he passed over every link of the logic of the discussion, completed its method in his own mind, and assured his perfect recollection of it, so as to be prepared to teach it on the morrow. This study completed in one or two hours, he pleasantly wheeled his chair towards the fire, removed the

9

injunction which he laid, at beginning, against addressing conversation to him, and passed into whatever topic engaged the
attention of his family. His instructions in the class-room were
accordingly conducted without ever referring to books, although
very closely conformed to them. Not only was his recollection
of their contents perfect, but even of the place upon the page
where each proposition might be found. Now, when his department of instruction is remembered, which involved the constant
use of the most refined mathematical analysis, and discussion
of figure, dimensions, motions, and relations of bodies in space,
which most minds comprehend with difficulty, even by the aid
of diagrams and models, the best scholar will best understand
how astonishing was the exercise of memory, abstraction,
imagination, and logical power in these studies. Some may
notice with incredulity the word imagination, included in this
enumeration, and may rejoin, that Jackson was notoriously
unimaginative and prosaic. If the name of this noble faculty,
the imagination, be degraded, as it is popularly, to express
the habitude of employing many tropes, either invented, or
recollected and borrowed, in the expression of the thoughts,
then it is conceded that he was not imaginative. He was
not prone to indulge his fancy; but, whether through inca-
pacity, the reader will perhaps discover. If, however, imagination is used in its proper sense, to express the creative power
of the mind, the ability to reproduce in the chambers of the
soul, and without the aid of sensation, the elements of conception, and to combine them, with a vivid distinctness, in new
relations, then Jackson had the faculty in great strength. And,
hence, it becomes true, that there is no better cultivation of this
faculty, than in the distinct comprehension of the subjects of the
applied mathematics, in their higher branches, by this purely
mental study. The great mathematician may not be accustomed

to bedizen his discourses with similes concerning purling brooks and silvery moonbeams; * but he can map out in conception the great circles of the heavens, equinoctial and ecliptic, with the orbits of the planets, and grasp the related movements of the worlds in his thought, as they wheel ih intricate, yet orderly labyrinths; a task under which the feeble mind of the poetaster collapses in hopeless confusion. The former knows how to body forth, with the distinctness of actual vision, the combinations of all the elements of thought which the mind gathers, in her illimitable excursions beyond the regions explored by the senses. He can so produce, before his thought, things that are not seen, and things that shall be, with the palpable reality of things that are seen, and of things that are, as to awaken by them all the strong emotions of the soul, which in natures less noble wait upon the actual information of sensation. And this is most essentially that faculty of the intellect which raises man from the sensuous animal toward the all-knowing Spirit, in whose image he is made. This is the faculty which, in the great statesman and commander, groups the data for the inspection of the profound judgment, which enables him for the clear comprehension of vast and multiplex affairs, and which ministers to his soul the stimulus of grand resolves.

One can now comprehend how valuable was the training which Jackson's mind received, in these meditations without book upon abstract truths, for his work as a soldier. Command over his attention was formed into a habit which no tempest of confusion could disturb. His power of abstraction became unrivalled. His imagination was trained and invigorated, until it became competent for grouping the most extensive and complex considerations. The power of his mind to endure its own ten-

* Purpureus, late qui splendeat, unus et alter
Assuitur pannus.   HOR. *Ad Pisones.*

sion, in the labors of reflection and volition, was drilled like the strength of the athlete. His self-concentration became unsurpassed. Having fixed upon his mind the positions of his forces and of the enemy's, and the relations of the routes, rivers, mountains and fortresses, by the inspection of a map; he could study all the possible combinations of movements as he rode, rapt in thought, at the head of his columns, with as much maturity as though alone in his chamber. Hence, in part, it resulted, that while no commander gave more scope to his own versatility and resource in the progress of events, there was never one whose foresight was more complete. Nothing emerged which had not been considered before in his mind; no possibility was overlooked; he was never surprised.

Jackson's life at the military school in Lexington was regular, and marked by few incidents. It was, however, the season when his personal character received its shape. It therefore appears a suitable place in this narrative, to proceed with its delineation, illustrating it by the few events of the period.

He was, without doubt, of a nature intensely ambitious and aspiring. The depression of his poverty and orphanage, in his youth, had only stimulated this passion in him. The evidences of its existence have been already given, in his zeal for military distinction during the Mexican War, and for scholarship at West Point, as well as in his ulterior purposes of life. To his intimate friend he once remarked, that the officer should always make the attainment of rank supreme, within honorable bounds, over every other consideration. Some sacrificed advancement to convenience, to secure service in a post where residence was pleasant, or to evade the authority of a harsh or unpopular superior; but his rule had been to secure promotion, if possible, at the cost of all such considerations; because, with the advancement in rank, the chances for distinction must usually improve. But his love of truth and rectitude was too strong and instinctive to permit his thirsting for any other than deserved distinction. He drew broadly the mark between notoriety and true fame. His passion deserved, as nearly as any man's could, the poet's description as —

"The last infirmity of noble minds."

Yet it was, as he himself avowed, an infirmity; that is to say, it was unquestionably an unsanctified principle, and inconsistent with Christian holiness — as it is in the breasts of all natural men. His Christian character was then in its germ, and the spirit of the military profession in which he had long been immersed, far away from all churches and their influences, blinded him to the nature of his aspirations. Very soon, he listened to no other than a sanctified ambition. In June, 1854, the Visitors of the University of Virginia held an election for Professor of Mathematics, to succeed Mr. Courtenay, himself an *alumnus* of West Point, who had long filled that place usefully and respectably. This University was the first in America, in the thoroughness of its instructions, and the dignities and emoluments of its professors. Jackson presented himself as a candidate, and procured many testimonials in support of his claims from persons of distinction, in which they concurred in ascribing to him competent scholarship, while they dwelt on his energy, devotion to duty, and courage. Among these were many teachers of the West-Point Academy, and Lieut.-Col. Robert E. Lee, then its Superintendent. When Jackson mentioned his project to his friend, he said to him: "Have you not departed here from what you told me, upon coming to this military school, was the purpose of your life?" [He referred to the declaration that war was his proper vocation.] Jackson, who seemed never to forget his own most casual remarks, or to overlook the obligation to maintain consistency with what he had once said, replied, "I avow that my views have changed." He then proceeded to explain, that while he should ever retain the same conviction concerning his own adaptation to the soldier's life, his convictions concerning war as a pathway to distinction were greatly modified; and that he would now by no means accept a commission in any war which the United States might wage, irrespective of its morality. He had never, he said, while an ungodly man, been inclined to tempt Providence by going in advance of his duty; he had never seen the day when he would have been likely to *volunteer* for a forlorn hope, although indifferent to the danger of a service to which he was legitimately *ordered*. But now, that he was endeavoring to live the life of faith, he would engage in no task in which he did not believe he should enjoy the Divine approbation; because, with this, he should feel perfectly secure under the disposal of Divine Providence; without it, he would have no right to be courageous. If, then, his country were assailed in such a way as to justify an appeal to defensive war in God's sight, he should desire to return to military life; but unless this happened, he should continue a simple citizen. But as such he regarded it as every man's duty to seek the highest cultivation of his powers, and the widest sphere of activity within his reach; and therefore he desired to be transferred to the State University. In this desire, however, he was disappointed; another gentleman was elected, and he acquiesced with perfect cheerfulness.

In politics, Jackson was always a Democrat. This term, in Virginia, always had reference more to the principles of Federal polity, the assertion of the sovereignty and reserved rights of the States, and the strict limitation of those of the Central Government, with the advocacy of a simple and unambitious exercise of its delegated powers, which were inculcated by Mr.

Jefferson, than to a government for the individual States, strictly popular, and founded on universal suffrage. To the latter, the most of the Virginian statesmen of the States' Rights school were no friends; and the State-constitution of South Carolina, the most thoroughly democratic of all the States as to Federal politics, is the farthest removed from literal democracy. But it is probable that Jackson would have accepted the name of a Democrat in more of its literality than the statesmen we have described. In Federal politics he was certainly a strict constructionist of the straitest sect. He voted with his party uniformly. To political discussions, in conversation, he was not given; and, while exceedingly exact in maintaining candor, he would usually content himself, when assailed by a political opponent, with a firm and polite declaration that he could not concur in his opinions, relapsing then into a silence from which no pertinacity could tempt him. With one or two intimates he conversed on public measures freely and with animation. And they always found his thoughts original and profound. He read little of the political journals; had there been no other reason for his disregard of them, his conscientious belief that it was his duty to employ his feeble eyesight in more important things, would have prevented him. His political opinions were, therefore, very far from being the echo of other men's. He approached each subject from his own point of view, and this was usually found to be as conclusive as it was original.

Unaffected modesty was imprinted upon his countenance, and every trait of his manners. No man ever lived who was further removed from egotism. Even his most intimate friend never heard him mention his own brilliant military career, of his own accord; nor did he ever speak of his family or kindred, many of whom, by their talents and social position, might have afforded topics for a boastful man. Yet his self-reliance was strong; as was proved by his favorite maxim. Mentioning to a friend, one day the omission in his academic education at West Point, which left him ignorant of Latin, he added: "But I think it probable that I shall some day repair this, and become as familiar with that language as with the Spanish." His friend replied, that perhaps he might acquire a partial knowledge of it by great effort; but it was generally held, that one who had not imprinted the forms of the language on the plastic memory in childhood, could never repair that loss, so as to become a familiar master of the tongue. He answered, "No; if I attempt it, I shall become a master of the language; I can accomplish whatever I will to do." When he was a candidate for the Chair of Mathematics in the University of Virginia, one of his few intimates suggested a fear that he had mistaken his own capacities, in seeking that place; because the method of teaching there was so largely by lecture; whereas his method was by the use of text-books; and he must be aware that he had little facility in extempore discourse. He acknowledged that he well knew that fact, and never dreamed of becoming eloquent; but, said he, "by effort I shall succeed as a lecturer, for I can accomplish anything I will to perform." It may be added, that there is no instance known in which he failed of realizing his boast.

The strength of his will was shown in his unfailing punctuality, in the vigor of his self-discipline — both bodily and mental, and in the energy of his actions. Among other improvements of his powers, he determined that he would acquire the art of speaking in public. To this end he became a member of the "Franklin Society," a respectable literary association in Lexington — endowed with a handsome hall and library — where the gentlemen of the town and of its scholastic institutions met for forensic debates, and other intellectual exercises. Here he was always a punctual attendant, and always spoke in his turn. His first essays were as painful to his audience as they probably were to himself; confused, halting, and frequently ending in an abrupt silence, when the power of controlling his thoughts for the time deserted him. Thus arrested by his own embarrassment, he would sit down, nowise abashed; and so powerful was the impress of his modesty and manly purpose upon his fellow-members, that none were ever seen to smile at these failures, although sometimes repeated a second and a third time, in the same evening. At a suitable moment he would rise again, and renew his effort, perhaps to end it with a similar painful halt. But before the close of the debate he would succeed in expressing the substance of what he had in his mind. By this dogged resolution, he gradually learned to control his diffidence, and became an effective speaker. His manner was rapid and emphatic, his thoughts marked by great directness, and his discourse began and ended with exceedingly little of exordium and peroration. So complete was his success, that he was said to have made, in a popular assemblage of his neighborhood, one of the most effective speeches ever heard. It was but ten minutes long; but it produced unanimity in an assembly before divided. He might have said, like the patriarch of Uz, "Unto me men gave ear, and waited, and kept silence at my counsel: after my words, they spake not again."

During nearly his whole life in Lexington, Jackson was a valetudinarian, and his regimen of body contributed no little to his character for singularity. He was ever scrupulously neat, and having, in one of his vacations, visited a hydropathic establishment in New England with supposed benefit, he became afterwards a still greater votary of cold water. He seems to have studied physiology and the laws of health in the same conscientious and business-like manner in which he performed all his tasks, and to have formed his own conclusions as to diet from

10

observing his own sensations. When these results were reached, he followed them out with an absolute self-denial, and without a particle of regard to their singularity. Yet, unlike most invalids, he was as catholic towards others as he was strict to himself; and, allowing each person to be a law unto himself, never denounced their indulgences as excesses, because they would have been such if committed by him. Some of his self-denying customs appeared very odd to those around him; but their defence may be found in the fact, that this temperance repaired an enfeebled constitution, and made it capable of great endurance. The most learned physiologists now admit, that the surd antipathies and appetencies of the corporeal tastes are often the most profoundly accurate indications of the wants of the system. Thus, when Jackson for a season refused the least trace of anything saccharine in his food, his conduct was probably wiser than that of the observers who called him whimsical. It is noteworthy that, at all times, he preferred the simplest food, and that he lived absolutely without any stimulant; using neither tea, coffee, tobacco, nor wine. This abstinence, however, was from principle, not from insensibility. Thus, reconnoitering the enemy's front on an occasion, in the winter of 1862, when prudence forbade the use of fire, he became so chilled, that his medical attendant, in real alarm for his safety, urged him to take some stimulant. There was nothing at hand except ardent spirits, and so he consented to take some. As he experienced a difficulty in swallowing it, and it seemed to produce the sensation of choking, his friend asked if it was very unpleasant. "No," said he; "no, I like it; I always did; *and that is the reason I never use it.*" At another time he took a long and exhausting walk with a brother officer, who was also a temperate and God-fearing man. The walk terminating at his quarters, he proposed to General Jackson, in consequence of their fatigue, to join him in a glass of brandy and water: "No," said he; "I am much obliged, but I never use it; I am more afraid of it than of Federal bullets." What a rebuke is here to that vain conceit and pride of character, which resents the friendly caution, and the call to watchfulness as disparaging to one's strength. This mighty man of God acknowledged that he was afraid of temptation. "When he was weak, then was he strong." How many a young man would have escaped the drunkard's grave if he had acted on this manly philosophy! Jackson always professed his ability to exert an absolute control over his appetites; and declared that he could feel little sympathy with suffering in others, which was caused by self-indulgence. When the people about him complained of headaches, or other consequences of imprudence, he would say: "Do as I do; govern yourself absolutely, and you will not suffer. My head never aches; if a thing disagrees with me, I never eat it."

His hours were early and regular; and rare must be the social obligation which induced him to depart from them. For in all these regulations, imposed on himself for the preservation of his health, he was accustomed to argue, that having determined any rule to be necessary, he was under a moral obligation to observe it. In vain did any friend plead that the one instance of relaxation in his system could not possibly work an appreciable injury. His uniform answer was: "Perfectly true; but it would become a precedent for another, and thus my rule would be broken down, and health would be injured, which would be a sin." Thus he carried out his self-denial in the use of his eyesight so rigidly, that even a letter received on Saturday night, if it was only one of compliment or friendship, was not read by him until Monday morning; for his Sabbaths were sacredly reserved from the smallest secular distractions. If his friend exclaimed, "Surely, Major, your eyes would not be injured by the reading of one letter now;" his answer was, "I suppose they would not; but if I read this letter to-night, which it is not truly necessary to do, I shall be tempted to read something else that interests me to-morrow night, and the next, so that my rule will be broken down. Then my eye-sight will undoubtedly be injured. But if I thus incapacitate myself, by acts not really necessary, for my duties to my employers and my pupils in the institute, I shall commit sin." And once, when his most intimate friend knew that he had received a letter of affection late on Saturday night, the question was asked, as they were walking to church on Sabbath morning, "Major, surely you have read your letter?" "Assuredly not," said he. "Where is it?" asked his friend. "Here," said he, tapping the pocket of his coat. "What obstinacy!" exclaimed his friend. "Do you not know that your curiosity to learn its contents will distract your attention from divine worship, far more than if you had done with reading it? Surely, in this case, to depart from your rule would be promotive of a true Sabbath observance, instead of injurious to it?" "No," answered he, quietly, "I shall make the most faithful effort I can to govern my thoughts, and guard them from unnecessary distraction; and as I do this from a sense of duty, I expect the divine blessing on it." Accordingly, he afterwards declared, that his soul was on that day unusually composed and devout, and his spiritual enjoyment of the public and private worship of the day peculiarly rich.

Under a similar sense of moral responsibility, he acquitted himself punctually of all social obligations. When a single man, he went into society as frequently as other young men of regular habits, saying that he was constrained to do so by a sense of justice and humanity; for when an acquaintance took the trouble to prepare an entertainment, and honored him with an invitation, to attend, where no duty interposed, was the only equitable return due for the kindness. In such assemblages he was never entirely at ease; but it may be said with truth, that there, as everywhere, his courtesy was perfect. No attention due to the host and hostess was ever omitted; no salutation ever failed to meet the most polite return; the very slightest favor never went without thanks. No female ever came short of her fair share of the attentions of the other sex, that he did not at once relinquish his own preferences, and devote himself to her entertainment. But when his early hour of retirement came, no allurements could detain him; and sometimes the ingenious plans laid by fair enemies to keep him, which he was too courteous to break through, placed him for a moment in amusing embarrassment. One of his most rigid rules was, never to eat a morsel after his frugal supper. Hence, in the refreshments offered at a later hour, he refused to have any part, to the distress of his hostesses. Amidst the clatter of china and conversation, and the sparkle of wines and ices, the tall form of the Major stood firm; polite, yet constrained; in the gay throng, but not of it. When a friend urged him at least to avoid the awkwardness of the position for himself and the hostess, by seem ing to participate, his answer was that he did not consider it truthful to seem to do what he was not really doing. Indeed, his care not to transgress the strict truth seemed to others excessive. He never talked at random, even in the most unguarded moment, or on the most trivial subject. All his statements were well-considered. On rare occasions something might have escaped him which he regarded as an exception; and then, it mattered not how unessential the subject of it might be, and how impossible it might appear that any actual evil could emerge out of his mistake, he made it a part of the serious business of the next day to give a full explanation.

His person was tall, erect, and muscular, with the large hands and feet characteristic of all his race. His bearing was peculiarly English; and therefore, in the somewhat free society of America, was regarded as constrained. Every movement was quick and decisive; his articulation was not rapid, but distinct and emphatic, and, accompanied by that laconic and perspicuous phrase to which it was so well adapted, it often made the impression of curtness. He practised a military exactness in all the courtesies of good society. Different opinions existed as to his comeliness, because it varied so much with the condition of his health and animal spirits. His brow was exceedingly fair and expansive; his eyes were blue, large, and expressive, reposing usually in placid calm, but able none the less to flash lightning. His nose was Roman, and exceedingly well chiselled; his cheeks ruddy and sunburnt; his mouth firm and full of meaning; and his chin covered with a beard of comely brown. The remarkable characteristic of his face was the contrast between its sterner and its gentler moods. As he accosted a friend, or dispensed the hospitalities of his own house, his serious, constrained look gave place to a smile, so sweet and sunny in its graciousness, that he was another man. But hearty laughter, especially, was a complete metamorphosis. His blue eyes then danced, and his countenance rippled with a glee and *abandon* literally infantile. This smile was indescribable to one who never saw it. Had there been a painter with genius subtile enough to fix upon his canvas, side by side, the spirit of the countenance with which he caught the sudden jest of a child romping on his knees, and that with which, in the crisis of battle, he gave his generals the sharp and strident command, " Sweep the field with the bayonet!" he would have accomplished a miracle of art, which the spectator could scarcely credit as true to nature.

In walking, his step was long and rapid, and at once suggested the idea of the dismounted horseman. It has been said that he was an awkward rider, but incorrectly. A sufficient evidence of this is the fact that he was never thrown. It is true that on the march, when involved in thought, he was heedless of the grace of his posture; but in action, or as he rode with bare head along his column, acknowledging the shouts which rent the skies, no figure could be nobler than his. His judgment of horses was excellent, and it was very rare that he was not well mounted.

Such was the man as he left the quiet walks of the Military Academy, in the spring of 1861, to begin a career which was to fill the world with his fame. Most of those who were conversant with him were unconscious of his power. A few intimates, indeed, were well aware of his capacity, and predicted for him an exalted destiny (for which they were usually held to be as singular as Jackson himself); but, with the many, he passed for a sensible, odd man, of undoubted courage, energy, and goodness; competent to a respectable success in anything to which he might bend his determined will, but to nothing more. Yet the cadets of his school gloried in his military prowess, of discussing which they were never weary; and the universal feeling among them was, that if ever they were called into actual service, he was the man whom they would prefer for their leader. The incorrect estimate which the many formed of him can be readily explained. Major Jackson was a man whom it was no easy matter to know; not because he sought to hide himself from scrutiny, nor because he was in the slightest degree covert in what he said or did, but because there was a breadth and depth of character about him, that would never be suspected by the superficial and bigoted. He was pre-eminently modest, and inexpressibly opposed to self-display, and equally consider-

ate of the taste and character of those with whom he held intercourse. He moulded his share of that intercourse accordingly.
His scrupulous and delicate politeness made it always his aim
to render others easy and comfortable in his presence. His
first thought on meeting with them seemed to be — what subjects
of conversation would be most familiar to their thoughts, and
most consonant to their feelings. He never introduced a subject merely because it was one with which he was most at home,
or on which he could best exhibit his talents, or parade his
information. With a clergyman or lady, he never introduced
party politics or military science. Having led the conversation, with polite deference to that topic upon which his guest
seemed best fitted to shine, he became usually an attentive but
almost silent listener, and made no disclosure of his own stores
of knowledge, or of profound and original reflections on the
same subject; although they were often far more complete than
those of the person whom he thus accepted as an instructor.
And had not subsequent facts evinced his superiority, his acquaintance would have felt it almost incredible that one who
was so well qualified to speak with confidence, should so entirely
suppress the desire to speak. Thus many a minister of the
gospel has been led by him to speak on ethical, ecclesiastical,
or theological subjects, and has carried away the impression
that the modest soldier, although almost ignorant of the alpha-
bets of those sciences, had at least the merit of an earnest
appetite for the knowledge of them, when in truth Jackson had
read as much upon them as he had, and with more close attention, and possessed more matured opinions concerning them.
The young person of literary tastes would be led to talk of the
British classics, or the great writers of romance, and would
leave him with the belief that he was innocent of all classical
reading, except the great masters of holy writ; for his honesty

was so strict, that if his knowledge of any author or literary fact were taken for granted, he would never rest in a tacit acquiescence, but would stop his interlocutor to undeceive him, by declaring his ignorance. Yet, while his feeble eye-sight and conscientious improvement of time had forbidden a promiscuous course of literary reading, he had studied the most important poets and historians with far more thorough judgment and taste than he permitted his young friends to divine.

In the sphere which of right belonged to him, he rarely if ever asked advice. No man knew his proper place better, or held it more tenaciously; and no man ever accorded this right to others more promptly or scrupulously. As a member and officer of the Church, he was eminently deferential to his pastor, as his superior officer. But, as a commander in camp, he would no more defer to the judgment of that pastor, than to that of the humblest of his own soldiers.

Americans being inordinately given to speech-making — an art which has acquired importance from their popular institutions — have set an overweening value upon eloquence as a test of ability; but Jackson professed to be no talker. He had no peculiar gift for teaching; yet teaching was, at Lexington, his profession. In finding a solution of the erroneous estimate of Jackson to which we have referred, something is also to be attributed to the character of the little society in which he moved. It was cultivated, but limited in extent; and, accordingly, it had its own closely-defined standard, by comparison with which every man was tried. In a society more cosmopolitan, such characters as Jackson are less apt to be misapprehended, because it consists not of one, but of many coteries, and because contact with diversified forms of talent and cultivation, gives breadth and tolerance to the views. This is but saying, in substance, what the voice of Fame has since pronounced, that

11

the wider the arena on which he acted, the greater his capacity
appeared.

But there were always a few, and they the most competent to
understand a gifted nature, who declared Jackson to be a man
of mark. To these chosen intimates he unbosomed himself,
modestly, yet without reserve. His views of public affairs were
broad, and elevated far above the scope of the party journals
which assumed to dictate public opinion. His mind was one
which would have made him a subtile and profound jurist. The
few who attributed to him this type of intellect, had their estimate fully sustained, by the manner in which he discussed those
numerous questions of a judicial nature which claim the attention of the leader of great armies. In the interpretation of
orders and army regulations; in the settlement of rank between
competing claimants; in the proceedings of courts-martial; in
the discrimination between military and civil jurisdiction, which
is often so difficult; his mind always approached the question
from an original point of view, and rarely did it fail to be
decisive to every attentive understanding. But it was especially
in the discussion of military affairs that the mastery of his
genius appeared. When these topics were introduced, his mind
assumed its highest animation, he disclosed a knowledge which
surprised his auditors, and his criticisms were profound. One
instance may be noted among many. In the summer of 1856,
he employed his long vacation in a European tour, in which he
visited England, France, and Switzerland. During this journey
he carefully examined the field of Waterloo, and traced out
upon it the positions of the contending armies. When he
returned home, he said that although Napoleon was the greatest
of commanders, he had committed an error in selecting the
Château of Hougomont as the vital point of attack upon the
British line, it should have been the village of Mont St. Jean.

This opinion has subsequently been corroborated by high authority in the military art.

But the most important feature of Jackson's character was the religious; and this is the most appropriate topic for illustration at this place, because it was mainly developed at Lexington. His peculiar posture towards Christianity upon coming there, has been described. He had been baptized, upon profession of his faith, by an Episcopal clergyman, but refused to be considered as committed to Episcopacy. In this state of opinion he had been admitted, at least once, to the communion of the Lord's Supper. While his religious knowledge was defective, and his Christian character consequently failed at that time in symmetry, it was sincere and honest, and, from the purity of his morals and his devotional habits, it was consistent.

Upon removing to Lexington, where the Christian people were divided among the Presbyterians, Episcopalians, Wesleyan Methodists, and Baptists, he at first attended the public worship of all their churches indiscriminately, listening with exemplary respect and attention. But after a time he discontinued this promiscuous worship. The pastor of the Presbyterians was the Rev. William S. White, D. D., a venerable man, who speedily became so intimately related to the religious life and tenderest affections of the great soldier, that an allusion to his devout eloquence, genial heart, and apostolic piety, is unavoidable in this narrative. Jackson sought an introduction to him in the autumn of 1851, and very soon paid him a confidential visit in his study, to lay before him his spiritual interests. He told him the steps he had taken, and declared his hope of his acceptance with God through our Lord Jesus Christ; but said that he had not then been able to determine with what branch of the Church to connect himself. Popery he had examined under the most favorable auspices, and he had been constrained to reject it as

an apostasy from the system of Holy Writ. Of Episcopacy he
had learned something from his friends Colonel Taylor and the
Rev. Mr. Parks, whose religious principles and feelings he, to a
great extent, approved and embraced; but with some of the
features of that system he was not satisfied. He had given
equal consideration to the claims and peculiarities of other
branches of the Church. He now, for the first time, had a fair
opportunity to observe the genius and working of Presbyterianism under its better auspices; and he found its worship
congenial to his principles, and desired to know more of its
character.

The result of his inquiries was, that on the 22d of November,
1851, he was received, by profession of his faith, as a member
of that church. His accession in that mode was an avowal that
he came in, not as one transferred from some other denomination in the visible church to the Presbyterian, but as a new
recruit from the world without. He did not, however, take this
step until he had thoroughly studied the catechisms and Confession of Faith, which constitute the doctrinal standards of that
church. To some things embodied in these standards he strongly
objected; and these objections he stated with the utmost clearness and frankness, not only to the pastor but to several intelligent laymen of the church. His chief difficulty was found in
the great truth of God's absolute sovereignty, in His purposes
regarding the calling and government of His church. His
opinions, at that time, leaned strongly to the system known as
Arminianism, nor were they immediately changed. Being
informed, however, that the Presbyterian Church expected uni-
formity of belief on these points, of none but its officers, and
only exacted of its private members a profession of those vital
doctrines of redemption, in which all Christians agree, he preferred to adopt it as his own. Many months after, in conversa-

tion with an intimate friend, he disclosed so serious a difficulty
in his views concerning the doctrines of God's decree and
sovereign providence, that the latter concluded with the half-
jocular remark, — "Major, if you have these opinions, you had
better become a Methodist." This suggestion, the intense honesty of his nature made him take seriously; and he answered,
"If you think so, then come with me, and let us see Dr. White
about it." They went to the pastor's study, and had a long
interview, as candid as it was kind. At the end of it the latter
remarked, "Well, Major, although your doctrinal theory is not
in perfect accord with ours, yet in your practical life you are so
good a Presbyterian, that I think you may safely remain where
you are." In this conclusion he acquiesced; and it was not very
long before all his difficulties gave way before his honest, persistent, and prayerful inquiries. He became one of the firmest
though least bigoted advocates of the Calvinistic as distinguished
from the Arminian scheme.

In these proceedings, his candid and eclectic spirit was characteristic, and honorable to himself, as well as a valuable testimony to the denomination which he selected. It would be hard
to find a man reared in a Christian country, more uncommitted
than he was, by education and association, to any sectarian
preference. His conscientiousness would not permit him to
decide the matter as so many do, by the accidents of social
relations, convenience, or taste. He made his church connection
the subject of deliberate comparison, serious study, and prayer;
and what Christian can justify himself for acting in any other
way? It may be assumed, therefore, that Jackson's conclusion
was dispassionate, and that he believed it to be the result of the
force of truth. To make this remark in an aggressive party
spirit against other denominations which Jackson passed over,
in selecting the Presbyterian, would be most inconsistent with

his liberal and just temper towards them all; for he was as catholic in his heart as he was decided in his principle. But to demand the suppression of this fact in his life would be yet more invidious on the other hand. That would be an extravagant temper indeed which would impose, in narrating the truth, a reserve which left upon Jackson's memory the implication that he was either not honest, or not intelligent in his ecclesiastical opinions. It is hoped that Presbyterians will not be so foolish as to claim that all the good and great are of their communion, or to hold that its true honor depends upon man, however exalted he may be.

It may be safely declared, that, from the beginning, Jackson's religious character was strictly sincere, and conscientious, above that of most Christians. This was a trait to be expected from the operation of the Holy Spirit upon a nature so decided in temper and clear in judgment as his. But his opinions concerning Christian duties were not wholly free from defect. It would have been wonderful indeed if they had been perfectly correct, when he was reared with so little instruction, and when his manhood had been moulded under the very peculiar moral influences of the military caste. But his exactness in performing what he perceived to be his duty, was always the same; some things which he afterwards saw to be obligatory, he had at first failed to see in this light. His aspirations for honorable fame were at first less chastened than became a saint. His deliberately expressed feelings concerning the resenting of injuries, were inconsistent with those inculcated by the law of love, as understood by the best Christians. While his conviction of the sacredness of the Sabbath was, from the beginning, unusually clear, his interpretation of the exceptions made for " works of necessity " differed somewhat from those current among evangelical Christians. But never was the healthy and cleansing influence of a right conscience over the under standing, more clearly displayed than in him. The head could not long remain misguided, when presided over by so guileless a heart. He very soon attained the most firm and distinct perceptions of duty, which differed usually from those of the great body of God's best people, only in being more strict. One of the most marked traits of his religious character then, was conscientiousness. It ruled in every act and word; in things great, and things minute; in his social relations, and his most unrestrained remarks; in the regulation of his appetites; in his observance of the courtesies of life; in the disposition of his time and money. Duty was with him the ever present and supreme sentiment. Such was his dread of its violation, that no sin appeared to him small; and the distinction between great and little obligations, which most Christians make the pretext for a certain remissness of conduct, seemed scarcely to have any place in his mind. To him, all duties were great, however trivial the affairs about which they were concerned, in human judgment. The prominent trait of his mind was the sentiment of reverence directed supremely to God, as the standard of perfection, the rightful source of all authority, and the embodi-ment of infinite greatness. It was this sentiment, in its lower aspects, which constituted his remarkable spirit of subordination. As God's nature and will were to him the standard of that which is right, and the fountain-head of obligation, so, whenever he found a fellow-creature clothed by the sanction of right, with legitimate authority over his conscience, he honored and obeyed him within his proper sphere, as a bearer of a delegated portion of the majesty of heaven; and his respect became a religious sentiment. Hence as a soldier no man was so prompt and exact in his military obedience; as a citizen none cherished so sacred a reverence for law, and for the offices of its magistrates

As a Christian layman, he honored and obeyed the pastor who had care of souls; and, while there was no man so little priest-ridden, there was none who so punctually paid to the ministers of religion, the captains in God's sacramental host, however humble in person and talents, deference for their work's sake.

Instances of his conscientiousness have already been given, but many others may be added. His convictions of the sin committed by the Government of the United States, in the unnecessary transmission of mails, and the consequent imposition of secular labor on the Sabbath day, upon a multitude of persons, were singularly strong. His position was, that if no one would avail himself of these Sunday mails, save in cases of true and unavoidable necessity, the letters carried would be so few that the sinful custom would speedily be arrested, and the guilt and mischief prevented. Hence, he argued, that as every man is bound to do whatever is practicable and lawful for him to do, to prevent the commission of sin, he who posted or received letters on the Sabbath day, or even sent a letter which would occupy that day in travelling, was responsible for a part of the guilt. It was of no avail to reply to him, that this self-denial on the part of one Christian would not close a single post-office, nor arrest a single mail-coach in the whole country. His answer was, that unless some Christians would begin singly to practise their exact duty, and thus set the proper example, the reform would never be begun; that his responsibility was to see to it that he, at least, was not *particeps criminis;* and that whether others would co-operate, was their concern, not his. Hence, not only did he persistently refuse to visit the post-office on the Sabbath day, to leave or receive a letter, but he would not post a letter on Saturday or Friday which, in regular course of transmission, must be travelling on Sunday, except in cases of high necessity. And believing, as he did, in the special superintendence of Providence over all affairs, and His favorable oversight of the concerns of those who live in His fear, he delighted to recount the fact, that God had always protected him and his affairs in this particular, so that he had never suffered any loss or real inconvenience by these self-imposed delays. One instance he related with peculiar satisfaction. It was, that proceeding on the Sabbath day to Divine worship with a Christian associate, his friend proposed to apply at the post-office for his letters, on the plea that there was probably a letter from a dear relative, whose health was in a most critical state, and might, for aught he knew, demand his immediate aid. But he dissuaded him by the argument, that the necessity for departing in this from the Sabbath rest was not known, but only suspected. They went together to church, and enjoyed a peaceful day. On the morrow it was ascertained there was a letter to his friend, from his afflicted relative, announcing a most alarming state of disease; but there was also a later one, arrived that day, correcting all the grounds of distress, and stating that the health of the sufferer was restored. "Now," said Jackson, "had my friend causelessly dishonored the Sabbath, he would have suffered a day of harrowing anxiety, which the next day's news would have shown utterly groundless; but God rewarded him for his obedience, by mercifully shielding him from this gratuitous suffering: He sent him the antidote along with the pain."

He always acted on the principle that he was as really bound to report the condition of himself and his family to his pastor, as the latter was to minister to their spiritual wants. In passing through several seasons of domestic sorrow, he called for his instructions and sympathy with equal delicacy and promptitude. Again, he called one evening to say to Dr. White, that in the sermon preached the preceding Sabbath, he had not been able to discover whether the discussion of a certain duty, was to be

12

regarded in the light of mere advice, or as authoritative. If it was the former, he was not clear that he should regard the duty as obligatory on him; but if the latter, then whatever his personal preferences might be, he should feel bound to comply with it, inasmuch as he could not plead conscience against doing it. Thus his pastor was to him the spiritual officer, under whose "orders" he was, and whom he therefore felt bound to obey, in all his admissible commands, for the sake of the authority and discipline of the spiritual host.

He engaged one day, with a Christian friend, in a conversation on the Hebrews' system of religious oblations, and was much interested in the assertion that, while the tithe was no longer enjoined, by express precept, on God's people under the new dispensation, the usage of worshipping God with stated offerings of our substance was in no degree abrogated; and that the tenth was probably, in most cases, a suitable proportion to be self-imposed by Christians, for this voluntary thank-offering. After much inquiry and friendly discussion, Jackson closed the conversation. The next day, on meeting his friend, he said that he had convinced him of a duty, not hitherto as fully understood as it should have been; and, with his usual courtesy, thanked him for the benefit thus conferred. Thenceforward he scrupulously gave a tenth of his whole income to charitable uses (until he adopted a greatly enlarged ratio).

The Presbyterians and other evangelical churches in Virginia, have long had the usage of meeting about the middle of the week in a social assemblage, under the superintendence of the pastor, for the especial purposes of concerted prayer and praise. This custom has had the happiest effects, in promoting devotional habits, and fraternity and sympathy, among the Christian people. Jackson was, of course, from the beginning, the most punctual of attendants on these meetings. The prayers were usually offered, under the pastor's direction, by the elders of the church, or other experienced Christians. Dr. White took occasion, in his Sabbath instructions, to enforce the advantages of these meetings, and said something of the duty of those who could appropriately lead the devotions of others, to render their aid in that way, overcoming, if necessary, false shame. In the course of the week, Jackson called to ask him if he thought him one of the persons to whom the latter exhortation was applicable. He proceeded to say that he was unused to all forms of continuous public speaking; that his embarrassment was extreme, especially upon so sacred a topic, in expressing himself before a crowd; and that he had therefore doubted whether it was for edification for him to attempt the leading of others at the throne of grace. Yet, he knew that, inasmuch as these concerts of prayer were of eminent utility, the general duty of participating in their exercises was indisputable, as to Christian heads of families, and other suitable persons. "You," he said, "are my pastor, and the spiritual guide of the church; and if you think it my duty, then I shall waive my reluctance, and make the effort to lead in prayer, however painful." He closed by authorizing him to call upon him for that service, if he thought proper. And his diffidence in all this was so clearly unaffected, that no mortal could have mistaken it. After a time, the pastor called upon him to pray. He obeyed, but with an embarrassment so great, that the service was almost as painful to his brethren as it obviously was to himself. The invitation was not repeated for a number of weeks, when, meeting Dr. White, he noted that fact, and indicated that he supposed the motive for sparing him was an unwillingness to inflict distress through his excessive diffidence. The good minister could not but admit that he had thought it best not to exact so painful a duty of him, lest his comfort in the meeting should be seriously marred. "Yes," said Jackson, "but my comfort or discomfort is not the question; if it is my duty to lead my brethren in prayer, then I must persevere in it, until I learn to do it aright; and I wish you to discard all consideration for my feelings in the matter." He was again called on; he succeeded in curbing his agitation in a good degree; and, after a time, became as eminent for the gift, as he was for the grace of prayer.

Another instance of his courage in doing good was given soon after he connected himself with the Presbyterian Church. Visiting his native country during a vacation, he perceived that infidel opinions were prevalent among many, and had infected several of his friends and relatives. He was anxious to do something to remedy this evil, but knew not what was best. He held private conversations with some, and gave tracts to others, but this only increased his anxiety to attempt something on a larger scale. He accordingly determined to announce a brief course of public lectures on the evidences of Christianity, notwithstanding his diffidence and inexperience as a public speaker. They were delivered in a church in the village of Beverley, Randolph county, where his only sister resided; and as he declared, his success greatly exceeded his expectations. It may be supposed that curiosity to see the novel spectacle of the young soldier and professor discussing such a theme, attracted many. But his argument was declared to be excellent, and his manner far from bad, by the most competent hearers. Doubtless the impression of his evident modesty, sincerity, and courage, was more valuable than would have been the most learned discussion from a professed divine. The interest aroused in his mind concerning the evidences of Christianity led him, on his return to Lexington, to ask of Dr. White leave to collect a class of young men for the study of this subject in connexion with the Sabbath school. This class he taught with his accustomed earnestness and fidelity, and several of them served under him as soldiers in the war.

He next proposed to gather the African slaves of the village in the afternoon of the Sabbath, and speedily he had a flourishing school of eighty or a hundred pupils, with twelve teachers; the latter of whom were recruited from among the educated ladies and gentlemen of the place. This he continued to teach successfully from 1855 until the spring of 1861; when he reluctantly left it to enter the army. And to the end of his life, he inquired of every visitor at the camp from his church at home, how his black Sabbath-school was progressing; and if the answer was favorable, he did not fail to express his gratitude. But no other person could sustain it as efficiently as he did. His health required him to spend most of his vacations in journeys; and, upon setting out, he was accustomed to leave his school in the charge of some member of the church, for the time. On his return, he usually found it dwindled from eighty to fifty scholars; but his efforts soon restored it to its wonted prosperity. His method was to make the sessions extremely short, continuing from three P. M. to a quarter to four P. M. At a quarter to three the bell was rung, and precisely at three o'clock he began. The exercises were first, singing and prayer, and then a brief, pointed, and perspicuous exposition of an assigned passage of the Scriptures, addressed by him to the whole school. The several teachers then took charge of their classes, and devoted the rest of the session to teaching them orally the Shorter Catechism, or some other suitable formula of truth. The exercises ended with the singing of a hymn, previously committed to memory, by the whole school, and a short prayer. Once a month he made a report of the punctuality and demeanor of each pupil, calling in person at the houses of their masters for this purpose; and if any servant was frequently absent or inattentive, he was sure to inquire into the cause during the week.

The African character is ever dilatory. In his native jungle, the negro has no conception whatever of the value of time; and in his civilized state, he retains too much of this weakness. Hence, at all religious meetings which they frequent, they are usually found arriving at every moment, from the beginning to the very close. Jackson speedily began to experience the same annoyance, and the lack of punctuality was unhappily countenanced by some of his teachers. He gave notice that the bell would ring the next Sabbath a quarter of an hour before the opening as usual, and that when the assigned moment arrived, he should lock the doors and proceed immediately to the duties of the school. Accordingly, the next Sunday, precisely at three o'clock, he locked the doors and commenced. Knocks were unheeded; and when, at the conclusion, the doors were opened, there was found a group in the street, consisting of a number of servants and a few mortified-looking ladies and gentlemen, whom he saluted as he passed on his way with his customary politeness. There was no more lack of punctuality.

While thus exacting in his discipline of the school, he was rendered extremely popular among all the more serious servants by these labors for their good. He was indeed the black man's friend. His prayers were so attractive to them, that a number of those living in his quarter of the town, petitioned to be admitted on Sabbath nights, along with his own servants, to his evening domestic worship. Before making them an answer, he called on Dr. White and stated their request to him, asking his sanction, and declaring that the assent of the masters of those servants must, of course, be also a necessary condition of his gratifying them. The approbation of the pastor and the masters was gladly given.

To his own slaves, he was a methodical and exact, but conscientious master. Absolute obedience was the rule of his household; and if he found chastisement was necessary to secure this, it was faithfully administered. He required all his slaves to attend the domestic worship of his family morning and evening; and succeeded, where so many Christian masters have found entire success apparently impossible, in securing the presence of every one. After his household was scattered by his absence in the camp, he found time to write to those to whom his servants were hired, inquiring into their spiritual state, urging their employers to see that they attended church regularly, and giving minute directions for their welfare. On hearing of the death of one of his female servants, he wrote expressing his gratitude for the attentions bestowed upon her in her illness and at her burial.

It may be accepted as a significant dispensation of Providence, that Jackson, the best type of the Christian master in the South, should be made the hero of this war for Southern independence. The people of the Southern States will cheerfully consent that this holy man, with his strong convictions of the righteousness and beneficence of their form of society, may stand forth to the world as their exemplar. He had no pretensions to a righteousness more righteous than that of prophets, apostles, and Jesus Christ. His understanding was too honest to profess belief in God's inspired Word, and yet hold that relation to be a sinful one, which Moses expressly allowed and legislated for; which the Bible saints sustained to their fellow-men; which the Redeemer left prominent and unrepealed amidst his churches, as well as in secular society; and which the apostles continued to sanction, by admitting those who held it, without any disclaimer, or pledge of reformation or repentance, to church membership and church office. His conscience was too sensitive to tolerate known sin, at any prompting of conscience or interest. It will be a difficult problem for those who revile us, if they remember how gregarious vices are, and how surely even a sin of ignorance pollutes the soul and grieves the Holy Spirit, to explain how this most decided of slaveholders came to be so eminent for sanctity, and so richly crowned with the noblest graces and joys which God ever conferred on man. Especially, let the happy condition which the benevolence of such masters confers on their servants, be contrasted with that degradation and ruin to which our enemies intentionally consign them. Southern masters, with very few exceptions, provide generously for the welfare of their servants, at the prompting of affection, conscience, self-respect, and interest, while they exact only a moderate labor; and many of them, like Jackson, strive conscientiously for their spiritual good. Northern anti-slavery men, under the pretence to the negro of being his disinterested liberator, seduce him from his protector, and leave him, without provision for body or soul, either to perish in pestilential indolence, or to wear out his frame in the severest toils, in entrenchments or factories, under the compulsion not of stripes, but of a bayonet in the hands of a brutal foreign mercenary. Not seldom does this hypocrisy find its candid and exact expression, in the conduct of the more shameless of our invaders; when the same men, after wheedling the servants with fine promises, pretended sympathies, and the terms "brother, sister," pass from their cabins to the master's dwelling, to insult him with the declaration that they despise the Africans as much as they hate him, and have no other purpose in seducing them from his service except to "humble his Virginian aristocracy."

On the 26th of December, 1857, Major Jackson was unanimously elected a deacon of his church. The reader will bear in mind that the Presbyterians, following what they believe to be the primitive institute of the Apostles, assign the care of souls to the order of Presbyters alone, of whom some rule only, and some also labor in word and doctrine; while the Deacon's function is "to serve tables," or, in other words, to collect and disburse the money and alms of the church, and to distribute to the destitute. This humble office Jackson promptly assumed at the call of his brethren, and fulfilled its duties with his accustomed fidelity. He was the best deacon the church had. The system of that congregation concerning almsgiving was unusually complete. Monthly, the deacons met for consultation, and the distribution of their labors. Every two months, a collection was solicited from all the people for some charitable or pious use; and for this purpose, to each deacon was allotted a district, in which he visited personally every adult worshipper, or at least every householder, at his own home, explained the object to be furthered, and received the gifts of the benevolent. At the monthly meetings, Jackson was always present. His idea of the duty was aptly expressed by his reply to a brother deacon, who excused his absence by saying that he had not time to attend. "I see not," said he, "how, at that hour, we can possibly lack time for this meeting, or can have time for anything else, seeing it is set apart for this business." His regularity in calling upon the pastor to relate the result of his diaconal labors, or, in his phrase, "to report," was perfectly military. Indeed his conception of the matter was, that he came to him, as his superior, for his orders. At one collection the gifts were solicited for the American Bible Society, and Jackson sallied forth, armed with the list of names for his district, furnished him by the clerk of the congregation. When he came to the pastor to report, he had a number of additional names written in pencil-marks at the foot

13

of his list, with small sums opposite to them. "What are these?" asked the good Doctor. "Those at the top," said Jackson, "are your regulars, and those below are my militia." On examining the names, they were found to be those of the free blacks of the quarters, all of whom he had visited in their humble dwellings, and encouraged to give a pittance of their earnings to print Bibles. He argued that these small sums were better spent thus than in drink or tobacco; that the giving of them would elevate their self-respect, and enhance their own interest in the Holy Book; and that they being indebted to it as well as others, should be taught to help in diffusing it.

There was another trait of his religious character so conspicuous, that it demands here full illustration, — his constant recognition of a particular Providence. No man ever lived who seemed to have a more practical and living sense of this truth of Christianity. He earned, indeed, thereby, the title of superstitious, from some of the unthinking, and of fatalist from others. But he was neither: his belief in the control of Divine Providence was most rational and scriptural. The only difference between him and other enlightened Christians here was, that his faith was "the substance of things anticipated, and the evidence of things not seen;" while theirs is, so largely, an impractical theory. That doctrine is, that God's special providence is over all his creatures and all their actions, to uphold and govern them; and that it is over His children for their good only. By that omniscient and almighty control all events are ordered, permitted, limited, and overruled. There is no creature so great as to resist its power, none so minute as to evade its care. But yet, by a mode which is perhaps beyond the cognizance of the human reason, it secures the action designed by God's intelligent purpose, from each created agent, in strict conformity with its nature and powers. The Christian doctrine of Providence does not reduce the universe into a pantheistic machine, with God for the sole power and only real cause of its every motion. It teaches that the property which creatures have of acting as second causes is real, that their powers are actual powers, inherent in them, and not merely seeming; conferred, indeed, by God, as Creator, and regulated in each specific action by his perpetual superintendence; yet, when conferred, intrinsic and efficient in the created agents, whenever the suitable relations or conjunctions for their action have place. And especially when those creature-agents are rational, voluntary spirits, does God by His providence order the rise of those free purposes in them, which his eternal plan includes, in strict conformity with their free agency.

The doctrine of Fate is, that all events, including the acts of free agents, are fixed by an immanent physical necessity in the series of causes and effects themselves; a necessity as blind and unreasoning as the tendency of the stone towards the earth, when unsupported from beneath; a necessity as much controlling the intelligence of God as of creatures; a necessity which admits of no modification of results through the agency of second causes, but renders them inoperative and passive as the mere stepping-stones in the inevitable progression. The doctrine of Providence teaches that the regular, natural agency of second causes is sustained, preserved, and regulated by the power and intelligence of God, and that, in and through that agency, every event is directed by His most wise and holy will, at once according to his plans and to the laws of nature which He has ordained. Fatalism tends to apathy, to absolute inaction; a belief in the Providence of the Scriptures, to intelligent and hopeful effort. It does not overthrow, but rather establishes the agency of second causes; for it teaches that God's method and rule of effectuating events only through them (save in the case of miracles), is as steadfast as His purpose to carry out His decree. Hence this faith produces a combination of courageous serenity, with cheerful diligence in the use of means. Jackson was as laborious as he was trustful, and laborious precisely because he was trustful. Everything that preparation, care, forecast, and self-sacrificing toil could do to prepare and earn success he did. And therefore it was that God, without whom "the watchman waketh but in vain," usually bestowed success. His belief in the superintendence of God was equal to his industry. In every blessing or calamity of private life, as well as in every order or despatch announcing a victory, he was prompt to ascribe the result to the Lord of Hosts; and these brief devout ascriptions were with him no unmeaning formalities. In the very flush of triumph he has been known to seize the juncture for the earnest inculcation of this truth upon the minds of his subordinates; and, in the anxieties of great and critical moments, his soul drew composure and assurance from it. Especially did he love to recognize the hand of God in the results of strategy and battles. While thé most pains-taking of commanders, he well knew that in these great operations many things must be done beyond the oversight of the commander, each of which by the manner of its performance may absolutely determine the event. Hence when the issue was according to his prayers, he recognized the presence of an Eye more comprehensive than that of any creature, and ascribed all wisdom, power, and glory to it.

His perpetual recurrence to this special providence was displayed in his prayers for the divine guidance of his own judgment. It was well known that he was accustomed to seek this guidance not only in general terms, but most directly and particularly on specific occasions. And the frequent answers which he seemed to receive to these prayers, suggested to the unreflecting the idea of his actual inspiration.

He would have modestly given an explanation less superstitious, and more scriptural. Mind has its natural laws as well as matter, to be learned in the same way, by correct induction from our observations; and they are just as regular in their operation as those of the stars, the waters, or the vegetable world. For instance, conception follows conception in our thinking, by certain laws of suggestion, which we ascertain and know, at least to a good degree. By another law, the volition put forth upon a conception, in the act of spontaneous attention, tends to fix and brighten that conception before the mind, in preference to any other competing suggestion, just as regularly as sunlight promotes chemical action in matter. Now, the very doctrine of Providence is, that the God who conferred upon spiritual substances these laws and powers of causation, as their inherent properties, regulates their action in strict consistency with their nature, with a constant superintendence. The mode may be inscrutable to us, even as all His workings in providence are; but the fact is taught by the Scriptures and experience, and the consistency of it with our own reasonable and voluntary nature, as is assured to us by our consciousness. Now then, when God, in answer to prayer, leaving the mind to act strictly according to all its natural laws, yet gives such providential supervision to its functions, as to order that the judgment shall, of itself, come to a prosperous conclusion, why should men be more incredulous, or suppose a more supernatural interference, than when God answers the prayers of his people with "fruitful seasons, and rain from heaven," through the regular course of those meteoric laws, which before brought drought and blight? No devout reader of the Scriptures can refuse the conviction that Satan, as a personal agent, has some mode consistent with the laws of mind, by which he often modifies the suggestions which arise, and thus the free determinations of the judgment and will. This fact assists us to establish, and in part illustrates, the contrasted fact of God's providential concern in the thoughts and purposes of the children of men.

There was at least one influence which Jackson's faith and habits of prayer in this matter exercised upon his judgment, which may be made intelligible to every virtuous mind. It was the cause of an intense sincerity of motive. He who goes before the Searcher of hearts with petitions for His light and guidance, can scarcely cherish there those corrupt and double purposes which he knows must be equally clear to His intelligence and hateful to His holiness. There is then, an obvious natural influence which makes the very act of prayer as "the euphrasy and rue" to purge the mental vision. But faith teaches us that there is, moreover, a divine answer to prayer; and in what form is the Christian's heart more familiar with this gracious power from above than in the purifying and chastening of its affections? Jackson was made by God's Spirit the most disinterested of men, in all his efforts to judge and act aright in His service. No collisions of guilty desire with conscience, no side-views of selfish ambition, no itchings of avarice, no sensuality, no cravings for notoriety, no weakness of moral cowardice remained to disturb or jostle the steady adjustments of his judgment. The functions of his understanding were actuated by one supreme emotion, the sentiment of duty; a motive-power as pure as forcible, and hence they were almost perfectly correct and true, and at the same time full of intense vigor. His "eye was single, and his whole body was full of light." This is the best explanation which can be given of that almost infallible judgment in practical affairs, which he never failed to display, whenever he felt it his duty to examine and decide. And this refers his greatness primarily to his Christianity; a solution which Jackson would have been himself most prompt to offer, if his modesty had permitted him to recognize greatness in himself.

Prayer implies a Providence. For if God hath not a present means of influencing the course of natural events, it is a waste of breath to petition for His intervention. Hence it will be anticipated, that he who was so clear in his recognition of Providence was also eminently a man of prayer. This was one of the most striking traits of Jackson's religious character. He prayed much, he had great faith in prayer, and took much delight in it. While his religion was the least obtrusive of all men's, no one could know him and fail to be impressed with the regularity of his habits of private devotion. Morning and night he bent before God in secret prayer, and rare must be the exigency which could deprive him of this valued privilege. There was in him an unusual combination of courage and modesty in this duty. If the presence of others was unavoidable, it had no effect whatever, be they who they might, however great or profane, to cause him to neglect his secret orisons. Yet, it is presumed, no one ever had the idea of ostentation suggested who witnessed one of the sacred scenes. He was accustomed, during the active campaigns, to live in a common tent, like those of the soldiers. Those who passed it at early dawn and at bed-time were likely to see the shadow of his kneeling form cast upon the canvas by the light of his candle; and the most careless soldier then trod lightly and held his breath with reverent awe. Those who were sceptical of the sincerity of other men's prayers, seemed to feel that, when Jackson knelt, the heavens came down indeed into communion with earth.

This spirit of prayer was manifested by the change which it wrought in his whole manner. Everywhere else his speech was decided and curt; at the throne of grace all was different; his enunciation was soft and deliberate, and his tones mellow and supplicatory. His prayers were marked at once by profound reverence and filial confidence, and abounded much in ascriptions of praise and thanks, and the breathings of devout affections towards God. Besides his punctual observance of his private and domestic devotions, and of the weekly meetings for social prayer, he was accustomed to select from time to time some one Christian, with whom he held stated seasons of devotion, in order to avail himself of the promise, " that if two of you shall agree on earth, as touching anything that they shall ask, it shall be done for them of my Father which is in heaven." And his partners in these fellowships were selected, not so much for their social as for their spiritual attractions. This narrative would be unjust to the truth, and to the memory of one of God's most honored servants, if it omitted the mention of the chief instrument for cultivating in him this spirit of prayer. When Major Jackson became a member of the congregation in Lexington, there was among its presbyters a man of God, whose memory yet smells sweet and blossoms in the dust, John B. Lyle. He was a bachelor, of middle age, well connected, but of limited fortune, who devoted nearly the whole of his leisure to the spiritual interests of his charge. He was constantly the friend of the afflicted, the restorer of the wayward, the counsellor of the doubting, a true shepherd of the sheep; and his inner Christian life was as elevated, as his outward was active. To him Jackson early learned to resort for counsel; for his spiritual state was not, at first, marked by that established comfort and assurance which shed such a sunshine over his latter years. He confessed to Mr. Lyle great spiritual anxieties, and seasons of darkness. The good man taught him that connexion between hearty obedience and access to the throne of grace, which is declared by the Psalmist when he says: " If I regard iniquity in my heart, the Lord will not hear me." It was largely due to his guidance, that Jackson attained to that thoroughness which marked all his subsequent Christian life. Henceforward, like Joshua and Caleb, "he had another spirit with him, and followed the Lord fully." His pious counsellor taught him by his example, by his instructions, and by suitable reading which he placed in his hands, to cherish a high value of prayer, and to expect, according to the scriptural warrant, a certain answer to it.

This prayerfulness was a profound inward spirit yet more than it was an outward manifestation. How he compelled his own diffidence to pray with others, under a sense of duty, has been described. But he was never forward to assume the lead of others at the throne of grace, where his station did not obviously make it proper. It has been said of him, that he was as often found leading his men in the prayer-meeting as in the field of battle; and those who knew not whereof they affirmed, have loved to represent him as a sort of Puritan Independent, of the school of Cromwell, Harrison, and Pride, assuming the functions of a preacher among his troops. No Christian could possibly be further from all such intrusions, both in principle and in temper. When called on by proper authority to lead his brethren in social prayer, he always obeyed. But he loved best to mingle with his rough and hardy soldiers, in the worship of God, as a simple lay-worshipper; with them to sit in the seat of the learner, with them to sing, with them to kneel, and with them to gather around the Lord's table. He would not pronounce the blessing over the plain food of his own mess-table, if a clergyman, or even an older Christian than himself, were present to do it. His whole nature and convictions were penetrated by a reverence for all constituted authority, and for right order in Church and State; the license of Independency was at least as opposed to his tastes as the restrictions of Prelacy.

It was in the secret communings of his heart that this spirit of

14

prayer was most prevalent. Devotion was the very breath of his soul. Once only was he led to make a revelation of these constant aspirations, to a Christian associate peculiarly near to him; and his description of his intercourse with God was too beautiful and characteristic to be suppressed. This friend expressed to him some embarrassment in comprehending literally the precept to "pray always," and to "pray without ceasing," and asked his help in construing it. He replied that obedience ought not to be impracticable for the child of God. "But how," said the other, "can one be always praying?" He answered, that if it might be permitted to him, without suspicion of religious display, he would explain by describing his own habits. He then proceeded, with several parentheses, deprecating earnestly the charge of egotism, to say that, besides the stated daily seasons of secret and social prayer, he had long cultivated the habit of connecting the most trivial ánd customary acts of life with a silent prayer. "When we take our meals," said he, "there is the grace. When I take a draught of water, I always pause, as my palate receives the refreshment, to lift up my heart to God in thanks and prayer for the water of life. Whenever I drop a letter into the box at the post-office, I send a petition along with it, for God's blessing upon its mission and upon the person to whom it is sent. When I break the seal of a letter just received, I stop to pray to God that He may prepare me for its contents, and make it a messenger of good. When I go to my class-room, and await the arrangement of the cadets in their places, that is my time to intercede with God for them. And so of every other familiar act of the day." "But," said his friend, "do you not often forget these seasons, coming so frequently?" "No," said he, "I have made the practice habitual to me; and I can no more forget it, than forget to drink when I am thirsty." He added that the usage had become as delightful to him as it was regular.

He had a higher and more unaffected sense of the value of the prayers of other Christians than of his own. To one who did not know how abhorrent all cant and pretence were to the sincerity and truthfulness of his nature, the frequent assertions of this feeling in his letters would almost appear as unmeaning verbiage. He never seemed to let slip an opportunity to urge Christians to prayer, for the Church and for their country. Here are examples, which only express his habitual language and spirit. Writing to a near Christian connexion, he says :—

" My dear Sister, — Do not forget to remember me in prayer. To the prayers of God's people I look with more interest than to our military strength. In answer to them, God has greatly blessed us thus far, and we may sanguinely expect him to continue to do so, if we and all His people but continue to do our duty."

He usually concluded his letters to his pastor during his campaigns, thus :—

"And now, present me affectionately to all my friends and brethren, and say to them, the greatest kindness they can show me is to pray for me."

When he had completed the series of brilliant victories in the Valley of Virginia, having utterly routed five Federal generals in quick succession, he entered upon a forced march of more than a hundred miles, to join the armies below Richmond. When about half of this march was completed, he stopped to rest his army during the Sabbath; and one use which he made of the respite was to write to his pastor upon two subjects. One was the supply of chaplains for the army; and the other may be stated in his own words :—

" I am afraid that our people are looking to the wrong source

for help, and ascribing our successes to those to whom they are
not due. If we fail to trust in God, and to give Him all the
glory, our cause is ruined. Give to our friends at home due
warning on this subject."

To another friend he wrote, Dec. 5, 1862 (eight days before
the great battle of Fredericksburg):—

"Whilst we were near Winchester, it pleased our ever-merciful
Heavenly Father to visit my command with the rich outpouring
of His Spirit. There were probably more than one hundred
inquiring the way of life in my old brigade. It appears to me
that we may look for growing piety and many conversions in the
army; *for it is the subject of prayer.* If so many prayers were
offered for the blessing of God upon any other organization,
would we not expect the Answerer of prayer to hear the petitions, and send a blessing?"

And again, January 1, 1863:—

"MY DEAR FRIEND,—Your last letter came safe to hand, and
I am much gratified to see that your prayer-meeting for the
army is still continued. Dr. White writes that in Lexington
they continue to meet every Wednesday afternoon for the same
purpose. I have more confidence in such organizations than in
military ones as the means of an early peace, though both are
necessary."

In the autumn of 1861, after the first battle of Manassas, his
pastor, with another venerable minister, visited his brigade at
his invitation, to preach to his soldiers, and to lodge in his quarters. They arrived at nightfall, and found the Commander-in-
Chief on the spot, communicating in person some important
orders. General Jackson merely paused to give them the most
hurried salutation consistent with respect, and without a moment's dallying passed on to execute his duties. After a length
of time he returned, all the work of the evening completed, and

renewed his welcome with a beaming face, and warm *abandon* of manner, heaping upon them affectionate attentions, and inquiring after all their households. Dr. White spent five days and nights with him, preaching daily. In the General's quarters, he found his morning and evening worship as regularly held as it had been at home. Jackson modestly proposed to his pastor to lead in this worship, which he did until the last evening of his stay; when, to the usual request for prayers, he answered, " General, you have often prayed with and for me at home, be so kind as to do so to-night." Without a word of objection, Jackson took the sacred volume, and read and prayed. "And never while life lasts," said the pastor, " can I forget that prayer. He thanked God for sending me to visit the army, and prayed that He would own and bless my ministrations, both to officers and privates, so that many souls might be saved. He gave thanks for what it had pleased God to do for the church in Lexington, 'to which both of us belong,' especially for the revivals He had mercifully granted to that church, and for the many preachers of the gospel sent forth from its membership. He then prayed for the pastor, and every member of his family, for the ruling elders, the deacons, and the private members of the church, such as were at home, and especially such as then belonged to the army. He then pleaded with such tenderness and fervor, that God would baptize the whole army with His Holy Spirit, that my own hard heart was melted into penitence, gratitude, and praise. When we had risen from our knees, he stood before his camp fire, with that calm dignity of mien and tender expression of countenance for which he was so remarkable, and said, 'Doctor, I would be glad to learn more fully than I have yet done, what your views are of the prayer of faith.' A conversation then commenced, which was continued long after the hour of midnight, in which, it is candidly confessed, the pastor received more instruction than he imparted."

But perhaps the most impressive exhibition of his prayerful spirit was that which was sometimes witnessed on the field of battle. More than once, as one of his favorite brigades was passing into action, he had been noticed sitting motionless upon his horse, with his right hand uplifted, while the war-worn column swept, in .stern silence, close by his side, into the storm of shot. For a time, it seemed doubtful whether it was mere abstraction of thought, or a posture to relieve his fatigue. But at length those who looked more narrowly were convinced by his closed eyes and moving lips, that he was wrestling in silent prayer for them! His fervent soul doubtless swelled with the solemn thoughts of his own responsibility and his country's crisis, of the precious blood he was compelled to put in jeopardy, and the souls passing, perhaps unprepared, to their everlasting doom; and of the orphanage and widowhood which was about to ensue. Recognizing the sovereignty of the Lord of Hosts, he interceded for his veterans, that "the Almighty would cover them with his feathers, and that his truth might be their shield and buckler." The moral grandeur of this scene was akin to that when Moses, upon the Mount of God, lifted up his hands while Israel prevailed against Amalek.

The Christian reader will easily comprehend that one so conscientious, and believing, and devout, was a happy man. He had, while in Lexington, his domestic bereavements, and he felt them as every man of sensibility must; but the consolations of the gospel abounded in him at those seasons. His habitual frame was a calm sunshine. He was never desponding, and never frivolous. It is manifest, that in all the later years of his religious life, his soul dwelt continually in the blessed assurance of his acceptance through the Redeemer; and this steady spiritual joy purified and elevated all his earthly affections. It is the testimony of his pastor, that he was the happiest man he ever knew. The assurance that "all things work together for good to them that love God, to them who are the called according to his purpose," was, to him, a living reality. It robbed suffering of all its bitterness, and transmuted trials into blessings. To his most intimate Christian associate, he was one day expressing his surprise that this class of promises did not yield to other Christians a more solid peace. The suggestion arose in the mind of his friend hereupon to try the extent of his own faith, with the question, whether the trust in God's love, and purposes of mercy to his own soul, would be sufficient to confer on him abiding happiness under the privation of all earthly good. He answered, "Yes; he was confident that he was reconciled and adopted through the work of Christ; and that therefore, inasmuch as every event was disposed by omniscience guided by redeeming love for him, seeming evils must be real blessings; and that it was not in the power of any earthly calamity to overthrow his happiness." His friend knew his anxious care of his health, and asked, "Suppose, Major, that you should lose your health irreparably, do you think you could be happy then?" He answered, "Yes; I should be happy still." His almost morbid fear of blindness was remembered, and the question was asked: "But suppose, in addition to chronic illness, you should incur the total loss of your eyesight; would not that be too much for you?" He answered firmly, "No." His dislike of dependence was excessive; he was therefore asked once more: "Suppose that, in addition to ruined health, and total blindness, you should lose all your property, and be left thus, incapable of any useful occupation, a wreck, to linger on a sick-bed, dependent on the charities of those who had no tie to you, would not this be too much for your faith?" He pondered a moment, and then answered in a reverent tone: "If it were the will of God to place me there, He would enable me to lie there peacefully a hundred years."

Such was the man, as he appeared to those who knew him best. The attempt has been made to enable the reader to see his Christian character just as it manifested itself, without conceal-ing, abating, or exaggerating any traits. Some of these will be pronounced by many to be singular, and some, perhaps, little worthy of applause or imitation; for, among those who observed it for themselves, there were not a few who regarded his con-science about little things as over-scrupulous, if not morbid. And some affected to regard him as a sincere, odd, weak man, to be admired for his honesty, but for little else. Whether his particularity concerning what have been called "the minor morals," was unreasonable, or whether it was but the rectitude which the Saviour inculcates, when He says, "He that is faithful in that which is least, is faithful also in much," may be left to each Christian to decide for himself, with the remark, that this strictness in little duties was attended with most noble fruits in the graver concerns of his life, and that God crowned this relig-ious character, such as it was, with peculiar honor. In view of these facts, it is hoped there will be many to join in the prayer, that, if Jackson's was a morbid conscience, all Christians may be infected with the same disease.

He has been often compared to Cromwell and to Havelock, but without justice in either case. The latter he certainly resembled in energy, in directness, in bravery, and in the vigor of his faith; but his spiritual character was far more symmetrical, mellow, and noble. His ambition was more thoroughly chastened. He had risen to a calm and holy superiority to all the glitter of military glory, to which Havelock never attained. Had Jackson reared sons to succeed to his name, he would never, like him, have directed them to the bustling pursuits of arms in preference to the sacred office of the gospel ministry. He would have said that, if his sons were clearly called by the providence of God to fight, and even to die, for the necessary defence of their country, then he should desire to see them brave soldiers; but that otherwise, his warmest wish for them would be, that they might share the honor of winning souls, the calling which he most coveted for himself. Nor had he, either in manners or character, any of that abnormal vivacity which made Havelock as peculiar as he was great. The field on which his military genius was displayed, and the armies he wielded, were so large compared with those of the British captain, that a comparison on this point would be equally difficult and unfair.

To liken Jackson to Cromwell is far more incorrect. With all the genius, both military and civic, and all the iron will of the Lord Protector, he had a moral and spiritual character so much more noble that they cannot be named together. In place of harboring Cromwell's selfish ambition, which, under the veil of a religiousness that perhaps concealed it from himself, grew to the end, and fixed the foulest stain upon his memory, Jackson crucified the not ignoble thirst for glory which animated his youth, until his abnegation of self became as pure and magnanimous as that of Washington. Cromwell's religion was essentially fanatical; and, until it was chilled by an influence as malign as fanaticism itself—the lust of power, it was disorganizing. Every fibre of Jackson's being, as formed by nature and grace alike, was antagonistic to fanaticism and radicalism. He believed indeed in the glorious doctrines of providence and redemption, with an appropriating faith; he believed in his own spiritual life and communion with God through His grace, and lived upon the Scripture promises; but he would never have mistaken the heated impulses of excitement for the inspirations of the Holy Ghost, to be asserted even beyond

15

and against His own revealed word; nor would he have ever presumed on such a profane interpretation of His secret will, as to conclude that the victory of Dunbar was sufficient proof, without the teachings of scriptural principles of duty, of the righteousness of the invasion of Scotland. There was never, in Jackson's piety, a particle of that false heat which could prompt a wish to intrude into clerical functions. Every instinct of his soul approved the beauty of a regular and righteous order. His religion was of the type of Hampden, rather than of the Independent. Especially was his character unlike Cromwell's, in its freedom from cant; his correct taste abhorred it. Sincerity was his grand characteristic. With him profession always came short of the reality; he was incapable of affecting what he did not feel; and it would have been for him an impossibility to use speech with the diplomatic art of concealing, instead of expressing, his true intent. His action, like Cromwell's, was always vigorous, and at the call of justice could be rigid. But his career could never have been marked by a massacre like that of Drogheda, or an execution like that of the King. The immeasurable superiority of his spiritual life over that of Cromwell, may be justly illustrated by the contrast between their last days. The approach of death found Cromwell's religion corrupted by power and riches, his faith tottering, his communion with God interrupted, his comfort overclouded; and at last he faced the final struggle with no better support for his soul than a miserable perversion of the doctrine of the perseverance of the saints, by which he claimed the comfort of a former assurance, long since forfeited by backslidings. But the piety of Jackson continually repaired its benignant beams at the fountain of divine light and purity, becoming brighter and brighter unto the perfect day. His nature grew more unselfish, his aims more noble, his spirit more heavenly; while his eager

feet ran with ever hastening speed and joy in the way of godli-
ness to its close.   And his end, sustained by the peaceful triumphs of faith, was rather a translation than a death.

This portraiture of Jackson's character will be concluded with
some notice of his domestic life in Lexington.   Thus the foliage
will be added to the crown of the column, lest the reader should
err by assigning to it a Doric severity.   After two years' residence at the Military Academy, he was married to Eleanor
Junkin, the daughter of the president of the adjoining college,
on August 4th, 1853.   The memorials of his short connexion
with this accomplished lady are scanty; but enough is known
to show that he was a tender husband.   After fourteen months
of married life he lost her by death; and the bereavement
was peculiarly harrowing, because it came without warning,
and just as he hoped the circle of his domestic joys was to
be completed instead of ruptured.   It is related that his grief
was so pungent, as not only to distress, but seriously to alarm
his friends.   Yet even then he was most anxious not to sin by
questioning in his heart the wisdom and rectitude of God's dealings with him.   His endeavors after self-control were strenuous,
and he never for a moment lost the dignity of the Christian in
his grief.   But for a long time his taste for secular occupations
and pleasures was lost, and his only aspirations pointed to the
other world.   During this season of discipline his health suffered
seriously, and his friends induced him, in the summer of 1856, to
make a European tour, in the hope that the spell might be
broken which bound him in sadness.   He visited England,
Belgium, France, and Switzerland, spending about four months
among the venerable architectural remains, and mountain scenery
of those countries.   This journey was the source of high enjoyment to him.   But the opposition of his nature to all egotism
was as strikingly shown here as elsewhere; he was no more

inclined to speak of his travels than of his exploits. It was only at rare times, when with some intimate friend who could appreciate his sentiments, that he launched out, and related with enthusiasm his delight in the grandeur of the mediæval temples and the Alps; of York Minster and Mont Blanc. He returned from this holiday with animal spirits and health completely renovated. Although he resorted no more to society, he resumed his scientific occupations with zest, and his religious life again became as sunny and cheerful as was his wont. A little incident attending his arrival at home illustrates the temper of the man. The full session of the military school had begun, at which time he had promised to return. His classes were awaiting him; week after week passed, and everybody wondered that the exact Major Jackson had not returned to his post. At length he reached Lexington unexpectedly; and his first act was to visit the family of his deceased wife. After the first joyful greetings and explanations of his delay, a sister exclaimed: "But, Major, have you not been miserable, have you not been perfectly wretched since the beginning of the month?" "Why, no!" said he, with amazement; "why should I be?" "You know," she replied, "that you are so dreadfully punctual, and as the session had begun, and the time you promised to return had passed, we just supposed you were beside yourself with impatience." "By no means," he replied; "I had set out to return at the proper time; I had done my duty; the steamer was delayed by the act of Providence; and I was perfectly satisfied."

He was married again, on July 15th, 1857, to Mary Anna Morrison, the daughter of Dr. R. H. Morrison, an eminent Presbyterian divine of North Carolina, and niece of the Honorable William Graham. This lady, with one living daughter, born in November 1862, survives him. Another infant, born in the early years of this marriage, was cut off at the age of a month.

In no man were the domestic affections ever more tender and noble. He who only saw the stern self-denying soldier in his quarters, amidst the details of the commander's duties, or on the field of battle, could scarcely comprehend the gentle sweetness of his home life. There the cloud which, to his enemies, was only night and tempest, displayed nothing but the "silver lining" of the sunlight upon its reverse; and that light came chiefly from the Sun of righteousness. He was intensely fond of his home, where all his happiness and every recreation centred. As his foot crossed its threshold, care lifted itself from his brow, his presence brought cheerfulness, and, by his example of childlike gaiety, he allured its inmates to every innocent enjoyment. His tongue, elsewhere so guarded in its speech, seemed to luxuriate in a playful variety of terms of endearment borrowed often from the Spanish, which he always said was richer and more expressive in these phrases than the English; and in these he loved to address, and be addressed by the members of his family. In his household, the law of love reigned; his own happy pattern was the chief stimulus to duty; and his sternest rebuke, when he beheld any recession from gentleness or propriety, was to say, half tenderly, half sadly: "Ah, that is not the way to be happy!"

It was in his own house, also, that the social aspects of his character shone forth most pleasingly to his acquaintances. Although the most unostentatious of men in his mode of living, he was generous and hospitable. Nowhere else was he so unconstrained and easy, as with the guests at his own table. A short time after his second marriage, he wrote thus to a near friend:—

"We are still at the hotel, but expect, on the 1st of January, to remove to Mr. ———'s house as boarders. I hope that in the course of time we shall be able to call some house our home; where we may have the pleasure of receiving a long visit from you. . . . . I shall never be content until I am at the head of an establishment in which my friends can feel at home in Lexington. I have taken the first important step by securing a wife capable of making a happy home. And the next thing is to give her an opportunity."

Before very long these purposes were realized; he was settled in his own house, where he delighted to entertain his select friends with unpretending but substantial comfort. An instance of his considerate kindness will show his character better than many words. One of his friends, having occasion to take his little daughter of four years upon a considerable journey without the attendance of its mother, called on the way to spend the night with Major Jackson. At bed-time, he proposed that Mrs. Jackson should take charge of the little one for the night; but the father replied that she would not be contented with a comparative stranger, and would give least trouble if he kept her in his own bosom. At a dead hour of the night, he was awakened by a gentle step in the room, and a hand upon his bed. It was Jackson, tenderly adjusting the bed-clothes around the infant's face; and when the father spoke, he replied that, knowing she was accustomed to a mother's watchfulness, he had lain awake thinking of the danger of her becoming uncovered and catching a cold; and had thought it best to come to his chamber and see that all was safe. This was also the mighty hand which guided the thunders of war at Sharpsburg and Chancellorsville!

Upon becoming the proprietor of a house with a garden, and soon afterwards of a farm of a few acres, his rural tastes revived in full force. He devoted his hours of recreation to gardening with his own hands, and was, from the first, very successful. Indeed, the ability of his mind displayed itself, as in Washington, by the practical skill with which he handled everything which claimed his attention. His vegetables were the earliest and finest of the neighborhood. His stable and dairy were stocked well and cared for in the best possible manner. His little farm of rocky hill-land was soon perfectly enclosed and tilled, and became a fruitful field. He used to say that the bread grown there, by the labor of himself and his slaves, tasted sweeter than that which was bought. Although he seemed to be absolutely indifferent to wealth, and gave from his modest means with an ungrudging hand, yet they grew under his energy and practical sense, as it were in spite of his generous profusion. The chief cause which he would have assigned for this prosperity, was the blessing of Him who declares that " the liberal soul shall be made fat." The secondary causes, which his neighbors assigned, were the moderation of his own habits, and the soundness of his judgment, which never admitted a mistake or a useless waste.

His life here was so methodical, that its picture may be taken from that of one day. He always rose at dawn; and his first occupation was secret prayer, followed, if the weather permitted, by a solitary walk. His family prayers were held at seven o'clock, summer and winter, and all his domestics were rigidly required to be present. But the absence of no one was allowed to delay the service. Breakfast then followed, and he went to his class-room at eight o'clock. Here he was usually engaged in instruction until eleven o'clock, when he returned to his study. The first book which engaged his attention was the Bible, which was not merely read, but studied as a daily lesson. The time until dinner was then devoted to his text-books. Between that meal and supper, the interval was occupied by his garden, his farm, or the duties of the church. The evening was devoted first to the mental review of the studies of the day, made without book, and then to literary reading or conversation, until ten o'clock, P. M., when he retired. He never chose works of fiction, but the classic historians and poets of the

English tongue; but this avoidance of works of mere fancy was from principle, not from indifference. If he was once entrapped into an interest in their narrative, he betrayed all the keenness of the veteran novel-reader; and only restrained it from a sense of the duty of husbanding his time. As the weakness of his eyes forbade the use of them at night, these readings for recreation were usually by some member of the family, while he sat an interested listener and critic. And such was the tenacity of his memory, that what was thus acquired was never parted with.

But the best conception of his domestic character will be gained from his own words; and, to enable the reader to form this, a few extracts will be given from his correspondence with his wife, so selected as to disclose his interior life, but not to violate the proprieties of a sacred relationship.

April 18*th*, 1857, upon hearing of the painful death of the son of a friend, greatly lamented by his parents, he says: — "I wrote to Mr. and Mrs. —— a few days since; and my prayer is that this heavy affliction may be sanctified to them. I was not surprised that little M. was taken away, as I have long regarded his father's attachment to him as too strong; that is, so strong that he would be unwilling to give him up, though God should call for His own. I am not one of those who believe that an attachment ever is, or can be absolutely too strong for any object of our affections; but our love for God may not be strong enough. We may not love Him so intensely as to have no will but His."

"*April* 25*th*, 1857. — It is a great comfort to me to know, that though I am not with you, yet you are in the hands of One who will not permit any evil to come nigh to you. What a consoling thought it is, to know that we may, with perfect confidence, commit all our friends in Jesus to the care of our

Heavenly Father, with an assurance that all shall be well with them."

"I have been sorely disappointed at not hearing from you this morning; but these disappointments are all designed for our good. In my daily walks I think much of you. I love to stroll abroad after the labors of the day are over, and indulge feelings of gratitude to God for all the sources of natural beauty with which He has adorned the earth. Some time since my morning walks were rendered very delightful by the singing of the birds. The morning carolling of the birds, and their notes in the evening, awaken in me devotional feelings of praise and gratitude, though very different in their nature. In the morning, all animated nature (man excepted) appears to join in active expressions of gratitude to God; in the evening, all is hushing into silent slumber, and thus disposes the mind to meditation. And as my mind dwells on you, I love to give it a devotional turn, by thinking of you as a gift from our Heavenly Father. How delightful it is, thus to associate every pleasure and enjoyment with God the Giver! Thus will he bless us, and make us grow in grace, and in the knowledge of Him, whom to know aright is life eternal."

"*May 7th*, 1857. — I wish I could be with you to-morrow at your communion [the Sacrament of the Lord's Supper]. Though absent in body, yet in spirit I shall be present, and my prayer will be for your growth in every Christian grace."

"I take special pleasure in the part of my prayers, in which I beg that every temporal and spiritual blessing may be yours, and that the glory of God may be the controlling and absorbing thought of our lives in our new relation. It is to me a great satisfaction, to feel that God has so manifestly ordered our union. I believe, and am persuaded, that if we but walk in His commandments, acknowledging Him in all our ways, He

16

will shower His blessings upon us. How delightful it is, to feel that we have such a Friend, who changes not! I love to see and contemplate Him in everything. The Christian's recognition of God in all His works, greatly enhances his enjoyment."

"*May* 16*th*, 1857. — There is something very pleasant in the thought of your mailing me a letter every Monday, and such manifestation of regard for the Sabbath must be 'well-pleasing in the sight of God.' O that all our people would manifest such a regard for His holy day! If we would all strictly observe all His holy laws, what would not our country be?

"When in prayer for you last Sabbath, the tears came to my eyes, and I realized an unusual degree of emotional tenderness. I have not yet fully analyzed my feelings to my satisfaction, so as to arrive at the cause of such emotions, but I am disposed to think that it consisted in the idea of the intimate relation existing between you, as the object of my tender affection, and God, to whom I looked up as my Heavenly Father. I felt that day as though it were a communion-day for myself."

"*June* 20*th*, 1857. — I never remember to have felt so touchingly as last Sabbath, the pleasure springing from the thought of ascending prayers for my welfare, from one tenderly beloved. There is something very delightful in such spiritual communion."

Mrs. Jackson being absent upon a distant visit. he wrote, April 13th, 1859 : —

"Is there not comfort in prayer, which is not elsewhere to be found?"

"*Home, April* 20*th*, 1859. — Our potatoes are coming up. . . . . We have had very unusually dry weather for nearly a fortnight, and your garden had been thirsting for rain till last evening, when the weather commenced changing, and to-day we have had some rain. *Through grace given me from above*, I felt that rain would come at the right time, and I don't recollect having ever felt so grateful for a rain as for the present one.

" Last evening I sowed turnips between our pease.

" I was mistaken about your large garden-fruit being peaches; it turns out to be apricots; and I enclose you one which I found on the ground to-day. And just think! my little —— has a tree full of them. You must come home before they get ripe."

He playfully applied the pronoun *your* to all the common possessions of his family when addressing his wife. It was "your house," "your garden," "your horse," "your husband," or, more generally, "your hombre," and even "your salary."

" *May* 11*th*, 1859. — I wrote you this morning that you must not be discouraged. 'All things work together for good' to God's children. I think it would have done you good to hear Dr. —— on this last Sabbath: 'No affliction for the present seemeth to be joyous, but grievous; nevertheless, afterward, it yieldeth the peaceable fruit of righteousness to them who are exercised thereby.' See if you cannot spend a short time each evening after dark in looking out of your window into space, and meditating upon Heaven with all its joys unspeakable and full of glory; and think what the Saviour relinquished in glory when he came to earth, and of His sufferings for us; and seek to realize with the Apostle, that the afflictions of the present life are not worthy to be compared with the glory which shall be revealed in us.

" Try to look up and be cheerful, and not desponding. Trust our kind heavenly Father, and by the eye of faith see that all things with you are right, and for your best interest. . . . . The clouds come, pass over us, and are followed by bright sunshine; so, in God's moral dealings with us, He permits us to have trouble awhile, but let us, even in the most trying dispensations of His providence, be cheered by the brightness which is a little ahead.

" Try to live near to Jesus, and secure that peace which flows like a river."

"*Home, May* 12*th*, 1859.—I have had only one letter this week, but 'hope springs immortal in the human breast.' So you see that I am becoming quite poetical, since listening to a lecture on that subject last night by ——, which was *one grand failure.* I should not have gone; but as I was on my way to see Capt. —— at Major ——'s, I fell in with them going to the lecture, and I could not avoid joining them. After the lecture, I returned with them and made my visit, and, before committing myself to the arms of Morpheus, your clock, though behind time, struck 12 A. M., so I retired this morning instead of last evening. I send you a flower from your garden, and could send one in full bloom, but I thought that this one, which is just opening, would be in a better state of preservation when you get it."

"*October* 5*th*, 1859.—I am glad and thankful that you received the draft and letters in time. How kind is God to His children especially! I feel so thankful to Him that He has blessed me with so much faith, though I well know that I have not that faith which it is my privilege to have. But I have been taught never to despair, but to wait, expecting the blessing at the last moment. . . . . Such occurrences should strengthen our faith in Him who never slumbers."

Such was the peaceful and pure life in which the days of Jackson glided by at Lexington. But the time was short. Events were ripening which called him into scenes more stirring, and to deeds that have brought his name before the world, and shed an imperishable lustre on his memory.

CHAPTER V.

SECESSION.

THE type of Major Jackson's political opinions has been already described, as that of a States'-Rights' Democrat of "the most straitest sect." This name did not denote the attachment of those who bore it to the dogmas of universal suffrage and radical democracy, as concerned the State Governments; but their advocacy of republican rights for these Governments, and a limited construction of the powers conferred by them on the Federal Government. Their view of those powers was founded on the following historical facts, which no well-informed American hazards his credit by disputing:—That the former colonies of Great Britain emerged from the Revolutionary War distinct and sovereign political communities or commonwealths, in a word, separate nations, though allied together, and as such were recognized by all the European powers: That, after some years' existence as such, they voluntarily formed a covenant, called the Constitution of the United States, which created a species of government resting upon this compact for its existence and rights; a government which was the 'creature of the sovereign States, acting as independent nations in forming it: That this compact conferred certain defined powers and duties upon the Central Government, for purposes common to all the States alike, and expressly reserved and prohibited the exercise of all other powers, leaving to the States the management of their own affairs. They, therefore, did not sacrifice their nature as sovereignties, by acceding to the Federal Union; but, by compact, they conceded some of the functions of an independent nation, particularly defined, to the Central Government, retaining all the rest as before. These facts and this inference were uniformly held by the Commonwealth of Virginia at all times, being solemnly asserted when she joined the copartnership, and frequently reaffirmed by her Government down to the present day. They were, in substance, embodied in the Constitution of the United States itself, by a formal amendment, immediately after it went into effect. Since the era of the elder Adams, when the centralizing doctrine was utterly overwhelmed by the election of Mr. Jefferson, they have been professed in theory, though often violated in act, by every Administration of whatever party it might be, and by nearly every State.

The party of the States'-Rights usually taught, from these principles, that the Federal Government ought to continue what it was in the purer days of Washington and Jefferson, unambitious in its claims of jurisdiction, simple and modest in its bearing, restricted in its wealth and patronage, and economical of expenditures, save in the common defence against external enemies. They held that all acts of legislation which interfered with those functions appropriate to the States as Commonwealths, and all those acts which turned aside from the general interests common to the States alike, to promote particular or local interests, were partial, usurping, and in virtual violation of the spirit of the Constitution. Among these, they classed all bounty laws designed to favor the inhabitants of a section, all protective tariffs, the chartering of a vast Banking Corporation in one of the States, and all meddling with the institution of domestic slavery in the States. They also held that the very Government, being the creation of commonwealths which acted as independent

nations in forming it, and originating in a covenant which they
voluntarily formed as such, derived its whole authority from its
conformity to the terms of that covenant: that, if the covenant
were destroyed, the Government was destroyed, and its rightful
title to allegiance from any person was annihilated — that being
gone which was the sole basis of it; and that, in the *dernier
ressort* upon any vital instance of usurpation, the States themselves must be the judges whether the covenant was destroyed,
and judges too of the necessity and nature of their redress.
This right, to be exercised, indeed, under those moral obligations
which should govern all international intercourse, they held to be
inherent in the States as originally sovereign; while to suppose
their federal compact divested them of it was preposterous, and
what was, in the nature of the case, impossible. It would
represent their voluntary act in acceding to the covenant as a
political suicide. And it would have been equally preposterous
for the Federal Constitution formally to confer it; it would have
been the absurdity of the offspring's attempting to confer on its
own parent the rights of paternity. Hence the absolute silence
of the Federal Constitution concerning this inalienable right of
the States was logically consistent, and is as incapable of implying anything against, as for, its just exercise. How natural
and fair this construction is, may be shown by the argument of
the great English moralist, Paley, against the theory which founds
the government of States over individuals upon the fiction of a
social compact. He reasons unanswerably, that if this were so,
the violation of the original compact by the government of a
commonwealth, in any one point, would destroy the binding force
of that covenant on the other party, the citizen, and so annihilate
all right to allegiance. Whence we should reach the ruinous
and absurd proposition, that any one unconstitutional act in the
ruler would release every citizen, in the future, from all rightful

obligation to obey any law he enjoined, just or unjust. The argument is perfectly sound against the theory of a social contract between individuals, because the government of a State over them is not founded on any such contract, but on the ordinance of God. But in the case of the United States the fact was precisely opposite, for the whole Central Government actually did originate avowedly in " a social contract," to which the parties were States instead of persons. So that Paley's deduction is, in this case, perfectly true. But its results are, here, in no wise absurd or disorganizing; because the creation of the Federal Government did not originate a social order or civic life for the States, and its destruction, therefore, would not destroy nor even relax it. The jurisdiction of the States themselves — older and more sovereign societies, indestructible save by the hand of political murder from without — preserved and regulated the whole social order; and the few functions which had been by them lent to the Federal Government, upon the fall of the latter, would not perish, but naturally revert to the States which had granted them. In the integrity of their powers, therefore, was the civic life of the American people.

The conception which the fathers of the Federal Constitution formed of their confederation, was that of a Common Agent for the equal benefit of the parties confederated, exercising no powers except those derived from their consent, and neither possessing nor needing any guarantee for those powers as against the parties, the States, save the obvious beneficence towards them of all its action. The Union was not a prison owned by some despot, within which the unwilling inhabitants were to be kept by force, making residence there the infliction, and escape the privilege; it was to be the home, created for their common happiness by a family of freemen, where residence would be the privilege, and exclusion the penalty; where each member of the brotherhood abode only because he chose to do so; and yet there was no danger that the membership would be prematurely dissolved, because the advantages of its just and beneficent rules would insure on the part of each member the desire to continue in it; and the threat of exclusion would be the sufficient discipline to reduce a capricious party to reason. And such was the Federal Union during the life of its founders; a government more deeply seated in the love of its people, and therefore stronger than any in Christendom; more productive of public wealth and happiness in its action; weak for aggression against the rights of its citizens, yet powerful for their defence against external enemies. In this point was intended to be the essential wisdom of its structure; that, being forbidden to enforce, by the strong hand, even its legitimate will (much more its illegal) upon the parties to it, the States, it was compelled to foster the motive for compliance by making its authority a minister of good only, and not of evil. Thus did our patriotic fathers attempt to solve the problem, hitherto unsolved, of securing the freedom of the parts, and yet giving sufficient unity to the whole, for protection against unprincipled power from without. Had all the parts possessed public virtue enough to understand and keep their obligations, the American Union would have continued a great, because a benign government. But with this great balance-wheel of free consent struck from its fabric, it became at once the most mischievous, cruel, and impracticable of all institutes, a centralized democracy, owning no law save the caprice of the numerical majority.

The States' Rights party could prove that their conception of the government was the true one, not only by the closest deduction of reasoning, but by notorious facts. One of these was, that the framers of the Constitution themselves left the Federal Government unclothed with any powers of coercion over the

17

States, not from oversight, but of set purpose. The proposal to give this power was made by one, and was rejected by the rest. In this, the men who were afterwards claimed as the leaders of the party of centralization, such as Alexander Hamilton, agreed precisely with the men who thenceforward asserted the rights of the States, represented by Mr. Madison.* All agreed in declaring, that to give such a power over States, was inconsistent with the nature of the government designed, would infallibly corrupt it, and would make it justly odious to the States, and impracticable to be maintained, save by the utter banishment of republican freedom out of the land. What more complete proof is needed of this truth, than the fact displayed in 1861, that in the very attempt to coerce States, the Constitution immediately perished? The Constitution was therefore, of purpose, left silent as to any such power; and on the completion of the document, the lack of it was expressly avowed in the words: " The powers not delegated to the United States by the Constitution, nor prohibited by it to the States, are reserved to the States respectively, or to the people."

Another fact was, that when the State of Virginia, then the leading one in fame, power, and the ability of her statesmen, gave her reluctant and chary adhesion to the Federal Union, she coupled it, in the very act accepting the Constitution, with this condition: that she should be for ever free to retract her adhesion, whenever she found the Union inconvenient, of which juncture she was to be sole judge; and to resume her separate independence, unmolested. Her reception upon these declared

---

* In the Convention on the 31st May, 1787, Madison declared that " the use of force against a State would be more like a declaration of war, than an infliction of punishment, and would probably be considered by the party attacked, as a dissolution of all previous compacts: a Union of States containing such an ingredient seemed to provide for its own destruction." In one of the debates on the New York State Convention, Hamilton said, " To coerce a State would be one of the maddest projects ever devised." We have lived to see an attempt to coerce not one State but eleven.

terms, the only ones upon which she would have entered, was virtually a promise that her condition should be granted. Nor was she the only State which made the same reservation. New York and Rhode Island, the latter the smallest, and the former the most powerful State, next to Virginia, both now among the covenant-breakers, which are persecuting the Old Dominion with a malignant treachery, for claiming her covenanted right, accepted the Union on the same condition. Their admission on such terms not only seals their right to retire at their option, but also demonstrates that all the other States understood the compact as, of course, implying such a right. The attempt has been made to break the force of this fact, by the miserable subterfuge: That Virginia, New York, and Rhode Island, only stipulated for this right to retire if they found the Union inconvenient, because they feared it might prove a failure; and that since its splendid success, that condition had become antiquated, and expired. It would be enough to expose this unprincipled sophism, to ask, how long a time might not be required to demonstrate that the Union had been successful? Do not the events which are now transpiring, keep that question yet in suspense: leading the most experienced minds in Europe to doubt whether such a scheme of government is not impracticable? But the very point of the stipulation made by Virginia was, that she was to judge for herself, when, and how far, the Union proved inadequate to confer those benefits she sought under it. And, if anything further is needed to explode the wretched pretext, it is found in the fact, that Virginia has always taken express care that this condition in her covenant should not grow antiquated, by re-affirming it from time to time, to this day, in the most formal manner.

It is thus abundantly proved that the right of the States to retire from the Federal Union, when the compact was broken, was inherent in them; and that the Constitution could neither give nor take away this privilege. The same thing appears equally from the manner in which the Colonies first acquired their independence. Their revolution was a secession from the British Empire. They declared themselves to be the only rightful judges of its necessity. So that every shadow of claim which they have to their present position is derived from the doctrine that the people of a commonwealth are entitled to change their form of government whenever they judge it necessary for their welfare. Nothing, therefore, can be more monstrous than the attempt of the States of the North to obstruct the exercise of this right by an inhuman war; when it is only by its exercise that they themselves exist.

Once more; the formation of the United States under their present Constitution, was an act of secession from the confederation previously existing. It was made all the more glaring by the fact, that the articles of Confederation had very recently been perfected, and had been accepted by all the States, with the express injunction — "And the Union shall be perpetual." That confederation did not dissolve itself: it did not grant its members leave to desert it, and form a new combination; on the contrary, it claimed an immortal existence. Yet one, and another, and another State deserted it to enter the new Union, when it saw fit; and one, Rhode Island, did not transfer itself from the old compact to the new, for three years. Yet neither the new nor the old confederation dreamed of assailing the other: both recognized the sovereign rights of the States, to secede or to accede. Accession to the new could only take place, by means of secession from the old Union; which had precisely the same claims to the adhesion of its members. So that, when Washington and his illustrious associates of the Convention of 1787, proposed a new Constitution to the States, they were proposing secession.

It is plain, then, that to speak of a State committing treason against the Government of the United States, is just as absurd as to describe a parent as being guilty of insubordination to his son. There might be injustice or violence; there could be no treason. To speak of resistance organized by the sovereign States against the Federal Government as rebellion, is preposterous. It was just as easy for Great Britain to rebel against Austria, while they were members of the great coalition against Napoleon. He who pretends to liken the secession of Virginia from the Union, to a rebellion of the county of York or Kent against the British throne, a simile advanced by the chief magistrate of the United States himself, is either uttering stupid nonsense or profligate falsehood; for the relations in the two cases have no ground in common, on which the pretended analogy can rest. What English county possessed sovereignty or independence, or in the exercise of such powers entered into any union or confederation?

It is objected again, that the admission of the right to retire from the Union renders its authority a rope of sand, and its character as a government a mere *simulacrum*, which dissolves at the first touch of resistance. The triumphant reply of Virginians is, that our State has always had this right as a condition of her membership in the Union; and yet this Government was to her, for eighty years, anything else than a "rope of sand." It was a bond which held her for that period in firm affection and loyalty, which nothing but the most ruthless despotism could relax, which retained its strength even when it was binding the State to her incipient dishonor and destruction. It is a strange and disgraceful proposition to be asserted by Republicans, that no force is a real force except that which is sustained by an inexorable physical power. It would seem that with its assertors, honor, covenants, oaths, affections, enlightened self-interest, are only a rope of sand. The truth is, that the physical power of even the most iron despotisms reposes on moral forces, and if these are withdrawn from beneath, the most rigid tyranny becomes but a *simulacrum*, which dissolves at the touch of resistance. How much more, then, must all free governments be founded on the affections, the common interests, and the consent of the governed? While the Government of the United States conciliated these, it was strong and efficient for good; when they were gone, it became impotent for good, and existed only for evil   This was all the strength which its founders ever meant to assign it, or which its nature permitted; if this species of strength failed it, then that fact was the evidence that it had ceased to fulfil the purposes of its creation, and ought to perish.

It has been urged, that if the right be denied to the United States to coerce a seceding State, it is equivalent to the absurd proposition, that the Union never had any other title to the allegiance of any State than its own caprice chose to yield it; that unless the right forcibly to resist secession is granted to the former, the right to withdraw for any cause, or for no cause, is asserted for the latter. This *dilemma* was charged upon Mr. Buchanan, the last President of the United States, when he ventured to reaffirm the established doctrine of the Constitution, that it gave Congress no power to coerce a State. Such pretended reasoners can never have heard of the well-known class of *imperfect rights* in ethics; they cannot conceive that a suffering Christian may have a claim in morals upon the alms of his fellow-Christian, and yet not have a moral right to take relief by force of arms. The right of the United States to the adhesion of the States, while the compact with them was faithfully kept, was precisely one of these imperfect rights. Their inherent right to withdraw for just cause, and to judge for themselves when that cause exists, does not imply a right to withdraw for no cause, or for a trivial cause, any more than the fact that the Christian must be left free in giving alms to the distressed, implies that he has a right to withhold alms from every person, however distressed. It is asked what guarantee the Union would then have against the secession of its members for trivial causes, or mere caprice? The answer is: It would have as guarantee the force of public opinion, habits, and affections; and above all, the fact that in every capricious secession the larger share of the inconveniences would fall upon the seceding member. If the Federal Government were equitable and beneficent, this safeguard would be always omnipotent.

Akin to this is the objection, that if the Union may not forcibly prevent the secession of a State, then it has no rightful mode of self-protection against any wrongful acts which the departing member may commit in her exit, such as appropriating the common property, or against any detrimental or even destructive use which she may make of her independence afterwards. But is not this State, the moment she resumes her separate independence, bound by the comity of nations to her former partners, as any other nation is? Just as any other independent neighbor may be required so to exercise its sovereignty as not to infringe the sovereignty of others, in the same way may she be, even by force of arms. But then the coercion must be applied only to compel her to act as a just equal and neighbor; not to enforce by violence a union which, in its very nature, can only be voluntary.

The clamor concerning the inconvenience and loss which the remaining United States experience by the just secession of a part, in the diminution of territory, departure from natural boundaries, severance of rivers and mountain chains, and interruptions of advantageous commerce, admits of an easy

answer to any honest mind. In all this, the North is but paying
the righteous penalty of the wrongs which justify the secession
of the South. If the former does not like the loss, why did it
commit the crime? Do the territories, the boundaries, the
mountains, the rivers of Virginia belong to her, or do they
belong to a parcel of States without her, which never claimed to
be more than her co-ordinates?

An excellent proof of the justice of all these reasonings may
be seen in the fact, that the most of those politicians at the
North who now deny them, were the violent assertors of them,
when they considered themselves aggrieved. So obvious were
they, that the most did not dare to deny their application to the
Southern States, in case they demanded the right of withdrawal.
The general opinion was, that in that case the Constitution
would require them to allow us to go in peace. But after the
thirst for plunder and revenge was awakened, and frantic
passions had seized on the minds of the North, all this was
changed, and sophistical pretexts were sought for war.

Such were the doctrines which the party of the States' rights
had always maintained, and to which Major Jackson was committed by the firmest convictions. If they appear to the reader
to present the conception of a government very singular, very
far removed from all European ideas, or even very impracticable,
still, if he has a particle of fairness of mind, he will see, at a
glance, that his estimate of the government has nothing whatever to do with the righteousness or propriety of the action
taken by the advocates of States' rights. This species of fed-
eration, be it wise or foolish, good or bad, was the one to which
they were actually bound in covenant. This, and no other form
of government, was what they had pledged themselves to obey.
In this way they had uniformly explained the obligations which
they considered themselves as assuming. This explanation had

been at first accepted by all parties; Virginia, declaring it in
the sovereign act by which she made herself a member of the
Federal Union, and repeating it in her famous resolutions of
1798–99, had never ceased to reiterate her claims; and in this
she had been followed by the other Southern States, her sisters
and daughters.

Secession, then, was no dishonest after-thought, suggested by
a growing sectional ambition, but the ancient, righteous remedy,
to which the Southern States were reluctantly driven, by a long
course of treachery and oppression. Ever since 1820, they had
seen with grief that the true balance of the Constitution was
overthrown, the Government centralized, and the rights of the
States engrossed by the Federal Congress. It was equally clear
that the practical advantages of these usurpations were all inur-
ing to the North against the South. A bounty on fisheries was
granted from the first, which was as plainly for the partial
advantage of New England, as though the tax-gatherer had,
with his own hand, plucked the money out of the pockets of the
rest of the citizens, to place it in 'theirs. This bounty, varying
from one to two millions annually, and continued for eighty
years, will account for the transfer of many hundreds of millions
to New England from the other States. The Northern were
maritime States; the Southern were, by population, climate,
habits, and geographical position, inclined to agricultural pursuits. A code of navigation laws was immediately passed,
which operated as a perpetual tax on Southern industry, for the
bribing of Northern adventure upon the seas. Under the first
President, the Constitution was violated by the assumption of a
power in Congress to create an overshadowing Banking corporation, with special privileges, within the territory of a State;
and this bank being, moreover, immediately employed as the
agent for funding and paying the Federal debt contracted for

18

the War of Independence, at once, and irrevocably, removed the financial centre from the Southern States, the richer portion, and paying the larger share of the taxes, to the poorer North, which paid less. A system of partial taxation by tariffs was also commenced, for a motive glaringly unconstitutional, namely, to foster local enterprises for home manufactures, seated almost exclusively in the Northern and Middle States. These tariffs were constantly pressed to a more exorbitant height, throwing millions of unequal burden annually upon the South; and never for one moment were they removed, although sometimes they received a momentary and deceitful relaxation, when the South seemed about to awake to a stern demand for justice.

But the chief sectional outrage was that aimed against the property of the Southern States in the labor of the African race, held to servitude within them. As soon as the Confederation began to acquire new territory, the Northern States disclosed a fixed purpose of sectional aggrandizement therein, by means of the general and ignorant prejudice against the African race, and the institution of slavery. Finding African labor unsuited to their climate, they had extinguished slavery among themselves from motives purely pecuniary, not generally by the emancipation of their slaves, but by selling them to the South. And the tendency of the landless population of Europe to flow to the Western Continent, showed them an indefinite supply of labor, population, and wealth; while a relative expansion of the Southern States was absolutely forbidden by the extinction of the slave-trade; a measure in which the South heartily concurred, against their obvious sectional interests, because of their conviction of the immorality of the traffic. The plan of the North was to engross the whole of the new territories for their population, by the exclusion of African labor; and the contest, which began from the very first, was never relaxed. But the South was then too powerful to be oppressed with entire success. After a threatening contest in 1820, concerning the admission of Missouri as a slave State, she was received as such; but the South unwisely permitted her entrance to be coupled with an enactment, that thenceforward all territory to the north of the Southern boundary of that State, latitude 36° 30′, *must* be settled by white labor, while the remnant to the south of it *might* be settled by slave-labor. But in 1849, upon the acquisition of new territory from Mexico, the State of California was immediately closed against the South, though lying in part south of that line; and the intention was boldly declared thenceforward to engross the whole territory for the North. So flagrant a wrong, coupled with the perpetual agitation of abolition in the States, and the perpetual, unrestrained theft of slaves by Northern interlopers, naturally inflamed the resistance of the South to an alarming height. After many discussions, a delusive pacification was made, chiefly through the influence of the veteran politician, Henry Clay, and Senator Douglas of Illinois. The sum of the measures adopted, under their advocacy at different times, was, that, on the one hand, the South should acquiesce in engrossments of territory already committed, and that, on the other, laws should be passed, in accordance with the Constitution of the United States, to prevent negro-stealing. As to the territory yet lying unappropriated, the Missouri Compromise (of 1820) was declared to be, as it was indeed, unconstitutional and null; and the apparently fair principle was adopted, of leaving the common territory open to immigration from all sections alike, and allowing the people settled there to decide for themselves, whether the State which grew up should exclude African labor or not. The latter subject was apparently disposed of in the Kansas-Nebraska law, the favorite project of Senator Douglas.

But no sooner was this law passed, than the South found that, while it "kept the word of promise to the ear," it was designed "to break it to the sense." The whole free-soil party, a majority of the whole North, openly proclaimed that they disdained to obey it; just as the whole Abolition party, now nearly a majority, defied the law against negro-stealing. (Here was an instance of insubordination, sufficient of itself to justify the secession of the South.) But more: under the Kansas-Nebraska law, the practical question immediately emerged: How, and when, the people settling upon a common territory should exercise the discretion of determining whether African labor should have place in the State there growing? The one party, aptly called that of squatter-sovereignty, said that they should wield this power as soon as they began to assemble there. This assured the victory in every case to the North, because landless free labor will, of course, ever anticipate capital and slave labor in mobility. The other party, including all the South, said, with obvious truth, that the people of the new State could only exercise the power of deciding for or against the African labor, when they became a State, a true *populus*, a full formed political society. To claim the opposite, was to make the rights of American citizens—rights recognized by both State and Federal Constitutions — dependent on the caprice of any rabble of paupers, foreigners, and free negroes, the majority of whom would probably not be citizens at all, assembled by sufferance upon the common domain. These territories, they argued, were the joint property of the United States; and, therefore, while held as such, should be administered (as usual in the case of territories) by Congress, for the impartial benefit of all the owners. No man becomes a citizen of the United States, save as he is the citizen of some State. To the citizens of all the States, therefore, those territories should belong; and whenever any of these chose to exercise his right of emigrating to a new part of the common domain, it was the duty of Congress to follow his person and all his lawful possessions, with the impartial shield of legal protection. The same equal measure should be meted out to the clock-factory of the Connecticut man, and the African labor of the Carolinian, when transported to the common domain. And this would not be intrusion into the sovereignty of a new State, as to its admitting or excluding African labor; because the moment it becomes a State, Congress withdraws, and leaves it, if it sees fit, to expel every African from its borders. The South saw clearly enough, that if this just view prevailed, they would still win no practical gain but merely preserving their honor. The emigration of white labor is mobile, quick, adventurous; that of the slave-owner is cautious, sensitive, and slow. The North, by virtue of its actual numerical superiority, and its European immigration, stood ready to pour in thousands, where the South could only furnish hundreds, for the new lands. The South had disinterestedly cut off its corresponding means of increase, by assenting to, and even demanding the extinction of the African slave-trade. Hence, it well knew, that, in claiming the constitutional construction of the Kansas-Nebraska law, it was making a demand which could save it nothing but its rights; and that, practically, every territory, fertile enough to be worth seeking, would henceforward be occupied by exclusive white labor, and belong to the North. They could justly inquire of the latter, "Why enforce a useless aggression, to win what is already virtually yours, where the only actual result is to fix a stigma of subjection upon us, your constitutional equals? Is it to teach us significantly that henceforth we are to be your slaves?" But the odious construction was generally adopted by the North; and at length, even the author of the law, Senator Douglas, deserted his own ground, and accepted it, becoming thus the leader of the larger number of Northern Democrats.

The long course of usurpation and aggression has now been traced near to its culminating point. The lawless events in Kansas helped to illustrate these differences, and to embitter the passions; but their description need not detain us. Meantime, the children of the South may say with pride and truth, that, on their side, the covenant of the Confederation was always observed. There have been at the South many corrupt, and some factious persons. Individuals have often asserted Southern rights in an intemperate, and sometimes in a wicked mode. But it will ever remain the glory of the South, that in no instance did any Southern State, or prevalent political party of the South, ever commit itself to any usurpation of power, through the Federal Government, to any sectional ends, or to any unconstitutional breach of the compact with the other sections, save perhaps in the instance of nullification—a defensive one. Our detractors are defied to produce from history one exception to this illustrious record. Moreover, although the South knew that the Federal institutions were all working partially, and against them, they constantly sustained the honor and common interests of the Confederation, with a loyalty unknown at the North; pouring out their blood in every war, and perpetually contributing, from their scantier resources, the major part of the support of the Government. They were conservative by temper, and determined to be faithful to their engagements to the end.

The reader will now be prepared to understand the political conclusions adopted by Major Jackson, in common with the most of his fellow-citizens. Secession has been so often charged upon us as a grave crime, that the defence of his memory demands these explanations. The chief lesson of his life would be neglected, were not the solution of the fact given,—that the purest and holiest of men became the hero of the war for

Southern independence. The statement has been insinuated that Jackson was seduced by factitious influences into the advocacy of a cause condemned by his own conscience; but the assertion that he was capable of this is a slander equally against his head and his heart. His political opinions were maturely formed, and were exceedingly fixed. Few who witnessed the deferential silence with which he listened to the talk of more dogmatical acquaintances, were aware how distinct and firm his conclusions were. He was pre-eminently given to forming his own resolves, especially upon every question of duty; and, even where he listened to advice, it was weighed with a sturdy independence equal to his politeness. In 1856, the question of free-soil had assumed somewhat of its angry importance, and the defection of the professed supporters of the rights of the States at the North had begun, under the pretext of squatter-sovereignty. To the few friends to whom Jackson spoke of his own opinions, he then declared that the South ought to take its stand upon the outer verge of its just rights, and there resist aggression, if necessary, by the sword; that, while it should do nothing beyond the limits of strict righteousness to provoke bloodshed, yet any surrender of principle whatever, to such adversaries as ours, would be mischievous.

In the Fall of 1859, the first angry drops of the deluge of blood which was approaching, fell upon the soil of Virginia. The event known as the *John Brown Raid* occurred at Harper's Ferry, in which that Border assassin endeavored to excite a servile insurrection and civil war, from that point. He and all his accomplices, save one, were either slain, or expiated their crime upon the scaffold. As his rescue was loudly threatened, a military force was mustered at Charleston, the seat of justice for Jefferson county, to protect the officers of the law in the exercise of their functions. Virginia then had scarcely any regular force, except the cadets of her military school. They with their officers were accordingly ordered to this place; and Major Jackson went with them, leading his battery of light pieces. His command, while there, was conspicuous for its perfect drill and subordination; and he diligently improved their time, in manœuvring them upon the roughest ground to be selected in that beautiful region. He was a spectator of the stoical death of Brown, and gave his friends a graphic account of the scene.

This mad attempt of a handful of vulgar cut-throats, and its condign punishment, would have been a very trivial affair to the Southern people, but for the manner in which it was regarded by the people of the North. Their presses, pulpits, public meetings and conversations, disclosed such a hatred to the South and its institutions, as to lead them to justify the crime, involving though it did the most aggravated robbery, treason, and murder; to deny the right of Virginia to punish it; to vilify the State in consequence with torrents of abuse perfectly demoniacal; to threaten loudly the assassination of her magistrates for the performance of their duty; and to exalt the blood-thirsty fanatic who led the party, to a public apotheosis. The pretext for this astounding outrage upon public opinion was, that it was the right of masters to property in the labor of their slaves, which John Brown sought to assail through this career of rapine and blood; a right, nevertheless, recognized by the laws of nearly every State in the Union, when at least as virtuous and Christian as now; by the laws of Virginia, and by the Federal Constitution itself, to which all alike avowed a common allegiance. And while this insult was eagerly given by every professed Abolitionist, they were seconded by so many of the free-soil party, that it was doubtful if the secret sympathizers did not constitute a majority of the Northern people. When the people of the

South witnessed these things, it caused a shock of grief and indignation. The most sober men saw in the event, insignificant in itself, a symptom of momentous importance, and recognized the truth that the grand collision was near at hand. Loyalty to the Union was, however, still unbroken; and the purpose was universal, to act only on the defensive, and to fulfil to the end every obligation of the Constitution.

Major Jackson spent the summer vacation of 1860 in New England, in the pursuit of health. On his return, he said he had seen and heard quite enough in the North, to justify the division which had just occurred in the Democratic party, and which resulted in the defeat of Douglas and the election of Lincoln; a division, he predicted, which would render the dissolution of the Union inevitable. This great schism among the Democrats was perfected in the spring of 1860, when they met in the city of Charleston, South Carolina, in grand *caucus*, to select a candidate for the office of President, to be presented for the votes of their party. The two sections then pressed their rival interpretations of the Kansas-Nebraska law, which had been left ambiguous by the similar *caucus* in Cincinnati, four years before. The Democrats of the South demanded that the party should propose no candidate, unless he held their view, that the people of a territory should not interfere with slavery in the public domains until they became a sovereign State; and that, meantime, African labor and white labor should enjoy common and equal privileges. The Democrats of the North, with a few exceptions, boldly avowed the doctrine of squatter-sovereignty. Various attempts were made at conciliation, but the utmost which the Northern party would concede was, a promise to abide by the decision which might be made upon that question afterwards, by the Supreme Court of the United States. This was rejected as nugatory, because that

19

Court had already decided, in the famous Dred-Scott case, as in others, that the legislature of the settlers in a territory had no right to impair the property of citizens of the United States in their slaves, residing among them; and that it was the duty of the Federal Government, in all its departments, to protect these rights of its citizens. If those partisans had ever intended to be governed by the authority of that pure and exalted tribunal, these questions would have been already settled for them; and the hope which they harbored was manifest, so to change the membership of that Court, in time, as to exact of it an *ex parte* decision which would strip the South of all legal defences. After a stormy discussion and an adjournment to Baltimore, the *caucus* was severed into two fragments, of which the Southern, with a few Northern Democrats, nominated John C. Breckinridge of Kentucky, then the vice-President; and the other, Senator Douglas. To the former of these, called Breckinridge Democrats, Major Jackson adhered with his usual quiet decision, speaking little concerning his political opinions, save to a few intimates, but voting in every case for men of this shade of opinion.

Meantime the party of the free soil, or as they called themselves Republicans (impudently assuming the name of the party founded by Jefferson, whose every principle in Federal politics they outraged!) nominated a purely sectional ticket, headed by Abraham Lincoln of Illinois. Their opponents called them Black Republicans; aptly expressing at once their negro-philism, and the monstrous nature of their pretensions. Their platform of principles embodied, on the old issues of politics, the most oppressive Federal usurpations; and on the question of the rights of the South in the common domain (the territory out of which future States should be formed), roundly declared that the North should henceforward engross absolutely the whole. It is true that they proposed to appease the alarm of the South, by declaring that the Federal Government had no power to interfere directly with slavery in the States. But how little solace any reasonable mind would discover in this deceptive pledge could be seen in the fact, that Mr. Lincoln and Mr. Seward, who, though not the candidate, was the *coryphæus* of the party, had declared that these United States could not exist part free and part slave; that there was an irrepressible conflict between the two systems; and that slavery in the States must therefore be put under a process of extinction. He was simply a fool who could not see what all this meant in the mouths of the advocates of a pretended "higher law;" which these men interpreted into a license to violate their own official oaths, and to disobey the precepts of a constitution they had sworn to support, where they were adverse to their prejudices; while they swallowed its emoluments, and enforced the parts advantageous to themselves against their fellow-citizens with unrelenting rigor; and all under pretence of conscience for God's revealed law. This doctrine Mr. Seward had openly proclaimed from his place as a Senator; and it had been generally accepted as the ethics of the party. The whole amount of the guarantee which the Lincoln platform gave the South was, that the Black Republicans, if victors, would refrain from issuing an immediate edict of abolition, in glaring violation of the Constitution. But, after depressing and weakening the South for a few years, by other usurpations and exactions, and plying against slaveholders all the artillery of Federal power, it was expected that she would become too weak to resist an amendment of that Constitution, laying all her rights at the feet of the tyrant section. Indeed, this plan was everywhere proclaimed by the populace, more candid than their demagogues. Another significant fact was that the open Abolitionists, who had previously run their own candidate for President, giving him at each quadrennial period a small, but increasing vote, now went over in a body to the support of Lincoln.

The result of the election, held in November, 1860, was that Lincoln became President by a vote of the States strictly sectional (*i. e.*, not a single State in the South voted for him), and in the North he failed to carry New Jersey. Of the popular vote he received about 1,800,000, while Douglas received about 1,276,000, and Mr. Breckinridge 812,000. The Whig party, retaining their old organization, cast about 735,000 votes for Senator Bell of Tennessee. Thus the popular vote for Lincoln included less than half of all the citizens; and that for Douglas, if joined to that for Mr. Breckinridge, would have been larger than the vote for Lincoln. But this fact brought no consolation to the South. The party of squatter-sovereignty in the North had also become manifestly a free-soil party. It was true they used the delusive catch-word of non-intervention with slavery; and adduced the specious plea of "popular sovereignty" to cloak the odious pretension, that an accidental rabble of adventurers, who might probably not be citizens at all, should overstep the sacred authority of Constitution, Congress, Supreme Court, and sovereign States, to trample upon a right of recognized citizens. Their cry of "no intervention either way," was explained by them to mean, that Congress should become derelict to its positive duty of protecting everywhere the equal rights of all the citizens, in order that a mob might be free to intervene, most fatally, against a part. They openly argued at home that their scheme was the more politic, because it effectually deprived the South of every inch of the common domain, while it was better concealed against constitutional objections. The South perceived it to be, in the strong phrase of one of her statesmen, "but a short cut to all the ends of the Black Republicans."

During the canvass, many patriotic voices were raised at the South, and a few at the North, in solemn remonstrance. Our enemies were reminded that Washington, Jefferson, and the other fathers of the Government, had predicted, that the triumph of a sectional party in the Confederation would be the knell of its existence; and that their own best statesmen had declared the South neither would nor could remain in the Union, under a domination so utterly subversive of the objects of the Union. But such was the temper of the Northern people, that warnings only inflamed their arrogance. And when they ascertained that they had elected their candidate, they burst forth, in belief of their irresistible power, into declarations of purposes of usurpation and tyranny so monstrous, that many just men at the North wrote eagerly to their Southern friends, to hasten and seek their only safety in a separate independence. In the South, at a distance from these scenes, few indeed comprehended their full danger, but all were painfully aroused, and many prepared for immediate defence. At the head of the latter was the State of South Carolina. Immediately after Lincoln's election was known, her Legislature called a sovereign convention of the people, which, on the 20th of December, 1860, formally retracted the connexion of the State with the Union, and resumed its independence. This action was had without discussion, and with perfect unanimity; the people of that State were convinced that the season for discussion had passed, and the season for action had arrived. But, in all the other Southern States, while there was no respectable party anywhere which wavered in the purpose of vigorous resistance, there was a division of opinion concerning the time and mode of commencing it, denoted by the terms, Separate

Secession, and Co-operative Secession. The advocates of the former prevailed at first in the planting States, bordering upon the Gulf of Mexico; of the latter, in the States lying next to the Free States, and in Virginia. With these Major Jackson sympathized. Although this class of patriots embraced many shades of opinion, their distinctive views were these: — That while the sectional action, and especially the temper of the Northern people, would justify before God and man an immediate separation, yet it was not politic to make it upon this provocation, because the South was so unprepared for that tremendous war which would probably follow. It was further contended that it would give her enemies the pretext — unfair, indeed, yet plausible — to rob her of a part of her moral strength, by charging her with a factious appeal from the polls to violence, prompted only by the loss of the powers and emoluments of office: That, inasmuch as this iniquitous election was yet made under the forms of the Constitution, it would be better to await the first aggression which plainly violated it, in form as well as in fact, and make that the signal of resistance: That the power of our enemies dictated the necessity of acting only in concert, so that the Southern cause might possess the full strength arising from the union of all these States: And that, since the collision of one with the Federal Government would inevitably decide the question of peace or war for all, and no State would stand idly, and see her Southern sisters crushed in detail by the common enemy, however erring by a generous precipitation, both courtesy and justice required that they should only act in concert. The advocates of immediate separate secession replied, that this act was, in its nature, that of a State acting sovereignly, and therefore singly: That, although the South was unprepared, yet it was best to act at once, because the time consumed in consulting and preparing, would be so improved by our enemies in the work of corrupting, intimidating, and encroaching, with all the potent enginery of the Federal Government in their hands, that the South would soon be disabled for any resistance: That, if action were postponed until full concert were secured, it would be postponed indefinitely; the partial apathy of the people under so many wrongs, having shown that nothing would effectually rouse them except the precipitating of the issue: And that the South had nothing to fear, because the unwarlike character of the North would deter them from attacking a chivalrous and determined people, and the preciousness of the Southern commerce would speedily procure from abroad potent mediation. It is plain, also, that some of the Carolinians were not unwilling to seize that accidental power, of committing their neighbors to a forcible resistance without asking their assent, which has been explained above; and therein they gave serious offence to many of their friends in Virginia.

It is not important that the historian should decide whether the advocates of immediate or of co-operative secession were right. The purpose to coerce South Carolina illegally was, at once, indicated by the retention of the strongest work commanding her chief city and harbor, Fort Sumter; and the manner in which this threatening act was accompanied, aggravated the indignation of the people. On the 9th of January, 1861, Mississippi left the Union; Alabama and Florida followed on the 11th; Georgia on the 20th; Louisiana on the 26th; and Texas on the 1st of February. On the 9th of February, a Provisional Government of the six seceding States was instituted at Montgomery, in Alabama, with Jefferson Davis for President, and Alexander H. Stephens for Vice-President.

Meantime the border Slave States, headed by Virginia, while declaring that they would not remain passive spectators of an attempt to chastise the seceding States for thus exercising their unquestionable right, continued in the Union, and made strenuous efforts at conciliation. The General Assembly of Virginia proposed a conference of the Free and Slave States by their ambassadors, to devise some terms of mutual concession. This body met in Washington, February 4th, and the members of Congress from the Border States continued their anxious exertions to mediate in the Federal Legislature. But every attempt was utterly vain. No sooner had the Peace Conference, as it was called, assembled, than it was found that the Commissioners from the North, instead of coming with the moderate and dispassionate wisdom of statesmen, to heal the wounds of their country, were as full of the *virus* of party as the demagogues who had led the popular elections. Nothing was done, save to devise a deceptive compromise to be recommended to the Congress, — a compromise so worthless, that the larger number of the Southern Commissioners refused to accept it. But even this the Congress, now under the domination of a Black Republican majority, disdained to grant, and almost to notice. The Legislature of Virginia had also called together a Convention of the people, containing delegates from every city and county. So far was it from the purpose of the people to precipitate themselves rashly into violent measures, that when this Convention met, only about twenty-five of its members advocated immediate secession. The remainder (with the exception of a few, who afterwards disclosed their original slavish intentions by their treason) were, on the one hand, unwilling to sacrifice the last hope of peace, until driven to self-defence by intolerable usurpations, but, on the other, resolved to maintain the rights of the South intact, and to resist every attempt of the United States to coerce the seceders by unconstitutional violence. Their expectation of being able to remain in the Union was slight, but they were resolved that the guilt of extinguishing this spark of hope, and compelling a

separation, should rest upon their assailants. To this number
adhered Major Jackson, with the larger part of the Christian
people of the State, of all political parties. They had hailed
the assembling of the Peace Conference with a gleam of hope,
but when its consultations ended so abortively, nearly all
accepted the stern conclusion, that nothing remained except that
alternative between base submission or resistance, in which no
honest man ever hesitates.

Still, they were reluctant to despair of the Union. They
appreciated the infamy which would attach to the Christianity of
America, if, after all its boasts of numbers, power, influence, and
spirituality, it were found impotent to save the country from
fratricidal war. Their cry was, " Christians to the rescue!"
They asked: Should there not be enough of the power of love in
these millions of the professed servants of the Prince of Peace,
to renew the bonds of friendship; to say to the tempests of
passion, "Peace, be still;" to keep down the hands which sought
their brothers' throats, and rather to receive the sword into their
own bosoms than allow their common country to be slain?
They said, as long as there was a spark of life, yea, even though
it were uncertain whether this spark was but an illusion, it would
be better to wait till it was extinguished by necessity, than incur
all the miseries of the extreme remedy, when it was possible
that they might afterwards be haunted by the remorseful discovery, that it was invoked without sufficient cause. They
determined that the mountainous aggregate of crime and woe
which impended — of a ruined Constitution, of cities sacked, of
reeking battle-fields, of scattered churches, of widowed wives
and orphaned children, of souls plunged, unprepared, into hell—
should not be chargeable to them. None strove more earnestly
to deprecate the crime than Major Jackson. A month before the
catastrophe, he called upon his pastor, and spoke substantially
20

as follows: — "If the general Government should persist in the measures now threatened, there must be war. It is painful to discover with what unconcern they speak of war, and threaten it. They seem not to know what its horrors are. I have had an opportunity of knowing enough on the subject, to make me fear war as the sum of all evils. Should the step be taken which is now threatened, we shall have no other alternative; we must fight. But do you not think that all the Christian people of the land could be induced to unite in a concert of prayer, to avert so great an evil? It seems to me, that if they would unite thus in prayer, war might be prevented, and peace preserved." To this his pastor promptly assented, and promised to do what he could to bring about the concert of prayer he proposed. "Meantime," said he, " let us agree thus to pray." And henceforward, whenever he was called on to lead the devotions of others, one petition prominently presented and fervently pressed, was, that God would preserve the whole land from the evils of war.

Between the leading Christians of the North and those of Virginia, several pacific communications passed, to some of which Jackson's name was appended, although with but faint hope of good results. On the Northern side, the actors were either impotent to carry out the fraternal feelings which they professed, against the prevalent fury, or else their overtures were only like the deceitful caresses with which the driver soothes a restless horse, while the harness is fastened on his neck. It was clearly perceived, that while these smooth-sounding missives were sent, invoking the Christian forbearance of the South, it was expected that all the forbearance should be on that side; and not one of the pacificators had the honesty or courage to propose that the simple expedient should be tried, for healing the unholy strife, of yielding to the South her just rights. While pretended meetings of sympathy were held for Southern wrongs, no practical measure was taken, and Black Republican majorities increased at every election. But the Christian people of Virginia strove to avert the storm with a generous sincerity, more glorious than their subsequent heroism in breasting it. Their influence was felt in the magnanimous efforts of the old Commonwealth to stand in the breach between the angry elements. They entreated her to endure wrongs, until endurance became almost a vice, to hold out the olive-branch after it had been spurned, to study modes of compromise and conciliation, until the verge of dishonor was touched, to refuse to despair of the Republic when hope had departed from all others, and to decline even acts of self-defence, which might provoke collision, until the cloud had risen over her very head. So reluctant was Virginia to behold the ruin of the Union she had so loyally adorned, that many of her sons and her allies were driven almost to fury by the nearness of the danger, and the taunts of her enemies.

But these were madly hurrying to take upon their own heads all the guilt of the giant crime, and thus to unite Virginia as one man, and render her justification as clear as the sunlight. The State of South Carolina had been soliciting, first of Mr. Buchanan and then of Lincoln, an equitable settlement of all questions in dispute between her as an independent power, and the Federal Government. Especially had she demanded that Fort Sumter, the only post in her territory held by that Government, should be restored to her on the obviously just ground, that being designed only for her local protection against foreign aggression, when she relieved the central administration of that function, it had no longer any concern in her fortresses. The attempt was made, first, to amuse and deceive her ambassadors, by declarations which cannot be correctly named by any term short of this — that they were a series of reiterated falsities, uttered by the Secretary of State; and this attempt at official treachery was rendered more loathsome by his ingeniously prostituting the sanctity of the ermine of the Supreme Court, to give credit to his assurances. But, on the 8th of April, a powerful armament being ready to reinforce the intrusive garrison of Fort Sumter, the mask was removed, and the Governor of South Carolina was bluntly informed that it should be done, "peaceably if they could, forcibly if they must." The Confederate authorities had not been hoodwinked; and they proceeded, on the 12th and 13th of April, to reduce the post by their forces under General Beauregard. Thus the Federal Government assumed the guilt of the first military aggression.

But they did not stop here: on April 14th, Lincoln made a proclamation, without the authority of a shadow of law from Congress, declaring war against South Carolina and the Confederate Government, and calling upon the States for seventy-five thousand soldiers to invade them. The Governors of all the Southern States, except Maryland, refused compliance. In Virginia all remains of hesitation were instantly extinguished; the Convention, which was in session, on the 17th of April, passed an ordinance resuming the separate independence of the State; and the Governor immediately began to prepare for war. On the fourth Thursday of May, at an election held with perfect respect for the freedom of opinion, the people of Virginia ratified this separation almost unanimously, except in a part of the north-western counties, where the intrusion of a foreign element had corrupted the public sentiment.

Virginia was recognized on all hands as the leader of the border Slave States. Her enemies evidently mistook her magnanimous forbearance and struggles for peace, as signs of conscious weakness. They said, the old "Mother of States and statesmen" was decrepit, that her genius was turned to dotage, that her breasts were dry of that milk which suckled her Henrys and Washingtons. They thought her little more than a cowering beldame, whom a timely threat would reduce to utter submissiveness. And thus they dared to stretch over her head the minatory rod. But when the tyrant tried the perilous experiment, he was startled by a result as unexpected as that which followed the touch of Ithuriel's spear. She, whom he thought a patient, hesitating, helpless paralytic, flamed up at the insolent touch, like a pyramid of fire, and Virginia stood forth again in her immortal youth, the unterrified Commonwealth of 1776, a Minerva radiant with the terrible glories of policy and war, wielding that sword which ever flashed before the eyes of her aggressors, the "*Sic semper Tyrannis.*" * The point of farthest endurance was at length passed; her demands for constitutional redress were all refused; her too generous concessions of right, met by a requisition for the unconditional surrender of honor and dignity; her forbearance abused to collect armaments and equip fortresses on her borders, and on her own soil, for her intimidation; the alternative forced upon her, either to brave the oppressor's rod, or to aid him in the destruction of her sisters and children, for no other cause than that they contended nobly, if too rashly, for rights common to them and her; and to crown all, the Constitution of the United States was rent in fragments by the assumption of the President to levy new forces, to wage war, without authority of any law of Congress, and to coerce sovereign States into adhesion, in the utter absence of all intentions and powers to that effect, in the Federal compact. Hence, except in the breast of a few traitors, there was now but one mind and one heart in Virginia. In one week, the whole State was converted into a camp, and the

* See the Seal of the Commonwealth.

gauntlet of deathless resistance was flung back with high disdain.

The world has learned to consider Jackson as the hero of the Virginia of 1861. The Commonwealth is proud to accept him as her representative man, and the attitude which he held was the true type of hers; as he stood conscientious, cautious, but fearless, pure and unselfish in motive, elevated in principle, with an eye raised in religious faith to the righteous heavens, awaiting the signal from the Divine approval for his resistance, profoundly sad for the mournful necessity, yet as sternly resolved to defend the right. In all classic and sacred story, there is no spectacle more affecting and sublime than that presented by this Christian man, and his Christian people, in this emergency. They did not share the delusion, cherished by many of . the immediate Secessionists, that the North would be restrained from striking; but they knew the history of passion and fanaticism enough to expect a fearful war. They saw the mighty beast gathering his forces for the bound upon his prey, yet they calmly stepped before his jaws. How grandly does the action of Virginia contrast with that of Maryland and Kentucky, which, professing attachment to the right, subsided into a pitiful "neutrality," that was, in fact, slavish co-operation with their enemies; the one, on the plea that the military highway to the tyrants' capital lay through her heart; and the other, on the ground that one-third of her border was only separated by a great river from the assailants! The defection of Kentucky left Virginia exposed on three sides to her invaders, and one of these the sea, vexed with the countless keels of the enemy; while his mercenaries had stolen, and now held her greatest place of arms, Fortress Monroe, which commanded the approach to the wharves of her chief sea-port and her capital city. Her border lay under the muzzles of the cannon which frowned from the ramparts of Washington, and it was plain to friend and foe, that her smiling fields must be the chief *arena* for trampling armies. But these men did not quail on account of this; having taken counsel only of God and the right, Virginia stepped into " the imminent deadly breach," baring her own fair bosom to the fiercest strokes of the swords lifted against her sisters.

History will some day place the position of these Confederate States, in this high argument, in the clearest light of her glory. The cause they undertook to defend was that of regulated, constitutional liberty, and of fidelity to law and covenants, against the licentious violence of physical power.   The assumptions they resisted were precisely those of that radical democracy, which deluged Europe with blood at the close of the eighteenth century, and which shook its thrones again in the convulsions of 1848; the agrarianism which, under the name of equality, would subject all the rights of individuals to the will of the many, and acknowledge no law nor ethics, save the lust of that mob which happens to be the larger.   This power, which the old States of Europe expended such rivers of treasure and blood to curb, at the beginning of the century, had transferred its immediate designs across the Atlantic, was consolidating itself anew in the Northern States of America, with a wealth, an organization, an audacity, an extent, to which it never aspired in the lands of its birth, and was preparing to make the United States, after crushing all law there under its brute will, the fulcrum whence they should extend their lever to upheave every legitimate throne in the Old World. Hither, by emigration, flowed the radicalism, discontent, crime, and poverty of Europe, until the people of the Northern States became, like the rabble of Imperial Rome, the *colluvies gentium.* The miseries and vices of their early homes had alike taught them to mistake license for liberty, and they were incapable of comprehending, much more of loving, the enlightened structure of English or Virginian freedom. The first step in their vast designs was to overwhelm the Conservative States of the South. This done, they boasted that they would proceed, first, to engross the whole of the American continent, and then to emancipate Ireland, to turn Great Britain into a democracy, to enthrone Red Republicanism in France, and to give the crowns of Germany to the Pantheistic humanitarians of that race, who deify self as the supreme end, and selfish desire, as the authoritative expression of the Divine Will. This, in truth, was the monster whose terrific pathway among the nations, the Confederate States undertook to obstruct, in behalf not only of their own children, but of all the children of men.

To fight this battle, eleven millions, of whom four millions were the poor Africans, lately feeble savages, prepared to meet twenty millions. The gigantic adversary was not impeded by distance, but lay everywhere alongside his proposed victim, ready to grasp him with his long arms. He held prepared, a veteran army of twenty thousand men, a navy, and vast arsenals and armories; while the Confederate States had everything to create. He had the administration of all the departments of a government; he had revenues, a treasury recruited perpetually with the gold of the modern Ophir, and huge accumulations of financial wealth: they had none. In his favor was a great commercial marine, second to none in the world, and manufactories teeming with productive labor fostered by the previous oppression and taxation of the South; while she had agricultural communities, possessing only the rudiments of commerce and of the arts. And to sustain these elements of Northern power, there was the well-known pertinacity of the Yankee character, infuriated now by a sectional hatred all the more incredible because unprovoked, and by a fanaticism set on fire of hell.

But had this been all the odds which the Confederate States had to meet, their prowess would, before this, have ended the contest. The ships of the Federals, availing themselves of the avarice and injustice of Europe, made all the workshops, ship-yards, and factories of the Old World tributary to their malice. The radicals, the *proletaires*, the robbers, the outlaws, of all other lands, flocked to their standards, taught by their ready instincts that their cause was the same. One-half of the prisoners of war, registered by the victorious armies of the South, have been foreign mercenaries. Mr. Smith O'Brien, warning his race against the unhallowed enterprise, declares that the Moloch of Federal ambition has already sacrificed two hundred thousand Irishmen to it. And still, as the flaming sword of the South mows down these hireling invaders, fresh hordes throng the shores. Last, our country has to wage this strife, only on these cruel terms, that the blood of her chivalrous sons shall be matched against the sordid streams of this *cloaca populorum*. In the words of Lord Lindsay, at Flodden Field, we must play our " Rose Nobles of gold, against crooked sixpences."

So that the Confederate States, while, in truth, fighting for the cause of the world, have the whole world to fight against. But how has their heroism been regarded from without? It must be declared (and this fact completes the grandeur of their attitude), that while thus bleeding for the common behoof of mankind, they have received aid from none, even idle sympathy from few, and only neglect and injustice from the governments of Europe. Men have seen fit to adopt the slanders of our known enemies as the only description of our institutions, and have refused us the poor privilege which even the criminal has, of being heard before he is condemned. The word *slave-owner* has been the talisman to evoke everywhere an ignorant prejudice,

21

too conceited to learn correction; and men have been willing to accept the rendering which it suits the malice of our enemies to give, falsely, as they know — that we are contending, not to preserve our own freedom, but to perpetuate the bondage of our fellow-men, unjustly enslaved. It is by this device our enemies have sought to hide the enormity of their attacks, and to rob us of even the sympathy of mankind. The Confederate States have, indeed, never complained of the refusal of aid to fight their battles, for they have never asked it. But they have a right to complain, that the interested slanders of their enemies should be echoed abroad without even examination; that the moral support of a recognition should be withheld, when it is a historical fact that the independence of several of those same States was recognized by all Europe eighty years ago, and, as is known to all the world, has never since been forfeited; that the maritime law, so recently and solemnly established for all nations, should be compelled to receive a new and deceitful interpretation for the benefit of our enemies, the moment it began to apply in our favor; and that a pretended neutrality should be so observed, as to make every advantage accrue to them. The people of the South well know, that, if they are overwhelmed, the greedy democracy, whose threats have exacted from the European governments these shabby compliances, will make them in due time rue their short-sighted injustice; but this is the concern of their people; ours is to endure, and to strive to the death.

The great career of Jackson is identified with the cause of Southern independence. To this he committed himself with solemn prayers and searchings of heart, ready, if he should die in this quarrel, to present his soul confidently before the judgment-bar, and ask the Divine approval. In it he wrought all his world-famous exploits. In it he died, professing in the last struggle the same confidence in the righteousness of the war.

If then the secession of Virginia was a crime, Jackson was the most amazing of self-deceivers, or the most profound of hypocrites. Therefore, his character cannot be appreciated, nor its fame receive its just estimate from history, without a full understanding of the merits of the case. This is the reason that the reader's attention has been so largely occupied with an exposition of it, and for this reason he is besought to weigh these concluding arguments.

First, The most determined anti-slavery man, if he have fairness of mind, will grant, when he understands the case, that African slavery is not the cause, but only the occasion, of the Southern resistance. The cause for which this people contend is constitutional right. It is but a circumstance that the right to the labor of their slaves happened to be the particular in which the sacred authority of law was assailed; and it may be asked, How can it appear that the object of the South was to perpetuate the bondage of the African, unless it appear that the object of Northern aggression was to end that bondage? But the Black Republican party expressly declared, that they proposed no interference with slavery in the States. Their defenders can only rescue them from this logical dilemma, by imputing to them deliberate falsehood on this point. They only proposed to limit the African population to its present home, so that their policy would not have made one slave less in all America, unless by so enhancing the miseries of their condition as to exterminate a part. Nor would the demand of the South, that the African race should be allowed to labor in the new domain, if granted, have made one slave more in all America, unless it had done it by ameliorating their condition, so as to save some alive who otherwise would have perished. Clearly, then, the policy of free-soil was not friendship to the black man, but only enmity to his white protector, and desire to rule over him.

But further, Black Republicanism is a system of intense hos‧ tility to the African race. Its inconsistency can only be equalled by its inhumanity. It persists in saying, contrary to the Consti‧ tution of the United States, that the African is a citizen of the Union; but it forbids these black fellow-citizens to enjoy the common territory in any form. It says they must not come as slaves, in the mode best adapted to their present welfare (as the most of the Black Republicans admitted). It says also, that they must not come as free negroes; for every Black Republican State, formed out of the national territory, with perhaps a single exception, has legislated sternly and absolutely against the immi‧ gration of this unfortunate class; and, of course, new States to be formed under the same creed, may be expected to do the same. In a word, Black Republicanism always means, that the African shall not exist at all on American soil. The uniform *shibboleth* of the party was the assertion, that this continent must belong exclusively to the white race. The proposal universally made by its demagogues to the agrarian hordes whom they deceived, was not: "Let us overthrow the institutions of the South, in order that you may share its industry with free negro competitors;" but, "Let us overthrow the institutions of the South, in order that you may exclude the negro from its indus‧ try, and take his place." If they were pointed to the wretched and waning caste of free blacks in the North, as proof that this race cannot thrive in competition with the whites, without the protection of domestic slavery, and asked what was to be the destiny of the millions of Africans, when their policy of free- soil was everywhere established; the usual answer was a sar‧ donic shrug, and the sneering declaration, that this was no concern of theirs. Others, more candid, pointed for answer, to the fate of the Indian tribes, who have wasted to nothing before the greater energies and crimes of the white race; and coolly said, that the Africans, deprived of the fostering shield of that southern slavery, under which they were now thriving so happily, must tend to extinction, under the pressure of their own miseries and degradation; and then the whole Union would be free, prosperous, and glorious, (?) belonging to the white man alone. Such was the hideous meaning of Black Republicanism, to oppress and enslave the humane master, in order to exterminate the contented and comfortable servant!

Any honest man, who has been so unlucky as to imbibe the false dogma, that the relation of master and slave is essentially unrighteous, will therefore admit, if he knows the truth, that the citizen of the Confederate States is not contending, in this quarrel, to perpetuate an unjust oppression. He will say: " Be the relation wrong as it may, it was not instituted by the Confederates, nor at their option, but by the greed of the Federal and British slave-traders, and the tyranny of Great Britain, thrusting the Africans upon the unwilling colonies. These citizens found it existing, recognized by the laws, guaranteed by the Constitution which the people of the North were pledged to observe, and which alone gave them any right to legislate for the South. It was, therefore, natural, yea right, that they should resist these usurpations; and the more, as they saw that the motive was, not to exalt the slave, but to oppress the master; to trample upon the liberties of the latter, in order to visit upon the former, a fate a thousandfold worse than slavery — lingering extermination."

But every citizen of the Confederate States, in the second place, like General Jackson, would disdain to argue this cause from the premiss, that the relation of the master to his slave is unrighteous in itself. They assume the high position that this relation is, for their circumstances, as innocent and lawful in itself as any other relation of government, and recognized as such by God and sound ethics, as well as by all the laws of their country. When pointed to the almost universal condemnation of this proposition by the rest of Christendom, they boldly declare, that this results from an exclusion of the Southern people from a hearing in their own defence, and a perverse and indolent reception from their enemies, of the most monstrous tissue of slanders and falsehoods, which ever confounded a human mind. The world has been told a myriad times until the world believes it, that Virginian slavery makes a human being a chattel, a piece of property, thus violating the first intuitions of justice. Yet, all this is absolutely false; every slave-law of Virginia treats the slave as a person, a responsible, reasonable being, and not a thing; the only property which the laws recognize in him, is the property in his involuntary labor. And if the involuntary labor of a human being cannot be property, then every parent, husband, and master of an apprentice, in the civilized world, is made a transgressor. It is uniformly asserted that slavery proceeds upon the assumption that it is the master's privilege to expend and exhaust the labor, welfare, and very being of his fellow-man, for his own selfish behoof, without equivalent; and that hence, it is a flagrant violation of that great law of love and equity, the golden rule. All this is alsolutely false: this form of servitude is defended only on the ground, demonstrated so fully by experience, that it secures for the servant the greatest practicable amount of well-being. The laws all make the duties and benefits of the relation reciprocal, and oblige the master to render to his servant a liberal return for his labor, in the form of a life-long maintenance of himself and his family, secured against every contingency of decrepitude and sickness; just as much as they oblige the servant to render his labor to his master. That this is, in the general, a better recompense than the

African could win as a free negro, is the justification always pleaded.

It has been charged that Virginian slavery makes the master the irresponsible possessor of the chastity of the female slave. This is again an absolute falsehood; the law fences around the chastity of the servant, even against the violence of her own master, by the same sanctions which protect that of the white lady. It has been charged that the laws of Virginia forbid the slave to lift his hand for the defence of life or limb, in obedience to the instincts of self-preservation, against any white man. This is absolutely false; while the laws require the servant to accept the chastisement of his master, they recognize in him the same discretion of self-defence, even against his owner, when assailed in life and limb, which is granted to the white freeman. It has been said that we prohibit the slave all access to letters, and do not permit him to learn to read even the book of life. This, again, is unmingled falsehood; there is no law in Virginia, forbidding a master to teach his slaves literature; and as many of them can read, and do read God's Word, as of the agricultural peasantry of boasted England. It has been said that Virginian slavery forbids the marital and parental relations among slaves, consigning them to a brutal concubinage, like that of animals. In the sense charged, this is absolutely false; conjugal and parental bliss is as much recognized, and as little interrupted among them, as among any people of the same civilization. It has been said that their discipline and treatment are inhuman. This is transcendently false. No peasantry on earth is treated with as much humanity, and bears tasks so light. There are instances of barbarity, even of murder; but they are punished by the laws and public opinion, at least as regularly as any crimes against free persons in this country. Are there no cases of wife-murder, and child-murder, in New and Old England? It is asserted, in ten thousand forms, that slavery has degraded the African; but this is also false : it has civilized and elevated him, more rapidly than any other philanthropy has raised any pagan race in the world.

This introduces the affirmative truth, that the relation of servitude is a righteous, because a beneficent one, for the African among white men.   Let the tree be known by its fruits.   It has conferred a higher physical well-being than is enjoyed by any other laboring population, as is proved by their increase of numbers, cheerfulness, and immunity from bodily infirmities. The Virginian servant is lifted in the scale of manhood so high above his fellows of the African wilds, that, when by rare chance he meets them, he is ashamed and indignant at the assertion of a community of race.   American servitude has made nearly half a million out of four millions (one in eight) members of Christian churches, from being, three generations ago, besotted Pagans. All the Christian philanthropy of the rest of the world has not done as much for heathendom.   Our system has created an affectionate union between the two races, elsewhere so hostile, which has astounded our enemies and the world, with their quietude in these times of convulsion.

And when we look into the ethics of the relation, we find that it was never suspected of immorality by any of the great masters of moral science, classic or scholastic, nor by any of the luminaries of the Church, patristic or reformed, until the dogma of modern abolition was born of atheistic parentage, amidst the radical disorganizers of France, in the Reign of Terror.   In the Word of God, the only infallible standard of morality, that doctrine finds no support.   Moses legalized domestic slavery for God's chosen people, in the very act of setting them aside to holiness.   Christ, the great Reformer, lived and moved amidst it, teaching, healing, applauding slaveholders; and while He assailed every abuse, uttered no word against this lawful relation. His apostles admit slaveholders to the church, exacting no repentance nor renunciation. They leave, by inspiration, general precepts for the manner in which the duties of the relation are to be maintained. They command Christian slaves to obey and honor Christian masters. They remand the runaway to his injured owner, and recognize his property in his labor as a right which they had no power to infringe. If slavery is in itself a sinful thing, then the Bible is a sinful book.

Strong in the truth of God and history, the people of the Confederate States therefore calmly breast the adverse opinion of the world. They fortify their position by the fact that their right to the labor of their slaves is not only protected by the laws they inherited from their fathers, but by the laws of God, and by eternal rectitude. Had they been unable to assert the latter truth, their resistance to anti-slavery aggressions would have been proper; because the Constitution, which alone united the States, recognized and protected it. But now their attitude is in every respect impregnable; for God protects it as well as the Constitution. To infringe the rights of slaveholders under the laws, was therefore a usurpation, and a violation of the primary compact. But a covenant broken by one party is broken for the other. The Southern States therefore had the clearest right to select their own redress. And especially is their secession justified, when the malignant intentions of the aggressors, and the ruinous nature of the wrongs they sought to inflict, are considered. Their purposes were evidently ruthless; they intended nothing less than our destruction. He who has observed the silent, yet potent influence of opinion on the conduct of political bodies, well knows how absurd would be the expectation, that the Southern people could consent to lie under

22

the stigma of a social crime, and of a standing moral delinquency and yet expect to receive of their supercilious accusers, equal and fair treatment in a political partnership. The sentiment of contempt and superiority will inevitably express itself in attempted domination. Had the dogma, which asserted the immorality of our institutions, professed itself the most unpractical abstraction, the South would have been wise and righteous in saying to the North: "It is time to part; we cannot live peaceably together."

But that sentiment was intensely practical. It proposed no less than to uproot our whole society, to plunder our citizens, at one stroke, of more than a thousand millions of their property, and thus to impoverish the whole land; to hurl back the prosperous and happy African race to barbarism, crime, and misery; to turn our plantations into one vast jungle, and our cities into deserted ruins; and to people this blighted region with a dispirited and disorderly medley of bankrupt whites, and degraded black savages. The people of the South know the African character. They have seen the bitter fruits of a general emancipation; and they well know that this picture of the results of Yankee usurpation would be verified in every lineament. If, then, self-preservation can ever justify resistance, in this instance it was a righteous, a sacred duty. Now the form of resistance adopted by the Southern people was the most moderate and equitable that could be conceived. A covenant repudiated by one party is annulled for the other. It was the Constitution of the United States alone, which constituted the Union, and gave any right to the Northern States to legislate for the South. When the former declared, as the North in substance did, that their conscience forbade their fulfilling the obligations of that covenant for the protection of slavery, the only conclusion to which honesty could have led them was this: Let the parties then separate, and restore to each other their mutual independence. And this was the very least which the most Christian forbearance on the part of the South could ask. But this was precisely what the South demanded, in claiming the right of peaceable withdrawal. Technical justice would have authorized her to say to the North: "You have bargained; you have appropriated the advantages of the bargain, and you shall be compelled to stand to its terms, whether you like them or not." It would have sustained her in demanding reparation for the heavy wrongs already sustained. It would have sanctioned her claim to the properties of the Union, which the North had really deserted, and not the South. But she asked none of these things; she made only the modest request to have her pledges restored, since they were so irksome to her partner, and to be let alone. But this the North refused; their claim was that they should be free to violate the mutual compact whenever its conditions were irksome to their interests, or passions or caprice, and absolutely vital to the rights of the South, while we, their equals, should yet be held to it at the point of the sword, and under the threat of the most atrocious outrages ever visited by barbarians on their victims! Was ever the ear of a just God vexed with wickedness more monstrous than this? " It is rank, and smells to heaven."

But, it is objected, the sectional party which had seized the general government, disclaimed the purpose of forcible emancipation in the States; and the South, in resisting, took counsel of their own angry suspicions alone. The crushing refutation of this plea is given by the developments of the Black Republican party since. In three years, they have attempted to consummate every outrage which the statesmen of the South imputed to their ulterior intentions; yea, they have left no tyranny or usurpation untried, which the wildest suspicion could have imagined. Thus

have they themselves justified the resistance of the South to God
and man, and made it clearer than the sun, that it was not one
whit too early or too strenuous.

The great charge made against the South by the Northern
Democrats was, that she had sought defence by leaving the
Union, instead of remaining in it, and trusting to their great
conservative party for the protection of their rights.   Said they:
"We guarantee you, in the Union, every privilege which the
Constitution gives you; but if you attempt to leave it, we become
your enemies."   On this pretext that party have, with a baseness beyond that of the Black Republicans, betrayed every
principle of their own creed, to join them in their persecution of
us.   Our answer is in the question: Have they been able to
protect their own rights in that Union?   And, is this the extent
of our offence, that we were not willing to commit our precious
liberties to the sole guardianship of those who have surrendered
every right of their own, without one blow in their defence,
with a folly and poltroonery unexampled in the history of reptiles,
not to say of men, at the first demand of a despicable and upstart
despotism?   Never was there a rejoinder so biting or so righteous as that which the cowardice of the Northern Democracy
puts into our mouths, against this, their favorite accusation.
For, which of the privileges of freemen is it which we have not
seen them betray in their own case; freedom from illegal arrest,
the benefit of the writ of *habeas corpus*, liberty of speech, liberty
of printing, free and untrammelled suffrage, liberty of conscience in the worship of God, rights of property, or freedom of
their own persons from military rule?

It has been clamorously asserted that the insolence of the
South in taking the aggressive by the first acts of violence, and
firing upon the national flag, left the Government no option, consistent with self-respect, save to resist.   The statement is false.

The violation of the Federal compact by the. North, restored to the South its inherent right to a peaceable withdrawal; and they who attempted to obstruct it were the first aggressors. The first act of war was committed by the Government at Washington against South Carolina, when fortresses intended lawfully only for her protection, were armed for her subjugation. That act of war was repeated, when armed preparations were twice made to reinforce these means of her oppression. And, at last, when she was imperiously warned that these forcible aggressions would be consummated, after a forbearance far greater than the Confederate Government was bound to exercise, it proceeded to what was an act of strict self-defence, the reduction of Fort Sumter.*

---

* Fort Sumter has become so celebrated, both by its being the scene of the first hostilities between the contending parties, and by the splendid and successful defence which it has since made in the hands of the Confederates, against the fleet and armies of the North, that the whole story connected with its original capture deserves to be better known than it is, generally, in Europe. It was on December 20, 1860, that the State of South Carolina, by the unanimous vote of a Convention, called by her Legislature, formally seceded from the Union. At this time Major R. Anderson was commandant of the Federal forces at Charleston. His head-quarters were at Fort Moultrie on the mainland; Fort Sumter, the strongest of all the defences, and placed in the middle of the bay, not being occupied. A grand banquet was given in honor of the Ordinance of Secession, on the evening of the day (Dec. 20), on which it passed. At midnight, Anderson, who must have received secret orders how to act, having spiked the guns, abandoned Moultrie, and conveyed all his men and stores to Sumter. Next morning, to the amazement of the South Carolinians, they saw the Union flag floating over it, and found Anderson in possession. As was to be expected, this act of treachery greatly incensed them; for the authorities of South Carolina had received a pledge from President Buchanan that the existing military *status* should undergo no change in their State, during the expiring term of his administration. That pledge was violated by this seizure and military occupation of Sumter; and, notwithstanding all remonstrances, Buchanan, probably under the pressure of Northern clamor, refused to order Anderson back again to Moultrie. The Secretary of War, J. B. Floyd, who had been a party to the promise, felt his honor so compromised by this gross breach of faith, that he instantly and indignantly resigned. Immediately after Mr. Lincoln had entered

But, it is replied, the Seceding States made themselves robbers, by seizing Federal ships, posts, arms, and money, by violence! It may be asked in rejoinder: Had the South no share in these appliances, provided with her money, and, when in her borders, having no other legitimate use than her defence? But she did not secede in order to commit a robbery. The proof is, that her ambassadors haunted the gates of the Federal Capitol for months, entreating to be permitted to make an equitable settlement of all these properties, until they were spurned away. And why were they forcibly seized, except that she was well assured the purpose was entertained to employ them for her ruin? Our neighbor and partner attempts to obstruct us in the prosecution of our unquestionable rights, by

on his office as President, in March 1861, Commissioners from the South proceeded to Washington, to urge a peaceable separation, and to negotiate for the transfer of Government property, and, in particular, for the removal of the Federal garrison from Forts Pickens and Sumter. But under the pretext that to treat with them avowedly and officially might embarrass the administration of Mr. Lincoln, they were assured through an intermediate party, that all would yet be well, that the military status of the South would be undisturbed, and that Sumter would be evacuated. These assurances were given by Secretary Seward himself, verbally and in writing, through Judge Campbell of the Supreme Court; but they were only meant to deceive. There never was any intention to keep faith, or to evacuate Sumter. It was a dishonest manœuvre to gain time for collecting armaments, and preparing coercive measures. The military reinforcement of Sumter was pronounced by General Scott, and other advisers of Lincoln, to be impracticable, except by artifice or surprise. Hence the deceit practised, to throw the Confederates off their guard. Meanwhile unusual activity was perceptible in the Northern dockyards and depots. Even down to the 7th of April, it was pretended that the evacuation would take place.

On that very day, Judge Campbell, uneasy as to Mr. Seward's good faith, wrote to him on the subject, and received the emphatic reply: — " *Faith as to Sumter fully kept — wait and see.*" The very next day (April 8th) the expedition started to convey " provisions to a starving garrison ; " but it consisted of eleven vessels, with an aggregate force of 285 guns, and 2400 men. It arrived in time to witness the bombardment and fall of Sumter on April 13th; lying at anchor, in the distance, during the action, and never firing a gun. The people brandishing a dagger before our eyes, purchased partly with our money. When we wrench it from his hand to save our own lives, shall he accuse us of stealing his dirk? Yet such was the insulting nonsense which was everywhere vented to make the South an offender for acts of self-defence, which the wicked designs of the tyranny at Washington justified more and more every day.

All the pretexts of coercion have thus been reviewed and exposed. The crime of the North stands forth without excuse, and black with every trait of guilt. Its motive, impiously cloaked under the sacred profession of sustaining the law, was to replace, by the more speedy means of the armed hand, that legislative and commercial plunder which had been so long practised, and to indulge a festering hatred. Its perpetrators were the people who claimed the largest share of the light and religiousness of the nineteenth century. Its victims were not aliens, but countrymen, brethren, and fellow-citizens. Its conduct

of Charleston had put the intended surprise out of the question; but the Lincoln Administration, nevertheless, accomplished one great object for which they had been scheming. They had procured the battle of Sumter; they had got the South to take the initiatory step of resistance. Henceforth the Federal Government, while in reality commencing a war which they had fully resolved upon, could make it appear that they were involved in it by the force of circumstances, rather than of their own choice, and that the South having fired the first shot was responsible for all the consequences. Such was the impression produced, and intended to be produced, in Europe; while the attack on the national flag, it was foreseen, could not fail to stir public sentiment to its lowest depth, and create a united war party in the North. Hence it was enough that the Federal forces in Sumter should make a mere show of resistance. Anderson accordingly just held the place as long as the rules of military honor required, and then surrendered it unconditionally, without having lost a man; whilst the fleet looked on, at a distance, and never attempted to come to his aid. We are entitled therefore to repudiate the charge of having commenced the war, by making the first appeal to arms. Granted that the first shot was fired by the South, the first military aggression was on the side of the North. The Federal Government are responsible for all.

has embodied every barbarity which could be practised by Hun, or Vandal, or Scythian. It has already shed more human blood, and crushed more hearts, than any war of modern ages. Reciting all these aggravations, the people of the Confederate States believe that no blacker national crime has challenged the lightning of heaven's wrath; therefore it is, that among this people, the best men are most resolved to resist it. If there are any of the children of the soil who excuse it, they are either the cowards, or the stupidly ignorant, or the mercenary, whose souls are bartered for filthy lucre. Every pure and noble man, like Jackson, every most devout soldier, the generous Southern women, the virtuous and cultivated citizens, the incorruptible judges of the law, the venerable and holy ministers of religion, these have committed their lives, and fortunes, and sacred honor to the defence of the Confederate States, as one man.

CHAPTER VI.

FIRST CAMPAIGN IN THE VALLEY.

THE reduction of Fort Sumter aroused at the North a general paroxysm of fury and revenge. Wherever there was enough of the spirit of moderation and justice to dissent, violent mobs were collected, which intimidated not only the press, but the pulpit, and exacted a pretended approval of the war-frenzy. The cry was, that the flag of the Union had been insulted, the Government assailed by treason, and the very life of the nation threatened. But even then, the enormity of the purposed crime of subduing free and equal States by violence, was so palpably felt, that the public mind, passionate as it was, acknowledged the necessity for a pretext. This was found in the false assertion that the Confederate States had inaugurated war, and thus justified a resort to force, — a misrepresentation which has already been refuted. It was claimed for the North, that its temper was just and pacific; and the contrast between the seeming calmness of her people before, and their tumultuous excitement after the first conflict, was pointed to as proof that they meditated no violence, and were only driven to a forcible defence of the Government, by the wickedness of the South. But the true explanation of the tempest is, that the North had just awakened to the fact, of which it was incredulous before, that the South was in earnest in the assertion of its rights. The difficulty of believing this arose in part from the many concessions of right

23

which the long-suffering South had made, from her long-continued, but futile expostulations, together with the ill-judged and passionate threats which her wrongs had often provoked from some of her politicians, and, in part, from the unspeakable vanity of the North, and its overweening conceit of its own power. The whole preparation of the Confederate States for self-defence, and the solemn warnings uttered by Virginia and the other Border States, were mocked at as only a new phase of political manœuvre. Often they affected a sort of good-natured forbearance, and spoke of not " whipping the spoiled children back into the Union," until they were obliged to do it. In the political slang which degraded the deliberations of the Capitol, it was currently asserted that those States " could not be kicked out of the Union." But, now, the North awoke out of this insane dream of delusion, to find that the South meant, and always had meant, what it said. Two purposes had long since grown up, and become fixed in the Northern mind : One was, not to surrender the legislative plunder which they had long gathered from the South, and which would be lost to them by its independence; the other was, not to make it contented in the Union, by a just concession of its rights. So long as the South could be kept quiet by mock compromises which secured it nothing, and by wheedling words, the North was very willing to expend these cheap means for that end; but so soon as it learned that the South was at last in earnest in asserting its rights, it became thoroughly in earnest also. The ruthless purpose of domination was at once revealed. Not only did the fragment of the Federal Government diligently prepare for a great war, but the people and the States began to provide munitions and raise troops, on a vast scale.

The prognostications indulged by speakers and newspapers, were as vainglorious, as their purposes were revengeful. The common language breathed threatening and slaughter, and demanded the sack, ruin, and extermination of the Southern people. To effect this, they thought the mighty North had only to lift up its little finger. The South was disdainfully described as poor, semi-barbarian, cowardly, unfurnished for war, and sunk in effeminacy; and the common expectation was, that nothing more was needed to wrap the whole country in the flames of a servile insurrection, than the signal of a Yankee invasion. In this spirit, equally fool-hardy and fiendish, the North rushed to the tremendous conflict.

Before Virginia seceded, the sword had been definitively drawn; indeed, it was this crime, which decided her to assert her independence. The legislative act was therefore accompanied, and immediately followed, by prompt preparations for defence.

The only standing army which the State possessed, was a single company of soldiers, who guarded the public property of the Commonwealth· at the Capitol. Her old militia system, which only required three exceedingly perfunctory drills a year, had, for some time, fallen into desuetude, and was just revived. The State had no men, who possessed any tincture of military training, except a few volunteer companies in her cities, and a few hundred *alumni* of the military academies at West Point and Lexington. Very few of these companies were armed. The armory of the State was in decay, its machinery rusting, and its arsenal only furnished with a few thousand muskets of antiquated make. The enterprise of private citizens, and the spirit of the country, more advanced than that of their rulers, had indeed led to the arming of a number of volunteer companies, after the attack of John Brown; and for these, a few thousand rifles had been purchased by the parties themselves. But the authorities of the State now set themselves, in earnest, to repair these omissions. The Convention, having passed the Ordinance of Secession the 17th of April, proceeded to appoint a Council of Three, to assist the Governor of the Commonwealth in his military duties. Orders were issued to the volunteer companies, which were springing into existence in every part of the State, to assemble in camps of instruction. The manufacture of cannon, projectiles, and muskets was resumed. Colonel Robert E. Lee, having resigned his commission from the Federal Government, had been invited to Richmond, immediately after the withdrawal of Virginia, and offered his services to his native State. His high character, patriotism, professional knowledge, and executive ability, were, fortunately, appreciated, and he was at once appointed Major-General and Commander-in-Chief of all the forces of the Commonwealth, by land and sea. Under his vigorous and sagacious management, order instantly began to arise out of chaos, and the excited masses of patriotic citizens assumed the proportions of an army. The most important of the camps of instruction was that named after him, Camp Lee, a mile beyond the western suburbs of Richmond. Here, several thousands of volunteers were assembled; and, to provide for their instruction, it was resolved to bring the more advanced Cadets of the Military School from Lexington, to perform the duties of drill-serjeants. The senior teachers of the school were already in Richmond, and this circumstance devolved the duty of conducting the cadets thither upon Major Jackson.

The bursting of the storm, which he had so long foreseen, found him calm, but resolved. About this time, a Christian friend, in whose society he greatly delighted, passed a night with him, and, as they discussed the startling news which every day brought with it, they were impelled to the conclusion that the madness of the Federal Government had made a great and disastrous war inevitable. The guest retired to his bed depressed by this thought, and, in the morning, arose harassed and melancholy. But, to his surprise, Jackson met him at the morning worship, as calm and cheerful as ever, and when he expressed his anxieties, replied, "Why should the peace of a true Christian be disturbed by anything which man can do unto him? Has not God promised to make all things work together for good to them that love him?"

The county of Rockbridge, like the rest of the State, was in a blaze of excitement, and its volunteers were arming and hurrying to the scene of action. Now it was that the hold which, notwithstanding his reputation for singularity, Major Jackson had upon the confidence of his countrymen, revealed itself. To his practical wisdom and energy they looked, in every difficulty of their organization and equipment. These calls, with the care of the Military Academy, occupied all his time. On Wednesday, April 17th, the presbytery of Lexington met in his church to hold its semi-annual session. These meetings, with their frequent opportunities for public worship and preaching, and their delightful hospitalities, have ever been, in Virginia, religious festivals. Major Jackson had been anticipating this reunion with great pleasure, and was preparing to entertain some of its members in his house. But the absorbing occupations of the week deprived him of every opportunity to attend either their meetings, or their worship. As he retired to rest on Saturday night, he remarked that he hoped for a quiet Sabbath-day, in which it would be his privilege to worship undisturbed, and to participate in the sacrament of the Lord's Supper, which was to be dispensed in the church; and he requested that politics and the troubles of the country might be banished from their conversation, that he might enjoy communion with God and his people undisturbed. But at day-break, on Sabbath morning, April 21st, an order arrived from the Governor of the State, to march the Cadets that day for Richmond.

Having given his wife some directions touching his own preparations for the journey, he immediately hurried to the Institute,
and busied himself in the arrangements for his pupils' departure.
One of these was to call upon his pastor, and request him to
attend at twelve o'clock A. M., to give them some Christian
counsels and a parting prayer. At eleven o'clock A. M., he
returned to his house, took a hurried breakfast, and retired
with his wife to their chamber, where he read the 5th chapter
of 2d Corinthians, commencing with the sublime and consoling
words: "For we know, that if our earthly house of this tabernacle be dissolved, we have a building of God, an house not
made with hands, eternal in the heavens." He then knelt, and
poured out a fervent prayer for themselves and for the country,
imploring God, in accents choked with tears, if it was compatible
with His holy will, that the storm might yet be calmed, and war
averted. He thus departed; and this happy home he never saw
again. Although he left his affairs thus unsettled, he never
asked nor received one day of furlough. From that time, he
never lodged one night outside the lines of his command. His
next return to Lexington was as a corpse, bedewed by a nation's
tears. After a few days, his family removed, by his advice, to
the house of a friend, his furniture was packed, his dwelling-
house closed, and his servants placed out for the war.

Having mustered the Cadets, and made everything ready for
their departure, at twelve o'clock, he invited Dr. White to begin
the religious service which he had requested, remarking significantly, "Doctor, we march at one o'clock precisely." This
hint against an undue prolongation of the worship was so well
observed, that the services were concluded fifteen minutes before
that hour. One of his officers, after a few moments' pause,
approaching him, said: "Major, everything is now ready, may we
not set out?" To this he made no reply, save to point to the

dial-plate of the great clock; and when it was upon the stroke of one, he gave the word: "Forward! March!" The corps of Cadets was conducted to Staunton, and thence, by railroad, to Richmond, and turned over to the commandant of Camp Lee. During a momentary pause in their journey, on the eastern slope of the Blue Ridge, he wrote to his wife: "Here, as well as at other points of the line, the war-spirit is intense. The cars had scarcely stopped here before a request was made that I would leave a Cadet to drill a company."

From Richmond he wrote, April 23d: "Colonel Lee of the army is here, and has been made Major-General. His (services) I regard as of more value to us than General Scott could render as commander." (This was an allusion to a report, by which the people had just been excited, that General Winfield Scott, the conqueror of Mexico, and a son of Virginia, was about to return, to espouse the cause of his native State.) "It is understood that General Lee is to be Commander-in-Chief. I regard him as a better officer than General Scott."

"The Cadets are encamped at the Fair Grounds, which are about one and a half miles from the city. We have excellent quarters. So far as we can hear, God is crowning our cause with success; but I do not wish to send rumors to you. I will try to give facts as they become known; though I may not have time to write more than a line or so. The governor, and others holding responsible offices, have not enough time for their duties; they are so enormous at this date."

The Camp of Instruction near Richmond being in charge of another officer, Major Jackson had no responsible duties to perform there during his short stay. He was exceedingly anxious for active employment; and, it must be added, distrustful of his prospects of obtaining it. For, his acute, though silent perspicacity taught him plainly enough, that the estimate formed of his powers by the major part of the people and the authorities, was depreciatory. But he disdained to agitate, or solicit for promotion; and busied himself quietly in assisting, at the camp, informally, in the drill and discipline of the mass of new soldiers there collected. One day he was accosted by one of these, an entire stranger, who told him that he had just been assigned as corporal of the guard for the day, that he was absolutely ignorant of the details of his duties, that the officer who had given him his orders, as ignorant, perhaps, as himself, had left him without instructions; and that seeing, by his uniform, he was an officer of rank, he wished to beg him for some aid. Major Jackson at once assented. He went with the soldier around the whole circuit of sentry-posts, taught him practically all the salutes, the challenges, and the instructions to be observed, and displayed such thorough knowledge and goodness at once, that he declared from that hour Jackson had won not only his respect but his love. It was these, not arts of popularity, but actual virtues, which bound the hearts of his men to him.

When the State had such urgent need of practical talent, it was impossible that an officer of Major Jackson's reputation should be wholly overlooked. A few days after he reached Camp Lee, it was determined by the Executive War Council to employ him in the engineer department, with the rank of Major. This arrangement his advocates justly regarded as unfriendly to him, for it gave him no actual promotion, while the State was showering titles and rank on scores of men who had never seen service; and it assigned him a branch of duty for which he always professed least taste and qualification. For placing a battery, an earthwork, or a line of battle, indeed, his judgment was almost infallible; but he was no draughtsman, and to set him to the drudgery of compiling maps, was a sacrifice of his

reputation and of his high capacities for command. But as soon
as this purpose was made known, and before it was reported to
the Convention for their approval, influential friends from Jackson's native district, by whom his powers were better esteemed,
remonstrated with the Council, and showed them that he was the
very man for a post of primary importance for which they were
then seeking a commander. By their advice, seconded by that
of Governor Letcher, this appointment was revoked, and he was
commissioned, Colonel of the Virginia forces, and ordered to
take command at Harper's Ferry. The next day this appointment was sent to the Convention for their sanction, when some
one asked, "Who is this Major Jackson, that we are asked to
commit to him so responsible a post?" "He is one," replied
the member from Rockbridge, "who, if you order him to hold a
post, will never leave it alive to be occupied by the enemy."
The Governor accordingly handed him his commission as Colonel, on Saturday, April 27th, and he departed at once for his
command. On the way he wrote thus to his wife:—

"*Winchester, April 29th.*—I expect to leave here about half-
past two P. M. to-day, for Harper's Ferry. I am thankful to say
that an ever-kind Providence, who causes 'all things to work
together for good to them that love him,' has given me the post
which I prefer above all others, and has given me an independent
command. To His name be all the praise.

"You must not expect to hear from me very often, as I expect
to have more work than I have ever had, in the same length of
time, before; but don't be concerned about me, as an ever-kind
Heavenly Father will give me all needful aid."

This letter is a truthful revelation of his character; on the
one hand, full of that self-reliance and consciousness of power,
which made him long for a conspicuous position and an independent command; and on the other, recognizing the gratification of

24

this wish as a mark of God's favor, and resting upon His aid, with an eminent faith, for all his success and fame.

On the 19th of April, two notable events had occurred in Virginia, of which one was the evacuation of the great naval depot in Norfolk Harbor by the Federal authorities, after its partial destruction; and the other was, the desertion of Harper's Ferry.

This little village, which events have rendered so famous, is situated on the tongue of land between the junction of the Potomac and Shenandoah rivers. The former of these is the boundary between Virginia and Maryland. The latter, collecting its tributaries southwest of Harper's Ferry, in the great valley of Virginia, flows northeastward along the western base of the Blue Ridge, until it meets the Potomac where that river forces its passage through this mountain range, to find its way towards the sea. The abundant water-power, the interior position, and its proximity to a plentiful country, had led to its selection by the Federal Government, for the manufacture and storing of fire-arms. The banks of the two streams were lined with factories, where muskets and rifles of the most approved patterns were made in large numbers; and in the village were the arsenals, where many thousands were stored. The space between the two rivers is also filled by a mountain of secondary elevation, called Bolivar Heights, and on the lower declivities of this ridge, as it descends to the junction of the two streams, the town is built in a rambling fashion. East of the Shenandoah the Blue Ridge rises immediately from the waters, overlooking the village, and the sides of Bolivar Heights. Here the mountain, lying in the county of Loudoun, is called Loudoun Heights. North of it, and across the Potomac, the twin mountain, bearing the name of Maryland Heights, rises to an equal altitude, and commands the whole valley of the Potomac above. From this description, it is manifest that Harper's Ferry is worthless as a defensive military post, when assailed by a large force, unless it were also garrisoned by a great army, and supplied with a vast artillery, sufficient to crown all the triangle of mountains which surround it, and to connect those crests effectually with each other. It had never been designed for a fortress, and there was nothing whatever of the character of fortifications around it. But as a preliminary point, it was of prime importance to hold it, both to protect Virginia against incursions, and to restrict the convenience of her enemy. Through the gorge opened in the Blue Ridge by the Potomac, passes also the Chesapeake and Ohio Canal, the great turnpike road from the regions of the Upper Potomac to the cities of Washington and Baltimore, and the railroad, which constitutes the grand connexion of those cities with the coal-fields whence they draw their fuel, and with the great West. Besides this, the railroad leading southward to Winchester, diverges from Harper's Ferry, and ascends the valley of the Shenandoah. Hence, the occupation of this point, as a focus, was regarded by the government of Virginia, as of radical importance, and it was obviously the advanced post of all her defences.

As soon as war became imminent, the minds of the people were turned to the value of the arms stored at Harper's Ferry, because they were precisely what Virginia lacked. Almost without prompting from the authorities, the militia was assembling in the neighborhood to capture the place; when the officer in command of the Federal guard attempted to destroy the factories and arsenals, and fled to Carlisle, in Pennsylvania. His designs against the former were abortive, and a quantity of machinery and materials, which proved of priceless value to the Commonwealth, was rescued; but when the militia entered the village, the storehouses, which had contained thousands of valuable arms, were wrapped in flames. It was indeed ascertained, that the larger part of the muskets were not consumed with the buildings, but were stolen and secreted by the inhabitants of the place. Of these, a few thousands were discovered, hidden in every conceivable place of concealment, and gathered for the State by the officers of the militia, while many of the privates armed themselves, by traffic with the venal populace. Meantime, other companies of volunteers flocked from the valley of Virginia to the place, until the materials of a little army were assembled there. But they were " without form and void."

It was at this juncture that Colonel Jackson took command. He was ordered by Major-General Lee to organize the companies of volunteers, assembled at Harper's Ferry, into regiments, and to instruct them diligently in military drill and discipline, to retain control of the great thoroughfares leading towards Washington city, and prevent their use by the Federal authorities for offensive purposes, even by their partial destruction, if necessary; to urge on the completion of fire-arms out of the materials already partially prepared at the factories, until such time as the machinery could be removed to the interior; and to defend the soil of Virginia from the invasion threatened from that quarter. About this time, there were assembled at Harper's Ferry, 2100 Virginian troops, with 400 Kentuckians, consisting of Imboden's, Rogers', Alburti's, and Graves'. batteries of field artillery, with fifteen guns of the lightest calibre; eight companies of cavalry without drill or battalion organization, and nearly without arms; and a number of companies of infantry, of which three regiments, the 2d, 5th, and 10th, were partially arranged, while the rest had no organization. The Convention had just passed a very necessary law, revoking the commissions of all the militia officers in command of volunteer forces; for their appointments, made long before, when the military system of the State was only a name, on every conceivable ground of political or local popularity, were no evidence whatever of fitness for actual command. These decapitated generals and colonels were, naturally, disaffected to the new order in military affairs. Of discipline there was almost none, and the force was apparently about to disintegrate and separate as rapidly as it had been gathered. Everybody wanted a furlough, for they had come as to a frolic. There was no general staff, no hospital, nor ordnance department, and scarcely six rounds of ammunition to the man.

To this confused mass Colonel Jackson came a stranger having not a single acquaintance in the whole command. He brought two of his colleagues in the military school, Major Preston and Colonel Massie, who virtually composed his staff, and two young men whom he employed as drill-masters. With their aid, his energy, impartiality, fairness and courtesy, speedily reduced the crude rabble to order and consistency. The little army, like the generous young courser, recognized a master in the first touch of the reins; and speedily the restive temper, which had been provoked by the incompetent hands that essayed to guide it, gave place to joy and docility. The reputation of Colonel Jackson as a stark fighter in the Mexican War, laid the foundation for his influence; for, among new soldiers, it clothed his person and authority with a fascination which charmed and stimulated their fancy. His justice engaged the approbation of every man's conscience; his unaffected goodness allured their love, and, if insubordination was attempted, his sternness awed them into submission. Once or twice only some wilful young officer made experiment of resisting his authority; and then the snowy brow began to congeal with stony rigor, the calm blue eye to kindle with that blaze, steady at once and intense, before which every other eye quailed; and his penalties were so prompt and inexorable, that no one desired to adventure another act of disobedience. His force was ultimately increased by the accession of volunteers from Virginia, and of a few Southern troops, to forty-five hundred men. Ammunition was forwarded to him, additional cannon of heavy calibre were procured, and the Pendleton battery, from his own village, afterwards famous on many a hard-fought field, was added to his command.

Several questions of peculiar delicacy were to be handled by him. One was the control of the Baltimore and Ohio Railroad. From the western boundary of Maryland to the Ohio river, this great thoroughfare passed through the territory of Virginia by two branches. It had opened up to the inhabitants valuable access to the eastern cities, which many of them prized more than liberties, or the claims of either the Union or Virginia. If commercial intercourse along this road were hindered, it was feared that the vacillating allegiance of the Northwest to the State would be utterly overthrown. Colonel Jackson therefore resolved to leave the road uninterrupted for all peaceful travel and traffic for the present.

The Maryland Heights overlooked the village from the north, and, if they were occupied by the enemy with artillery, his position there would be rendered untenable. But Maryland then professed to be neutral; it was hoped that she would, before long, espouse the cause of the South; and the authorities of Virginia wished to respect her territory, and all her rights, so long as she did not become one of our enemies. One expedient proposed by General Lee was, to induce Marylanders to enlist in the war, in sufficient numbers to hold the crest of the mountain, and commit its guardianship to them. But the people of that region were too timid and undecided to concur in such a plan. Another was, to postpone the occupancy of the mountain until the near approach of the enemy rendered it a military necessity; when this would constitute the justification of the act. But against this the obvious objection lay, that the enemy's advance might be too sudden to permit those preparations which were necessary to make the post tenable. Colonel Jackson therefore decided the matter for himself, and seized the Maryland Heights; constructing upon them a few block houses, and quartering there a few companies of troops.

He was his own engineer, and reconnoitred all the ground for himself. He constructed very few entrenchments; and, to the end of his career, it was characteristic that he made almost no use of the spade and pick. On the 8th of May he wrote as follows to his wife:—

"I am living at present in an elegant mansion, with Major Preston in my room. Mr. Massie is on my staff, but left this morning for Richmond, as bearer of despatches, and is to return in a few days. I am strengthening my position, and, if attacked, shall, with the blessing of the kind providence of that God who has always been with me, and who, I firmly believe, will never forsake me, repel the enemy. I am in good health, considering the great labor which devolves on me, and the loss of sleep to which I am subjected."

In the despatches which he sent to the Government, he announced his conviction that his post should be so defended, as to make it a Thermopylæ. His command was the advanced-guard of all the Southern forces; a collision was expected first at Harper's Ferry, which was threatened by a large force under Major-General Patterson; and, through that pass, it was supposed the invaders would attempt to pour into the State. Such a resistance, Colonel Jackson declared, should be made to this first assault, as would convince our enemies of the desperate determination of the people of the South, and would set, to our soldiers, an example of heroism in all future combats. As Leonidas and his three hundred judged that the moral effect of their sacrifice would be worth more to Greece, in teaching her citizens how to die for their country, than any subsequent services which they could hope to render, so Jackson determined, if necessary, to die at his post at Harper's Ferry, in order to elevate the spirit of Southern resistance.

From the beginning, he manifested that reticence and secrecy as to all military affairs, for which he was afterwards so remarkable. It was his maxim, that, in war, mystery was the key to success. He argued, that no human shrewdness could foretell what item of information might not give some advantage to an astute adversary, and that, therefore, it was the part of wisdom to conceal everything, even those things of which it did not appear how the enemy could make use. And since the channels by which intelligence may pass, are so numerous and unforeseen, those things which he did not wish divulged to the enemy he divulged to no one, except where necessity compelled him. Not long after he took command at Harper's Ferry, a dignified and friendly Committee of the Legislature of Maryland visited him to learn his plans. It was deemed important to receive them with all courtesy, for the co-operation of their State was earnestly desired, and every one was watching to see how Colonel Jackson would reconcile his secrecy, and his extreme dislike to be questioned upon military affairs, with the demands of politeness. Among other questions, they asked him the number of his troops. He replied promptly, "I should be glad if Lincoln thought I had fifteen thousand."

The character of his thinking was illustrated by the declaration which he made upon assuming this command, that it was the true policy of the South to take no prisoners in this war. He affirmed that this would be in the end truest humanity, because it would shorten the contest, and prove economical of the blood of both parties; and that it was a measure urgently dictated by the interests of our cause, and clearly sustained by justice. This startling opinion he calmly sustained in conversation, many months after, by the following considerations, which he prefaced with the remark, that, inasmuch as the authorities of the Confederate States had seen fit to pursue the other policy, he had cheerfully acquiesced, and was as careful as other commanders to enjoin on his soldiers the giving of quarter and humane treatment to disarmed enemies. But he affirmed this war was, in its intent and inception, different from all civilized wars, and therefore should not be brought under their rules. It was not, like them, a strife for a point of honor, a diplomatic quarrel, a commercial advantage, a boundary, or a province; but an attempt on the part of the North against the very existence of the Southern States. It was founded in a denial to their people of the right of self-government, in virtue of which, solely, the Northern States themselves existed. Its intention was a wholesale murder and piracy, the extermination of a whole people's national life. It was, in fact, but the "John Brown Raid" resumed and extended, with new accessories of horror, and, as the Commonwealth of Virginia had righteously put to death every one of those cut-throats upon the gallows, why were their comrades in the same crime to claim now a more honorable treatment? Such a war was an offence against humanity so monstrous, that it outlawed those who shared its guilt beyond the pale of forbearance. But as justice authorized their destruction, so wisdom and prudence demanded it, for it is always wisest to act upon principle, in preference to expediency. He argued further, that this enormous intent of the war, together with the infuriated temper of the Northern people, and the circumstances of the contest, would inevitably lead them, before its close, even if they observed some measure at first, to barbarities and violations of belligerent rights, which would

25

compel our authorities, by every, consideration of righteous retribution and duty to their own injured citizens, to a bloody retaliation. But this would probably be then retorted, and the internecine policy would only assume a wider extent. The arrogance of the Federal Government would be sure to add political persecution of our citizens to the other rigors of war, under the pretext of punishing rebellion. The Administration at Washington was indebted to Abolitionism for its real strength, and would find itself impelled, whether it willed it or not, to conduct the war in accordance with the demands of that fell fanaticism. It would be seen, before this contest was over, inciting slave insurrections in the South, arming the servile class against their masters, and setting them on to perpetrate all the horrors of savage warfare. The Confederate States ought not to submit to these enormities, and could not; but the measures of retribution which the protection of their outraged citizens would require, should be directed rather against the instigators than the ignorant tools. By the time, however, this stern necessity had manifested itself, the Federal Government might have many of our soldiers, and much of our territory, in their clutches, so that retaliation would be encumbered with additional difficulties. It would be better, therefore, to begin upon a plan of warfare which would place none of our citizens in their power alive. And lastly, if quarter was neither given nor asked, our soldiers would be only the more determined, vigilant, and unconquerable, for they were fighting under an inevitable necessity for liberties, homes, and existence; while the soldiers of our enemies would be intimidated, and enlistments would be prevented, because they contend only for pique, revenge, and lust of gain. Indeed, it was in every way for the advantage of the Confederate States, that the war should be made to unmask its murderous nature, most practically, to the apprehensions of our citizens, for then they would be more likely to rise to the exercise of those radical and primary instincts of the human soul, which are commensurate in intensity with the magnitude of the stake at issue. This war was, in its true nature, internecine; it were better that it should be understood as such. Its real meaning was destruction to the South; better have each citizen and soldier understand this for himself, in the most personal sense. Then, instead of seeing a people waging so dire a contest for the primary objects of existence, with divided zeal, and with only the secondary motives of their nature, the most powerful moral forces of the soul would be evoked to sustain the struggle.

Such, in substance, were the reasons which he rendered for his conclusion. They were given with an unpretending simplicity, which no other can reproduce; for it was a characteristic of his mind, that the most profound considerations were seen by him so clearly and simply, that they were expressed without logical parade or pomp, as though they had been easy, and obvious to every understanding. Those who have watched the subsequent course of the war can decide, how accurately all his predictions have been verified. And every thoughtful man now anticipates nothing else, than to see mutual acts of retaliation precipitate the parties into an unsparing slaughter; a result which has only been postponed thus far, by the unexampled forbearance of the people and government of the Confederate States.

Meantime, on the 2d of May, Virginia had adopted the Constitution of the Confederate States, appointed Commissioners to their Congress, and thus united her fortunes with theirs. The secession of Virginia gave a second impulse to the revolution, by which the States of North Carolina, Tennessee, Arkansas, and Missouri, and afterwards, in name, Kentucky, were added to the Confederation. On the 20th of May, the Confederate Congress adjourned from Columbia to Richmond, which they had selected as their future capital, and on the 29th of the same month, Mr. Jefferson Davis, the President of the Confederacy, was received in Richmond with unbounded enthusiasm. By a treaty between Virginia and the Confederate Government, the State transferred all her troops and armaments to that power; which engaged, in return, to defend her, and to pay and govern the forces. One of the earliest acts of the Confederate Government was to appoint a Commander of higher rank and greater experience to Harper's Ferry, which they justly regarded as a post of prime importance. General Joseph E. Johnston was selected by them for this office, May 23d, and proceeded thither immediately, to take command. The Virginian authorities afterwards assured Colonel Jackson, that they were fully satisfied with his administration there, and would have been well pleased to increase his rank until it was adequate to the extent and responsibility of the command; but they properly acquiesced in the appointment made by the Confederate Government. When General Johnston, however, arrived at Harper's Ferry, and claimed to relieve Colonel Jackson of his command, the latter had received no directions from the State Government to surrender his trust. And here arose a momentary collision between the two authorities, which displayed the inflexibility of Jackson's character. He replied that he had been intrusted by Major-General Lee, at the command of the State of Virginia, with this charge; and could only relinquish it by his orders. In this position, he was, while respectful, immovable; and as the Confederate commander was equally firm, a mischievous strife was anxiously feared. But very soon, the mails brought an application from some person pertaining to Colonel Jackson's command, upon which was endorsed, in the hand-writing of

Major-General Lee, a reference to the authority of General Joseph E. Johnston, as commanding at Harper's Ferry. This furnished Colonel Jackson all the evidence which he desired, to justify his surrender of his trust; and he hastened, with cordial pleasure, to transfer his whole powers to General Johnston. The purity of his motives, and the absence of ambition, were appreciated by the latter, in a way equally honorable to both; Colonel Jackson became at once a trusted subordinate, and a zealous supporter. The Virginia regiments, at the different posts, were now separated and organized into a brigade, of which he was made commander. Thus began his connexion with the Stonewall Brigade. It was composed of the 2d Virginia regiment, commanded by Colonel Allen, who fell at Gaines' Mill; the 4th, commanded by Colonel Preston; the 5th, commanded by Colonel Harper; the 27th, commanded by Colonel Gordon; and, a little after, the 33d, commanded by Colonel Cummings. The battery of light field-guns, from his own village of Lexington, manned chiefly by the gentlemen of the college and town, and commanded by the Rev. Mr. Pendleton, Rector of the Episcopal congregation of that place, formerly a graduate of the West Point Academy, was attached to this brigade, and was usually under Jackson's orders. His brigade staff was composed of Major Frank Jones (who also fell as Major in the 2d regiment, at Gaines' Mill), Adjutant; Lieutenant-Colonel James W. Massie, Aide-de-camp; Dr. Hunter M'Guire, Medical Director; Major William Hawkes, Chief Commissary; Major John Harman, Chief Quartermaster; and Lieutenant Alexander S. Pendleton, Ordnance Officer. It is due to the credit of Jackson's wisdom in the selection of his instruments, and to the gallant and devoted men who composed this staff, to add, that all of them who survived, rose with their illustrious leader to corresponding posts of usefulness and distinction. It may be added, that every brigadier who has com-. manded this famous brigade, except its present gallant leader, has fallen in battle, either at its head or in some other command. General Jackson was succeeded as its commander, by General Richard Garnett, who, having been appointed to another brigade, fell at the head of his command, at Gettysburg. The next General of the Stonewall Brigade was the chivalrous C. S. Winder, who was killed at its head, at Cedar Run. He was succeeded by the lamented General Baylor, who speedily, in the second battle of Manassas, paid, with his life, the price of the perilous eminence; and he, again, by the neighbor and friend of Jackson, General E. F. Paxton, who died on the second of the bloody days of Chancellorsville, thus preceding his commander by a week. This fatality may show the reader what kind of fighting that brigade was taught, by its first leader, to do for its country.

General Johnston, having speedily learned the untenable nature of his position at Harper's Ferry, and having accomplished the temporary purposes of its occupation, by the removal of the valuable machinery and materials for the manufacture of fire-arms, determined to desert the place. The Federal commander, General Patterson, had now approached the Potomac northwest of Harper's Ferry, by the way of the great valley of Pennsylvania, so that against him the tenure of that post had become no defence. His purpose to effect a junction at Winchester with the forces of General M'Clellan, advancing from northwestern Virginia, was suspected. That town, situated in the midst of the champaign of the great valley, about thirty miles southwest of Harper's Ferry, is the focus of a number of great highways, from every quarter. Of these, one leads north, through Martinsburg across the Potomac at the little village of Williamsport, the position then occupied by General Patterson. Another, known as the northwestern turnpike, passes by

Romney, across the Alleghany Mountains, throughout north-western Virginia to the Ohio River. And others, leading east-ward, southward, and southwestward into the interior of the State, Winchester, was therefore the true strategic point for the defence of the upper regions of Virginia, and thither General Johnston determined to remove his army. Having destroyed the great railroad bridge at Harper's Ferry, and the factories of the Government, and removed all his heavy guns and stores, he left that place on Sunday, June 16. About this time, the advance of the Federal army from the northwest was reported to be at Romney, forty miles west of Winchester; and General Patterson was crossing the Potomac at Williamsport, nearly the same distance to the north, with 18,000 men. General Johnston having marched to Charlestown, eight miles upon the road to Winchester, turned westward to meet Patterson, and chose a strong defensive position at Bunker Hill, a wooded range of uplands between Winchester and Martinsburg. Upon hearing of this movement, Patterson precipitately withdrew his forces to the north bank of the Potomac. Colonel Jackson thus described these movements in his letter to his wife:—

"*Tuesday, June* 18. — On Sunday, by order of General John-ston, the entire force left Harper's Ferry, marched towards Win-chester, passed through Charlestown, and halted for the night about two miles this side. The next morning we moved towards the enemy, who were between Martinsburg and Williamsport, Ma., and encamped for the night at Bunker Hill. The next morning we were to have marched at sunrise, and I hoped that in the evening, or this morning, we would have engaged the enemy; but, instead of doing so, General Johnston made some disposi-tion for receiving the enemy, if they should attack us, and thus we were kept until about twelve A. M., when he gave the order to return towards Winchester. At about sunset, we reached this place, which is about three miles north of Winchester, on the turnpike leading thence to Martinsburg. When our troops on Sunday were marching on the enemy, they were so inspirited as apparently to forget the fatigue of the march, and though some of them were suffering from hunger, this and all other privations appeared to be forgotten, and the march continued at the rate of about three miles per hour. But when they were ordered to retire, their reluctance was manifested by their snail-like pace. I hope the General will do something soon. Since we have left Harper's Ferry, something of an active movement towards repelling the enemy is, of course, expected. I trust that, through the blessing of God, we will soon be given an opportunity of driving the invaders from this region."

From this time Colonel Jackson's brigade formed the advanced body of the infantry of the army of the Valley, and was continually near the enemy. He thus speaks of the command:—

" The troops have been divided into brigades, and the Virginia forces under General Johnston constitute the first brigade, of which I am in command. I am very thankful to our kind heavenly Father, for having given me such a fine brigade. He does bless me beyond my expectations, and infinitely beyond my deserts. I ought to be a devoted follower of the Redeemer."

About this time, Colonel A. P. Hill, afterwards Lieut.-General, was sent towards Romney with a detachment of Confederate troops. The Federalists there retired before him, and having occupied that village, he proceeded along the Baltimore and Ohio Railroad, eighteen miles west of the town of Cumberland, assailed a detachment which guarded an important bridge, dispersed them, capturing two cannon and their colors, and destroyed the bridge. On the 19th of June, Colonel Jackson was sent with his brigade north of Martinsburg, to observe the enemy, who were again crossing the Potomac. They retired before him, evidently afraid to hazard a collision. On this expedition Colonel Jackson was ordered by General Johnston to destroy the locomotives and cars of the Baltimore Railroad at Martinsburg. At this village there were vast workshops and depots for the construction and repair of these cars; and more than forty of the finest locomotives, with three hundred burden-cars, were now destroyed. Concerning this he writes:—"It was a sad work; but I had my orders, and my duty was to obey. If the cost of the property could only have been expended in disseminating the gospel of the Prince of peace, how much good might have been expected!"

That this invaluable property should have been withdrawn to Winchester by the way of Harper's Ferry, before this point was evacuated, is too plain to be argued. Whose was the blunder cannot now be ascertained; that it was not Colonel Jackson's appears from the extract of his letter just inserted. The bridges across the streams, between Martinsburg and Harper's Ferry, were by this time burned. So desirable did it afterwards appear that the railroads of the Confederate States should be recruited with the remaining stock at Martinsburg, that a number of locomotives and burden-cars were drawn along the turnpike roads by long teams of horses to Winchester, and thence to the Central Virginia Railroad.

Colonel Jackson remained with his brigade a little north of Martinsburg, with Colonel J. E. B. Stuart in his front, then commanding a regiment of cavalry, until July 2d. On that day, he first fleshed his sword in actual combat with the Federal army. Patterson had, at last, ventured to cross the Potomac again in force, and to advance towards Jackson's camp. The latter immediately struck his tents, and ordered his command under arms. The instructions given him by his commander were to observe the enemy, and, if he advanced in full force, to

26

retire until he found a supporting body of his friends. He therefore advanced to meet the Federalists with the 5th Virginia Regiment, a few companies of cavalry, and one light field-piece of Captain Pendleton's battery, leaving orders to the remainder of his command to be ready to march either way, and to commence sending their baggage to the rear. Near Falling Water Church, a rural house of worship half-way between Martinsburg and the Potomac, he met the advance of the enemy, assailed and repelled them. Receiving reinforcements, they again advanced, and were again repulsed. Perceiving by this time the smallness of the force which was holding them in check, the enemy displayed a large body of infantry, which extended its wings, and then advanced them, with the design of enveloping Jackson in their folds. But he had posted his infantry behind the buildings and enclosures of a farm-house and barn, which occupied both sides of the highway, and thence poured a galling fire upon the enemy, until they were about to surround him. Bringing up his field-piece to cover the retreat of his men, he then withdrew them. The first fire of his gun cleared the highway of the advancing column of Federals, and he retired, skirmishing with them until, four miles south of Martinsburg, he met the army advancing to his support. In this combat, known as that of Haines' Farm, Colonel Jackson employed only 380 men (for the whole of the 5th Regiment was not engaged), with one piece of artillery. The enemy brought into action the whole of Cadwallader's Brigade, containing 3000 men and a battery of artillery. Yet it occupied them from nine o'clock A. M. until mid-day to dislodge this little force, and it cost them a loss of forty-five prisoners, captured by Colonel Stuart in a dash of his cavalry, and a large number of killed and wounded. Jackson's loss was two men killed and ten wounded. He was probably the only man in the detachment of infantry who had ever been under fire; but he declared that "both officers and men behaved beautifully." On the other hand, his coolness, skill, care for the lives of his men, and happy audacity, filled them with enthusiasm. Henceforward, his influence over them was established. General Patterson reported to his Government that he had repulsed 10,000 rebels, with the loss of one man killed. The numerous covered wagons of the Dutch farmers, which went to the rear, with the blood dripping through the seams of the boards, told a different story of his loss. The dead of the Federal army were carefully concealed from their comrades, lest the sight should intimidate the unwarlike rabble.

General Patterson occupied Martinsburg while General Johnston remained at the little hamlet of Darkesville, four miles distant, and offered him battle daily. This challenge the Federal general prudently declined. The Confederate commander, on the other hand, refused to gratify the eagerness of his men by attacking him in Martinsburg; for the massive dwellings and warehouses of that town, with the numerous stone-walled enclosures, rendered it a fortified place, of no little strength against an irregular approach. At the end of four days, General Johnston retired to Winchester. On the 15th of July General Patterson advanced to Bunker Hill, but, when his adversary again offered battle, he paused there, and began to extend his left eastward towards the little village of Smithfield. To the uninformed, the meaning of this movement seemed to be, to surround General Johnston by his larger forces. But the superior sagacity of the latter discerned the true intention, viz., to prepare for co-operation with the army of General M'Dowell, the Federal commander, who was about to assail the Confederate forces under General Beauregard at Manassa's Junction, and at the same time, to prevent the army of the Valley from extending that aid which would be so much needed by him.

Upon his return to Winchester, Colonel Jackson received the following note : —

"RICHMOND, 3d *July*, 1861.

"My dear General, — I have the pleasure of sending you a commission of Brigadier-General in the Provisional army; and to feel that you merit it. May your advancement increase your usefulness to the State. — Very truly,

"R. E. Lee."

General Johnston had recommended him for this promotion, immediately after the affair of Haines' Farm; but it had been already determined upon by the Confederate Government, and the letter of appointment was dated as early as June 17th. General Jackson was exceedingly gratified by this tribute to his merit, and by his permanent assignment to his Brigade. Ignorant of the generous intentions of the Government, he had been led by his modesty to fear, that his possession of that command would only be temporary. Other colonels in command of Brigades had just been relieved by officers of higher rank; and he anticipated the same event for himself. He had, indeed, written, just before, to an influential member of the State Government, earnestly requesting him to procure for him such promotion as would prevent this fate. His advancement, therefore, brought him all the pleasure of an agreeable surprise. To the constant sharer of his joys, he wrote : —

"I have been officially informed of my promotion to be a Brigadier-General of the Provisional Army of the Southern Confederacy. My promotion is beyond what I anticipated, as I only expected it to be in the volunteer forces of the State. One of the greatest [grounds of] desires for advancement is the

gratification it will give you, and serving my country more efficiently.

"Through the blessing of God I now have all that I ought to
desire in the line of promotion. I would be very ungrateful if
I were not contented, and exceedingly thankful to our kind
heavenly Father. May his blessing ever rest on you, is my
fervent prayer!"

The reader will see here, the same remarkable union of
honorable professional aspirations, with faith and dependence on
God, which distinguished his whole course.

CHAPTER VII.

MANASSAS.

THE movement of General Johnston from Harper's Ferry to Winchester was dictated, not only by the circumstances within his own field of operations, but by his relations to the Confederate commanders on his right and left. In the northwest was General Garnett, who, with five thousand men, confronted a Federal army of four times that number, commanded by Generals M'Clellan and Rosecranz. Had this army been overpowered, as it was during the month of July, while General Johnston was at Harper's Ferry, the victorious forces of M'Clellan would have been in a condition to threaten his rear at Winchester. East of the Blue Ridge, General Beauregard was organizing an army at Manassa's Junction, to cover that approach to the capital of the confederacy, and was confronted by the strongest of all the Federal armies, under General M'Dowell. The fearful preponderance against Beauregard could at any time have been increased, by suddenly withdrawing General Patterson's army from the Upper Potomac to Washington, for which the vast resources of the Baltimore Railroad offered ready means; while, from Harper's Ferry to Manassa's Junction, General Johnston must have travelled a more circuitous line; but, by placing his head-quarters at Winchester, he tempted General Patterson to Martinsburg. The advantages for concentration were now all reversed. General Johnston possessed the interior line, and was able to move by the shorter route to the support of General Beauregard.

The traveller who left the town of Alexandria, upon the Potomac, to go southwestward into the interior of Virginia, at the distance of twenty-five miles, found the Manassa's Gap Railroad dividing itself on the right hand from the main stem, and turning westward towards the peaks of the Blue Ridge, which are visible in the horizon. This road sought a passage through those mountains at Manassa's Gap, a depression which received its name from an obscure Jew merchant named Manassa, who, years ago, had fixed his home in the gorge of the ravine. From this the railroad was called the Manassa's Gap Road, and the junction with the Alexandria Railroad the Manassa's Junction. Thus the name of an insignificant Israelite has associated itself with a spot, which will never cease to be remembered, while liberty and heroism have votaries in the world. This Junction was manifestly the strategic point for the defence of Northeastern Virginia. It was at a convenient distance from the Potomac, to observe the course of that river; for the Confederate generals were too much masters of the art of war, to adopt the stupid policy of attempting to hold all the banks of a long stream, on the stationary defensive, against a superior assailant. It was manifest that the command of railroads, by reason of their capacity for the rapid transportation of troops and supplies, must ever be a decisive advantage in campaigns. The general who is compelled to move all his forces and material of war over country roads, by the tedious and expensive agency of teams, in the presence of an adversary who effects his advance on a railroad, must be at his mercy. To hold Manassa's Junction, covered two railroads, of which one led southwestward to Gordonsville, and thence, by two branches, to Charlottesville, and Richmond; and the other led westward, through the Blue

Ridge, into the heart of the Great Valley, the granary of the State; but worse, the possession of the Manassa's Gap Railroad by the Federalists uncovered General Johnston's rear to them equally whether he were at Harper's Ferry or at Winchester, and at once required the evacuation of the whole country north of that thoroughfare.

For these reasons, the Confederate Government made every effort to hold, and the Federal, directed by the veteran skill of General Winfield Scott, to seize this point. It is situated three miles south of Bull Run (a little stream of ten yards' width, almost everywhere fordable), in a smiling champaign, diversified with gentle hills, woodlands, and farmhouses.

The water-course takes its rise in a range of highlands, called the Bull Run Mountains, fourteen miles west of the Junction, and, pursuing a southeast course, meets Broad and Cedar Runs five miles east of it, and forms, with them, the Occoquan. The hills near the stream are more lofty and precipitous than the gentle swells which heave up the plain around the Junction; and, on one side or the other, they usually descend steeply to the water, commanding the level meadows which stretch from the opposite bank. Where the meadows happened to be on the north bank, the stream offered some advantages of defence for the Confederates; but where the lowlands were on the south side, the advantage for attack was with the Federalists.

No works of any description defended this line. The Junction, three miles in its rear, was surrounded with a single circuit of common earthworks, consisting of a ditch and an embankment of a few feet in height, with platforms for a score of cannon. A journey of six miles from the Junction, northeastward by the country road, brings the traveller to the hamlet of Centreville, seated on a high ridge. Through this little village passes the paved highway from Alexandria to Warrenton, in a direction almost due west; and, at a point five miles northwest of the Junction, this thoroughfare crosses the channel of Bull Run obliquely upon an arch of stone. Here a little tributary, called Young's Branch, enters the stream from the southwest, and the hills from which it flows rise to even a bolder elevation than the other heights of Bull Run. Upon those hills was fought the first Battle of Manassas.

On the 16th of July, the hosts of General M'Dowell left their entrenched camps along the Potomac, and drove in the advance of General Beauregard from Fairfax Court House on the 17th. The Federal army consisted of about sixty thousand men, including nearly all the United States regulars east of the Rocky Mountains, and sixty pieces of artillery. It was equipped with all that wealth and art could lavish, and armed throughout with the most improved implements of destruction.

The whole army and people of the North were inflated with the assurance of victory. The Generals had labelled the packages of supplies "for Richmond." The fanatical volunteers had supplied their pockets with halters with which to hang the "Southern Rebels," as soon as they were captured in battle. The Federal Congress, then in session in Washington, was adjourned, in order to enable the members to go with the army, and feast their eyes with the spectacle of the rout of the Confederates; and long lines of carriages, filled with females bedecked with their holiday attire, followed the rear of the Federal army, with baskets of champagne, and all the appliances for the feast and the dance, with which they proposed to mock the groans of the dying thousands on the evening of their victory. The newspapers of the North scouted with disdain the ideas of defeat; and declared that, in ten days at the utmost, their triumphant army must be established in Richmond, and

27

the Confederate Government drowned in the blood of its leaders.*

On the evening of July 17th, General Beauregard assembled all his forces along the line of Bull Run, from the Stone Bridge to the Union Mills, a distance of eight miles.   He thus presented to the enemy a body of about twenty thousand combatants, with thirty field-pieces, of which the heaviest were twelve-pounder howitzers.   These forces were divided into eight brigades.   The infantry was armed, with a few excep-tions, with the smooth-bore musket; and the cavalry, with fowl-ing-pieces and sabres.   On the 18th of July, the enemy, having assembled in force at Centreville, made a tentative effort with a heavy detachment of all arms, to force the line of Bull Run, at Mitchell's and McLean's* fords, upon the direct road to the

---

* It may be well to recall to memory the boastful spirit and arrogant self-con-fidence, with which the North entered upon the struggle with the South.   The *Tribune* said :   " The hanging of traitors is sure to begin before the month is over.   The nations of Europe may rest assured that Jeff. Davis & Co. will be swinging from the battlements of Washington, at least by the 4th of July.   We spit upon a later and longer deferred justice."   The *New York Times* said: " Let us make quick work.   The 'rebellion,' as some people designate it, is an unborn tadpole.   Let us not fall into the delusion of mistaking a 'local commotion,' for a revolution.   A strong active 'pull together' will do our work effectually in thirty days."   The *Philadelphia Press* declared that " no man of sense could, for a moment, doubt that this much-ado-about-nothing would end in a month." The Northern people were " simply invincible."   " The rebels, a mere band of ragamuffins, will fly, like chaff before the wind, on our approach."   But who can wonder that the press of America should pander thus to the ignorance and the arrogance of the North, when Seward himself, just a month before the Battle of Manassas, wrote thus in a public document, addressed to Mr. Dayton, the Minister at the French Court: "France seems to have mistaken a mere casual and ephemeral insurrection here, such as is incidental in the experience of all nations, for a war, which has flagrantly separated this nation into two co-existing political powers, who are contending in arms against each other, after the sepa-ration."   And again: "It is erroneous to suppose that any war exists in the United States.   Certainly there cannot be two belligerent powers, where there is no war."   Read in the light of subsequent events, ean anything appear more grotesque, more contemptible ?

Junction. Meeting with a bloody repulse in this essay, he occupied Friday and Saturday, the 19th and 20th, with explorations of the country, for the purpose of devising a flank movement.` The desired route was discovered, leading to Sudley Church, on Bull Run, two miles above the extreme left of the Confederates at the Stone Bridge; and the morning of Sunday, July 21st, was chosen for the second attempt.

Meantime, indeed at the first appearance of the Federal advance, General Beauregard had given notice to General Johnston, that the time had arrived for him to render his aid. Accordingly, on the forenoon of Thursday the 18th, the army of the Valley, numbering about eleven thousand men, was ordered under arms at its camp, north of Winchester, and the tents were struck. No man knew the intent, save that it was supposed they were about to attack Patterson, who lay to the north of them, from Bunker Hill to Smithfield, with twenty thousand men; and joy and alacrity glowed on every face. But at midday, they were ordered to march in the opposite direction, through the town, and then to turn southeastward towards Millwood and the fords of the Shenandoah.

As they passed through the streets of Winchester, the citizens, whose hospitality the soldiers had so often enjoyed, asked, with sad and astonished faces, if they were deserting them, and handing them over to the Vandal enemy. They answered, with equal sadness, that they knew no more than others whither they were going. The 1st Virginia brigade, led by General Jackson, headed the march. The cavalry of Stuart guarded every pathway between the line of defence which Johnston had just held and the Federalists, and kept up an audacious front, as though they were about to advance upon them, supported by the whole army. The mystified commander of the Federalists stood anxiously on the defensive, and never discovered that his adversary was gone until his junction with General Beauregard was effected, when he sluggishly drew off his hosts towards Harper's Ferry. As soon as the troops had gone three miles from Winchester, General Johnston commanded the whole column to halt, and an order was read explaining their destination. " Our gallant army under General Beauregard," said this order, "is now attacked by overwhelming numbers; the commanding general hopes that his troops will step out like men, and make a forced march to save the country." At these nervous words, every countenance brightened with joy, and the army rent the air with their shouts. They hurried forward, often at a double-quick, waded the Shenandoah River, which was waist-deep to the men, ascended the Blue Ridge at Ashby's Gap, and, two hours after midnight, paused for a few hours' rest at the little village of Paris, upon the eastern slope of the mountain. Here General Jackson turned his brigade into an enclosure occupied by a beautiful grove, and the wearied men fell prostrate upon the earth without food. In a little time an officer came to Jackson, reminded him that there were no sentries posted around his bivouac, while the men were all wrapped in sleep, and asked if some should be aroused, and a guard set. "No," replied Jackson, "let the poor fellows sleep; I will guard the camp myself." All the remainder of the night he paced around it, or sat upon the fence watching the slumbers of his men. An hour before daybreak, he yielded to the repeated requests of a member of his staff, and relinquished the task to him. Descending from his seat upon the fence, he rolled himself upon the leaves in a corner, and in a moment was sleeping like an infant. But, at the first streak of the dawn, he aroused his men and resumed the march.

From Winchester to Manassa's Junction the distance is about sixty miles. The forced march of thirty miles brought the army to the Piedmont Station, at the eastern base of the Blue Ridge, whence they hoped to reach their destination more easily by railroad. General Jackson's infantry was placed upon trains there, on the forenoon of Friday (the 19th July), while the artillery and cavalry continued their march by the country roads.

The president of the railroad company promised that the whole army should be transported on successive trains to Manassa's Junction by the morning of Saturday; but by a collision which was, with great appearance of reason, attributed to treachery, the track was obstructed, and all the remaining troops detained, without any provision for their subsistence, for two precious days. Had they been provided with food, and ordered to continue their forced march, their zeal would have brought the whole of them to the field long before the commencement of the battle. General Jackson's whole command reached the Junction at dusk on Friday evening, and were marched, hungry, weary, and dusty, to the pine-coppices near Mitchell's Ford, where they spent Saturday in refreshing themselves for the coming conflict. All of Saturday night again, their indefatigable general was afoot, busy in the distribution of food and ammunition, and in the review of his preparations.

It was no part of General Beauregard's plan to occupy the defensive attitude absolutely, along so weak and extended a line as that which he held on Bull Run. To do this, was to give the enemy leisure and opportunity to concentrate his forces, at any point which he might select, in such preponderance as inevitably to crush the portion of the Confederate army guarding that place; and then the line of the water-course, being lost at one part, must be relinquished everywhere, or the army defending it would be cut in two. The Confederate general proposed, if General Johnston's reinforcements had arrived in time, to mass his troops, take the aggressive, and strike the unwieldy body of the Federal army near Centreville. But Saturday passed, and they had not arrived. Nothing remained for him but to retain his defensive attitude, and await the development of the enemy's purposes. The morning of July 21st dawned with all the beauty and softness befitting a summer Sabbath-day, and the birds greeted the rising sun with as joyous a matin hymn as though the lovely quiet had been destined for nought but the worship of the Prince of peace. But the invaders had consecrated it, with an impiety equal to their malice, to the bloody orgies of the Moloch of their ambition. The sun had not begun to exhale the dew, when, along the Warrenton turnpike, every more pleasing sound was hushed into terror by the rumbling of the wheels of a great park of artillery, and the hoarse oaths of the officers hurrying it towards the extreme left of the Confederates. Columns of dust, rising into the quiet air in several directions, disclosed the movements of heavy masses of infantry. The Federal general, leaving one strong division to guard his rear at Centreville, paraded another opposite Mitchell's Ford, and still another in front of the Stone Bridge, each accompanied with batteries of rifled cannon; while the mass of his army made a detour through an extensive forest to the west, to cross Bull Run at Sudley Church, and thus to commence the assault in the rear of the Confederate left. They proposed to amuse the right and centre by a cannonade and a pretended assault, so as to detain those troops while the flanking force marched down the south side of Bull Run, crushed the brigade which guarded the Stone Bridge, and opened a way for the division attacking it to cross, and thus beat the patriot army in detail. Had the prowess of the Yankee troops been equal to the strategy of the chieftain, this masterly plan would have given them a great victory. The Confederate generals anticipated a flank attack, but were unable to decide at first, whether it would be delivered against their extreme right or left. Their hesitation, and the friendly concealment of the forest, enabled the enemy to effect his initial plan, and throw 20,000 men across Bull Run, at and near Sudley Ford, without a show of opposition. Colonel Evans, with a weak brigade of 1100 men, held the Confederate left, and watched the Stone Bridge. A mile below, Brigadier-General Cocke, with three regiments, guarded the next ford. When Evans ascertained that the enemy were already threatening his rear, he left the bridge and turnpike to the guardianship of two small pieces of artillery, wheeled his gallant brigade towards the west, and advanced a mile to meet the coming foe. Here the battle began, and soon the roar of musketry, and the accelerated pounding of the great guns, told that the serious work of the day was to be upon the left.

The cruel dilemma in which the superiority of the enemy's numbers, and their successful manœuvre, placed the Confederate commanders, can now be comprehended. If they disfurnished their centre or right, while threatened with an imminent attack in front, the direct road to victory was surrendered to the enemy. If they permitted their left to remain unassisted it was inevitably crushed, and the remainder of the Confederate army was taken in reverse. They had three brigades in reserve, of which one was not available, because of its distance in the rear of the extreme right. But the other two were those of Generals Bee and Jackson, and the heroism of these two was sufficient to reinstate the wavering fortunes of the day. The plan of battle which was adopted, after the designs of the enemy were fully disclosed, was worthy of the genius of Beauregard, who suggested, and of Johnston who accepted it. This was, to send the two reserve brigades which were at hand to sustain the shock upon the left, and to enable that wing of the army to hold its ground for a time, while the centre and right were advanced across Bull Run, and swung around into a position parallel to the enemy's line of march, towards the Stone Bridge, with the view of assailing their rear-guard and their line of communications, at Centreville.

The movement was to begin upon the extreme right, which would have the segment of the largest circle to traverse, and to be propagated thence to the centre, so as to concentrate all the brigades below Cocke's, in front of Centreville, in a formidable line of battle. This fine conception promised every advantage. It offered most effectual relief to the laboring left wing; for the Federal army would be sure to relax its assault, when the thunder of the Confederate battle on the north side of Bull Run and in their rear, told them that their line of communications was threatened. At the same time, it obviated the difficulty, otherwise insuperable, of employing the right and centre, now inactive, in deciding the fortunes of the day, without stripping the lower fords of Bull Run of their defences, and thus opening an unobstructed way for the enemy to the Junction. For as the Federal troops threatening those fords were pushed back, and the Confederates interposed between them and the stream, that access to the Junction was more effectually barred than before. But chiefly, this manœuvre promised a magnificent completeness in the victory which it seemed to secure; because it placed the strength of the Confederate army in the rear of their enemies, and in a formidable position commanding their only line of retreat. He who considers the panic which their actual discomfiture caused in the Federal army, will not doubt that, with the capture of Centreville, it would have dissolved into utter rout, and been dissipated or captured.

The two generals despatched the orders for this movement to

the commanders of the right and centre, and then galloped to the scene of action on the left where the furious and increasing fire showed that their presence was so urgently needed. The orderlies, by whom they were sent, miscarried; and Beauregard, after listening in anxious suspense to hear his guns open upon the heights of Centreville, until the day and the battle were too far advanced for any other resort, relinquished the movement, and devoted himself to sustaining the struggle before him. The only Confederate line seriously engaged was now at right angles to Bull Run, and facing westward. The Federal forces continuing to pour across at Sudley Ford, and extending their right wing perpetually farther to the south, pressed back their opponents by their fearful superiority of numbers and artillery, and by threatening to overlap their left. The only tactics which remained to the Confederate generals were, to bring up such reinforcements as could be spared from the centre and right successively, and as their line of battle was borne back from west to east, to repair its strength, and to increase its front by placing fresh troops at its south end, until it had sufficient extent and stability to breast the avalanche of Federal troops.

The reader is now prepared for an intelligent view of the important part borne by General Jackson in the battle. At four o'clock on the morning of the 21st, he was requested by General Longstreet, whose brigade formed the right of the centre, to reinforce him with two regiments. With this he complied, until the appearance of an immediate attack was rumored. He was soon after ordered by General Beauregard to support Brigadier-General Bonham at Mitchell's Ford, then to support Brigadier-General Cocke above, and then to take an intermediate position where he could extend aid to either of the two. About ten o'clock A. M., General Cocke requested him to move to the Stone Bridge, and assume the task of

28

guarding it, in place of Evans, who had gone westward to meet the enemy descending from Sudley. But as Jackson advanced in this direction, the firing became more audible, and taught his superior judgment where was the true point of danger. He hastened towards it, sending forward a messenger to General Bee, who had already reinforced Evans, to encourage him with the tidings, that he was coming to his support with all his force. It was, indeed, in good time. For two hours, these two officers, with five regiments and six guns, had breasted the Federal advance, often nearly surrounded, but stubbornly fighting as they retired, inflicting and receiving heavy losses, until their commands were disheartened and almost broken. As Jackson advanced to their assistance, he met the fragments of Bee's regiment sullenly retiring, while the heavy lines of the Federalists were surging forward like mighty waves. He proposed to that general to form a new line of battle, assuming the centre for himself, while Bee rallied his men in the rear, and then resumed his place upon his right. The ground which Jackson selected for standing at bay, was the crest of an elevated ridge running at right angles to Bull Run, between Young's Branch and another rivulet to the eastward, which flowed by a parallel course into the former stream. The northern end of this ridge overlooked the Stone Bridge. Its top and its western slopes were cleared of timber, and swept down in open fields to a valley, which divided Jackson at the moment from the advancing enemy; but the reverse side of the hill, towards the Confederate rear, was clothed with a tangled thicket of pines, impenetrable, save by two pathways, to artillery or cavalry. Before the Confederate line, were two homely cottages, with their enclosures and stables; and a country road descended obliquely across the front, at the distance of a few hundred yards, enclosed on both sides with the heavy wooden fences of the country, and

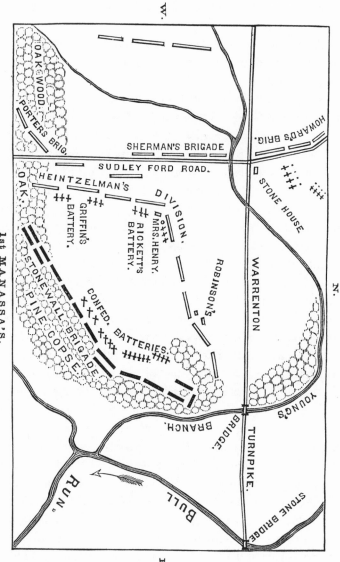

1st MANASSA'S.
Confederate Centre, 3 o'clock P. M., July 21.

worn, by the action of the elements, into an excavation of a yard in depth.

The soldierly eye of Jackson, at a glance, perceived that this was the spot on which to arrest the enemy's triumph. In the rear of this, the country approached more the character of a plain, and offered no marked advantages. It was true that the two little farm-houses in front of his right and left respectively, offered shelter to the enemy should they succeed in approaching his position, and the road which descended beyond gave them almost the advantage of an entrenchment; but the thickets on his right, left, and rear, protected them from the assault of any other force than skirmishers, — a vital point to one so fearfully outnumbered. The swelling ridge gave his artillery a commanding elevation, whence every approach of the enemy in front could be swept with effect, and, by placing his guns a little behind the crest, he gave the cannoneers who served them a protection from the adverse fire. The infantry supports in the rear of the batteries were still better shielded. Here, then, he began the new formation, by putting in position two guns of Stanard's battery, with the regiments which headed his column of march, and, while the remainder came to the ground designed for them, these two pieces held the enemy in check by their accurate fire. The opposing batteries were then upon the hill beyond the valley in front, which was also swarming with heavy masses of Federal infantry. Jackson recalled Imboden's battery, which had entered the action with General Bee's command, and gallantly maintained a perilous position until all its supports were routed. He brought up the other two guns of Stanard, and also the Pendleton battery, so that twelve pieces, which a little after were increased to seventeen, were placed in line under his command behind the crest of the eminence. Behind this formidable array he placed the 4th and 27th Regiments, commanded respectively by Colonel Preston and Lieut.-Colonel Echols, lying upon their breasts to avoid the storm of cannon-shot.   On the right of the batteries, he posted Harper's 5th Virginia, and on the left the 2d Regiment commanded by Colonel Allen, and the 33d led by Colonel Cummings.   Both ends of the brigade, when thus disposed, penetrated the thickets on the right and left, and the 33d was wholly masked by them.   On the right of Jackson's Brigade, General Bee placed the remains of the forces which, under him and Evans, had hitherto borne the heat and burden of the day, while, on the left, a few regiments of Virginian and Carolinian troops were stationed.   At this stage of affairs, Generals John- ston and Beauregard galloped to the front, inspiriting the men by their words and fearless exposure of their persons, and assisted in advancing the standards of the rallying regiments.   Their appeals were answered by the fierce cheers of the Confederates; and a new battle now began, to which the former was but a skirmish.   Jackson's Brigade numbered 2600 bayonets, and all the troops confronting the enemy, about 6500.   The Fed- eral commander, according to his own declaration, marshalled 20,000 of his best troops, with twenty-four guns, for the attack upon this position.   Successive lines of infantry were pressed across the valley and up the ascent of the ridge; they filled the fences of the roadway with sharp-shooters, who picked off the Confederate gunners with their long-range rifles; they crowded onward, and got foothold in the buildings before their lines. The Federal artillery poured a tempest of missiles upon our batteries, while they as furiously cannonaded the advancing lines of infantry.   From 11 o'clock A.M. to 3 P.M. the artillery shook the earth with its incessant roar, while the more deadly clang of the musketry rolled in peals across the field.   To the spectator in the rear, the smoke and dust rolled sullenly upward beyond the dark horizon of pines, like the fumes of Tophet.   Through the long summer hours, Jackson's patient infantry stood the ordeal, which even the hardiest veterans dread, lying passive behind their batteries while the plunging shot and shells of the enemy ploughed frequent gaps through their lines.   He rode, the presiding genius of the storm, constantly along his lines, between the artillery and the prostrate regiments, inspiring confidence wherever he came.   In the early morning, while he was ordered first to one post and then to another, but always in the rear, and it seemed as if he were destined for no decisive share in the great struggle, his men noticed that his cheeks were wan and his eye haggard with anxiety and suspense.   But now, all was changed, the ruddy glow had returned to his face, his whole form was instinct with life; and while his eye blazed with that fire which no other eye could meet, his countenance was clothed with a serene and assured smile.

As the grim wrestle continued, for the key of the Confederate position, the enemy perceived that they could make no impression upon Jackson's front.   They therefore extended and advanced their wings.   On his left, they brought a formidable battery of six guns within musket range, intending to enfilade his line, while on his right their irresistible numbers overwhelmed the shattered ranks of Bee.

It was then that this general rode up to Jackson, and with despairing bitterness exclaimed, " General, they are beating us back!"   "Then," said Jackson, calm and curt, "we will give them the bayonet."   Bee seemed to catch the inspiration of his determined will, and, galloping back to the broken fragments of his over-tasked command, exclaimed to them, " *There is Jackson standing like a stone wall.   Rally behind the Virginians.   Let us determine to die here, and we will conquer.   Follow me.*"   At this trumpet-call a few score of his men reformed their ranks.   Placing himself at their head, he charged the dense mass of the enemy, and in a moment fell dead, with his face to the foe. From that time Jackson's was known as the *Stone-wall Brigade*, a name henceforward immortal, and belonging to all the ages; for the christening was baptized in the blood of its author, and that wall of brave hearts has been, on every battle-field, a steadfast bulwark of their country.

Meantime, the battery which advanced upon Jackson's left had paid dearly for its temerity. It formed itself close upon the masked position of the 33d regiment, which, after a well-directed volley from the unerring mountain riflemen that slaughtered the larger part of the horses, dashed upon it with the bayonet, and captured every gun. But the excavated road-way was just beyond, and, from its depressed banks and zig-zag fences, the Federal infantry poured in such a fire, that it was impossible to retain the prize. The struggle for the crest of the eminence had now continued three hours, and was evidently approaching its crisis. Both of Jackson's flanks were threatened. Upon his front the enemy was pressing with overwhelming numbers; the ammunition and the strength of his cannoneers were failing together; and the red cloud of dust, in which the advancing line of the Federalists shrouded itself, was rolling perilously near to his batteries. Jackson saw that the moment had come to appeal to his supreme arbiter, the bayonet. Wheeling his guns suddenly to the rear by his right and left, he cleared away the arena before his regiments, and gave them all the signal. Riding up to the 2d regiment, he cried, "Reserve your fire till they come within fifty yards, then fire and give them the bayonet; and, when you charge, yell like furies!" Like noble hounds unleashed, his men sprang to their feet, concentrating into that moment all the pent-up energies and revenge of the hours of passive suffering, delivered one deadly volley, and dashed upon the enemy. These did not tarry to cross bayonets with them, but recoiled, broke, and fled headlong from the field. The captured battery was recaptured, along with a regimental flag; the centre of the enemy's line of battle was pierced, and the area, for which they had struggled so stubbornly, cleared of their presence.

This was, for the Confederates, the critical success. For nearly four hours, Jackson had held the enemy at bay; and the precious season had been diligently improved by the commanding Generals, in bringing up their reserves. As the pressure upon their lines below was relaxed, regiments and brigades were detached, and hurried up to the scene of action. A perpetual stream of fresh men was pouring on towards the smoking pine-woods, the chasms made in the scanty host on the crest were refilled, and the Confederate line of battle extended towards the south, by new batteries and brigades. The decisive hour was saved, and saved chiefly by Jackson's skill and heroism. It is true that, even when he charged the enemy's centre, their sharp-shooters found an inlet through the breaches of the line upon his right and left, and almost enveloped his rear; that his brigade was partially broken and dissipated, by the eagerness of its pursuit of the fugitive foe; and that their teeming numbers enabled these to return again and re-occupy a portion of the contested arena, and the battery which Jackson had twice taken. But the other troops which were now at hand, were formed by him, under the direction of General Johnston, and speedily regained the lost ground; a few well-directed shots from the artillery which Jackson posted farther to the rear, cleared away the encumbrances of his right flank; and the fresh regiments killed or captured the audacious skirmishers, who had insinuated themselves into the thickets behind him.

It was now four o'clock in the afternoon, and the Federalists were as yet only repulsed, and not routed. They were still

bringing up fresh masses, and, on the eminences fronting that
from which they had just been driven, were forming an imposing
line of battle, crescent-shaped, with the convex side toward the
Confederates, for a final effort. But their hour had passed.
The reserves from the extreme right, under Early and Holmes,
were now at hand; and better still, the Manassa's Gap Railroad, cleared of its obstructions, was again pouring down the
remainder of the Army of the Valley. General Kirby Smith
led a body of these direct to the field, and receiving at once a
dangerous wound, was replaced by Colonel Arnold Elzy, whom
Beauregard styled the Blucher of his Waterloo. These troops
being hurled against the enemy's right, while the victorious Confederates in the centre turned against them their own artillery,
they speedily broke, and their retreat became a panic rout.
Every man sought the nearest crossing of Bull Run. Cannon,
small arms, standards, were deserted. The great causeway,
from the Stone Bridge to Centreville, was one surging and mad-
dened mass of men, horses, artillery, and baggage, amidst which
the gay equipages of the amateur spectators of the carnage,
male and female, were crushed like shells; while the Confederate cavalry scourged their flanks, and Kemper's field-battery
from behind, pressed them like a Nemesis, and ploughed through
the frantic medley with his bullets. In this pursuit Jackson
took no share, except to plant a battery upon a rising ground
at his rear, whence he could speed the flight of the enemy with
some parting shots. He retired then to seek relief for a painful
wound in the hand, which he had received early in the action;
while his officers collected their wearied and shattered men, and
ministered to their disabled comrades.

Along a little rivulet, fringed with willows, which ran behind
the hill that received the farthest cannon-shot of the enemy,
many hundreds of wounded Confederates were gathered, with

many more of shameless stragglers, who had deserted the field under the pretext of assisting disabled comrades. During all the afternoon, the surgeons were busy here, under the grateful shade, plying their repulsive but benevolent task, and the green sward was strewn for half a mile with men writhing in every form of suffering, and the corpses of those just dead. Here Jackson found the Medical Director and the surgeons of his brigade. A rifle-ball had passed through his bridle-hand, breaking the longest finger and lacerating the next. He was seen at the time to give his hand an impatient shake, and wrap his handkerchief around it, but, during the remainder of the action, he took no further notice of it. When he came up, his friend, Dr. M'Guire, said, "General, are you much hurt?" "No," replied he; "I believe it is a trifle." "How goes the day?" asked the other. "Oh!" exclaimed Jackson, with intense elation, "we have beat them; we have a glorious victory; my brigade made them run like dogs." And this was the only instance in which he was ever known to give expression to these emotions, upon his most brilliant triumphs. Several surgeons now gathered around to examine him, but he refused their services, saying, "No, I can wait; my wound is a trifle; attend first to these poor fellows." And he persisted, against their earnest entreaties, in compelling them to dress the hurts of all the seriously wounded belonging to their charge, while he sat by upon the grass holding up his bloody hand, evidently suffering acute pain, but with a quiet smile on his face. After the common soldiers were attended to, he submitted to their examination, and, as they passed judgment upon the nature of the wound, he looked intently from one speaker to another, while all, except their chief, concurred in declaring that one finger at least must be removed immediately. Turning to him, he said, "Dr. M'Guire, what is your opinion?"

He answered, " General, if we attempt to save the finger, the cure will be more painful; but if this were my hand, I should make the experiment." His only reply was to lay the mangled hand in Dr. M'Guire's, with a calm and decisive motion, saying, "Doctor, then do you dress it." The effort was a successful, though a tedious one, and his hand was restored, after a time, nearly to its original shape and soundness.

While he was at this place, the President of the Confederate States, with a brilliant staff, galloped by towards the battle-field, and called upon the idlers to return with him to the assistance of their comrades. General Jackson arose, waved his cap, and exhorted the men to give him a lusty cheer, and to respond with alacrity to his orders. The men who had shed their blood for the cause were much more hearty in their greeting than the stragglers. Jackson, describing the manifest rout of the enemy, remarked to the physicians, that he believed " with 10,000 fresh men he could go into the city of Washington."

The actual results of this victory were the capture of twenty-eight cannon, with several thousands of muskets, and a vast store of ammunition, equipments, and clothing; a number of army-wagons and ambulances, and a thousand or two of prisoners of war. The State was delivered from the immediate danger of invasion, and, while the Federal army and capital, with the rabble of the nation, were thrown into a panic as abject as their previous boasting had been arrogant, the Confederate people and armies received the news of their deliverance with an unwonted quiet, made up of devout gratitude to God, and solemn enthusiasm. No bells were rung in Richmond, no bonfires lighted, no popular demonstrations made. From the solemn acts of religious thanksgiving, the people turned at once to eager ministrations to the wounded heroes, who had purchased the victory with their blood. For these, the preparations made by the Confederate

Government were crude and scanty, but the generosity of the people amply supplemented the lack of public service. The commanding generals reported, on the Confederate side, a loss of 369 killed on the field, and 1483 wounded. The Federal commander never confessed his real loss, covering up the number of his killed in a vague statement of the missing; but the greater masses engaged on his side, the superior accuracy of the Confederate fire, and the appearance of the field of battle, proved that the enemy's killed and wounded must have been twice or thrice as numerous as ours.

The portion of the Confederate loss borne by Jackson's brigade was the best evidence of the character of their resistance, and of its importance to the general result. Out of less than 2700 men present it lost 112 killed and 393 wounded. The object of this narrative has been to give such a sketch of the whole battle, as to make the part borne by the Stonewall Brigade and its leader intelligible, and to give fuller details of the conduct of the general whose life is the subject of this work. The reader will not infer from this that all the stubborn and useful fighting was done by Jackson and his command. Other officers and other brigades displayed equal heroism, and contributed essentially to the final result. But the divine Providence which he delighted so much to recognize assigned to him the maintenance of the critical post, during the critical hours. Had the enemy overpowered his brigade and occupied the eminence, which was the key of the Confederate position, or had they not been held at bay until forces could be assembled to cope with them, no other stand could have been made, save within the entrenchments around the Junction, where the lack of water and the confined limits would speedily have made surrender inevitable. In this sense Jackson may be said to have won the first Battle of Manassas.

But no narrative of the event will be so full of interest to the reader as the disclosure of his own secret emotions in view of the battle. To his wife he wrote, July 22d: —

"Yesterday we fought a great battle, and gained a great victory, for which all the glory is due *to God alone*. Though under a heavy fire for several continuous hours, I only received one wound, the breaking of the largest finger of the left hand, but the doctor says the finger can be saved. My horse was wounded, but not killed. My coat got an ugly wound near the hip. My preservation was entirely due, as was the glorious victory, to our God, to whom be all the glory, honor, and praise. Whilst great credit is due to other parts of our gallant army, God made my brigade more instrumental than any other in repulsing the main attack. This is for your own information only; . . . say nothing about it. Let another speak praise, not myself."

To complete this view of his magnanimous and modest temper, two other letters will be anticipated. In reply to some expression of impatience at the silence of rumor concerning his valuable services, while so many others were vaunting their exploits in the newspapers, he wrote, July 29th: —

"You must not be concerned at seeing other parts of the army lauded, and my brigade not mentioned. 'Truth is powerful, and will prevail.' When the reports are published, if not before, I expect to see justice done to this noble body of patriots."

"*August 5th.* — You think that the papers ought to say more about me. My brigade is not a brigade of newspaper correspondents. I know that the 1st Brigade was the first to meet and pass our retreating forces, to push on with no other aid than the smiles of God, to boldly take its position with the artillery that was under my command, to arrest the victorious foe in his onward progress, to hold him in check until reinforcements arrived, and, finally, to charge bayonets, and, thus advancing, pierce the enemy's centre. I am well satisfied with what it did, and so are my Generals, Johnston and Beauregard. . . . I am thankful to our ever kind heavenly Father, that He makes me content to await His own good time and pleasure for commendation, knowing that all things work together for my good. *Never distrust our God*, who doeth all things well. In due time He will make manifest all His pleasure, which is all His people should ever desire. If my brigade can always play as important and useful a part as in the last battle, I shall always be very grateful, I trust."

The pursuit of the enemy was not continued beyond Centreville, and this was the first error which made the laurels of the Confederate army, so fair to the eye, barren of substantial fruit. It was accounted for, in part, by the paucity of the cavalry; but this excuse was no justification, because the cavalry in hand, of which only two companies had been engaged in the actual combat, was not pertinaciously pressed after the fugitives, but paused even before it met with any solid resistance from them. Another cause of the interrupted pursuit was a rumor brought at sunset to the commanding generals, by some alarmed scout, who had seen a bewildered picquet of the enemy wandering through the country, — that a powerful Federal force was about to attack the lines of Bull Run near the Union Mills, where they were now denuded of defenders. This caused them to recall the fresher regiments from the chase, and send them upon a forced march of seven or eight miles, by night, to meet an imaginary enemy, and to return next morning to the field of battle. It would have been better had those regiments marched an equivalent fourteen miles upon the track of the fugitives. It should have been remembered also, that, even if full credit were given to the rumor of a fresh force advancing from the east, the masses which General M'Dowell had that day displayed on the left and front, all of which were now discomfited, were too large to permit the supposition that this detachment could be itself a formidable array. But, if it were, obviously enough its proposed attack was intended to be only in concert with the one already made by M'Dowell, so that the most speedy and certain way to repel it was to precipitate the rout of the latter. The true policy of the Confederate generals should therefore have been to leave this supposed assault to take care of itself, for the moment, and to hurry every man after the beaten enemy.

The whole army and country naturally hoped, that so splendid a victory would not be allowed to pass, without prompt and energetic efforts to gather in all the fruits. It was expected that the Confederate commanders would at least pursue the enemy to the gates of their entrenchments before Alexandria and Washington; and it was hoped that it might not be impracticable, in the agony of their confusion, to recover the Virginian city, to conquer the hostile capital, with its immense spoils, and to emancipate oppressed Maryland, by one happy blow. The toiling army, which had marched and fought along the hills of Bull Run through the long July day, demanded, with enthusiasm, to be led after the flying foe, and declared that they would march the soles off their feet in so glorious an errand without a murmur. But more than this; the morning after the battle saw an aggregate of 10,000 fresh men, composed of the remainder of the Army of the Valley, who had at length reached the scene, and of reinforcements from Richmond, arrive within the entrenchments at Manassa's Junction, who were burning with enthusiasm, and expected nothing else than to be led against the enemy at once. In a few days, the patriotic citizens of Alexandria sent authentic intelligence of the condition

of the beaten rabble there, and in Washington, which a true
military sagacity would have anticipated, as Jackson did, without actual testimony. When Bee and Evans were repulsed in
the forenoon, the Federalists had telegraphed to Washington
that the "rebels" were beaten in the open field; that the Grand
Army was marching triumphantly upon the Junction; and that
victory was assured. This premature boast the vain confidence
of the Federals accepted as sufficient, and they spent the remainder of the Sabbath-day in exultation; but the dawn of
Monday revealed to the citizens of Alexandria a different story.
Already the streets were full of a miserable, jaded, and unarmed rabble, whose fears had given them wings to flee the thirty
miles, within the short summer night. They sat cowed, upon
the curbstones and door-steps, and begged the citizens, over
whom they had so lately boasted, in pitiful tones, for a morsel
of bread and a few rags to bind up their wounds. As the
morning advanced, the stream increased into a torrent. They
had run until their laboring breath compelled them to fall into
a languid walk, and yet, at every sound in the rear, they burst
into fresh speed. Stalwart men were seen to throw themselves
upon the pavement, upon reaching the town, and give vent to
their sense of relief, in floods of tears. To the questions of the
citizens, some replied that Beauregard, with his bloody horsemen, was just beyond the last hill; while some were too frightened and eager to pause for any answer. For days, there was
neither organization nor obedience, nor thought of resistance,
on the south side of the Potomac; and the confused crowd
heeded only two wants, food for their present hunger, and means
to cross the river, that they might at once desert, and return
to their homes. The steam ferry-boats were crowded nearly
to sinking, until the authorities of Washington arrested their
journeys altogether. Sentry or picket-guard there was none

on the front next the enemy; the whole energies of the military authorities were directed to guarding the other side, to prevent their brave soldiers from running away. Nor was the capital city in a more hopeful condition. Confusion and uncertainty reigned there; nothing was needed but a few cannon-shots upon the southern bank, to turn their alarm also into a panic rout.

Now, then, said the more reflecting, was the time for vigorous audacity. Now, a Napoleonic genius, were he present, would make this victory another Jena, in its splendid fruits; and, before the enemy recovered from his staggering blow, would concentrate, into one effort, the labors and successes of a whole campaign. He would fiercely press upon the disorganized masses; he would thunder at the gates of Washington; and, replenishing his exhausted equipments with the mighty spoils, would rush blazing, like the lightning that shineth from the one part under heaven to the other, through the affrighted North, until the usurper was crippled, humbled, and compelled to relinquish his iniquitous designs. Especially was this boldness the true prudence now, because of the revolutionary nature of the war. Such struggles are so much moral convulsions, that military success is usually the prize of that party which knows how to impress, and mould the vacillating mind of the public, by its initial policy. Nowhere else is it more true, that the use made of the first tide of fortune decides the whole issue. In the North, the coercive policy of the Lincoln Government was an acknowledged innovation upon the established doctrines of the Republic. Up to that year, all schools of politicians had condemned it as wicked and absurd. The rage and pride of the Black Republicans had impelled them to adopt it, but it was a confessed novelty; and with all their heat, there was no solid assurance of its success. The triumphs of the patriots against

30

it would have taught multitudes to reconsider the rash and bloody experiment, and to return, though with reluctance, to the creed which founded the Union on the consent of the sovereign States. But especially were decisive results at the outset important to determine the wavering judgments of Maryland, Kentucky, and Missouri. The occupation of Washington would have transferred the former of these States from the Northern to the Southern side, and have united the divided allegiance of the other two; and such a change in the balance of strength, would have decided the whole subsequent success, had the North thereafter endeavored to continue the struggle.

With these views of the campaign, General Jackson earnestly concurred. His sense of official propriety sealed his lips; and, when the more impatient spirits inquired, day after day, why they were not led after the enemy, his only answer was to say, "That is the affair of the commanding Generals." But to his confidential friends he afterwards declared, when no longer under the orders of those officers, that their inaction was a deplorable blunder; and this opinion he was subsequently accustomed to assert, with a warmth and emphasis unusual in his guarded manner. He was then compelled to sit silent, and see the noble army, with its enthusiastic recruits, withering away in inaction on the plains of Bull Run, now doubly pestilential from the miasma of the August heats, and the stench of the battle-field, under camp-fevers tenfold more fatal than all the bullets of the enemy. Regiments dwindled, under the scourge, to skeletons; and the rude, temporary hospitals acquired trains of graves, far more numerous and extended than those upon the hills around the Stone Bridge. The enemy recovered from their terror, which was replaced, again, by a mocking contempt for the Government, which could be capable of so impotent a policy. A new commander was installed by them, and the gigantic North set itself, with energies only quickened by its shame, revenge, and consciousness of danger just escaped, to equip more enormous fleets and armies, and to carry the scourge of war to every coast and river of the South. Jackson had the mind to comprehend the inestimable value of the opportunity thus wasted, and the heart to feel a grief commensurate with the evils it was destined to cost his country. He knew that when God's providence gives either to a man or a people rare occasion for securing the blessing, it is not for nought; and His goodness cannot be slighted or misunderstood with impunity. The question may be asked, with scarcely less emphasis in the affairs of providence than in those of redemption, "How can ye escape, who neglect so great salvation?" He foresaw that the country would be called to pay the penalty of this mistake in future arduous and protracted struggles. But his lips were silent. He busied himself as diligently, and, to outward appearance, as cheerfully, in the duties assigned to him, as though the policy of the campaign had been his own.

Those who justified the inactive policy, affected, indeed, to treat the hope that the Confederate forces might now occupy Washington, as fanciful. They urged that the utter disorganization of the Yankee army could not be immediately known, and was not naturally to be inferred from losses so moderate as theirs; that the dreary rain which succeeded the battle hindered immediate pursuit, and that, to be effective, the pursuit of so powerful a foe must be prompt; that the Commissary's warehouse was empty, and the troops must have marched without rations; that the army, after its large increase, had not adequate transportation to enable it to move; and that, if it went towards Washington, it could expect nothing else than to meet the unbroken army of General Patterson, which, it was well known, was effecting a junction with that of McDowell. The reply to these pleas is, that the military intuitions of Jackson told him, before the battle was ended, what the rout and disorganization of the enemy would be. The wearied Confederate soldiers did not find the rain any the less dreary on the next day, because they were either countermarched up and down Bull Run, or left to crouch on the battle-field in fence-corners, without tents, instead of engaging in the inspiring pursuit of the enemy; and it would have been well to begin teaching them, even for no other object, the lesson they have since so abundantly learned, of marching and fighting in all weathers. Rations were not created by sitting still, and the appropriate supply for the victorious army was that which was in the magazines of their enemies. The country was then teeming with supplies; herds of bullocks were feeding in the pastures around Centreville, and the barns of the farmers were loaded with grain, which was denied its usual outlet to Washington and Baltimore. A march of twenty-five miles could surely have been accomplished without baggage or rations, especially when the short effort might lead them to the spoils of a wealthy capital. If the arrival of General Patterson's army was suspected, it was not known. At the most, it was only the army which, before it was appalled by disaster, had so often recoiled before the 11,000 of General Johnston. How then could it meet 40,000 Confederates flushed with victory? But in truth, at the hour Jackson was piercing the centre of M‘Dowell, with a fatal thrust, at Manassas, Patterson was haranguing his mutinous troops at Charleston, within a few miles of the lines in which Johnston had left him the Thursday before; and the Confederate forces would have reached Washington before him. The recital of these numerous obstacles, which were surmised (and with probable reason) to exist, but which the event showed did not exist, teaches what was the true fault of the Southern commanders. They are not to be condemned by history because they did not actually take Washington, but because they did not try. Their inexcusable error was, that they were not adventurous enough to explore the extent of their own good fortune. It is ever the duty of a leader of armies to hope that obstacles may be superable, unless he has proved them insuperable. It is early enough for him to arrest his career, when he has found them actual, and not merely possible.

The true solution of the enigma, how men, capable of winning such a victory, could prove so incompetent to improve it, is probably to be found in their mistrust of their own irregular soldiery. They were officers of the regular army of the United States, accustomed to prize its professional accuracy, and to depreciate the uninstructed militia, and they were unable to understand the capacities of the peculiar force which they handled. This was an army of volunteers, who had been drilled, at most, for eight or twelve weeks, and were led by company-officers who had never seen a battle, nor heard the whistling of a bullet. Subordination was slight, and the feeble bond of order which they had acquired, although it sufficed to give them on the parade-ground the semblance of a gallant army, was not as yet habitual enough to endure the strain of battle. Under the pressure of either success or repulse, it was dissolved, and regiments reverted almost into mobs. This body was pervaded by a large infusion of personal heroism, and, even after its exact order was lost, the major part of its men continued to fight with admirable gallantry; but their impulse was personal, and not common. In their tactics, — intelligence, patriotism, and chivalry supplied the place of methodical concert and mutual dependence. In the *mêlée*, each man found opportunity to do what was right in his own eyes, and, while the larger number, the brave men, fought on in their irregular fashion, and won the day, the remainder of poltroons straggled shamefully to the rear.

Hence, doubtless, these great professional soldiers were horrified when they saw their army so disorganized by its own success. They shuddered when they asked themselves what would have been its condition in defeat? They felt as though a victory with such an army was only a lucky accident; and that their wisdom would be to "let well enough alone," and tempt the Fates no more with so uncertain an instrument.

But Jackson was more than the professional soldier. Leaving the army, he had become the citizen, the philosophic scholar, the statesman. He knew both the vices and virtues of this citizen-soldiery. He knew that, penetrated by such a moral sentiment as animated the larger number, it would be even less disorganized by defeat than by victory. While he reprobated the base stream of stragglers, and was as anxious as any to super-induce upon the good men all the advantages of a thorough discipline, in addition to a generous *morale*, he knew how to take those thin, irregular lines, decimated by the laggards, and so to launch them against the enemy as to pluck a brilliant triumph from the midst of numbers. His hardy and sober judgment reminded him that, if battle had loosened the bonds of order in our ranks, it had destroyed them in those of our enemies; for their army also was a militia, composed, not of gallant gentlemen and their reputable dependants, but of unwarlike mechanics. He foresaw that, while the thorough drill would benefit our gallant soldiery, relatively it would advance the mercenary hordes of the enemy yet more. The more nearly both were brought to the mechanical perfections of a regular army, the more would the difference between them be narrowed. And, therefore, notwithstanding the imperfections of the Confederate army, the present was its opportunity, and its earliest blows would be successful at least cost to it.

A few days after the battle of Manassas, General Jackson

moved his brigade to a pleasant woodland, a mile in advance of Centreville. There he busied himself in perfecting the discipline of the troops. After a time the Confederate generals, whose forces had grown to about 60,000 men, pushed their lines forward to Munson's and Mason's Hills, within sight of the Federal capital, and erected slight earthworks upon these eminences. Their object was to tempt General M'Clellan to an assault. But this leader was too well taught by the disasters of Bull Run to risk a general action. He occupied the attention of the Confederates with skirmishes of pickets and occasional feints, which required the advance of heavy supports to the front. In these alarms the 1st Brigade was always conspicuous for the promptitude with which it appeared at the threatened point, and for its martial bearing. This season of comparative quiet was largely employed by General Jackson in religious labors for the good of his command. His correspondence showed the same humility and preference for the quiet enjoyments of home which characterized him before he became famous.

August 22d, he wrote to his wife : — " Don't put any faith in (the assertion) there will be no more fighting till October. It may not be till then; and God grant that, if consistent with His glory, it may never be. Sure, I desire no more, if our country's independence can be secured without it. As I said before leaving you, so say I now, that if I fight for my country it is from a sense of duty, a hope that, through the blessing of Providence, I may be enabled to serve her, and not merely because I prefer the strife of battle to the peaceful enjoyments of *home*."

September 24th, he says : — " This is a beautiful and lovely morning, beautiful emblem of the morning of eternity in heaven. I greatly enjoy it, after our cold, chilly weather, which has made me feel doubtful of my capacity, humanly speaking, to endure the campaign, should we remain longer in tents. But *God, our*

God, will do, and does all things well, and if it is His pleasure that I should remain in the field, He will give me the ability to endure all its fatigues."

This hope was fully realized. The life in the open air proved a cordial to his feeble constitution. Every appearance of the scholastic languor vanished from his face, his eye grew bright, and its vision, so long enfeebled, was so fully restored that thenceforward it endured, by night and by day, all the labors of his burdensome correspondence, and the business of his command. His cheek grew ruddy and his frame expanded, so that to his former acquaintances he appeared a new man.

The period is now reached when it is necessary to narrate the views and efforts of General Jackson, in reference to his native region, Northwestern Virginia. The communications of all the region between the Ohio River and the Alleghany Mountains, are much more easy with the States of the Northwest than with the remainder of Virginia. A large portion of the population was, moreover, from this cause, disaffected. The type of sentiment and manners prevailing there, was rather that of Ohio than of Virginia. To the military invasions of the enemy it lay completely open, while direct access from the central parts of the Confederacy could only be had by a tedious journey over mountain roads. The western border is washed by the Ohio River, which floats the mammoth steamboats of Pittsburg and Cincinnati, save during the summer-heats. The Monongahela, a navigable stream, pierces its northern boundary. The district is embraced between the most populous and fanatical parts of the States of Ohio and Pennsylvania. Two railroads from the Ohio eastward, uniting at Grafton, enabled the Federalists to pour their troops and their munitions of war, with rapidity, into the heart of the country. The Confederate authorities, on the contrary, had neither navigable river nor railroad by which to transport their troops, or to subsist them there, but could only effect this by a long wagon-road crossing numerous mountain-ridges from Staunton, upon the Central Virginia Railroad. It was manifest, therefore, that the Government had little prospect of being able to cope with the Federalists for the occupation of the country. The traitorous partisans of the region, intimidating the loyal people by the bayonets of the invaders, set up a usurping government, and adhered to the Lincoln dynasty. But the same difficulties of transportation would evidently press the enemy, so soon as he, not content with the occupation of Northwestern Virginia, sought to invade the central parts of the State; for, then, it would be the Federal army which would have the long and laborious line of communication to sustain, and the Confederate force would be brought near its railroad and its supplies. The obvious military policy for Virginia, therefore, was to make no attempt to hold the Northwest, in the face of such difficulties; but to tempt the enemy to involve himself in the arduous mountain-roads, and to await his enfeebled attacks on the nearer side of the wilderness, where the means of more rapid concentration would give the power to crush him. But this policy was forbidden by a generous pride, and an unwillingness to leave a loyal population exposed, even for a time, to the oppressions of a clique of traitors, backed by invaders. A small army was sent thither, under General Garnett, through vast difficulties. It numbered about 5000 men, and, as might have been expected, found itself confronted by a force of fourfold numbers and resources, under General M'Clellan. On the 11th of July, the little army, indiscreetly divided into two detachments, was assailed at Rich Mountain. Both parts were compelled to retreat across the Alleghanies with the loss of their baggage and a number of prisoners, and, at the skirmish at Cannock's Ford, their unfortunate leader was killed. It was this

31

easy triumph which procured for General M'Clellan, from the
Yankee people, the title of "The Young Napoleon," the most
complete misnomer by which the rising fortunes of a young
aspirant were ever caricatured.

General Jackson held, that there was one plan of campaign by
which the difficulty of contesting this country with the enemy
might probably be solved, and, during the first year of the war,
he was eager to be engaged in it. His scheme embraced two
parts. One was, the sending of a commander into the northwest, to rally as many of the population as possible to the
Confederate cause, and thus find a large part of the men and
materials for sustaining the contest, in the country itself. The
leader, therefore, must be one who was known to the people, and
possessed their confidence, and who knew how to conciliate their
peculiar temper. He believed that nearly all the more respectable people of that region were loyal to their State and duty;
and, in this, events sustained his opinion; for, after a year's
experiment, the most which the usurping Government could
assert was, that among the forty counties which they claimed for
their pretended State, they had dared to collect revenues in
eleven only. And it has been shown that, with a few exceptions,
the county majorities, polled in their favor at elections, were
composed of the intrusive votes of the soldiers encamped there,
to intimidate the people; while the true voters, not being permitted to speak their real wishes, almost unanimously stayed at
home.

The other part of General Jackson's plan was, to retain, by
force of arms, that section of the great Baltimore and Ohio
Railroad, which lies on the territory of Virginia, from Harper's
Ferry westward, and to employ it as the line of operations for
the major force employed in the northwest: For, he argued,
this road being the great military and commercial thoroughfare

connecting the enemy's capital with the West, whence he drew so many of his men and supplies, it was at all times a vital matter to us to deprive him of it. Next, its use as a line of operations would cover, from the ravages of the enemy, a most important part of central and northern Virginia, the counties of the lower Valley, and of the south branch of the Potomac — a magnificent region teeming with precious resources, and inhabited, in the main, by a gallant and loyal people. But the chief reason for maintaining this line was, that it was the only one by which it was practicable for us to move men and materials in sufficient masses, and with speed enough, to cope with the Federalists, entering the contested district by two navigable rivers and two railroads. A strong force, he said, should be pushed along the railroad, so far west as to place itself in the rear of the Federal army, operating against the little detachment which we so painfully sustained at the western side of the mountains. This would compel the retreat of our enemies, and make their capture probable. The country, being thus cleared of their presence, and reassured against their return by the occupation of the great railroad, would, in consequence, revert to its proper allegiance, and by its resources make this part of the war nearly self-sustaining. A reference to the map will show that this scheme was in appearance liable to a capital objection: The Baltimore and Ohio Railroad, thus made the line of operations for the Confederate forces, would be parallel to the frontier of Pennsylvania, which the enemy might at once make the base of their operations against us. But such an arrangement is likely to be fatal to the party pursuing the aggressive (in this case the Confederates), because their communications are ever within the reach of their enemy's blows. Here, however, the objection was more seeming than real. The true base from which the Federalists must have operated against this line of advance, was not the Pennsylvanian frontier, but the Central Pennsylvania Railroad, parallel thereto, and a hundred miles distant. Now, to operate from that base against the Confederate line of advance, they would have had not railroads, but only the country roads of a mountainous region. Thus the superior mobility of our forces along their line of operations would have compensated, in great measure, for their exposure to the enemy's advance across it.

From the beginning of the war, General Jackson was anxious to be sent to the Northwest. It was the land of his birth and his kindred. The oppressions of the enemy and the traitorous defection of a part of its people, filled him with grief and indignation. The patriots who fled thence before the Federal bayonets and domestic informers, looked to him as their natural avenger. They knew that he was the pride of his numerous race — everywhere stanch in its loyalty to Virginia, and wielding the wealth and influence of the district; and that they would have secured for him a popular support which no other commander could have received. Hence, when General Jackson was placed at the head of the 1st Brigade, in June, he expressed to his wife an earnest hope that the Government would despatch it to the Northwest, and the modest belief, that he could march with it to the Ohio River. He declared that he was willing to serve in any capacity under General Garnett, then commanding there. After that unfortunate commander was killed, and his army expelled from the country, the Confederate Government sent out from Staunton a much more powerful expedition, under General Robert E. Lee. This commander endeavored to shorten the arduous line of communication over the mountain roads, by leaving the Central Virginia Railroad, at a point forty miles west of Staunton, and penetrating the northwest through the counties of Bath and Pochahontas at the Valley Mountain.

But the intrinsic difficulties of his line, aggravated by a season of unusual rains, robbed him of solid success. From his great reputation, and the fine force entrusted to him, brilliant results were expected. In this hope General Jackson concurred. He wrote, August 15th, to his wife: — "General Lee has recently gone west, and I hope that we will soon hear that *our God* has again crowned our arms with victory. . . . If General Lee remains in the Northwest, I would like to go there and give my feeble aid, as an humble instrument in the hand of Providence, in retrieving the down-trodden loyalty of that part of my native State. But I desire to be wherever those over me may decide, and I am content to be here (Manassas). The success of my cause is the earthly object near my heart, and, if I know myself, all that I am and have is at the service of my country."

To his friend, Colonel Bennet, first auditor of the Commonwealth, he wrote, August 27th: —

" My hopes for our section of the State have greatly brightened since General Lee has gone there. Something brilliant may be expected in that region. Should you ever have occasion to ask for a brigade from this army for the Northwest, I hope that mine will be the one selected. This of course is confidential, as it is my duty to serve wherever I may be placed, and I desire to be always where most needed. But it is natural for one's affections to turn to the home of his boyhood and family." In a few weeks, the unavoidable obstacles surrounding General Lee's line of operations disclosed the truth, that, although he might check the enemy, he could do nothing aggressive. The second failure of the campaign, in hands so able, only demonstrated more fully than before that General Jackson's was the proper conception. He returned therefore to this with redoubled strength of conviction, and in the month of September endeavored, through every appropriate channel, to infuse his ideas into the rulers of the country. While he did this, he strictly charged his friends to make no reference to his name or authority, both because he would not be suspected of craving any power or distinction in a new field of enterprise, and because his punctilious subordination forbade his even seeming to criticise his military superiors. His plans were submitted to some civilians, that, as the authorized counsellors of the Government, they might recommend them for adoption if approved by their judgment. He urged that, inasmuch as six precious weeks had been wasted since the victory at Manassas, and the enemy had been allowed to recover from his panic so far as to render an attack upon Washington city hazardous, the Army of the Valley, under General Johnston, should be again detached and sent westward; that General Beauregard should be left near Manassas with his corps, to hold the enemy in check, supported, if need be, by General Lee, who, by falling back to the Central Railroad, could reinforce him in a few days; that General Johnston meantime should re-occupy the lower Valley about Winchester, Harper's Ferry, and Martinsburg, and, making it his base, push his powerful corps, by the Baltimore and Ohio Railroad, direct to the Ohio River; and that thence he should cut off the retreat of General Rosecranz and his whole force, whom General Lee had drawn far eastward into the gorges of the Alleghanies. The capture of the larger part of the Federal army, and the deliverance of the country, he thought, could hardly fail to reward the prompt execution of this project. But it was not brought to the test of experiment. The fine army of North Virginia expended the remainder of the year in inactivity, neither attempting nor accomplishing any-thing. General Lee was held in check, not by the enemy, but by the mud, and the Northwest remained in the clutches of the oppressor. Whether General Jackson would have succeeded in that difficult region, or whether Providence was kind to him and his country in crossing his desires, and preserving him for future triumphs in more important fields, must remain undecided.

On the 7th of October, 1861, the Minister of War rewarded General Jackson's services at Manassas with promotion to the rank of Major-General in the Provisional Army. The spirit in which this new honor was received, is displayed in the following letter to his wife : —

" *October 14th*, 1861. — It gives my heart an additional gratification to read a letter that hasn't travelled on our holy Sabbath. I am very thankful to that good God who withholds no good thing from me (though I am so utterly unworthy and so ungrateful), for making me a major-general of the provisional army of the Confederate States. The commission dates from October 7th.

" What I need is a more grateful heart to the ' Giver of every good and perfect gift.' I have great reason to be thankful to our God for all His mercies which He has bestowed, and continues to shower upon me. Our hearts should overflow with gratitude to that God who has blest us so abundantly and over-abundantly. O that my life could be more devoted to magnifying His holy name ! "

Soon after came an order assigning him, under General Johnston, to the Valley District, a military jurisdiction embracing all the country between the Blue Ridge and the Alleghany Mountains. The force assigned him would be still under the general supervision of the Commander-in-Chief; yet it constituted a separate, and, to a great degree, an independent command. When this appointment reached him, his venerable pastor was present, upon that visit to his soldiery which has been mentioned. He handed him the order, and, when he had read it, said with a simplicity and candor which could not be mistaken : — " Such a

degree of public confidence and respect as puts it in one's power
to serve his country, should be accepted and prized; but, apart
from that, promotion among men is only a temptation and a
trouble.   Had this communication not come *as an order*, I should
instantly have declined it, and continued in command of my
brave old Brigade."

To his wife he wrote thus:—

" *Nov. 4th*, 1861. — I have received orders to proceed to Winchester.   My trust is in God for the defence of that country.   I
shall have great labor to perform, but through the blessing of
an ever-kind heavenly Father, I trust that He will enable me
and other instrumentalities to accomplish it.   I trust that you
feel more gratitude to God than pride, or elation at my promotion.   Continue to pray for me, that I may live to glorify God
more and more by serving Him and our country."

His brigade was ordered to remain with the Army of the Potomac, and it became necessary for him to part from his comrades-
in-arms.   On the day fixed for beginning his journey to his
new scene of labor, he directed the regiments to be paraded
in arms, and rode to their front with his staff.   No cheer
arose, like those which usually greeted him, but every face was
sad.   Ranging his eye along their ranks, as though to say an
individual farewell to each familiar face, he addressed them thus:
"I am not here to make a speech, but simply to say farewell.
I first met you at Harper's Ferry in the commencement of this
war, and I cannot take leave of you without giving expression
to my admiration of your conduct from that day to this, whether
on the march, in the bivouac, or the tented field; or on the
bloody plains of Manassas, where you gained the well-deserved
reputation of having decided the fate of the battle.   Throughout
the broad extent of country over which you have marched, by
your respect for the rights and the property of citizens, you

have shown that you were soldiers, not only to defend, but able and willing both to defend and protect. You have already gained a brilliant and deservedly high reputation, throughout the army of the whole Confederacy, and I trust, in the future, by your deeds on the field, and by the assistance of the same kind Providence who has heretofore favored our cause, you will gain more victories, and add additional lustre to the reputation you now enjoy. You have already gained a proud position in the future history of this, our second War of Independence. I shall look with great anxiety to your future movements; and I trust, whenever I shall hear of the First Brigade on the field of battle, it will be of still nobler deeds achieved, and higher reputation won."

Then pausing, as though unable to leave his comrades-in-arms without some warmer and less official words, he threw the rein upon the neck of his horse, and, extending his arms, exclaimed,—

"In the army of the Shenandoah you were the First Brigade; in the army of the Potomac you were the First Brigade; in the Second Corps of the army you are the First Brigade; you are the First Brigade in the affections of your general; and I hope, by your future deeds and bearing, you will be handed down to posterity as the First Brigade in this our second War of Independence. Farewell."

Thus saying, he waved his hand, wheeled, and left the ground at a gallop, followed by a shout in which his brave men poured out their whole hearts. He repaired immediately to Winchester, and entered upon his duties as General commanding in the Valley district.

This chapter will be closed with four passages from his correspondence, which show how thoroughly public spirit and disinterestedness ruled in his heart. The new and enlarged sphere to which he was promoted called for a re-arrangement of his

32

staff. Application was made to him by dear friends, to make this the occasion of advancing persons near to his affections, as well as to theirs. His reply was the following: —

"My desire, under the direction and blessing of our heavenly Father, is to get a staff specially qualified for their specific duties, and that will, under the blessing of the Most High, render the greatest possible amount of service to their country."

And his personal friends were not appointed. To another kinsman he replied, by stating that qualification must be, with him, in every case, the first requisite; and inasmuch as the prosperity of the service, and even the fate of a battle, might depend on the fitness of a staff-officer for his post, he could not gratify personal partialities at his country's expense. The habits into which he made most anxious inquiry, were *early rising* and *industry;* and, upon the whole subject of seeking promotion, his views were expressed with characteristic wisdom and manliness to another friend thus: —

"Your letter, and also that of my much esteemed friend, Hon. Mr. —— in behalf of Mr. ——, reached me to-day; and I hasten to reply, that I have no place to which, at present, I can properly assign him. I knew Mr. —— personally, and was favorably impressed by him. But if a person desires office in these times, the best thing for him to do is at once to pitch into service somewhere, and work with such energy, zeal, and success, as to impress those around him with the conviction that such are his merits, he must be advanced, or the interest of the public service must suffer. If Mr. —— should mention the subject to you again, I think that you might not only do him, but the country, good service, by reading this part of my letter to him. My desire is, to make merit the basis of my recommendations and selections."

The next extract is upon a different topic: —

"*Nov. 9th*, 1861. — I think that, as far as possible, persons should take Confederate State bonds, so as to relieve the Government from any pecuniary pressure. You had better not sell your coupons from the bonds, as I understand they are paid in gold, but let the Confederacy keep the gold. Citizens should not receive a cent of gold from the Government, when it is so scarce. The only objection to parting with your coupons, is, that if they are payable in gold, it will be taking just so much out of the treasury, when it needs all it has."

To appreciate the self-denial expressed in the following passage, it must be known how dear his home was to him. In reply to a suggestion that he should obtain a furlough, he says: — "I can't be absent, as my attention is necessary in preparing my troops for hard fighting, should it be required; and as my officers and soldiers are not permitted to visit their wives and families, I ought not to see mine. It might make the troops feel that they are badly treated, and that I consult my own comfort, regardless of theirs. Every officer and soldier who is able to do duty ought to be busily engaged in military preparation, by hard drilling, etc., in order that, through the blessing of God, we may be victorious in the battles which, in His all-wise providence, may await us. If the war is carried on with vigor, I think, under the blessing of God, it will not last long."

CHAPTER VIII.

WINTER CAMPAIGN IN THE VALLEY. 1861–62.

THE appointment of General Jackson to the command of a separate district under General Joseph E. Johnston, consisting of the Valley of Virginia, was made on October 21st, 1861. On the 4th of November he took leave of his brigade, and set out, in compliance with his orders from the Commander-in-Chief, for Winchester, by railroad, and reached that place on the same day.   On his arrival there, the only forces subject to his orders, in the whole district, were three fragmentary brigades of State militia, under Brigadier-Generals Carson, Weem, and Boggs, and a few companies of irregular cavalry, imperfectly armed, and almost without discipline or experience.   The first act of the General was to call out the remaining militia of those brigades from the adjoining counties.   The country people responded with alacrity enough to raise the aggregate, after a few weeks, to 3000 men.   To the disciplining of this force he addressed himself with all his energies.

A brief description of the country composing his district is necessary to the understanding of the remaining history.   The Great Valley extends through much of the States of Pennsylvania and Virginia, and crosses Maryland, at its narrowest part.   This district is widest and most fertile just where the Potomac passes through it, from its sources in the main Alleghany range to its outlet into Eastern Virginia, at Harper's

Ferry. It is bounded on the southeast by the Blue Ridge, which runs, with remarkable continuity, for many hundred miles from northeast to southwest; and on the other side there is a similar parallel range, called the Great North Mountain. The space between the bases of these mountains varies from thirty to fifteen miles in width, but it is by no means filled by a level vale. The intervening country is one of unrivalled picturesqueness, variety, and fertility, whose hills, in some places, sink into gentle swells of the most beautiful arable lands, and, in others, rise into mountains, only inferior to the great ranges which bound the district. Of these mountains, the most considerable is the Masanutthin, or Peaked Mountain, which is itself a range of fifty miles in length, and which, beginning twenty miles southwest of Winchester, runs parallel to the Blue Ridge, including between them, for that distance, a separate valley of the same character. This space is occupied by the populous counties of Page and Warren, and watered by the main stream of the Shenandoah. It is only when the traveller, standing upon some Peak of the Blue Ridge or of the Great North Mountain, looks across to the other boundary, and, ranging his eyes longitudinally, sees the grand barriers extending their parallel faces to a vast distance, and losing themselves in the blue horizon, that he fully comprehends the justness of the name, Valley of Virginia. The romantic hills and dales of the intermediate space are then, by comparison, lost to view, and the whole district presents itself as a gigantic vale. The streams which descend from the abounding ranges of mountains, as well as those which rise between the Great North Mountain and the Alleghanies, pass along and across the valley obliquely, until they gather into sufficient volume to force their way to the ocean, as the Potomac, the James, and the Roanoke. The outlets from the Valley on either side are by railroad, or by turnpike roads, which pass through depressions of the mountains, called, in the language of the country, Gaps. The soil is almost uniformly calcareous, and the roads, where they are not paved, of heavy clay. The population at the beginning of the war was dense, industrious, and loyal, the agriculture was skilful, and the whole goodly land teemed with grain, pasturage, horned cattle, swine, sheep, and horses. The manufacturing industry of this region was also prosperous, every county boasting of its numerous mills or furnaces, for the production of woollen cloths, iron wares, and other staple supplies of an agricultural people.

Between the Great North Mountain and the Alleghany is a rugged region, more extensive than the Valley proper, which is sometimes included under that term. It is almost filled with parallel ranges of mountains, which increase in altitude as the traveller proceeds westward, until he crowns the parent ridge itself. But hidden between these chains are a thousand valleys of unrivalled beauty and fertility, peopled with a happy and busy population. The most extensive of these is the far-famed valley of the south branch of the Potomac, which forms the garden of three counties, Pendleton, Hardy, and Hampshire. The wide meadows which line this stream from its source to its mouth are fruitful beyond belief; their prodigal harvests of hay and Indian corn, together with the sweetness of the upland pastures by which they are bordered, make them the paradise of the grazier. As Winchester is the focal point and metropolis for the lower Valley, so Romney, forty miles northwest of it, is the key to the valley of the south branch (of the Potomac) and the capital of the great county of Hampshire. The north-western turnpike, an admirable, paved road, beginning from the former place, passes through the latter on its way to the Ohio River, and crosses the highways which ascend the valleys of the streams.

All this country, to the Alleghany crest, was included in General Jackson's military district. The frontier, which he was required to guard against the enemy, was the whole line of the Potomac, from Harper's Ferry to its source in the mountain last named, and from that ridge to the place where the troops of General Lee were posted, after their ineffectual attempt upon Northwest Virginia. That commander had been recalled, to be employed in a more important sphere; and his troops were left along the line which he had occupied under the command of Brigadier-Generals Henry Jackson and Loring. The first of these, with a detachment of that army, had, on the 8th of October, repulsed the Federalists with the aid of Colonel Edward Johnson, in a well-fought battle upon the head of the Greenbrier River, in Pochahontas county. But the only fruit of this victory which the Confederates gathered, was an unobstructed retreat to a stronger position, upon the top of the Alleghany mountains: another striking evidence of the soundness of General Jackson's theory concerning the campaign in the Northwest. Yet more surprising proof was furnished a few weeks later. On December 13th, the same gallant little army was attacked in its new position on the Alleghany; and, under Edward Johnson, now Brigadier-General, the result was a brilliant victory over their assailants. As soon as General Jackson heard of it, he again wrote, to urge that this force should be sent to him, and predicted that, if it remained where it was, it would, before long, have no enemy in its front, and find the foe which it had beaten, threatening its communications by the way of the South Branch. This was exactly verified. His advice was rejected; and it was not many weeks until the victorious army was retreating to another position, on the Shenandoah mountain, forty miles to the rear. The explanation was, that the Federalists being in undisturbed possession of the Baltimore and Ohio Railroad, were able to occupy Hampshire and Hardy, and to threaten thence the communications of the Confederates.

General Jackson had not reached Winchester, before his foresight of these results induced him to urge upon the Government that plan of campaign which was explained in the last chapter. Possessed of the keen appreciation of the value of time in war, he begrudged the loss of every day. On the route to Winchester, he paused at a station, to write to an influential friend in Richmond, asking his aid to further his views; and, through every proper channel, he continued to press them, until events forbade their execution. He proposed the immediate organization of a winter campaign in the Northwest, to be conducted from Winchester, by the way of the railroad and northwestern turnpike. He requested that all the forces of Generals Loring and Johnson should be hurried to him, so as to constitute a body sufficient to sustain itself. If it was suggested that the Federalists might take advantage of their withdrawal, to invade the central parts of the State, by crossing the mountains, his reply was, that it would be so much the worse for them. While they were marching eastward, involving themselves in those interminable obstacles, which had proved so disastrous to our arms there, he would be rapidly pouring his masses westward by railroad and turnpike, would place himself upon their communications, would close behind them, and would make their destruction so much the more certain, the farther they advanced towards their imaginary prize. If the Confederate Government, he argued, delayed its efforts to recover the Northwest, it would then find the Federalists more firmly seated there; the loyalty of the inhabitants would be more corrupted by their blandishments and oppressions; the supplies, which should feed our soldiers, would be consumed by our enemies, and the country too much exhausted to sustain a vigorous campaign from its own resources; fortified posts would be created where none now existed; and, above all, the constant development of the military power of the United States under the management of General M'Clellan, might occupy all our forces elsewhere.

His representations were so far successful, that about the middle of November, his old Brigade was sent to him, with the Pendleton battery, now under the command of Captain M'Laughlin. Early in December, Colonel William B. Taliaferro's brigade from the army of the Northwest, consisting of the 1st Georgia, 3d Arkansas, and 23d and 37th Virginia regiments, reached Winchester. Near the close of December, the last reinforcements arrived from that army, under Brigadier-General Loring, consisting of the brigades of Colonel William Gilham, and Brigadier-General S. R. Anderson. The former of these brigades embraced the 21st, 42d, and 48th regiments of Virginia, and the 1st battalion of State Regulars, with Captain Marye's battery; the latter, the 1st, 7th, and 14th regiments of Tennessee, and Captain Shurmaker's battery. He now, at the end of December, found himself in command of about eleven thousand men, of whom three thousand were militia, while the remainder were the volunteer forces of the Confederacy. But the delay in assembling these was such, as nearly to blast his hopes. He had continued to urge that the command of Brigadier-General Edward Johnson, from the Alleghany, should be sent to him, or else directed to march northward through Hardy and Hampshire counties, to effect a junction with him near Romney; but his advice was not adopted. This subtraction from his expected means, he declared, would be decisive against his cherished plan of penetrating to the Northwest. For, contemplating the repeated failures to which the Confederate cause had been condemned in that quarter by inadequate means, he was determined

33

not to make an attempt without such forces as would make success possible.

Just before General Jackson came to the Valley, Romney was occupied by a Federal force, which was speedily increased to 6000 men. At Williamsport, and neighboring points, were as many more. Beyond Harper's Ferry, General Banks was organizing a force of 26,000 men, for the invasion of the Valley. Before the arrival of General Loring's command, General Jackson had to oppose nearly 40,000 enemies, with only 4000 men, inclusive of his undisciplined militia; yet, if this force was increased to so many as 15,000, he had resolved to attempt the audacious enterprise of clearing away the foes who hung around his own district, and then invading another, occupied by an army as strong as his own.

But his genius taught him that his safety lay in audacity. Winchester is the centre to which great thoroughfares converge, from Harper's Ferry on the northeast, from Martinsburg and Williamsport on the north, and from Romney on the northwest; while another highway from the south branch would place his enemies twenty miles in his rear, at Strasburg. He said that unless Romney and the south branch were held, Winchester was untenable. It was true that his central position gave him the interior line of operations; but, to employ this advantage, it was necessary for him to strike one of his adversaries promptly. If he waited until they approached near enough to co-operate, and to hem him in by their convergent motions, he would have no alternative except precipitate retreat or surrender; hence his burning anxiety to be in motion. His purpose was to assail the Federal General Kelly at Romney, first, so as to secure the western side of his district, as a preliminary, either to his expedition into the Northwest, or, if that were surrendered, to his approaching contest with General Banks. It has already been indicated, that the late arrival of General Loring's brigades, and the refusal of the Government to send General Edward Johnson's, doomed the hopes of General Jackson to disappointment as to the former enterprise. It may be useless to speculate upon the results which he would have attained, if it had been undertaken in good time. He never concealed his belief that the attempt was hazardous; but many would perhaps conclude that it was utterly rash; and, in the latter opinion, it would appear the War Department concurred. The facilities which the Federalists enjoyed for pouring troops and supplies into Northwest Virginia, must ever have rendered its occupation by a Confederate force, an arduous task. Had General Jackson gone thither with 15,000 men, the countless hordes of United States troops, who, a little later, crushed the Confederates at Fort Donelson, in spite of most heroic fighting, might have been directed upon him. If the skill and courage with which he evaded similar dangers in the famous campaign of the ensuing spring were forgotten, the conclusion would be reached, that in such an event his situation in the Northwest would be desperate. But the issue of that campaign has taught the world, that there is no limit to be set to the possibilities which genius, united to generous devotion, may achieve. Success would have turned mainly upon the degree of support which the people of the Northwest would have given to the cause, when rallied under their favorite leader. And these speculations may be most safely dismissed, with a thankful acquiescence in the orderings of Divine providence, which forbade Jackson's making the great experiment, and preserved him for the service of his country on a still more important and glorious field.

About the middle of November, General Jackson, busying himself, while he awaited his reinforcements, in organizing his command, adverted to the condition of his cavalry. This

consisted of several companies, raised in his district, which had
no regimental formation. He found serving with them Lieut.-
Colonel Turner Ashby, and, recognizing in him a kindred spirit,
he assigned to him the chief command. From that day to his
death this chivalrous officer served his general, as commander of
cavalry, with untiring zeal and intelligence. He was a gentleman of Fauquier county, of the best connexions, of spotless and
amiable character, devoted to field sports and feats of horsemanship, and known to be as modest and generous as he was
brave. At the first outbreak of the war, he had flown to his
country's service, had raised a company of cavalry, had assisted
at the first capture of Harper's Ferry, and, during the summer
campaign of 1861, had distinguished himself by his devotion
and vigilance, upon the outposts of the army, below that village.
After it ceased to be an important position to the Confederates,
he was transferred to the Upper Potomac. There occurred the
first of those daring exploits which soon surrounded his name
with a halo of romance. A part of his command, under his
beloved brother, Captain Richard Ashby, was assailed, in the
county of Hampshire, by an overpowering force of Federal
cavalry; and, in the retreat which followed, Captain Ashby was
overtaken, at an obstruction presented by the railroad track to
the career of his horse, and was basely murdered, while prostrate and helpless under his fallen steed. A few moments after,
Turner Ashby, attracted by the firing, came up with a handful
of fresh horsemen, and the enemy retired. He found his brother
mortally wounded and insensible, and, kneeling beside his body,
he raised his sword to heaven, and made a sacred vow to consecrate his life afresh to delivering his country from the assassin
foe. The assailants had retired to an island in the river, covered
with shrubbery and driftwood, and there stood on the defensive,
concealed in these hiding-places. Ashby now gathered a dozen

men, and, fording the stream under a shower of bullets, dashed among them, slew several men with his own hand, and dispersed or captured the whole party. From the day he paid this first sacrifice to the *manes* of his murdered brother, he appeared a changed man. More brave he could not be; but while he was, if possible, more kindly, gentle, and generous to his associates than before, there was a new solemnity and earnestness in his devotion to the cause of his country. He evidently regarded his life as no longer his own, and contemplated habitually its sacrifice in this war. He was, in his own eyes, as a man already dead to the world. His exposure of his person to danger became utterly reckless, and, wherever death flew thickest, thither he hastened, as though he courted its stroke. Yet his spirit was not that of revenge, but of high Christian consecration. To his enemies, when overpowered, he was still as magnanimously forbearing, as he was terrible in the combat. Henceforward, his activity, daring, and seeming immunity from wounds, filled the Federal soldiers with a species of superstitious dread. At the sound of his well-known yell, and the shout of "Ashby" from his men, they relinquished every thought of resistance, and usually fled without pausing to count the odds in their favor. To General Jackson he was eyes and ears. Ever guarding the outposts of his army with rare discretion, and sleepless vigilance, he detected the incipient movements of the enemy; and his sobriety of mind, which was equal to his daring, secured implicit confidence for his reports.

In December, General Jackson determined to employ his enforced leisure in a local enterprise, which promised much annoyance to the enemy. This was the interruption of the Chesapeake and Ohio Canal. The Potomac not being navigable above Washington city, a great canal had been begun from tide-water below that point, which was carried along the valley of

the river, with the proud design of threading its highest tributaries, piercing the Alleghany ridge, and connecting the waters
of Chesapeake Bay with those of the Ohio. It was not completed farther than Cumberland, in western Maryland; but this
place is within the verge of the great coal-fields of that country,
whence the cities of Washington and Baltimore, the furnaces
of the military factories at the Federal capital, and many of their
war-steamers, were supplied with fuel. Besides, this canal offered
the means for the speedy transportation of large masses of troops
and supplies. Although the Confederates had interrupted the
great railroad, by destroying the bridge at Harper's Ferry, and
the whole track to Martinsburg, the Federal authorities had
the unobstructed use of it from the Ohio River eastward to
Cumberland. The destruction of the canal was therefore
needed, to make the interruption complete. This work, ascending the left, or north bank of the Potomac, receives its water
from that river, which is raised to a sufficient height to feed it
by a series of dams thrown across its channel. The most important of these was the one known as Dam No. 5, built within
a sharp curve of the river, concave towards the south, north of
the town of Martinsburg. The sluices from above this barrier
filled a long level of the canal, and its destruction left it dry,
and useless for many miles; while no force would be adequate
to rebuild it amidst the ice and freezing floods of winter.

Jackson therefore marched to Martinsburg, December 10th,
with a part of his militia, his cavalry, and the Stonewall Brigade, and thence made his dispositions to protect the working
party, who were to attempt the task of demolition. It was
necessary to guard the whole circuit of the curve upon which
the dam was situated, lest the enemy, who were in force on the
other bank, should cross behind the detachment. General
Jackson, sending the militia to make a diversion towards

Williamsport, entered the peninsula, posted the veteran brigade near the work, but behind a hill which protected them from the cannon planted upon the opposite bank, and, by night, he advanced his working party to the brink of the stream.   A guard of riflemen occupied a strong mill, whence they could deliver a murderous fire upon any detachment advancing to a near attack upon the workmen, while these speedily shielded themselves from the more distant sharpshooters in the cavities which they excavated in the doomed structure.   Although the Federal General, Banks, assembled a large force on the other side, and cannonaded the Confederates, the work was continued from the 17th to the 21st of December, until a great chasm was made, through which the whole current of the river flowed down towards its original level, leaving the canal far above it drained of its waters.   The most essential parts of the work were done by the gallant men of Captain Holliday, of the 33d, and Captain Robinson, of the 27th Virginia regiments.   These generous fellows volunteered to descend, by night, into the chilling waters, and worked under the enemy's fire, until the task was completed.   The amount of fatigue which the men endured, laboring, as they constantly did, waist-deep in water, and in the intense cold of winter, can never be sufficiently appreciated.   The only loss, at the hand of the enemy, was that of one man killed, a member of the infantry guard which watched the work, but the effects of such exposure could hardly fail to tell ruinously on the health and lives of many of those who executed the difficult and dangerous task.

General Jackson returned to Winchester on December the 25th, and had the pleasure of meeting there the reinforcements which have been already mentioned, under Brigadier-General Loring.   It was settled by the Government, that he should retain command of all the troops which he had brought with him, and be second to General Jackson.   The weather was most propitious for the season, and the roads were still firm. He, therefore, determined to carry out that part of his original scheme, which was still feasible, and to drive the Federalists from the western part of his district. At Bath, the seat of justice for Morgan County, a village forty miles north of Winchester, was a detachment of fifteen hundred Federal soldiers, with two pieces of artillery, who grievously tyrannized over the loyal part of the inhabitants. At the village of Hancock, upon the opposite side of the Potomac, was another detachment. Romney upon the south branch, at a distance of about forty miles, was occupied by a force of the enemy now increased to at least ten thousand, who were fortifying themselves there, and ravaging all the fertile country about them. General Jackson intended to march rapidly upon the detachment at Bath and capture them, next, crossing the Potomac, to disperse the party at Hancock, and then, having cleared his rear, to proceed to Romney. The 1st day of January, 1862, an April sun was shining, and the dust was flying in the roads. The whole army, with the exception of the necessary detachments, began its march for Bath, numbering about 8500 men, with five batteries of artillery, and a few companies of cavalry. But, before the day was ended, a biting northwester began to blow, and this was succeeded by a freezing rain and snow, which sheathed the roads in ice. The hardships of the troops now became most severe. The march was pressed forward notwithstanding the inclement weather; the soldiers were often unable to keep their footing upon the slippery mountain sides; and, along the column, the accidental discharge of muskets frequently announced the fall of their owners. The country was one of the roughest, and the roads selected were the most unfrequented, in order that the movement might be kept a secret. For several nights, the wearied troops bivouacked in the sleet and snow, without tents, rations, or blankets, because he baggage-train was unable to overtake them, and with the recklessness of new soldiers, they had refused, against orders, to carry them. The Stonewall Brigade bore these trials without murmuring, for their beloved General shared them all; but, among the reinforcements, the discontent was excessive, and was openly encouraged by a part of their officers, who pronounced the expedition rash, unreasonable, and out of season. General Jackson was cursed by many of them, for this adventure, and looked on as a maniac, for dragging his command through such a region, and at such a season. Many of the troops, taking countenance from the unsoldierly complaints of their leaders, deserted the ranks under plea of sickness, and returned to Winchester. That town was soon thronged with many hundreds of these pretended invalids, who roamed the streets without control, and taxed the generous hospitality of the citizens. Jackson, nevertheless, pressed on, and the third day, met the enemy's outposts a few miles from Bath. They were speedily driven in, and the army proceeding a little farther, encamped for the night. In the morning, January 4th, General Jackson made his dispositions to surround and capture the enemy. A body of militia had already been detached, to cross the mountain behind the village, and then approach it from the west. The main column was now pushed along the direct road, headed by General Loring, while Colonels Maury and Campbell advanced upon the hill sides, on the left and right respectively, to surround the village. General Jackson complained much of the dilatory movements and repeated halts of the column. It seemed as though the whole day would be consumed in marching a few miles, until at length the wings were impelled forward with more energy, and a detachment of cavalry, headed by Lieut.-Col. Baylor of the General's staff, dashed into the town. At their approach the enemy fled without any resistance, leaving all their stores and camp

34

equipage in the hands of the victors. General Jackson himself entered the place in advance of the skirmishers of the main column; but so sluggish had been their movements, that the enemy was already out of sight. Their escape filled him with chagrin, and he instantly urged the pursuit, along the route by which they had fled.

Bath is situated three miles from the Potomac, from which it is separated by a small mountain-ridge. Two roads lead to the river, one to the nearest railroad station, that of Sir John's Run, and the other to Hancock, which is seated upon the opposite bank. By one of these two routes the Federalists must have escaped, but so dilatory had been the movements of General Loring's command, that even his skirmishers were not in sight of the rear of the fugitives, when they disappeared. It was not immediately apparent, therefore, by which of the roads the main body had gone. General Jackson, accordingly, divided his forces, sending a part of his cavalry, and General Loring's column, towards Hancock; the second Virginia brigade, under Colonel Gilham, and Captain Wingfield's company of cavalry, towards Sir John's Run; and Colonel Rust with his and the 37th Virginia regiments, and two field-pieces, by the western road, towards an important railroad bridge over the Great Capon river. The first of these detachments General Jackson accompanied. It speedily overtook the rear of the enemy, and drove them, with some loss, into Hancock. The General then crowned the southern bank of the river with artillery, and fired a few shots into the town. This was in retaliation for the crime of the Federalists, who had repeatedly shelled the peaceful village of Shepherdstown, on the south bank of the Potomac, when it was not used as a military position by the Confederates, and even when there was not a soldier near it. Jackson declared that they should be taught, such outrages could not be perpetrated with impunity; and he added, that, while he was in command of that district, the lesson was efficacious upon their dastardly natures. The 4th of January was now closed by night, and the troops opposite the town again bivouacked in the snow.

Meantime, the second column, directed towards Sir John's Run, had overtaken a considerable detachment of the enemy; but although the ground offered facilities for turning the position on which they stood at bay, no improvement was made of the opportunity, and the Federalists were allowed to escape unmolested over the river, when they probably joined their comrades at Hancock. The third detachment under Colonel Rust proceeded with more vigor. When near the Capon Bridge, they met a party of Federalists guarding that important structure, with whom they skirmished until night, suffering some loss, and inflicting upon the enemy a more serious one. The next morning, January 5th, having been reinforced by General Loring, they drove away the guard, destroyed the bridge and station-houses, and pulled down a long tract of the telegraph wires, besides capturing great spoils. Thus, both railroad and telegraph communication between the Federal commander at Romney and General Banks below, was effectually severed. The Confederates could now pursue their designs against the former without molestation from the latter, and beat each of them in detail. Such were the promising results, which seemed to be about to reward the vigorous use of the interior line of movements by Jackson.

But he did not propose to leave the party at Hancock so near his line of communications. On the morning of January 5th, he summoned the place to surrender, and notified the Federal commander, that if he declined to accept this proposal he must remove the non-combatants, as he proposed to cannonade the place in good earnest. The bearer of the summons was the gallant Colonel Ashby. As he was led, blindfold, up the streets, he overheard the Federal soldiers whispering the one to the other, " That is the famous Colonel Ashby; " and soon the suppressed hum of a crowd told him that they were thronging around, to catch a sight of the warrior, whose name had so often carried confusion into their ranks. The Federal commander refused either to evacuate the place, or to remove the females and children, and claimed that, if the cannonade took place, the guilt of shedding their blood would rest upon the Confederates, — a preposterous and impudent pretension, especially when coming from a party which has burned so many peaceful dwellings, and so often shelled unresisting towns without notice. The true motive of the claim was obvious. The Yankee thought that the humanity of General Jackson was so great, it would permit him to skulk safely behind the skirts of the women. But the Confederate General was as clear-sighted and vigorous as he was humane. After the time had elapsed which he had announced in his challenge, he opened a hot cannonade from a score of guns, and speedily drove every Federal soldier out of the town, or into some invisible hiding-place. At the same time, a detachment was busy preparing to construct a bridge across the Potomac, two miles above, that the Confederates might attack them on the Maryland side; but before this work was completed, they received reinforcements so numerous, that General Jackson judged it inexpedient to risk the loss which would be incurred in defeating them, when every man was needed for the attainment of his great object, the deliverance of Romney and the South Branch. Believing, therefore, that the enemy in this quarter were sufficiently chastised to cause them to respect his further movements, and, secure in another line of communication with Winchester, far to the south of

Bath, even if the latter place were re-occupied by them, he determined to move westward without further delay.

Having destroyed all the spoils which he lacked means to remove, he left Hancock on January 7th, and returned to the main Romney highway, reaching a well-known locality called Unger's Store, the same evening. On that day his advanced forces, consisting of a regiment of militia and a section of artillery, had an unfortunate affair with the Federalists at Hanging Rock, fifteen miles from Romney, in which two guns were lost by the Confederates; but the difficulties of the roads and season compelled General Jackson to halt here, to collect and refresh his wearied men, and to prepare the horses of his artillery and baggage-trains for their labors. The roads over the mountain-ranges were now sheeted with firm and smooth ice, upon which the wearied animals could keep no footing. Bruised, and sometimes bleeding from their falls, they had struggled thus far, only dragging the trains a few miles daily, by the most cruel exertions. The order was now given to replace their shoes with new ones, constructed so as to give them a firm foothold upon the ice. In this way the time was consumed until the 13th, when the army resumed the march, and the General, with the advanced infantry, entered Romney on the 14th of January. But on the 10th, the Federal commander had taken the alarm, and retreated precipitately to the northwestern part of Hampshire. The hope of making a brilliant capture of prisoners was again disappointed. The flight of the enemy was only witnessed by two of Ashby's cavalry companies, which were pressing close upon their rear. It was some solace, however, to the conquerors, to find their tents standing, with all their camp equipments, and their magazines filled with valuable military stores, which fell into the hands of the Confederates. This retreat was·an emphatic testimony to the dread which the vigor of Jackson already inspired in his enemies. With a force larger than his own, they feared to meet him in a most defensible position, which they had selected and entrenched at their leisure. When he was yet more than a day's march distant, they fled in such panic as to leave behind them the larger part of their equipage!

But cowardice like this was the natural sequel to the barbarities by which they had disgraced the name of soldiers. As soon as the Confederates passed Hanging Rock, they began to see marks of desolation, then new, but now, alas! familiar to their eyes. Nearly every dwelling, mill, and factory, between that place and Romney, was consumed; the tanneries were destroyed, and the unfinished hides slit into ribbons; the roadside was strewed with the carcasses of milk-kine, oxen, and other domestic animals, shot down in mere wantonness. As they came in view of the town, lately smiling in the midst of rural beauty, scarcely anything appeared, by which it could be recognized by its own children, save the everlasting hills which surround it. Gardens, orchards, and out-buildings, with their enclosures, were swept away; the lawns were trampled by cavalry horses into mire; many of the dwellings were converted into stables, and the blinds and wainscot torn down for fuel; and every church, save one, which the Federal commander reserved for the pious uses of his own chaplains, was foully desecrated. And these outrages had no pretext, for the despoilers had found Romney a defenceless town, and had entered it at their leisure, without resistance. Their crimes are detailed here, not because the fate of this once charming village has been peculiar among the towns cursed by Federal occupation. If every such instance, which has been added in the progress of the war, were detailed with a similar truthful particularity, the narrative would only be extended, and marked with a dreary and repulsive monotony.

But it is just, that this beginning of sorrows should be fixed in history, for the everlasting infamy of the Federals, and as an example of the never-to-be-forgotten acts of barbarity which the Southern people have endured at their hands. Let the solemn testimony of Jackson against the perpetrators stand recorded, as long as his great name is revered among men. His official report of the campaign is closed with these words : — " I do not feel at liberty to close this report without alluding to the conduct of the reprobate Federal commanders, who, in Hampshire county, have not only burned valuable mill-property, but also many private houses. Their track from Romney to Hanging Rock, a distance of fifteen miles, was one of desolation. The number of dead animals lying along the roadside, where they had been shot by the enemy, exemplified the spirit of that part of the Northern army."

On the 16th of January, the whole Confederate army was again assembled near Romney. It was ascertained that the retreating force had gone to the neighborhood of Cumberland, in Maryland, a town on the north side of the Potomac, and opposite to the northwestern border of Hampshire county. Three important railroad bridges required their oversight in that region. One of these crossed Patterson's Creek, near its entrance into the river. A little west of this spot, the railroad, which pursues the southern bank for more than fifty miles, crosses to the other side, and continues upon the northern margin to Cumberland; above which it returns to the soil of Virginia. Two massive and costly bridges span the river at these crossings. By destroying these bridges, communication between the Federalists at Cumberland, and the army of General Banks in the lower Valley, would be more effectually severed. But more than this : since the force which had invaded Hampshire drew its supplies from the west by the railroad,

these breaches in its continuity would restrict their future operations to the eastward, inasmuch as they would entail upon them,
as they advanced, a continually lengthening line of transportation
by wagons. On the arrival of the main body of his troops,
General Jackson instantly prepared to press onward to New
Creek. This stream, flowing northward, enters the Potomac at
the western extremity of Hampshire county, and above Cumberland; but in consequence of its situation upon the apex of a
great angle of the river, the road which conducts to that town
from Romney is much longer than the one leading to the mouth
of New Creek. He purposed, therefore, to proceed to the
latter spot, and, placing himself above the enemy, to destroy
the bridge across the Potomac, above Cumberland, first, thus
insulating them from their western base. He selected the Stonewall Brigade, and that of Colonel Taliaferro, from the army of
General Loring, to perform this service under his own eye; but
when he was ready to march, he discovered that the discontent
and disorganization had proceeded so far in the latter brigade,
that they were not to be trusted for so responsible a service.
With deep mortification and reluctance, he therefore relinquished
further aggressive movements, and prepared to defend what he
had already won; and this, although less than he believed a
more efficient army would have realized for him, was by no
means little. In sixteen days, he had driven the enemy out of
his whole district, except a few miles which they occupied at its
extreme corner; had liberated three counties from their tyranny,
securing for the Confederate cause their riches of corn and cattle;
had rendered the railroad useless to the enemy for a hundred
miles; and had captured stores almost equal to the equipment
of an army like his own. On the first day of January, scarcely
a man in those counties, loyal to his State, could remain at his
home, without danger of persecution or arrest. The dominion

of law and peace was now restored to all the citizens. All this had been accomplished with a loss of four men killed, and twenty-eight wounded.

General Jackson now proceeded to place the command of General Loring in winter quarters, near Romney, and to canton Boggs' brigade of militia along the south branch, from that town to Moorefield, with three companies of cavalry for duty upon the outposts. The remainder of the cavalry and militia returned to Bath, or to the Valley, to guard its frontier; and the Stonewall Brigade was placed in winter quarters as a reserve, near Winchester. Having begun these dispositions, General Jackson returned to the latter place on the 24th of January. He was uneasy lest General Banks should initiate some movements in his absence. General Loring was left in command at Romney, with his three brigades, and thirteen pieces of artillery. The militia force upon his left placed him in communication with the army of General Edward Johnson, upon the Alleghany Mountain; for a forced march of three days would have brought those troops to Moorefield. At Winchester, forty miles from Romney, was the Stonewall Brigade, ready to launch itself from its central position upon any point of the circumference which was assailed, and it was to be immediately connected with General Loring's forces by a new line of telegraph. Romney itself offers an exceedingly defensible position. It is situated in the Valley of the south branch, twenty miles from the Potomac, and it could be approached, from the direction of the enemy, only by two roads. Of these, one ascends the valley of the river, and the other crosses the mountain-ridge separating it from the vale of Patterson's Creek by a narrow defile. Both these routes pass through gorges in approaching the town, where the sides are utterly impracticable for artillery, and a regiment might hold a host at bay. East of Romney lies a low mountain, not commanded from any

35

other height, but commanding the town completely, as well as the highway to Winchester. The General who knew how to use these advantages, might reasonably count on defending himself against threefold odds, long enough to receive succor from the latter place. Finally, the loyal farmers of the south branch offered, from their magnificent plantations, abundant supplies for the whole winter; or, if these failed, the way was open, by a drive of twenty-five miles, to the broad fields and teeming granaries of the Great Valley. General Jackson designed that the troops, after the construction of their winter quarters, should at once strengthen their position by entrenchments; and, to this end, he urgently requested that an able engineer should be sent to him.

Upon his return to Winchester, he found the country full of debate and difference concerning his movements. No one presumed to dispute his courage and devotion, and many had perspicacity enough to perceive, in his administration, the promise of a great commander. But the larger number professed to depreciate his capacity, and not a few declared that he was manifestly mad. They said that the man had a personal disregard of danger, a hardihood of temper, and a stubbornness, which made him a good fighter, where he was guided by a wiser head; that he was competent to lead a brigade well on the parade ground, or the battle-field, but had no capacity adequate to the management of a separate command, and an extensive district; that his headstrong and unreasoning zeal, with his restless thirst for distinction, thrust him into enterprises which he lacked discretion to conduct to a prosperous issue, and that it was only good fortune, or the better judgment of his reluctant subordinates, in lagging behind his rash intentions, which saved his army from a catastrophe. His wintry march, with the hardships of his men, exaggerated in every form by the interested falsehoods of the stragglers, was denounced as inhuman. They forgot that the unreasonable period to which the expedition was delayed was the fault of others, and was deplored and condemned by him more than by any one else. They refused to consider that he had shared all the hardships of the freezing sleet, and snowy bivouac, and the cold vigils, with his men, and had endured them cheerfully. They were ignorant of the careful and able arrangements which he had made for their comfort. So anxious was he that every supply for their wants should accompany them, that when his chief commissary was consulting him as to the selection of the rations to be transported behind the army, and proposed to take no rice along, inasmuch as it was a species of food seldom preferred by the troops, he dissented, and ordered several tierces to be carried, saying that his soldiers must lack for nothing which they were accustomed to enjoy, so long as it was practicable to furnish it. He was also charged by his critics with being partial to his old brigade, Jackson's pet lambs, as they were sneeringly called; it was said that he kept them in the rear, while other troops were constantly thrust into danger; and that now, while the command of General Loring was left in mid-winter in an alpine region, almost within the jaws of a powerful enemy, these favored regiments were brought back to the comforts and hospitalities of the town, whereas, in truth, while the forces in Romney were ordered into huts, this brigade was three miles below Winchester, in tents, and under the most rigid discipline. And what would have been the outcry of the objectors had General Jackson left the old brigade with General Loring, and brought away a part of his troops, which had been assured to him by special pledge of the Government? His secrecy, which was absolute as that of the grave, piqued the

curiosity and self-importance of these cavillers. But had he
condescended to explain, they would not have been able to
comprehend his policy. Necessities which were plain in
the future to his prophetic eye, they could not see. His
far-reaching combinations were beyond their grasp; hence,
to their imperfect view, the movements, which are now recognized as the promptings of a profound and original genius,
appeared to be the erratic spasms of rashness. And truth
requires the statement, that not a few of his subordinates so far
forgot the proprieties of their honorable profession, as to echo
these criticisms and lend them all their credit. Especially were
such persons found among those who had lately come under his
command. They were unaccustomed to a military regimen so
energetic as his. For while he was, personally, the most modest
of men, officially, he was the most exacting of commanders;
and his purpose to enforce a thorough performance of duty,
and his stern disapprobation of remissness and self-indulgence,
were veiled by no affectations of politeness. Hence, those who
came to serve near his person, if they were not wholly like-
minded with himself, usually underwent, at first, a sort of
breaking in, accompanied with no little chafing to restive spirits.
The expedition to Romney was, to these officers, just such an
apprenticeship to Jackson's method of making war. All this
was fully known to him; but while he keenly felt its injustice,
he disdained to resent it, or to condescend to any explanation
of his policy.

On the 31st of January, he was astounded by the receipt of
the following order, by telegraph, from the Secretary of War:
— "Our news indicates that a movement is making to cut off
General Loring's command; order him back to Winchester
immediately." The explanation was, that a number of officers

from that command, as soon as it was ordered into winter quarters, had obtained furloughs and repaired to Richmond, where they busily filled the ears of the public and the Government with complaints of the exposed and hazardous position assigned them, and the rashness and severity of General Jackson's rule. A petition for the recall of the troops was actually signed among them, and the General complained, with justice, that it was not more positively discountenanced by their commander. It filled him with indignation, to see men bearing their country's commission, assigning the presence of danger as the ground of their complaints, as though it were not a soldier's profession to brave danger; and when the withering rejoinder was at hand, that, if indeed the men intrusted to their care were in such peril, then it was no time for a gallant officer to be wasting his days on a furlough, amidst the luxuries and cabals of a far-distant capital. The demand for the recall of the troops, without reference to the commander of the district, directly impugned his vigilance and good judgment. Yet the Secretary of War, misguided by the urgency of the discontented officers, gave the peremptory order, without consultation either with General Jackson, or General Joseph E. Johnston, the Commander-in-Chief of the whole department. The injury thus done to the authority and self-respect of both these officers is too obvious to need illustration. Of the personal element of wrong, Jackson seemed to feel little, and he said nothing. But, considering his usefulness in his District at an end under such a mode of administration, he instantly determined to leave it. The reply which he sent to the War department is so good an example of military subordination, and, at the same time, of manly independence, that it should be repeated.

"HEAD-QUARTERS, VALLEY DISTRICT,

"Hon. J. P. BENJAMIN,   January 31st, 1862.
                    Sec. of War.

"SIR, — Your order requiring me to direct General Loring
to return with his command to Winchester, immediately, has
been received, and promptly complied with.

"With such interference in my command, I cannot expect to
be of much service in the field, and accordingly respectfully
request to be ordered to report for duty to the Superintendent
of the Virginia Military Institute, at Lexington; as has been
done in the case of other professors. Should this application
not be granted, I respectfully request that the President will
accept my resignation from the Army. — Respectfully, etc., your
obed. serv.,

                                           "T. J. JACKSON."

This conditional resignation he forwarded through the appointed channel, the head-quarters of his Commander-in-Chief.
At the same time, to make one more effort for preventing the
injury, he wrote requesting that General Johnston would coun-
termand the order for the retreat.   To his adjutant he said,
"The Secretary of War stated, in the order requiring General
Loring's command to fall back to this place immediately, that he
had been informed the command was in danger of being cut off.
Such danger, I am well satisfied, does not exist, nor did it, in my
opinion, exist at the time the order was given; and I therefore
respectfully recommend that the order be countermanded, and
that General Loring be required to return with his command to
the neighborhood of Romney." But the Commander-in-Chief,
although concurring in his opinions of the campaign, did not
think it best to assume the responsibility of giving the order;
and all the troops returned to the vicinity of Winchester.
General Johnston detained the resignation for a time, and

immediately wrote to General Jackson, in terms alike honorable
to his own magnanimity, and to the reputation of the latter.
Descending from the position of his commander to that of a
friend and brother-in-arms, he declared his full approval of his
disposition of the forces, and his belief that the order of which
he complained was injurious to the country, and to his official
rights; yet, expressing an exalted appreciation of his value to
the cause, he besought him to waive every personal interest,
to hold even his just rights in abeyance, and to sacrifice everything for his native land.

The news of his resignation aroused a vivid excitement in the
army, the capital, and the State at large, which showed that, notwithstanding the criticisms of his enemies, he had gained a firm
hold upon the affections of his countrymen. Their sympathies
were warmly with him against the Government. They were
outraged, that the only army which had marched, and which had
won anything from the enemy, should be thus arrested. Indeed
the decision and dignity of his attitude silenced at once the voices
of the fault-finders; and they seemed to concur in the general
feeling of the people of his district, which regarded him as their
bulwark and deliverer. He was besieged with solicitations
from soldiers, citizens, and clergymen, far and near, appealing
to his patriotism, to subordinate his sense of injustice to the
public good, and assuring him that, with his resignation, the
hopes of the people would sink. The Governor of the State,
besides writing to urge his continuance in the service, sent a
friend of the greatest weight in the Commonwealth to expostulate in person against his intended retirement. To all these
General Jackson made the same reply. To the Governor, he
had tersely stated the grounds of his decision in the following
words: — "The order was given without consulting me; it is
abandoning to the enemy what has cost much preparation,

expense, and exposure to secure; it is in direct conflict with my military plans; it implies a want of confidence in my capacity to judge when General Loring's troops should fall back; and it is an attempt to control military operations in detail, from the Secretary's desk at a distance." To his ambassador, he now added, that he had no personal pique to satisfy; for, however he might feel at another time, that he himself was wronged, the hour of his country's extremity was no occasion to weigh private grievances. Neither had he any complaint to lodge against his superior, the Secretary of War; but, presuming that he was a considerate and firm man, he must infer that the order given in this case was an example of his intended system of management. And, then, he was satisfied that he could not hope to serve his country usefully or successfully under such a system. But it was the rule of his life never to hold a position where he could not be useful; his conscience forbade it. He had not sought command because it was sweet to him; he had no ambition to gratify; the soldier's stormy career had no allurements for him; and nothing on earth, save the hope of being useful to his injured country, had ever persuaded him to forego the happiness of a beloved home, and a congenial occupation, for the daily martyrdom of his present cares. Now that this hope was extinguished, he felt that the voice of duty, which alone had driven him out from his happy privacy, not only permitted, but commanded his return to it. It was answered that he should be willing to make sacrifices to serve his country, in her hour of need. "Sacrifices!" he exclaimed; "have I not made them? What is my life here but a daily sacrifice? Nor shall I ever withhold sacrifices for my country, where they will avail anything. I intend to serve her, anywhere, in any way in which I am permitted to do it with effect, even if it be as a private soldier. But if this method of making war is to prevail, which they seek to establish in my case, the country is ruined. My duty to her requires that I shall utter my protest against it in the most energetic form in my power; and that is, to resign." And then, traversing the floor of his chamber with rapid strides, he burst into an impetuous torrent of speech, in which he detailed his comprehensive projects with a Napoleonic fire and breadth of view; his obstacles, created by the reluctance and incompetency of some, with whom he had been required to co-operate; his hardships, and the heroic spirit of his troops; the brilliant success with which Providence had crowned his first steps, and the cruel disappointment which dashed the fruit of all his labors. For a long time he was inexorable; but at last, when he was told that the Governor had, in the name of Virginia, withdrawn his resignation from the files of the War Department, and requested that action should be suspended upon it until an attempt was made to remove his grounds of difficulty, he consented to acquiesce in this arrangement.

In a few days he received the assurance, that it had never been the purpose of the Government to introduce the obnoxious system against which he protested.   Accepting this as a sufficient guarantee that his command would not hereafter be subjected to such a system of interference, he quietly left his resignation in the hands of the chief magistrate of the State, and resumed his tasks.

In this transaction, General Jackson gained one of his most important victories for the Confederate States.   Had the system of encouragement to the insubordination of inferiors, and of interference with the responsibilities of commanders in the field, which was initiated in his case, become established, military success could only have been won by accident.   By his firmness, the evil usage was arrested, and a lesson impressed both upon the government and the public opinion of the country, which

36

warrants that it will not soon be revived. Whether he had
any expectation of this result, when he demanded a release
from the service, it is useless to surmise: if he had, his sound
judgment taught him that the way to secure this issue was
to seem not to expect it, but to offer an explicit resignation,
and to act as though he anticipated nothing else than its certain acceptance.

The one instance in which he betrayed the emotions which
were aroused by the affair, has been related. In no other case
did he show a shade of feeling, and the grandest impression
which the people about him ever received of the greatness of
his moral nature, was that made by his demeanor under this
trial. He uttered no complaint against his detractors or his
superiors, and calmly refused to listen to those who endeavored,
in that form, to express their sympathy with his wrong. While
he thanked them for their partial estimate of his value to the
country, he exhorted them, for his sake, not to relax anything of
their own zeal; and he showed the same care and diligence in
preparing everything for the advantage of his unknown successor, as though he had expected to continue in permanent
command of the district. Concerning the operations of his
army he had always been obstinately silent, and repelled inquiry with sternness. It appeared that this reserve was dictated, not by pride or love of power, but by a sense of duty.
Now that the concern respected his own interests, he had no
secrecy, and invited the most candid expressions of opinion;
save that he would not permit any denunciations of those who,
as his friends supposed, had sought to injure him. As soon as
the affair was terminated, it was banished from his conversation,
and he was never again heard to allude to the actors in it, except where he could honestly applaud them. He appeared to be
elevated wholly above all the infirmities of passion; and the

only human emotion which was apparent, even to his wife, who was then on a visit to him, was the revival of his genial gaiety, at the prospect of their speedy return to their home.

His domestic tastes led him, whenever his duties confined him to the town, to take his meals with the family of a congenial Christian friend. To them there appeared, during these trials, the most beautiful display of Christian temper. His dearest relaxation from the harassing cares of his command, were the caresses of the children, and the prayers of the domestic altar. When he led in the latter, as he was often invited to do, it was with increasing humility and tenderness. A prevalent petition was that they "might grow in gentleness;" and he never spoke of his difficulties, except as a kind discipline, intended for his good, by his Heavenly Father.

The inexpediency of the evacuation of Romney was soon manifested. The ice of January was now replaced by the mud of February; and the deficiency of transportation, with the timid haste of the retreat, caused a loss of tents and military stores, equal to all which had been won in the advance. The enemy immediately assumed the aggressive again, and reoccupied Romney in force. February 12th they seized Moorefield, and on the 14th they surprised and routed the advanced force, composed of a small brigade of militia, stationed at Bloomery Gap, twenty-one miles from Winchester, capturing a number of prisoners. Two days after, Colonel Ashby, with his cavalry, recovered the pass, which the Federalists had left in the keeping of a detachment; but they remained firmly established beyond it, with a force of 12,000 men. The whole valley of the South Branch was now open to their incursions. Good roads led up this stream from Moorefield to its head, far in the rear of General Edward Johnson's position on the Alleghany, which the enemy had found so impregnable in front. The prediction of

General Jackson was now verified, and that force, to save its communications, was after a little compelled to retire to the Shenandoah mountain, only twenty-five miles from Staunton, thus surrendering to the inroads of the Federalists the three counties of Pendleton, Highland, and Bath. Winchester was again exposed to the advance of the enemy from four directions.

The difficulties of General Jackson's position were, at the same time, aggravated by a diminution of his force. General Loring having been assigned to a distant field of operations, his command was divided between the Valley and Potomac districts. The brigade of General Anderson, composed of Tennessee troops, was sent, with two regiments from that of Colonel Taliaferro, to Evansport, on General Johnston's extreme right. The brigade of Colonel Gilham, now commanded by the gallant Colonel J. S. Burks, was retained by General Jackson, and was henceforth denominated the 2d Brigade of the Army of the Valley. Two Virginia regiments only, the 23d and 37th, remained to Colonel Taliaferro. These, increased afterwards by the addition of the 10th Virginia, composed the 3d Brigade of the Army of the Valley. The three militia brigades were continually dwindling through defective organization, and before the opening of the active campaign they were dissolved. The conscription law of the Confederate Congress was passed not long after, which released the men over thirty-five years old, and swept the remainder into the regular regiments of the provisional army. When the Tennessee regiments were sent away, February 22d, General Jackson informed the Commander-in-Chief that his position required at least 9,000 men for its defence, threatened as it was by two armies of 12,000 and 36,000 respectively. His effective strength was now reduced to about 6,000; but he still declared that, if the Federalist generals advanced upon him, he should march out and attack the one who approached first. The force on the south branch was now commanded by General Lander, and was concentrated about a locality on the Baltimore and Ohio Railroad called Paw Paw, thirty-five miles from Winchester. The importance of the expedition which Jackson had been so anxious to make in January, to destroy the great bridges about Cumberland, was now manifest. This force was able to draw its supplies by railroad from the west, and to bring them unobstructed to the Great Capon Bridge. That work they were rapidly rebuilding, and nothing could be anticipated but that, on its completion, they would break into the valley, in concert with General Banks, from the northeast. The latter commander had been hitherto inactive, but it was known that he had a large force cantoned at Frederick City, Hagerstown, and Williamsport, in Maryland. His first indications were, that he was moving his troops up the northern bank of the Potomac, and effecting a junction with General Lander, by boats constructed at Cumberland and brought down the stream. But this movement, if it was not a feint, was speedily reconsidered. On the 25th of February he crossed at Harper's Ferry with 4000 men, and by the 4th of March had established his head-quarters at Charlestown, seven miles in advance. The remainder of his force was brought over, from time to time, until he, with General Shields, had now collected about 36,000 men at that place, Harper's Ferry and Martinsburg.

A General of less genius than Jackson would have certainly resorted to laborious entrenchments, as an expedient for repairing the inequality of his force. But he constructed no works for the defence of Winchester. To an inquiry of General Hill, he replied, "I am not fortifying; my position can be turned on all sides." Knowing that, if he enclosed himself in forts, the superior forces of the Federalists would envelop him, he refused to construct works for them to occupy, after his enforced evacuation. He hoped to return upon them some day, and did not desire to have the necessity of reducing his own fortifications. His strategy sympathized always with that of the Douglas, who "preferred rather to hear the lark sing, than the rat squeak."

General Jackson, perceiving that the Commander-in-Chief would not be able to give him the aid he desired, looked next for co-operation to the force stationed at Leesburg, in Loudoun county, under General D. H. Hill. By providing means of rapid transit across the Shenandoah at Castleman's Ferry, and establishing a telegraph line between Leesburg and Winchester, he proposed to secure a concentration of the two forces by two days' march at most. He also advised that General Hill should proceed to the Loudoun heights, in the northwest corner of that county, and station some artillery upon the mountain there overlooking Harper's Ferry, so as to make the ferry across the stream so hazardous, and the village so untenable, as to compel General Banks to relinquish that line of approach. But the duty of guarding his own position forbade General Hill to extend to him the proposed assistance. He therefore busied himself in removing his sick, and his army stores to Mount Jackson, in Shenandoah county, in order to be prepared either for a desperate resistance at Winchester, or for a safe retreat. While he was thus occupied, the winter ended, and the spring campaign opened in good earnest; and, before the summer was over, General Jackson, up to this period comparatively unknown, won for himself a world-wide reputation, by a series of the most brilliant achievements; in which, with a mere handful of troops, he again and again swept thousands of the enemy before him, and, passing swiftly and silently from point to point, burst like a thunderbolt upon the foe, when least expected, and at the decisive hour.

CHAPTER IX.

GENERAL VIEW OF THE CAMPAIGNS OF 1862.

THE campaigns of 1861 had been but a prelude to the gigantic struggle which was to be witnessed in 1862. The prowess and superiority which the Confederates everywhere displayed, rudely awakened the people of the United States from their dreams of an easy conquest, and exasperated their pride and revenge. The Washington Government now resolved upon a new policy. This was, to raise armies so vast, and to add to their *momentum* by such deliberate preparation, as to overwhelm their gallant enemies by material weight. Under the industrious management of General M'Clellan, their levies reached, if they were to be believed, the enormous number of seven hundred thousand men; and it is probable that more than half a million were actually under arms, and drilling with the greatest care. Hitherto, the different campaigns had been detached, but in 1862 they assumed connexion with each other. The movements in Virginia were related to those in the Great West, and the brilliant events in the district commanded by General Jackson had a vital influence upon the campaign in Virginia.

In writing the military history of this great commander, two objects must be kept in view. One will be to explain the strategic grounds which support the propriety of his own movements: the other, to show the intimate connexion of his successes with the fortunes of the war. Many persons have claimed his career as an illustration of the uselessness of the science of warfare, and an instance of success in defiance of it. They have conceived of him as a leader who discarded rules, and trusted only to his fortunate star, to rapidity of movements, and to hard blows. They suppose his victories were the results of his boldness only, with that inexplicable chance, which, to man's natural reason, appears good luck, and which a religious faith, like that of Jackson, terms Providence. But while the perpetual and essential influence of the divine power is asserted, which alone sustains the regular connexion of means with ends, it will be shown that these conceptions are erroneous; that General Jackson's campaigns were guided by the most profound and original applications of military science, as well as sustained by the vigor of their execution; and that they are an invaluable study for the leader of armies.

The reader has now reached the commencement of that wondrous campaign in the Valley of Virginia, which created his fame. Before the narrative is begun, it will not be unprofitable to pass in review the general theatre of the war, and the posture and advantages of the two parties. This survey, as well as the subsequent history, will involve the use of a few technical terms, whose definition may be helpful to the unprofessional reader. In accordance with the best usage the word *Strategy* will be employed to denote the art of giving the proper direction to the movements of an army upon the theatre of war. A *Strategic Point* is a place, which, from geographical or other reasons, secures for its occupant some advantage in strategic movements, and thence, some control over a part of the theatre of war. Thus, Manassa's Junction was an important strategic point for the Confederates in 1861, because the two railroads meeting there gave them the decisive advantage in all movements over the territory through which they pass. So, an important fortress, a *focus* where many highways meet, a mountain defile constituting the main entrance to a region, may be such a point. The phrase *General Tactics* expresses the art of arraying and using an army successfully upon a field of battle; while special tactics is the drill which is taught to the single soldier, the company, or the battalion, in the several branches of infantry, cavalry, or artillery. A *Base of Operations* is that line, or series of neighboring points, in secure possession of an army, whence it sets out to assail its enemy, whence it continually draws its supplies and reinforcements, and to which it may retreat for safety. Its *Line of Operations* is the zone along which an army advances from its base toward the object of its attack; and its *Line of Communications* is but the same tract, usually, viewed in the inverted direction. It might appear from this definition, that an army's line of operations would be projected always at right angles to its base, or in a direction approximating this; but while this is often true, it is not necessarily so, and instances arise in which the most successful line of operations may be oblique, or even almost parallel to the base. Other terms which occur will now easily explain themselves to the attentive reader, without the formality of definitions.

The one decisive advantage, to which the North owes all its successes over the South, has been, not its larger territories, or population, or armies, or geographical position, but its superiority upon the water. And this is true, as will be made clear, notwithstanding that it has been chiefly a war upon land. At the division of the Union, the Government of Washington retained all the Federal Navy. Many of its States were maritime and manufacturing communities; while those of the South were chiefly agricultural; hence the multiplication of ships and sailors, from the river transport up to the man-of-war, was far more

37

rapid among them. This inequality was made more ruinous to the naval force of the South, by the further fact, that the initial superiority of the North excluded her rival from all foreign sources of supply, for equipping and manning ships. The result has been, that the Confederates have had no oppor-tunity to cope with their invaders upon the water; and where-ever an entrance was open to Federal ships, either upon sea or river, the former have been expelled.

It has also been the misfortune of the Confederate States, to have the hitherto unsettled question, whether shore-batteries can prevent the passage of ships of war, decided, in novel instances, of the most serious importance to them. When ships were only propelled by the winds, a motive power never so forcible as steam, save in tempests, variable, uncertain, liable to desert the mariner at the critical moment, and leaving him no option save that of moving in a direction somewhat conformed to its own, or else, of casting anchor, artillerists might well boast, that the stationary battery would usually destroy the vessel which chal-lenged its fire. But our generation has witnessed the introduc-tion of steam-ships of war, having a regular and unfailing motive power within themselves, propelling them irrespective of winds and tides, in any direction desired, and capable of a speed as safe and steady, at once, as that of the gentle breeze, and as rapid as the hurricane. When to these advantages is added the iron plating, which, if not impenetrable, at least delays the ruin of the ship's frame-work until after a series of blows, it becomes probable, that such a vessel of war might brave the bullets of shore-batteries, and pass them with impunity without silencing them. But the old authorities of the land service, confident in the former precedents, still declared that such batteries must ever be a secure protection against the entrance of ships of war into rivers and harbors; and it required the disastrous events of

Island No. 10, of New Orleans, and at last, of Vicksburg, in each of which the batteries were passed, and thus rendered useless, without being silenced, to teach the Confederate Government this new fact in warfare.

Let it be remembered, then, that the oceans which bound two sides of the Confederate States, belong to their enemy, affording them a way of approach, cheap, speedy, and secure from assault. This fact renders the whole sea-shore, wherever harbor or inlets gave access to Federal ships, a base of operations to their armies. It has made it all an exposed frontier, and brought the enemy upon it all, as though he had embraced its whole circumference with coterminous territories of his own. Popular readers may form to themselves some conception of the disastrous influence of this fact, by representing to themselves the inland kingdom of Bavaria, assailed at once on four sides, by Austria, Switzerland, and the German States, all united under a single hostile will. The similitude is unequal only in this, that the Confederate States have a larger area than Bavaria. The professional reader will comprehend our disadvantage more accurately, by considering that our enemies thus had two pairs of bases of operations, at right angles to each other; whence it resulted, that from whatever interior base a Confederate army might set out, to meet the invading force advancing from one of these sides, the Confederate line of operations must needs be exposed, at a greater or less distance, to a Federal advance from another base, threatening to strike it at right angles. And the cheap and rapid transit of large masses by water, from one line of operations to another, gave to the exterior lines all the advantages for concentration usually possessed by the interior.

But this was not the worst: the Confederate territories are penetrated in every part by navigable rivers, either opening into the sea, which is the territory of the Federal, or into his own frontiers.

From the east and south, the Potomac, the Rappahannock, the James, the Roanoke, the Neuse, the Cape Fear, the Savannah, the Alabama, the Brazos, pierce the country from the sea, while the Mississippi, itself an inland sea, which floats the greatest men of war, passes out of the United States, through the middle of the Confederacy, to the Gulf of Mexico. The Tennessee and the Cumberland, with their mouths opening upon the Federal frontier, and navigable in winter for war-ships as well as transports, curve inward, deep into the heart of the southeastern quarter; and the Arkansas and Red Rivers open up the States west of the Mississippi. Now, the naval supremacy of the Federalists having been asserted upon all these streams, it is the least part of the evil, that their fertile borders have all been exposed to ravage, and the wealthy cities which grace them, have been wrested from the Confederates. The margins of all these rivers are thus made capable of becoming new bases of operations for invading armies, as secure as their own frontiers. The difficulties of distance, arising from the great extent of the Confederate territories, are reduced, and worst of all, no interior base remains to the Confederates, from which strategic operations can proceed in any direction, but that line is found parallel to some one of these bases of Federal operations; and so, exposed at no great distance, to their advance at right angles upon it. Or, if there is an exception, it is only found in the regions surrounding the Appalachian Range, in Virginia, the Carolinas, and Georgia, equally removed from the navigable waters' of the Ohio, the Tennessee, and the Atlantic streams. And here, accordingly, the Confederates may be expected to make their most successful resistance, and the Federalists to find their accidental advantages lost, and their true obstacles beginning.

The true strategic difficulties of the Confederates, have ever arisen more from their enemies' command of the water, than from their superior numbers. A review of the crowd of disasters with which the year 1862 opened, will be the best illustration of these reasonings.

The first of these was the battle of Mill Spring, or of Somerset, in the southeastern part of Kentucky; where the Confederates, at first victorious, were struck with discouragement by the death of their beloved commander Gen. Zollicoffer, and suffered a defeat. This insulated event was without consequence, save as it showed improved spirit and drill in the Federal soldiery. February 8th, a Federal fleet and army, entering Albemarle Sound in North Carolina, overpowered the feeble armament on land and water, by which the Confederates sought to defend Roanoke Island, the key to all the inland waters of the region. The enemy established himself there; and this naval success was one of the causes, which led to the evacuation of Norfolk at a later day; because it gave a base for offensive operations against the rear of its defences. The Confederate General Albert Sidney Johnston, to whom the defence of Kentucky and Tennessee was entrusted, had stationed his main force at Bowling Green, in Kentucky, a position in itself strong and well chosen. But his retention of it depended upon his closing the Mississippi, Tennessee, and Cumberland Rivers, to the enemy; because the former ran parallel with his line of communications, and the two latter actually passed behind his rear. He attempted to close the Mississippi by batteries at Columbus, the Tennessee by Fort Henry, and the Cumberland by Fort Donelson. The first of these posts was supposed by friends and enemies, to be of adequate strength. But the second fell after a feeble defence, February 6th, and the third after a bloody and heroic resistance, February 15th. These events at once compelled the evacuation

of Columbus, on the Mississippi, because they gave the Federalists, on the margin of the two rivers now opened to them, a base
of operations parallel to the line of communications which connected the Confederate army, at Columbus, with their base.
The next defence was attempted at Island No. 10, between that
place and the city of Memphis.   The Federalists, after an expensive and futile bombardment, made an essay to pass the
batteries with their gunboats, without waiting to silence them;
and being partially successful in this, compelled the evacuation
of the post, which they could not reduce, by threatening the
communications of the garrison.   The necessary corollary was
the fall of Memphis without a defence.   There now remained
for the Confederates, no practicable line of operations, in all
West and Middle Tennessee: for the reason that the three
streams, diverging from points near Cairo, the great naval depot
of the Federalists, and open to their fleets, gave them bases of
operations on all their banks, parallel to any line upon which
the other party might move.   The determination of Generals
A. S. Johnston and Beauregard to transfer the campaign to the
southern bank of the Tennessee, was therefore in strict conformity with military principle; although it required the loss of
the Capital of the fine State of Tennessee, and two-thirds of its
territory.   The result of their wise strategy was the victory of
Shiloh, April 6th: yet even this was almost neutralized by the
facility of concentration, which the naval resources of the enemy
gave them.   The selection of Corinth as the strategic point for
the protection of the State of Mississippi was also correct: for
it gave the command of the railroads diverging thence eastward
and southward.   But the advantage of river transportation for
troops and munitions of war, to the neighborhood, speedily
enabled the Federalists to assemble so enormous a preponderance of means in front of General Beauregard's position there,

as to compel his retreat to an interior point. Had he withstood this motive for retreat, another, still more controlling, would in time, have appeared: the Mississippi River, now open to the enemy to Vicksburg, offered them a base, parallel to General Beauregard's line of communications from Corinth with his rear; so that it was practicable to assail that line by advancing from the water.

The extravagant joy of the Federalists at the fall of Forts Henry and Donelson was generally ridiculed. It was said that the capture of two hastily-constructed earthworks, mounting a few cannon, was no exploit to justify the boastings of a great fleet and army, employed in their reduction. The results of these successes were far greater than their glory; and they spoke far more strongly against the providence of the Confederate rulers, than for the prowess of the Federal armies. The true gravity of the events was not in the fact, that the reduction of such works was a difficult or honorable task: but in the fact that the Confederates lacked either the wisdom or the means to interpose more stable defences in avenues of such vital importance to their campaign. It is now manifest, that the possession of the three rivers decided that of the theatre of war. It is not intended that the mere access to the margins of these streams, and the opportunity to use them as bases of operations on land, would have been enough, without a preponderance of military means to be employed thence; but that, without the advantage of these bases, even the great superiority of the Federal numbers would not have availed to give them the campaign.

But the most fatal of all these advantages was the occupation of New Orleans. This success also resulted from the discovery, whose novelty was so unfortunate for the Confederate cause, that war steamers could pass batteries with impunity. After the chief of the naval force had despaired of the reduction of the forts which guarded the approaches to the city, Commodore Farragut, April 24th, essayed, what was then esteemed the rash experiment of passing them by night, with perfect success. The rich and unarmed city then lay at his mercy; for the Confederates had no fleet adequate to resist his approach, and the surrender of the forts was the obvious sequel to the loss of that, which they were intended to protect. The Mississippi River was now open to the Federal navies through all its length, except the section embraced between the fortresses of Port Hudson and Vicksburg. Thus, their strategic advantages were extended indefinitely for operating in all the States on both sides of its waters. The greater success of the Federalists in their southwestern campaigns is explained by the position of these great rivers. When the advantage which they possessed in them is considered, the only wonder will be, that they did not accomplish more, with their vast military resources. Their failure to conquer the whole is only to be explained by their own timidity and feebleness in execution, coupled with the bravery and talent of the Confederates. It is no small glory to the latter, to have saved any part of their country from an enemy possessed of strategic advantages so deadly.

The policy which should have been adopted for defence by the Confederate Government, is also indicated by these events. They should have understood that there were four vital points, —the mouth of the Mississippi, its course at the western extremity of Kentucky, the mouth of the Tennessee, and the mouth of the Cumberland, to the defence of which every energy should have been bent from the first day of the war. The loss of one of these, and especially of one of the last three, rendered nugatory the defence of the others; because the invading army, penetrating along the one stream which it had opened, could base itself upon its banks, far in the rear of the forces defending the other two, and, by threatening their communications, compel their retreat. The obstacles placed upon all of them should, therefore, have been equally impregnable. It had been better to neglect anything else, and to suffer any incursions by land, than to fail in this. And since the recent introduction of steam into ships of war, with the earnest warnings of enlightened naval men, ought to have aroused at least a mistrust of shore-batteries, as a sufficient defence against ships, other and more certain means of resistance should have been provided at these essential points. To the construction of enough efficient war-ships to hold these four avenues, the energies of the Government and people should have been directed, at the earliest hour, with an activity akin to that of desperation. The Confederates then possessed the wealth, the skilled labor, and the material supplies, of Nashville, Memphis, New Orleans, and Norfolk; by neglecting to expend a part early and wisely, they lost the whole of them.

At the place last named, the Confederates were employed during the winter, in one enterprise, which pointed in the right direction; the construction of the iron-clad steamer, Virginia. This powerful and unique ship, armed with the most formidable rifled cannon, was prepared for action early in March, and on the 8th of that month, attacked the Federal fleet in Hampton Roads, destroying three frigates and several gunboats, and putting the remainder to flight.

This brilliant action filled the people with delight, and the noble ship was accepted as a sufficient defence for the mouth of James River, against all the men-of-war which the Federalists could at that time bring against her. Her prowess showed that a few such vessels in the Mississippi might have saved the disasters of the southwest, and the occupation of a third of its territory.

The disparity of the strength of the two parties was pointed out at the beginning of the war. The geographical position of the Confederate States, it has been now shown, rendered them yet weaker for a defensive war; but to this species of resistance they were shut up. At the beginning of the campaign of 1862, they had experienced a farther diminution of strength, in the virtual loss of Kentucky and Missouri. A few of the chivalrous citizens of these States, accepting banishment rather than subjugation, followed the fortunes of the Confederacy; but their territories, their revenues, and their wealth were now in the hands of the oppressors. The military events which induced this result need not be detailed here; for they would lead too far away from the proper subject — the Virginian campaign. After this loss, which occurred before the struggle reached its acmé, the Confederates States had about eight and a half millions of people, including among them nearly all the Africans of the South, with whom to resist twenty millions. This statement declares, more forcibly than any eloquence of words, the heroic character of the defence which they have since made.

Comparisons of present with past events assist us to appreciate the merit of the latter, by the help of the estimate established for the former in history. Let the defence of the Southern Confederacy against the United States, be illustrated, for instance, by that of Spain, in the Peninsular War, against the designs of Napoleon, which were not unlike the aggressions of the Federals in iniquity. Spain then possessed about eleven millions of people, an army of one hundred and twenty-seven thousand men, and a navy superior to that of the United States, at the opening of this war. Her soil was open to the invader only at one quarter, for the sea which surrounds her was held by the fleets of England, in conjunction with her own; and these reduced the navy of France to an absolute inactivity. Access to her wealthy colonies was open throughout the struggle, and no blockade obstructed the entrance of the British arms and supplies. On the other hand, the population of the French Empire was double that of the Federal States, but the armies of the Emperor were not more numerous than those employed for our conquest. The vast difference against Napoleon was, that during the whole Spanish struggle, his strength was also tasked with gigantic wars elsewhere while the malice of the Federal has met no diversion from any other nation in its concentration upon the work of our destruction, and to his armies, equal to all the imperial legions, must be added the efforts of a great navy. Yet, with these relative means of aggression, Napoleon overran the whole territory of Spain, occupied her capital, and compelled her to a war of six years, in which she was seconded by the whole military power of Great Britain, to shake off his grasp. What, then, must have been the energy of the Southern character, as compared with the Spanish, or what the impotency of the Federal administration as compared with the French, to reduce the consequences of their invasion to so partial a limit, at the end of three years of lavish expenditure and bloodshed?

The opening of the campaign of 1862 found the Federalists firmly seated upon the coast of South Carolina at Beaufort, and of North Carolina at Fort Macon, Newberne, and Roanoke Island. On the eastern borders of Virginia, they occupied Fortress Monroe, and Newport News, all the lower peninsula between the James and York Rivers, and the mouth of the Rappahannock. Near the ancient towns of Williamsburg and York, General Magruder, with a few thousand men, held their superior numbers at bay: and his guns maintained a precarious command over the channels of the two rivers. Around Washington, swarmed "the Grand Army" of General M Clellan, upon both banks of the Potomac; while its wings extended from the lower regions of the State of Maryland, to the Alleghanies. It was confronted by the army of General Joseph E. Johnston, with its right wing resting upon the Potomac to Evansport, and commanding the river by a formidable battery, its centre about Manassa's Junction, and its left at Winchester under General Jackson. This army was composed of volunteers enlisted for one year; and the hour when their term of service expired, was now fast approaching.

Neither State nor Confederate Government had yet adopted any permanent system for raising or recruiting armies. The Congress was just moving, under the impulse of threatening disasters, towards the adoption of a general conscription, which placed all the male white population, between the ages of eighteen and thirty-five, in the military service.

But this law, while it promised ultimately to bring a multitude of new soldiers into the service, released a number of veterans, who were more than thirty-five years old. It moreover involved the reorganization of every regiment, by the election of new officers; a work which was in progress throughout the early months of the campaign. All the forces of the Confederacy, being volunteers, had claimed the republican privilege of election. The fruits of this vicious system of appointment were now becoming more painfully manifest; when to its other relaxations of authority were added the desire on the part of the officers to propitiate the favor of their soldiers by indulgence, in view of the approaching vote, and the disposition of other aspirants to oppose their pretensions to a re-election, by every species of cabal. The troops were chiefly raised by authority of the States: during the remainder of the war, they were to be governed by that of the Confederacy. That power therefore proposed to introduce, along with their conscription, a uniform system for its armies. The 3rd of March, General Jackson, through a member of Congress from his Military District, urged the adoption of two principles: of which one was, that the right of electing should be arrested, save for the lowest rank of commissioned officers, third lieutenants: and that above that grade, all vacancies should be filled by promotion. The second was, that promotion should not be obtained by seniority, unless the applicant was approved by a Board of Examiners, whose rejection, when sanctioned by the Commander-in-Chief of a Department, should be final. Although the reorganization of the Virginia regiments, for the second year, was completed under laws of the State, without these wholesome regulations, they were soon after embodied in the laws of Congress. Their effect has been steadily to raise the efficiency of the officers, and thus, the discipline of the army. But during the first, and the greater part of the second campaign, the lack of competent and energetic officers for companies and regiments, was the bane of the service, and the constant grievance of the commanders. In many, there was neither an intelligent comprehension of their duties, nor zeal in their performance.

Appointed by the votes of their neighbors and friends, to lead them, they would neither exercise that rigidity in governing, nor that detailed care in providing for the wants of their men, which are necessary to keep soldiers efficient. The duties of the drill and the sentry-post were often negligently performed; and the most profuse waste of ammunition, and other military stores, was permitted. It was indeed seldom that these officers were guilty of cowardice upon the field of battle; but they were often in the wrong place, fighting as common soldiers, when they should have been directing others. Above all, was their inefficiency marked by their inability to keep their men in the ranks. "Absenteeism" grew under them to a monstrous evil; and while those who were animated by principle were bravely in their places on the day of action, every poltroon and laggard found a way to creep from the ranks. Indeed, it was no·rare thing to hear these leaders reason, that efforts to keep the latter class in their places were injudicious; because they would be of no use, if present! Hence the frequent phenomenon, that regiments which, on the books of the commissary appeared as consumers of five hundred or a thousand rations, were reported as carrying into action two hundred and fifty, or three hundred bayonets. The thinness of these ranks must needs be repaired by the greater devotion and gallantry of the true men. They were compelled to take their own share of the bullets, and those of the cowards in addition: and thus, the blood which was shed in battle was almost exclusively that of the noblest and best, while the ignoble currents, in the veins of the base, were husbanded.

At the approach of the spring campaign, other causes, less discreditable, concurred to diminish the armies in Virginia. Furloughs were liberally given, in order to encourage the men to re-enlist with cheerfulness. A majority of the officers were at their homes, professedly engaged in collecting absentees, or in recruiting new men. The fevers of the previous autumn had decimated the most of the regiments. While, therefore, the diligence of the Federal Government was swelling the host of M'Clellan to two hundred and thirty thousand men, the command of General Johnston was absolutely diminished more than one half, when the season of activity arrived. It was manifest that he would be in no condition to cope with his adversary, in his present positions. His chief protection against a catastrophe had been, for some time, the condition of the roads, which forbade campaigning. A winter and early spring of unprecedented rains had so softened the argillaceous soil of the Bull Run, that the two armies lay immovable, like two hostile ships fast grounded in a shoal of mud, a little too remote for combat. General M'Clellan was anxiously awaiting the first drying suns of March, to move his gigantic army forward to that triumph, for which he had been so assiduously preparing them for eight months; and General Johnston was watching for the same juncture, to retire to a more interior line of defence.

The goal of the Federal advance was, of course, to be Richmond; and to its capture, every movement was to converge. General M'Clellan was to drive back the left wing of the Confederate army at Winchester, by the forces under Shields and Banks, to insulate and overpower the right wing resting on the Potomac at Evansport, and to surround and crush General Johnston at Manassas, or else to force him toward Richmond, and pursue him. The army on the Peninsula, setting out from Fortress Monroe, was to press back General Magruder, and assail the capital from the East. The forces in the Valley, having beaten General Jackson, were either to converge towards the rear of Manassa's Junction, by crossing the Blue Ridge, or else to march southwestward up that District, and at Staunton, meet a powerful force from the Northwest, which was preparing to advance from Wheeling, under General Fremont. Staunton was manifestly one of the most important strategic points in Central Virginia. It is situated on the Central Railroad, and at the intersection of the great Valley Turnpike (a paved road which extends from the Potomac continuously to the extremity of Southwestern Virginia). It is also the *terminus* of the Turnpike to Parkersburg, in Northwest Virginia, and the *focus* of a number of important highways. Its possession decided that of the whole interior of the State, and of another avenue, the Central Railroad, leading to Richmond from its western side. As this road, on its way to the capital, passes by Gordonsville, the intersection of the Orange and Alexandria road, on which General Johnston now depended as his sole line of communications, its possession by the Federalists would at once endanger that line, and compel him to seek a position still more interior. Moreover, Eastern Virginia, south of Gordonsville, was the great tobacco-planting region, and consequently, yielded no large supplies for the capital or armies. The great central counties, to which Staunton was the key, were the granary of the Commonwealth. There was, then, little hope that the capital, with the large armies necessary for its defence, when thus insulated from its sources of supply, and open only to the south, would endure a very long investment. Considering these things, and remembering that if Staunton were surrendered, the concentration of General Banks' and General Fremont's columns there must inevitably occur, thus placing a third army of commanding strength far in the rear of General Johnston's left, and of his temporary base, General Jackson declared that the defence of the Valley was essential to the defence of Virginia. Geographically, it is the heart of the State. Its vast resources were essential to our strength; and if seized by the enemy, would enable them to deal deadly blows. If they seated themselves in force there, they could not be dislodged, save at great cost; because no favorable base and line of operations against them, would remain to the Confederates.

The retreat of General Johnston from Manassa's Junction implied that of General Jackson from Winchester, for reasons already explained (in Chap. VII.); and for the latter, no practicable line of operations would remain north of Front Royal and Strasbourg. These two villages, both on the line of the Manassa's Gap Railroad, marked the opening of the twin valleys, into

which the Masanuttin Mountains divide the Great Valley for
fifty miles. The strategic question for General Jackson was,
whether he should move to Front Royal, at the mouth of the
Eastern Valley, or to Strasbourg, at the beginning of the Western, and on the great road leading to Staunton. At the beginning of March, this question was receiving careful discussion by
letters between his Commander-in-Chief and him. The former
advised that he should retire to Front Royal, and thence, up the
south branch of the Shenandoah, because it was in the direction
of his own intended retreat, and therefore upon convergent
lines; because thus, the retreating wings would be prepared for
a more rapid concentration than those of the invading army, and
for a vigorous blow at each of them in turn : and because it was
contrary to all sound discretion to allow the enemy to attain a
point between the Manassa's Army and the Army of the Valley,
from which he might act against them on interior lines. General Johnston accordingly enjoined on General Jackson, not to
permit the Federalists to insinuate themselves between Winchester and the Blue Ridge. Had there been no armies on the
theatre of war, save those of M'Clellan and Johnston, Banks
and Jackson, these views would have been correct. But General Jackson declared his preference for a retreat up the main
Valley, in the direction of Staunton. That place, he argued,
would be the object of Banks's endeavors, rather than a junction
with M'Clellan in front of General Johnston; because, by approaching Staunton, he threatened General Edward Johnson's
rear, and compelled his retreat without a blow; he thus opened
the way for General Fremont's unobstructed advance, and
effected a junction with him; and he placed himself, in redoubled force, so far in the rear of General Johnston's left,
and so near his line of communications, as to necessitate his
retiring without battle, and yielding to M'Clellan the vast and

precious circuit of country which has been described. For this reason, he said the main Valley must not be left open to General Banks. But unless the Confederates from Winchester moved so decisively towards the Blue Ridge, as to leave the road to Staunton undefended against him, they could not effect General Johnston's purpose, of converging on lines shorter and more concentric than those of the enemy's advance. Indeed, since a short march from Charlestown, by the way of Berryville and Milwood, would place General Banks at the fords of the Shenandoah, and on the main roads from Winchester to Manassa's, if that purpose were to be the dominant one, the Confederate army ought to move that very day, not towards Front Royal, but directly towards Manassa's. If such an object were in view as dictated the masterly strategy of July, 1861 [to make an immediate concentration, and fight a successful battle for the retention of Manassa's Junction], then this would be the proper movement; but in no other case. On the other hand, he declared that he did not believe General Banks could cross the Blue Ridge, to bear upon General Johnston, while he remained in the Valley near him, acting upon the line of communications with Staunton, and continually threatening his right. General Jackson therefore desired to be permitted to retire to Strasbourg; but he closed his manly argument with the assurance, that he should promptly and cheerfully obey the wishes of his Commander-in-Chief, whatever they might be. General Johnston conceded to him the exercise of his own discretion; and he made preparations to retreat, when it became necessary, up the Valley, by sending his stores and sick to Mount Jackson, forty-five miles above Winchester. It will appear how far events confirmed his speculations.

To a friend in the Confederate Congress, General Jackson thus disclosed his own wishes. Speaking of the Valley of Virginia, he says:—"What I desire is, to hold the country as far as practicable, until we are in a condition to advance; and then, with God's blessing, let us make thorough work of it. But let us start right. . . .

"In regard to your question as to how many troops I need, you will probably be able to form some idea, when I tell you that Banks, who commands about 35,000 has his head-quarters in Charlestown, and that Kelly, who has succeeded Lander, has probably 11,000, with his head-quarters near Paw Paw. Thus you see two Generals, whose united force is near 46,000, of troops already organized for three years or the war, opposed to our little force here; but I do not feel discouraged. Let me have what force you can. M'Clellan, as I learn, was at Charlestown on Friday last: there may be something significant in this. You observe then, the impossibility of saying how many troops I will require, since it is impossible for me to know how many will invade us. I am delighted to hear you say *Virginia* is resolved to consecrate all her resources, if necessary, to the defence of *herself*. Now we may look for war in earnest."

"You ask me for a letter respecting the Valley. I am well satisfied that you can say much more about it than I can, and in much more forcible terms. I have only to say this; that if this Valley is lost, Virginia is lost.

"Very truly, your friend,

"T. J. JACKSON."

CHAPTER X.

KERNSTOWN.

BY the 11th of March, 1862, General Jackson had removed all his sick and supplies to Mount Jackson, and had gathered in all his troops from the outposts to Winchester. He now had only the First, Second, and Third Virginia Brigades, the last containing two small regiments, Colonel Ashby's regiment of horse, and six batteries of field artillery. On that day, General Banks approached within four miles of Winchester, on the north, and General Jackson went out and offered him battle. This challenge Banks declined, although his force present on the field was fourfold, and preferred to await the arrival of General Shields with his reserves. The Confederates, therefore, returned in the evening to their camp around the town, and General Jackson assembled the commander and colonels of the Stonewall Brigade, as a council of war, to lay before them a daring project which he had conceived. While he was awaiting them, he went to take his supper with the hospitable family whose board he frequented, and appeared in their parlor with his military cloak, spurs, sword, and haversack. His spirits were unusually bright and genial, and his countenance glowed with animation. His friends, on the contrary, were oppressed with gloom; for they could not but see that the movement of stores to the rear, which had been so complete, portended the evacuation of Winchester, and their surrender to the hated oppressions of the enemy. To the inquiries of the ladies, he replied by a polite evasion, while he evidently sought to relieve their apprehensions. According to the usage of the family, the domestic devotions were to follow the meal; but the master, presuming that General Jackson must be too busy on this occasion to be delayed by them, paused to give him an opportunity to retire. He, however, requested the privilege of joining in them. At their close, he arose, asked that a lunch be placed in his haversack, and went away with a cheerful good evening, — merely saying that he hoped to dine with them on the morrow as usual. His friends, re-assured by his air, and by their implicit confidence in his prowess, went out to make a call. In an hour, the General returned, with a rapid stride, and gave the door-bell an energetic ring. Upon learning that the family were out, he left with the servants a request that their master should repair to his head-quarters immediately after his return; and they said that he looked anxious and hurried. His friend hastened down to his office, and found him prepared for mounting, striding across the room with rapid steps, and depressed with an inexpressible weight of sadness. General Jackson then explained that it was his plan to march the army back by night, after allowing them time to refresh themselves, to General Banks's front, and, having made his dispositions in profound silence, to begin a fierce attack upon him at the "small hours" of the morning. General Shields had not yet come within a supporting distance; but by the next day he would be united with his commanding general, and the odds would then be so enormous that it would be madness to resist them. General Banks had an army of new and unsteady troops, half intimidated by the fame and valor of the Confederates, while the latter were animated by a towering enthusiasm and confidence. He believed that the darkness, the suddenness and fury of his attack, the lack of experience in evolutions among the Federalists, would throw them into confusion; and, by the vigorous use of the bayonet, and the blessing of the Providence in which he trusted, he should inflict upon them a great overthrow. He was exceedingly loath to leave the gallant, loyal, and generous town, with all the fine country around it, to their ruthless sway, without a struggle. But when he consulted his officers, he found them too reluctant, to permit him to hope for a successful execution of his plan. They argued that the troops had already marched ten miles to and fro that day, and the night attack would require a farther journey of six miles, after which they would reach the scene of action too much wearied to effect anything; and that there was at least a probability of an advance of the enemy from Berryville; which would place them, at the critical moment, upon the right and rear of the Confederates.

As he detailed these facts, General Jackson paced his floor in painful indecision, and repeated an expression of his bitter reluctance to leave Winchester without one brave stroke for its defence. Then passing full before the candles, he lifted up his face with a look of lofty determination, and his hand convulsively grasped the hilt of his sword, while he slowly hissed through his clenched teeth words to this effect: "But—Let me think—may I not execute my purpose still?" As he uttered this, his eye burned with a fire before which his friend, who had never seen the light of battle in his face, confessed he could not but tremble. Then releasing his sword, he dropped his head, and said, "No: I must not do it: it may cost the lives of too many brave men. I must retreat, and wait for a better time." The air of grief again possessed him, and he proposed to return to his friend's dwelling, to take leave of his family. He bade them a sad farewell, but said he hoped a good Providence would enable him soon to return, and bring them deliverance. The next morning,

at dawn of day, the Confederate army left Winchester for Strasbourg, and at 9 o'clock, A. M., the column of General Banks
began cautiously to enter it.   As they approached, Colonel Ashby slowly withdrew his troopers into the streets, and then
through the town, while he remained the last man, and sat
quietly upon his horse, until the enemy had approached within a
short distance; when he gave his defiant shout, and galloped
away.   The Federalists found not a single prisoner, horse,
musket, or wagon, to enrich their conquest.   The citizens of
Winchester, who, saw their nervous timidity at the thought of
Stonewall Jackson's proximity, and their ignorance of his real
numbers, were convinced that, had the night attack been made,
they would have been utterly routed.   General Shields's troops
were so far in the rear, that they did not begin to arrive until
2 o'clock, P. M., and it is therefore manifest that the affair would
have been decided, before they reached the scene of action.   But
the panic among their friends would not have been slow to
propagate itself among them.

General Jackson wished, after once surrendering the lower
Valley, to draw the enemy farther into the country, and thus
both to relieve General Johnston of their pressure, and to diminish the numbers with whom he would be required to deal in
his front.   After marching to Strasbourg, twenty miles above
Winchester, the 12th of March, he retreated slowly to the neighborhood of Mt. Jackson, reaching it the 17th.   There he received
a despatch from General Johnston, dated March 19th, stating that
it was most desirable the enemy's force in the Valley should be
detained there, and prevented from reinforcing General M'Clel
lan.   To effect this, he requested General Jackson to return
nearer the enemy, and remain in as threatening attitude as was
practicable without compromising the safety of his army.   The
Commander-in-Chief was completing that hazardous retreat

from Manassa's Junction to the south side of the Rappahannock, begun March 10th, by which he so skilfully delivered his army, and its whole *materiel*, from the jaws of his powerful enemy. M'Clellan was also endeavoring to envelop him with his multitudinous hordes, and, to this end, was just drawing a number of regiments from the army of Banks, to aid in turning General Johnston's left. They had already begun their march, and were preparing to cross the Blue Ridge at Snicker's Gap, while their General, regarding Jackson as a fugitive whom it was vain to pursue, had returned to Washington to boast of his bloodless conquest, leaving the remainder of his army in charge of General Shields. Upon receiving the orders of his Commander-in-Chief, the Confederate General prepared for a rapid return towards Winchester. Leaving the neighborhood of Mount Jackson, March 22d, he marched that day to Strasbourg, twenty-six miles; while Colonel Ashby, with his cavalry and a light battery of three guns, advanced before him, and drove the enemy's outposts into Winchester. The rapidity of this movement took them by surprise. The troops which remained with General Shields were encamped below the town, and Ashby found only a feeble force in his front. With these he skirmished actively and successfully; and, in the combat, an exploding shell from one of his guns broke the arm of the Federal Commander. So audacious was Ashby's pursuit, that his scouts privately penetrated the town of Winchester, and communicated with the citizens. The latter, knowing that many regiments had been sent towards Manassa's, by Snicker's Gap, and seeing very few remaining near the town, assisted to confirm him in the impression of the paucity of the enemy's numbers. He accordingly sent back to General Jackson the assurance that there were but four regiments of infantry occupying Winchester, and that they were preparing to return to Harper's Ferry: which encouraged him, in turn, to push forward his whole force on the morning of the 23d. But the alarmed enemy had advanced all the forces encamped below the town, and had sent couriers to recall all those which were on their march towards Manassa's. When the General, therefore, reached Barton's Mills, five miles from the town, at noon of that day, he found Ashby pressed back to the highlands south of Kernstown, and confronted by considerable masses of the enemy.

It was the Sabbath day; and if there was one principle of General Jackson's religion, which was more stringent than the others, it was his reverence for its sanctity. He had yielded to the demands of military necessity, so far as to march on the sacred morning, that he might not lose the advantages which opportunity seemed to place within his reach; but now a more inexorable necessity was upon him. It was manifest that Colonel Ashby had been deceived in his estimate of the force opposed to him; and Jackson had reason to anticipate that General Johnston's desire to have the powerful army of Banks recalled, was fulfilled too efficaciously for his own safety. The region about him, and in his rear, was a beautiful champaign, swelling with gentle hills: and on that side of Cedar Creek, twelve miles behind him, there was no defensible position against superior masses. The whole country was practicable for the manœuvres of cavalry and artillery. To delay, therefore, was to incur the hazard of being enclosed in the overwhelming numbers of the enemy: already it was doubtful whether a prompt retreat would be safely concluded. General Jackson's resolution was therefore immediately taken, to assail the enemy on the spot, and win, if not a decisive victory, at least the privilege of an unmolested retreat, before the preponderance against him became more alarming than it already was. In the force with which he proposed to attack them, more than half the commissioned officers

40

were absent, either on furloughs or recruiting service; for a few days before, it was supposed that the cessation of the enemy's pursuit would allow a period of quiet, to be devoted to the needed work of reorganization. Many of the men were also at their homes; so that after deducting the stragglers lurking with the baggage train, the foot-sore, whom the rapid march had left behind, and a regiment detained to guard the equipage, there were but two thousand seven hundred of the little army left, to meet the enemy.

The great road crossing the Opequon Creek, a quiet mill stream, five miles from Winchester, proceeds thither over a series of long and gentle slopes, through a country smiling with fertility, and almost denuded of its forests. Two miles from the Opequon, after surmounting a moderate ridge, it reaches Kernstown, a hamlet of a dozen houses, seated in the midst of meadows, three miles from Winchester. All the vicinity was divided into farms, by stone fences, which also lined the highway continuously. Here, there was nothing in the nature of the ground to offer advantage to the smaller force. A mile to the left, or west of the Turnpike, is a country road, which also crosses the Opequon, and passing through gently undulating farms, converges towards Winchester, in such a direction as to meet the main thoroughfare at the nearer side of the town. And west of this country road, there is an elevated ridge parallel to it, terminated at its rear, or southwestern end, by the Opequon, which curves around it. This range of hills, after running forward for two miles towards the town, sinks into the plain. Although elevated enough to command the whole neighborhood, it is not craggy, but so rounded, as to permit the ascent of artillery; and it is clothed with forests, with a few small fields interspersed, and notched by successive depressions, which descend into ravines between the lateral spurs of the hill. West of this ridge is another vale, filled with meadows and farm-houses, among which the ascending course of the stream threads its way parallel to the main crest. The larger part of the fields here, likewise, were enclosed by fences of limestone, which, rising to the height of four feet, offered a very adequate breastwork against the fire of musketry. A mile west of the region last described, still another road passes in the direction of Winchester, called the Cedar Creek Turnpike. This route manifestly gave the enemy access to the left and rear of the Confederates.

General Jackson's plan was to contest the wooded ridge with the enemy; for upon it rested their right flank, and its heights gave their artillery commanding positions whence they could sweep all the champaign between it and the great road. With their wings thus supported, the one by the hills, and the other upon Kernstown, and their centre strengthened with fourfold numbers of infantry and artillery, an attack in front gave no promise of success. The only hopeful project for the inferior force taking the aggressive, was, to amuse the enemy's centre and left, while the main body availed itself of the covert and strength of the same heights, which were occupied at their northern end by them, and to direct the whole weight of the assault against their right. The obvious mode for effecting this would have appeared to be to ascend the ridge at its southwestern end, and thus proceed along its crest; but such a movement was forbidden by an extensive pond, formed on the Opequon for feeding a mill, whose waters embraced that extremity of the hill. General Jackson was compelled, therefore, to march his infantry and artillery obliquely from the great road to the hills, under a hot cannonade from the enemy, without the ability to return his fire at that time. But the movement was effected without loss, and without confusion. About 4 o'clock in the afternoon, the following dispositions were completed. On his

extreme right, which rested upon the turnpike in front of Kernstown, he posted Colonel Ashby, with his battery of three guns,
all his cavalry, except four companies detached for the left, and
four companies of infantry from the Stonewall Brigade. These
were ordered to occupy the attention of the enemy's left by a
constant cannonade, and to press them as opportunity might
permit. Next to the turnpike was placed the 5th Virginia
regiment, to hold a mile of space, and to watch the enemy's
centre. Effective resistance from so small a force was, of
course, not to be expected; but General Jackson relied upon
his artillery, commanding the country along which they must
advance if they assumed the aggressive from the centre, and yet
more upon the engrossing occupation which he expected to give
them upon their right wing, to hold that part of their army in
check. Nor was he disappointed of this hope. His main line
of battle was finally formed, with no small interval between it
and the regiment last named, obliquely across the wooded ridge,
with his left advanced. Next the right were the 42d and 21st
regiments of Virginia Volunteers, and the 1st battalion of
Virginia Regulars, composing the 2d brigade, under the command of Colonel Burks. Next to these on the left, was the
Stonewall Brigade, with the 2d regiment on its right, and then
the 33d, the 27th, and the 4th. The left of the infantry line
was composed of the two regiments of the 3d brigade, the 37th
and 23d, under the command of Colonel Fulkerson. These
occupied the farther, or western, side of the ridge. Beyond the
meadows which lay at its base, four companies of cavalry were
stationed on a hill which overlooks the country to the Cedar
Creek turnpike, to check the insults of the enemy's horse. The
batteries were posted in the centre in front of the Stonewall
Brigade; for their line passed across the higher grounds, most
suitable for the position of artillery.

Thus disposed, the little army advanced against the enemy, with its left continually thrown forward, through the alternate woods and fields which covered the sides and crest of the highlands. After a spirited cannonade, by which several batteries of the enemy were silenced, the infantry engaged with inexpressible fury, at close quarters, the 27th regiment leading off. In some places, the lines were advanced within twenty paces, partially shielded from each other by the abrupt little ravines, where the Confederates, lying upon their breasts behind the protuberances of the ground, or retiring a few steps into the hollow places to reload, held their enemies at bay by their scathing discharges. As regiment after regiment came into position, their heroic General led them into the hottest of the fire; and wherever the line wavered under overwhelming numbers, he was present, to cheer the fainting men, and bring up the reinforcements. But he had no reserves, save the 5th Virginia, which was speedily released from its first position by the inactivity of the enemy in that quarter, and the 48th, left as a baggage guard. Only the former of these came up in time to share in the action, and was introduced to reinforce the 2d brigade between the 42d and 21st, where it bore its full share of the glories and dangers of the combat. On the Federal side, the superior numbers enabled them perpetually to bring up fresh troops. As one regiment recoiled, reeling and panicstruck, it was replaced again and again by another; and the officers, secure of victory from their preponderating force, were seen riding madly behind the wavering lines, goading their men to the work with the sabre. The Confederates, on the other hand, having no succors, fought until they exhausted their ammunition. As the men fired their last cartridge, their officers allowed them to go to the rear; and after a time, the thinned lines presented no adequate resistance to the fresh crowds of enemies. Near nightfall, General Richard B. Garnett, com manding the Stonewall Brigade, in the centre, seeing his fire dying away for lack of ammunition, and his line pierced on his right, assumed the responsibility of authorizing a retreat of his command, without orders from General Jackson; and nothing now remained, but to protect the movement from more serious disaster.

Where every regiment fought with steady heroism, and none retired until they had fired the last round from their cartridge-boxes, detailed exploits can scarcely be singled out, without injustice to the men passed over in silence. But a few particulars, in which the actors possessed, not more courage, but more opportunity, should be described, as having a decisive influence on the battle. On the right, Colonel Ashby cannonaded the enemy continually with his three guns, with such audacity, as to win ground all the day from their multitudes. They advanced their infantry through a tract of woodland, to seize his pieces; when his four infantry companies, thrown forward as skirmishers, scoured the forest with enthusiastic courage, and repulsed the attacking party, until the artillery was again posted in a more secure position. Later in the day, this daring leader executed a cavalry charge against the extreme left of the Federalists, drove their .first line back upon their reserves, and captured a few prisoners. In that quarter, they advanced no more during the day. Upon the left, where the advance was first confided to the 27th and 21st regiments, supported by Colonel Fulkerson, and Carpenter's and McLauchlin's batteries, the guns were advanced with great spirit under the eye of General Jackson, delivering an effective fire towards the right and front. The infantry engagement was opened by the 27th, seconded by the 21st; and these two regiments sustained the whole brunt of the fire with unsurpassed heroism, until Colonel

Fulkerson passed to their left, and the remainder of the Stone-wall Brigade came up. Twice they routed their assailants in quick succession, and held the Federalist army in check while the line of battle was completed. In the centre, the 5th and 42nd regiments, with the batteries of McLauchlin and Carpenter, were the last upon the field. While the enemy pressed up to close quarters, and shot down the horses and gunners at the pieces, the latter replied with murderous discharges of canister shot, at the distance of a hundred paces. This determined resistance saved the batteries, with the exception of two guns, of which one was disabled, and the other entangled in a fence, and of four caissons, whose horses were slaughtered. On the left, Colonel Fulkerson, upon becoming warmly engaged, perceived between him and the enemy, a long stone fence, to which each party was advancing, intending to employ it as a breastwork against the other. The boldness of the Confederates secured them that advantage. Reaching the covert a moment in advance of the enemy, they fell upon their knees, and delivered a volley so withering, that the whole line before them seemed to sink into the earth. The larger part of the Federalists were indeed killed or wounded by that unerring fire; and the remainder, to escape instant death, prostrated themselves, and attempted to crawl to the rear. But in this endeavor, nearly all perished; the mountain riflemen picked them off with deadly aim, before they reached the shelter of the wood. The regiment thus annihilated was said to be the 5th Ohio. A New York regiment, coming to their aid, escaped with a fate little less terrible; for when they sheltered themselves behind another stone fence running to that occupied by Colonel Fulkerson at right angles, and endeavored to fusillade the Confederates from its shelter, that skilful commander moved a part of his line down, along his own defence, to a point below the juncture of the two walls, whence he delivered an enfilading fire upon the exposed rear of the astonished Federalists. But finding the centre of the Confederate line broken, at nightfall he retired in good order, bringing off his two little regiments in safety. The four companies of cavalry upon the extreme left had been instructed by General Jackson to hold themselves prepared to charge the enemy should he retreat, or to protect the Confederate infantry, should it be forced to that alternative. They now rendered good service, by holding in check, and ultimately putting to flight, the Federal cavalry, which had made a circuit by the Cedar Creek turnpike, and sought to interrupt the retreat of their friends. But on the eastern side of the Opequon, a number of the fugitives found themselves enclosed, at dark, between the mill-pond and the enemy, and were thus captured. The infantry retreated a few miles to the neighborhood of Newtown, while the cavalry of Colonel Ashby took its station at Barton's Mills, a mile in the rear of the field of combat, and held the enemy in check until 10 o'clock of the next morning. General Jackson himself, begging a morsel of food at the bivouac fire of the soldiers, lay down in the field, to snatch a few hours' repose, a little in the rear of his outposts.

Such was the battle of Kernstown, — in which twenty-seven hundred Confederates, with eighteen guns, attacked eleven thousand Federalists, and almost wrested the victory from their hands. For General Jackson estimated their force actually engaged at that number, besides heavy reserves upon their left which were not brought into action. The next morning, while remarking upon the struggle, he said: "Had I been able to bring up two thousand more men, I should have beaten them." The officer to whom he spoke replied by referring to the dense masses of unbroken infantry hanging behind Kernstown, and expressed the opinion that any success won by so small a force

must have been unavailing, because these reserves, by threatening his right, would have compelled him to arrest his career.
Jackson answered: "No; if I had put the men engaged to flight,
they would all have gone together." The troops marshalled
against him were unquestionably the best in the Federal army,
composed chiefly of hardy Western men, habituated from childhood to field sports and the use of fire-arms; and while those
who have a visible odds of four to one upon their side deserve
but little credit for their boldness, and would have no excuse for
their panic, the perseverance with which the Federal regiments
brought their weight of numbers to bear against the Confederates, notwithstanding bloody losses, is some testimony to their
manhood. General Jackson's loss was eighty killed outright,
three hundred and seventy-seven wounded, and two hundred and
sixty captured, — making a total of seven hundred and seventeen, or more than one fourth of the whole force engaged. The
loss of the enemy was never divulged; but there are reasons for
believing that it was nearly quadruple that of the patriots. Their
officers reported their killed as four hundred and eighteen. The
loyal citizens of Winchester were permitted to perform the last
offices to the Confederate dead upon the field of battle; and, as
they collected the glorious remains, they had an opportunity to
observe that the slain invaders lay four times as thick. Hundreds
of corpses were sent by railroad to their northern friends for
interment, and many more must have remained, unhonored and
forgotten, to find their common tomb in the pits of the battle-
field. The generous women of Winchester demanded and
obtained leave to carry their ministrations of love to the Confederate wounded in the hospitals of the enemy, — for many of the
captives were also wounded, — and thus they were enabled to
estimate the numbers of disabled men belonging to the other
party. The unfortunate 5th Ohio, in particular, filled hundreds

41

of cots with its wounded. From the testimony of these witnesses, it is believed that as many men were disabled by Jackson in the enemy's ranks as he had soldiers in his own. Their greater loss is to be accounted for by his skill in handling his forces, by the superior accuracy of the Virginians' aim, by their discipline and deliberate courage, and by the density of the enemy's ranks, which hardly permitted a well-directed shot to miss its object.

This was the first pitched battle in which General Jackson had supreme command, and it was fought exclusively by Virginians, except that a few Marylanders participated in its dangers. Its effect was to raise the estimate of the prowess both of soldiers and leader to an exalted height; and from this day, the great qualities of the Virginian soldiery, depreciated at first by their own Southern brethren, but illustrated and redeemed at Manassa's, have shone forth unquestioned by all. Kernstown has remained, among the many more bloody days, when greater hosts pursued the work of slaughter in this sanguinary war, a name expressive of the sternest fighting, to the Confederates, to spectators, and to the Federalists. The soldiers of the old Jackson division, when describing the horrors of some subsequent struggle, are wont to say that it almost reminded them of Kernstown. The peaceful citizens of Winchester, who have met the strange fate of having their ears grow more familiar with the sounds of battle than those of many a veteran, still declare that none of the tempests of war which have howled around their devoted town raged like that of Kernstown, with cannonade so fast and furious, and such reverberating roars of musketry. The Federal soldiery, after timidly pursuing the Confederates the next day for a few miles, returned to their quarters, with no triumph upon their tongues, or in their countenances. Their commander, with the usual gasconade of the Federal Generals, claimed a brilliant victory; but his boasts awoke no answering enthusiasm among his followers. The deadly energy of Jackson's blows filled them with gloom and dread, as they asked themselves, what was the task which they had undertaken, in seeking to conquer this people in their consolidated strength, whose resistance, in their weakness and disorganization, was so terrible. To this sombre impression, the spirit of the captives and the oppressed people contributed no little. The former, as they passed through the streets to their prisons, were joyous and defiant, the sympathies of the patriotic multitude converted their progress rather into an ovation than a defeat, and they rent the air with shouts for their country and General, which their gloomy captors, durst not suppress. The very scenes upon the field of blood, harrowing as they were, intimidated the Federal spectators. The regiments which suffered most in Jackson's command, were raised in the lower Valley, and in the town itself. As soon as the permission was given to the Mayor and citizens, to bury the dead of their defenders, they flocked thither upon this errand of grief and mercy. The cultivated and accomplished female, the minister of religion, the tottering grandfather, were seen together, in all the *abandon* of their anguish, running to and fro, pouring water into the parched lips of the wounded, composing the convulsed limbs of the slain into decency, and looking eagerly into every begrimed and haggard face of dead or dying, to recognize a son, a husband, or a brother. Yet, amidst all these horrors, the very women were as determined as the brave men whose fate they bewailed, and arose from beside the corpses whose discovery had just informed them of their bereavement, to declare to their invaders that none of these miseries, nor death itself, should bend their souls to submission. Yet these same women, with a generosity equal to their heroism, divided their cares and gifts between wounded friends and foes in the hospitals where they languished together.

General Jackson had directed his wounded to be gathered at the village of Middletown, eight miles above the field of battle. Intending to retreat to a strong position above Cedar Creek, and there stand on the defensive, he had instructed his Medical Director to collect every vehicle which was available, and send the sufferers to the rear, before the army retired. The morning was approaching, and that officer, after working all the night at the humane task, and employing every carriage which he could procure, found a large number of wounded awaiting removal still. On meeting the General, he informed him of this, and added that he knew not where the transportation was to be obtained, and that unless some expedient were discovered these brave men must be left to the enemy. General Jackson ordered him to have the necessary vehicles impressed from the people of the vicinage. "But," said the surgeon, "that requires time; can you stay to protect us?" "Make yourself easy," said Jackson, "about that. This army stays here till the last wounded man is removed." And then, with a glow of passion suffusing his face, he cried; "Before I will leave them to the enemy, I will lose many men more." It was such traits as these, which made him the idol of his soldiery. It is related of the great Bruce, that, while retreating before his enemies, in his expedition to Ireland, the distress of a poor laundress, who was too helpless to follow the army, and was therefore about to be abandoned to the savage pursuers, touched his heart. He halted the host, and said; "Gentlemen, is there one of us who was born of a woman, so base as to leave this poor soul to her fate? No: let us rather die with her." And he then drew up his men in line of battle, to await the enemy; but they, supposing he had received reinforcements, or was more powerful than his former retreat indicated, recoiled, and feared to assault him. In like manner, the bold front which Jackson assumed, held the enemy at a respectful distance. They did not venture to annoy him, save by a few cannon-shot; and, after the first day, discontinued their pursuit. He retired to the neighborhood of Woodstock; and thus, in three days, his army marched seventy-five miles, and fought a hardly contested pitched battle.

The battle of Kernstown, was technically, a victory of the Federalists. They held the field, the dead, and the wounded. But, like those of Pyrrhus at Heraclea, and of Cornwallis at Guilford, it was a victory with the results of a defeat. The conquerors, crippled by their losses, and terrified by the resistance which they met, dared not press the retreating Confederates. But above all, the object of the battle was won by General Jackson. The Federal army in the Valley was detained there, and the troops which were on their way to Manassa's to increase the embarrassments of General Johnston, were recalled. The army of the latter extricated itself from its perilous situation, and retired in safety behind the Rappahannock, while M'Clellan, foiled in his plans, arrested his advance at Manassa's, and began to consider the policy of transferring the campaign to the Peninsula.

Yet, General Jackson was not satisfied with the results, and insisted that a more resolute struggle for the field might have won it, even against the fearful odds opposed to him. The chief error of the battle, he believed, was the unexpected retreat of the Stonewall Brigade from the centre; for this necessitated the surrender of the field. His disapprobation was strongly expressed against its brave General, Garnett, nor was he willing to accept the justification, that their ammunition was expended. A regiment of reserves was at hand, and the bayonet, his favorite resource, yet remained to them; and he

did not consider all the means of victory as exhausted, until the
naked steel was employed.   Justice to one now dead, requires
that these facts should also be stated: that General Garnett's
gallantry was declared by the officers of his brigade, to be
conspicuous on this bloody field; that they concurred with him
in the opinion, that the troops were not withdrawn too soon to
save them from destruction; and that proceedings against him
were dismissed, and he was again employed by the Government
in a most honorable post, in which he surrendered his life at the
battle of Gettysburg.   It is neither necessary nor practicable
to pass a correct judgment upon the question, whether General
Jackson's animadversions upon his conduct at Kernstown were
erroneous.   It is enough to testify, that all men regarded them
as consistent with the justice of his intentions.   This instance
may serve to show Jackson's rigid ideas of official duty, which
were always more exacting, as men rose in rank.

On the 1st of April, the army retreated to a range of highlands overlooking the North Branch of the Shenandoah, five
miles below the town of Newmarket, called Reede's Hill.   The
stream is bordered here by a wide expanse of fertile meadows,
over which this hill dominates; and artillery posted upon it
commands the bridge by which the great highway crosses
it.   The Federal forces, again under the command of General
Banks, now advanced by slow and cautious steps to the opposing
hills, whence, for many days, they cannonaded the Confederates
without effect.   General Jackson, meantime, keeping Colonel
Ashby in front, busied himself in refitting his crippled artillery,
and recruiting his forces.   The 10th Virginia regiment joined him,
and was assigned to the 3d brigade, to which Brigadier-General Wm. B. Taliaferro was now promoted.   His men returned
rapidly from hospitals and furloughs, and a multitude of new
recruits poured in, inspired by the growing fame of the General,

and the urgency of their country's danger. Especially was the enthusiasm of the people stimulated by the chivalrous and modest courage of Ashby, whose name roused the thrilling hearts of the youth, like the peal of a clarion. His regiment of troopers was speedily swelled to twenty-one companies, and more than two thousand men. Including these, General Jackson's aggregate force now mounted up to more than eleven thousand. But the irregularities and official neglects which have been described were still lurking in all the regiments, and prevalent in the cavalry. Colonel Ashby had little genius for organization and discipline; tasks which, at best, are arduous in a force continually scattered upon outposts, and harassed by hardships, and which were impracticable for a commander seconded by few competent officers, and compelled to launch his raw levies at once into the employments of veteran troopers. The continuance of this imperfect organization was caused by the indiscreet action of the War Department itself. The Secretary, dazzled by Colonel Ashby's fame and exploits, had given him independent authority to raise and command a cavalry force. When General Jackson attempted to stretch his vigorous hand over that part of his army, so as to bring order out of confusion, he was met with a reference to this separate authority, and a threat of resignation. Knowing Colonel Ashby's ascendancy over his men, and finding himself thus deprived of legitimate power, he was constrained to pause, and leave the cavalry unorganized and undisciplined. Colonel Ashby and a Major were the only field-officers for the twenty-one companies; nor had they any regimental organization whatever. The evils and disasters growing out of the crude condition of this force will manifest themselves in the subsequent narrative. They give a valuable illustration of the importance of those principles of military order and subordination, established by experience,

and of the danger of such departures from them as that of the
Secretary of War in making Colonel Ashby independent of his
commanding General. Of his great command, one half was
rarely available for duty, while the remainder were roaming
over the country, imposing upon the generous hospitalities
of the citizens, or lurking in their homes. The exploits of their
famous leader were all performed with a few hundreds, or
often scores, of men who followed him from personal devotion
rather than the force of discipline. Thus, the effective force
which General Jackson was now able to wield against the
enemy, may be correctly estimated as seven or eight thousand
men, with thirty guns.

The position on Reede's Hill, with so strong an artillery,
was impregnable in front. But while, on the right, it was
supported upon the Masanuttin Mountain, on the left it could
be turned with facility by fords of the North River, above
the main bridge, which were practicable in all dry seasons.
Luckily, the melting snows of the western mountains concurred
with the rains of spring, to swell the current, and General
Jackson continued to hold the position until he should be more
seriously menaced by Banks. Its chief value to him was in
the fact, that it covered the juncture of the great Valley turnpike, at New Market, with that which leads across the Masanuttin,
by Luray, the seat of justice for Page County, to Culpepper.
The head-quarters of General Johnston, with the army of
North Virginia, were now at that place, about fifty miles
distant from General Jackson; and it was desirable to hold
possession of the route, that a speedy union of the two armies
might be effected, should necessity demand it. The next
movements thence inaugurated a new arrangement of the
forces upon the theatre of war. The chapter will therefore
be closed with a few brief extracts from General Jackson's

le.ters to his wife, illustrating the events which have just been narrated.

March 24th, just after the battle of Kernstown, he wrote:

"Our God was my shield. His protecting care is an additional cause for gratitude." . . . . "My little army is in excellent spirits: it feels that it inflicted a severe blow on the enemy."

April 7th. "I trust you and all I have in the hands of an ever kind Providence, knowing that all things work together for the good of his people. So live that your sufferings may be sanctified to you; remembering that our light afflictions, which are but for a moment, work out for us a far more exceeding and eternal weight of glory." [In allusion to the illness of his wife.]

"Our gallant little army is increasing in numbers, and my prayer is, that it may be an army of *the living God*, as well as of its country. Yesterday was a lovely Sabbath day. Though I had not the privilege of hearing the word of life, yet it felt like a holy Sabbath day, beautiful, serene, holy and lovely. All it wanted was the church bell, and God's services in the sanctuary, to make it complete. . . . . After God, *our God*, again blesses us with peace, I hope to visit this country with you, and enjoy its beauty and loveliness."

No Christian reader can fail to note here, the parallelism between these sentiments, and those of the ancient warrior-saint, in similar circumstances. "How amiable are Thy tabernacles, O LORD of hosts! My soul longeth, yea, even fainteth, for the courts of the LORD: my heart and my flesh crieth out for the living God."

April 11th. "I feel much concerned at having no letter this week, but my trust is in *the Almighty*. How precious is the consolation flowing from the Christian's assurance, that "all things work together for good, to them that 'love God.'"

42

" God gave us a glorious victory in the S. W. (Shiloh), but the loss of the great Johnston is to be mourned. I do not remember having ever felt so sad at the loss of a man whom I had never seen."

In explanation of his Sabbath attack at Kernstown, he wrote :

" You appear greatly concerned about my attacking on Sunday. I was greatly concerned too ; but I felt it my duty to do it, in consideration of the ruinous effects that might result from postponing the battle until the next morning. So far as I can see, my course was a wise one ; the best that I could do under the circumstances, though very distasteful to my feelings, and I hope and pray to our *Heavenly Father,* that I may never again be circumstanced as on that day. I believed that so far as our troops were concerned, necessity and mercy both called for the battle."

" I hope that the war will soon be over, and that I shall never again have to take the field. Arms is a profession that, if its principles are adhered to for success, requires an officer to do what he fears may be wrong, and yet, according to military experience, must be done, if success is attained. And this fact, of its being necessary to success, and being accompanied with success, and that a departure from it is accompanied with disaster, suggests that it must be right. Had I fought the battle on Monday, instead of Sunday, I fear our cause would have suffered ; whereas, as things turned out, I consider our cause gained much from the engagement."

For his achievement at Kernstown, the Confederate Congress rewarded him with the first of those honors, which were afterwards showered so thickly upon him. The following Resolutions of Thanks were unanimously passed :

1. " Resolved by the Congress of the Confederate States, That the thanks of Congress are due, and are hereby tendered

to Major General Thomas J. Jackson, and the officers and men under his command, for gallant and meritorious services, in a successful engagement with a greatly superior force of the enemy, near Kernstown, Frederick Co., Va., on the 23d day of March, 1862."

2. "Resolved, That these resolutions be communicated by the Secretary of War to Major General Jackson, and by him to his command."

CHAPTER XI.

M'DOWELL.

FROM April 1st to April 17th, General Jackson occupied the position already described, upon Reede's Hill. Meantime, the grand armies of the Potomac had wholly changed their theatre of war. April 1st, General M'Clellan appeared at Fortress Monroe, on the eastern extremity of the peninsula between the James and York Rivers, and began to direct the approaches of his mighty host against Richmond from that point. On the 4th, he appeared before the lines of General Magruder, at Young's Mill, while at the same date, the troops of General Johnston were pouring through Richmond, from their lines behind the Rappahannock, to reinforce their brethren defending the peninsula. General Jackson's prospect of a junction with the main army in Culpepper were, therefore, at an end; and his movements were thus rendered, for a time, more independent of the other Confederate forces. The correctness of his reasonings upon the probable movements of the Federalists was now verified. He was convinced that Staunton would be the aim of General Banks, if he were guided by a skilful strategy; and the Official Report of General M'Clellan, since published, shows that his instructions to that General were, to press to that point as soon as his means would permit. The forces at his disposal now amounted, according to General M'Clellan, to 25,000 men, besides General Blenker's Division of 10,000 Germans, which,

having been just detached from the Federal Army of the Potomac, to reinforce General Fremont in the Northwest, was ordered
to pause at Strasbourg, and support General Banks during the
critical period of his movement. For the rest, the position of
the Federal forces in Virginia was the following: General
Fremont, in command of the Northwestern Department, was
organizing a powerful force at Wheeling, while General Milroy,
under his orders, confronted the Confederates upon the Shenandoah Mountain, twenty miles west of Staunton, and considerable reserves, under General Schenck, were ready to support
him in the Valley of the South Branch. At, and near Manassa's
Junction, were stationed forces amounting to about 18,000 men,
guarding Washington City against an imaginary incursion of the
dreaded Rebels; while the 1st Army Corps of General M'Dowell,
detached from the grand army, against the urgent remonstrances
of General M'Clellan, lay near Fredericksburg, to protect the
capital in that direction.

On the side of the Confederates, were found the six regiments of General Edward Johnston, impregnably posted on the
Shenandoah Mountain; the army of General Jackson at Reede's
Hill; the Division of General Ewell upon the Rappahannock,
confronting the Federalists upon the Orange and Alexandria
Railroad; and the command of General Anderson, about 10,000
strong, watching Fredericksburg. The whole remainder of the
forces in Virginia was collected upon the peninsula, to resist the
advance of M'Clellan.

By the 17th of April, the fords of the North Fork of Shenandoah, above Reede's Hill, were becoming practicable; and General Jackson's position there was no longer secure. He therefore
resumed his retreat on that day, and retired, by two marches, to
Harrisonburg, the capital of Rockingham county, upon the great
Valley Turnpike; while General Banks timidly pursued him.

From Harrisonburg, he turned aside to the east, and passing the southern end of the Masanuttin Mountain, which here sinks into the plain, crossed the South, or main Fork of the Shenandoah River, at Conrad's Store, and posted himself in the valley of Elk Run, at the gorge of Swift Run Gap in the Blue Ridge. The highway to Staunton was now seemingly open to General Banks; but he durst not pursue it. This was indeed, one of the most adroit manœuvres of the great strategist. His position in the mouth of the mountain gorge was unassailable, and deprived his adversary of all the advantage of his superior numbers. Yet he threatened thence the Federal rear, the moment they attempted to advance upon Staunton; and thus arrested him as completely as though a superior force had been planted in his front. From his own rear, a good turnpike road led over Swift Run Gap, into Eastern Virginia, and to the Central Railroad, forty miles distant, at Gordonsville; thus providing him supplies, a secure line of retreat, and communication with General Ewell in Culpepper. There was, indeed, one grave objection to the movement; but the manner in which General Jackson's insight into his adversary's character here modified his application of the maxims of the military art, most clearly displayed his genius. Had his enemy been enterprising, this objection would have been decisive; but knowing his slowness and timidity, he safely disregarded it. From Harrisonburg, a turnpike road leads southwestward to the Warm Springs, passing through Jennings' Gap in the Great North Mountain, which was not guarded by any adequate force, along the eastern base of the Shenandoah Mountain, in the immediate rear of General Edward Johnson's position there. A forced march of little more than one day would have conducted General Banks to this spot; where proper concert with General Milroy, in front, would have ensured the destruction of the little army of Confederates. The two Federal forces united would then have easily occupied Staunton, and made the Valley untenable for Jackson, thus deprived of the expected co-operation of Johnson. But the fear of leaving his rear exposed for a moment to the terrible Stonewall, together with the difficulty of passing the Shenandoah at Bridgewater, where the citizens had destroyed the bridge, were enough to deter General Banks from so promising a movement. General Jackson stated in his correspondence, that he foresaw the danger of such a manœuvre, and calculated the timidity of his opponent, as a sufficient defence.

About the time of his march to Swift Run Gap, an incident occurred which showed his decision. The elevated valleys of the Blue Ridge Mountain are inhabited by a poor, rude, and hardy people, little amenable to law, in the best times, who live as much by hunting as by agriculture. Among a part of these, an insurrectionary movement arose against the conscription; and a few score of the men assembled in one of their fastnesses, and prepared for a forcible resistance to the laws. General Jackson at once sent a force and dispersed them, capturing some of the more daring. For this act of promptitude he received the thanks of the authorities.

In the previous winter, General R. E. Lee had been stationed next the President in Richmond, as general director of the operations of all the armies in the field. The high estimate held by General Jackson of his character and accomplishments was pleasantly illustrated by the manner in which he received the news of this appointment, at Winchester. Much had been said by his friends there, of the desire that he should receive reinforcements. One evening, at supper, he said, with a smile, to the lady whose hospitality he was sharing: " Well, Madam, I am reinforced at last;" and pointed her to a paragraph in the newspaper from Richmond just received, which announced the appointment of General Lee as Commander-in-Chief. It was his wisdom and counsel, which he regarded as equivalent to new forces.

While General Jackson held Banks thus check-mated for a fortnight at Harrisonburg, he was busily corresponding with General Lee concerning the proper direction to be given to his, and the neighboring Confederate forces. Three movements were discussed by them, of which the first was, to draw General Ewell to Swift Run Gap, in order to hold General Banks in check, while General Jackson combined with General Edward Johnson to deliver a crushing blow against Milroy, and then associated his and General Ewell's forces against Banks. The second was, to leave General Johnson for a little while, with a detachment from General Jackson's force intended to mask his withdrawal from Banks, to hold the Valley as best they might; while he marched with General Ewell across the Rappahannock and made a vigorous onslaught against the Federalists upon the Manassa's Railroad, and at its Junction. It was hoped by General Lee, that the news of this attack, so far towards his base, would cause Banks's immediate retreat to Winchester, or even to the Potomac. The third project was to leave the same dispositions for the defence of the Valley, effect a junction with General Ewell at Gordonsville, and marching thence to Fredericksburg, unite with the forces of Generals Anderson and Field, and attack the Federal army in that neighborhood. This assault gave promise of alarming the Government at Washington, of recalling Banks, and of disturbing the arrangements of General M'Clellan on the peninsula. As General Lee remarked, the dispersion of the enemy's forces clearly indicated the policy of concentration, to attack some one or other of their detachments. But he gave General Jackson full discretion to select the project which he preferred. He decisively chose the first. The secret history of this movement is related here, because many have asserted, according to their *hypothesis*, that General Jackson was a mere fighter, and no strategist, that the plan of the Valley campaign was due to another mind.   On the contrary, the choice was left wholly to his judgment; and the first among the three schemes, the one adopted, and so gloriously effected, was of his suggestion. It is easy to argue for his preference of it, after it was so sanctioned by complete success.   But the considerations which seem to have decided General Jackson to prefer it were such as these: That it made a more complete concentration of our strength, in that it included General Edward Johnson, who, upon the other plans, would have been left aside, with a detachment, also, of General Jackson's own army; that it provided a more complete protection for the Valley and Staunton, of which he so highly appreciated the strategic importance; and that, if successful, it would as effectually neutralize the Federal forces on the Rappahannock, through the fears excited for Washington City, and thus assure the left flank of the army protecting Richmond against an assault from the direction of Fredericksburg.

General Ewell was accordingly withdrawn from the Rappahannock towards Gordonsville, and then, towards the eastern outlet of Swift Run Gap.   He brought with him three brigades, those of Brigadier-Generals R. Taylor, Trimble, and Elzey, with two regiments of cavalry, commanded by Colonel Th. S. Munford, and Lieutenant-Colonel Flournoy, with an adequate supply of field artillery.   The whole formed an aggregate of about 8,000 men, in an admirable state of efficiency.   The afternoon of April 30th, General Ewell entered Swift Run Gap, and took the position which General Jackson had just left to march towards Staunton.   General Banks had been deceived by feints of an attack in force in the direction of Harrisonburg, on the previous day, and on that morning; so that he received

43

no knowledge of the true direction of General Jackson's move-ment. The object of the latter was to reach Staunton by a route, which, while not so circuitous as to consume invaluable time, should be sufficiently so, to conceal his march from the enemy, and protect him from an attack on the road. The incessant rains of a late and ungenial spring had rendered all the roads, which were not paved, almost impracticable. After careful explorations, General Jackson determined to ascend the eastern or right bank of the Shenandoah river to Port Republic, a village seven miles from Harrisonburg, and then, instead of proceeding direct to Staunton by a road of twenty-five miles, to cross the Blue Ridge into Albemarle County, by Brown's Gap, and go thence to Staunton along the line of the Virginia Central Railroad. This route made three marches; but it completely masked his movement, and mystified both friends and foes; for no one, except the General's chief engineer, knew whether he was on his way to the east or the west.

In the midst of a dreary rain, the army left its comfortless *bivouac* on the Elk Run, and made a half march, between the river and the western base of the Blue Ridge, towards Port Republic. The stream is here separated from the declivities of the mountain by a plain of two or three miles in breadth, whose flat, treacherous soil, softened by the rains, was speedily converted by the trains of baggage and artillery, into a quag-mire without apparent bottom. If the teamsters attempted to evade this by turning aside into the woodlands, as soon as the fibrous roots of the surface were severed, the subsoil proved even more deceitful than the mire of the roads, and a few vehicles made the track impassable. The rivulets descending from the mountain were swollen into broad rivers, and the glades of the forest were converted into lakes. The straggling column toiled along through water and mud for a few miles, yet enthusiastically cheering their General when he passed along it; and then *bivouacked* in the woods, while he, with his suite, found shelter in the hospitable mansion of General Lewis. In the morning, the clouds were gradually dispersed by the struggling sun; and General Jackson, having established his head-quarters in the little village of Port Republic, and having assigned to a part of his staff the duty of arresting all transit between his line of march and the enemy, returned with the remainder, and addressed himself to the arduous task of extricating his trains from the slough, which would have been to any other, a "slough of despond." Each detachment was preceded by a large party of pioneers, who, with excessive toil, so far repaired the effects wrought by the wheels of the preceding one, as to pass, over another train. Whole road-beds formed of stones and brush-wood sunk into the quicksands, and others were placed above them, again and again. The General and his staff were seen dismounted, urging on the laborers; and he carried stones and timber upon his own shoulders, with his uniform bespattered with mud like a common soldier's. From Thursday afternoon until Saturday morning, the trains struggled along, sorely scattered and travel-soiled, until at length, all were assembled at the western opening of Brown's Gap. The energy and determination required to drive them, in a day and a half, through those sixteen miles of incredible difficulties, were equal to any display of these qualities, ever made upon the field of a great victory.

The mountain-sides afforded a road-bed so stony, that no floods could soften it; and on Saturday, the army passed over to Whitehall in Albemarle, by a track rough, but firm, cheered by a brilliant sun, and full of confidence and elation. The Sabbath morning dawned upon them clear and soft, in their pleasant bivouacs along the green meadows of Moorman's river; and the General, after hard debate with himself, and with sore reluctance, gave the order to march again, surrendering the day of holy rest, which he would have so much enjoyed, to military necessity. General Johnston reported himself closely pressed by the enemy west of Staunton; and the crisis forbade the expenditure of a precious day. When General Jackson had left the Great Valley Turnpike at Harrisonburg, to turn aside to Swift Run Gap, the people of Staunton, in their panic, supposed that he was gone to reinforce the army near Richmond, leaving them to their fate; and unauthorized messages from officers near head-quarters confirmed this erroneous construction of his movement. The consequence was a fit of alarm, in which public military stores were hastily removed or destroyed, and the most exciting news of the certain occupation of Staunton by the enemy was sent to the force on the Shenandoah Mountain. General Johnson was detained from his command at the time; but the officer next in rank concluded that the juncture required immediate action, to rescue the army from capture. He therefore evacuated his strong position on the mountain, and retired to West View, only six miles west of Staunton, prepared to evade the approach of Banks, on that place, and retire to the Blue Ridge. Thus the advanced forces of Milroy were brought within ten miles of Staunton, and he was about to establish his communications with the Federalists at Harrisonburg. General Jackson therefore pressed forward from Whitehall to Staunton, reaching the latter place at evening on the Sabbath; to the unspeakable delight of the inhabitants, who had only heard that the army had disappeared again into Eastern Virginia, no one knew whither. By Monday evening, the whole army came up, and the junction with General Johnson was virtually effected.

Meantime, General Banks no sooner learned that General

Ewell had reached Elk Run, and that General Jackson had vanished thence, than he hastily evacuated Harrisonburg; and retreated to Strasburg, followed by the cavalry of Ashby. The imagination of the Federal leader was affrighted with the notion of an attack in front from Ewell, while the mysterious Jackson should fall upon his flank or rear, from some unimagined quarter. Yet his force present at Harrisonburg, about twenty thousand men, was superior to that of both generals united!

On Wednesday morning, May 7th, a day having been employed in collecting and refreshing the troops, General Johnson broke up his camp at West View at an early hour, and marched against the enemy, followed by General Jackson in supporting distance, with the brigade of General Taliaferro in front, that of Colonel Campbell next, and the Stonewall Brigade, now commanded by General Charles S. Winder, in the rear. The Corps of Cadets, from the Military Academy, forming a gallant battalion of four companies of infantry, under their teachers, was also attached to the expedition. The spruce equipments and exact drill of these youths formed a strong contrast with the war-worn and nonchalant veterans, as they stepped out, full of enthusiasm, to take their first actual look upon the horrid visage of War, under their renowned Professor.

The first collision with the enemy occurred about mid-day, at the intersection of the Harrisonburg and Parkersburg turnpikes. There a Federal picket was surprised, and nearly captured, escaping with the loss of a few men and horses. Their advanced posts at the eastern and western bases of the Shenandoah Mountain were immediately deserted, with some military stores, and the position upon the top of the mountain, lately held by the Confederates; and they retired across the Bull Pasture Mountain to M'Dowell, making no other resistance to the advance of the Confederates, than a few ineffectual cannon shots. The latter paused for the night upon both sides of the Shenandoah Mountain, with the rear brigades many miles behind the front. On Thursday morning, May 8th, the march was resumed early, with General Johnson's regiments still in advance, and the ascent of the Bull Pasture Mountain was commenced. This ridge, unlike its neighbors, has a breadth of a couple of miles upon its top, which might be correctly termed a table-land, were it not occupied by clusters of precipitous hills, which are themselves almost mountainous in their dimensions and ruggedness. The Parkersburg turnpike, proceeding westward, ascends to this table land, passes across it, and descends to the Bull Pasture River, by a sinuous course, along the ravines which seam the sides and top of the mountain alike; so that it is almost everywhere commanded, on one or both sides, by the steep and wooded banks of the valleys which it threads.   On the right and left of the road, the western portions of the rough *plateau* which has been described, were occupied by pasture lands, covered with the richest greensward, with here and there the prostrate trunk of a forest tree long since girdled and killed.   The chasm which separates the higher reaches of these lofty pastures, is a mile in width; and far down in its bottom, the turnpike descends toward the river, until it debouches through a straight gorge of a few hundred yards in length, upon the bridge.   Artillery, planted upon a hillock beyond the river, commanded this reach of the road with a murderous fire.

Generals Jackson and Johnson having cautiously ascended the mountain, and driven away a picket of the enemy which quartered its top, proceeded to the western ridge of the pasture lands on the left of the road, and occupied the forenoon in examining the position of the enemy.   The grounds here belonged to a patriotic citizen named Sitlington; while the rival heights, on the right of the turnpike, fed the cattle of a proprietor named Hull. The latter were found to be occupied by two regiments of Federal riflemen; but the distance was too great for effective volleys. Beneath them lay the smiling hamlet of M'Dowell, crowded with Federal troops, stores, and artillery, while beyond, the champaign stretched away with a smooth and gentle ascent to the westward, for a number of miles. The edges of the vale next to the position of the Confederate Generals were fringed by a forest, which covered the steeper and more barren slopes of the mountain's foot. This wood was speedily found to be infested by the enemy's skirmishers; but a detachment of General Johnson's riflemen easily kept them at bay, and chastised their audacity whenever they attempted to advance from cover. The open field itself, of a mile's length, was heaved into confused and billowy ridges, presenting, on the whole, the concavity of an irregular crescent toward the west. The ravine by which the Confederates reached this field from the turnpike, is narrow and precipitous, and occupied both by the forest and by a stream of rude boulders, which the rains had precipitated from the ridge above. Yet it was judged that, by the strenuous exertions of men and horses, field guns might have been carried up after several hours' labor.

From the ridges of the pasture-field, General Jackson quietly watched the enemy far below him, for a number of hours; while they cannonaded him and his escort from a battery on the farther side of the vale, whose guns had their muzzles elevated toward the sky, and their trails thrust into trenches in the ground. It was no part of his purpose to engage them that day, nor on that ground. He had reason to hope that they were ignorant of his junction with General Johnson, and that they supposed they had only the six regiments of the latter to deal with. His troops had not all come up; and the 'Stonewall Brigade especially, was many miles in the rear. His purpose was to amuse the enemy, while his engineers diligently explored the mountain to the right and left, for a road which might lead him to their rear. To the zeal of his artillery officers, who offered to bring up batteries, he quietly replied: "Thank you; not yet;" and at length added to one of them: "Perhaps Providence may open a way toward Monterey for you tomorrow." (Monterey is the next village ten miles west of M'Dowell; and was in the enemy's rear.) In truth, his explorations had already been successful in leading him to a rude mountain road, practicable for artillery, which, passing far to the right of Hull's mountain pastures, enters the highway five miles in the rear of M'Dowell; and his orders were just issued to move a formidable park of artillery, with sufficient escort, by this road, during the night; who were to assume a good position behind the enemy. His preponderance of force would have enabled him thus to envelop and crush the army of Milroy.

But that officer had astuteness enough, though ignorant of these formidable preparations, to apprehend something of the danger of his position. If once the lofty fields occupied by Generals Jackson and Johnson were crowned with artillery, their plunging fire would have made the whole valley of M'Dowell untenable for him; and the altitude forbade an effective reply. At mid-day General Schenck arrived with three thousand additional bayonets: and they resolved to take the initiative, and drive the Confederates from their threatening position at once. How little purpose General Jackson had of commencing the action that evening, appears from the fact, that as the afternoon advanced, he had dismissed all his staff, save two members, upon different errands, with kindly instructions to seek the repose of their quarters when they had fulfilled those functions, and had sent orders to the Stonewall Brigade, which was at length approaching the top of the mountain, to descend again, and seek a suitable encampment. But the advance of the enemy did not, for all this, find him unprepared. Although he had carefully avoided making any display of force upon the open hills, the regiments of General Johnson were close at hand, and the brigades of Taliaferro and Campbell within supporting distance. The aggressive intentions of the enemy now becoming manifest, the 52d Virginia regiment was brought upon the field, and posted upon the left, speedily followed by the 58th and 44th Virginia, and the 12th Georgia regiments. The 52d Virginia having been disposed as skirmishers, were speedily engaged in a brisk encounter with the enemy's skirmishers, whom they handsomely repulsed. The other three regiments then arriving, were soon afterwards posted as follows: the 12th Georgia on the crest of the hill, and forming the centre of the Confederate line, the 58th Virginia on the left to support the 52d, and the 44th Virginia on the right near a ravine.

General Milroy's advance now began in good earnest. He was protected in his approach by the convexity of the hills, and by the wood interposed in the Confederate front, until he emerged from it, and engaged their skirmishers. These he drove before him, and poured a galling fire into the Confederate right, which was returned, and a brisk and animated contest was kept up for some time; when General Johnson's two remaining regiments, the 25th and 31st Virginia came up and were posted on the right. The fire was now rapid and well sustained on both sides, and the conflict fierce and sanguinary. The narrow and rough ravine by which the Confederate troops ascended from the left side of the turnpike to the field of battle, has been described. If the enemy advanced along the highway and seized its mouth, the results would be disastrous. To prevent the possibility of such a movement, the 31st Virginia

44

was posted on both sides of the road, between that point and the enemy. It was, not long after, ordered to join its brigade in action; and its place was taken by the 21st Virginia. To the commander of this regiment General Jackson gave his orders in person. They were, that he should avail himself of every inequality of the ground to protect his men, and then hold the turnpike against all odds, and at every cost.

The engagement had now not only become general along the entire line, but so furious, that General Jackson ordered General Taliaferro to the support of General Johnson. Accordingly, the 23d and 37th Virginia regiments were advanced to the centre of the line which was then held by the 12th Georgia, with heroic gallantry; and the 10th Virginia was ordered to support the 52d Virginia, which had already driven the enemy from the left, and had now advanced to make a flank movement on him. At this time the Federalists were pressing forward in strong force on the extreme right of the Confederates, with a view of turning that position. This movement was speedily detected, and met by General Taliaferro's brigade, and the 12th Georgia, with great promptitude. Further to check it, portions of the 25th and 31st Virginia regiments were sent to occupy an elevated piece of woodland on the right and rear, so situated as fully to command the position of the enemy. The brigade commanded by Colonel Campbell, coming up about this time, was ordered, together with the 10th Virginia, down the ridge into the woods, to guard against designs upon the right flank. This duty they, in connexion with the other force, effectually performed. The battle had now raged from half past four to half past eight o'clock P. M., and the shades of night had descended. Every attempt of the enemy by front or flank movement, to attain the crest of the hills where General Jackson's line was formed, was signally and effectually repulsed;

and they finally ceased firing and retired from the field. During all the earlier portions of the engagement, the enemy's artillery on the farther side of the valley was actively employed in throwing shot and shell, until their infantry approached too closely. But the elevation of the mountain, and the shelter of the sharp ridges rendered their fire ineffectual. Only one of the Confederate slain lost his life by a cannon shot. General Jackson brought up no artillery; assigning as his reason, that in case of disaster, there was no road by which it could be promptly withdrawn. The battle may therefore be said to have been fought with musketry alone.

By nine o'clock, the roar of the struggle had passed away; and the green battle-field reposed under the starlight, as calmly as when it had been occupied only by its peaceful herds. Detachments of soldiers were silently exploring the ground for their wounded comrades, while the tired troops were slowly filing off to their *bivouac*. At midnight the last sufferer had been removed, and the last picket posted; and then only did General Jackson turn, to seek a few hours repose in a farm-house at the eastern base of the mountain. The valley of M'Dowell lay beneath him in equal quiet. The camp-fires of the Federals blazed ostentatiously in long and regular lines, and their host seemed to be wrapped in sleep. At one o'clock A. M., the General reached his quarters, and threw himself upon a bed. When his faithful servant, knowing that he had eaten nothing since morning, came with food, he said, "I want none; nothing but sleep"—and in a minute, was slumbering like a healthy infant. The dawn found him in the saddle, and ascending the mountain again. When he reached the crest of the battle-field, he saw the vale beneath him deserted; the foe had decamped in the night, leaving their dead, and partially destroying their camp-equipage and stores. The pebbly bottom

of the neighboring stream was found strewn with tens of thou
sands of musket-cartridges, and vast heaps of bread were still
smoking amidst the ashes of the store-houses which had sheltered
them. After marching west for a few miles, General Milroy
sought the sources of the South Branch of the Potomac, and
turned northward down that stream, along which a good highway led toward Franklin and Romney. His aim was to meet
the reinforcements of General Fremont, which, he hoped, were
approaching by that route, from the Baltimore and Ohio Railroad. The line of his retreat was marked by the graves of his
wounded, and the wreck of an occasional carriage.

The loss of the Confederates in this engagement was sixty-
nine killed, and three hundred and ninety-one wounded; making
a total of four hundred and sixty men. The greatest carnage
occurred in the ranks of the famous 12th Georgia regiment,
which had thirty-five killed, and one hundred and forty wounded.
This noble body, trained under the eye of General Edward Johnson, when Colonel, held the centre of the battle from the beginning to the end. But their heavy loss was also due to their own
zeal and chivalry. Having been advanced at first, in front of the
crest of the hills, where their line showed to their enemies from
beneath, in bold relief against the sky, they could not be persuaded to retire to the reverse of the ridge, where many of the
other regiments found partial protection without sacrificing the
efficiency of their fire. Their commander, perceiving their
useless exposure, endeavored again and again to withdraw them;
but amidst the roar of the musketry his voice was lifted up in
vain; and when by passing along the ranks he persuaded or
entreated one wing of the regiment to recede, they rushed again
to the front while he was gone to expostulate with the other. A
tall Georgia youth expressed the spirit of his comrades, when he
replied the next day to the question, why they did not retreat to

the shelter of the ridge behind them, whence they could fight the battle equally well: "We did not come all this way to Virginia, to run before Yankees."

Just before the close of the engagement, General Johnson received a painful wound in the ankle, which, breaking one of its bones, compelled him to leave the field. General Jackson paid him the following merited tribute in his report: "General Johnson, to whom I had entrusted the management of the troops engaged, proved himself eminently worthy of the confidence reposed in him, by the skill, gallantry, and presence of mind, which he displayed on the occasion." Colonel Gibbons, commanding the 10th Virginia, a Christian gentleman and soldier, beloved by all his comrades, fell dead as he was bringing his men into position; and he was the only person in his regiment who was struck. Colonel Harman, of the 52d Virginia, Colonel Smith, and Major Higginbotham, of the 25th, and Major Campbell, of the 42d Virginia, were wounded. At the beginning of the action, General Jackson was, for the reason stated above, accompanied by only two of his staff: Captain Lee, his ordnance-officer, and Lieutenant Meade, his Aide. These two, by their zeal and courage, temporarily supplied the place of all; and Captain Lee received a severe wound in the head. The Federal loss was estimated by General Johnson, who witnessed nearly the whole struggle, to be double that of the Confederates; but this reckoning was probably too large. Few prisoners were taken on either side; but among those captured by Jackson was a Colonel of an Ohio regiment. Some Quarter-Master's and Commissary stores, arms, ammunition, and cavalry equipments remained for the victors. The force of General Milroy was supposed to be 8,000 men. Of General Jackson's, about 6,000, or only half his force, were engaged.

From M'Dowell, General Jackson sent the following modest

and laconic despatch, the first of those missives which, during the remainder of his career, so frequently electrified the country with joy:

VALLEY DISTRICT, MAY 9th, 1862.

To GEN. S. COOPER:

" God blessed our arms with victory at M'Dowell yesterday."

T. J. JACKSON, *Major-General.*

This announcement was received by the people of Virginia and of the Confederate States with peculiar delight, because it was the first blush of the returning day of triumphs after a season of gloomy disasters. The campaign had opened with the fall of Fort Donelson and the occupation of Nashville. The fruitless victory of Shiloh had been counterpoised in April by the fall of New Orleans, a loss as unexpected to the Confederates as it was momentous. On the 4th of May, while Generals Jackson and Johnson were effecting their junction at Staunton, York-town was deserted by the Confederates, and, on the next day, Williamsburg fell into their hands after a bloody combat. On the 9th, Norfolk surrendered to the enemy, and, on the 11th, the gallant ship Virginia, the pride and confidence of the people, was destroyed by her own commander. The victory of M'Dowell was the one gleam of brightness athwart all these clouds; and the eyes of the people turned with hope and joy to the young soldier who had achieved it, and recognized in this happy beginning the vigor and genius of the great commander.

General Jackson immediately threw forward a few companies of cavalry under Captain Sheetz to harass the enemy's rear, and collected his infantry in the valley beyond M'Dowell to prepare for a close pursuit. The mountain passes by which General Banks might have communicated succors to Milroy were imme-diately obstructed, and an active officer was sent by a circuitous

route to the northern parts of Pendleton county, below Franklin,
to collect the partisan soldiers of the mountains in the enemy's
rear. They were exhorted to fill the roads with felled timber,
to tear down the walls which supported the turnpike along
the precipitous cliffs, and to destroy the bridges, in order that
the retreat of Milroy might be retarded, and the advance of
Fremont to his aid checked, until his flying army was again
beaten and dispersed. Saturday morning, the victors resumed
their march, refreshed by a night of quiet rest, and pressed the
enemy so hard, that General Jackson hoped in the afternoon to
bring them to bay. Their rear-guard assumed a position, and
held the Confederate cavalry in check. General Jackson disposed his troops, and issued his orders for battle with a stern
joy; but the slippery game soon continued its flight. The next
morning was the Sabbath; but after anxious deliberation, the
Confederate General concluded that the importance of over-
taking the enemy, who would certainly not pause from any
reverence for the sacred day, and of inflicting another disaster
before the reinforcements of General Fremont arrived, required
him to disregard its claims. When he began to urge the enemy
again, the Federals resorted to the expedient of setting fire to
the forests upon the mountain sides, in order to envelop their
flight in obscurity. Soon the sky was overcast with volumes of
smoke, which almost hid the scene, and wrapped every distant
object in a veil, impenetrable to the eyes and the telescopes of
the officers alike. Through this sultry fog the pursuing army
felt its way cautiously along, cannonaded by the enemy from
every advantageous position; while it was protected from ambuscades only by detachments of skirmishers, who scoured the
burning woods on each side of the highway. As fast as these
could scramble over the precipitous hills, and through the blazing
thickets, the great column crept along the main road, like a lazy

serpent; their General often far in advance of its head, in his eagerness to overtake the foe. He declared that this smoke was the most adroit expedient, to which a retreating army could resort, to embarrass pursuit, and that it entailed upon him all the disadvantages of a night attack. By slow approaches, and constant skirmishing, the enemy were driven to the village of Franklin; when the double darkness of the night, and the fog, again arrested his progress.

When the morning of Monday arrived, General Jackson resolved to discontinue his pursuit of Milroy, and return to pay his respects to General Banks. Several considerations weighed together, to determine his judgment. He ascertained that his orders for obstructing the turnpike below Franklin had been disregarded by the citizens; and their supineness and timidity filled him with disgust. It was now obvious that his cunning adversary, with an unobstructed road for retreat, and all the advantages of a mountainous country for defence, would not be brought to a battle, until he had received the support of General Fremont. On the other hand, the concentration of the Confederates was only half completed, for the excellent division of General Ewell, was still to be associated with the forces of Jackson; and prudence dictated that the risk of such a collision as that, with Fremont and Milroy united, should not be taken without the advantage of all the strength attainable by him. Moreover, time was precious; for he knew not how soon a new emergency at Fredericksburg or at Richmond, might occasion the recall of General Ewell to the East, and deprive him of the power to strike any effective blow against General Banks. The motive last mentioned was perhaps the most operative of all; for he knew that the loan of General Ewell's aid to him by the Confederate authorities at Richmond, was not entirely hearty, and that they did not wholly concur in his estimate

of the importance of protecting his District from invasion. But
the conclusive reason, was a despatch from General Lee, May
11th, requiring his return. The same day General Jackson sent
a courier to General Ewell, to announce his coming, who was
commanded to ride post-haste with his message.

General Jackson, therefore, prepared to turn his face eastward again. He granted the soldiers the half of Monday as a
season of rest, in lieu of the Sabbath, which had been devoted
to warfare; and issued the following order to them.

" Soldiers of the army of the Valley and North West." " I
congratulate you on your recent victory at M'Dowell. I request
you to unite with me, this morning, in thanksgivings to Almighty
God, for thus having crowned your arms with success; and in
praying that He will continue to lead you on from victory to
victory, until our independence shall be established; and make
us that people whose God is the Lord."

" The chaplains will hold divine service at 10 o'clock A. M.,
this day, in their respective regiments."

The different groups were accordingly soon assembled, beneath
a genial sun, along the verdant meadows of the South Branch;
and the neighboring mountains, which, on the Sabbath, had
reverberated with the bellowings of cannon, now echoed the
Sabbath hymns. The commanding General attended reverently
the worship of a company of artillery near his tent. After mid-
day, the camps were broken up, and the march was resumed for
M'Dowell; which the army reached Wednesday evening. The
next day's journey brought them to the Lebanon Springs, on the
road to Harrisonburg; where they paused for a day, Friday,
May 16th, to observe a season of national humiliation and
prayer, appointed by the Confederate Government, for all the
people and armies. On Saturday, an easy march was ended,
in the beautiful region of Mossy Creek; where the troops, no

45

longer pressed by a military exigency, were allowed to spend a quiet Sabbath.

One incident remains to be mentioned, illustrating Jackson's iron will, which occurred while the army paused on this march, at M'Dowell. A part of the men of the 27th regiment, in the Stonewall Brigade, who had volunteered for twelve months, now found their year just expired. Assuming that the application of the late conscription to them was a breach of faith, they demanded their discharge, and laying down their arms, refused to serve another day. Their gallant Colonel Grigsby referred the case to General Jackson for instructions. On hearing it detailed, he exclaimed, his eye flashing, and his brow rigid with a portentous sternness, "What is this but mutiny? Why does Colonel Grigsby refer to me, to know what to do with a mutiny? He should shoot them, where they stand." He then turned to his adjutant, and dictated an order to the Colonel to parade his regiment instantly, with loaded muskets, to draw up the insubordinate companies in front of them, disarmed, and offer them the alternative of returning to duty, or being fusilladed on the spot. The order was obeyed, and the mutineers, when thus confronted with instant death, promptly reconsidered their resolution. They could not be afterwards distinguished from the rest of the regiment in their soldierly behavior; and this was the last attempt at organized disobedience in the army.

CHAPTER XII.

WINCHESTER.

WHILE General Jackson was hurrying back from Franklin, critical events were occurring at Richmond, which must be known in order to appreciate the value of his victories, and their effect upon the public mind. The destruction of the ship Virginia by her crew, on the 11th of May, has been narrated. This blunder left the River James open to the enemy's fleet, up to the wharves of the city. The Confederate engineers had indeed projected an earthwork upon an admirable position, seven miles below, where the lands of a planter named Drewry overlooked a narrow reach of the stream, in a lofty bluff or precipitous hill. But so nerveless and dilatory had been their exertions, that when the river was thus opened to the enemy, there were neither guns mounted upon the unfinished ramparts of earth, nor obstructions completed in the channel beneath. The Legislature of Virginia had urged upon the Confederate War Department, the vast importance of defending this avenue to the Capital of the Commonwealth, and had received promises; but they remained unfulfilled. The hurried removal of military stores to the Southwest; the packing of the archives of the Confederate Departments, and the significant movements of their occupants, now indicated the purpose of the Government to desert Richmond to the enemy. Not only was it left approachable by water; but the grand army of M'Clellan had pressed from the

peninsula up to the neighborhood of the city on the east, while
a strong and increasing army under General M'Dowell, at
Fredericksburg, threatened it by a northern route of only three
marches, with no adequate force to oppose him. It was in this
gloomy hour, that the spirit of the General Assembly of Virginia, and of the citizens of her Capital, flamed up with a lofty
and unshaken heroism, worthy to be compared with the noblest
displays of patriotism in all the ages. The former body
addressed to the President of the Confederate States, a Resolution, requesting him to defend the city, if necessary, until one
stone was not left upon another, and proposing to lay it as a
sacrifice, with all its wealth, upon the country's altar. The
Town-council met, and amidst the stern and unanimous enthusiasm of the citizens, seconded this resolve. They were determined, that if the city could not be successfully defended, it
should only be yielded to the enemy as a barren heap of rub-
bish, the sepulchre, and glorious monument at once, of its
defenders. The General Assembly sent its Committee to lay
their wishes before the President; who thanked them for their
devotion, and assured them that the evacuation of Richmond, if
it occurred, would by no means imply the desertion of Virginia.
Even while they conferred together, a courier brought him news,
that some Federal ships of war, availing themselves of the
absence of the Virginia, were ascending the river, with the
evident intention of reaching Richmond. Rising from his seat,
he dismissed the Committee, saying, "This manifestly concludes
the matter;" and proceeded to arrange for the removal of his
family. But the timidity of the Federalists, afraid of torpedoes,
or some other secret annoyance, and incredulous that so vital a
point could indeed be left open for them, for this time saved the
city; which, so far as its proper defenders were concerned, was
already lost. The ships paused to make soundings, and to

reconnoitre the banks; and meantime, the citizens went to work.
The City Council called upon the Confederate Engineers, to
know what they lacked for the immediate completion of their
works; and pledged themselves to supply everything. The citizens themselves turned laborers, and drapers and bankers were
seen at the port, loading barges with stone. Two or three
excellent guns were mounted; great timbers were hewn, floated
to the foot of Drewry's Bluff, and built into a row of cribs;
which, when ballasted with stone and bricks, promised to resist
the momentum of the heaviest ships. By the 15th of May,
when the advance of the Federal fleet appeared, after their
cautious dallying, these beginnings of defences were made; and
the three guns, manned by Confederate marines, gloriously beat
off the gunboats Monitor and Galena, with no little damage of
their boasted invulnerability.

The benefit wrought by these events upon the temper of the
people, which was before tending fast to abject discouragement,
cannot be described by words. The Confederate authorities
had doubtless decided with perfect correctness, according to the
technical maxims of war, that Richmond was untenable; but
fortunately, the great heart of the "Unterrified Commonwealth"
was wiser than the intellect of the Government. Her glorious
example sent a quickening pulsation of generous shame, of hope,
and of courage, through the veins of the army and of all the
States. Throughout the Confederacy, her high determination
was re-echoed; the people everywhere resolved rather to sacrifice their homes to the magnanimous work of defence, than to
yield them a coveted prey to the enemy; the Government and
Generals began, in good earnest, to prepare for holding the
Capital against every assault.

This was, properly, the main object of the campaign, and
all other movements were auxiliary to it. General Jackson's

command was expected to concur in securing the Capital, by so dealing with that of General Banks, as to neutralize his co-operation in movements against Richmond, whatever might be the form they assumed. General Lee, reasoning from the strategic principles which he thought should have governed M'Clellan and Banks, and from news of partial movements of the forces of the latter towards Eastern Virginia, anticipated the sudden withdrawal of his whole army from the Valley, to Fredericksburg, for a combined movement with M'Dowell against Richmond; or even to the peninsula. General Jackson was steadfast in the opinion, that Banks's objective point was still Staunton, and the command of the Central Railroad; and he therefore confidently expected to fight him in the Valley. General Joseph E. Johnston, who, as commander of the Depart-ment of North Virginia, was still General Jackson's immediate superior, constantly instructed him and General Ewell, in his despatches to them, to observe these two injunctions: If Gen-eral Banks moved his army to M'Dowell at Fredericksburg, to march immediately by way of Gordonsville, and join General Anderson at some point in front of the former town; or if he remained in the Valley, to fight him there immediately, only avoiding the effusion of blood in assaults of a fortified position. But he left it to them to decide which of these alternatives was about to become necessary. In the case that they were com-pelled to follow Banks to Fredericksburg, General Edward Johnson was to be left with his six regiments, to hold the Valley against Fremont, as he best might. Two more fine brigades were sent from Richmond to Gordonsville, to assist General Jackson in his movement against Banks; but before a junction was effected with him, they were suddenly ordered back to the neighborhood of Richmond, to defend the approaches on the side of Fredericksburg; where they soon after suffered a disastrous defeat from M'Clellan's advance, at Hanover Court House. Jackson was also very nearly deprived of the assistance of General Ewell, by the same uneasiness concerning an attack from the side of Fredericksburg. After a series of despatches, varying with the appearances of danger, the latter General was finally instructed by the Commander-in-Chief, that it would be necessary for him to move at once from Swift Run Gap towards Gordonsville. But he had just been informed by General Jackson, that he was hastening back, to effect a junction with him near Harrisonburg, and to assail Banks. Mounting his horse, without escort, General Ewell rode express, night and day, and met Jackson on the Sabbath, May 18th, at Mossy Creek, to inform him of this necessity for inflicting so cruel a disappointment upon him. The latter uttered no complaint, and made no comment; although the sleepless energy with which he had been pressing forward, told how dear the project was to his wishes. He meekly replied; "Then Providence denies me the privilege of striking a decisive blow for my country; and I must be satisfied with the humble task of hiding my little army about these mountains, to watch a superior force." The warm and generous heart of Ewell was touched with such an exhibition of unselfish devotion, and was unwilling to desert him. He therefore proposed that if Jackson, under whose immediate orders he was, as ranking Major-General, would assume the responsibility of detaining him until a remonstrance could be uttered against his removal, he would remain. The contingency under which General Johnston had authorized him to leave the Valley had not yet occurred; and the discretion which their general instructions conceded to General Jackson, for regulating his movements according to circumstances, authorized such an exercise of power. It was therefore concluded between them, that the junction should be completed at New Market, a day's

march below Harrisonburg. The unwearied Ewell, after resting
his limbs during public worship, again mounted his horse
and returned to hurry on his division.

It is now time to pause, and explain the proceedings of
General Banks. His precipitate withdrawal from Harrisonburg, upon the movement of Generals Jackson and Ewell, has
been described. He retired first to New Market, and then,
leaving a heavy rear-guard in that region, to Strasbourg, twenty
miles above Winchester; where he began fortifying himself in a
strong position, commanding at once the great Valley Turnpike
leading to Winchester, and the Manassa's Railroad leading
towards Alexandria. The cavalry of Ashby, following close
upon his rear, watched all the roads of the main Valley;
while that of General Ewell guarded the communications
between the Masanuttin Mountain and the Blue Ridge. A
system of strategy was now begun by the Federalists, dictated
by the senseless fears of the Executive at Washington, and by
the judicial blindness dispensed to them from a Divine Providence merciful to the Confederates, in which every movement
was a blunder. The aggressive attempt upon Staunton was
postponed, at the precise juncture when it should have been
pressed with all their forces combined; and General Banks was
consigned to the defence of Strasbourg. Whereas, if Staunton
was not won at once, then his whole force should have been
transferred without delay to aid an aggressive movement from
Fredericksburg, as General Lee anticipated. Milroy having
been caught, beaten, and chased, like a hunted beast, through the
mountains, Blenker's division was now hurried to the support of
him and General Fremont. It arrived just when Jackson had
left them alone, and it left General Banks just when he was
about to be assailed by him. Worse than all: as though an
army of nearly forty thousand men, under Generals M'Dowell

and Augur, were not enough to protect the road from Fredericksburg to Washington against the embarrassed Confederates,
Banks detached the best brigades he had,— those of Shields and
Kimball, containing seven thousand men, — and sent them on
the 14th of May, by way of Luray and Front Royal, to support
the forces on the Rappahannock. It was this movement, so
unaccountable in its folly, which, being observed by General
Ewell, led him to believe, for a moment, that Banks's whole force
had gone to assail Richmond from that quarter. This unlucky
General thus reduced himself to about eighteen thousand men,
at the critical moment when the storm was about to burst upon
him. And he completed the chapter of errors in this, that by
sending away General Shields he evacuated the New Market
Gap, and gave to General Jackson the fatal option to assail him
either in front or in flank. The latter watched all his mistakes
with a silent intelligence; and while nothing escaped his eagle
eye, it never betrayed his purposes by even a sparkle of elation.

That the measures now taken by General Jackson may be
comprehended, the reader must recall the outline already given
of the topography of the Valley of Virginia. From the neighborhood of Elk Run, General Ewell's recent position, to that of
Strasbourg, — a distance of fifty miles, — the Valley is divided
by the Masanuttin, a high and precipitous mountain, parallel to
the Blue Ridge, which, at both its ends, terminates suddenly in
lofty promontories dominating the plains. The valley between
it and the Blue Ridge is more narrow and rugged than that west
of it; but it is watered throughout its whole length by the South
Shenandoah, and gives space enough for the fertile and populous
county of Page, with its seat of justice at the village of Luray.
One good road only connects this subordinate valley laterally
with the main Valley — the turnpike across New Market Gap.
But, longitudinally, the county of Page is traversed by several

46

excellent highways, parallel to the general course of its river and mountain barriers. Just west of the base of the New Market Gap is seated the village of that name, upon the great Valley Turnpike, and in the midst of a smiling champaign. The force which occupied this Gap, and commanded this village, was, in a sense, master of both valleys. This was the position which Banks deserted without cause, when he detached General Shields to Eastern Virginia. As the traveller proceeds northeast down the county of Page, he enters the county of Warren, lying just where the lesser valley merges itself again in the greater. The north fork of the Shenandoah River, which coasts the western base of the Masanuttin Mountain, turns eastward around its northern end from the neighborhood of Strasbourg, and meets the south fork emerging from the other valley, near Front Royal, the seat of justice of Warren county. The excellent paved road from this village to Winchester leads by a course of eighteen miles, across both branches of the river, just above their union, and through a country of gentle hills, farms, and woodlands, converging towards the great Valley Turnpike as it approaches the town.

When Shields evacuated New Market, Colonel Ashby advanced his quarters to it, and extended his pickets to the neighborhood of Strasbourg, where he closed the whole breadth of the great Valley, there much contracted, by a *cordon* of sentries. Every movement above was thus screened effectually from the observation of General Banks. General Jackson, leaving Mossy Creek Monday, the 19th of May, proceeded by two marches, to the neighborhood of New Market. He there met the fine brigade of General Richard Taylor, which had marched from Elk Run valley by the Western side of the Masanuttin Mountain. On Wednesday, the 21st he crossed the New Market Gap, and in the neighborhood of Luray, completed his union with the

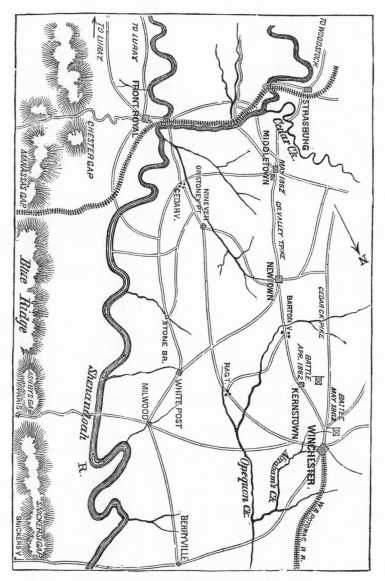

VALLEY OF THE SHENANDOAH.

remainder of General Ewell's forces. His army now contained about sixteen thousand effective men, with forty field guns. It was composed of his own division, embracing the brigades of Winder, Campbell, and Taliaferro, of General Ewell's division, which included the brigades of Taylor, Trimble, Elzey, and Stewart, and the cavalry regiments of Ashby, Munford, and Flournoy, with eight batteries of artillery. At Mossy Creek, he had been met by Brigadier-General George H. Stewart, a native of Maryland, whom the Confederate Government had just commissioned, and charged with the task of assembling all the soldiers from that State into one *Corps*, to be called The Maryland Line. To begin this work, General Jackson at once assigned to his command the First Maryland regiment of Colonel Bradley T. Johnson, and the Brockenborough Battery, which was manned chiefly by citizens of Baltimore, as the nucleus of a brigade.

He had determined to march by ᴌuray and Front Royal, in order to avoid the necessity of attacking Banks in his strong fortifications. This route offered other advantages: it placed him between his enemy and Eastern Virginia, whither General Lee feared he was moving: it enabled him to conceal his march from Banks more effectually, until he was fairly upon his flank: and it ensured the issuing of that General from his entrenched position in order to save his communications. Leaving the picket line of Ashby in Banks's front, he marched with all his other forces towards Front Royal: where, he was aware, a Federal detachment of unknown force was stationed. The advance of the army, consisting of the First Maryland regiment and the battalion of Major Wheat from Taylor's brigade, under the command of General Stewart, reached the village about two o'clock P. M., on Friday, May 23d. They had been ordered to diverge from the main road which enters the village from the

south, into a rugged pathway across the hills, which led them
into another road descending into the village from the mountains
on the east. The surprise of the Federalists was complete, and
it was evident that the first news they received of the presence
of a hostile army, was the volley fired by Stewart into their
picket, a mile from the village. Yet they showed themselves
prepared to make a spirited resistance. Their advance was
speedily driven through the town, with the loss of some prisoners, when their main force took up a position upon a commanding height on the side next Winchester, overlooking the village,
and the approach of the Confederates from the opposite side.
From this hill they cannonaded the troops as they approached,
but without effect. The commands of Colonel Johnson and
Major Wheat, deployed as skirmishers, with a company of
Cavalry accompanying them, dashed through the streets, and
across the fields in front, with impetuosity; while General
Jackson ordered Taylor's Louisiana brigade to support them
by a movement on the left flank, through a wood which lay on
that side of the village. Before this effort could be completed,
however, the gallant skirmishers had dislodged the enemy, and
the General galloped forward to the height they had just occupied. On the nearer side of the South Shenandoah, which
flowed just beyond this hill, was the enemy's camp, pitched in a
charming meadow along the water-side, but now wrapped in
flames, and sending up volumes of smoke to the skies, while
under its cover, their whole infantry was marching, in excellent
order, up the road which obliquely ascended from the other
bank, every rank distinctly displayed to view. Their guns
were again posted on the rival height to that on which Jackson
stood, far above the infantry, prepared to protect its retreat.
As the General beheld this picture, he was seized with uncontrollable eagerness and impatience, and exclaimed: "Oh, what

an opportunity for artillery ! Oh, that my guns were here ! " Then turning almost fiercely to the only aid who accompanied him, he commanded him to hasten to the rear, and "order up every rifled gun, and every brigade in the army." Some guns were, after a little, brought up; but the enemy had meantime passed the crest of the ridge, and the pursuit was resumed; the General riding among the skirmishers and urging them on.

Here occurred a striking effect of a vicious usage, which it was the honor of General Lee to banish from the armies in Virginia. This was the custom of temporarily attaching to the staff of a General commanding a division or an army, a company of cavalry to do the work of orderlies and couriers. By this clumsy contrivance, the organization of the cavalry regiments was marred, the men detached were deprived of all opportunity for drill, and the General had no evidence whatever of their special fitness for the responsible service assigned them. Nay, the Colonel of cavalry required to furnish them, was most likely to select the company least serviceable to him by reason of deficient equipments, or inexperience. At the time of the combat of Front Royal, the duty of couriers was performed for General Jackson, by a detachment from one of Colonel Ashby's undisciplined companies, of whom many were raw youths just recruited, and never under fire. As soon as the first Federal picket was driven in, and free access to the village won, orders were despatched to the rear brigades, to avoid the laborious and circuitous route taken by the advance, and to pursue the direct highway to the town, a level tract of three miles, in place of a precipitous one of seven or eight. The panic-struck boy, by whom the orders were sent, thought of nothing but to hide himself from the dreadful sound of the cannon, and was seen no more. When General Jackson sent orders to the artillery and rear brigades to hurry to the pursuit, instead of being found near at hand, upon the direct road, they were at length overtaken, toiling over the hills of the useless circuit, spent with the protracted march; for they had received no instructions, and had no other guide than the footprints of those who preceded them. Thus night overtook them by the time they reached the village; and they lay down to rest, instead of pursuing the enemy. This unfortunate incident taught the necessity of a picked company of orderlies, selected for their intelligence and courage, permanently attached to head-quarters, and owning no subordination to any other than the General and his staff. Such is the usage now prevalent in the Confederate armies.

But on this occasion the enemy did not escape through this accident. In the forenoon, Colonel Ashby and Colonel Flournoy had been detached with all the cavalry except a company or two, to cross the south fork of the Shenandoah at McCoy's Ford, above the position of the Federalists, for the purpose of destroying the telegraphic and railroad communications between Front Royal and Strasbourg, and of preventing the passage of reinforcements or fugitives between the two posts. Colonel Flournoy, with his own and Colonel Munford's regiments, kept a short distance west of the river, and having executed his orders, now appeared upon the Winchester road, in the most timely manner, to join in the pursuit. At the north fork of the Shenandoah, the retreating Federalists made an abortive attempt to burn the bridge. Before they could fully accomplish this purpose the Confederates were upon them and extinguished the flames, but not until they had made one span of the bridge impassable for horsemen. Colonel Flournoy, however, accompanied by the General, with difficulty passed four companies of his own regiment across the river, and ordering the remainder to follow, hurried in pursuit. The Federals were overtaken near a little hamlet named Cedarville, five miles from Front Royal, where their whole force, consisting of a section of artillery, two companies of cavalry, two companies of Pennsylvania infantry; and the 1st Maryland regiment of Federal infantry, now placed themselves in order of battle to stand at bay. General Jackson no sooner saw them than he gave the order to charge with a voice and air whose peremptory determination was communicated to the whole party. Colonel Flournoy instantly hurled his forces in column against the enemy, and broke their centre. They, however, speedily reformed in an orchard on the right of the turnpike, when a second gallant and decisive charge being made against them, their cavalry broke and fled, the cannoneers abandoned their guns, and the infantry threw down their arms, and scattered in utter rout. Other Confederate troops speedily arriving, the fields and woods were gleaned, and nearly the whole opposing force was killed or captured. The result was, the possession of about seven hundred prisoners, immense stores, and two fine ten-pounder rifle guns. The loss of the patriots, in the combat and pursuit; was twenty-six killed and wounded.

Thus, two hundred and fifty men were taught, by the dash and genius of Jackson, to destroy a force of four times their number. His quick eye estimated aright the discouragement of the enemy, and their wavering temper. Infusing his own spirit into the men, he struck the hesitating foe at the decisive moment, and shattered them. A glorious share of the credit is also due to the officers and men of the detachment. General Jackson declared with emphasis to his staff, that he had never, in all his experience of warfare, seen a cavalry charge executed with such efficiency and gallantry; commendation, which, coming from his guarded and sober lips, was decided enough to satisfy every heart.

While these occurrences were in progress, Colonel Ashby, after crossing at McCoy's ford, inclined still farther to the west, so as to skirt the northern base of the Masanuttin Mountain. His route led him to Buckton, the intermediate station of the railroad, between Front Royal and Strasbourg, where he found a body of the enemy posted as a guard, behind the railroad embankment, and in a store-house or barn of logs, which afforded them secure protection from his fire. Dismounting his men, he led them in person against the Federals, and speedily dispersed them. The track of the road was then effectually destroyed, so as to prevent the passage of trains. But in this hazardous onset, several of his soldiers were lost, and among them, his two best captains, Fletcher and Sheetz. The latter especially, although the year before but a comely youth taken from the farm of his father, had already shown himself a man of no common mark. Collecting a company of youths like himself in the valleys of Hampshire, he had armed them wholly from the spoils of the enemy, and without any other military knowledge than the intuitions of his own good sense, had drilled and organized them into an efficient body. He speedily became a famous partisan and scout, the terror of the invaders, and the right hand of his Colonel. Sheetz was ever next the enemy; if pursuing, in command of the advanced guard; or if retreating, closing the rear; and Jackson had learned to rely implicitly upon his intelligence; for his courage, enterprise, sobriety of mind, and honesty, assured the authenticity of all his reports.

The skirmishers of General Ewell had now penetrated within four miles of Winchester, and the whole Confederate army, collected along the turnpike leading from Front Royal to that place, commanded Banks's communications, by numerous easy approaches. On the morning of Saturday, May 24th, that ill-starred General, who was beaten before he fought, had only three practicable expedients. One was to retreat to the Potomac by

47

the Winchester road: another to defend himself at Strasbourg: the other, to avail himself of the Confederate advance on the former town to pass their rear at Front Royal, and so seek a refuge towards Manassa's Junction and Alexandria.   But he was now in the clutches of a master, who had his wary eye upon every contingency.   Jackson determined to move the body of his army neither to Strasbourg nor to Winchester, but to Middletown, a village upon the great Winchester road, five or six miles from Strasbourg, and thirteen from the latter place.   General Ewell, with Trimble's brigade, the 1st Maryland regiment, and the batteries of Brockenborough and Courtney, was directed to pursue his movement upon Winchester by the Front Royal road, observing appearances of the enemy's retreat, and prepared to strike him in flank.   Brigadier-General Stewart, in temporary command of the cavalry regiments of Munford and Flournoy, was directed to strike the Winchester road at the village of Newtown, nine miles from that town, with directions to observe the movements of the enemy at that point.   General Jackson himself, with all the remainder of the army, marched by a cross road from Cedarville towards Middletown.   Colonel Ashby's cavalry was in front, supported by Chew's battery, and two rifled guns from the famous battery of Pendleton, now commanded by Captain Poague.   Next followed the brigade of Taylor, and the remainder of the infantry.   Colonel Ashby kept his scouts on his left extended to the railroad, so as to note any signs of a movement towards Front Royal.   All the detachments of the army were in easy communication; and whether the enemy attempted to make a stand at Strasbourg, at Winchester, or at any intermediate point, the whole force could be rapidly concentrated against him.   Before the main body was fairly in motion, Brigadier-General Stewart had already sent news of his arrival at Newtown, where he captured a number of ambulances, with prisoners and medical stores, and found evident signs of a general retreat upon Winchester.

General Jackson now advanced upon Middletown, confident that his first surmise would be confirmed, and that he should strike the retreating army upon the march. Half-way between that place and Middletown, his advance was confronted by a body of Federal cavalry, evidently sent to observe him. Captain Poague's section of artillery being then in front, the General ordered him instantly to gallop forward, take a position at short range, and fire into them. This was done with perfect success, and the detachment scattered; which was a novel instance of a charge effected by field artillery. When the little village of Middletown came in view, across the broad and level fields, the highway passing through it, at right angles to the direction of General Jackson's approach, was seen canopied with a vast cloud of gray dust, and crowded beneath, as far as the eye could reach, with a column of troops. At the sight, the artillery dashed forward in a gallop for a rising ground, whence to tear their ranks with shell. Ashby swooped down upon the right like an eagle; cut through their path, and arrested their escape on that side; while General Taylor throwing his front regiment into line, advanced at a double quick to the centre of the village, his men cheering and pouring a terrific volley into the confused mass which filled the street. Never did a host receive a more mortal thrust. In one moment, the way was encumbered with dying horses and men; and at every fierce volley, the troopers seemed to melt by scores from their saddles; while the frantic, riderless horses, rushed up and down, trampling the wounded wretches into the dust. But the astute cowardice of the Federals, made the real carnage far less than the apparent; they fell from their horses before they were struck, and were found, when the victors leaped into the road, squat behind the stone fences which bordered it, in long and crowded lines, where they all surrendered at the first challenge. Among the remainder of the Federal cavalry, the wildest confusion ensued, and they scattered in various directions. Two hundred prisoners and horses with their equipments, remained in the hands of the Confederates at this spot. But it did not yet appear what part of the retreating army was above, and what below, the point of assault. As soon as the bullets ceased to fly, the astonished citizens gathered around; and when they saw the miserable, begrimed, and bloody wreck of what had just been a proud regiment of Vermont cavalry, they exclaimed with uplifted hands; "Behold the righteous judgment of God; for these are the miscreants who have been most forward to plunder, insult, and oppress us!" By some of them, General Jackson was informed, that dense columns of infantry, trains of artillery, and long lines of baggage-wagons, had been passing from Strasbourg since early morning.

Many wagons were seen disappearing in the distance towards Winchester, and Colonel Ashby, with his cavalry, some artillery, and a supporting infantry force from Taylor's brigade, was sent in pursuit. But a few moments elapsed before the Federal artillery, which had been cut off with the rear of their army, began to shell the village from the direction of Strasbourg. General Jackson, regarding this as an indication of a purpose to cut a way for retreat through his forces, immediately formed Taylor's brigade south of the village, and advanced it, with a few guns, to meet their attempt. The brigade of Colonel Campbell soon after arriving, was brought up to support it. But the enemy's courage was not adequate to so bold an exploit; the cannonade was only tentative; and, after a short skirmish, a column of flame and smoke arising from the valley of Cedar Creek told that they had fired the bridge over that stream, in order to protect themselves from attack. This fragment of the broken army, which was probably small in numbers, finally fled westward; and either took refuge with General Fremont in the valley of the South Branch, or made its way, piecemeal, to the Potomac, along the base of the Great North Mountain. A large amount of baggage fell into the hands of the victors at the scene of this combat; entire regiments, apparently in line of battle, having laid down their knapsacks, and abandoned them.

General Jackson was now convinced that the larger game was in the direction of Winchester, and returned with his whole force to pursue it. The Stonewall Brigade, which had now come up, took the front, and the whole army advanced towards Newtown. The deserted wagon-train of the enemy was found standing, in many cases with the horses attached, and occupied the road for a mile. Upon approaching Newtown, the General was disappointed to find his artillery arrested, and wholly unsupported by the cavalry; while the enemy, taking heart from the respite, had placed two batteries in position on the left and right of this village, and again showed a determined front. Nearly the whole of Colonel Ashby's cavalry present with him, with a part of the infantry under his command, had disgracefully turned aside to pillage; so that their gallant commander was compelled to arrest the pursuit. Indeed, the firing had not ceased, in the first onset upon the Federal cavalry at Middletown, before some of Ashby's men might have been seen, with a quickness more suitable to horse-thieves than to soldiers, breaking from their ranks, seizing each two or three of the captured horses, and making off across the fields. Nor did these men pause until they had carried their illegal booty to their homes, which were, in some instances, at the distance of one or two days' journey. That such extreme disorders could occur, and that they could be passed over without a bloody punishment, reveals the curious inefficiency of officers in the volunteer Confederate army.

The rifled guns of Captain Poague were immediately placed in position upon arriving near Newtown, on an opposing eminence, and replied to the Federal battery upon the right of the village with effect; but it was sunset before they were dislodged, and the pursuit resumed. The enemy had improved this pause to set fire to a large part of their train containing valuable stores; and, as the army advanced, the gathering darkness was illuminated for a mile by blazing wagons and pontoon boats; while blackened heaps of rice, beef, and bread, intermingled with the bands and bars of glowing iron, showed where carriages laden with these stores had been consumed.

General Jackson's perfect knowledge of the ground surrounding Winchester, suggested to him the fear that the Federalists would occupy the range of hills to the left of the turnpike and southwest of the town, so as to command his approaches. He therefore determined to press them all night, in the hope of seizing the contested heights during the darkness. Without a moment's pause for food or sleep, the army marched forward in perfect order, some of the brigades enlivening their fatigues from time to time with martial music, while ringing cheers passed, like a wave, down the column for four miles, until their sound was lost in the distance. The last time Jackson's division had passed over this road, they were making their slow and stubborn retreat from the bloody field of Kernstown; and they were now eager to wipe out the disgrace of that check. The night was calm, but dark. All night long, the General rode at the front, amidst a little advanced guard of cavalry, seeking the enemy's bleeding haunches with the pertinacity of a blood-hound. Again and again he fell, with his escort, into ambuscades of their riflemen, posted behind the stone fences, which here line the road almost continuously. Suddenly the fire appeared, dancing along the top of the wall, accompanied by the sharp explosion of the rifles, and the bullets came hissing up the road. The first of these surprises occurred soon after the burning wagons were passed. No sooner had the fire begun, than the General, seeing his escort draw rein and waver, cried in a commanding tone: "Charge them! Charge them!" They advanced unsteadily a little space, and then, at a second volley, turned and fled past him, leaving him in the road with his staff alone. But the enemy, equally timid, also retired, seemingly satisfied with their effort. The conduct of these troopers filled Jackson with towering indignation; and turning to the officer next him, he exclaimed: "Shameful! Did you see anybody struck, sir? Did you see anybody struck? Surely they need not have run, at least until they were hurt!" Skirmishers from the 33d Virginia infantry of Colonel Neff, were now thrown into the fields right and left of the turnpike, and advancing abreast with the head of the column, protected it for a time from similar insults. But as it approached Barton's Mills, five miles from Winchester, the enemy, posted on both sides of the road, again received it with so severe a fire, that the cavalry advance retired precipitately out of it, carrying the General and his attendants along with them, and riding down several cannoneers, who had been brought up to their support. So pertinacious was the stand of the Federalists here, the 27th, 2nd, and 5th Virginia regiments were brought up, and the affair grew to the dimensions of a night-combat, before they gave way. A similar skirmish occurred at Kernstown also, in which a few of the enemy were killed and captured. The army was now not far from its goal; and the General, commanding the skirmishers to continue a cautious advance, caused the remainder to halt, and lie down upon the road-side, for an hour's sleep. He himself, without a cloak to protect him from the chilling dews, stood sentry at the head of the column, listening to every sound from the front.

Meanwhile, the wearied skirmishers pressed on, with a patient endurance beyond all praise, drenched with the dews, wading through the rank fields of clover and wheat, and stumbling across ditches, until their tired limbs would scarcely obey their wills. When the early dawn came to their relief, the heights commanding Winchester were in sight, and against the faint blush of the morning sky the figures of the Federal skirmishers upon the crest were distinctly relieved. The tired Confederates having rested a short time, General Jackson, in a quiet undertone, gave the word to march, which was passed down the column; and the host rising from its short sleep, chill and stiff with the cold night-damps, advanced to battle.

The town of Winchester is seated upon ground almost level; and such also is the surface south and east of it, through which the great roads from Strasbourg and Front-Royal approach. The former, especially, passes through smooth fields and meadows, by a smiling suburb and mill-house, a mile from the town; after which it surmounts a gentle ascent, and enters the street. But toward the southwest, a cluster of beautiful hills projects itself for a mile toward the left, commanding the town, the turnpike, and the adjacent country. They were then enclosed with fences of wood or stone, and covered with luxuriant clover and pasturage, with here and there a forest-grove crowning the eminences farthest west. Why the enemy did not post their powerful artillery upon the foremost of these heights, supported by their main force, can only be explained by that infatuation which possessed them, by the will of God, throughout these events. When General Jackson arrived near them at early dawn, with the main column, he found them occupied by a skirmish line only. After a careful examination of a few minutes, he ordered General Winder to bring forward the Stonewall Brigade; which, forming in line of battle with the 5th Virginia on the right, advanced, and speedily dislodged the enemy from the first line of eminences. The General immediately advanced a strong detachment of artillery, composed of the batteries of Poague, Carpenter and Cutshaw, and posted them advantageously just behind the crests of the hill. The enemy's main force now disclosed itself, occupying a convex line upon the high grounds, south, and southwest of the town; and while the Stonewall Brigade, with that of Colonel John A. Campbell, were disposed as supports to the batteries; a fierce cannonade, intermingled with a sharp, rattling fire of riflemen, greeted the rising sun. The May dews, exhaled by his beams, wrapped a part of the landscape in a silvery veil, into which the smoke of the artillery melted away. Just at this moment, General Jackson rode forward, followed by two field officers, Colonel Campbell and another, to the very crest of the hill, and amidst a perfect shower of balls, reconnoitred the whole position. Both the officers beside him were speedily wounded, but he sat calmly upon his horse, until he had satisfied himself concerning the enemy's dispositions. He saw them posting another battery upon an eminence far to his left, whence they hoped to enfilade the ground occupied by the guns of Poague; and, nearer to his left front, a body of riflemen were just seizing a position behind an oblique stone fence, whence they poured a galling fire upon the gunners, and struck down many men and horses. Here this gallant battery stood its ground, sometimes almost silenced, yet never yielding an inch. After a time, by direction of General Winder, they changed their front to the left, so as to present a more successful face to their adversaries; and while a part of their guns replied to the opposing battery, the remainder shattered the stone fence which sheltered the Federal infantry, with solid shot, and raked it with canister. Carpenter and Cutshaw also kept up so spirited a contest with

48

the batteries in the direction of the town, as to silence their fire. General Jackson was hard to be convinced that the enemy would be so foolish as to yield the contest, without an attempt to drive his artillery from this vital position, and to occupy it with their own.   At this stage of the battle, he rode up to Colonel Neff, of the 33d Virginia, supporting the battery of Carpenter, and after ordering the latter not to slacken his fire, said to the former; " Colonel, where is your regiment posted ?"   " Here," he replied ; " the right masked in this depression of ground, and the left behind that fence."   Said the General, " I expect the enemy to bring artillery to this hill ; and they must not do it ! do you understand me, sir !   *They must not do it !*   Keep a good look out ; and your men well in hand ; and if they attempt to come, charge them with the bayonet ; and seize their guns : *Clamp them, sir,* on the spot."   As he gave this order, his clenched hand and strident voice declared the energy of his fiery will, in such sort as to make the blood of every beholder tingle.

But the narrative must pause here, to return to the movements of General Ewell.   During the previous evening, he had pressed the enemy back from the direction of Front Royal, until his advanced regiment, the 21st North Carolina, Colonel Kirkland was within two miles of Winchester.   Here he rested his advance at 10 o'clock P. M., and his command slept upon their arms.   At dawn he moved simultaneously with General Jackson, and the first guns of Carpenter were answered from the east, by those of his batteries.   He advanced his left, Colonel Kirkland still in front, until he was met by a fire of musketry from the enemy's line, posted behind a stone fence, so destructive that the field officers were all wounded, and the gallant regiment compelled to recoil.   This check was speedily retrieved by the 21st Georgia regiment, which in turn drove the enemy's infantry from their cover. But General Ewell, upon the suggestion of Brigadier-General Trimble, was convinced that his better policy would be to move by his right. Bringing the remainder of his regiments forward, he executed this movement, and the enemy began at once to give way from his front.

The battle had now reached a stage which General Jackson perceived to be critical; the hour for striking the final blow had arrived. The enemy were evidently moving, by a still wider circuit, towards the wooded heights which commanded his extreme left. He now sent for the fine brigade of General Taylor, which was at the head of the column of reserve, in the rear of the mill-house. Before the messenger could bring it up, his eagerness overcame him, and he was seen riding rapidly to meet it. Conducting it by a hollow way, around the rear of his centre, he directed its rapid formation in line of battle, with the left regiments thrown forward to the westward of the enemy's position. Under a shower of shells and rifle-balls, this magnificent body of troops wheeled from column into line, with the accuracy and readiness of a parade. As soon as General Jackson saw them in motion in the desired direction, he galloped along the rear of his line toward the centre, giving the word for a general advance. When he reached the hill occupied by the battery of Carpenter, where he had so exposed himself at the beginning, he mounted it again, with an air of eager caution, peering like a deer-stalker over its summit, as soon as his eyes reached its level. His first glance was sufficient; setting spurs to his horse, he bounded upon the crest, and shouted to the officers near him: "Forward, after the enemy!" No more inspiring sight ever greeted the eyes of a victorious captain. Far to the east, the advancing lines of Ewell rolled forward, concealed in waves of white smoke, from their volleys of musketry, and were rapidly overpassing the

suburbs of the town. On the West, the long and glittering
lines of Taylor, after one thundering discharge, were sweeping
at a bayonet charge up the reverse of the hills, with irresistible
momentum.   Nearer the General, came the Stonewall Brigade,
with the gallant 23d Virginia, who sprung from their lairs, and
rushed panting down the hill-sides. Between him and the town
the enemy were everywhere breaking away from the walls and
fences where they had sheltered themselves, at first with some
semblance of order, but then dissolving into a vast confusion, in
which the infantry, mounted officers, and artillery crowded and
surged toward the streets. But they found neither shelter nor
respite there; the eager Confederates were too close upon them
to allow time for any arrangements for defence. For a few
moments, pursuers and pursued were swallowed from view, and
the rout roared through every street, with rattling rifle-shots,
and ringing cheers of the victors, until it disgorged itself upon
the commons north of the town. The General, with his face
inflamed with towering passion and triumph, galloped amidst
the foremost pursuers, and urged them upon the enemy. The
sidewalks and doorways were thronged with children, women,
and old men, who rushed out, regardless of the balls, to hail
the conquerors. Of these, some ran in among the horses, as
though to embrace the knees of their deliverers; many were
wildly waving their arms or handkerchiefs, and screaming their
welcome in cheers and blessings, while not a few of the more
thoughtful were seen, standing upon their doorsteps, with their
solemn faces bathed in tears, and spreading forth their hands
to heaven, in adoration. To complete the thrilling scene, two
great buildings, in different places, were vomiting volumes of
flame and smoke, which threatened to involve all in one common
ruin; for the enemy, in cowardly spite, lighted them, and left
them in flames in the midst of the town. But not one of the

endangered citizens sought to arrest any pursuing soldier for
this; and after the first frenzy of their joy was passed, the old
men and the females set to, and extinguished the fires. Delicate
women were seen bringing water, and rushing into the burning
building, stored with the ammunition of the enemy, to drag out
the Federal sick and wounded, who had been left there by their
comrades, to be overwhelmed in the explosion which they
expected to follow.

When General Jackson issued into the open ground again at
the Martinsburg Turnpike, all the fields, which the depredations
of the enemy had converted into a waste denuded of fences and
crops, were dark with a confused multitude of fugitives, utterly
without order or thought of resistance. From the head of every
street, eager columns of Confederates were pouring, and deploy-
ing without awaiting the commands of their officers, into an
irregular line, in order to fire upon the retreating mass. As
this surged wildly away it left scattered over the common its
human wrecks, in the shape of dead and dying, intermingled
with knapsacks, arms, and bundles of stolen goods. Upon
glancing around this picture, the General exclaimed; "Never
was there such a chance for cavalry; oh that my cavalry were
in place!" When an officer near him remarked that the best
substitute for a cavalry pursuit would be the fire of the field
artillery, he replied; "Yes; go back and order up the nearest
batteries you find." After despatching this order, he sent another
member of his staff, with the characteristic command, "to order
every battery and every brigade forward to the Potomac." In
his official report he says; "Never have I seen an opportunity
when it was in the power of the cavalry, to reap a richer harvest
of the fruits of victory." And again; "There is good reason
for believing that, had the cavalry played its part in this pursuit
as well as the four companies under Colonel Flournoy, two days

before, in the pursuit from Front Royal, but a small portion of Banks's army would have made its escape to the Potomac." The cause of this untimely absence of the cavalry may be surmised by the reader, as to that part under Colonel Ashby. Disorganized by its initial success, it was so scattered that its heroic leader could gather but a handful around him on the morning of the battle. With these he had undertaken an independent enterprise, to cut off a detachment of Federalists on their left; and passing around the scene of action he joined in the pursuit many hours after, at Bunker Hill. The 2d and 6th regiments had been placed under the temporary command of Brigadier-General George H. Stewart, of General Ewell's division. As they did not appear after the pursuit had been continued for some time, General Jackson sent his Aide, Captain Pendleton, after them. General Stewart replied that he was awaiting the orders of General Ewell, under whose immediate command he was, and could not move without them. While these were obtained, precious time was wasted, and two hours elapsed before the two regiments were upon the traces of the enemy. That a superior officer, addressing his commands to persons under the orders of his inferior, should direct them through him, if he is present, is a proper mark of consideration, and a means of regularity in governing. But it is a most effectual way to rob a commanding general of his command, to assume that he may not claim the services of the subordinate of his own subordinate, in the absence of the latter; when, if he were present, he could legitimately control him and all under him. The utmost which the former could ask, when receiving orders without the intervention of his immediate superior, would be, that his commanding general should remember to explain to that officer the orders thus given in his absence.

After pursuing for a few miles with infantry and artillery,

General Jackson perceived that the interval between his men and the enemy was continually widening. The warm mid-day was now approaching, and since the morning of the previous day, the troops had been continually marching or fighting, without food or rest. Nature could do no more. At every step some wearied man was compelled to drop out of the ranks by overpowering fatigue. The General therefore ordered the infantry to cease their pursuit, and return to the pleasant groves of Camp Stevenson, three miles north of Winchester, for rest and rations, while the cavalry, which had now arrived, assumed the duty of pressing the enemy. This General Stewart performed with skill and energy, picking up a number of prisoners, and driving the Federalists through Martinsburg, and across the Potomac at Williamsport. General Banks was one of the first fugitives to appear at Martinsburg, having deserted his army long before the conclusion of the battle. His forces were thus driven without pause, and within the space of thirty-six hours, a distance of sixty miles. At Martinsburg, enormous accumulations of army stores again fell into the victors' hands. When the cavalry drove the last of the fugitives across the Potomac, a multitude of helpless blacks were found cowering upon the southern bank, who had been decoyed from Winchester and the adjacent country, by the story that Jackson was putting to death all the slaves whom he met, upon the charge of fraternizing with the Yankees. Many of these unhappy victims of fanaticism, deserted in the hour of alarm by their seducers, were cared for, and brought back to their homes, by the horsemen.

The remainder of the day was devoted by the army as well as their Commander, to repose. The tired men, disencumbered of their arms, reclined under the noble groves interspersed among their camp, while the famished horses grazed busily upon

the rich sward.   The thunder of the battles and the shouting of
the captains were soon followed by a Sabbath stillness, amidst
which the General slowly rode back to the town.   Having procured quarters in the chief hotel, he refused all food, and throwing himself across a bed upon his breast, booted and spurred, was
sleeping in a moment, with the healthy quietude of infancy.

The next day was devoted to a religious rest, in order to pay
that honor which General Jackson ever delighted to render to
Almighty God, and to repay the troops, in some sort, for the
interruptions of the holy day by battle.   This purpose was announced to the troops in the following General order:

"Within four weeks this army has made long and rapid
marches, fought six combats and two battles, signally defeating
the enemy in each one, captured several stands of colors, and
pieces of artillery, with numerous prisoners, and vast medical,
ordnance, and army stores; and, finally, driven the boastful host
which was ravaging our beautiful country, into utter rout.   The
General commanding would warmly express to the officers and
men under his command, his joy in their achievements, and his
thanks for their brilliant gallantry in action and their patient
obedience under the hardships of forced marches; often more
painful to the brave soldier than the dangers of battle.   The
explanation of the severe exertions to which the Commanding
General called the army, which were endured by them with
such cheerful confidence in him, is now given, in the victory of
yesterday.   He receives this proof of their confidence in the
past with pride and gratitude, and asks only a similar confidence
in the future.

"But his chief duty to-day, and that of the army, is, to recognize devoutly the hand of a protecting Providence in the brilliant
successes of the last three days (which have given us the results
of a great victory without great losses); and to make the oblation

of our thanks to God for his mercies to us and our country, in heartfelt acts of religious worship. For this purpose the troops will remain in camp to-day, suspending as far as practicable all military exercises; and the Chaplains of regiments will hold divine service in their several charges at 4 o'clock, P. M. "

At the appointed hour the General attended public worship with the 37th Virginia regiment, and presented an edifying example of devotion to the men.

Winchester had been the great resort of Federal sutlers, who had impudently occupied many of the finest shops upon its streets, and exposed their wares for sale in them. The headlong confusion of Banks's retreat left them neither means nor time to remove their wealth. All was given up to the soldiers, who speedily emptied their shelves. It was a strange sight to see the rough fellows, who the day before had lacked the ration of beef and hard bread, regaling themselves with confectionery, sardines, and tropical fruits. Their spoils, however, were about to produce a serious evil. The stores of clothing captured by the men in these shops, and in the baggage of the fugitives, were so enormous, that in a day the army seemed to be almost metamorphosed. The Confederate grey was rapidly changing into the Yankee blue. Had this license been permitted, the purposes of discipline would have been disappointed, and the dangers of battle multiplied. General Jackson speedily suppressed it by this adroit and simple measure. He issued an order that every person in Federal uniform should be arrested, and assumed to be a prisoner of war going at large improperly, until he himself presented adequate evidence of the contrary. The men of the Provost-Marshal had not acted upon this order many hours before the army became grey again as rapidly as it had been becoming blue. The men either deposited their gay spoils in the bottom of their knapsacks, or sent them by the baggage-trains

49

which were carrying the captured stores to the rear, and donned their well-worn uniforms again.

General Jackson was not the man to lose the opportunities growing out of such a victory by inaction. The use to be made of his present successes was dictated by the authorities at Richmond; but it is believed their designs met the full approbation of his own judgment. Immediately after the battle of Winchester he had sent a trusty officer to the Capital with despatches explaining his views. The decision of the government was, that he should press the enemy at Harper's Ferry, threaten an invasion of Maryland, and an assault upon the Federal capital, and thus make the most energetic diversion possible, to draw a part of the forces of M'Clellan and M'Dowell from Richmond. After allowing his troops two days of needed rest, the army was moved, Wednesday morning, May 28th, toward Charlestown, by Summit Point, General Winder's brigade again in advance. Charlestown is a handsome village, the seat of justice of Jefferson county, eight miles from Harper's Ferry. When about five miles from the former place, General Winder received information that the enemy was in possession of it in heavy force. Upon being advised of this, General Jackson ordered General Ewell with reinforcements to his support. But General Winder resolved not to await them, and advanced cautiously toward Charlestown. As he emerged from the wood, less than a mile distant from the town, he discovered the enemy in line of battle about fifteen hundred strong, and decided to attack them. Upon the appearance of our troops, the enemy opened upon them with two pieces of artillery. Carpenter's battery was immediately placed in position, with the 33rd Virginia regiment as support; and was so admirably served that in twenty minutes the enemy retired in great disorder, throwing away their arms and baggage. The pursuit was continued rapidly with artillery and infantry to

Hall-town, a hamlet a couple of miles from the Potomac. A short distance beyond that point, General Winder observing the enemy strongly posted on Bolivar Heights, and in considerable force, concluded that prudence required him to await his supports; and he therefore arrested the pursuit, and returned to the vicinity of Charlestown.

On the following day, the main body of the army took position near Hall-town, and the 2nd regiment, Virginia infantry, was sent to Loudon heights, with the hope of being able to drive the enemy from Harper's Ferry, across the Potomac. But this movement was no sooner made, than General Jackson received intelligence which imperiously required him to arrest it, and provide for his own safety. The Federal Government, awakened by its disasters, to a portion of sense and activity, gave orders to General Shields, to move upon General Jackson's communications from the Rappahannock, and General Fremont from the valley of the South Branch. Both these bodies were now threatening to close in upon his rear, with a speed which left not a moment for delay. At Front Royal, the 12th Georgia regiment, so distinguished for its gallantry at M'Dowell, and previous engagements, had been stationed to watch the approaches of the enemy from the east, and to guard the prisoners and valuable stores captured there the previous week. Through the indiscretion of its commander, it was driven from the place, with the loss of all the prisoners, and a number of its own members captured; while the stores were only rescued from falling again into the hands of the Federalists, by the energy of a Quartermaster, who fired the warehouses containing them. Thus a loss of three hundred thousand dollars, in provisions and equipments, was incurred at the outset.

In the afternoon of the 30th, the whole army was in motion, retreating upon Strasbourg, the point at which it was expected

Shields and Fremont would attempt their junction. General Winder was ordered to recall the 2nd regiment from Loudon heights, and with the cavalry, to protect the rear of the army. On arriving at Winchester, General Jackson learned that the approach of the enemy to Strasbourg was so imminent, that it was essential his rear should reach that place by mid-day of the 31st, in order to avoid separation from the main body, and capture. He, therefore, sent back orders to the Stonewall Brigade, not to pause in its march on the 30th, until it passed Winchester. It travelled, in fact, from Hall-town, to the neighborhood of Newtown, a distance of thirty-five miles: and the 2nd Virginia regiment, which had its steps to retrace from the heights beyond the Shenandoah, accomplished a march of more than forty miles, without rations. This astonishing effort was made also over muddy roads, and amidst continual showers! The next morning the rear-guard arose from their wet *bivouac*, stiff and sore of limb, and completed the march to Strasbourg in the forenoon. When they arrived there, they found the army halted and awaiting them; while General Ewell, with his division, facing toward the west, was sternly confronting Fremont, and offering him gage of battle. The latter had arrived in the neighborhood of Strasbourg, by way of Wardensville, and issued from the gap of the great north mountain, as though to attack the retreating army. But when it stood thus at bay, he prudently withdrew, after a desultory skirmish, into the gorge from which he had issued. General Jackson now resumed a deliberate retreat, with his rear covered by his cavalry; seeking some position in the interior, where he could confront his foes without danger to his flanks.

During the week which embraced these brilliant events, the Quartermasters' and Ordnance departments of the army were laboriously engaged in collecting and removing the captured stores. The baggage trains of the army, and those captured from the enemy were laden with the precious spoils, and sent toward Staunton. Every carriage which could be hired or impressed from the vicinity of Winchester, was also employed; and yet a vast and unestimated mass which could not be removed, was consigned to the flames. Only those things which were brought safely away will be enumerated. It has been related how the soldiers themselves were permitted to dispose of the contents of the sutlers' stores. A large part of the army was thus equipped with clothing, boots and shoes, blankets, oil cloth coverings, and hats. One of the largest storehouses in Winchester was found filled with medicines, surgical instruments, and hospital appliances, of the choicest description. Of these a small portion were distributed to the surgeons for the immediate wants of their brave men; and all the remainder were sent to Richmond, where they were found abundant enough to replenish the medical stores of the great army. The mercy of Providence in this supply, was as manifest as His rebuke of the barbarity of the enemy. With an inhumanity unknown in modern history, they had extended the law of blockade to all medicines and hospital stores; hoping thus not only to make the hurts of every wounded adversary mortal, (where brave men would have been eager to minister to a helpless foe,) but to deprive suffering age, womanhood, and infancy of the last succors which the benignity of the universal Father has provided for their pangs. This cold and malignant design was in part disappointed by the victory of Jackson. The stores captured at Winchester not only supplied the conquering army, but carried solace and healing to the sick and wounded throughout the approaching campaign of Richmond. In bright contrast with this barbarity of the enemy, stands the magnanimity of Jackson. Finding a large and well provided hospital at Winchester, filled with seven hundred Federal sick and wounded, he ordered that nothing of their stores or medicines should be removed, and having ministered to the sufferers with generous attention during the week they were in his power, he left everything untouched, when Winchester was again evacuated. The seven hundred enemies were paroled, not to fight again until exchanged.

The 31st of May, the 21st Virginia regiment left Winchester, in charge of twenty-three hundred prisoners of war. The whole number of the enemy captured was about three thousand and fifty. One hundred beeves, thirty-four thousand pounds of bacon, and great masses of flour, biscuit, and groceries, were secured by the Chief Commissary, while the Quartermasters removed stores in their department, to the amount of one hundred and twenty-five thousand dollars. Two hundred wagons and ambulances, with a number of horses, which would have been very great, but for the rapacity of the Confederate cavalry, were also secured. But the most precious acquisition was the ordnance stores, containing, besides ammunition, nine thousand, three hundred and fifty small arms, perfectly new, and of the most approved patterns.

These results of the week's campaign were won with small expenditure of blood by the patriot army. In all the engagements, from Front Royal to Strasbourg, sixty-eight men were killed, three hundred and twenty-nine were wounded, and three were missing; making a total loss of four hundred men. The General closed his official narrative with these words: " Whilst I have had to speak of some of our troops in disparaging terms, yet it is my gratifying privilege to say of the main body of the army, that its officers and men acted in a manner worthy of the great cause for which they were contending, and to add that, so far as my knowledge extends, the battle of Winchester was, on our part, a battle without a straggler."

It was while reposing after his victory at Winchester, that he wrote thus to Mrs. Jackson:

"Winchester, May 26th, 1862. An ever kind Providence blessed us with success at Front Royal on Friday, between Strasbourg and Winchester on Saturday, and here with a successful engagement yesterday. . . . . I do not remember having ever seen such rejoicing as was manifested by the people of Winchester, as our army yesterday passed through the town in pursuit of the enemy. The town was nearly frantic with joy. Our entrance into Winchester was one of the most stirring scenes of my life. Such joy as the inhabitants manifested, cannot easily be described. The town is greatly improved in its loyalty."

A few days after, while threatening Harper's Ferry, he sent messages to the Confederate Government by his zealous supporter and assistant, the Hon. Mr. Boteler of the Congress, begging for an increase of his force. He pointed out again that an assault upon the enemy's territory, indicating danger to their capital, was the most ready and certain method to deliver Richmond from the approaches of General M'Clellan. "Tell them," he said, "that I have now but fifteen thousand effective men. If the present opening is improved as it should be, I must have forty thousand." But the Government was unable to advance these reinforcements, and Divine Providence reserved to him the glory of assisting in the deliverance of our capital in a more direct manner.

This chapter will be closed with a reference to a fact which assists in fixing the seal of infamy upon the Federal Government, generals, and armies; the authorized robberies now begun in the valley of Virginia. Not only were the inhabitants plundered by the Federal soldiers as they marched through the peaceful country, but they were systematically robbed of their horses, and other live-stock by General Banks, in his march to and from Harrisonburg. This commander officially boasted to his Government, that the results of his conquest had supplied his artillery and trains with enough of excellent horses, besides many other valuable resources. Now none of these were prize of war; for so accomplished a leader was Jackson, in retreat as well as in triumph, that nothing belonging to his army fell into his enemy's hands. These horses, and other animals, were simply stolen from the rich and peaceful farmers of Rockingham and Shenandoah. Here was the beginning of a system of wholesale robbery, since extended to every part of the Confederate States which the enemy has reached! But if the reader assigned to General Banks any pre-eminence of crime or infamy, above his nation, he would do him injustice. The Federal Congress and Executive had already, by formal and unblushing legislation, ordained that the war should be a huge piracy, as monstrous as the rapacity of any of their lieutenants could make it. Under pretexts which could be used by any other nation, in any other war, with equal plausibility, to steal any species of private property whatever, laws had been passed, declaring all tobacco, cotton, and labor of slaves, in the Confederate States, or coming thence, to be "contraband of war," and liable to confiscation. The true intent of this law was to subject these three kinds of property, the most important in our country, to systematic theft, and this purpose has since been most diligently and consistently carried out.

CHAPTER XIII.

PORT REPUBLIC.

IT has been related how General Jackson . assembled his army at Strasbourg before the occupation of that place by Fremont, and thus eluded the combination designed by him and Shields, in his rear.   On the evening of June 1st, he resumed his retreat up the Valley.   The object immediately demanding his attention was the rescue of his army from its perilous situation.   The indirect purpose of the campaign was already accomplished; his rapid movements and stunning blows had neutralized the efforts of General M'Dowell against Richmond — Banks was driven from Winchester the 25th of May, and the Federal authorities were panic-struck by the thought of a victorious Confederate army, of unknown numbers, breaking into Maryland by Harper's Ferry, and seizing Washington City. Just at this juncture, M'Clellan had pushed his right wing to a point north of Richmond, at Hanover Court House, and within a single march of M'Dowell's advanced posts.   On the 27th of May, the Confederate General Branch was defeated at that place with loss, and the fruit of this success was the occupation of all the roads, and of the bridges across the waters of the Pamunkey, connecting Richmond with Fredericksburg and Gordonsville, by the Federalists.   Had the advice of M'Clellan been now followed, the result must have been disastrous to General Lee, and might well have been ruinous.   The Federal

50

commander urged his Government to send General M‘Dowell, with all the forces near Manassa's, under Sigel and Augur, by the route thus opened to them, to effect an immediate junction with his right wing, to hold permanently these lines of communication between Lee and Jackson, and to complete the investment of Richmond. These operations, which the Confederates had no means to resist, with the addition of the forty thousand troops which they would have brought to M‘Clellan's army, already so superior in numbers, would have greatly endangered Richmond and its army. .But the terror inspired by Jackson caused the President to refuse his consent; he was unwilling to expose his Capital to a sudden blow from this ubiquitous leader; and instead of sending General M‘Dowell forward, he commanded him to retire nearer to Washington. General M‘Clellan was further ordered by telegraph, to burn the bridges across the south Pamunkey, won by his recent victory, and by which his reinforcements should have joined him, lest the Confederates should move by them against Washington! Thus Providence employed the movements of General Jackson's little army to paralyze the forces of Fremont, Banks and M‘Dowell, amounting to eighty thousand men, during the critical period of the campaign. It is therefore with justice, that his successes in the Valley are said to have saved Richmond and Virginia. When the small means, the trivial losses, and the short time, with which this great result was wrought, are considered, it will be admitted that military genius has never, in any age, accomplished a more splendid achievement. It was indeed so brilliant, that the doubt has been suggested, whether the mind of Jackson or of any other strategist, was prophetic enough to forecast and provide for so grand a conclusion, or whether it was the fortunate and unforeseen dispensation of chance, or of Providence. To the latter he delighted to attribute all his success; and he would

have been the first to concur in the estimate, which made him
only an humble instrument in the hand of an omniscient Guide,
who superintended his fallible judgment, overruled the efforts
of his enemies, and, among the variety of possible effects, connected his measures with those consequences which were most
beneficial to his country.   But while this Christian solution is
fully admitted, the honor of General Jackson, as an instrument,
is vindicated by these facts, that, from the first, he strongly urged
the movements which were at length made, as the surest means
for these ends, and that he continued steadfastly of the same
mind amidst all the mutations in others, produced by the fluctu-
ating appearances of the campaign.   The wisdom of his plan
was seconded by a devotion and energy in action, which gave it
such success as no other could have commanded.

A more glorious sequel yet remains to be narrated, in which
General Jackson extricated himself from his baffled enemies, and
assisted in crushing the remainder of the Federal forces near
Richmond.   The former of these results was effected at Port
Republic; and to this spot the narrative now leads.   When
General Jackson, on the evening of June 1st, resumed his retreat
from Strasbourg, he was aware that Shields had been for nearly
two days at Front Royal.   The fact that he had not attempted
an immediate junction with Fremont suggested the suspicion that
he was moving for a point farther upon the rear of the Confederates, by way of Luray and New Market Gap.   To frustrate
this design, General Jackson now sent a detachment of cavalry to
burn the White House bridge across the South Shenandoah, by
which the Luray turnpike passed the stream, and also the
Columbia bridge, a few miles above it.   He knew that Shields
had no pontoon train, for Banks had been compelled to sacrifice
it at Newtown; and the rivers were still too much swollen to be
forded.   Having taken this precaution, he retreated up the

Valley turnpike in his usual stubborn and deliberate fashion, with his cavalry and Chew's light battery in the rear. It was the saying of his soldiers, that his marches were always easy when in retreat, but hard when pursuing. This calmness of movement not only promoted order, and gave time to bring off his supplies, but wrought an invaluable effect upon the spirits of the troops. A hurried march in retiring from the enemy suggests insecurity, and ministers a constant excitement to the minds of the men akin to panic, and easily converted into it. General Jackson's deliberation reassured his army; and they never lost confidence or spirit because they were compelled to retire for a time. It was by this means that he was enabled to preserve the order of his troops equally in retreat and in advance.

General Fremont, having ascertained that the Confederates were withdrawing, pursued with spirit; and, after nightfall, a portion of his horse came so near the rear-guard that they were challenged by them. They replied, "Ashby's cavalry"; and, having thus deceived our forces, availed themselves of the advantage to charge the 6th regiment of cavalry, which was next the rear. These were thrown into disorder; and a few of them were ridden down, and wounded, or captured. Confusion was also communicated, to some degree, to the 2nd regiment next it; but the commander, Colonel Munford, soon reformed it, gallantly charged the enemy, repulsed them, and captured some prisoners. On the 2nd of June, the enemy succeeded in taking position where their artillery was able to cannonade the Confederate rear. The cavalry was thrown into disorder by the shells, and fled, carrying a part of its supporting battery with them. The Federal cavalry now pushed forward to reap the fruits of this success, when Ashby displayed that prompt resource and personal daring which illustrated his character. Dismounting from his horse, he collected a small body of riflemen who were lagging, foot-sore and weary, behind their commands, and posted them in a wood near the road-side. Awaiting the near approach of the enemy, he poured into their ranks so effective a fire that a number of saddles were emptied, and a part of the survivors retired in confusion. The remainder were carried past by their *momentum*, and even broke through the ranks of the rear regiment in a brigade of infantry, — that of Colonel Campbell, — commanded since his wounding at Winchester by Colonel J. M. Patton. But that officer, filing his next regiment from the road in good order, made way for the onset of the enemy, and, as they passed, gave them a volley which terminated their audacity. Only one of the party returned alive to his comrades, the remainder being all killed or captured. Colonel Patton, while reporting the events of the day to the General, at nightfall, remarked that he saw this party of foes shot down with regret. He seemed to make no note of these words at the time, but pursued his minute inquiries into all the particulars of the skirmish. After the official conversation was ended, he asked: "Colonel, why do you say that you saw those Federal soldiers fall with regret?" It was replied, that they exhibited more vigor and courage than anything which had been attempted by any part of the Federal army; and that a natural sympathy with brave men led to the wish that, in the fortunes of the fight, their lives might have been saved. The General drily remarked: "No; shoot them all: *I* do not wish them to be brave." It was thus that he was accustomed to indicate, by a single brief sentence, the cardinal thought of a whole chapter of discussion. He meant to suggest reasonings which show that such sentiments of chivalrous forbearance, though amiable, are erroneous. Courage in the prosecution of a wicked attempt does not relieve, but only aggravates, the danger to the innocent party assailed, and the guilt of the assailants. There is, then, a sense in which the most vigorous are the most worthy of death; and the interests of those who wage a just defence prompt them to visit retribution, first, upon those who are most dangerous.

The 2nd and 6th regiments of cavalry were now transferred from the command of General Stewart, to that of Ashby. When the latter returned to Winchester the week before, from the pursuit of Banks, he was met by his commission of Brigadier-General of cavalry; an honor well earned by his arduous and important services. He was now raised to that position best adapted to his powers. While unsuited for the drudgery of the drill and the military police, General Ashby had every quality of a brilliant commander in the field. Seconded by diligent and able Colonels in his regiments, he would have led his brigade to a career of glory surpassing all his previous successes. But such a destiny was not in store for him; and his sun was now about to set in its splendid morning.

On the 3rd of June, the Confederate army placed the north fork of the Shenandoah behind it; and General Ashby was entrusted with the duty of burning the bridge by which it passed over. Before this task was completed, the Federalists appeared on the opposite bank, and a skirmish ensued, in which his horse was struck dead, and he himself very narrowly escaped. The necessity of replacing this bridge, arrested Fremont for a day, and gave the tired Confederates a respite, which they employed in retiring slowly and unmolested, to Harrisonburg. A mile south of that village, General Jackson left the valley road, and turned eastward, towards Port Republic; a smaller place upon the south fork of the Shenandoah, and near the western base of the Blue Ridge. It was not until the evening of June 6th, that the Federal advance overtook his rearguard, which was still within two miles of Harrisonburg,

posted at the crest of a wooded ridge, commanding the neighboring fields. General Ashby, as usual, held the rear; and the
division of General Ewell was next. In part of the Federal
army was a New Jersey regiment of cavalry, commanded by
one of those military adventurers, whose appetite for blood presents so monstrous and loathsome a parody upon the virtues of
the true soldier. A subject of the British crown, and boasting
of his relationship to some noble English house, this person had
offered his services to the Federal Government, siding with the
criminal and powerful aggressors, against the heroic and righteous patriots, without one of those pleas of native soil and sentiments, which might rescue his acts from the criminality of naked
murder. It had been his blustering boast, that at the first
opportunity, he would deal with the terrible Colonel Ashby;
and for this he sought service in this part of the Federal armies.
His opportunity was now come; he advanced his regiment to
the attack, when General Ashby, taking a few companies of his
command, met them in the open field, and at the first charge,
routed them, and captured their Colonel with sixty-three of his
men. The remainder fled into Harrisonburg in headlong panic;
and the braggart mercenary found his fitting recompense in a
long captivity.

The sound of the firing now brought General Ewell to the
rear; and General Ashby assuring him that the Federal attack
would be speedily renewed in force, asked for a small body of
infantry, and proposed a plan, most brilliantly conceived, for
turning their onset into a defeat. General Ewell entrusted to
him the 1st Maryland regiment, of Colonel Bradley Johnston,
and the 58th Virginia, under Colonel Letcher. Ashby disposed
the Marylanders in the woods, so as to take the Federal advance
in flank, while he met them in front at the head of the 58th.
Indicating to General Ewell the dispositions of the enemy, which

he had exactly anticipated, and his own arrangements to meet them, he seemed to the spectators, to be instinct with unwonted animation and genius. At this moment, the enemy's infantry advanced; and a fierce combat began. They, approaching through the open fields, had reached a heavy fence of timber; whence, under the partial cover, they poured destructive volleys into the ranks of the 58th regiment. Ashby seeing at a glance their disadvantage, galloped to the front, and ordered them to charge, and drive the Federals from their vantage ground. At this moment his horse fell; but extricating himself from the dying animal, and leaping to his feet, he saw his men wavering. He shouted, " Charge men; for God's sake, charge!" and waved his sword; when a bullet pierced him full in the breast, and he fell dead. The regiment took up the command of their dying General, and rushed upon the enemy, while the Marylanders dashed upon their flank. Thus pressed, the Federals gave way, the Confederates occupied the fence, and poured successive volleys into the fleeing mass, who were fully exposed to them until they passed out of musket range. If blood, by comparison so vile, could have paid for that of the generous Ashby, he would have been fully avenged. The Lieutenant Colonel commanding the foremost Federal regiment, remained a prisoner in the hands of the Confederates, and the field was sprinkled over with killed and wounded.

With this repulse, the combat ceased: resulting in a loss to the confederates of seventeen killed, and fifty wounded, which fell chiefly on the 58th Virginia. The place where it occurred was not the one selected by General Jackson to stand the brunt of a general action, and it was therefore necessary to remove the wounded and the dead at once. The oversight of this humane task he entrusted to General Ewell. All the wounded who could bear a hasty removal were set on horses, and carried to a place of safety. A few remained whose hurts were too painful to endure the motion; and of these General Ewell was seen taking a tender leave, replenishing their purses from his own, that they might be able to purchase things needful for their comfort in their captivity, and encouraging them with words of good cheer. The glorious remains of Ashby were carried to Port Republic, and prepared for the grave. After all the sad rites were completed, General Jackson came to the room where he lay, and demanded to see him. They admitted him alone; he remained for a time in silent communion with the dead, and then left him, with a solemn and elevated countenance. It requires little use of the imagination to suppose that his thoughts were, in part, prophetic of a similar scene, where his corpse was to receive the homage of all the good and brave. But the duties of the hour were too stern to give a longer time to grief. At a subsequent day, his official report paid this brief but emphatic tribute to his companion in arms.

"In this affair, General Turner Ashby was killed. An official report is not an appropriate place for more than a passing notice of the distinguished dead; but the close relation which General Ashby bore to my command, for most of the previous twelve months, will justify me in saying that, as a partisan officer, I never knew his superior. His daring was proverbial, his powers of endurance almost incredible, his tone of character heroic, and his sagacity almost intuitive in divining the purposes and movements of the enemy."

General Ashby was of a spare and graceful figure, irregular features, and swarthy complexion. His hair and beard were profuse, and of jetty black, while his eye was a clear, piercing gray. Accomplished from his youth in all the feats of horsemanship and wood-craft, he was already trained for irregular warfare, before he girded on his sword. His private life had

51

been marked by purity, generosity, and a chivalrous spirit; and the modest dignity and cultivation of his manners showed him the true gentleman. These qualities remained untarnished, and shone only the more, when he became a military commander. No coarse excess soiled for a moment the maidenly delicacy of his morals; no plunder ever stained his hands, nor did woman, nor disarmed enemy, ever meet anything but magnanimous kindness from them. He was necessarily entrusted, as commander of outposts and patrols, in a district subject to martial law, with a large discretion in dealing with private rights; but his measures were always directed with such wisdom and equity, as to command the approval of friends and foes. His was an understanding formed by nature for war. As a citizen, he would have passed through life unmarked, save for his virtues, modesty, and high breeding. But when his native State called her sons to the field, he found his proper element. Excitement roused his powers, danger only invigorated and steadied them; and his comrades instinctively recognized in his decision, unerring judgment, magnanimity, and resource, one born to command. When he fell, the presence of the enemy in his native county forbade his burial among his kindred; so that although his venerable mother, who had now given to her country her last son, with the devotion of a Roman matron, anxiously awaited his remains there, it was necessary to seek for them another resting place. His friends selected the grave-yard of the State University: thither they were conveyed with martial pomp, and buried while the thunders of the distant battle at Port Republic tolled a fitting knell for the great soldier. There, the tomb of Ashby should remain, a memorial to the generous youth of Virginia, to suggest to them in all future times, the virtues and patriotism which he illustrated by his life and death.

In all the qualities of the citizen, the young man could find no nobler or purer exemplar.

On the 7th of June, the main body of the army was assembled in the neighborhood of Port Republic. General Jackson was now repeating with Fremont the manœuvre by which he had confounded Banks, by turning aside toward the base of the Blue Ridge. But his ready skill dictated some important differences in his strategy, to meet the different conditions of the case with which he now had to deal. The mountain was, to the Confederates, not only a fastness, but a base of operations; for the regions of Eastern Virginia beyond it offered them, by the various roads crossing it, both supplies, and a safe place of retreat. The line of operations of the Federalists was along the great Valley Turnpike; and this was parallel to the mountain. Hence, when Jackson took a position at the western foot of the Blue Ridge, he gained the advantage of a military base parallel to his enemy's line of operations, which enabled him to strike it at right angles, if it were prolonged by further advance into the country. Twice he resorted to this strategy, and each time it arrested the career of the superior army. His march from Swift Run Gap in May had taught him another advantage, belonging to the point which he now selected. A good road led from Port Republic across the mountain into Albemarle by Brown's Gap, offering him a safe outlet in case of disaster, and a means for drawing supplies from that fertile country. Before this road crowns the summit of the Blue Ridge, it passes through a valley, which constitutes the most complete natural fortress in all these mountains. Two arms of the mountain, lofty and ragged as the mother ridge, project from it on the right and left hand, embracing a deep vale of many miles' circuit, watered by a copious mountain stream; and while the mighty rim of this cup is everywhere impracticable for artillery and cavalry, the narrow gorge through which the road enters it from the west, affords scarcely room to set a regiment in battle array, between the two promontories of the mountains. Here was obviously the place for a small army to stand at bay against superior numbers.

But General Jackson did not purpose to withdraw into this fortress, save in the last resort; for to do this, he must sacrifice the advantage which the unscientific strategy of his adversaries gave him, by keeping their two armies apart, and attempting to approach him upon convenient lines, while his army was already concentrated. Befooled with the old fallacy of crushing an inferior force by surrounding it from different directions, Fremont and Shields were pursuing this method, instead of uniting their troops before the collision; and they were destined to illustrate again, by their disasters, the correctness of the maxim, that the inferior force possessing the interior position between its enemies, must have the advantage, if it strikes them in detail while separated. The two Federal Commanders had neglected a junction below Strasbourg. By burning the Columbia and White House Bridges, General Jackson had prevented their union at New Market; and he was now prompt to make them continue their error. Shields was still east of the Shenandoah, and there remained but two bridges, above or below, by which he could cross to the west side, to reach Fremont. One of these was at Port Republic, and was in Jackson's possession; the other was at the mouth of Elk Run valley, fifteen miles below. This General Jackson now sent a detachment of cavalry to burn; when there occurred one of those manifest interpositions of Providence, which from time to time shewed the answer to his prayers for the divine blessing. A quarter of an hour before the Confederate troopers reached the bridge, the advanced guard of General Shields arrived there, sent by him to ascertain whether

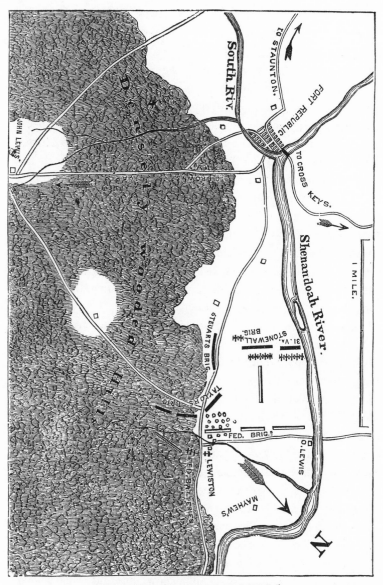

BATTLE OF PORT REPUBLIC.

the structure was still standing; for he had now awakened to some conception of its importance to him. They found it safe; but hearing that there was a corporal's guard of Confederate soldiers a few miles above, watching a parcel of stores, they dashed off to capture them, instead of remaining to guard the bridge, or else returning to report its condition to their commander. The stores were captured, and the guard escaped; but when the head of Shields's main column reached the bridge, the Confederates had arrived, and the work was hopelessly involved in flames. The Shenandoah, still swollen by the rains of a late and ungenial spring, was nowhere fordable, and the construction of a bridge in the presence of such a foe as Jackson was not an inviting enterprise. He was now master of the situation: he had comprehended all the conditions of the critical problem upon which he staked the very existence of his army; and while all others were full of anxious forebodings, he awaited the issue with calm determination.

• The part which remained to him in the coming tragedy was to hold fast his command of the brigade at Port Republic, and to seize his opportunity to crush the one of his assailants, now approaching from opposite directions, whom he judged it most judicious to attack. But the nearness of both of them, (within less than a day's march,) left little room for seeking the advantage which he knew so well how to use, by rapid movements, and successive blows. To any inferior leader, the danger would have been imminent of a simultaneous attack in front and rear; for if the converging detachments of enemies are allowed time to make such attacks, then indeed, all the success expected from the bungling plan of thus surrounding an army, may be realized. To understand the consummate union of skill and audacity with which Jackson obviated this danger, and still compelled his enemies to fight him in detail, although within sight of the smoke

of each others' guns; a more particular description of the ground
is necessary.   Between Harrisonburg and Port Republic the
country is occupied by the wooded ridges characteristic of a
limestone region, elevated but rounded, and practicable for
the movements even of artillery; and these are interspersed
with farms and fields which fill the vales.   These bold hills
extend to the river's brink on that side; while between the
waters and the mountain, where Shields was approaching, the
country stretches out in low and smooth meadows, everywhere
commanded from the heights across the stream.   Between these
level fields and the mountain itself, is interposed a zone of
forest, of three miles' width, broken into insignificant hillocks,
and interposed with tangled brush-wood, which stretches parallel
with the river and the Blue Ridge, for a day's march above and
below.   The little village is seated on the southeastern side of
the Shenandoah, in the level meadows, and just within the angle
between the main stream and a tributary called South River.
The only road to Brown's Gap, descending from the bold highlands of the northwest bank, over the long wooden bridge,
passes through the hamlet, crosses the South River by a ford,
and speedily hides itself, upon its way to the mountain-base, in
the impenetrable coppices of the wood.

General Shields, disappointed in the hope of joining Fremont
by the bridge at Elk Run valley, continued his march up the
southeastern bank of the river, by the same difficult road which
the Confederates had followed in their march from Swift Run in
April.   On the evening of Saturday, the 7th of June, his advance appeared at Lewiston, the country-seat of General Lewis,
three miles below the village.   The main object dictated by
General Jackson's situation now was, to keep his enemies apart,
separated as they were by the swollen stream, and to fight first
the one or the other of them, as his interest might advise him.

The defeat of one would obviously procure the retreat of both; for their cautious and timid strategy required the concert of the two armies to embolden them for coping with their dreaded adversary. It was manifest that good generalship should select Shields as the victim of the first blow. His force was smaller than that of Fremont, and so it was reasonable to expect an easier victory over it. If he were beaten, his retreat would be hemmed in between the river and the mountain, to a single scarcely practicable road; whereas General Fremont would be able, if overthrown, to withdraw by a number of easy highways. If, on the other hand, the attack of the Confederates upon Shields were unsuccessful, they would be able to retire into their own country, and nearer their supplies; while if they were defeated in an assault on Fremont upon the other side of the river, they would have that barrier to a retreat in their rear, with Shields's army unbroken, threatening them with destruction. It might appear, at first thought, that the obvious way to carry out the purpose of attacking Shields and defeating him separately, was to withdraw the whole Confederate army at once to the same side of the river with him, burn the bridge, thus leaving Fremont alone and useless upon the other bank, and then fall with full force upon the former. This, any other good soldier than Jackson would probably have done; but his designs were more audacious and profound still. With whatever promptitude he might attack Shields, he saw that the battle-field must be upon the southeastern margin of the Shenandoah, and under the heights of the opposite bank; which, if he yielded all the country on that side to Fremont, would of course be crowned by his artillery. And then, the struggle would have been virtually against both his foes combined; although the waters still flowed between their troops. In addition, his powerful artillery, the right arm of his strength, would then

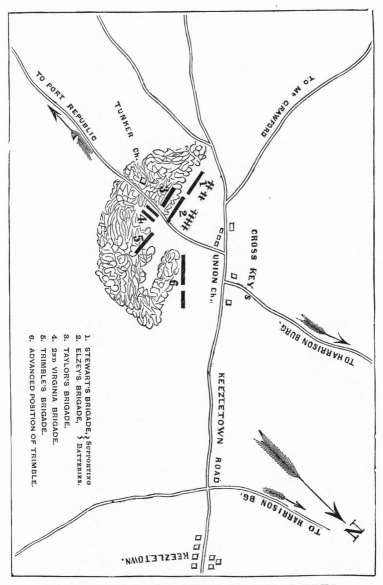

CONFEDERATE POSITION AT CROSS-KEYS.

have been paralyzed by the inferiority of its positions as com·
pared with those ceded to Fremont upon the northwestern
bank. Further, General Jackson was not willing to deprive
himself of the power to take the aggressive against Fremont,
after disposing of Shields, should his success in assailing the
latter prove sufficiently crushing to encourage him to a second
battle.

For these reasons, General Jackson neither ceded the northwestern bank to Fremont, nor burned the bridge. Where an
inferior genius would have purchased the full union of his forces
at the expense of allowing to his two enemies a virtual concert
as injurious as an actual junction; he accepted a nominal separation of his own troops, perceiving that he would thus have the
most effective co-operation. He purposed thus to hold both
his adversaries at bay, until the propitious moment arrived to
strike one of them a deadly blow. For this end, he selected for
General Ewell an excellent position upon the road leading to
Harrisonburg, five miles from the bridge, while he posted the
other division of his army, with several batteries of artillery,
upon the heights next the river, but still upon the northwest
side. Thence his guns could overlook and defend the bridge,
the village, the narrow champaign extending towards Brown's
Gap, and all the approaches on the side of Shields. In Port
Republic itself he stationed no troops save a detachment of
horse, which guarded the roads towards Lewiston, and protected
his own quarters in the village. His dispositions were completed by bringing all his trains across the bridge and placing
them near by, where they might be withdrawn either to the
mountain or to Staunton. Two companies of cavalry were
detached to watch the approach of General Shields, of which
one was sent to reconnoitre, and the other was stationed as a
picket guard upon the road to Lewiston.

The morning of June 8th, which was the Sabbath day, dawned with all the peaceful brightness appropriate to the Christian's sacred rest; and General Jackson, who never infringed its sanctity by his own choice, was preparing himself and his wearied men to spend it in devotion. But soon after the sun surmounted the eastern mountain, the pickets next the army of Shields came rushing to the head-quarters in the village, in confusion, with the Federal cavalry and a section of artillery close upon their heels. So feeble was the resistance which they offered, the advance of the enemy dashed across the ford of the South River almost as soon as they, and occupied the streets. The General had barely time to mount and gallop towards the bridge, with a part of his staff, when the way was closed; two others of his suite, attempting to follow him a few moments after, were captured in the street; and one or two, perceiving the hopelessness of the attempt, remained with the handful of troops thus cut off. But out of this accident, to them so involuntary, Providence ordained that a result should proceed essential to the safety of the army. As the captured Confederate officers stood beside the commander of the Federal advance, some of his troopers returned to him, and pointed out the long train of wagons hurrying away, apparently without armed escort, just beyond the outskirts of the village. He immediately ordered a strong body of cavalry in pursuit; and the hearts of the Confederates sank within them; for they knew that this was Jackson's ordnance train, containing the reserve ammunition of the whole army; and that all its other baggage was equally at the mercy of the enemy. But as the eager Federals reached the head of the village, they were met by a volley of musketry, which sent them scampering back; and when they returned to the charge, two pieces of artillery opened upon them, to the equal surprise and delight of their anxious captives, and speedily cleared the streets with showers of canister. The explanation was, that one of the officers separated from the General's suite, seeing the impossibility of joining him, had addressed himself to rallying a handful of the fugitive picket guards, and with these, and a section of raw artillerists from the reserves, had boldly attacked the enemy. Thus the trains were saved, and a diversion was made, until the General could bring forward more substantial succors.

Nor was it long before these were at hand. Galloping across the bridge, and up the heights, to the camp of the 3rd and 1st brigades of his own division, he ordered the long roll to be instantly beaten, and the artillery to be harnessed. The horses were still grazing in the luxuriant clover-fields, and the men were scattered under the shade of the groves; but in a few moments the guns were ready for action, and two or three regiments were in line. Jackson ordered the batteries of Poague, Wooding, and Carpenter to crown the heights overlooking the river, and placing himself at the head of the leading regiment of the 3rd brigade, — the 37th Virginia of Colonel Fulkerson, — rushed at a double-quick toward the all-important bridge, now in the enemy's possession. When he approached it, he saw the village beyond crowded with Federal cavalry, but now checked in their pursuit of his trains; while one of their two field-pieces was replying to the Confederate artillery, and the other was placed at the mouth of the bridge, prepared to sweep it with murderous discharges of grape. One lightning glance was enough to decide him. Ordering Captain Poague to engage with one of his pieces the gun at the southern end of the bridge, he led the 37th regiment aside from the high road, so that they descended the declivity obliquely against the upper side of that structure, marching by the flank. Without pausing to wheel them into line, as they came within effective distance, he commanded them, with a tone and mien of inexpressible authority, to deliver one round upon the enemy's artillerists, and then rush through the bridge upon them with the bayonet. They fired one stinging volley, which swept every cannoneer from the threatening gun, and then dashed with a yell through the narrow avenue. As soon as Jackson uttered his command he drew up his horse, and, dropping the reins upon his neck, raised both his hands toward the heavens while the fire of battle in his face changed into a look of reverential awe. Even while he prayed, the God of battles heard; or ever he had withdrawn his uplifted hands the bridge was gained, and the enemy's gun was captured. Thus, in an instant, was a passage won, with the loss of two men wounded, which might have become a second bridge of *Lodi*, costing the blood of hundreds of brave soldiers. So rapid and skilful was the attack, the enemy were able to make but one hurried discharge, before their position and their artillery were wrested from them. To clear the village of their advance was now the work of a moment, for the batteries frowning upon the opposite bank rendered it untenable to them; and the Confederate troopers next the baggage trains, plucking up heart, scoured the streets of every foe. Their retreat was so precipitate that they left their other piece of artillery behind them also, and dashed across the fords of South River by the way they came.

As they retired toward Lewiston, they met the infantry of Shields's army advancing to their support. But it was too late: the batteries were now all in position, and greeted their approach with a storm of projectiles from the farther side of the river, before which they were compelled to recoil with loss. The novel sight was now presented, of a retreating army pursued by two or three batteries of field guns, and retiring before them in helpless confusion. For as the Federal troops withdrew along the south side of the stream, the Confederates limbered their guns and galloped over the swelling fields upon the north side, to other lofty positions, whence they still commanded the ground occupied by the retreating foe, until he concealed himself behind the forest near Lewiston. He thus verified the judgment of General Jackson, by finding himself as effectually debarred, by these masterly dispositions, from co-operating in the contemplated attack of Fremont, as though he had been separated from him by many days' marches. And although the most urgent motives prompted Shields to renew his attack in concert with his associate on the other side, so manifest was the triumph of Jackson's generalship, he did not again venture the hopeless attempt; but sat all day idle, within sound of the cannonade, which told him that Fremont was compelled to risk and lose the field, without his aid. One element of General Jackson's greatness and success was the decision and confidence with which he held the conclusions of his own judgment after he had once matured them. His reflection was careful, his caution in weighing all competing considerations great; but when his mind once adopted its verdict, it held to it with unwavering and giant grasp. This characteristic was strongly illustrated in these events. As the reader viewed the considerations detailed above, by which the plan of action was dictated at Port Republic, some of them have probably appeared to him so nice and delicate, that he was inclined to deem it rashness, to stake the existence of an army upon deductions drawn from them. But when General Jackson had weighed them all, his decision was made with an absolute confidence, and he was calmly prepared to risk everything upon it. When it was argued with him that, surely, General Shields would not suffer the critical hour to pass, without attempting again to co-operate with Fremont by a more serious and persistent attack, his only answer was, to wave his hand towards the commanding positions of his artillery, and say; "No sir! No! He cannot do it; I should tear him to pieces." And he did not do it! During all the remainder of the day's struggle, he remained passive; visited, doubtless, by misgivings not very comfortable, as to his own coming share in the attentions of the Confederate General. The latter now placed the third brigade, under Brigadier-General Taliaferro, in the village, to watch the fords of South River and the roads toward Lewiston, on the one hand, while on the other, he guarded the course of the Shenandoah above the village and opposite to General Ewell's left, by a few pickets. The first brigade of General Winder was sent down the river with a portion of the artillery, and posted upon the north side, to observe the discomfited enemy about Lewiston. The remainder of his division was disposed so as to be ready for the support of Ewell.

These dispositions had not been completed, when the firing to the north told that he was seriously engaged with Fremont. This General had moved out to the attack from Harrisonburg, (doubtless expecting the assistance of Shields upon the other side,) with the divisions of Blenker, Milroy and Schenck, making seven brigades of infantry, a brigade of cavalry, and a powerful train of artillery. This army was correctly estimated by General Ewell, at eighteen thousand men. His own division had now been recruited, by the addition of the six regiments of General Edward Johnson, known as the army of the northwest. Of these, the 12th Georgia, and the 25th and 31st Virginia, had been attached to the Brigade of Elzey; and the 52nd, 58th and 44th Virginia, lately under Colonel Scott, had been given to General George Stewart, and associated with the Maryland line. The position chosen for meeting Fremont was a continuous ridge, a little south of the point where the Keezletown road crosses that from Harrisonburg to Port Republic. This range of hills crosses the latter highway obliquely, in such manner that

General Ewell's left, occupying it, was much advanced beyond his right, and rested, at its extremity, very near the prolongation of the Keezletown road, toward the west. The hills are elevated, but occupied by arable fields. In front runs an insignificant rivulet, while the rear and flanks of the position are covered by woods of noble oaks, penetrable even by a column of artillery, in many places, but yet affording excellent cover for sharpshooters. On this ridge, then, General Ewell deliberately posted his troops to receive the shock, while Colonel Canty, with the 5th Alabama infantry, stubbornly contested the advance of the enemy along the road from Harrisonburg. In the centre, upon the best positions, he placed four picked batteries, those of Courtney, Lusk, Brockenborough, and Rains, with General Elzey's brigade in their rear, as a reserve force. On his right was the brigade of General Trimble, in advance of the centre, and on his left, that of General Stewart. The guns were placed on the reverse of the hills, a little behind the crest, where the cannoneers were protected from all missiles which came horizontally; and the lines of infantry lay in the valleys behind them, almost secure from danger.

About ten o'clock A. M., the Federal artillery was posted opposite to this position, and a spirited cannonade began, which continued for several hours. Indeed, the battle was chiefly one of artillery; for this arm was the only one which the Federalists employed with any perseverance or courage. After feeling the Confederate lines for a time with this fire of cannon, Fremont advanced a part of Blenker's German division, upon his left. Finding no enemies near the front of his left, save a few videttes, who were easily repulsed, he sent back glowing accounts of his success, in driving in the Confederate right wing. When he had thus swung around for nearly a mile, he was rudely undeceived. The veteran General Trimble, held his excellent brigade well in hand, behind the crest of a forest ridge, which, in front descended by a gentle declivity, to the margin of a wide meadow, and was there bounded by heavy fence of timber. He commanded the troops to reserve their fire until the enemy appeared above the hill, within point-blank range, when he poured a deadly discharge into their ranks. The Germans recoiled in disorder, and Trimble, seizing the moment, charged them with the bayonet, and drove them down the slope and across the meadow. It was then, especially that the foe paid the penalty of his assault. The Confederates pausing at the fence, and firing from it in security, and with deliberate aim, continued their murderous discharges, until the enemy had crossed the open ground, and taken refuge in the opposite wood. The green vale was strewn with hundreds of the dead and wounded; and the remainder left the field, to be rallied no more that day. The Federals now attempted to arrest Trimble's career, by posting a battery a half mile in front of his extreme right. But having received the 25th and 13th Virginia regiments, of Elzey's brigade, as reinforcements, he at once advanced with the purpose of capturing it. After several spirited skirmishes with its infantry supports, he forced his way to the ground, and found it deserted. General Trimble had now advanced more than a mile from his original position, while the Federal advance had fallen back to the ground occupied by them before the beginning of the action.

The enemy then developed a strong movement toward General Ewell's left, for which the Keezletown road, proceeding westward from Cross Keys, provided such facilities. This advantage, with the superior numbers of the opposing army, manifestly suggested the fear of such a movement, and nothing but the most impotent generalship on their part, could account for the fact that they allowed the day to close, disastrously for

them, without making it. General Ewell's left being neces
sarily thrown strongly forward, would have been enfiladed by
troops advancing from that quarter. Hence, he wisely guarded
that wing, and employed the most of his reinforcements to
strengthen it. A little after mid-day, when the battle was at its
height, General Jackson rode to the field, from his post near
Port Republic, and calmly examined the progress of the struggle.
Returning, he sent back to Ewell the Louisiana brigade of
Taylor, which had been moved to his support during the alarm
at the bridge, and also detached the second brigade of his
division, under Colonel Patton. The remainder of General
Elzey's brigade was then moved to the left, leaving their post in
the rear of the centre to these troops. Thus prepared, General
Ewell awaited for a long time the expected onset upon his
flank. It resulted in nothing more than a feeble demonstration,
which was easily repulsed by two or three regiments of Elzey.
Seeing this, Ewell advanced his own line just before night-fall,
drove in the enemy's skirmishers, and assumed a new position
on ground which they had held during the battle. Thus the
day closed, and his troops lay upon their arms, upon the
vantage-ground they had won, ready to resume the strife, and
hoping to rout Fremont at dawn on the morrow.

In this combat of Cross Keys, Ewell had about six thousand
men in his line of battle, and only three thousand five hundred
actually engaged. Yet Fremont reported to his government
that he was compelled to yield to superior force, and found
himself outnumbered at every point where he attempted a
movement. The veteran Ewell remarked, that he felt all day
as though he were again fighting the feeble, semi-civilized armies
of Mexico. The loss with which the Confederates achieved this
success, was surprisingly small, being only forty-two (42) killed,
and two hundred and thirty-one wounded. The chief loss of

the enemy was probably in front of Trimble, where it amounted to many hundreds.

General Jackson, regarding Fremont as only repulsed, and not routed, still adhered to his purpose to risk his first decisive blow against Shields, for the reasons which have been explained; and he deemed the present the proper hour to strike it, while the former was reeling and confused from his rude rebuff, and the latter was standing irresolute in an exposed attitude. He therefore summoned General Ewell, after he had completed his dispositions for the night, to his quarters; and instructed him to send the trains over to the troops, for the purpose of issuing food to them; to have them again withdrawn to the south side of the Shenandoah, and at break of day to march to Port Republic, leaving a strong rear-guard to amuse and retard the enemy. Then, awaiting the rising of the moon, which occurred about midnight, he collected his pioneers; and caused them, under his own eye, to construct a foot-bridge across the fords of the South River, by which he designed to pass his infantry down toward Lewiston. This structure was hastily made by placing wagons, without their bodies, longitudinally across the stream. The axles formed the cross-beams for the support of the floor; and the latter was composed of long boards, borrowed from a neighboring saw-mill, laid loosely from one to another. This bridge, on the morrow, furnished an instance of the truth, that very great events may be determined by very trivial ones. It was intended that the flooring should occupy the whole breadth between the wheels of the wagons, giving passage to several men abreast. But by an oversight, just at the deepest and angriest part of the stream, the hinder axle of a large wagon was placed next the foremost axle of the next. The inequality in the height, with the increasing depth of the current, made a space of nearly two feet, which, when the flooring was placed in order, presented a step, or sudden descent, of that amount; and all the boards of the higher stage proved to be unsupported at their ends, and elastic, but one. As the men began to pass over in column, several were thrown into the water by this treacherous and yielding platform, until, at length, growing skittish of it, they refused to trust themselves to any except the one solid plank; and thus the column was converted, at this point, into a single file.

The actual achievements of General Jackson at Port Republic were as brilliant as anything in the history of war. But his secret design embraced still more. It has already been explained that he did not arrest the pursuit of Fremont by at once burning the bridge across the Shenandoah, because he was unwilling to deprive himself of the ability to take the aggressive against that General. He now formed the bold purpose to concentrate his army, and fight both Shields and him, successively, the same day. Hence his eagerness to begin the attack on the former at an early hour. Stronger evidence of this startling design will be given. During the night he held an interview with Colonel Patton, commanding the 2nd brigade, which he then proposed to employ as a rear-guard to cover the withdrawal of General Ewell's forces from the front of Fremont. This officer found him, at two o'clock in the morning of the 9th, actively engaged in making his dispositions for battle. He immediately proceeded to give him particular instructions as to the management of his men in covering the rear, saying: "I wish you to throw out all your men, if necessary, as skirmishers, and to make a great show, so as to cause the enemy to think the whole army are behind you. Hold your position as well as you can; then fall back, when obliged; take a new position; hold it in the same way; and *I will be back to join you in the morning.*" Colonel Patton reminded him that his brigade was small, and that the country between Cross Keys and the Shenandoah offered few advantages for protracting such manœuvres. He therefore desired to know for how long a time he would be expected to hold the army of Fremont in check. He replied: "By the blessing of Providence, I hope to be back by ten o'clock."

Here then, we have revealed his whole purpose: He allotted five hours to crushing the army of Shields, and expected the same day to recross the Shenandoah and assail Fremont, or at least re-occupy his strong position upon the north bank, and again defy his attack. The Stonewall Brigade was accordingly ordered to begin the movement at the dawn of day; and by five o'clock it had crossed the South River, and was ready to advance against Shields. The Louisiana brigade of General Taylor came next, and as soon as they had passed the foot-bridge, the General eagerly moved with them to the attack, directing the trains to be passed toward Brown's Gap in the mountain, and the remainder of the troops to be hurried across as rapidly as they arrived, and sent to his support. But now the defect which has been described in the footway disclosed itself; proposals to arrest the passage of the troops long enough to remedy it effectually, or else to disuse the bridge, and force the men through the water, were all neglected by the commanders of brigades; and while six or eight thousand men were passed over in single file, ten o'clock arrived and passed by. The consequence was, that the first attack made upon the Federalists, being met with a stubborn resistance, and unsustained by adequate numbers, was repulsed with loss, and the battle was protracted far beyond the hour which permitted a second engagement that day on different ground. Thus three ill-adjusted boards cost the Confederates a hard-fought and bloody battle, and delivered Fremont from a second defeat far more disastrous than that of the previous day.

When General Jackson led the brigades of Winder and

Taylor against the Federalists, he found their main army posted advantageously at Lewiston. The level tract which intervenes between the Shenandoah and the forest-zone which girdles the mountain's base, has been described. The whole space was here occupied with smooth fields of waving clover and wheat, divided by the zigzag wooden fences of the country. Near the edge of the forest stood the ample *villa* of General Lewis, surrounded by substantial barns and stables, and orchards; while a lane, enclosed by a double fence, led thence direct to a mill and dwelling upon the margin of the stream. This lane marked the basis of the enemy's line of defence. His right was supported upon the river, and his left upon the impenetrable wood, while his centre was defended by the extensive enclosures and buildings of Lewiston. Upon a hillock just at the edge of the thickets were planted six field-pieces, which commanded the road from Port Republic, and all the fields adjacent to it.

General Jackson's plan of battle was now promptly formed. He placed the Stonewall Brigade, commanded by Brigadier-General Winder, in front, supported on its right by one of the regiments of Brigadier-General Taylor, and on its left by the 52nd and 31st Virginia regiments. The battery of Poague was posted in its front, while that of Carpenter was ordered to make its way through the tangled forest upon the right and find some commanding position, whence they could silence the enemy's guns above Lewiston. The brigade of General Taylor was also sent to the right, by a detour through the woods, to capture those guns, and then to turn the position of the Federalists. But the almost impenetrable thickets rendered their progress slow, and by a slight mistake of their direction in these pathless coverts, they approached the left front, rather than the flank of the dangerous battery. Meantime the Stonewall Brigade, with its supports, had advanced across the level fields, without any shelter from the animated fire of artillery and rifles, from the orchards and fences about Lewiston, and after a stubborn contest with overpowering numbers, was compelled to retire, leaving one six-pounder in the enemy's possession. As the Louisiana troops emerged from the woods on the hill-sides above, they saw with admiration the Virginians sustaining the unequal combat with heroic courage, until they were at length forced back, their ammunition exhausted, by sheer weight of numbers. The Federalists now advanced from their cover, with loud and taunting cheers, pierced the centre of Jackson's feeble line, and threatened to throw back the fugitives against the river which was upon their left, and thus to cut them off from retreat. But the regiments of Taylor, nothing daunted, charged the Federal battery, and driving the supports away, seized the six guns, which they held for a short time. General Ewell, who had now passed the whole of his division across the South River, was also hurrying to the front. He had just placed the 44th and 58th Virginia regiments, as a reserve, on the right of the road-way, and fronting towards it, under cover of the wood. Seeing Winder forced back, and two brigades of the enemy impetuously advancing through the Confederate centre, he now most opportunely launched the two regiments against their flank, and poured in a galling fire. The Federalists wheeled and confronted them, and, after a furious conflict, forced them back also with heavy loss. But a saving diversion had been made. The attack of Taylor upon their left had silenced their artillery for the time, and placed him far in rear of their advancing lines. The indefatigable Winder rallied his scattered infantry, and sought new positions for the remaining guns of Poague, and for the battery of Carpenter, who had now returned from his ineffectual struggle with the thickets; and the batteries of Chew, Brockenborough, Courtenay and Rains contributed, to reinstate his battle, with such pieces as had not been crippled in the contest of the previous day. Thus the inso-lent foe was steadily borne back toward his original position at Lewiston, and the buildings, orchards and fences, which he occu-pied there, were scourged by a pitiless storm of cannon-shot.

But it is time to return to General Taylor, who was left in pos-session of the Federal battery of six guns, upon the right. He was now, in turn, driven from them, by a brigade which made a detour through the thicket, and fell upon his right flank. At this critical juncture, General Ewell brought up the 44th and 58th Virginia regiments to his support, which· had been rallied after their bloody contest on the centre, and advanced under Colonel Scott, with a steadiness unexampled in volunteer troops, after losses so severe as theirs. By their assistance, and that of the 2nd Virginia regiment from the Stonewall Brigade, Taylor's attack was renewed. Twice more was the contested battery lost and won. The Confederates, driven off for a time by the enfilading fire of the enemy in the woods above them, and the murderous volleys of canister in front, rushed again and again to the charge; and after the third capture, the prize remained in their possession, while the Federalists sullenly retired. The dead of both armies were intermingled around the guns, while nearly all the horses belonging to them, lay slaughtered behind them.

Meantime, General Jackson perceived that the struggle had become too protracted and serious to permit another collision with Fremont that day. The brigade of General Trimble, with two regiments from that of Colonel Patton, were slowly retiring before him from Cross Keys toward the river. At 10 o'clock A. M., a messenger was despatched to them by the General, with orders to hasten their march to his assistance, and to burn the bridge behind them. The brigade of General Taliaferro, which had been left to occupy the village, was also hurried to the front, and arriving with great celerity, gave the parting volley to the retreating foe. The cavalry of Ashby was now launched after them, and their flight became a rout. Nearly half of an Ohio regiment were separated from their comrades by General Taliaferro, and surrendered in a body; and the pursuit was continued eight miles farther by the cavalry, who gathered, as spoils of war, small arms and vehicles, with many prisoners.

In the battle of Port Republic, the Federalists had eight thousand men engaged, and the Confederates three small brigades of infantry, with three regiments of cavalry, and a superior artillery. The enemy fought with a steadiness and courage unwonted, and inflicted upon the troops of General Jackson, a serious loss of ninety-one officers and men killed, and six hundred and eighty-six wounded. They owed their escape from ruin, only to the narrow road by which they retreated, and the impenetrable wilderness by which it was bordered; which made the manœuvres of cavalry impossible, and enabled a small rear-guard to cover their flight successfully. It was said that General Shields was fifteen miles in the rear with his reserves, when the battle occurred, and that the forces engaged were commanded by Brigadier-General Tyler.

As the evening approached, General Jackson recalled his jaded men from the pursuit, and led them by a side way, from Lewiston, towards the mouth of Brown's Gap, in the Blue Ridge. As they passed the field of battle on their return, they saw the hills opposite to Port Republic, black with the troops of Fremont, who had arrived in time to be impotent spectators of the flight of their friends. That commander now vented his disappointed malice in an act of inhumanity, for which he will be execrated until his name sinks into its merited oblivion. The tall wheat and the tangled thickets were full of the dead and of

54

mangled wretches, difficult to be discovered, and scattered over a length of three miles. A dreary and chilling rain was commencing. The Confederates were busy searching out and relieving the sufferers, and collecting the dead for a decent burial. Many wounded men had been carried into a farm-house near the river, and its surrounding buildings, and the yellow flag, the sacred badge of suffering, was conspicuously displayed from its roof, while the surgeons and chaplains were busily plying their humane labors. Suddenly Fremont advanced his artillery and riflemen, to the heights from which General Jackson had cannonaded the troops of Shields the previous day, and swept the whole field, and the hospital, with a storm of shot. The ambulances, with their merciful attendants, were driven away, and the wounded fled precipitately from their cots. The design of this outrage was obvious; it was supposed that the humanity of General Jackson, would prompt him to demand by flag of truce, an unmolested opportunity to tend the wounded; and on that request, the Federal General designed to found a pretext for claiming, in his despatches, the command of the field and the victory; which he knew belonged to Jackson. But the latter was as clear-sighted, and as determined, as he was humane. No flag of truce, no request was sent. Thanks to the affectionate zeal of the soldiers, all the Confederate dead and wounded had been already removed; and they were just proceeding to extend the offices of humanity to their enemies, when this treacherous interruption occurred. So that the only result of Fremont's savage generalship was, that his own suffering comrades lay under the drenching rain, until he retired to Harrisonburg. By that time, many had died miserably of hemorrhage, exhaustion and hunger, whom their generous enemies would have rescued; and not a few of their dead, with some, perchance, of the mangled living, were partially devoured by swine before their burial!

It was as General Jackson was returning on this day from the pursuit of the routed Federalists, that he first saw their diabolical explosive rifle-balls. A soldier presented him several which he had found in the dust of the road, unexploded. On examination they were found to be composed of two pieces of lead, enclosing a cavity between them, and cemented together by pressure. The hollow space was filled with fulminating powder, which was intended to explode by percussion, upon the impact of the ball against the bone of the penetrated body. Thus the fragments of lead would be driven in various and erratic directions through the mangled flesh, baffling the surgeon's probe, and converting the wound into a mortal one.

While Jackson sought a season of secure repose for his over-tasked men within the mountain cove of Brown's Gap, Fremont made pretence of bridging the Shenandoah River in order to assail him again. The Confederate pickets reported that on the evening of the 9th he was bringing timber to the bank, and on the morning of the 10th he was using it for some structure in the water. But soon after, he seemed to think better of his dangerous position, and disappeared from the neighborhood. Doubtless, he had now learned the true condition of General Shields's army. The Confederate cavalry, under Colonel Munford, crossing the river above Port Republic, pursued to Harrisonburg, which they entered June 12th, Fremont having retired precipitately down the Valley, leaving his hospitals, and many arms and carriages, to capture. Four hundred and fifty prisoners were taken upon the field; and the sick and wounded found in the hospitals swelled the number to nine hundred. One thousand small arms, and nine beautiful field-pieces, with all their apparatus, fell to the victors as prize of war. On the 9th of June, the loss of the Federalists in killed and wounded did not much differ from that of the Confederates. On the 8th the disproportion was enormous. In front of General Trimble's brigade alone, the dead were two hundred and ninety. When the most moderate addition is made for the loss inflicted by the terrific cannonade of the centre, and the spirited skirmishing on the left of General Ewell's line, the whole number of Federal killed and wounded cannot be placed at less than two thousand. And to this agreed the testimony of the prisoners and of the citizens.

The heavy loss of the Confederates on the 9th was due to the superior position occupied by the Federalists, to the fact that General Shields's brigades fought better than Fremont's, and to the detention of General Jackson's column at the imperfect footbridge across South River, which caused his first attack to fail through deficient numbers. His zeal and eagerness led him to forget that no subordinates could be expected to urge their commands to the field with his fiery energy; and, in this sense, he required them to undertake too much. If there had been no bridge, and the infantry had been required to ford the summer stream in dense columns, so as to reach the field more simultaneously, the victory would have been more promptly and cheaply won. Again, if the Louisiana brigade of General Taylor had been more accurately directed by its guides, through the tangled wilderness to the right of the battle-field, so as to strike the rear of the enemy's left, as was the purpose of their commander, instead of their left front; and if they had arrived at the moment of the front attack by Brigadier-General Winder, in place of appearing after he was repulsed, the army of Shields would have been destroyed. For, just below Lewiston, the champaign suddenly terminates, the hill-side thickets approach the river-bank, and to the mouth of the single narrow woodland track, by which the Federalists must have all retreated, General Taylor would have been nearer than they; while he would have commanded their approach to it from a superior and a sheltered position. The discomfited enemy, thus arrested on the one side, and driven on the other, by the whole weight of the Confederate army, into the neck of such a funnel, would have been crushed to pieces. Such was Jackson's masterly plan: natural obstacles, and the mistakes of some subordinates, caused the performance to fall short of it.

But enough was accomplished to cover General Jackson with a blaze of glory. Fifteen days before, he was a hundred miles from his base, with a little army of fifteen thousand men, while forty thousand enemies were on his immediate front and flanks. Now, he was disembarrassed of them all, with a loss of not more than one thousand five hundred men; while two armies, whose aggregate was double his own, were flying from him, quivering with disaster, leaving his victorious hands full of trophies. From this hour, doubt and detraction were silenced; he stood forth acknowledged by all as a General of transcendent abilities. His mere name, henceforth, brought assurance of triumph to his friends, and panic to his enemies. Within forty days he had marched four hundred miles, fought four pitched battles, — defeating four separate armies, — with numerous combats and skirmishes, sent to the rear three thousand five hundred prisoners, killed and wounded a still larger number of the enemy, and defeated or neutralized forces three times as numerous as his own, upon his proper theatre of war, besides the *corps* of M'Dowell, which was rendered inactive at Fredericksburg by the fear of his prowess.

On the 12th of June, before the dawn, the army were marched out from their confined and uneasy *bivouac* in Brown's Gap, to the plains of Mount Meridian, upon the middle fork of the Shenandoah, a few miles above Port Republic. The two days' rain was now succeeded by the brilliant suns and genial warmth of June. The troops were encamped in a range of woodland

groves between the two rivers, surrounded with the verdure of
early summer, and the luxuriant wheat fields whitening for the
harvest.   In this smiling paradise they solaced themselves
five days for their fatigues, the men reposing under the shade,
or bathing in the sparkling waters of the Shenandoah, and the
horses feeding in the abundant pastures.   The Saturday following the battle, was proclaimed by General Jackson as a day of
thanksgiving and prayer, and all the troops were called to join
with their General and their chaplains, in praises to God for his
deliverances.   The next day, a general communion was observed
in the 3rd Virginia brigade, at which the Lord's supper was dispensed, in the wood, to a great company of Christian soldiers
from all the army.   At this solemnity the General was present,
as a worshipper, and modestly participated with his men in the
sacred feast.   The quiet diffidence with which he took the least
obtrusive place, and received the sacred emblems from the hands
of a regimental chaplain, was in beautiful contrast with the
majesty and authority of his bearing in the crisis of battle.

The following brief extract from his correspondence with his
wife exhibits the same humble and devout temper, which ever
characterized him ·

"NEAR WIER'S CAVE, June 14th.

"Our God has thrown his shield over me in the various apparent dangers to which I have been exposed.   This evening
we have religious services in the army, for the purpose of rendering thanks to the Most High for the victories with which he
has crowned our arms; and my earnest prayer is that our ever
kind Heavenly Father will continue to crown our arms with
success, until our independence shall, through his divine blessing,
be established."

CHAPTER XIV.

THE RICHMOND CAMPAIGN.

AFTER the victory of Winchester in May, General Jackson had requested his friend Hon. A. R. Boteler to represent to the authorities near Richmond, his desire for reinforcements, that he might carry the war toward the Federal Capital. " Tell them," said he, " that I have now fifteen thousand men. I should have forty thousand; and with them I would invade the North." When this message was delivered to General Lee, the Commander-in-Chief, he replied: " But he must help me to drive these people away from Richmond first." Thus it appears that his sagacious mind had already formed the design of concentrating the army of Jackson with his own, in order to take the aggressive against M'Clellan. Had the battle of Port Republic been a disaster, this would have been impossible, and Richmond would probably have fallen into the hands of the assailants. As soon as the news of Jackson's victory there was received in Richmond, it was judged that the proper time had arrived for the great movement. To make it successful, it was necessary to mask Jackson's removal from the Valley, lest his enemies, lately defeated, should assail some vital point, and to continue the diversion of General M'Dowell's army from a union with M'Clellan. To further these objects, a strong detachment, consisting of the brigades of Whiting, Hood, and Lawton, which made an aggregate of seven thousand men, was sent to Jackson by the way of Lynchburg and Charlottesville. It was so arranged that the captives from Port Republic on their way to the military prisons of Richmond, should meet all these troops upon the road; and on their arrival there, General Lee dismissed the officers among them upon parole. He knew that they would hasten to Washington and report what they had seen. The report of General M'Clellan reveals the success of the expedient. He states that the answer made by Mr. Lincoln to the next of his repeated requests for the co-operation of General M'Dowell, was the following: that he could not now need that aid, inasmuch as the army of General Lee was weakened by fifteen thousand men just sent to General Jackson, and the dangers of Washington City were to the same extent increased: (the Federal officers, with their customary exaggeration, had doubled the number of Jackson's reinforcements.)

He, meanwhile, was deceiving the enemy in the Valley with equal adroitness. As soon as Colonel Munford established his cavalry at Harrisonburg, he sent him orders to arrest all transit up and down the Valley, and even to limit the communication between his own troops on the outposts and the Confederate infantry, to the narrowest possible bounds; so that no intelligence might steal through to the enemy. He also instructed him to press his outposts with energy against those of the enemy, and to drive him as far below as practicable. He desired thus to produce in Fremont the persuasion, that the whole Confederate army was about to advance upon him, to improve its victory in that direction. Last, he requested Colonel Munford to do all in his power, by other means, to foster this belief. Opportunity was already provided for carrying out this order. As the advance of the Confederates pressed toward Fremont, they met, twelve miles north of Harrisonburg, a Federal flag of truce, in the hands of a major, followed by a long train of surgeons and ambulances bringing a demand for the release of their wounded men.   Colonel Munford had required the train to pause at his outposts, and had brought the major, with one surgeon, to his quarters at Harrisonburg; where he entertained them with military courtesy, until their request was answered by the commanding General. He found them full of boasts and arrogance: they said that the answer to their flag was exceedingly unimportant, because Fremont and Shields were about to effect a junction, when they would recover, by force, all they had lost, and teach Jackson a lesson which would cure his audacity.   When Colonel Munford received the instructions we have mentioned, he called for Mr. William Gilmer of Albemarle, a gentleman of infinite spirit and humor, who was serving with his young kinsman as an *amateur* trooper, and gave him his cue.   He silently left the village, but presently returned, in very different fashion, as an orderly, with despatches from General Jackson and from Staunton.   With an ostentatious clanking of spurs and sabre, he ascended to Colonel Munford's quarters, and knocked in a hurried manner.   "Come in," said the gallant Colonel.   "And what answer do you bring, orderly, from General Jackson?"   At this word, the Yankee officers in the adjoining chamber were heard stealthily approaching the partition, for the purpose of eavesdropping.   "Why," said Gilmer, "the General laughed at the demand for the surrender of the wounded prisoners.   He has no notion of it."   "Do you bring any good news?" asked the Colonel.   "Glorious news," he answered.   "The road from Staunton this way is chock-full of soldiers, cannon, and wagons, come to reinforce Jackson in his march down the Valley.   There is General Whiting, General Hood, General Lawton, and General I-don't-know-who.   I never saw so many soldiers and cannon together in my life.   People say there are thirty thousand of them."   After a few such questions and answers, framed for the edification of the eavesdroppers,

55

Colonel Munford dismissed him, and he descended, to fill the hotel and the town with his glorious news. The whole place was speedily in a blaze of joy and excitement. Citizens came to offer supplies for the approaching hosts; and bullocks, flour, and bacon were about to be collected for them in delighted haste. After leaving his guests to digest their contraband news, for several hours, Colonel Munford at length sent for them, and told them that he had a reply from his General, respectfully declining to accede to their request; so that nothing now remained but to send them back to their friends, in the same honor and safety in which they had come. They departed much humbler, and as they imagined, much wiser men. He pushed his advance soon after them, to New Market; and upon their arrival at the quarters of General Fremont near Mount Jackson, the Federal army precipitately broke up its camp, and retreated to Strasbourg; where they began busily to fortify themselves. The Confederate cavalry then drew a *cordon* of pickets across the country just above them, so strict that the befooled enemy never learned General Jackson's whole army was not on his front, until he discovered it by the disasters of M'Clellan.

The larger part of the reinforcements sent from Richmond had halted near Staunton. On the evening of June 17th, General Jackson began to move his troops from Mount Meridian, and leaving orders with his staff to send away the remainder the next morning, he went to the town to set the new brigades in motion. No man in the whole army knew whither it was going. General Ewell, the second in command, was only instructed to move towards Charlottesville, and the rest were only ordered to follow him. Two marches brought them to the neighborhood of the latter town, where General Jackson rejoined them, and confiding to his chief of staff the direction of his movement, with strict injunctions of secrecy, departed by railroad, to hold a preliminary conference with General Lee in Richmond. He directed that an advanced guard of cavalry should precede the army continually, and prohibit all persons, whether citizens or soldiers, from passing before them toward Richmond. A rear-guard was to prevent all straggling backward, and when they encamped, all lateral roads were to be guarded, to prevent communication between the army and country.

But on reaching Gordonsville, whither the brigade of General Lawton had gone by railroad, he was arrested for a day by a groundless rumor of the approach of the enemy from the Rappahannock. Then, resuming the direction of the troops, he proceeded to a station called Frederickshall, fifty miles from Richmond, where he arrested his march to give the army its Sabbath rest. No General knew better than he, how to employ the transportation of a railroad in combination with the marching of an army. While the burthen trains forwarded his stores he caused the passenger trains to proceed to the rear of his line of march, which was chosen near the railroad, and take up the hindmost of his brigades. These were forwarded, in a couple of hours, a whole day's march; when they were set down, and the trains returned again, to take up the hindmost, and give them a like assistance.

After a quiet Sabbath, the General rose at 1 o'clock A.M., and mounting a horse, rode express with a single courier, to Richmond. A few miles from his quarters, a pleasing evidence of the fidelity of his pickets was presented to him. He endeavored to pass this outpost, first as an officer on military business, and then as an officer bearing important intelligence for General Lee. But the guard was inexorable, and declared that his instructions from General Jackson especially prohibited him to pass army men, as well as citizens. The utmost he would concede was, that the captain commanding the picket should be called, and the appeal made to him. When he came, he recognized his General; who, praising the soldier for his obedience to instructions, bound them both to secrecy touching his journey. Having held the desired interview with the Commander-in-Chief, he returned the next day to the line of march pursued by his troops, and led them, the evening of June 25th to the village of Ashland, twelve miles north of Richmond.

To understand the subsequent narrative, the reader must have a brief explanation of the position of the two great armies. The Chickahominy River, famous for the adventures and capture of Captain John Smith, in the childhood of Virginia, is a sluggish stream of fifteen yards width, which flows parallel to the James, and only five miles north of Richmond. It is bordered by extensive meadows, which degenerate in many places into marshes, and its bed is miry and treacherous; so that it constitutes an obstacle to the passage of armies far more formidable than its insignificant width would indicate. During this year, especially, the excessive rains and repeated freshets had converted its little current into an important stream, its marshes into lakes, and its rich, level cornfields into bogs. But at the distance of half a mile from the channel, the country on each side rises into undulating hills, with farms interspersed irregularly among the tracts of forest, and the coppices of young pine. General M'Clellan, taking his departure from the White House, on the Pamunkey, and using the York River Railroad as his line of supply, had pressed his vast army to the east and north of Richmond. Its two wings, placed like the open jaws of some mighty dragon, the one on the north and the other on the south side of the Chickahominy, almost embraced the northeast angle of the city. To connect them with each other, he had constructed three or four elaborate bridges across the stream, with causeways leading to them, and along the length of the valley,

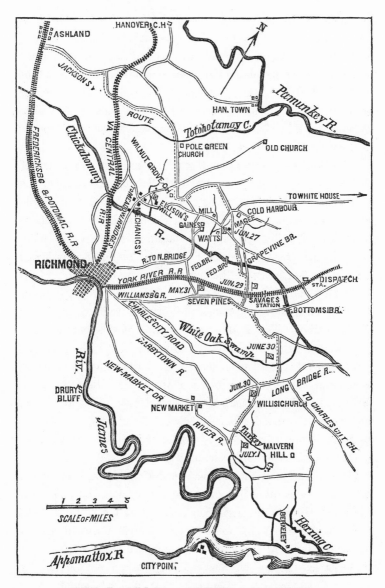

THE BATTLES AROUND RICHMOND.

by which he hoped to defy both mire and floods. On both sides, his front was so fortified with earthworks, abattis, and heavy artillery, that they could not be assailed, save with cruel loss. These works, on his left, were extended to the front of the battle-field of Seven Pines, and on his right to the hamlet of Mechanicsville; which, seated upon the north bank of the Chickahominy, six miles from Richmond, commanded the road thence to Hanover Court House.

The Confederate army, now under the immediate order of General Robert E. Lee, confronted M'Clellan, and guarded the course of the Chickahominy, as high as the half sink farm, northwest of Richmond, where Brigadier-General Branch, of Major General A. P. Hill's division, was stationed within a few miles of Ashland. General Lee, after the battle of Seven Pines, had fortified his front, east of Richmond, in order that a part of his forces might hold the defensive against the Federal army; while, with the remainder, he attempted to turn its flank north of the Chickahominy. To test the practicability of this grand enterprise, and to explore a way for General Jackson's proposed junction, he had caused General J. E. B. Stuart, of the cavalry to make his famous *reconnoissance* of the 12th of June; in which that daring officer had marched a detachment of cavalry from north to south around M'Clellan's whole rear, and had discovered that it was unprotected by works, or by proper disposition of forces, against the proposed attack.

The conception of the Commander-in-Chief is thus developed in his own general order of battle, communicated to General Jackson. He was to march from Ashland on the 25th of June, to encamp for the night, west of the Central Railroad, and to advance at three A. M., on the 26th, and turn the enemy's works at Mechanicsville, and on Beaver-Dam Creek, a stream flowing into the Chickahominy a mile in the rear of that hamlet, where he had a powerful reserve entrenched. Major-General A. P. Hill was to cross the Chickahominy, to the north side, at the meadow bridges, above Mechanicsville, and associating to himself Branch's brigade, which was to advance so soon as the march of General Jackson opened a way for it, was to sweep down against the enemy's right. As soon as the Mechanicsville bridge should be uncovered, Longstreet and D. H. Hill were to cross, the latter to proceed to the support of Jackson, and the former to that of A. P. Hill. The four commands were directed to sweep down the north side of the Chickahominy, toward the York River Railroad; Jackson on the left and in advance, Longstreet nearest the river and in the rear. Huger and Magruder were to hold their positions south of the Chickahominy, against any assault of the enemy, to observe him closely, and to follow him should he retreat. General Stuart, with his cavalry, was thrown out on Jackson's left, to guard his flank, and give notice of the enemy's movements.

The evening of June 25th found the army of General Jackson a few miles short of their appointed goal—at Ashland—instead of the line of the Central Railroad. The difficulties of handling so large a force with inexperienced subordinates, concurred with the loss of the bridges on his direct line of march, (lately burned by order of the Federalists,) to delay him thus much. No commander ever sympathized more fully with the spirit of Napoleon's answer, when he replied to one of his marshals, in view of a similar combination of his armies for a great battle: "Ask me for anything but time." Jackson's ardent soul, on fire with the grandeur of the operations before him, and with delight in their boldness and wisdom, and chafing at the delays of blundering and incompetent agents, forbade rest or sleep for him on this important night. He deliberately devoted the whole of it to the review of his preparations, and to prayer. Rations were to be distributed and prepared by the men for three days. The lead ers of the different divisions, encamped around Ashland, were to be instructed in their routes, so that the several commands might take their places in the column without confusion or delay. After all his staff were dismissed for a short repose, he still paced his chamber in anxious thought, or devoted to wrestling with God the intervals between the visits of his officers. In the small hours of the night, two of the commanders of divisions came to suggest that he should move the army by two columns, on parallel roads, instead of by one. He listened respectfully, but requested that they would await his decision until morning. When they left him, the one said to the other: " Do you know why General Jackson would not decide upon our suggestion at once? It was because he has to pray over it, before he makes up his mind." A moment after, the second returned to Jackson's quarters to fetch his sword, which he had forgotten; and, as he entered, found him upon his knees! praying, doubtless, for Omniscient guidance in all his responsible duties, for his men, and for his country.

Notwithstanding his efforts, the army did not move until after sunrise; when, all being ready, it advanced in gallant array toward the southeast, crossed the Central Railroad, and, meeting here and there the vigilant cavalry of General Stuart, which came in from the left at the cross-roads, approached the Pole-Green church, a century before sanctified by the eloquence of the Rev. Samuel Davies, at 4 o'clock in the afternoon. Jackson was now abreast of the enemy's right flank at Mechanicsville, and but a few miles north of it. Between him and the church was the Tottopottamoy, a little stream which still bears its Indian title. The pickets of M'Clellan occupied the opposite bank, and had destroyed the light wooden bridge, and obstructed the road beyond with prostrate trees. The Texan brigade of Hood, which was in front, deployed a few skirmishers, who speedily cleared the opposing bank with their unerring rifles; and the wood beyond was shelled by one of Whiting's batteries while the bridge was rapidly repaired. This initial cannonade was intended to subserve the additional purpose of a signal, by which the Confederates before Mechanicsville might be advertised of his presence.

For many hours' the brigades of A. P. Hill had been patiently awaiting the expected sound, before the enemy's works. They now pressed forward, and a furious cannonade opened on both sides. General Hill, supported by Ripley's brigade, of D. H. Hill's division, speedily carried the little village, with the field-works and camp of the enemy, while the latter retired a mile to the eastward, to their stronger lines upon Beaver-Dam Creek. Jackson's advance would in due time have turned this position, as it had Mechanicsville, and would thus have given to the two Hills an easy conquest; but the presence of the Commander-in-Chief and the President of the Confederate States upon the field, with their urgency that the place should be carried without delay, impelled them to the attack. The heroic troops pressed up to the stream, and held the nearer brink throughout the night, but could effect no lodgement within the hostile works; and thus, at nine o'clock, the cannonade died away, and the opposing forces lay down upon their arms, after a bloody and useless struggle. As General Jackson's forces passed the Pole-Green church, and went into camp a little below, at Hundley's Corner, the sound of the guns and the roar of the musketry told them that the gigantic struggle had begun.

Thus opened the seven days' tragedy before Richmond. The demeanor of its citizens during the evening of June 26th, gave an example of their courage, and their faith in their leaders and their cause. For many weeks, the Christians of the city had

given themselves to prayer; and they drew from heaven a sublime composure. The spectator passing through the streets saw
the people calmly engaged in their usual avocations, or else
wending their way to the churches, while the thunders of the
cannon shook the city. As the calm summer evening descended,
the family groups were seen sitting upon their door-steps, where
mothers told the children at their knees, how Lee and his heroes
were now driving away the invaders. The young people prome-
naded the heights north of the town, and watched the distant
shells bursting against the sky. At one church, a solemn cavalcade stood waiting; and if the observer had entered, saying to
himself: "This funeral reminds me that Death claims all seasons
for his own, and refuses to postpone his dread rites for any inferior horrors," he would have found a bridal before the altar.
The heart of old Rome was not more assured and steadfast,
when she sold at full price in her *Forum*, the fields on which the
victorious Carthaginian was encamped.

During the night, detachments of the enemy approached General Jackson's camps at Hundley's corner, but were checked by
Brockenborough's battery, and the 1st Maryland, 13th Virginia,
and 6th Louisiana regiments. At an early hour, the troops were
put in motion, and speedily crossed the higher streams of the
Beaver-Dam, thus turning the right of the enemy's position.
The way was now opened, by their retreat, for the advance
of General D. H. Hill, who crossing Jackson's line of march,
passed to his front and left. The evacuation of the lines of
Beaver-Dam also soon followed. At the dawn of day, the contest between the Federal artillery there, and that of General A.
P. Hill had been resumed; but perceiving the divisions of General Jackson approaching their rear, the enemy retreated precipitately down the Chickahominy towards Cold Harbor, pursued by Generals A. P. Hill and Longstreet, burning vast

quantities of army stores, and deserting many uninjured. As General Jackson approached Walnut Grove church, he met the Commander-in-Chief; and while he halted his column to receive his final instructions from him, the gallant division of A. P. Hill filed past, in as perfect array as though they had been unscathed of battle. General Lee presuming that the Federalists would continue to withdraw, if overpowered, toward the York River Railroad and the White House, directed General Jackson to proceed, with General D. H. Hill, to a point a few miles north of Cold Harbor, and thence to march to that place, and strike their line of retreat. Two roads led thither, the one direct, the other circuitous. The latter, which passed first eastward, and then southward, was the one which offered the desired route for General Jackson; for the former would have conducted him to ground in the rear of the retreating army, already occupied by General A. P. Hill. General Jackson had selected young men of the vicinage, found in a company of cavalry near him, for guides. When he asked them the road to Cold Harbor, his habitual reticence, in this instance too stringent, withheld all explanation of his strategic designs. They therefore naturally pointed him to the direct and larger road, as the route to Cold Harbor. After marching for a mile and a half, the booming of cannon in his front caught his ear, and he demanded sharply of the guide near him: "Where is that firing?" The reply was, that it was in the direction of Gaines's Mill. "Does this road lead there?" he asked. The guide told him that it led by Gaines's Mill to Cold Harbor. "But," exclaimed he, "I do not wish to go to Gaines's Mill. I wish to go to Cold Harbor, leaving that place to the right." "Then," said the guide, "the left-hand road was the one which should have been taken; and had you let me know what you desired, I could have directed you aright at first." Nothing now remained, but to reverse the column, and return to the proper track. It was manifest that an hour of precious time must be lost in doing this, while the accelerated firing told that the battle was thickening in the front, and every heart trembled with the anxious fear lest the irreparable hour should be lost by the delay. But Jackson bore the same calm and assured countenance, and when this fear was suggested to him, he replied: "No, let us trust that the providence of our God will so overrule it, that no mischief shall result." Nor was he mistaken in this confidence; for the time thus allowed to General D. H. Hill enabled him to reach the desired point of meeting north of Cold Harbor, just in front of Jackson, and brought them into precise conjunction. They then turned to the right and moved directly toward the supposed position of the enemy, with the division of Hill in front, followed by those of Ewell, Whiting, and Jackson in the order of their enumeration. After passing Cold Harbor, and arresting at that spot a few Federal carriages, they perceived the enemy about a half mile southward, drawn up in battle array, and fronting to the north. General Jackson, with a numerous suite, rode forward to observe their position; and at his suggestion a battery from Hill's division was posted opposite to them. But before they began to fire, several Federal batteries opened upon them a furious cannonade, by which the Generals were speedily driven to a distant part of the field, and the Confederate guns were silenced, after a gallant but unequal contest of half an hour.

It was now two o'clock in the afternoon. The firing west of Cold Harbor told that General A. P. Hill was fully engaged with the enemy there. In fact, he was fighting single-handed, the whole centre of the opposing host. For a time, General Jackson held his troops back in the margin of the woods looking toward the highway, and along the line of their march, in the hope that the enemy, retreating before Generals A. P. Hill and

Longstreet, would expose their flank to a crushing blow from him. But the firing on his right began evidently to recede, showing that Hill, instead of driving the savage game into his toils, was giving way before their overpowering numbers. He then determined to bring his whole *infantry into action. Assigning to General D. H. Hill the extreme left, he placed General Ewell's division next him, and sent orders to Generals Whiting and Lawton, and to the Brigadiers of his own original division, which brought up the rear, to form for battle along the road by which they were marching, and then moving in *echelon*, beginning on the left, to feel for the position of the enemy and engage him. The topography was unknown to Jackson and to his subordinates, the forests forbade a connected view of the country, and no time was left for *reconnoissances*. Nothing remained, therefore, but to move toward the firing, and engage the foe wherever he was found.

The expectations that the Federalists would continue their retreat, when hard pressed, toward the White House, was erroneous. Their commander proposed to himself another expedient: to concentrate his troops on the south of the Chickahominy, and relinquishing his connections with the York River, to open for himself communications with the River James below Richmond, now accessible to his fleets up to Drewry's Bluffs. Accordingly, his present purpose was to stand at bay upon the northern bank of the former stream, until he could withdraw his troops across it in safety. He chose, for this end, a strong position, covering two of his military bridges, and confronting with a convex array, the Confederates who threatened him from the north and west. His right, or eastern wing occupied an undulating *plateau*, protected in front by thickets of pine and the rude fences of the country, and presenting numerous commanding positions for artillery. In front of that wing a siuggish rivulet, speedily degenerated into a marsh, thickset with briers and brushwood, stretched away to the east, affording a seeming protection to that flank. An interval of a few hundred yards in front of his right was unprotected by any such obstruction; but the fields were here swept by a powerful artillery. And as his line passed westward, another rivulet commenced its course, and flowed in front of his whole centre and left wing, in an opposite direction to the first, until, merging itself into Powhite Creek, it passed into the Chicka-hominy above. His centre was enveloped in a dense forest, which, with the marshy stream in front, precluded the use of artil-lery by the assailants. His left was posted in a belt of woodland, which descended with a steep inclination from the plateau to a deep and narrow gully, excavated for itself by the rivulet. Three formidable lines of infantry held this hill-side, the first hidden in the natural ditch at its bottom, the second behind a strong barricade of timber a little above, and the third near the top. The brow of the eminence was crowned with numerous batteries, which screened by the narrow zone of trees, commanded every approach to the position. Last, a number of heavy, rifled cannon upon the heights south of the Chickahominy, protected the extreme left, and threatened to enfilade any troops advancing across the open country to the attack. These formidable disposi-tions were only disclosed to the Confederates by their actual onset, so that manœuvre was excluded, and the only resort was to stubborn courage and main force. And it was only on General Jackson's extreme left, that the Confederate artillery could find any position, from which the enemy could be reached effectively. The front upon which these two great armies were to contend was less than three miles in extent. Hence, as the brigades of Longstreet and A. P. Hill from the Confederate right, and of D. H. Hill and Jackson from the left, moved into the combat on con-vergent *radii*, they formed, in many places, an order of battle two

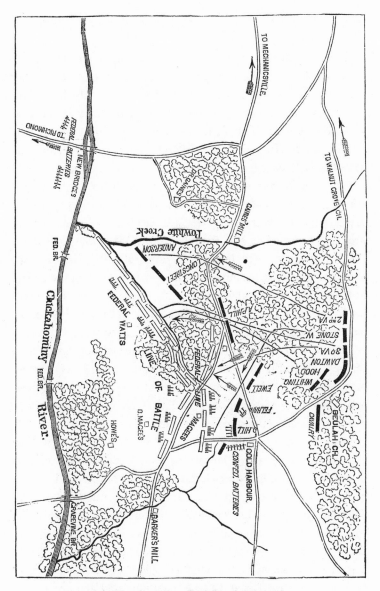

BATTLE OF CHICKAHOMINY.

or three lines deep; and those first engaged were supported by those which arrived later.

The road along which General Jackson drew up his line for battle, made with the enemy's front an angle of forty or fifty degrees.   Hence, the troops toward the right had the longer arc to traverse, in reaching the scene of combat, and all were required to incline toward their left, in order to confront the enemy. General D. H. Hill, on the Confederate left, moved first, and was soon furiously engaged.   For two or three hours he struggled with the enemy with wavering fortunes, unable to rout them, but winning some ground, which he stubbornly held against a terrible artillery and musketry fire.   General Ewell moved next, with one brigade upon the left, and two upon the right of the road which led from Gaines's Mill toward the Federal left.   Crossing the marsh, he ascended the opposing hill-side, and engaged the enemy in the forest.   Before their terrific fire, General Elzey, command-ing his left brigade, fell severely wounded, and Colonel Seymour, commanding the Louisiana brigade of Taylor, was slain.   Whole regiments were killed, wounded, or scattered, under this leaden tempest; but still their dauntless General rallied his fainting men, repaired his line, and held all his ground against the double and triple lines of the enemy; until just as his ammunition was exhausted, welcome succors arrived under General Lawton.

One cause of delay in the arrival of the remaining troops has already been seen, in the larger space which they were required to pass over in order to reach the enemy.   Another, and a more dangerous one, arose out of a fatal misconception of General Jackson's orders by his messenger.   Communicating to all the commanders in the rear of Ewell the plan for their advance, he had concluded by instructing them to await farther orders before engaging the enemy!   But another officer of the staff, compre-hending better the General's true intentions, and the urgency of the occasion, corrected the error, and at length moved the remaining brigades into action.   Their leaders could learn nothing of the country, to which they were all strangers; and their movements were partially concealed from each other by the numerous tracts of coppice and forest.   Hence, instead of advancing toward the enemy in parallel lines, they unconsciously crossed each other; and several of them, at last, went into action far aside from the points at which they were expected to strike. But the Providence of that God to whom their General ever looked, guided them aright to the places where their aid was most essential.

The Stonewall Brigade, under General Winder, was next the last in the line of march, and should therefore have formed almost the extreme right of General Jackson's battle.   Their General, so soon as he comprehended the error of the instructions which held him inactive, advanced with chivalrous zeal. But his neighbors on the left, with whom he should have connected his right, having already passed out of sight in the thickets, he had no other guide than the din of the battle.   Feeling his way rapidly toward this, he passed transversely from right to left, across the ground over which the *corps* had already swept, and found himself behind the struggling line of D. H. Hill. This indomitable soldier was just devising, with his two Briga diers, Garland and Anderson, upon his left, a daring movement, to break the stubborn resistance of the Federalists.   Garland proposed to swing around their extreme right with his brigade; and, taking them in reverse, to charge with the bayonet, while the rest of the division renewed their attack in front.   One formidable obstacle existed: a hostile battery at that extremity of the field threatened to enfilade his ranks while marching to the attack.   To obviate this danger, Hill determined to storm the battery with five regiments; but only one — that of Colonel

57

Iverson, of North Carolina — arrived at it. He was severely wounded; and, after ten minutes, his men were driven from it by overpowering numbers; but this interval, during which its guns were silenced, was decisive. For, meantime, Winder had advanced the famed Stonewall Brigade, in perfect order; had rallied to him all the shattered regiments of Elzey and Hill which he found lurking under cover, or waging a defensive struggle; and now swept with an imposing line and a thundering cheer across the whole *plateau* occupied by the enemy's right. Garland and Anderson dashed simultaneously upon their flank; the contested battery was in an instant captured a second time; and the whole wing of the Federal army, with their reinforcements, hurled back into the swamps of the Chickahominy. There they broke into a scattered rabble in the approaching darkness, and crouched behind the trees, or found their way across the stream to their friends. This brilliant movement, with simultaneous successes upon other parts of the field, decided the day. Nowhere were the panic and confusion of the beaten army more utter than here. The fields which were the scene of this terrific struggle composed the farms of two respectable citizens, named Maghee. The one of these farthest in the Federal rear was spectator of their rout. Regiments sent over by M'Clellan to support the wavering battle were seen to pause, even before they came under fire; to break, without firing a musket; and to throw away their arms, and fly to the swamp. As ordnance wagons and ambulances galloped toward the scene of action, they were arrested by the frantic fugitives, who snatched the animals from them, and, mounting two or three on each, fled toward the bridge, leaving ammunition and wounded comrades to their fate. One officer was seen, delirious with terror, with his hat in one hand, and his empty scabbard in the other, screaming as he ran: "Jackson is coming! Jackson is coming!"

Indeed, the baseness of the Northern soldiery was shown by the fact that, throughout this battle, it was usually the supporting regiments in the rear, unscathed as yet, which gave way first; while the resistance was sustained by the old United States regulars of Sykes and Porter in the front. In the volunteer regiments, the "will of the majority," which was usually a determination to retire at the critical moment, was sometimes expressed against the authority of the officers by a formal popular vote. To the entreaties of their commanders their answers were: "We 're tired out fighting;" "Got no more ammunition;" "Guess the rebels will be down to them bridges soon." And so they broke away, and the rout was propagated from the rear to the front.

The two other brigades of Jackson's old division, the 2nd and 3rd Virginia, under the lead of Colonels Cunningham and Fulkerson, also advanced with spirit as soon as they received correct orders. Having met messengers from the Commander-in-Chief, and General A. P. Hill, they obtained more correct guidance, and advanced to the Confederate right. The second brigade supported Brigadier-General R. H. Anderson, near General Longstreet's extreme right. Just as they arrived, the troops of Anderson were giving ground momentarily before the enemy. Colonel Cunningham proposed to take the front, and give him an opportunity to reform behind his lines; but the gallant Carolinian insisted upon completing his own work. The shout was raised; "Jackson's men are here," and his regiments answering with a cheer, rushed forward again, and swept all before them, leaving to the Virginians little more to do than to fire a parting volley. In like manner, the third brigade reinforced the line of A. P. Hill, near the centre, but only arrived in time to see the enemy give way before Whiting's division, which had come earlier to its help. As Colonel Fulkerson advanced to relieve these wearied and decimated troops of the labors of the pursuit, the retreating enemy fired a last volley, by which he was mortally wounded. In him General Jackson lost an able and courageous subordinate, who had proved himself equal to every task imposed upon him. Had he lived, the highest distinction must have crowned his merits; for his judgment, diligence and talent for command, were equal to his heroic courage.

Just before the three original brigades of Jackson, had marched the Georgia brigade of Lawton, nearly four thousand strong. The time had now come for them to fight their maiden battle. As they advanced towards the enemy's centre, they unconsciously crossed the line of march just before pursued by General Whiting, and passing under a severe fire from a battery upon the *plateau* near Maghee's they crossed the marsh, and entered the wood in rear of General Ewell, passing between two regiments which had retired from the contest after exhausting their ammunition. Here the brigade was thrown into line, and advanced firing, with imposing force. Their appearance was most timely; for the shattered remnant with which Ewell still stood at bay, were firing their last rounds of cartridges. As the grim veteran saw this magnificent line of thirty-five hundred bayonets sweeping through the woods, he waved his sword with enthusiasm and shouted; "Huzza for Georgia!" Lawton, receiving directions from him, pressed forward with a steady advance, drove the enemy's centre from the woods, into the open fields, nearer the river, and connecting with D. H. Hill and Winder on his left, assisted them in sweeping the Federalists, at nightfall, into the swamps.

But the most brilliant achievement of the day was reserved for the division of General Whiting, consisting of the Mississippi brigade of Colonel Law, and the Texan brigade of General Hood. In Jackson's initial order of battle, they filled the space

between Ewell and Lawton, thus being the third division, counting from the left.   Whiting, after being sorely embarrassed by
the confused and erroneous instructions received, was properly
informed of General Jackson's wishes, and put his two brigades in
motion.   Before they had advanced far, he met the Commander-
in-Chief, who directed him to the part of the field held, at the
beginning of the battle, by A. P. Hill.   Passing through the
forest from which this General had already driven the enemy,
he emerged into a broad, open field, in front of that ravine and
gully, which have already been described as covering the left-
centre, and left of the Federal army.   Farther toward the
Confederate right, Longstreet was bringing up his division
simultaneously, to storm this desperate line; and, after other
brigades had recoiled, broken by a fire under which it seemed
impossible that any troops could live, was just sending in his
never-failing reserve, Pickett's veteran brigade.   These troops,
after advancing heroically over the shattered regiments of their
friends, within point blank range of the triple lines before them,
unfortunately paused to return the fire of the concealed enemy.
The entreaties of their officers to charge bayonets were unheard
amidst the terrific roar of musketry.   It was as they stood thus,
decimated at every volley, unable to advance, but too courageous
to flee, that the brigades of Hood and Whiting were launched
against the Federal lines on the left.   The charge may be best
described in the language of General Jackson himself.

"Advancing thence, through a number of retreating and disordered regiments, he came within range of the enemy's fire;
who, concealed in an open wood, and protected by breastworks,
poured a destructive fire, for a quarter of a mile, into his advancing line; under which many brave officers and men fell.   Dashing on with unfaltering step, in the face of these murderous
discharges of canister and musketry, General Hood and Colonel

Law, at the heads of their respective brigades, rushed to the charge with a yell. Moving down a precipitous ravine, leaping ditch and stream, clambering up a difficult ascent, and exposed to an incessant and deadly fire from the entrenchments, these brave and determined men pressed forward, driving the enemy from his well-selected and fortified position.

"In this charge, in which upwards of a thousand men fell, killed and wounded, before the fire of the enemy, and in which fourteen pieces of artillery and nearly a regiment were captured, the fourth Texas, under the lead of General Hood, was the first to pierce these strong-holds and seize the guns." . . . . "The shouts of triumph which rose from our brave men as they, unaided by artillery, had stormed this citadel of their strength, were promptly carried from line to line, and the triumphant issue of this assault, with the well-directed fire of the batteries, and successful charges of Hill and Winder upon the enemy's right, determined the fortunes of the day. The Federalists, routed at every point, and aided by the darkness of the night, escaped across the Chickahominy."

The next morning, as Jackson inspected this position, and saw the deadly disadvantages under which the Texans had carried it, he exclaimed; "These men are soldiers indeed!" Here, and in front of Pickett's charge near by, all the Confederate dead were on the north side of the gorge. Just as soon as the enemy saw them determined to advance, in spite of their fire, and the first line was dislodged from the channel of the rivulet in front, the other two lines incontinently fled from their barricades, although well able still to have repulsed the shattered assailants twice over; nor did the artillery hold their ground with more firmness upon the brow of the ascent. But now, as the troops of Longstreet and Whiting drove the throng of their foes from cover into the open fields, they speedily reaped a bloody revenge for all previous losses. The Federal infantry, resigning all thought of battle, fled across the fields or huddled together in the open vales, where the furious Confederates mowed them down by hundreds. The Federal artillery flying to another position a few hundred yards in the rear, opened upon retreating friends and advancing foes, distinguished nothing in the gathering gloom; and as the victors rushed upon the guns again, they drove before them as a living shield, a confused herd of fugitives, whose bodies received the larger part of the volleys of canister.

During the afternoon, General Jackson, with his escort, occupied a position near Cold Harbor, where five roads met, in the rear of his left centre. Ignorant of the delay which had kept his reserves for two hours out of the strife, and of its unlucky cause, he grew more and more anxious as the sun approached the horizon, and the sustained firing told him that the enemy was nowhere broken. Sending first for Stuart, he suggested to him a vigorous charge of cavalry; but this was relinquished as impracticable. His gigantic spirit was manifestly gathering strength, and its rising tides were chafing stormily against their obstacles. Riding restlessly to and fro to the different points of interest, he issued his orders in a voice which rang with the deadly clang of the rifle, rather than the sonorous peal of the clarion. Cheek and brow were blazing with the crimson blood, and beneath the vizor of his old drab cap, his eye glared with a fire, before which every other eye quailed. But a half hour of sunlight now remained. Unconscious that his veteran brigades were but now reaching the ridge of battle, he supposed that all his force had been put forth, and (what had never happened before) the enemy was not crushed. It was then that he despatched messengers to all the commanders of his divisions, with these words: "Tell them this affair must hang in suspense no longer; sweep the field with the bayonet." The officers darted away with their messages; but before they reached the line, the ringing cheers, rising from every side out of the smoking woods, told that his will was anticipated, and the day was won. At this sound, no elation lighted up his features, but subduing the tempest of his passion, he rode calmly forward, to direct the pursuit of the enemy.

In this battle, General Jackson employed little artillery. Upon his wing a few of the batteries of D. H. Hill were put in action at the extreme left, with small effect at first, upon the enemy's fire. Later in the day, Major Pelham, of Stuart's horse-artillery, whose splendid courage Jackson then first witnessed took position in front of Cold Harbor, with two guns, and engaged the Federal batteries which obstructed the movements of Hill. One of his pieces was speedily disabled; but with the other, he continued the unequal duel to the close of the day. At sunset, the batteries upon the extreme left were reinforced by those of Courtenay and Brockenborough. Thirty guns now opened upon the retreating enemy, and contributed much to his final discomfiture.

In the battle of Chickahominy, the Confederates used about forty thousand men, of whom twenty thousand belonged to the command of General Jackson, exclusive of the division of D. H. Hill, temporarily associated with it. General M'Clellan asserted that he had but thirty-six thousand men engaged. The length of his triple lines of battle, and the superior numbers met by the Confederates at every point, show that if this statement was correct, it excluded the reserves engaged at the close of the day; and if a similar subtraction were made on the other side, their numbers also would be reduced far below that amount. General Lee declared that the principal part of the Federal army was engaged. When it is remembered that this force embraced all of their regulars, and that the adroit use of the position selected

by M'Clellan debarred the Confederates from the employment
of artillery, while it exposed them on both wings to that powerful implement of war, their victory will be received as a glorious
proof of their prowess. They captured twenty-five pieces of
artillery, and more than four thousand prisoners; while the field
showed that the carnage among the Federalists was considerably
heavier than among the patriots. The victory was purchased by
a loss of five hundred and eighty-nine men killed on the field,
two thousand six hundred and seventy-one wounded, and twenty-
four missing, in Jackson's *corps*. In the other divisions engaged, the
loss was also heavy. Several circumstances made the price paid
for the splendid advantages of this achievement, heavier than it
might have been, and the fruits more scanty. Of these, the one
most worthy of the attention of the Confederates, because susceptible of a remedy, was the lack of a competent general Staff,
by which the plans of the Commander-in-Chief might be carried
out with accuracy, and unity of action secured. Next, it should
be remarked, that the generals were possessed of no topographical surveys, and were therefore compelled to manoeuvre their
troops without any acquaintance with the ground, in an intricate
country, obscured by woodlands, and devoid of any elevated
points of view. The whole space over which Jackson's troops
moved, was occupied by a succession of thickets of pine, and
insignificant farms; so that scarcely anywhere did two brigades
move in sight of each other, and an advance of a quarter of a
mile invariably hid them from view. It was vain therefore, for
the General to depend upon his own eyes; and with a scanty
and ill-organized staff, he had no means of knowing, for a considerable time, whether his orders were executed or not.

On the morning of Saturday, June 28th, there was not a Federal soldier in arms north of the Chickahominy. The two
bridges by which M'Clellan had retreated were jealously guarded

58

by his sharpshooters, and by commanding batteries upon the southern heights, which forbade their passage, save at an expense of blood too great to be contemplated. Ewell's division, with the cavalry of Stuart, marched, early in the morning, for the York River Railroad; which they occupied without opposition, at Dispatch Station. The enemy thereupon retreated to the south side of the river, and burned the railroad bridge, while General Ewell destroyed a part of the track. Stuart, pursuing a detachment of cavalry toward the White House, found all the Stations in flames, including the dwelling and farm buildings of General Lee, at the latter place, and a vast amount of military stores destroyed. It was now manifest from the enemy's own act, that this line of retreat was finally surrendered. Two other alternatives remained to him: one was to cross the Chickahominy below, by the Williamsburg road and the neighboring ways; the other, to turn to the river James. To prevent the adoption of the former, General Ewell was ordered to guard Bottom's bridge, the next below the railroad, while the cavalry watched the lower course of the stream. To resist the latter, General Holmes's division was directed to watch the roads leading toward the James, with a portion of the cavalry, while Generals Magruder and Huger guarded his front, and stood prepared to press the Federalists upon the first appearance of retreat. The Confederate forces upon the north bank of the Chickahominy remained there until their purposes were developed.

M'Clellan, although still superior to Lee in numbers and *materiel* of war, was now in a situation which might well excite his solicitude. His vast army, cut off from its established line of supplies, must either move at once or starve. Before him, and on both his flanks was a determined and victorious foe. Behind him was a forest country, possessing few good roads, and intersected by sluggish water-courses, which the unprecedented rains had this year converted into swamps. But the forests were, ɯ another aspect, his friends; for they concealed his designs and prevented the watching of his movements. One vigorous day's march, moreover, would bring him to his powerful fleet, which would give him a secure refuge and the needed supplies. Saturday evening, there were manifest signs of movement behind the Federal entrenchments, and Sunday morning they were abandoned, and the bridges across the Chickahominy were broken down. General Longstreet now marched to the south side by the New Bridge; but the Grapevine Bridge opposite General Jackson's position was so destroyed that the pioneers consumed nearly the whole day in repairing it. Late in the afternoon, the Stonewall Brigade, with the General and his Staff, passed over, and inspected the country. At the Trent farm near by, were extensive bowers, ingeniously woven of cedar boughs, which had surrounded the headquarters where M'Clellan had recently resided, in a village of canvas, provided with every appliance of luxury. Here also was his telegraph office, whence lines diverged to each *corps* of his army and to Washington, with the floor littered with the originals of those fictitious despatches, with which his Government was wont to delude its people. A little farther, General Jackson found the forces of General Magruder, with the Commander-in-Chief, watching the retreating enemy; and, it was agreed, after consultation, that the evening was too far advanced for an effective movement, and that General Jackson should return to his *bivouac*, and commence his march in pursuit at dawn the next morning. As he rode across the fields this evening, he witnessed a spectacle of inexpressible grandeur. The attention was attracted toward the east by the roar of an invisible railroad train, which seemed to be rushing toward the Chickahominy, far beyond the distant woods, with a speed which was constantly accelerated until it became frightful.

Suddenly, as the beholders were speculating upon the cause of this sound, a vast pillar of white smoke was seen to spring upwards into the sky, which rose higher and higher, and continually unfolded itself from within, in waves of snowy vapor, until it filled that quarter of the heavens. And, a moment after, the atmosphere, slower than the sunbeams, brought to the ear an astounding explosion, in which a multitude of nearly simultaneous thunder-claps were mingled into a roar louder than cannon. The explanation was learned afterwards. The retreating foe had loaded a train with a vast bulk of ammunition, and, firing the engine to its most intense heat, had launched it from Savage's Station, without a guide, with a slow match lighted. Just as it plunged into the Chickahominy, at the chasm where the bridge had lately been, the powder caught; and ammunition, engine, and carriages were blown into one huge wreck.

This was not the only form of destruction which the Federalists employed to prevent their enemies from profiting by the spoils. Their industry in attempting to demolish was equal to the haste of their flight. The whole country was full of deserted plunder; and this, indeed, was equally true of the tracts over which they had been driven on the north side of the river, from Mechanicsville downward. Army wagons and pontoon trains, partially burned or crippled; mounds of grain and rice, and hillocks of mess-beef smouldering; tens of thousands of axes, picks, and shovels; camp-kettles gashed with hatchets; medicine-wagons with their drugs stirred into foul medley; and all the *apparatus* of a vast and lavish host, encumbered the roads; while the mire under foot was mixed with blankets lately new, and overcoats torn in twain from the waist up. For weeks afterwards, the agents of the army were busy gathering in the spoils; while a multitude of the country people found in them partial indemnity for the ruin of their farms. Great stores of fixed ammunition were saved, while more was destroyed.

Scarcely had General Jackson returned to the northern bank, when a rapid outbreak of firing told that General Magruder had attacked the enemy near Savage's station. Here were the last entrenchments behind which M'Clellan could stand at bay. By a vigorous attack in flank and front, he was driven out of them just at sunset, and pursued for a short space with great slaughter. The sound of this combat kindled again in Jackson's heart the fire of battle, and as he lay down under the open sky for a short repose, he gave orders that everything should be ready to move in pursuit at the earliest dawn. At midnight, however, a sudden shower awoke him, and finding himself wet through, he determined to sleep no more, but to precede the troops to the position of General Magruder, in order to have time for fuller conference. When the head of his column, composed again of the division of D. H. Hill, reached the scene of the evening's combat, the General was found drying himself by a camp-fire. Without procuring any food or refreshment, he now advanced through the troops of Magruder, and took the old highway which led to Williamsburg. When the station near Savage's came in view, a city of canvas was seen upon a distant hill-side, glittering in the morning sun. This was a vast field-hospital of M'Clellan, where twenty-five hundred sick and wounded, with their nurses, had been left by him to the care of the Confederates. General Jackson, having sent a suitable officer to receive the submission of these, advanced rapidly upon the enemy's traces. At every step the Federal stragglers issued from the thickets, and submitted themselves as prisoners of war, until a thousand additional men were sent to the rear. A vast drove of mules deserted by the Federal army, was gathered from the woods. Every hut and dwelling near the roadside was also converted into a refuge for the wounded, whose numbers showed the sanguinary nature of the struggle of the previous evening. An officer congratulating the General upon the great number of his prisoners, said jocularly, that they surrendered too easily, for the Confederacy would be embarrassed with their maintenance. He answered, smiling; "It is cheaper to feed them, than to fight them."

Before reaching White Oak Swamp, an inconsiderable stream which crossed the road, he diverged toward the right in the direction of the Court House of Charles' City County, pursuing still the wrecks of the enemy's flight. It now became manifest that he had relinquished all thought of a retreat toward Yorktown, and had turned decisively toward the river James. To explain the subsequent movements, the disclosure of M'Clellan's plans, still doubtful to the Confederate commander, must be a little anticipated. His purpose was to collect his army and all its *apparatus* upon the bank of the James, at some point below the mouth of the Appomattox: where the greater width and depth of the stream would enable his great fleets to approach him with convenience, and manœuvre for his defence. To disencumber the roads leading directly thither, and leave them free for the march of his columns, he sent his whole baggage trains down the way which Jackson had now reached, leading from the neighborhood of Savage's Station on the railroad, to Charles City Court House. Having followed this route until they were effectually protected, they made their way across from this thoroughfare, to the deep water at Harrison's Landing. To protect them, Franklin's *corps* was stationed on the eastern bank of White Oak Swamp; and when Jackson reached it, he stubbornly contested its passage with him during the whole of Monday, June 30th. On the other hand, the *corps* of Keyes, from M'Clellan's left, with the beaten troops of Porter, were rapidly marched to Malvern Hill, a range of highlands accessible by the shortest march from the southern end of the Federal line, and overlooking at once the river James, and the New Market, or river road, which leads from the city of Richmond down its northern side. The object of this movement on the part of M'Clellan, was to protect his communications with the deep water from an advance down the New Market road, which he had good reason to fear. The remainder of his great army was massed on Monday midway between the White Oak Swamp and Malvern Hill, under Generals Heintzelman and M'Call, to watch the roads going eastward; by which the Confederates might insinuate themselves between his right and left, and pursue his baggage trains. These judicious dispositions, made in a forest country, and chiefly by night marches, were not immediately disclosed in all their details to the Confederate leader. But his troops were now directed, with a masterly and comprehensive foresight, to meet every contingency, in such sort that had all his purposes been carried out, the adroit concealments of his adversary would have been vain. Major General Holmes was ordered to cross from the south bank of the river James, which he had been left to guard, on the 29th, and march down the New Market road, to prevent the enemy from reaching the water. He did not approach Malvern Hill until the 30th, when he found it already powerfully occupied by the enemy under Keyes and Porter, crowned by a formidable artillery, and flanked by gunboats in the river. Early on the 29th Major-Generals Longstreet and A. P. Hill were directed to cross the Chickahominy at the New Bridges, and march eastward by the Darby-town road, a highway parallel to the New Market road, and north of it. Major-Generals Huger and Magruder were directed to press the enemy in front, by the road leading direct from Richmond to Charles City; while Jackson was to advance rapidly upon the left, scour the south side of the Chickahominy, and endeavor to attain the enemy's rear.

Longstreet and A. P. Hill, who moved first on the 29th, first came up with the enemy's centre, upon the 30th, posted a little below the termination of the Darby-town road. Magruder, who advanced by the same road, was diverted by a request of General Holmes for reinforcements; and, thus unfortunately, was turned aside from the centre, where a fatal blow was practicable, toward the heights of Malvern Hill, which were now unassailable; and did not retrace his steps until the day was decided. But General Huger still remained to support the attack of Longstreet and Hill upon the right; and General Jackson, on the other hand, if able to force his passage across White Oak Swamp, would have found himself upon the enemy's flank and rear. Such was the attitude of the respective parties at mid-day of June 30th.

When Jackson approached the stream last named, at this hour, he found in the fields near it, extensive camps deserted, and full of spoils, and another field-hospital crowded with wounded. The hills descended by long and gentle declivities on both sides toward the little water-course, and the meadows along its margin were soft and miry from the recent rains. On the Confederate side, the right of the road was occupied by the open fields of an extensive farm, and the left by a dense forest of pines. On the side occupied by Franklin, the fields extended far both to the right and left of the highway; but the low margin of the stream opposite the Confederate right was covered by a belt of tall forest, in full leaf, which effectually screened all the Federal left from view. But the hills on their right were occupied by fifteen or twenty cannon in position, and were black with long lines of infantry. General Jackson, riding, as was his wont, with the advanced guard, no sooner saw the ground than he halted his army, and ordered twenty-eight guns to be brought up, by a little vale through the fields on his right, just deep enough to hide them effectually from the enemy's view. These, although upon his right wing, were directed to the batteries of the Federalists opposite his left. At a preconcerted signal, the guns, ready shotted, were now moved forward upon the brow of the eminence, and opened their thunders upon the enemy. So sudden and terrible was the revelation, they scarcely made an effort to reply, but galloped away, leaving two or three rifled pieces behind them; while the ranks of infantry melted swiftly into the woods far in their rear. After a little, several batteries upon the enemy's left, concealed behind the belt of forest, began to reply to this fire; and, from this time, the two parties kept up a desultory artillery-duel during the day. But as each was invisible to the other, much damage was neither given nor received.

The General now advanced a section of artillery near the crossing of the stream, which speedily drove the Federal sharp-shooters from the opposite bank and trees; and he ordered over the cavalry regiment of Colonel Munford. They found the wooden bridge broken up, and its timbers floating — a tangled mass — in the waters. But just above was a deep and narrow ford, by which they passed over, followed immediately by the General. They scoured, with drawn sabres, over the ground lately occupied by the Federal right wing, noted the deserted cannon, and picked up a few prisoners. But the enemy's left, behind the long screen of forest, was found standing fast, while they were bringing both artillery and infantry into position to command the crossing. Colonel Munford therefore passed down the stream to his left, and, finding a spot where it was practicable, returned to his friends without loss. Jackson, upon observing this, advanced the divisions of D. H. Hill and Whiting into the pine wood on his left, detailed a working party to act with their support, and attempted to repair the bridge, with the purpose of forcing his way by a simultaneous advance of his infantry and artillery. But the men could not be induced to labor steadily, exposed to the skirmishers of the enemy; and the attempt was abandoned. The remainder of the afternoon was spent in endeavors to discover some way, on the right or the left, by which the vexatious stream could be crossed, and the enemy's position turned; but the roads were so effectually obstructed with fallen trees, that no hope appeared of removing them in time to fight a battle that evening. The troops were then withdrawn out of reach of the enemy's shells, and bivouacked, to await a more propitious morning. On this occasion it would appear, if the vast interests dependent on General Jackson's co-operation with the proposed attack upon the centre were considered, that he came short of that efficiency in action for which he was everywhere else noted. Surely the prowess of the Confederate infantry might have been trusted, for such a stake as Lee played for that day, to do again what it had so gloriously done, for a stake no greater, on the 27th; it might have routed the Federal infantry and artillery at once, without the assistance of its own cannon. Two columns, pushed with determination across the two fords at which the cavalry of Munford passed over and returned, — the one in the centre, and the other at the left, — and protected in their onset by the oblique fire of a powerful artillery so well posted on the right, would not have failed to dislodge Franklin from a position already half lost. The list of casualties would indeed have been larger than that presented on the 30th, of one cannoneer mortally wounded. But how much shorter would have been the bloody list filled up the next day at Malvern Hill? This temporary eclipse of Jackson's genius was probably to be explained by physical causes. The labor of the previous days, the sleeplessness, the wear of gigantic cares, with the drenching of the comfortless night, had sunk the elasticity of his will and the quickness of his invention, for the once, below their wonted tension. And which of the sons of men is there so great as never to experience this? The words which fell from Jackson's lips, as he lay down that night among his Staff, showed that he was conscious of depression. After dropping asleep from excessive fatigue, with his supper between his teeth, he said: " Now, gentlemen, let us at once to bed, and rise with the dawn, and see if to-morrow we cannot *do something!*" Yet he found time, amidst the fatigues of this day, to write to Mrs. Jackson, with a heart full of piety and of yearning for domestic happiness: —

" NEAR WHITE OAK SWAMP BRIDGE, June 30th.

" An ever kind Providence has greatly blessed our efforts, and given us great reason for thankfulness in having defended Richmond as he has."

" I hope that our God will soon bless us with an honorable peace, and permit us to be together at home, in the enjoyment of domestic happiness."

Meantime, Generals Longstreet and A. P. Hill, after confronting the enemy's powerful centre until 4 o'clock P. M., heard firing upon the Charles City road, which they supposed indicated the near approach of Huger. The former placed a battery in position and discharged it against the enemy to give notice of his presence. The Federalists replied, and the old war-horse, whose mettle forbade his ever declining the gage of battle, rushed to the contest. None of his expected supports came up; and the advantage of position and numbers was wholly with his adversaries. But after a sanguinary conflict, he drove them from their whole line save at one point, and captured many prisoners, including a general of division, several batteries, and some thousands of small arms; when night arrested the furious struggle. This action has been known as the battle of Frazier's farm. So near did its issue bring the enemy's left wing to destruction, even without the expected assistance of Jackson, Huger, and Magruder, that when it closed, at dark, the victorious troops of Longstreet were, unconsciously, within sight of the cross road by which Franklin was required to march his *corps*, in the rear of the Federal centre, in order to reach the appointed place of concentration at Malvern Hill. Nay, the cornfields beyond that road were ploughed up with Longstreet's cannon-shot. What then might not the triumph have been, if the intended co-operation had been given? As soon as the night grew quiet, Franklin, informed of his critical position, moved off from White Oak Swamp, glided silently behind the shattered ranks which still confronted Longstreet, and retired, with them, to the protection of M'Clellan's lines at Malvern Hill. When the morning dawned, there was nothing in front of Jackson save the forsaken cannon of the enemy, and they had deserted to Longstreet a field ghastly with multitudes of their slain and wounded. His wearied troops, with those of A. P. Hill, were drawn off to seek the needed repose, and Magruder took his place.

General Jackson putting his *corps* in motion at an early hour, July 1st, with Whiting's division in front, crossed the White Oak Swamp; and, a little after, turning south, marched upon the traces of the enemy toward Malvern Hill. As he approached Frazier's farm, a Confederate line of battle was seen a little distance from the right of the road, with their skirmishers upon the opposite side, looking eastward. These were the forces of Magruder, which had relieved those of Longstreet during the night. Jackson passed between the line and the skirmishers, lustily cheered by them, and pursued the enemy swiftly. The road now plunged into an extensive woodland, with the Willis' Church upon the right hand, filled with the wounded of both armies. After advancing for a mile and a half through this forest, the General's suite was suddenly greeted with a volley of rifle-balls from the Federal outposts, and a moment after, by a shower of shells. Retiring to a safer spot, he now ordered up his troops, and prepared to attack. His *reconnoissance* showed him the enemy most advantageously posted upon an elevated ridge in front of Malvern Hill, which was occupied by several lines of infantry partially fortified, and by a powerful artillery. In short, the whole army of M'Clellan, with three hundred pieces of field artillery, was now, for the first time, assembled on one field, determined to stand at bay, and contend for its existence; while the whole Confederate army was also converging around it, under the immediate eye of the Commander-in-Chief and the President. The war of the giants was now about to begin, indeed! before which the days of Gaines's Mill and Frazier's Farm were to pale. The position of the Federalists had been selected by M'Clellan himself, with consummate skill. His line fronted north, covering the river road behind it, and presenting a convex curve toward the Confederates. His right was covered by a tributary of Turkey creek, and his left by the fire of his gunboats, which threw their monstrous projectiles beyond his whole front. The ground occupied by him dominated by its height over the whole landscape; and nowhere in his front was there a spot, where artillery could be massed to cope with his on equal terms. For, the country before him was not only of inferior altitude, but covered with woods and thickets, save within a few hundred yards of his own lines. And here, the open fields sloped gently away, offering full sweep to his murderous fire; while this approach was only reached, before his right and centre, by struggling across the treacherous rivulet in front.

General Lee now assigned the left to Jackson, and the right to Magruder, supported by Huger and Holmes. Longstreet and A. P. Hill, with their wearied divisions, were held in reserve. The only spot where open ground appeared in opposition to the enemy's, was upon Jackson's extreme left. Here an extensive farm, belonging to a gentleman named Poindexter, indented the forests, and its luxuriant wheat fields, partially reaped, descended to the stream from which the Federal position rose on the opposite side. This field offered the only ground for the manœuvring of artillery. After an examination of it, General Jackson ordered a few batteries to enter it from the covert of the woods, and engage the enemy. But the number of guns directed against them by him was too great; and after a short contest, they retired crippled. The batteries of Poague and Carpenter from the Stonewall Brigade, and of Balthis from the division of Whiting, were then ordered forward, and by approaching the enemy more nearly, found a position which, though of inferior altitude, offered some shelter. Here they maintained a stubborn and gallant contest with the numerous batteries opposed to them during the remainder of the day, and barred the way to the advance of the enemy's infantry. The infantry of Whiting was now disposed upon the left, the brigade of Colonel Law concealed in the tall wheat of the field, and that of General Hood in the adjoining forest, while the 3rd Virginia brigade, of Jackson's division, commanded by General Hampton, supported the guns. The centre was occupied by the Louisiana brigade of Taylor, and the right by D. H. Hill. The reserve was composed of the remainder of the division of Ewell, and the brigades of Lawton, Winder and Cunningham. These dispositions were completed by 2 o'clock, P. M., and the General anxiously awaited the signal to begin. But the *corps* of Magruder, moving after Jackson's and delayed by a misconception of the route, was later in reaching its position. Instructions were sent by General Lee, that the onset should begin upon the right, with the brigades of Magruder, and that when D. H. Hill heard the cheer with which they charged the enemy, he should attack with the bayonet, to be followed immediately by the leaders upon his left. To approach the Federal centre, Hill was compelled to emerge from the forest, and cross an open field, where he suffered a preliminary loss of no small amount, from their artillery. His own batteries had been left in the rear, their ammunition exhausted; and the Confederate artillery sent to his support was advanced, piece-meal, only to be crippled in detail and driven from the field. Fording the rivulet, however, in despite of his losses, he found a partial shelter for his division under a body of woodland within four hundred yards of the enemy's front. Accompanied by General Jackson, he then made a more particular examination of the ground, and found himself confronted by two or three lines of infantry and batteries, whose murderous fire commanded every approach. Five o'clock had now arrived, when suddenly Hill heard a mighty shout upon his right, followed by an outburst of firing. Regarding this as doubtless the appointed signal, and the beginning of Magruder's onset, he gave the word, and his men advanced devotedly to the charge under a storm of artillery and musketry. The first line of the enemy was forced, and their guns were compelled to withdraw to avoid capture; but the other points of their line, unoccupied by a simultaneous attack, advanced reinforcements to them; and Hill was beaten off, after inflicting and suffering a severe loss. Jackson reinforced him, by sending the brigades of Trimble, Lawton, Winder and Cunningham; but the difficulties

of the position, the approaching darkness, and the terrific fire
of the enemy, prevented their doing more than holding their
ground, and maintaining an uncertain conflict.

As sunset approached, and after the attack of Jackson was
checked, Magruder at length got his troops into position, and
advanced, with similar results. Much heroism was exhibited by
his men, some ground was won from the enemy, a bloody loss
was inflicted upon them, and received in his own command.
At these attacks, the fire of the Federal artillery, which had been
heavy, became inexpressibly furious. Along their whole line,
whether assailed or not, their countless field-pieces belched forth
their charges of flame with an incessant din, which was answered
back by the hoarser bellowings of the gunboats in the rear.
Wherever the eye turned, it was met by a ceaseless stream of
missiles shrieking and crashing through the forest. A moonless
night descended on the turmoil, and the darkness was lighted up
for miles with the glare flashing across the heavens, as when two
thunder clouds illuminate the adverse quarters of the horizon
with sheet lightning. Beneath, the fitful lines of light danced
amidst the dark foliage, showing where the stubborn ranks of infantry plied their deadly work; and the roar of the musketry
filled the intervals of the mightier din with its angry monotone;
while a fierce yell from time to time told of some hardly won
vantage ground gained by the Confederates. At ten o'clock, the
battle died away; for the Federalists were silently withdrawing
from the field, under the friendly veil of the darkness. Indeed,
much of the cannonade was doubtless intended to cover this
retreat; and no sooner had it sunk into silence, than the rumbling of the multitude of wheels began to tell that the artillery
was withdrawing from a field which was already abandoned by
their infantry. The Confederates lay down upon their arms
where the battle had ceased, in many places within a few paces

of the opposing pickets, and during the night they saw the lanterns flitting over the field, where they were busy removing the wounded.

When the battle had ceased thus, General Jackson retired slowly and wearily to the rear, to seek some refreshment and rest. In the midst of a confused multitude of wagons and stragglers, his faithful servant had prepared a pallet for him upon the ground; and here, after taking a morsel of food, he lay down and slept. At one o'clock his division commanders awoke him, to report the condition of their forces, and receive instructions for the morrow. None of them knew, as yet, those signs of retreat and discomfiture, which the advanced pickets were observing; they only knew what they had suffered in their own commands. Their imaginations were awe-struck by the sights and sounds of the fearful struggle, and every representation which they gave was gloomy. At length, after many details of losses and disasters, they all concurred in declaring that M'Clellan would probably take the aggressive in the morning, and that the Confederate army was in no condition to resist him. Jackson had listened silently, save as he interposed a few brief questions, to all their statements; but now he replied, with an inexpressible dryness and nonchalance: "No; I think he will clear out in the morning." These words reveal one element of his power and greatness. Such was the clearness of his military intuitions, and the soundness of his judgment, such the steadfastness of his spirit, that he viewed every fact soberly, without distortion or exaggeration. His excited fancy played no tricks with his understanding. Dangers never loomed into undue proportions before his steady eye. Hence, in the most agitating or even appalling circumstances, his conclusions were still correct. Such they proved to be now; for when morning dawned upon the battle-field,

60

M'Clellan was gone indeed, leaving every evidence of precipitate retreat.

The morning dawned with a dreary and pitiless rain, in contrast with the splendor of the harvest sun of the previous day, as though the heavens had clad themselves in mourning, and were weeping a flood of tears for the miseries of the innocent, and the crimes of the guilty aggressor. The woods, which, the evening before, were thick with sulphureous smoke, were now wreathed in vapor; and the deep dust of the roads trampled into ashes by the myriad feet of men and horses, was now as speedily converted into semi-fluid mire. All were of course without tents; and fatigued and hungry, they wore an aspect of squalid discomfort. The only activity visible was the humane labor of the surgeons and their assistants, who were still bringing in the wounded, exhausted by their sufferings and drenched with rain. General Jackson, however, arose, and without breakfast, hurried to the front to watch over his men. The air was too thick with mist to distinguish anything upon the opposite hill; but soon the reports from his outposts, and from the cavalry of Munford, convinced him that the enemy was gone. He now issued orders that the troops should form in the woods which they had occupied the day before, kindle liberal fires, cook their food, and refresh themselves after their fatigues; while he repaired to the house of Poindexter to meet the Commander-in-Chief. General Stuart, whom the latter had recalled from the north side of the Chickahominy, had reached Turkey Creek on the left of the lines of Jackson, just as the battle closed. He was now witness of the precipitate retreat of the enemy, and following him down the river road, found numerous carriages fast stuck in the mire, or wrecked, with ammunition, clothing, equipments and muskets strewn broadcast over the country. He was informed by the country people, that the Federal army reached the open fields of

Haxall's at morning, without the semblance of organization, observing no ranks nor obedience, spreading over the fields and woods at will, and lying down to sleep under the pelting rain. Instead of meditating the aggressive, the whole host would have surrendered to the summons of ten thousand fresh men. But, alas! the Confederates had not those men to pursue them. Every division of the army had been worn by marching and fighting, and a certain disarray prevailed throughout. It must also be declared that this inability to reap the fruits of their heroic exertions arose partly from that lack of persistence which is the infirmity of the Southern character. The army of Lee was as able to pursue, as that of M'Clellan was to flee; and to the true soldier, the zeal to complete a hardly-won victory, and to save his country by one successful blow, should be as pungent a motive for intense exertion, as the instinct of self-preservation itself. Another cause of delay in the pursuit was the hesitation of the Commander-in-Chief, who, uninformed as yet of all the signs of defeat given by his enemy, and prudently sceptical of the extent of his own success, was uncertain whether this was a flight, or a ruse of M'Clellan to draw him from his bridges and from Fort Drewry, in order that he might suddenly pass to the south side, now denuded of defenders, and occupy Petersburg and Richmond without resistance. The remainder of July 2nd was therefore consumed in replenishing the ammunition of the batteries, and in refreshing the men. Orders were given that on Thursday morning, the 3rd, all the army should pursue the enemy by way of Turkey Creek and the river road, with Longstreet in front. But after that General had put his troops in motion, General Lee determined to march toward Harrison's landing, where the Federalists were now assembled, by returning to the Charles City road, and making his way thence down to the river. His purpose was to avoid the obstructions which they were reported to have left behind them to cover their rear. The brigades of Longstreet were therefore countermarched by Willis' Church; and Jackson was directed to give him the road. The guides of the former proved incompetent to their duties, and he was compelled to halt his division before half the day's march was completed. Hence General Jackson only moved three miles on Thursday. Chafing like a lion at the delay, he moved his troops at early dawn of Friday, and pressing close upon the heels of Longstreet, reached the enemy's front by the middle of the day.

The opportunity was already almost gone. M'Clellan had now been allowed two unmolested days to select and fortify his position, and to reduce again the huge mob which followed him to the form of an army. The return of genial suns, with rest and rations, and the immediate proximity of their gunboats, were fast restoring their spirits. The ground occupied by them was a beautiful peninsula, between the river James and a tributary called Herring Creek, composing the two estates of Westover and Berkeley. The creek, which enters the river at the eastern extremity of this peninsula, is, first, a tide stream; then, an impracticable marsh; and, then, a mill-pond, enlarged by an artificial embankment. West of Berkeley, another stream of the like character descends to the river; so that the only access was through a space between the two creeks, of no great extent, and rapidly closing with earthworks. The fire of the gunboats, it was supposed, might also assist to cover this approach, over the heads of their friends.

"The Commander-in-Chief was disappointed to learn, on his arrival in front of the Federalists, that no opportunity had been found for striking a blow, either on their retreat, or in their present position. He immediately rode forward with General Jackson; and the two, dismounting, proceeded, without attendants to make a careful reconnoissance on foot, of the enemy's whole line and position. Jackson concurred fully in the reluctant opinion to which General Lee was brought by this examination,—that an attack would now be improper; so that, after mature discussion, it was determined that the enemy should be left, unassailed, to the effects of the summer heats and the malaria, which were now at hand."

To this the condition of his troops powerfully inclined him. On Saturday, General Jackson obtained returns of all his *corps* in front of the enemy, and ready for duty; and found them just ten thousand men, exclusive of the division of D. H. Hill, which had been left to bury the dead at Malvern Hill. Half his men appeared, therefore, to be out of their ranks, from death or wounds, from the necessary labors of the care of the wounded, from straggling, and from the inefficiency of their inferior officers. The army was therefore allowed to lie quiet in front of the enemy, and refresh themselves after their fatigues. The wagons of the General also arrived; and, for the first time in a fortnight, the Staff enjoyed the luxury of their tents. These were now pitched beside a beautiful fountain, under the shade of a group of venerable oaks and chestnuts; and here the quiet Sabbath was spent in religious worship, and in much-needed repose.

The battle of Malvern Hill was technically a victory for the Confederates, for they held the field, the enemy's killed and wounded, and the spoils; while the Federalists retreated precipitately at its close. But, practically, it was rather a drawn battle; because the loss inflicted on them was probably no greater than that of the assailants; and, especially, because the enemy would have retired to the same spot, and at the same time, if no assault had been made. The loss of Jackson's *corps* was three hundred and seventy-seven men killed, and one thousand seven hundred and forty-six wounded, with thirty-nine missing. The larger part of this bloodshed was in the division of D. H. Hill. The divisions under command of General Magruder lost about two thousand nine hundred men, killed and wounded.

The struggle for the possession of the Confederate Capital was now closed. The results of Lee's victories were, indeed, far less than the overweening hopes and expectations of the people; for Richmond was agitated with daily rumors that the Federal army was wholly dissipated; and, then, that it was about to surrender in a body. But, in the language of the Commander-in-Chief, "Regret that more was not accomplished, gives way to gratitude to the Sovereign Ruler of the universe for the results achieved. The siege of Richmond was raised; and the object of a campaign, which had been prosecuted, after months of preparation, at an enormous expenditure of men and money, completely frustrated. More than ten thousand prisoners, — including officers of rank, — fifty-two pieces of artillery, and upwards of thirty-five thousand stand of small arms were captured. The stores, and supplies of every description, which fell into our hands, were great in amount and value; but small in comparison with those destroyed by the enemy. His losses in battle exceeded our own, as attested by the thousands of dead and wounded left on every field; while his subsequent inaction shows in what condition the survivors reached the protection to which they fled."

But yet, the same exalted authority has declared, that, "under ordinary circumstances, the Federal army should have been destroyed." While that which was effected is creditable to the Confederates, yet the ruin of the enemy was within the scope of probability; and might have been effected by them, by a higher degree of skill and effort. It is therefore of interest to the student of the military art, to learn what were the obstacles and blunders which prevented the fullest success. Of these, some were unavoidable; and among these latter must be reckoned a large part of the ignorance concerning the movements of M'Clellan, and the proper directions to be taken by the Confederates, by which General Lee found himself so much embarrassed. There were no topographical surveys of the country, and all the general officers were strangers to it. It was a country of numerous intricate roads, of marshy streams, and of forests. Hence every march and every position of the enemy was enveloped in mystery, until it was disclosed in some way at the cost of the Confederates; and every movement made by them in pursuit was in some degree tentative.

Among the unavoidable difficulties may, perhaps, be also ranked that which was, directly or indirectly, the fruitful parent of every miscarriage. The army was not sufficiently instructed, either in its officers or its men, for its great work. The capacity to command, the practical skill and tact, the professional knowledge, the devotion to duty, which make the efficient officer, do not come in a day; and few are the natures which are capable of learning them to a high degree. When the Confederate Government attempted to produce *extempore* officers of all grades for armies so great, out of a people who had been reared in the pursuits of peace, it could only be partially successful. The company and field officers competent to instruct and govern their men thoroughly, and to keep them to their colors amidst the confusion of battle and the fatigues of forced marches, were far too few for the regiments to be commanded. There were not enough Brigadiers, who knew how to manœuvre a brigade quickly or vigorously; nor enough Major-Generals able to handle a great mass of troops. Hence that deficiency in the functions of the Staff which has been already explained, by reason of which the commander was ever in imperfect communication with his forces, and was never certain that his wishes were properly conveyed to all of them, or that he was possessed of their whole situation when out of his sight. Through so imperfect a medium perfect unison in action could never be gained, upon a theatre like that of Malvern Hill, extended over miles of wooded country, and including the convergent movements of several separate armies. It was from these causes the bungling combinations proceeded, upon every important field of this brief campaign. Enough officers always manœuvred their commands so slowly as to compel the Commander-in-Chief to let slip critical hours, and to wear away the day which should have been employed in attacking and pursuing. Thus it was ever: at Mechanicsville, at Cold Harbor, at Savage's Station, at Frazier's Farm, and especially at Malvern Hill; the prime of the day was spent in waiting for somebody, or in getting into position; the battle, which should have been the business of that prime, was thrust into the late afternoon; and when the bloody victory was won, no time remained to gather in its fruits fully by a vigorous pursuit.

The event also taught, what no forecast, perhaps, would have foreseen, that a more efficient employment of the cavalry upon the enemy's flanks would have put the Commander-in-Chief in earlier possession of essential information. It has been seen that General Stuart, after his return from the White House, was directed to remain upon the north side of the Chickahominy, guarding the Long Bridge, and the other crossings below; and that he only rejoined the army the night of July 1st. He should rather have been required to cross the Chickahominy immediately, and press as closely upon the line of the enemy's actual operations, let it be where it might, as was possible. He would thus have equally fulfilled the purpose of his stay upon the north side, to ascertain that they did not retire toward Yorktown by the lower roads; and he would probably have discovered at once, their real movement. It afterward appeared, that the whole bag-gage train of M'Clellan, with numerous stragglers, passed nearly to Charles City Court House, by a road parallel to the Chicka-hominy and only a few miles distant from it, on the 29th of June. Had this fact been reported to General Lee by the first of July, it might have thrown a flood of new light upon the momentous question, which he was required that day to decide: must M'Clellan be attacked in his almost impregnable position or not? It was known that he was assembling all the *corps* of his army at Malvern Hill; that his gunboats had ascended thither; that he was beginning to entrench himself there. Was it his purpose to convert this spot into a permanent entrenched camp, to defend it from all such assaults as he had just experienced on the Chickahominy, by his engineering skill; to provision it from his ships, and thus to establish himself again within fifteen miles of Richmond, upon a base which General Lee's wisdom taught him to be a better one than that which he had lost? If this was his design, then it was imperative that he should be dislodged; and the more speedily it was attempted, the less patriot blood would it cost. For if he were permitted to fix himself here, all the toil and loss of the glorious week would be vain. But now, add the fact that M'Clellan had sent all his trains to another spot, and that he stood upon Malvern Hill with nothing but his ammunition, and the supplies of a day; and it became probable that he would retreat from this place, whether he were attacked or not; that he would retreat whither his trains had preceded him, and that he was only standing at bay for a short time, to secure the privilege of that retreat. The ques-tion thus assumed a new aspect, whether it were better to assail him on his chosen ground, at such a cost of blood, or to wait for a fairer opportunity as he withdrew.

If it were granted that M'Clellan ought to have been attacked

at once, on his own ground, much yet remains in the management of the battle on the Confederate side, which, though
excused, cannot be justified.   The attack was made in detail,
first at one point, and then at another, instead of being simultaneous. Had the *corps* of Jackson and Magruder charged simultaneously, with the devoted gallantry which a part of each
exhibited, the Federal lines would doubtless have given way, and
a glorious success would have rewarded the Confederates, without any greater expenditure of blood than they actually incurred.
But it is worthy of question whether M'Clellan's advantage of
position could not have been neutralized.   Malvern Hill is upon
the convexity of a sharp curve in the river James, which just
below that neighborhood, flows away toward the south, while
the river road pursues still an easterly course.   If M'Clellan
moved eastward, he must either forsake the coveted help of his
gunboats, or, to continue near the water, he must leave the highlands, and descend to a level region commanded from the
interior.   These facts seemed to point to the policy of extending
the Confederate left, until his egress by the river road was so
violently threatened as to compel him to weaken his impregnable
front.   The great body of forest, which confronted his centre,
might have been safely left to the guardianship of a skirmish
line; for their weakness would have been concealed by the
woods, and the enemy was, on that day, in no aggressive mood.
A powerful mass of artillery and infantry displayed beyond their
extreme right, would probably have produced the happiest effects.
Last, the tardy and indirect pursuit which followed the battle,
was the least excusable blunder of all.   The two days which
were allowed to M'Clellan proved the salvation of his army.
But what are all these criticisms more than an assertion in
different form, of the truths that all man's works are imperfect,
and that every art must be learned before it is practised?

When it is remembered that the South had very few professional soldiers, that the men who formed the victorious army of Lee were, the year before, a peaceful multitude occupied, since their childhood, in the pursuits of husbandry, and that half the brigades into which they were organized had never been under fire before the beginning of the bloody week, the only wonder will be that the confusion was not worse, and that the failures were not greater. That so much was accomplished is proof of the eminent courage of the people, and their native aptitude for war.

It is a fact worthy of note in this narrative, that the fire of the gunboats, so much valued by the Federals and at first so dreaded by the Confederates, had no actual influence whatever in the battle. Their noise and fury doubtless produced a certain effect upon the emotions of the assailants; but this was dependent on their novelty. The loss inflicted by them was trivial when compared with the ravages of the field artillery, and it was found chiefly among their own friends. For more of their ponderous missiles fell in their own lines, than in those of the Confederates. Indeed, a fire directed at an invisible foe, across two or three miles of intervening hills and woods, can never reach its aim, save by accident. Nor is the havoc wrought by the larger projectiles proportioned to their magnitude. Where one of them explodes against a human body, it does indeed crush it into a frightful mass, scarcely cognizable as human remains. But it is not likely to strike more men, in the open order of field operations, than a shot of ten pounds; and the wretch, blown to atoms by it, is not put *hors du combat* more effectually, than he whose brain is penetrated by half an ounce of lead or iron. The broadside of a modern gunboat may consist of three hundred pounds of iron, projected by thirty or forty pounds of powder. But it is fired from only two guns. The effect upon a line of men is therefore but one fifteenth of that

which the same metal might have had, fired from thirty ten-
pounder rifled guns.

In conclusion, a statement of the numbers composing the two
armies in this great struggle, is necessary to estimate its merits.
Under the orders of General Lee there were, at its beginning,
about seventy-five thousand effective men, including the *corps*
brought to his aid by General Jackson. M'Clellan confidently
represented the numbers opposed to him as much larger than
his own; but the habitual exaggerations of his apprehensive
temper were patent, even to his own Government. He states
that his own force was reduced to eighty thousand effective
men. It must be remembered that during the campaign before
Richmond, the motives of M'Clellan's policy dictated a studied
depreciation of his own numbers. In the returns given by
himself in another place, his effective force present for duty is
set down at one hundred and six thousand men, inclusive of the
garrison of Fortress Monroe under General Dix. Halleck declared, in his letter of Aug. 6th, that M'Clellan still had ninety
thousand men at Berkeley, after all his losses ! These M'Clellan
had estimated at fifteen thousand, how truthfully may be known
from this : that he places the men lost by desertion and capture
under six thousand, whereas the Confederates had in their hands
more than ten thousand prisoners; and the woods of the peninsula were swarming with stragglers. Whatever may have been
his numerical superiority, it is indisputable that every advantage
of equipments, arms, and artillery was on his side.

But the arrival of General Jackson brought a strength to the
Confederates beyond that of his numbers. His fame as a warrior had just risen to the zenith; while all the other armies of
the Confederacy had been retreating before the enemy, or at
best holding the defensive with difficulty, his alone had marched,
and attacked, and conquered. A disaster had never alighted on

his banners. His assault was regarded by friends and foes as the stroke of doom, and his presence gave assurance of victory. Hence, when the army before Richmond learned that he was with them, they were filled with unbounded joy and confidence, while their enemies were struck with a corresponding panic.

CHAPTER XV.

CEDAR RUN.

WHILE the army lay near Westover, resting from its toils, General Jackson called his friend, the Honorable Mr. Boteler, to his tent, to communicate his views of the future conduct of the war, and to beg that on his next visit to Richmond, he would impress them upon the Government. He said that it was manifest by every sign, that M‘Clellan's was a thoroughly beaten army, and was no longer capable of anything, until it was reorganized and reinforced. There was danger, he foresaw, of repeating the error of Manassa's Junction; when the season of victory was let slip by an ill-timed inaction, and the enemy was allowed full leisure to repair his strength. Now, since it was determined not to attempt the destruction of M‘Clellan where he lay, the Confederate army should at once leave the malarious district, move northward, and carry the horrors of invasion from their own borders, to those of the guilty assailants. This, he said, was the way to bring them to their senses, and to end the war. And it was within the power of the Confederate Government to make a successful invasion, if their resources were rightly concentrated. Sixty thousand men could march into Maryland, and threaten Washington City, producing most valuable results. But, he added; while he wished these views to be laid before the President, he would disclaim earnestly the charge of self-seeking, in advocating them. He wished to follow, and not to lead, in this glorious enterprise: he was willing to follow anybody; General Lee, or the gallant Ewell. "Why do you not at once urge these things," asked Mr. Boteler, "upon General Lee himself?" "I have done so;" replied Jackson. "And what," asked Mr. Boteler, "does he say to them?" General Jackson answered: "He says nothing." But he added; "Do not understand that I complain of this silence; it is proper that General Lee should observe it: He is a sagacious and prudent man; he feels that he bears a fearful responsibility: He is right in declining a hasty expression of his purposes, to a subordinate like me." The advice of Jackson was laid before the President. What weight was attached to it, is unknown; but the campaign soon after took the direction which he had indicated.

He was extremely anxious to leave the unhealthy region of the lower James, where his own health, with that of his command, was suffering, and to return to the upper country. He longed for its pure breezes, its sparkling waters, and a sight of its familiar mountains. Events had already occurred, which procured the speedy gratification of his wish. After the defeat of Fremont and Shields, the Washington Government united the *corps* of these Generals, of Banks, and of M'Dowell into one body, under the name of the "Army of Virginia." These parts made an aggregate of fifty or sixty thousand men, who were now sent, under Major-General John Pope, upon the mission of making a demonstration against Richmond by the Orange and Alexandria Railroad, and thus effecting a diversion which would deliver M'Clellan from his duress. The former was directed to seize Gordonsville, the point at which the Orange and Central Railroads cross each other, and thus to separate Richmond from the interior. General Pope, who was supposed to have distinguished himself at New Madrid, on the Mississippi, was chiefly noted for his claim of ten thousand prisoners captured from General Beauregard in his retreat from Corinth, where the former commanded the advance of the Federalists (a boast which was reduced, by the truthful statement of the Confederate General, to one hundred). He was the most boastful, the most brutal, and the most unlucky of the Federal leaders who had yet appeared in Virginia. In a general order issued to his troops, he ostentatiously announced his purpose, to conduct the war upon new principles. "He had heard much," he said, "of lines of communication, and lines of·retreat. The only line a general should know anything of, in his opinion, was the line of his enemy's retreat." He declared also, that hitherto he had never been able to see anything of his enemies but their backs; and announced, that during his campaign, the head-quarters should be in the saddle. So coarse a braggart was sure to be in sympathy with the race for which he promised to fight, and they did not need to wait for any deeds actually accomplished to proclaim him "the coming man" of his day. The reader may easily imagine the quiet smile with which Jackson would hear these shallow threats of his antagonist, and the silence with which he accepted them as auguries of a certain victory. General Pope's method of dealing with the people of Virginia was to be as novel as his strategy. He deliberately announced his purpose to subsist his troops on the country, and authorized an indiscriminate plunder of the inhabitants. His army was let loose upon them, and proceeded like a horde of brigands, through the rich counties of Fauquier and Culpepper, stripping the people of food, live stock, horses, and poultry, and wantonly destroying what they could not use. Their General also ordained, that all the citizens within his lines must perjure themselves by taking an oath of allegiance to Lincoln, or be banished South, to return no more, under the penalty of being executed as spies.

Jackson was now moved toward Gordonsville, to meet this doughty warrior, who, as he left Alexandria to assume command of his army at Manassa's Junction, celebrated the triumphs to be achieved, before they were won, with banners and laurels. The *corps* returned from Westover to the neigborhood of Richmond, the 10th of July. There they remained until the 17th, preparing for their march; and it was during this respite that General·Jackson first made his appearance openly, in the city which he had done so much to deliver. He gives the following account of it in a letter to his wife.

"Richmond, July 14th.

"Yesterday I heard Doctor M. D. Hoge preach in his church, and also in the camp of the Stonewall Brigade. It is a great comfort to have the privilege of spending a quiet Sabbath, within the walls of a house dedicated to the service of God. . . . . People are very kind to me. How God, our God, does shower blessings upon me, an unworthy sinner !"

The manner of his entrance was this. He came to the church without attendants; and just after the congregation was assembled, they saw an officer who was manifestly a stranger, in a faded and sunburned uniform, enter quietly, and take his seat near the door. The immediate commencement of the worship forbade any notice or inquiry; they could only observe that he gave a devout and fixed attention to the services. When they were concluded, it began to be whispered that he was General Jackson; but he scarcely gave them time to turn their eyes upon him, before he was gone, after modestly greeting one or two acquaintances. After visiting a mother, whose son had fallen in his command, he returned to his tent.

On the 19th of July, he reached Gordonsville with his *corps*, and took quarters in the hospitable house of Reverend D. B.

Ewing, where he had before found a pleasant resting place, when passing through the village. He appeared jaded by his excessive labors, and positively unwell; and said that he had not suffered so much, since his return from Mexico. But the rest, the mountain breezes, and the fresh fruits in which he so much delighted, speedily restored the vigor of his frame. He loved to refresh himself here, after the labors of the day were finished, with the social converse of the amiable family which surrounded Mr. Ewing's board, and with the prattle of his children. One of these, while sitting upon his knee, was captivated with the bright military buttons upon his coat, and petitioned that when the garment was worn out, he should give her one as a keepsake. This he promised; and months afterward, amidst all his weighty cares, he remembered to send her the gift; which she ever after hoarded among her treasures. It was his greatest pleasure to share the family prayers of this Christian household, and he did not refuse to take his turn in conducting them. His host remarks of these services: "There was something very striking in his prayers—he did not pray to men, but to God. His tones were deep, solemn, tremulous. He seemed to realize that he was speaking to Heaven's King. I never heard any one pray, who seemed to be pervaded more fully by a spirit of utter self-abnegation. He seemed to feel more than any man I ever knew, the danger of robbing God of the glory due for our success." Although he was incapable of making an ostentatious display of himself, and would never permit the interruption of business by society, yet when time sufficed for social enjoyments, he was easily approached by all who sought to know him, and was careful to contribute to their entertainment by bearing a modest part in conversation.

After a few days spent near Gordonsville, he retired southward a few miles into the county of Louisa, whose fertile fields

offered abundant pasturage for his jaded animals. Here he
devoted himself to reorganizing his command, and recruiting his
artillery horses, for the approaching service. It was at this time
that he complained, in his letters to his wife, of being overbur-
thened with cares and labors: but he chided himself by referring
to the Apostle of the Gentiles, who "gloried in tribulation," and
declared that it was not like a Christian to murmur at any toil
for his Redeemer.

Learning that Pope was advancing toward the Rapid Ann
River in great force, he called upon General Lee for reinforcements; and the division of General A. P. Hill was sent to join
him. This fine body of troops continued henceforth to be a part
of his *corps*. On the 2nd of August, the Federal cavalry occupied the village at Orange Court House, when Colonel William
E. Jones, the comrade of Jackson at West Point, commanding
the 7th Virginia cavalry, attacked them in front and flank while
crowded into the narrow street, and repulsed them with loss.
They, however, speedily perceiving the scanty numbers of their
assailants, returned to the charge; and threatening to envelop
Jones, forced him back in turn. But he retired skirmishing with
so much stubbornness, that they pursued him a very short
distance, when they withdrew across the river. This affair
occurred ten miles north of Gordonsville. Pope's infantry
paused in the county of Culpepper, which lies over against
Orange, across the Rapid Ann. He indiscreetly extended his
army a few miles in rear of that stream, upon a very wide front,
while some of the troops designed to serve under his orders
were still at Fredericksburg, two marches below. This was an
opportunity which the enterprise and sagacity of Jackson were
certain to seize. He knew that the army of Lee, still detained
to watch M'Clellan upon the lower James, could not come to his
support before that of Pope would be assembled. The mass of

the latter would then be irresistible by his little army; and there was reason to fear that Gordonsville would be lost, the railroad occupied, and a disastrous progress made by Pope before he could be arrested. He therefore determined to strike his centre immediately at Culpepper Court House, and to cripple him so that he would be unable to advance, before other dispositions could be made for resisting him. Another powerful reason dictated an attack. Jackson's soldierly eye had shown him that the line of the Rapid Ann was the proper one to be held by a defensive army guarding the communications at Gordonsville, and the centre of Virginia; for the commanding heights of the southern bank everywhere dominated over the level plains of the Culpepper border. This judgment was afterward confirmed by the high authority of General Lee, who selected that line for defence against Generals Meade and Grant; and, by its strength, baffled every attempt to force it in front. Pope, then, must not be permitted to occupy it; put it suited the temper of General Jackson to prevent it by an aggressive blow, rather than by a dangerous extension of his inadequate force upon it. Hence, on the 7th of August, he gave orders to his three divisions to move toward Culpepper, and to encamp on that night near Orange Court House.

It was on this occasion that the striking witness was borne by his African servant, Jim, to his devout habits, which was so currently (and correctly) related. Some gentlemen were inquiring whether he knew when a battle was about to occur. "Oh, yes, Sir," he replied: "The General is a great man for praying; night and morning — all times. But when I see him get up several times in the night besides, to go off and pray, then I know *there is going to be something to pay;* and I go straight and pack his haversack, because I know he will call for it in the morning."

August 8th, the division of Ewell, which led the way, bearing off to the northwest, crossed the Rapid Ann at the Liberty Mills, as though to attack the extreme right of Pope. The other divisions crossed at Barnett's Ford, below; and Ewell, turning to the east, returned to their line of march, and bore toward Slaughter's Mountain. The division of A. P. Hill, delayed by the trains which followed the preceding troops, and by a misconception of orders, did not cross the river until the morning of the 9th. This derangement of the march arrested General Jackson many miles from Culpepper Court House, and he reluctantly postponed his attack to the next day. On the morning of August 9th, having ascertained that A. P. Hill was now within supporting distance, he moved early; and, with his cavalry in front, pressed toward the Court House. About eight miles from that place, the advance reported the enemy's cavalry before them, guarding the roads, and manœuvring in a manner which indicated a force behind them; and, a little after, the line of horse was discovered upon a distant ridge, drawn up as if for battle. A few cannon shot from a rifled gun dislodged them; but speedily the fire was returned by the Federal artillery from a distant position, and the line of cavalry re-appeared. General Jackson, convinced that he had a strong body of the enemy in his front, now made his dispositions for battle, a little after the middle of the day.

His army had by this time fallen into the main road, leading northeastward to Culpepper Court House; and to this quarter his front was directed during the remainder of the day. The neighborhood around him was a region of pleasant farms, of hills and dales, and of forests interspersed. But parallel with the road which he was pursuing distant about a mile on his right, was an insulated ridge, rising to the dignity of a mountain, running perfectly straight from southwest to northeast, and dropping into the plain as suddenly as it arose. This is called by the country-people, Slaughter's Mountain. The fields next its base are smoother and more akin to meadows than those along the highway at the distance of a mile. Across the northeastern end of the ridge, flow the rivulets which form, by their union, Cedar Run, and make their way thence to the Rapid Ann. General Early's brigade of Ewell's division, which held the front, was ordered to advance along the great road and develop the position of the enemy, supported by the division of Jackson, commanded by Brigadier-General Winder. The remainder of Ewell's division, consisting of the brigades of Trimble and Hays, (lately Taylor's) diverged to the right, and skirting the base of Slaughter's Mountain, by an obscure pathway, at length reached the northeast end, whence, from an open field elevated several hundred feet above the plain, they saw the whole scene of action unfolded beneath them. The battery of Lattimer, with half that of Johnson, was drawn up to this promontory, and skilfully posted, so as to cover with its fire the whole front of the Confederate right and centre. It was to the promptitude with which General Jackson seized this point, and the adroitness with which he employed its advantages, that he was chiefly indebted, in connection with the bravery of his troops, for his victory. The guns of Lattimer and Johnson, in consequence of the elevation of their position, commanded a wide range of the country below, and were themselves secure from the fire of the enemy. Every shot aimed at them fell short, and buried itself, without *ricochet*, in the hill-side beneath them; while their gunners, in perfect security, and in a clear atmosphere above the smoke of the battle-field, played upon the enemy with all the deliberation and skill of target practice. Thus the level and open fields next the mountain, which otherwise were most favorable to the display of the Federalists' superior numbers, were effectually barred

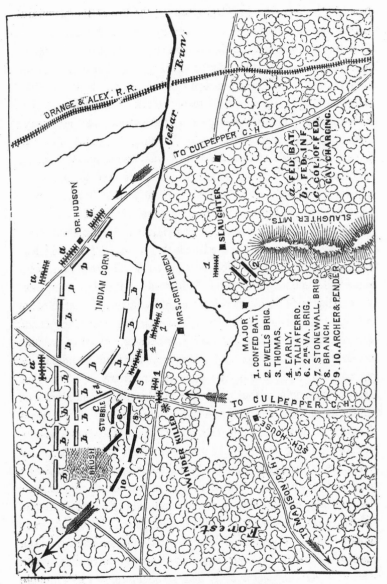

BATTLE OF CEDAR RUN.

from their approach; or, if they braved the fire of the mountain-battery, the two brigades of Ewell lay hid in the dense pine thickets which clothed the side of the ridge, ready to pour upon their flank a crushing fire from superior ground. These dispositions at once decided the security of Jackson's right wing for the whole day. He placed no troops in the meadows next the mountain-base; for on this ground the artillery of the enemy could play with best effect. But though this marked *hiatus* in his line seemed to invite attack, none was seriously attempted; the disadvantage imposed upon the assailants revealed itself to them so powerfully, at their first approach, that they observed the deadly trap afterward with respectful avoidance.

Before these dispositions upon the right were completed, General Early had become engaged with the enemy. Throwing his brigade into line of battle across the road, he advanced obliquely to the right, scouring the woods before him with his skirmishers and driving back the observing force of cavalry. A march of a half-mile brought him to the top of a gentle hill where the road emerged from the forest, and ran forward for a third of a mile farther, between the wood and a large pasture field of undulating ground. In other words, the open ground here cut into the forest by an angle, so that the traveller advancing thenceforward had the field upon his right, and the wood upon his left, for that distance. There the wood terminated, upon the brow of a hillock overlooking the rivulet; and there were open fields upon both sides of the highway. That on the right was covered, for a great extent, with a tall growth of Indian corn in all its summer glory. That on the left was a stubble field of narrow extent, with wheat in the shock; and still farther to the left of this, was another piece of ground of about equal size, which had been denuded of its timber. but was now densely overgrown with brushwood of the height of a man's shoulders. The stubble field and the clearing, together, constituted in fact but a species of bay, penetrating the surrounding forests to the left of the main road; for on their farther side the woods commenced again. The cornfield, the stubble field, the brushwood, and the angle of forest on the Confederate side, were destined to be the *Aceldama*. By the time General Early had reached the rear angle of the great pasture field just described, his whole line was, in consequence of his oblique advance, on the left of the road, and was soon, by his farther advance, separated from it by a considerable space. Sweeping the Federal skirmishers before him, he pushed his line, in perfect order, to the front of the declivity which descended to the rivulet and the Indian corn. Several batteries on his right and in front were now opened on him, and the wheat-field on the left of the highway was observed full of squadrons of cavalry. Withdrawing his men into a slight depression behind the foremost crest of the hill, he obtained partial shelter from the enemy's artillery, and brought up four guns from the batteries of Captains Brown and Dement, to a favorable position upon his right, whence they engaged the opposing batteries with great credit. But no line of infantry was yet visible before him, for it was masked in the thick corn.

The division of Winder had now arrived, and its commander was posting several of its best batteries in *echelon* along the road in the rear of Early's left, whence they delivered a most effective oblique fire toward the right and front. The second brigade of the division was advanced on the left of the road, to the further edge of the wood, presenting a convex line toward the cornfield and the stubble field; the third brigade was left in column parallel to the road and in rear of their artillery: and the first, or Stonewall Brigade, was disposed as a reserve to support the left. A rapid and continuous thunder of artillery now began on both sides, which was prolonged for two hours. Distant spectators perceived that the aim of the Confederates was much more accurate than that of the enemy. While the shells of the latter mostly exploded high in the air and above the tree-tops, those of the former were seen ploughing the ground among the guns of their adversaries, and throwing the dust, with their iron hail, in their midst. But one fated shot from the Federal batteries robbed the patriots of one of the chief ornaments of their army. While General Winder was standing beside the guns of Poague and Carpenter, directing their working with his customary coolness and skill, a shell struck him upon the side, dashed his field-glass from his hand, and inflicted a ghastly wound, of which he died three hours after. No more just or graceful tribute can be paid to his memory, than that of General Jackson's report. "It is difficult within the proper reserve of an official report, to do justice to the merits of this accomplished officer. Urged by the medical director to take no part in the movements of the day, because of the enfeebled state of his health, his ardent patriotism and military pride could bear no such restraint. Richly endowed with those qualities of mind and person, which fit an officer for command, and which attract the admiration and excite the enthusiasm of troops, he was rapidly rising to the front rank of his profession. His loss has been severely felt." Succeeding General Richard Garnett in the command of the Stonewall Brigade, after the battle of Kernstown, and coming to it wholly a stranger, he had unavoidably inherited some of the odium of that popular officer's removal. During the first two months of his connexion with it, he was respected and obeyed; for his dignity, bearing, and soldierly qualities were such as to ensure this everywhere; but he inspired no enthusiasm. It was at Winchester, when General Jackson assigned him the command of his left wing, that his prowess broke forth to the apprehension of his men, like the sun bursting through clouds. The heroism with which he shared their dangers, and the mastery with which he directed their strength, placed him thenceforth in their hearts.

At five o'clock in the afternoon, the struggle began in earnest, by the advance of the Federal infantry against Early, through the Indian corn. This General, handling his regiments with admirable coolness and daring, held the heavy masses in his front at bay, with slight loss to himself. Soon after, the enemy advanced a strong force of infantry to turn his right; but just as the movement was endangering the guns of Brown and Dement,· a brigade was seen advancing rapidly to their support. It was the command of Thomas (from the division of A. P. Hill, who had now arrived upon the scene); which, with two additional batteries, took post upon Early's right. The Confederate line of battle was thus extended within a half-mile of the mountain, and all the efforts made against it on this side were hurled back with loss. But, upon the other extremity of the field, grave events were occurring. It has been related, how the second brigade of the division of Winder, under Colonel Garnett, had been stationed on the left of the great road, with its line conformed to the convexity of the wood. The Stonewall Brigade, which was its reserve, was, unhappily, too far to the rear to give it immediate support. One moment it was declared that there was no hostile infantry visible in its front; but the next, the men at the extreme left beheld a formidable line, whose length overlapped them on either hand, advancing swiftly from the opposite woods, and across the stubble field, to assail them. The battalion at that end of the line, seeing themselves thus overmatched, fired a few ineffectual volleys, and gave way; the Federal right speedily swept around, entered and filled the· woods, and even threatened the rear of the batteries of the division, from which the third brigade of Taliaferro had a little before been removed to the front, to fill the interval between the second and that of Early. The whole angle of forest was now filled with clamor and horrid rout. The left regiments of the second brigade were taken in reverse, intermingled with the enemy, broken, and massacred from front and rear. The regiments of the right, and especially the 21st Virginia, commanded by the brave Christian soldier, Colonel Cunningham, stood firm, and fought the enemy before them like lions, until the invading line had penetrated within twenty yards of their rear. For the terrific din of the musketry, the smoke, and the dense foliage, concealed friend from foe, until they were only separated from each other by this narrow interval. Their heroic Colonel was slain, the orders of officers were unheard amidst the shouts of the assailants, and all the vast uproar; yet the remnants of the second brigade fought on, man to man, without rank or method, with bayonet thrusts and muskets clubbed, but borne back like the angry foam on a mighty wave, toward the high road. The third brigade, also, upon the right of the second, was broken, and on both sides of the way the enemy made a vast irruption, in which half of Early's brigade was involved. On his extreme left, next to Taliaferro stood the famous 13th Virginia, which, under the gallant leading of its sturdy Colonel, J. A. Walker, still showed an unbroken front, and fell back, fighting the flood of enemies. The right regiments of Early, under the immediate eye of their veteran General, held their ground like a rampart. But the Federalists were fast gaining their rear in the open field.

It was at this fearful moment that the genius of the storm reared his head amidst the tumultuous billows; and in an instant the threatening tide was turned. Jackson appeared in the mid torrent of the highway, his figure instinct with majesty, and his face flaming with the inspiration of battle; he ordered the batteries which Winder had placed to be instantly withdrawn, to preserve them from capture: he issued his summons for his reserves; he drew his own sword (the first time in this war), and shouted to the broken troops with a voice which pealed higher than the roar of battle: "Rally, brave men, and press forward! Your general will lead you. Jackson will lead you. Follow me!*" The fugitives, with a general shame, gathered around their adored general: and rushing with a few score of them to the front, he posted them behind the fence which bordered the roadside, and received the pursuers with a deadly volley. They recoiled in surprise; while officers of every grade, catching the generous fervor of their commander, flew among the men, and in a moment reinstated the failing battle. The fragments of Early and Taliaferro returned to their places, forming around that heroic nucleus, the 13th Virginia, and swept the open field clear of the enemy. The Stonewall Brigade had already come up and changed the tide of battle in the bloody woodland, for some of the regiments sweeping far around to the left through the field of brushwood, had taken the Federalists, in turn, upon their flank, and were driving them back with a fearful slaughter into the stubble field. Scarcely was this Titanic blow delivered, when the fine brigade of Branch, from the division of A. P. Hill, hardly allowing itself time to form, rushed forward to second them, and completed the repulse.

The Federal commander, loth to lose his advantage so quickly, now brought forward a magnificent column of cavalry, and hurled it along the highway, full against the Confederate centre. No cannon was in position to ravage their ranks; but, as they forced back the line for a little space by their *momentum*, the infantry of Branch closed in upon their right, and that of Taliaferro and Early upon their left. Especially did the 13th Virginia

---

* His own words, as repeated by a member of his staff, who was present.

now exact a bloody recompense of them for all their disasters. Wheeling instantly toward the léft, they rushed to the
fence beside the road; and, just as the recoil of the shock began,
poured a withering volley into the huddled mass from the distance of a few yards. On both sides of the devoted column, the
lines of Branch and of Taliaferro blazed, until it fled to the rear,
utterly scattered and dissipated. And now Jackson's blood was
up; and he delivered blow after blow from his insulted left
wing, with stunning rapidity and regulated fury. Scarcely was
the charge of this cavalry repelled, when he again reinforced the
ranks of Branch in front of the bloody stubble field, with the
brigades of Archer and of Pender, from the division of Hill,
extending them far to the left. These fresh troops, with the
remainder of the first and second brigades of Jackson's division
were ordered by him to advance across the field, throwing their
left continually forward, and attack the enemy's line in the opposite wood. They advanced under a heavy fire, when the foe
yielded the bloody field, and broke into full retreat. The brigade of Taliaferro also charged, bearing toward the right, and
pierced the field of Indian corn in front of General Early, where
they captured four hundred of the enemy, with Brigadier-General
Prince.

The two brigades which had hitherto remained with General
Ewell upon the mountain now advanced also upon the right,
turned the left flank of the Federalists, and captured one piece
of artillery. Thus, at every point, the foe was repulsed, and
hurled into full retreat. When night settled upon the field they
had been driven two miles, Jackson urging on the pursuit with
the fresh brigades of Stafford and Field. It was his cherished
desire to penetrate to Culpepper Court House, for he would
then have struck the centre of Pope's position, and his chief *depot*
of supplies; whence he hoped to be able to crush the fragments

of his army before the *corps* of M'Dowell could reach him. With this object, he purposed at first to continue the pursuit all night. Ascertaining by his scouts that the enemy had paused in their flight just in his front, he now placed the battery of Pegram in position, and opened a hot fire upon them at short range. This new cannonade threw them for a time into great confusion; and had the darkness of the night permitted the victor to see distinctly where his blows should be aimed, he would probably have converted the retreat of the Federals into a disastrous rout. But, after a time, three batteries began to reply to Pegram with such vigor as plainly indicated that Pope had received some fresh supports since the night fell. The indefatigable Colonel William E. Jones also, returning with his regiment of cavalry from a fatiguing expedition, had passed to the front, and ascertained the arrival of the remainder of the *corps* of Fremont, now commanded by Sigel. The General therefore determined not to hazard more in the darkness of the night, and commanded the troops to halt and bivouac upon the ground which they had won.

The long day, sultry with an August sun, and with the heats of battle, had now given place to a night, moonless but placid. Jackson at length gathered his wearied Staff about him, and rode languidly back through the field of strife, lately so stormy, but now silent, save where the groans of the wounded broke the stillness, seeking a place of repose. Applying at two or three farm-houses for shelter, he was informed that they were full of wounded men, when he persistently refused to enter, lest he should be the occasion of robbing some sufferer of his resting-place. Resuming his way, he observed a little grass-plot, and declared that he could go no farther, but must sleep then and there. A cloak was spread for him upon the ground, when he prostrated himself on it upon his breast, and in a moment forgot his toils and fatigues in deep slumber.

The morning of the 10th of August, General Jackson withdrew his lines a short distance, and proceeded to bury his dead,
and collect from the field the spoils of his victory. These consisted of one piece of artillery and three caissons, three colors,
and five thousand three hundred small arms. The loss of the
Confederates in this battle was two hundred and twenty-three
killed, one thousand and sixty wounded, and thirty-one missing,
— making a total of one thousand three hundred and fourteen.
General Jackson modestly estimated the loss of his enemy as
double his own. How moderate that estimate was will appear
in the sequel. The Federalists, according to their own returns,
had thirty-two thousand men engaged in this battle. The numbers of General Jackson were between eighteen and twenty
thousand. The prisoners captured from the enemy were chiefly
from the *corps* of General Banks; but a few from those of Sigel
and M'Dowell showed that parts of their commands were also
engaged. On the 11th of August, Pope requested, by flag of
truce, access to the field to bury his dead. This privilege was
granted to him; and General Early was appointed commandant
of the field, to enforce the terms of the temporary truce. Soon
the ground was covered with those who had lately been arrayed
against each other in mortal strife, mingling unarmed. While
the burying parties collected their bloody charge, and excavated
great pits in which to cover them, the rest were busy trading their
horses with each other, arguing upon the politics of the great con-
troversy, and discussing the merits of their respective Generals.
The Federals, with one consent, were loud in their praises of
Jackson; and declared that if they had such Generals to lead
them, they also could win victories and display prowess. Not a
few of them were prompt to draw parallels between the simplicity, self-reliance, and courage of the Confederate Generals, and
the ostentation and timidity of their own, little complimentary to

them. "See old Early," they said, "riding everywhere, without a single guard, among his enemies of yesterday. If it were one of our mutton-headed Generals, he must needs have half a regiment of cavalry at his heels, to gratify his pride, and defend him from unarmed men!" General Early saw them bury seven hundred corpses. How many were borne from the field by them during the progress of the battle, cannot be known. If they, like the Confederates, had five wounded for every one slain (the usual ratio), then their total loss was, at the least, four thousand six hundred. While the field of Indian corn was sprinkled over with dead, the most ghastly accumulation was in the stubble field and the brushwood in front of the Confederate left; which one of their own Generals (taking his metaphor from his own former trade) denominated "the slaughter-pens." The battle of Cedar Run, like all those where Jackson was the assailant, was remarkable for the narrowness of the front upon which the true contest was enacted. A space of a mile in width here embraced the whole of the ground upon which his centre and left wing had wrestled, for half a day, against thirty thousand men. When it is remembered that these were enough to man a line of battle, six miles long, this fact will appear a singular evidence of the incompetency of the Federal tactics,—that their boastful commander should have accepted defeat with all the advantage of his superior numbers, in an open country, without effecting any more extended development of his lines, or resort to the resources of manœuvre. General Jackson, on his part, pronounced this the most successful of his exploits. But he announced it to his superior, General Lee, in these devout and modest terms:—

"August 11th, 6½ A. M.

"On the evening of the 9th instant, God blessed our arms with another victory. The battle was near Cedar Run, about six miles from Culpepper Court House. The enemy, according to statements of prisoners, consisted of Banks's, M'Dowell's and Sigel's commands. We have over four hundred prisoners, including Brigadier-General Price. Whilst our list of killed is less than that of the enemy, we have to mourn the loss of some of our best officers and men. Brigadier-General Charles S. Winder was mortally wounded whilst ably discharging his duty at the head of his command, which was the advance of the left wing of the army. We have collected about 1500 small arms, and other ordnance stores."

Whilst General Jackson was engaged on the 10th, caring for his killed and wounded, he caused careful *reconnoissances* to be made under the care of General J. E. B. Stuart, who providentially visited his army on that day, on a tour of inspection. He was convinced by this inquiry, that the army of Pope was receiving constant accessions, and that before he could resume the offensive, it would be swelled to sixty thousand men. The bulk of the forces of M'Dowell, was upon the march to join the enemy, by a route which seemed to threaten his rear. He therefore determined that it was imprudent to hazard farther offensive movements. Having sent back all his spoils and his wounded, he retired from the front of the enemy the night of August 11th, and returned unmolested to the neighborhood of Gordonsville, hoping that Pope's evil star might tempt him to attack his army there, where the proximity of the railroad would enable him to receive adequate re-inforcements.

A part of the leisure of his day of truce was employed in writing to Mrs. Jackson a letter, from which the following extract is taken.

" On last Saturday our God again crowned our arms with

victory, about six miles from Culpepper Court House. All glory be to God for his unnumbered blessings.

"I can hardly think of the fall of Brigadier-General C. S. Winder, without tearful eyes. Let us all unite more earnestly in imploring God's aid in fighting our battles for us. The thought that there are so many of God's people praying for His blessing upon the army, which, in His providence, is with me, greatly strengthens me. If God be for us, who can be against us? That He will still be with us, and give us victory after victory, until our independence shall be established, and that He will make our nation that people whose God is the Lord, is my earnest and oft-repeated prayer. Whilst we attach so much importance to being free from temporal bondage, we must attach far more to being free from the bondage of sin."

His report of the battle is closed with these words:

"In order to render thanks to God for the victory at Cedar Run, and other past victories, and to implore His continued favor in the future, divine service was held in the army on the 14th of August."

This battle was claimed by the Federalists, with their usual effrontery, as a victory; under the pretext that General Jackson had after two days retreated and recrossed the Rapid Ann. Had these measures on his part been caused by anything that was done upon the battle-field by the forces engaged against him August 9th, that pretext would have worn the color of a reason. But since his withdrawal was caused by the arrival of fresh troops in great numbers, after the battle was concluded, it might with as much truth be said that any other victory in history was a defeat, because the material resources of the two parties were afterwards modified or reversed.

The opinion has been expressed that although Jackson fought well at Cedar Run, it would have been better not to have fought at all; because his victory, while glorious, was without other result; and thus the brave men lost were made a useless sacrifice. This criticism should be met by two answers. The battle was not without solid result, for it arrested the career of Pope until the army of Northern Virginia arrived, and prevented his gaining positions decisive of future operations. It must be remembered that on the 2nd of August, the vanguard of the invading army had crossed the Rapid Ann, and penetrated within twelve miles of Gordonsville. The troops which came to support Jackson did not move against the enemy from that place, until August 16th. What disastrous progress might not the invaders have made within that time, if Jackson had not arrested them by his timely blow? But second: designs, which must necessarily be made in advance, are entitled to be tried, when the question is of the wisdom of him who formed them, not by the strict rule of the actual event, but by the milder one of the probable result. General Jackson proposed to strike the enemy, not at Cedar Run, but at Culpepper Court House; and not upon the 9th, but the 8th of August. The space to be traversed to effect this, was not unreasonable, (but one day's rapid marching) and the blunder by which it was prevented was unforeseen. Had his wishes been attained, it is not unreasonable to say, that his victory would have been so much more complete as to silence every charge of fruitlessness. For we have seen that the supports which saved Pope from destruction only arrived at nightfall upon the 9th.

CHAPTER XVI.

SECOND MANASSA'S.

THE battle of Cedar Run was but the prelude to a more bloody struggle, which was destined, by a strange coincidence, for the historic plains of Manassa's. General Jackson had scarcely returned to his encampment near Gordonsville, when the gathering of the hostile masses in larger volume began. General Lee, convinced that M'Clellan was incapable of farther aggression, and that the surest way to remove him finally from the peninsula would be to threaten Washington more violently, began to remove the remainder of his army from Richmond to the Rapid Ann, August 13th; proposing to leave only a small force for observation upon his lines there, until the success of his experiment was verified. On that day, General Longstreet commenced his march for Gordonsville, and the remainder of the troops were moved in the same direction, the division of General D. H. Hill bringing up the rear, near the end of the month. Halleck, the new Federal *generalissimo*, was also eagerly dictating the same movement to M'Clellan. He found the "Grand Army" divided into two widely separated fragments, and trembled before the activity of Jackson, and the danger of his Capital. M'Clellan accordingly broke up his camps at Berkeley on the 17th of August, and with sore reluctance shipped the decimated remains of his troops to Aquia Creek on the Potomac. Disease had been carrying on the work which the sword had begun, and the fever and dysentery of the country had fearfully thinned his ranks. But meantime, General Burnside had brought his corps from North Carolina, and landing it at the same spot on the Potomac, had marched it to the support of General Pope in Culpepper.

That commander now had his forces tolerably concentrated along the line of the Orange Railroad. But ignorant of the first principles of strategy and possessed with the vain conceit of crossing the Rapid Ann nearer its source, and thus turning Jackson's left wing, he had extended his right toward Madison. He did not advert, seemingly, to the fact that this manœuvre gave him a line of operations nearly parallel to his adversary's base, and thus exposed his own left and his communications, to a more mortal thrust from him. The course of the Rapid Ann, which had now manifestly become Jackson's temporary base, is north of east; while the curvature of the Orange Railroad is such that its course, eastward of Culpepper Court House, is parallel to that river, or even brings its stations near the Rappahannock, nearer to it than at the Court House. Thus the Confederates, without exposing their own communications, had it in their power to strike those of Pope at Brandy Station by a march shorter than that which would fetch the Federal advance back to that place. So obvious an advantage could not escape any one except the doughty Pope. Jackson of course seized it upon the instant. Upon an elevated hill which is called Clarke's Mountain, east of Orange Court House, he had established a signal station. From this lofty lookout, all the course of the Rapid Ann and the plains of Culpepper, white with the enemy's tents toward Madison, were visible. As soon, therefore, as the troops from Richmond began to arrive, General Jackson left Gordonsville, and on the 15th of August, marched to the eastern base of Clarke's Mountain, where he carefully masked his forces near the fords of the Rapid Ann. His signal officer upon the peak above, reported to him that the enemy were quiet, or even extending their right still farther up the country, unconscious of their danger. The Commander-in-Chief, who was now upon the ground, appointed the morning of the 18th at dawn of day, for the critical movement; but the dilatoriness of a part of his subordinates disappointed the completeness of his combinations, and overruling the eagerness of Jackson, he postponed it until the 20th. He again issued orders for that day, that all the troops should be prepared to advance in light marching order, with three days' rations, and throw themselves that afternoon upon the enemy's rear. Jackson was to cross the stream at Somerville's ford, so as to occupy the left, supported by the division of General Anderson; while Longstreet passed below, at Raccoon ford, and formed the right. General Stuart, now Major-General of cavalry, was to cross with his two brigades of Robertson and FitzHugh Lee, and his flying artillery, at Morton's ford, march direct for the Rappahannock bridge, destroy it, and then turning back along the enemy's line of communication, destroy his trains, and fill every place with panic, until he connected with the infantry of Longstreet upon the extreme right. It was hoped that by these skilful dispositions, the enemy, cut off from his line of retreat, and fiercely attacked upon his left, would be routed. insulated and destroyed.

But the issue showed the importance of that element of strategic combinations, which Jackson so keenly estimated, time. The propitious moment was already forfeited by delay. On the night of the eighteenth of August, the day when the movement should have been made, a handful of fugitive negroes reached the army of Pope, and revealed to him enough of the movements of the Confederates, to open his eyes to his danger. On the nineteenth, as the Commander-in-Chief stood upon his lookout on Clarke's Mountain, the encampments of the enemy farthest west were seen to disappear, and as the day advanced, the rest vanished from view like a fleeting vision. Pope was in full retreat, eager to place the Rappahannock between himself and his adversary. This was his first lesson upon the soundness of his maxim, that a conquering General should leave his communications to take care of themselves; and he was destined to receive others still ruder. General Lee hastened to pursue, and put his army in motion on an early hour of the 20th of August, according to the plan already arranged. General Jackson, crossing the Rapid Ann at Somerville's ford, marched rapidly toward Brandy Station, while General Longstreet, crossing simultaneously below, pressed toward Kelley's Ford on the Rappahannock. No Federal infantry awaited their approach; before their arrival, all had crossed the latter stream. But their cavalry still occupied the Culpepper bank, and were driven across by the brigades of Stuart. One of these, the brigade of Robertson, formerly the lamented Ashby's, under the eye of its Major-General, had a brilliant combat with the enemy's horse near Brandy Station, and drove them across the river with loss. Pope's whole army was now found massed upon the northern bank of the Rappahannock, with a powerful artillery prepared to dispute the passage of General Lee. He therefore formed the plan of striking his rear at a point still farther north, and thus dislodging him, and fighting a general battle. But the conditions under which the second movement must be made, were far less favorable than those of the one projected from the Rapid Ann; and the results could not be expected to be so great. The Rappahannock, which was then in Pope's rear, and would have been a fatal obstacle to the retreat of his defeated army, was now in his front, and was his defence. His communications were no longer exposed to a direct blow, but could only be reached by a dangerous, arduous, and circuitous march. And when the battle was fought and won, the beaten army would be within a day's march of its place of refuge, the lines of Arlington. Yet the vigor and courage of Jackson were trusted to effect this difficult enterprise. It was determined to march up the Rappahannock River, until a practicable crossing was found; and then to throw the *corps* of Jackson, which, being on the left, became the front in this movement, by forced marches to Manassa's Junction; and when his threatening presence there had called Pope away, to follow with the remainder of the army.

The first essay in pursuance of this plan was made on the 21st of August. General Jackson, leaving the hamlet of Stevensburg, where he had *bivouacked*, crossed the railroad, and approached the river above it, at Beverly's ford. A lodgement was effected here by a regiment of cavalry, upon the northern bank, which was held until the evening; but the enemy was approaching in such force, that it was deemed inexpedient to make the passage in their presence, and the advanced party was withdrawn. The artillery of General Longstreet had meantime engaged that of the enemy at the railroad crossing, a few miles below, with such success as to compel them to withdraw to their works on the north side, and then to burn the bridge and desert the position. The morning of August 22nd witnessed a renewal of the same proceedings: the two armies advanced slowly up the Rappahannock, upon its opposite banks, contesting with each other every available crossing, by fierce artillery duels; and attempting upon each other such assaults as occasion offered. The *corps* of Jackson having passed the Hazel River, a tributary of the Rappahannock near its mouth, left its baggage train parked there, under the protection of Brigadier-General Trimble, of Ewell's division; while the main force pressed on to secure the bridge leading from Culpepper to Warrenton. The cupidity of the enemy was excited by this tempting prize, and they crossed to seize it, capturing a few ambulances. These were almost immediately regained, and Trimble, upon receiving the support of General Hood, who formed the van of Longstreet's *corps*, attacked the intruders, and drove them with loss to the north bank, filling the stream with their floating corpses. A similar enterprise attempted on the other hand, by the Confederate General Stuart, on this day, was as much more successful than the Federals, as it was more audacious. Crossing the Rappahannock, above the enemy's outposts, with a brigade of cavalry, he pressed on through the village of Warrenton, and struck the rear of their army at Catlett's Station after nightfall. Finding here a detachment of troops, with an extensive encampment, in the midst of a furious thunder-storm and Egyptian darkness, they dashed into it with a yell, scattering the astounded occupants to the winds, and capturing a great spoil, with a number of prisoners. This encampment was found to contain the headquarters of General Pope; and the baggage, clothing, horses, and money of his Staff, as well as his own, rewarded the boldness of the assailants. Great exertions were also made to destroy the important railroad bridge spanning a large creek near by; but the deluge of rain had saturated the timbers beyond the possibility of ignition, and the rising freshet underneath, with the intense darkness, forbade the men to ply their axes with success. Stuart therefore, gathering up his spoils and prisoners, returned the way he came, leaving the enemy confounded by his seeming ubiquity. Pope thus learned, in a second hard lesson, that the communications of an army are worthy of its commander's attention. The gravest loss which he experienced in this capture, was that of his letter book, which contained copies of his confidential despatches to Washington, and thus revealed to General Lee the most intimate secrets of his. numbers, his plans, and his pitiable embarrassments.

General Jackson, reaching the Warrenton road the afternoon of the 22nd, found the bridge destroyed, and other evidence that the enemy were in close proximity. But they were not yet prepared to dispute his passage. Opposite to him, on a beautiful hill, rose the buildings of a watering place, known as the Warrenton Springs, or Fauquier White-Sulphur; while to his right, a mile below, stretched a forest which clothed the ridge overlooking the river on that side. He sent the 13th Georgia from Lawton's brigade across, to occupy the Springs; while Early's brigade, supported by two batteries, was passed over on a ruinous mill-dam a mile below, and occupied the wooded ridge. But now the darkness of the approaching night and storm arrested the passage of other troops; the floods descended, and the current was speedily swollen so as to become impassable. This accident placed the command of Early in extreme peril. The advanced parties of the Federalists were hovering around him in the darkness, and he had nothing to expect but to be crushed at the dawn of day by the whole weight of their army, within sight of his friends, but beyond their reach. But his own skill, with the wise and firm support of Jackson, rescued him without the loss of a man. When the morning came, the latter sent word to General Early to associate the 13th Georgia with his own brigade, and form the whole across the highlands near the watering place, with his left upon the river, and his right upon a creek, now equally swollen and impracticable, which here approached from the north to mingle its waters with the Rappahannock. He urged forward, meantime, the construction of a temporary bridge; and, in the afternoon, passed the remainder of Lawton's brigade to the support of Early. But the freshet which had protected his right was now receding into its banks, and the whole army of Pope was manifestly at hand. Yet Early so adroitly concealed his force in the woods, and held his foes at bay with his artillery, that they were able to make no decisive attack before nightfall. During the darkness he retired safely to the southern bank, with his batteries, leaving not a man nor a trophy behind. The deliverance of Early was scarcely completed before the dawn of the 24th. The troops of Longstreet had now arrived, and relieved those of Jackson in the afternoon of that day. A fierce cannonade was kept up across the river, chiefly by the guns of A. P. Hill, by which the enemy was occupied, while Jackson retired a few miles from the river-bank to the village of Jeffersonton, relinquishing to Longstreet the task of amusing Pope by the appearance of a crossing at the Springs.

While the enemy was thus deluded with the belief that the race up the Rappahannock was ended, and that he now had nothing more to do than to hold its northern bank at this place, General Jackson was preparing, under the instructions of the Commander-in-Chief, for the most adventurous and brilliant of his exploits. This was no less than to separate himself from the support of the remainder of the army, pass around Pope to the westward, and place his *corps* between him and Washington City, at Manassa's Junction. To effect this, the Rappahannock must be passed on the upper part of its course, and two forced marches made through the western quarters of the county of Fauquier, which lie between the Blue Ridge and the subsidiary range of the Bull Run Mountains. Having made a hasty and imperfect issue of rations, Jackson disembarrassed himself of all his trains, save the ambulances and the carriages for the ammunition, and left Jeffersonton early on the morning of August 25th. Marching first westward, he crossed the two branches of the Rappahannock, passed the hamlet of Orlean, and paused at night, after a march of twenty-five miles, near Salem, a village upon the Manassa's Gap Railroad. His troops had been constantly marching and fighting since the 20th; many of them had no rations, and subsisted upon the green corn gathered along the route; yet their indomitable enthusiasm and devotion knew no flagging. As the weary column approached the end of the day's march, they found Jackson, who had ridden forward, dismounted, and standing upon a great stone by the road-side. His sun-burned cap was lifted from his brow, and he was gazing toward the west, where the splendid August sun was about to kiss the distant crest of the Blue Ridge, which stretched far away, bathed in azure and gold; and his blue eye, beaming with martial pride, returned the rays of the evening with almost equal brightness. His men burst forth into their accustomed cheers, forgetting all their fatigue at his inspiring presence; but, deprecating the tribute by a gesture, he sent an officer to request that there should be no cheering, inasmuch as it might betray their presence to the enemy. They at once repressed their applause, and passed the word down the column to their comrades: "No cheering, boys; the General requests it." But as they passed him, their eyes and gestures, eloquent with suppressed affection, silently declared what their lips were forbidden to utter. Jackson turned to his Staff, his face beaming with delight, and said: "Who could not conquer, with such troops as these?" His modesty, ever attributing his glory to his brave men rather than to himself, caused him to forget that it was his genius which had made them such soldiers as they were.

On the morning of the 26th, he turned eastward, and passing through the Bull Run Mountains, at Thoroughfare Gap, proceeded to Bristoe Station, on the Orange Railroad, by another equally arduous march. At Gainsville, he was joined by Stuart, with his cavalry, who now assumed the duty of guarding his right flank, and watching the main army of Pope, about Warrenton. As the Confederates approached Bristoe Station, about sunset, the roar of a railroad train proceeding eastward, was heard, and dispositions were made to arrest it, by placing the brigade of Hays, under Colonel Forno, across the track. The first train broke through the obstructions placed before it, and escaped. Two others which followed it were captured, but were found to contain nothing. The *corps* of Jackson, had now marched fifty miles in two days. The whole army of Pope was interposed between it and its friends. They had no supplies whatever, save those which they might capture from the enemy. But they were between that enemy and his capital, and were cheered by the hope of inflicting a vital blow upon him before he escaped. This movement would be pronounced wrong, if judged by a formal and common-place application of the maxims of the military art. But it is the very prerogative of true genius to know how to modify the application of those rules according to circumstances. It might have been objected, that such a division of the Confederate army into two parts, subjected it to the risk of being beaten in detail; that while the Federal commander detained and amused one by a detachment, he would turn upon the other with the chief weight of his forces, and crush it into fragments. Had Pope been a Jackson, this danger would have been real; but because Pope was but Pope, and General Lee had a Jackson to execute the bold conception, and a Stuart to mask his movement during its progress, the risk was too small to forbid the attempt. The promptitude of General Stuart in seizing the only signal station whence the line of march could possibly be perceived, and the secrecy and rapidity of General Jackson in pursuing it, with the energy of his action when he had reached his goal, ensured the success of the movement.

The first care of the General, after he reached Bristoe, was to secure the vast stores accumulated at the Junction, four miles North. He determined not to postpone this essential measure until the morning, lest the enemy should be able to destroy them; and he therefore accepted the offer of Brigadier-General Trimble, with the 21st North Carolina and 21st Georgia regiments, to volunteer for this service. Major-General Stuart was ordered to support the attack with a part of his cavalry, and as the superior officer in rank, to command the whole detachment. The two regiments of General Trimble had already marched twenty-five miles, and the additional distance to the Junction made them thirty; but they set out with an eagerness which emulated that of the cavalry. Stuart, having unmasked the enemy's pickets in front of the fortifications of Manassa's, and having sent the regiment of Wickham to the north, in order to arrest the retreat of the garrison, Trimble placed his regiments in line right and left of the railroad, and advanced steadily to the attack. The night was rayless, and the artillery of the place opened upon them at short range. They knew not what force awaited them in the darkness, but dashing forward, they surmounted the works, and seized two batteries of field guns, with all their men and horses, almost without loss to themselves. The whole entrenchments now fell into their hands without farther resistance, with vast spoils. This gallant attack was a happy illustration of the success which may usually be expected from bold and rapid movements. The place was found crowded with stores for Pope's army, all of which, with three hundred prisoners, eight field-pieces, and two hundred and fifty horses, fell into the hands of the victors, besides two miles of burden cars, laden with army stores and luxuries. The store-houses were found filled with bacon, beef, flour. and ammunition. Everything was here which the Confederates needed. The confessions of Pope show that the loss of these stores was a chief element of his subsequent disasters. It discouraged and intimidated his men, and compelled them to enter the arduous struggle of the three bloody days without adequate rations or ammunition.

On the morning of August 27th, the two regiments of General Trimble, who had been under arms all night were relieved by General Jackson's arrival from Bristoe. He brought with him the divisions of A. P. Hill and Taliaferro, leaving that of Ewell at Bristoe to watch for the approach of Pope, with orders to make head against him as long as practicable; but when pressed by his main force, to retire and join him at Manassa's. Scarcely had General Jackson come upon the ground, when a shot from a distant battery upon the left, announced the purpose of the Federalists to contest it with him, and a brigade made its appearance advancing along the railroad from Alexandria. This was the detachment of Brigadier-General Taylor, of New Jersey, sent out by Halleck to re-open Pope's communications, and to brush away what they supposed was a mere inroad of cavalry. They advanced with all the confidence of ignorance, until they found themselves almost enveloped in the toils. The captured guns were turned against them by Stuart and Trimble; the batteries of Poague and Carpenter poured destructive volleys upon them in front, and the infantry of A. P. Hill threatened them on both sides. General Jackson now pitying their desperate situation, rode toward them alone, waving a white handkerchief as a signal of truce, inviting them to accept quarter. Their answer was a volley of rifle balls. Seeing his compassion thus requited with treachery, he hastened back to his troops and commanded them to let loose their full fury against their foes. In a moment the detachment was routed, their commander slain, and the fugitives, pursued by Hill and Stuart, were cut to pieces and scattered.

The General now gave the wearied troops a respite, to recompense themselves with the spoils, for their labors. Knowing that means of transportation would be utterly wanting to remove the larger part, he allowed the men to use and carry away whatever they were able to appropriate. And now began a scene in ludicrous contrast with the toils of the previous forced march. Dusty Confederates were seen loading themselves with new clothing, boots, hats, and unwonted luxuries. The men who had for days fed on nothing but green apples and the roasted ears of Indian corn, now regaled themselves with sardines, potted game, and sweetmeats. For several hours the troops held carnival.

General Ewell was not allowed to remain unmolested at Bristoe all the day. In the afternoon, heavy columns of Federalists were seen approaching on the west of the railroad, from the direction of Warrenton. The 6th and 8th Louisiana regiments of Hays' brigade, with the 60th Georgia, were posted to receive them, masked in the edge of the pine thickets, and supported by several batteries. Two heavy columns of the enemy advanced against them, each consisting of not less than a brigade; but almost at the first volley, they broke and fled in confusion, many of them throwing away their arms. Fresh columns, however, speedily supplied their places, and it was evident that Pope's main force was at hand. General Ewell therefore gave the word to retire, in order to join his friends at Manassa's. This retreat, which must be conducted in the face of a superior force actually engaged with them, was a most delicate and difficult work; but was effected in perfect order, and without loss. As the three regiments which had received the enemy's first attack were withdrawn, the brigade of Early took their places, and held the enemy in check, with so much steadiness and adroitness, that the stream which separated Bristoe from Manassa's was crossed

66

safely without the capture of a single man.   The Federalists
then halted at the former point, and left Ewell to pursue his
way unmolested, his rear covered by the cavalry regiments of
Munford and Rosser.   The Railroad bridge across Broad Run
was now burned, and after all the troops had supplied their
wants from the captured stores, the remainder was destroyed.
This task was committed to the division of Taliaferro, which
devoted to it the early part of the night, and then retired toward
Sudley Church, across the battle-field of July 21st, 1861.   There
they were joined, on the morning of the 28th of August, by the
division of A. P. Hill, which had marched northward to Centreville, and then returned across the Stone Bridge, and by the
division of Ewell, which had crossed Bull Run and marched up
its north bank until it fell into the same route.   The cavalry,
which had scoured the country as far as Fairfax Court House,
also assembled on the flanks of the infantry, and the concentration of the *corps* was completed.

   General Jackson had now successfully executed the first part
of the task entrusted to him.   He had pierced the enemy's rear,
destroyed his supplies, and secured a position between him and his
Capital.   But in doing this, he had drawn upon himself the whole
of the Federal army, and until the remainder of General Lee's
forces should arrive, he must either bear the brunt of their
attacks with his single corps, reduced by straggling and casualties
to eighteen thousand men; or he must retire again toward his
friends, leaving Pope's operations unobstructed, and thus surrender the larger part of the advantages of his brilliant movements.   Jackson was not the man to do the latter; he therefore
selected a position where he could hope to stand successfully at
bay, and prevent Pope's retreat, until sufficient forces arrived to
deal with him successfully.   One alternative was to remain at
Manassa's Junction within the old Confederate entrenchments,

but to this there were many conclusive objections. The direct turnpike road from Warrenton, where Pope's army was massed, to Alexandria ran five miles northwest of the Junction, and would be still left open: an avenue more valuable to that General than the railroad, since its bridges and trains were destroyed. The Junction, moreover, was a post of limited extent, ill furnished with water, situated in a champaign every way favorable to the operations of the force having the numerical superiority, and denuded of all cover, by the presence of previous armies. The other alternative was to retire to the north side of the Warrenton and Alexandria turnpike, nearer to Thoroughfare Gap through which Longstreet was expected to advance, and there occupy the stronger ground, with the advantage of retreat upon the Confederate reserves in case of disaster. From this position, although the road was not directly obstructed, yet the passage of Pope was forbidden; for his army could not expose itself by marching past such a leader as Jackson, who sat, with eighteen thousand men, ready to pounce upon its exposed flanks.

If the reader will recall the description of the battle-field of the first Manassa's he will have before him the position assumed by Jackson. The Warrenton turnpike, running due east toward Alexandria, is crossed at right angles, a mile and half before it passes the Bull Run at the stone bridge, by the country road which proceeds northward from the Junction to Sudley ford, at which the Federal right first crossed the stream on the morning of July 21st, 1861. At this ford, Jackson now rested his left wing, protected by the cavalry brigade of Robertson, while his right stretched eastward across the hills, in a line oblique to the course of Bull Run, toward the road by which Longstreet was expected from Thoroughfare Gap. His front was nearly parallel to the Warrenton turnpike, and distant from it, between one

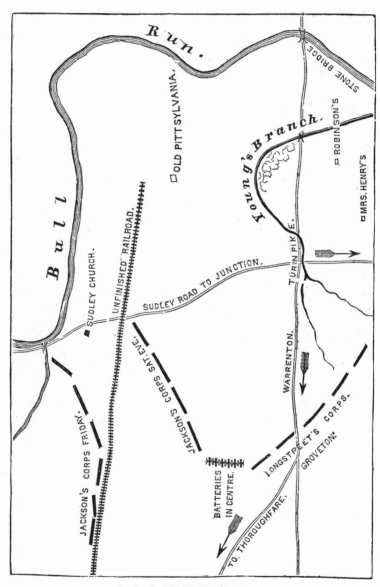

2nd MANASSA'S.

and two miles. The division of A. P. Hill formed his left, that of Ewell his centre, and that of Taliaferro, strengthened by the remainder of the cavalry and the horse-artillery of Pelham, his right.

Scarcely had these dispositions been completed, when the enemy was found to be advancing along the Warrenton turnpike in heavy masses, as though to force his way back to Alexandria. Mid-day had now arrived. The second brigade of Taliaferro's division, under the temporary command of Colonel Bradley T. Johnson, which had been detached to watch the turnpike, was directed to skirmish with the front of the Federal column, and obstruct their advance. The remainder of the division of Taliaferro, supported by that of Ewell, was marched by its right flank and toward the turnpike, to attack the enemy in flank. He, perceiving this movement, and the obstruction in his front, at first attempted to file his masses across the open country toward Manassa's Junction, as though to seek some passage over Bull Run below the stone bridge. But Jackson now threw forward his line with so much energy as to compel him to relinquish this movement, and make a stand. The batteries of Wooding, Carpenter, and Poague were advanced to an elevated hill upon the left and rear of Taliaferro's line of skirmishers, whence they delivered so effective a fire of shell and solid shot upon the dense lines of the Federalists, that their numerous batteries were halted, and placed in position to reply. The Confederate artillery was then promptly removed to another position upon Taliaferro's right, whence they were enabled to enfilade the Federal guns; and the infantry line was again pressed forward, with its front parallel to the Warrenton turnpike, and within a hundred yards of it. Sunset was now near at hand, when a struggle commenced unprecedented in its fury. On Taliaferro's right, the partial screen of an orchard and a cluster of farm-buildings separated him from the highway, which was occupied by the Federal infantry. But, on his left, his line occupied the open field, and received and returned their volleys at the distance of a hundred yards. Until nine o'clock at night, the first, third, and fourth brigades maintained a stubborn contest upon this ground with successive lines of the enemy, when the latter sullenly retired, and gave up the field. On the left of Taliaferro, Ewell, with a part of his forces, waged a contest of almost equal fury, and with the same results, when the darkness closed the battle, and the Confederates remained masters of the field. In this bloody affair, both the Commanders of the divisions engaged, with many field-officers, were wounded, Taliaferro painfully, and Ewell severely. The latter was struck upon the knee by a rifle-ball, and the joint was so shattered that amputation was necessary to save his life. During the remainder of Jackson's career he was unable to return to the field, and the General was deprived of his valued co-operation. The first of the three bloody days was now closed, and Jackson stoutly held his own. With one more struggle his safety would be assured; for the Commander-in-Chief, with the *corps* of Longstreet, leaving the neighborhood of Jeffersonton on the afternoon of the 26th, and following the route of Jackson through upper Fauquier, was now at the western outlet of Thoroughfare Gap, preparing to force his way through, the next morning, and come to the relief of the laboring advance. On the morning of the 29th this pass was forced; and the *corps* of Longstreet, stimulated by the sound of the distant cannon, which told them that Jackson was struggling with the enemy, hurried along the road to Gainesville, where they entered the Warrenton turnpike. Before they reached that village, the indefatigable Stuart, with his cavalry, met them, opened their communication with Jackson's right wing, and informed the Commander-in-Chief of the posture of affairs.

But the narrative must return to the lines of General Jackson. Anxiously did that General watch the distant road which led from Thoroughfare Gap down to the Warrenton turnpike, on the morning of the 29th. His little army was now manifestly confronted by the whole Federal host, which, concentrating itself more toward his left, was preparing to force him back from Bull Run, and to crush him before his supports could arrive. His lines, exhausted by their almost superhuman exertions, thinned by battle, and pallid with hunger, stood grimly at bay; but the stoutest hearts were anxious, in view of the more terrible struggle before them. In the early morning, clouds of dust arising along the Thoroughfare road had mocked their hopes; but they were raised by the Federalists, who, having occupied that pass the day before to obstruct the march of Longstreet, were now retiring upon their masses toward Bristoe Station. As the day verged toward the meridian, other and denser clouds again arose, along the same highway; and soon the couriers of Stuart came, with the welcome news, that it was the *corps* of Longstreet, advancing to connect with the right of Jackson. Already the Federalists, warned of the shortness of their time, had begun the attack by a heavy cannonade upon that part of his position, at ten o'clock. The batteries of Taliaferro's division now commanded by the brave General Starke, replied. But the head of General Longstreet's column was now at hand, and threatened to insinuate itself behind the Federal left. They therefore shifted their demonstration to Jackson's left, opening upon that part of his position with a furious cannonade, and preparing vast masses of infantry to force it. While Longstreet deployed his line across the Warrenton turnpike, and fronting toward the east, Jackson's *corps* was now disposed at right angles to it, along the excavations and embankments of an unfinished railroad, which, crossing Bull Run a half mile below Sudley, ran westward, parallel to the

Warrenton turnpike. This work had been begun to connect the city of Alexandria directly with the Manassa's Gap road near Thoroughfare. Running across the hills and vales of an undulating country, and presenting now an elevated embankment and anon a cut, it offered to the Confederates almost the advantages of a regular field-work. Here General Jackson had arranged his infantry in two lines of battle, with the artillery chiefly posted upon eminences in the rear. A. P. Hill formed his left, Ewell his centre, and Starke his right. An interval between his right and the left of Longstreet was occupied by a large collection of the artillery of the latter, posted upon a large hill, whence they assisted, by their fire, in the repulse of the enemy on either hand. Pope, now contenting himself with showing a front against Longstreet, began, at two o'clock, P. M., to hurl his infantry with fury and determination against the lines of Jackson. Especially did the storm of battle rage in front of the left, occupied by the division of A. P. Hill. In defiance of his deadly fire, delivered from the shelter of the railroad embankments, line after line was advanced to close quarters, only to be mowed down, and to recoil in confusion. Soon the second line of Hill was advanced to the support of the first. Six times the Federalists rushed forward in separate and obstinate assaults, and as many times were repulsed. At an interval between the brigade of Gregg, on the extreme left, and that of Thomas, the enemy broke across in great numbers, and threatened to separate the former from his friends, and surround him. But two regiments of the reserve, advancing within ten paces of the triumphant foe, poured such volleys into their dense masses that they were hurled back before this murderous fire, and the lines re-established. The brigade of Hays from the division of Ewell, now commanded by General Lawton, was first brought to the support of Gregg. The struggle raged until the cartridges of the infantry were in many places exhausted. When Hill sent to the gallant Gregg to ask if he could hold his own, he answered, "Tell him I have no ammunition, but I will hold my position with the bayonet." In several places, the Confederate lines, without a single round of cartridges, lay in the railroad cuts, within a few yards of their enemies, sternly defying their nearer approach with the cold steel, while the staff-officers from the rear sent in a scanty supply of ammunition, by the hand of some daring volunteer, who ventured to run the gantlet of a deadly fire to reach them. In other parts the men, laying aside their empty muskets, seized the stones which lay near, and with them beat back the foe. When the bloody field was reviewed, not a few were found whose skulls were broken with these primitive weapons. But the strength of the extreme left was now exhausted by seven hours of strife; nature could do no more; and General Jackson ordered Early, with his brigade and the 8th Louisiana and 13th Georgia, to relieve Gregg and Hays. The enemy had by this time occupied a considerable tract of the railroad, and the woods in front of it. Early advanced upon them, drove them out of the thickets and across the excavation with fearful slaughter, and pursued them for a distance beyond it, when he was recalled to the original line. With this magnificent charge, the struggle of the day closed. It had raged in similar manner along the centre, where that sturdy veteran, Brigadier-General Trimble, was severely wounded. But the carnage upon the left was most ghastly. Here might be seen upon the fields, the black lines of corpses, clearly defining the positions where the Federal lines of battle had stood and received the deadly volleys of the Confederates; while the woods and railroad cuts were thickly strewn for a mile with killed and wounded. In the division of Hill the loss was also serious; and among the severely wounded were two brigade commanders, Field and Forno. During the heat of the battle, a detachment of Federal troops had penetrated to Jackson's rear, near Sudley Church, and captured a few wounded men and ambulances. The horse artillery of Pelham, with a battalion of cavalry, under Major Patrick, speedily brushed the annoyance away, and recovered the captures. But this incident cost the army the loss of one of its most enlightened and efficient officers, the chivalrous Patrick, who was mortally wounded while pursuing the fugitives.

While this struggle was raging along Jackson's lines, the *corps* of Longstreet continued to confront the observing force of Federalists before them, and the batteries of his left engaged those of the enemy in a severe cannonade. As the afternoon advanced, Stuart reported to him the approach of a heavy column of the enemy upon his right and rear, from the direction of Bristoe. This was indeed a *corps* of the army of M'Clellan from the peninsula, which, landing on the Potomac, had been pushed forward to support Pope. Against this new enemy Longstreet showed a front, while Stuart, raising a mighty dust along the road near Gainsville, by causing a number of his troopers to drag bundles of brushwood along the highway, persuaded him that some heavy mass of fresh Confederate troops was advancing from Thoroughfare to meet his assault upon Longstreet's right. The Federal commander therefore recoiled, after a feeble demonstration; and, passing by a circuit to the eastward, sought to unite himself with the forces in front of Jackson. Longstreet now advanced several brigades to the attack, with those of Hood in the van, and until nine o'clock at night, drove back the enemy before him with great vigor, capturing a number of prisoners, a cannon, and three colors. Darkness then closed the bloody day, and the Confederates on every side withdrew to lie upon their arms upon their selected lines of combat. From this respite, the boastful Pope took the pretext to despatch to his masters a pompous bulletin of victory, claiming that the Confederates were repulsed on all hands! With a stupidity equal to his impudence, he concealed from himself the fact that this lull in the tempest was but the prelude to its final and resistless burst. The mighty huntsman now had the brutal game secure in his toils, and only awaited the moment of his exhaustion to despatch him.

As Jackson gathered his officers around him in the darkness, at the close of this second act of the tragedy, and prepared to lie down for a short repose under the open sky, their triumph wore a solemn hue. A week of marching and fighting, without any regular supply for their wants, had worn down their energies to a grade where nothing but a determined will could sustain them. Many of the bravest and best had fallen, and the sufferers and the dead were all around them. The Medical Director, Doctor M'Guire, recounting the many casualties which he had witnessed, said, " General, this day has been won by nothing but stark and stern fighting." "No," said Jackson, "It has been won by nothing but the blessing and protection of Providence." It was strong evidence of the devout spirit of the patriot troops, that amidst all these fatigues and horrors, they yet found time for acts of devotion. The Chaplains, after spending the day in attentions to the wounded, at nightfall returned to their regiments, and gathered such groups in the woods as could be spared from the watches, where they spent a season in prayer and praise. Many were the brave men who joined in these strange and solemn prayer-meetings, whose next worship was offered in the upper sanctuary.

The advance of Longstreet at nightfall, upon the Confederate right had disclosed the fact that the Federalists were posted, in heavy masses, upon a position of great natural strength. The

choice offered to General Lee now was, to leave the favorable
ground which he had chosen, and taking the aggressive, to dislodge them at a great cost: or else to await their attack, with
the prospect of turning their retreat into a disaster if they
attempted to cross Bull Run in his immediate front and retire
without fighting.   He well knew that Pope would scarcely be so
rash as to attempt the latter expedient; for the two armies were
now at such close quarters, that there was no room for either to
turn away without a deadly side blow from the other; and the
Federal commander had been so obliging, as to manœuvre himself into a position which had the stream immediately in its rear,
with two practicable crossings for artillery, of which one was a
stone arch which a few well directed round shot might have dis-
mantled.   General Lee, therefore, calmly awaited the final strug-
ple, standing on the defensive in his previous lines.   These
formed a vast, obtuse *fourchette*, presenting its concavity toward
the enemy.   The left of Longstreet did not touch the right of
Jackson at the angle; but a space of half a mile between the
two was occupied by an elevated ridge, which commanded the
fronts of both wings.   This hill was now crowned with the artillery battalions of Shumaker of Jackson's *corps*, and S. D. Lee of
Longstreet's, making an aggregate of thirty-six pieces.   From
this arrangement it resulted, first, that the troops of Pope, operating within the jaws of the Confederate army, would naturally
become more densely massed than their opponents, and would
thus afford a more certain mark for their accurate fire; which
no force on earth could ever face in close order, without murderous loss.   The second result was, that the superior *momentum*
of the Federal masses must yet result only in a bloody failure,
when hurled against either wing of the Confederates, because they
would be enfiladed from the other wing.   By these dispositions,
he battle was decided before it was fought.   The only gleam of

good sense which the ill starred Federal leader showed, was in delaying the decisive hour until the late afternoon; so that the friendly darkness might speedily supervene upon the disaster which was destined to follow, and save him from utter destruction. The forenoon of Saturday, August 30th, was therefore spent in a desultory cannonade, addressed first to one, and then to another part of the Confederate lines, with irregular skirmishes interspersed. He was employed in disposing his infantry, under cover of the woods and valleys, chiefly in Jackson's front; for against him he again destined his main attack. The infantry of the latter was still posted along the unfinished railroad, in two lines, the first sheltered, where the ground was favorable, by the excavations and embankments, and the second massed upon the wooded hills above. At half past three o'clock, the enemy made a show of attack along the lines of Longstreet. But scarcely had this begun, when they advanced, without preliminary skirmishing, in enormous masses, against Jackson. Three lines of battle surged forward like mighty waves, and rolled up to the Confederate position. As one recoiled before their fire, another took its place, with a dogged resolution, as though determined to break through by sheer weight of numbers. The Federal flags were planted sometimes within twenty paces of the excavations which contained the opposing line; and again the Confederates, after exhausting their ammunition, resorted to the stones of the field to beat back their assailants. When this furious struggle had raged for half an hour, and the wearied lines of Jackson was yielding at some points, he sent word to Longstreet to move for his relief. But his desire was already anticipated; the artillery in the centre was advanced, and wherever the attacking lines of Federalists exposed themselves before Jackson's front, it showered a crushing and enfilading fire upon them. The third and second lines were first broken, and the woods in which they attempted to rally searched with shells. Meantime, the artillery of Ewell's and Hill's divisions, from Jackson's rear and left, joined in the *melée* as position offered. Before this fire in front and flank, the Federal lines wavered, broke, and resolved themselves into huge hordes of men, without order or guidance. General Jackson now ordered the advance of his whole line of infantry; and the Commander-in-Chief, seeing that the moment for the final blow had come, sent a similar order to his right wing. But its energetic leader had divined his wishes, and had already begun the movement. Over several miles of hill and dale, of field and forest, the two lines now swept forward, with a terrible grandeur, closing upon the disordered masses of the enemy like the jaws of a leviathan; while Jackson upon the left, and Stuart upon the right, urged forward battery after battery at a gallop, to sieze every commanding hill whence they could fire between the gaps, or over the heads of the infantry, and plough up the huddled crowds of fugitives. But at many points, these did not yield without stubborn resistance. The brigades of Jackson dashed at them with fierce enthusiasm, and such scenes of close encounter and murderous strife were witnessed, as are not often seen on fields of battle. The supreme hour of vengeance had now come; in the expressive phrase of Cromwell, the victors "had their will upon their enemies." As they drove them for two miles toward Bull Run, they strewed the ground with slaughter, until fury itself was sated and fatigued with the carnival of blood. And now, night again closed upon the third act of the tragedy, black with a double gloom of the battle smoke and a gathering storm; but still the pursuers plied their work with cannon shot and fierce volleys, fired into the populous darkness before them. At ten o'clock they ceased their pursuit, for they found that amidst the confusion of the field, and the obscurity, friend could no longer be distinguished from foe. The army then lay down to rest upon the ground they had won; while all night long, the broken fragments of the Federalists were stealing across the stream, and retreating to the heights of Centreville.

In this three days' battle, the Confederate loss was heavy, but that of their enemies was frightful. Compared to it, the carnage of the Chickahominy was child's play. The bloody field told the story of the disproportion for itself, and when the Federal surgeons came upon it under a flag of truce, such was the multitude of the wounded lying helpless upon it, that days were exhausted in collecting them, while many wretches perished miserably of neglect during the delay. This disproportionate carnage was due to the masterly handling of the Confederate troops, to their advantageous position, to the density of the enemy's masses, and especially to the terrible moment of the rout, when the work of destruction was pursued, for a time, without resistance. The Sabbath morning dawned upon a scene in most fearful contrast with its peace and sanctity. The storm which had gathered during the night was descending in a comfortless rain, drenching the ghastly dead, the miserable wounded, and the weary victors. The soldiers of Jackson arose from the ground stiffened with the cold, and after devoting a few hours to refreshment, resumed the march, while those of Longstreet remained to bury the dead and collect the spoils. Stuart had reported that he found the enemy rallied upon the heights of Centreville, commanding the Warrenton turnpike, where General Joseph E. Johnston had constructed a powerful line of works, the first winter of the war, which were capable of defence either in front or rear. Here the fragments of Pope, supported by large reinforcements from the army of M'Clellan, again showed a front against the pursuers. Jackson was therefore directed to turn this position, and compel the retreat of the enemy from it

without a battle. To effect this, he crossed the Bull Run at
Sudley, and marching northward by a country road, came the
next day into the Little River turnpike, which leads eastward,
and intersects the Warrenton road at Fairfax Court House, far
in the rear of Centreville. No sooner was this movement perceived by the enemy, than they resumed a hasty retreat. But as
their crowded column approached Fairfax Court House, they
found Jackson at hand, prepared to strike their line of march
from the side. They therefore detached a strong force to make
head against him, and posted it upon a ridge near the little hamlet of Germantown. As soon as Jackson ascertained the position
of this force, he threw his infantry into line of battle, Hill on the
right, Ewell in the centre, and his old division on the left, and
advanced to the assault. The enemy, knowing that the salvation
of their army depended upon them, made a desperate resistance,
and the combat assumed a sudden fury in the front of Hill, equal
to that of any previous struggle. The enemy were encouraged
by a momentary success in breaking Hayes' brigade, but his lines
were immediately reinstated by the reserves, and after a short
but bloody strife, the battle died away as suddenly as it had
begun, and the enemy retired in the darkness. This affair,
which was known as the battle of Ox Hill, closed the evening of
September 1st. Its thunders were aggravated by those of a
tempest, which burst upon the combatants just before the battle
was joined, and the Confederates fought under the disadvantage of the rain, which was swept by a violent wind directly into
their faces. Two Federal Generals fell here, in front of Hill's
division, Kearney and Stephens, and their death doubtless completed the discouragement of their troops. The next morning,
the Federalists were within reach of their powerful works before
Washington, and the pursuit was arrested. The Commander-in-
Chief now purposed to transfer the strife to a new *arena*.

The total loss of the Confederate army in this series of battles was about seven thousand five hundred, of whom eleven hundred were killed upon the field. Of this loss, nearly five thousand fell upon the *corps* of Jackson; out of which number eight hundred and five officers and men were killed. The captures from him, in the whole of the long struggle, amounted to only thirty-five. The excessive loss in his command is explained by the fact that it was always the advance, and that the enemy continually directed the chief fury of his attacks upon him. The results of the battle of Manassa's were the capture of seven thousand prisoners, in addition to two thousand wounded left in the hands of the Confederates; with twenty thousand small arms, thirty pieces of artillery, numerous colors, and a large amount of stores; and the deliverance of Northern Virginia from the footsteps of the invader, save where he still clung to a few miles along the Potomac included within his works. General Jackson closed his Report of the Campaign with these words: —

"For these great and signal victories our sincere and humble thanks are due unto Almighty God. We should in all things acknowledge the hand of Him who reigns in Heaven, and rules among the armies of men. In view of the arduous labors and great privations the troops were called to endure, and the isolated and perilous position which the command occupied, while engaged with greatly superior numbers of the enemy, we can but express the grateful conviction of our mind, that God was with us, and gave us the victory; and unto His holy name be the praise."

Few words are needed to point out the share which Jackson and his *corps* merited, in the glory of the second victory of Manassa's. To the rapidity of his march, the promptitude and skill of his action in seizing and destroying the Junction, the wisdom which guided his selection of a position, and the heroic tenacity

68

with which he held it against fearful odds until the arrival of General Lee, was the splendid result chiefly due. It was so ordered, as if to illustrate the superior prowess of the Confederate soldiery, that in this battle the positions of the combatants in July, 1861, were almost precisely reversed. The ground held by Jackson in the second battle, was that held by McDowell in the first; and the ground from which the Confederates drove Pope, at nightfall, the 30th of August, was that from which McDowell could not drive them, on the 21st of July; while the preponderance of numbers was still upon the Federal side.

The blunders of Pope in this short campaign, — which were almost as numerous as it was possible to make them, — are an instructive study to the commanders of armies. First, it was little short of lunacy to adopt, in Culpepper, a line of operations along the Orange Railroad, and even west of it, which was parallel to the Rapid Ann — the temporary base of the Confederates — in the presence of such masters of the art of war as Lee and Jackson. Instead of extending his right so far toward Madison, with the preposterous design of turning Gordonsville, upon the west, he should have directed the head of his column toward the lower course of the Rapid Ann, and perpendicular to it. He would thus have covered his own line of advance; and, if he succeeded in crossing that river, would have uncovered the communications of his adversary, which would then have been by the Central Railroad. Nothing but the delay of Lee's reserves in reaching Raccoon Ford, saved Pope here from a disaster far worse than that of Manassa's. Second: after retiring across the Rappahannock, — which was a measure dictated by so stringent a necessity that a fool could not err therein, — he repeated the old, but seductive folly, of attempting to hold a river as a defensive line, by extending his whole force along its immediate bank, to watch and resist the passage of his opponent. Although a river is, to some extent, a barrier to the assailant attempting to cross it in the face of a force defending it; yet, if the latter consigns itself to the stationary defensive along its banks, the other is always enabled thereby to baffle his vigilance at some one point; or to mass at a single spot a preponderance of force, which will more than compensate him for the resistance of the natural obstruction, and break its way over it. Then the barrier, broken at one point, becomes useless, and must be forsaken at all. Such was the result here; the stream was passed above Pope's right, before he was in condition to prevent it. His next mistake was in the singular ~inefficiency of his cavalry, which seems to have been more busy in harrying the hen-roosts of the citizens, than in ascertaining whither the swift-footed Jackson was bent, when he disappeared to the northwest from his position before Warrenton Springs. Thus Pope was left in a shameful ignorance, even after his communications were cut at Bristoe Station, whether it was done by a serious force, or by an audacious incursion of horse. But on the evening of the 27th, at least, he was taught, in a bloody lesson by Ewell, that he had a formidable foe in his rear. The plainest deduction might have convinced him, that such a General as Lee would not have placed such a body of infantry and artillery, as he saw grimly confronting him across Broad Run at the close of that combat, so far from its base, without powerful supports.

From that moment the goal of safety for Pope should have been Centreville; and he should have lost no time in concentrating his whole army by forced marches, to strike the formidable obstruction from his rear, and secure his retreat thither. There he would have been front to front with his adversary once more, and within reach of the support of M'Clellan, by whose aid he might have advanced again, and quickly resumed his lost ground. But although it is but one march from Warrenton, where his headquarters were, to Manassa's, two and a half precious days were wasted, between the 26th, when Jackson struck Bristoe, and the 29th, when Longstreet reached his right; and neither was Jackson crushed, nor Thoroughfare Gap effectually held, nor the army safely transferred to Centreville. At mid-day, on the 29th, the arrival of Longstreet rendered his fortunes difficult enough; but, as though he were intent to make them desperate, when his left was incommoded by the appearance of Longstreet's column behind it, instead of retiring squarely from his antagonists, keeping his right upon Bull Run, until his left met the support of the approaching column of Fitz-John Porter, from Aquia, he weakly sought to disengage his left, by manœuvring to his right, and again confining his onset to the lines of Jackson. These were skilfully retracted, to lead him into the trap; and the result was, that on the third and decisive day, he was compelled to fight with the stream in his immediate rear, and with his whole army inclosed within the limits of the fatal *fourchette*. The Confederates might well pray that such leaders should ever command the armies of their enemies.

This chapter will be closed with a characteristic letter from General Jackson to his wife.

"SEPTEMBER 1st, 1862.

" We were engaged with the enemy at and near Manassa's Junction Tuesday and Wednesday, and again near the battle-field of Manassa's on Thursday, Friday, and Saturday; in all of which God was with us, and gave us the victory. All Glory be to His holy name! May He ever be with us, is my earnest prayer, and we ever be His devoted people. It greatly encourages me to feel that so many of God's people are praying for that part of our forces under my command. The Lord has answered their prayers; and my trust is in Him, that He will still continue to do so. God, in His providence, has again placed us across Bull Run; and I pray that He will make our arms entirely successful, and that the glory will be given to His holy name, and none of it to man.

"'God has blessed and preserved me through His great mercy.'"

Thus his soul dwelt habitually upon the plain and familiar promises of Gospel blessings, with a simplicity of faith like that of the little child. He did not entertain his mind with theological refinements and pretended profundities or novelties; but fed it with those known truths which are the common nourishment of all God's people, wise and simple, and which are, therefore, the greatest truths of redemption. The eminence of his Christian character was not in that he affected to see doctrines unknown or recondite to others; but in this: that he embraced the doctrines common to all, with a faith so entire and prevalent. This character of his religion often suggested to those less spiritually minded than himself the opinion, that his was a common-place understanding. They forgot that it is by receiving the kingdom of God as a little child that we must enter therein. When they met Jackson in council or in action, in his own profession, they soon learned their mistake, and recognized in him the original force and power of true greatness.

CHAPTER XVII.

THE CAMPAIGN IN MARYLAND.

THE Confederates had abundant reason to be satisfied with the results of the summer's operations. With an aggregate of about eighty thousand men in all Virginia, they had rescued the State from the grasp of M'Clellan, with his two hundred and twenty-three thousand. No invaders now polluted its soil, save at the fortified posts along the coast, where they were protected by their overwhelming naval forces, at Alexandria, and at Harper's Ferry, and Martinsburg in the Great Valley. The powerful expedition of Burnside had been recalled from North Carolina, leaving no fruits of its exertions in the hands of his Government, except the occupation of a few feeble places. The "grand army" had been reduced by battle, desertions, captures, and sickness, from its huge proportions, so that M'Clellan was now able to set in the field only ninety thousand men, by concentrating all those parts which had lately outnumbered and oppressed the Confederates, from the extreme west of Maryland to the capes of the Carolinian coast. The grateful people of the South might well exclaim with Jackson, in view of so grand a deliverance: "Behold! what hath God wrought!"

General Lee now determined to pursue his advantages by invading the country of his enemy in turn, and thus giving such occupation to him as would secure to Virginia, during the remainder of the season, a respite from the cruel devastations it had so long suffered. The temper of the South demanded it, swelling with the grief of its mighty wrongs, and hungering for righteous retribution. Wise policy dictated that the soil of Virginia should, if possible, be relieved of the burden of the invading and the patriot armies, which it had so long borne, and that their ravages should be retorted upon the aggressor. Maryland, it was known, had succumbed reluctantly to his yoke, and the hope was entertained that the presence of the southern army would inspirit its people to attempt something in aid of their own liberation: or that, at least, the well-grounded fears of the despot lest their discontent should endanger his Capital, would detain so large a force to defend it and to hold them prostrate, that his army in the field might be defeated upon their own soil, and a successful incursion might carry a wholesome terror into the heart of Pennsylvania. The two veteran divisions of R. H. Anderson and D. H. Hill had now overtaken the main army, diminished indeed by the losses of the peninsular campaign, but in excellent condition. Indeed, the former of these had reached Manassa's plains on the 30th of August, early enough to support Longstreet's centre, in its decisive advance against Pope. The fragments of his army, reinforced by M'Clellan, were now ensconced within their lines near Alexandria, under the skilful direction of the latter General; and to attack them there would be attended with too prodigal a waste of patriot blood. General Lee therefore determined to turn aside and promptly cross the Potomac. But notwithstanding the accessions he had just received, he was made conscious, in the very attempt, of that cruel disparity of means and numbers, which robbed the Confederates of the larger part of the fruits of their heroism. The invasion of Maryland, he well knew, would stimulate that recruiting of the depleted armies of the enemy, which their population made so easy; while he could expect no material increase of his force. They would operate along great railroads, and sustain their troops with a lavish supply of transportation, stores, and ammunition, from their vast depots just at hand. He had now left his railroad communication far behind, and must provide for the wants of his army with scanty trains of wagons; while ordnance, clothing, and shoes were deficient, and impossible to obtain in adequate quantities. No generals, therefore, ever adopted a bolder project than that of Lee and Jackson, or executed it with greater promptitude. The battle of Ox Hill ended at nightfall, September 1st, amidst thunder, tempest, and a deluge of rain. On the 2nd the last remains of the beaten Federals were whipped in under the shelter of their ramparts. On the 3rd the Confederate army was upon the march for the fords of the Potomac!

The invasion determined on, two places offered themselves to General Lee for penetrating into Maryland. If he removed his army directly across the Blue Ridge to the Lower Valley, he could easily brush away the force which occupied Martinsburg; when the valley of central Pennsylvania would lie open before him, and his own line of communication could be established with the Central Virginia Railroad at Staunton, along that still abundant country. Or else, he might cross the Potomac between the Federal fortifications and the Blue Ridge, and entering the middle regions of Maryland, proceed as the movements of the enemy should indicate. He adopted the latter plan. His purpose was, first to draw the Federal army from the Virginian bank by violently threatening their Capital and Baltimore, from the other side, so that his field hospitals at Manassa's Plains, his own communications toward Orange, and the important work of removing his prisoners, wounded and spoils, from the scene of his late triumphs, might be relieved from their incursions for a season. He also hoped, that when the head of his great column began to insinuate itself between Washington and Harper's Ferry, the Federal detachment at the latter place would act upon the obvious dictate of the military art, evacuate that place to him without a struggle, and retire into communication with their friends; thus clearing his left of that annoyance. His purpose was then to move toward Western Maryland and Central Pennsylvania, establish his communications with the valley of Virginia, and drawing the Federalists afar from their base at Washington, fight them beyond the mountains. He therefore put the army in motion, September the 3rd, with the cavalry of Stuart and the fresh division of D. H. Hill in front, followed by the *corps* of Jackson, which still formed the body of the advanced force. He marched to Drainsville that day, and to Leesburg, the county-seat of Loudoun, the 4th of September. On the 5th, the *corps* passed the Potomac, at White's Ford, near Edwards' Ferry, a few miles distant, just below the scene of the bloody repulse of Ball's bluff, and established themselves upon the soil of Maryland without opposition. At this place the great river spreads itself out to the width of more than half a mile, over a pebbly and level bed; and its floods, reduced in volume by the summer heats, were but two or three feet deep. The infantry, and even the cannoneers passed, by wading through the water. All day long the column poured across, belting the shining river with a thin, dark line; and as the feet of the men were planted upon the northern bank, they uttered their enthusiasm in hearty cheers. Many a gallant man, who now touched that soil, was destined to sleep, till the last day, within it, in a stranger's grave. The first care of the Confederates, after gaining the northern bank, was to interrupt the navigation of the canal effectually, by destroying its locks, and opening the embankments, so that the waters escaped and left its bed dry. Jackson then advanced northward, and on the 6th of September occupied the Baltimore and Ohio

Railroad, and the flourishing town of Frederick. The arrival of the Confederates in Maryland awakened in a part of the population a faint glow of enthusiasm. A committee of citizens met General Jackson with the present of a costly horse, and a few hundreds of the young men enlisted in the patriot army. But the opinions of the people in the upper regions of the State were divided, and the major part merely acquiesced in the occupation of the country, with a truckling caution. General Jackson employed the most stringent measures against straggling, and every outrage; and established in the town a police so strict, that its citizens were almost unconscious of the inconveniences of hostile occupation. Two appearances were now manifest in strong contrast, which have not failed to re-appear at every return of the Confederate army to the northern soil; on their part a generous forbearance and respect for private rights, almost incredible in men who had left their own homes desolated by outrages so diabolical; and on the part of the so called Union population, a disgusting brutality, which declared itself incompetent even to comprehend their magnanimity, by imputing it uniformly to fear.

All direct communication between Washington and Harper's Ferry was now severed. The first effect which General Lee hoped from his movement was immediately gained. M'Clellan, who was placed by the verbal request of Lincoln, in supreme command, began at once to withdraw his troops to the north bank of the Potomac; and the Confederate rear was delivered from all serious annoyance, save the insults of flying parties of cavalry. The other consequence, the evacuation of Harper's Ferry and Martinsburg, would also have followed, if the sound discretion of M'Clellan had prevailed. No sooner had he fully discovered General Lee's drift, than he requested of Halleck that the troops there and at Harper's Ferry, useless and in peril where they were, should be withdrawn and brought into connexion with him. His advice was disregarded, and the speedy capture of both those detachments evinced at once the soundness of his counsel and the soundness of General Lee's expectation, that his advance on Frederick ought naturally to result in the peaceable occupation of Harper's Ferry by the Confederates. The blunder of the Federalists in remaining there, did, indeed, exert an unforeseen and indirect influence in favor of their army, as will appear in the sequel; but, as it was one which was not designed by either Halleck or M'Clellan, it does not acquit the former of these Generals from the charge of an error of judgment. This commander was now seized with a panic for the safety of Washington, which obfuscated his own senses, and obstructed, for a time, every effort of M'Clellan to act with vigor against the invaders. He was haunted with the fear that the march into Maryland was a feint,— that only a small detachment was there, while the bulk of their army was somehow hidden away in some *limbus* in the woods of Fairfax, whence the terrible Jackson would suddenly emerge, seize the lines of Arlington while denuded of their defenders, and thunder with his cannon upon the White House. Again, he imagined that he would suddenly recross the Potomac somewhere in the mountains, march down its southern bank, pass it a third time below M'Clellan's army, and, approaching Washington by its north side, capture the place, with the precious persons of the President and his minions, before the latter General could turn about. A few days after, when he heard that Jackson was indeed passing to the south side of the Potomac at Williamsport, a hundred miles away, he was sure that the catastrophe was at hand. Hence, he detained M'Clellan in his march; he entreated him not to proceed far from the Capital; he warned him to look well to his endangered left. These fancies of the *Generalissimo* are of interest only as showing the conviction of Jackson's enemies, that there was nothing which was not within reach of his rapid audacity, and as evincing how happily his prowess confounded their counsels.

These uncertain and dilatory movements of the enemy gave General Jackson a respite from the 6th to the 10th of September, at Frederick, which he improved in resting and refitting his command. The day after his arrival was the Sabbath. Such was the order and discipline of the invading army, that all the churches were opened, and the people attended their worship, with their wives and children, as in profound peace. Jackson himself appeared in the German Reformed Church, as a devout worshipper. He expressed to his wife his lively delight in participating in the divine service again, after so many weeks of privation, with a regular Christian assembly, and in a commodious temple, consecrated to God.

Meantime his cavalry, under the gallant Colonel Munford, with some supporting force, observed the approaches of the enemy on the side of Washington. This officer, who had just distinguished himself on the plains of Manassa's in the most brilliant cavalry charge of the war, skirmished daily with the enemy's advance; and, as their masses began to press more heavily upon him, fell back toward Frederick. The whole Confederate army had arrived there, and was encamped near the town. General Lee now assembled his leading Generals in council, to devise a plan of operations for the approaching shock of arms. Harper's Ferry had not been evacuated, as he hoped. His first design, of withdrawing his army in a body toward Western Maryland, for the purpose of threatening Pennsylvania, and fighting M'Clellan upon ground of his own selection, was now beset with this difficulty: that its execution would leave the garrison at Harper's Ferry to re-open their communications with their friends, to receive an accession of strength, and to sit upon his flank, threatening his new line of supply up the valley of Virginia. Two other plans remained: the one was to leave Harper's Ferry to itself for the present, to concentrate the whole army in a good position, and fight M'Clellan as he advanced. The other was to withdraw the army west of the mountains, as at first designed, but by different routes, embracing the reduction of Harper's Ferry by a rapid combination in this movement; and then to re-assemble the whole at some favorable position in that region, for the decisive struggle with M'Clellan. The former was advocated by Jackson; he feared lest the other system of movements should prove too complex for realizing that punctual and complete concentration which sound policy required. The latter, being preferred by the Commander-in-Chief was adopted. It would be unjust to point to its partial results as proof of superior sagacity in Jackson, for the impartial reader would remember that the plan of his preference was never tried; and, if it had been, the test of experiment might have shown that it also was only capable of imperfect success. It should be added that the execution of the plan which was actually adopted was marred, in some measure, by the untimely disclosure of it to the enemy. Either project was bold, and its execution would have been delicate and hazardous. The purposes of General Lee cannot be so clearly set forth in any way as by the *order* which unfolded them to his Lieutenants, issued at Frederick, September 9th:—

" The army will resume its march to-morrow, taking the Hagerstown road. General Jackson's command will form the advance, and, after passing Middletown with such portion as he may select, will take the route toward Sharpsburg, cross the Potomac at the most convenient point, and by Friday night take possession of the Baltimore and Ohio Railroad, capture such of the enemy as may be at Martinsburg, and intercept such as may attempt to escape from Harper's Ferry.

" General Longstreet's command will pursue the same road as far as Boonesborough, where it will halt with the reserve, supply, and baggage trains of the army.

" General M'Laws, with his own division, and that of General R. H. Anderson, will follow General Longstreet; on reaching Middletown he will take the route to Harper's Ferry, and by Friday morning possess himself of the Maryland Heights, and endeavor to capture the enemy at Harper's Ferry and its vicinity.

" General Walker, with his division, after accomplishing the object in which he is now engaged, will cross the Potomac at Cheek's Ford, ascend its right bank to Lovettsville, take possession of Loudoun Heights, if practicable, by Friday morning; Key's Ford on his left, and the road between the end of the mountain and the Potomac on his right. He will, as far as practicable, co-operate with General M'Laws and General Jackson in intercepting the retreat of the enemy.

" General D. H. Hill's division will form the rear-guard of the army, pursuing the road taken by the main body. The reserve artillery, ordnance, and supply-trains, &c., will precede General Hill.

" General Stuart will detach a squadron of cavalry to accompany the commands of Generals Longstreet, Jackson, and M'Laws; and with the main body of the cavalry will cover the route of the army, and bring up all stragglers that may have been left behind.

" The commands of Generals Jackson, M'Laws, and Walker, after accomplishing the objects for which they have been detached, will join the main body of the army at Ꝫꝋ nsborough or Hagerstown."

It will be seen that the advance was again committed to General Jackson, together with the task of making the longer circuit, and reducing Harper's Ferry. On the morning of Wednesday, September 10th, he set out, and marched across the mountains to Boonsborough. The next day, leaving Hagerstown on his right, General Jackson marched to Williamsport; and crossing the Potomac at that place, re-entered Virginia a full day's march west of Harper's Ferry. Then, dividing his forces, he sent General A. P. Hill on the direct road to Martinsburg; while he, with the other two divisions, moved to the North Mountain Depot, the nearest station west of that town. The object of these movements was to prevent the garrison of Martinsburg from escaping by the west or north. Their commander, Brigadier-General White, finding no other outlet, deserted the place on the approach of the Confederates, and retired to Harper's Ferry. They entered Martinsburg on the morning of the 12th of September, and found many valuable stores abandoned by the enemy. By the patriotic part of the population of this oppressed town General Jackson was received with an uncontrollable outburst of enthusiasm. He was now in his own military district again, — his beloved Valley; and he appeared among the astonished and delighted people almost as a visitor from the skies. The females, especially, to whom his purity and domestic virtues made him as dear as his lofty chivalry, crowded around him with their affectionate greetings; while the foremost besieged him for some little *souvenir*. Blushing with embarrassment, he said: "Really, ladies, this is the first time I was ever surrounded by the enemy;" and disengaged himself from them. Allotting scanty time to the indulgence of this popular emotion, he pressed forward the same day toward Harper's Ferry, and approached it from the west at eleven o'clock on the morning of the 13th. His two partners in the enterprise, Generals M'Laws and

Walker, had not yet arrived; and it is striking evidence of his celerity, that while they had but the distance of a day's march to traverse, he completed a circuit of more than sixty miles, and arrived first. Placing his signal officer upon a conspicuous eminence, he began immediately to question the neighboring heights of Loudoun and Maryland, but received no response. He then sent by couriers; and, during the night of the 13th, received answer that General M'Laws had succeeded in seizing the Maryland Heights, after a spirited and successful combat, about four and a half o'clock, P. M., while General Walker had the same evening occupied the Loudoun Heights with two regiments, without opposition.

The village of Harper's Ferry has already been described, as occupying the angle between the Potomac and Shenandoah, where these two rivers unite, immediately before their passage through the gorge of the Blue Ridge. The town ascends, in a rambling fashion, a ridge which fills the space between the two rivers, and which is itself almost a mountain. This range of highlands, known as Bolivar Heights, upon its reverse, presents a regular acclivity, looking toward the southwest over the open country of the valley, which extends from the Shenandoah to the Potomac. The former stream separates them from the Loudoun Heights, and across the latter, they are confronted by the Maryland Heights. Along the crest of Bolivar Heights the Federalists had constructed a defensive line of earthworks, with heavy *abattis*, and many batteries of artillery. On the morning of September 14th, General Jackson placed himself in communication with his associates, and taking the chief direction as senior officer, proceeded to dispose everything for the capture of the place, with its entire garrison. Brigadier-General Walker carried four rifled cannon to the crest of Loudoun Heights, supported by a portion of his infantry; while with the remainder he guarded the roads by which the enemy might seek to escape eastward. Major-General M'Laws established himself in Pleasant Valley, a mountain vale embraced between the main crest of the Blue Ridge, and a subsidiary range parallel to it on the west, known as Elk Ridge. It is the southern promontory of this, which, immediately overlooking the river and village, is known as Maryland Heights. After seizing this commanding position, as has been related, he devoted the night of the 13th and the forenoon of the 14th, to constructing a road along the crest of Elk Ridge, by which cannon could be carried out upon its southern extremity. By two o'clock P. M. four pieces of artillery were established there, with great labor, overlooking the whole town, and a part of the enemy's works on Bolivar Heights. The remainder of General M'Laws' force was employed in watching the outlets from Harper's Ferry down the Potomac, where the main road, the railroad and the canal, passed under the mountain's foot, and to guarding his rear against the approach of the heavy force of M'Clellan; who sought to raise the siege by pressing him from the north. But while the guns of M'Laws and Walker upon the mountains now rendered the town untenable to the Federalists, they could not dislodge them from their main line upon Bolivar Heights; and here, it was plain, they would cling, in the hope of being relieved by M'Clellan, until the place was actually forced. So that the main struggle, after all, fell to the *corps* of General Jackson. He directed the division of Hill toward the Shenandoah, and that of Taliaferro, under Brigadier-General J. R. Jones, to the banks of the Potomac. The division of Ewell, under Brigadier-General Lawton, marched upon the Charlestown turnpike, and supported Hill. On the 14th General Jackson, observing an eminence upon the extreme right of the enemy's line, and next the Potomac, occupied only by horsemen, directed the Stonewall Brigade, under Colonel Grigsby, to seize it. This

was done without much difficulty; and the hill was at once
crowned by the batteries of Poague and Carpenter. On his
right, a similar operation, of still greater importance, was happily effected by General A. P. Hill. Perceiving an elevated
piece of ground, (whence the Federal position along Bolivar
Heights could be enfiladed at the distance of only a thousand
yards,) which seemed to be defended by infantry behind a
heavy *abattis* without artillery, Hill sent three brigades under
General Pender, to storm it. This was effected in most gallant
style, and with slight loss. During the night Major Walker,
director of his artillery, by indefatigable exertions, carried several batteries to the position thus won; while the remainder of
the infantry of the division, availing themselves of the darkness,
and the precipitous ravines which descend to the Shenandoah,
insinuated themselves down its left bank, and took post in rear
of the enemy's left. By these dispositions, the fate of the garrison was sealed. But General Jackson, to make sure of his
work, also directed his chief of artillery, Colonel Crutchfield, to
pass eleven pieces of artillery from Ewell's division across the
Shenandoah, and establish them upon its right bank, so as to
take a part of the Federal line in reverse. To the division of
Ewell was assigned the front attack, in the centre.

This arrangement of the Confederate forces has been described in its completeness, because there is no more beautiful
instance in the whole history of the military art, of a grand
combination absolutely complete and punctual, irrevocably deciding the struggle before it was begun, and yielding a perfect
result, which left nothing more to be desired. In the afternoon
of the 14th, the guns of M'Laws and Walker, upon the two
mountains, had given the enemy a foretaste of their overthrow,
by silencing their batteries nearer the Potomac, and searching
the whole encampment and barracks with their shells at will.

But Jackson was now ready also; and at dawn on the 15th he proceeded to give to his adversary the *coup de grace*. He ordered all the different batteries to open at once. M'Laws and Walker plunged their shot among the Federal masses from the heights; Poague and Carpenter scourged their right with a resistless fire; Lawton advanced to the attack with artillery and infantry in front; and the enfilading batteries of General Hill and Colonel Crutchfield swept their men from the ramparts by a storm of projectiles. After an hour of furious cannonading, all the Federal batteries were silenced. General Jackson had directed that at this signal, Hill should instantly advance, and storm the place upon the right. His brigades were just moving, the gallant Pender again in front, supported by two advanced batteries, when amidst the surges of smoke, a white flag was seen waving from a prominent height within the town. Hill arrested the tempest of battle at once; and sending an officer to ascertain the purpose of the enemy to surrender, soon after entered the town, and received the submission of its commander. The senior officer present, Colonel Miles, had just fallen by a mortal wound; Brigadier-General White, the next in command, surrendered at discretion, with a garrison of eleven thousand men, seventy-three pieces of artillery, thirteen thousand stand of small arms, a great number of wagons and horses, and a vast accumulation of stores of every description. When General Hill entered the place, all was confusion and panic, and the defenders had already lost every appearance of subordination.

General Jackson granted most liberal terms to the prisoners, although they had placed themselves at his will. The officers were dismissed with their side-arms and personal effects, upon their parole; and wagons, with horses, lent them to remove their baggage to the Federal lines. The privates also, were disarmed, and released upon parole. The force of General Lee was too small to permit, at this critical hour, the detachment of men to conduct them into the interior. This magnificent capture confirmed the judgment of General Joseph E. Johnston, who decided in 1861 that Harper's Ferry was an untenable position for a garrison menaced by a large army. The only resource for the Federal commander, when he saw his enemies approaching, was a retreat to the Maryland Heights. These commanded the Loudoun Heights, as they, in turn, commanded the village. He should have retreated thither at the beginning with his light artillery, destroyed his stores, and broken up the bridges between himself and Harper's Ferry. That place would have then been as untenable to Jackson as it had been to him, and he would have speedily restored communication between himself and M'Clellan, who was approaching from the north.

The surrender of Harper's Ferry was received at 9 o'clock A.M., the 15th of September. General Jackson, assigning to Hill the receiving of the captured persons and property, immediately resumed his march to rejoin General Lee at Sharpsburg with his two remaining divisions. By a toilsome night march, he reached that place on the morning of Tuesday, September 16th. He also ordered M'Laws and Walker to descend, pass through Harper's Ferry, and follow him. The Commander-in-Chief was now demanding their presence with urgency. To understand its cause, other lines of events must be resumed.

On the 12th of September, the advance of M'Clellan's grand army having discovered that all the Confederates had left Frederick, ventured to enter the place. The next day, a copy of General Lee's order, directing the movements of his whole army, which had been unfortunately dropped in the town, was discovered and sent to the Federal General. Satisfied at once of its authenticity, he perceived that he now had the clew for which he had been groping so cautiously, and determined to disregard the groundless fears of the despotism at Washington, and to press the Confederates, henceforward, with vigor. He saw correctly that celerity of movement might now make him master of the situation, and adopted a plan of operations dictated by the highest skill. This was to push his great army westward as rapidly as possible by several parallel routes so near together as to render a concentration on either rapid and easy; to feel all the passes across the mountain which were held by Lee, and as soon as he effected an entrance at any, to collect his whole force beyond that barrier between the Confederates near Harper's Ferry and the other wing, supposed to be tending toward Hagerstown; to crush the former first, delivering the beleaguered garrison, and then turn upon the latter. That all this was not effected, was due to the surprising promptitude with which Jackson reduced Harper's Ferry, and to the heroic tenacity of M'Laws and D. H. Hill in holding the Pleasant Valley and Boonsborough Gap against him, until the Confederate army could be concentrated. On the 14th, the Federal left wing, in great force, under General Franklin, forced Crampton's Gap, by which M'Laws had approached Harper's Ferry. But when they passed the first crest of the mountain, they found M'Laws, with a strong rear-guard, drawn up across the Pleasant Valley with so bold a front, that they feared both to attack him and to expose their flank by proceeding farther west. Here Franklin lost a day invaluable to his commander, by pausing to confront M'Laws until the fall of Harper's Ferry on the 15th opened to the latter a safe exit, by which he retired toward the appointed *rendezvous*. On the 14th of September, also, the remainder of the Federal army, moving from Frederick by the main road toward Boonsbororough hurled its vast masses all day against D. H. Hill, in the mountain pass in front of that place. This determined soldier held his ground with less than five thousand men, when General Longstreet coming to his support in the afternoon, sustained the onset until nightfall. They then withdrew their divisions toward Sharpsburg, under favor of the darkness, and arrived at that position on the 15th, while their enemies pursued sluggishly, bravely resisted by the cavalry of FitzHugh Lee. In the combat of Boonsborough Gap, M'Clellan, with that usual exaggeration of the numbers of his enemy to which his timid temperament inclined him, placed the force of D. H. Hill at fifteen thousand, and that of Longstreet at as many more. A large portion of his army arrived in front of the Confederate position at Sharpsburg on the same day with them, and he might have immediately attacked with the prospect of overwhelming the three divisions opposed to him. But the absence of Franklin with his whole left wing, which was detained in Pleasant Valley by M'Laws, the cumbrous size of his vast and sluggish host, and his own caution, consumed both that day and the 16th. Then, two divisions of the *corps* of Jackson and that of General Walker were in position, and the hope of beating the Southern army in detail was at an end.

The position selected by General Lee for his final concentration is marked by the little village of Sharpsburg, a cluster of German farm-houses, which had spent its quiet existence amidst the hills and woods, dreaming little of the fame which was to connect its name forever with the greatest battle of this gigantic campaign. It is situated at the intersection of six roads, two and a half miles east of the Potomac, and one mile west of Antietam Creek, a picturesque mill-stream, which descends from the north, and separates between the rolling hills of the great valley, and the long, sloping ridges which form the western bases of the Blue Ridge, or South Mountain. The roads which centre at the village lead southward to Harper's Ferry, northward to Hagerstown, westward to Shepherdstown, upon the Virginian

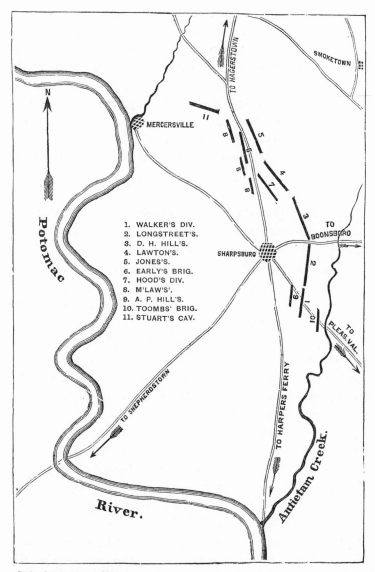

Scale, 3-4 Inch to a Mile.

CONFEDERATE POSITIONS AT SHARPSBURG.

shore of the Potomac, eastward to Boonsborough, and southeastward to Pleasant Valley. It was by the last two that M'Clellan's
army approached; and these highways passed the Antietam upon
substantial bridges of stone; while other practicable crossings,
above and below, were offered by fords and country roads of
less note. The country around Sharpsburg is elevated and
rolling, with woods, fields, farm-houses, and orchards interspersed,
divided by stone fences, and scarred here and there with ledges
of limestone which project a few feet from the soil. It offered,
therefore, a strong defensive position for an army receiving the
attack of its enemies; but the ground lay under two grave
objections, of which the one was, that this army had the Potomac
in its immediate rear, and the other, that its lines were almost
enfiladed by the heavy rifled artillery of the assailants, posted
upon the ascending ridges which rose from the eastern margin
of the Antietam toward the mountain. Here, however, General
Lee began the formation of his line of battle, on the 15th of
September, by placing the divisions of D. H. Hill, Longstreet
and Hood upon the range of hills in front of Sharpsburg, and
overlooking Antietam Creek. His line was nearly parallel to
this stream, and had Longstreet upon the right and Hill upon
the left of the road which led to Boonsborough: while Hood's two
brigades, stationed upon the left of Hill, extended that wing to
the highway leading to Hagerstown. The evening of that day
was expended by the Federalists in feeble *reconnoissances*. But
on the morning of the 16th they were evidently busy in posting
their batteries, and disposing their vast masses for a pitched
battle. At mid-day General Jackson arrived, with the two
divisions under the command of Brigadier-Generals Jones and
Lawton, and, after granting his men a few hours' repose, took
position on the left of Hood, nearly filling the space between the
Hagerstown road and the Potomac. To rest his extreme left in

the neighborhood of the river, he was compelled to retract it somewhat from the direct line.   This exposed him to two inconveniences, — that his position was thereby more completely enfiladed by hostile batteries in front of his right, and that space was thus left between him and the Antietam for the collecting of a heavy force of the Federalists before his left, and on the hither side of that barrier.   But no other choice was left him; the vast numbers of M'Clellan would otherwise have enabled that General to swing around between his extreme left and the river.   General Walker, arriving with his two brigades a little after Jackson, was posted on the right of Longstreet.   After spending the day in a heavy but useless cannonade, M'Clellan advanced to the assault about sunset on the 16th and attacked the two brigades of Hood, on the left of the centre, in great numbers.   These veteran commands received the onset with firmness, and inflicted serious loss upon the assailants.   The combat continued far into the night, and was suspended without result; when Hood's troops were relieved by the brigades of Trimble and Lawton, from the division of Ewell (now commanded by Lawton), that they might have a much needed respite during the night, to prepare food and replenish their ammunition.   The two divisions of Jackson now occupied the whole left, from that of D. H. Hill forth, and the command of Hood became the reserve.   Thus the troops lay down upon their arms, with the skirmishers immediately confronting the lines of the enemy, and sought such repose as· they might, amidst the alarms of a continual dropping fire.

The morning of the 17th of September dawned with all the mellow splendor of the American autumn; but scarcely had the sun arisen, when its quiet and beauty were obscured by the thunders and smoke of a terrific cannonade, which burst from the whole Federal line.   The plan of M'Clellan's battle was, to advance his right first, under the lead of Generals Hooker and

71

Mansfield, who had already made a lodgement west ot the Antietam, to overpower the Confederate left, and then to sweep down the stream, taking the remainder of General Lee's line in reverse, and forcing it simultaneously by a front attack. To effect the first part of this design, he hurled against the left the *corps* of Hooker, Mansfield, and Sumner, containing, by his own statement, forty-four thousand combatants, and supported by five or six batteries of rifled artillery from his reserves, besides the numerous guns attached directly to their movements. But so far was this force from proving adequate to his purpose, he relates that the *corps* of Franklin, then numbering twelve thousand men, was necessarily brought up as a reserve, and a part of it engaged, to prevent the Confederates from retorting his assault upon their left by a serious disaster. Thus, the post of danger and of glory again fell to the devoted *corps* of Jackson. The divisions present were now diminished by battle, straggling, and overpowering fatigues, to an aggregate of less than seven thousand men. With this little band, supported by five thousand reserves under Hood and M'Laws, of whom the latter only arrived from Harper's Ferry in the crisis of the battle, did Jackson hold his ground throughout the day, and breast every onset of the deluge of enemies. His dispositions have already been described in part. The brigades of Lawton and Trimble were between the Hagerstown road and the command of D. H. Hill. On the left of these, and parallel to that road, was the division of Jones. The brigades of Early and Hayes were at first detached to support the horse artillery of General Stuart, who, with a portion of his cavalry, had seized an elevated hill distant nearly a mile from the infantry, whence he proposed to threaten the extreme right of the Federalists. Hays was immediately recalled from this movement to the support of Lawton's brigade, leaving Early to guard the batteries of Stuart. This

General, finding that the wide interval between him and General Jackson's left allowed the intrusion of the enemy, almost immediately removed his guns to a height somewhat farther to the rear, and nearer to his friends. From this position he rendered essential service, not only in guarding their flank, but in repulsing the onsets of the Federalists, by a spirited cannonade. But the advance of their infantry had begun simultaneously with the furious fire of their batteries, and, by sunrise, the skirmishers were hotly engaged in the woods east of the Hagerstown road. Very soon the Confederates were driven out, and the position was occupied by large masses of Federal infantry, with several batteries of artillery, which assailed the Confederate line in front, while the rifled guns in the distance raked them with a murderous fire from their right. But under this double ordeal, the veterans of Jackson stood firm, and returned the fire, inflicting a terrible slaughter upon their enemies. For more than an hour this unequal contest raged with unabated fury. The brigade of Hayes was speedily called from the second line into the first. General Lawton, commanding the division, was severely wounded. Colonel Douglass, leading his brigade, was killed. Colonel Walker, commanding Trimble's brigade, was wounded and unhorsed. General J. R. Jones, commanding the old division of Jackson, was compelled to leave the field, and the gallant General Starke, succeeding him, was immediately slain. Trimble's brigade had one-third, and the others half their men *hors du combat*; and four out of five of their field officers were killed or wounded. The whole line was speedily reduced to a shattered remnant, which still fought with invincible tenacity, from hillock to hillock, and ledge to ledge, as they retired. It was in this terrific crisis that General Jackson commanded Hood to return to the front and relieve the division of Lawton, and recalled Early with his brigade, to assume the command vacated

by the wounding of the latter. With his accustomed prowess
the heroic Texan rushed forward against the teeming multitudes
of the enemy, and stayed the tide of battle. His two little
brigades engaged five times their own numbers; and in a deadly
grapple, of several hours' duration, drove them steadily back a
quarter of a mile, and re-established the Confederate lines.
After firing away all his cartridges, he caused his men to replenish their supply from the slain of both armies, and still maintained the struggle, until the Federalists, about mid-day, remitted
their exertions.

But General Early brought other succors to the failing line at
the same time with Hood. Marching his brigade by its right flank
over sheltered ground in the rear of the Confederate lines, he
brought it, at the moment when the division of Starke was
almost overpowered, to their assistance. They had been driven
from the Hagerstown road, across an elevated field, and into a
wood beyond, where the dauntless Colonels Grigsby and Stafford were endeavoring to rally a few score of their brigades.
The Federalists had already posted a battery in the road; and,
thinking the left successfully turned, were advancing heavy
columns of infantry against both the right and the left of the
ground which Early had just assumed. Informing General Jackson of his critical position, he assigned to Colonel Grigsby the
task of holding the left column in check for a few moments, and
moved his own brigade farther to the right, so as to confront the
other, concealed from them by the undulations of the ground.
Having gained the desired position, he suddenly disclosed his
line, advanced, and attacked them with fury. They gave way
before him, and he pursued them with great slaughter to the road.
At this opportune moment the brigades of General M'Laws began
to arrive to his support,—Kershaw and Barksdale upon his right,
and Semmes upon his left. The Federal column, threatening

that part of his line had just come far enough to endanger his left flank and rear, as he advanced against the routed enemy in his front. Early therefore arrested his men in the ardor of their pursuit, changed his front, and advanced upon this second body of enemies, in conjunction with Semmes, Grigsby, and Stafford. By this combined attack they were swept summarily, with great loss, from the woods, and the lines were finally restored. At the same time, the other brigades of M'Laws were advanced on Early's right with admirable skill and spirit, by their commander; and drove the enemy across the woods and fields for half a mile, strewing the ground with killed and wounded. The whole of General Jackson's line was then re-established by the united troops of Hood, M'Laws, and Early; and the conflict of the infantry sunk into a desultory skirmish of outposts. But the baffled Federalists kept up, during the remainder of the day, a furious cannonade upon his position, under which his men lay quiet behind the hillocks, rocky ledges, and fences, suffering but little loss. The share of his wearied troops in the glories of the day was now completed. In the afternoon, indeed, instructed by the Commander-in-Chief, he made an attempt to effect a diversion in favor of his comrades upon the right and centre, by attacking the extreme right of the Federalists in conjunction with General Stuart. But their lines were found to extend so near the Potomac, and to be so fortified with artillery, that the experiment was relinquished. During this terrible conflict General Jackson exposed his life with his customary imperturbable bravery, riding among his batteries and directing their fire, and communicating his own indomitable spirit to his men. Yet he said to a Christian comrade, that on no day of battle had he ever felt so calm an assurance that he should be preserved from all personal harm, through the protection of his Heavenly Father.

While M'Clellan was accumulating his chief strength against

the Confederate left, he was also diligently preparing for an attack in force upon the centre, by feeling its lines with a heavy artillery fire. No sooner had the tempest exhausted its fury upon Jackson, than it burst upon D. H. Hill and Longstreet, with almost equal violence; but it was met with the same determined resistance. To describe its course would lead the reader over a precisely parallel story of fourfold numbers, resisted by the thin Confederate lines, with a sublime heroism which supplied every defect of force; of the lamentable martyrdom of devoted officers and men, but avenged by bloody slaughters of the assailants; of shattered brigades reduced to handfuls, and of fearful onslaughts, turned back by the rally of these unconquerable men, when the effort seemed almost madness. At one moment, he would see vast masses of the enemy pouring through a breach in the single line of Hill, and about to seize the very key of the Confederate position, arrested and turned back by that General with four field-pieces, and a few hundreds of bayonets, rallied from several broken brigades. At another, he would see Longstreet, sitting alone upon his horse, near a battery of four field-pieces, which was supported by the North Carolina regiment of Cooke, without a single cartridge, and thus confronting and beating back a whole line of battle.

At four o'clock in the afternoon, M'Clellan transferred his attack to the Confederate right, and attempted with the *corps* of Burnside, to force the bridge over the Antietam, leading from the Pleasant Valley. This was immediately defended by several batteries, and two regiments of General Toombs's Georgia brigade, stationed near the stream. These troops held the enemy's advance in check until they had passed the stream in great numbers below; when they were necessarily withdrawn, to avoid capture. Burnside now crossed the bridge in great force, and attacked Longstreet's right, under General D. R. Jones, forcing him from the range of hills which commanded the approaches. An advance of a few hundred yards more would have given the enemy control of the roads leading from Sharpsburg to the Potomac; but here also through the providence of the Commander-in-Chief, timely succor was at hand. The remaining division of General Jackson's *corps*, under General A. P. Hill, having been ordered up from Harper's Ferry, had just reached the field, and was now sent to the support of the right wing. This General, advancing four of his brigades, with his batteries, attacked the Federalists, flushed with confidence, but disordered by the rapidity of their advance, and immediately arrested their career. Assailed in flank by Toombs, and in front by Branch, Gregg and Archer, they wavered, broke, and fled in confusion to the banks of the Antietam, where they sought protection under the fire of the numerous artillery upon the opposite hills. In this splendid combat, two thousand men of Hill's division, assisted by the brigade of Toombs, routed the fourteen thousand of Burnside, and drove them under the shelter of M'Clellan's reserves.

The General was now compelled to pass from the aggressive to the defensive, and was happy to be able to prevent the Confederates from crossing the bridge in turn, forcing back his left, and separating him from the mountain base which he destined for his refuge in case of disaster. To the anxious appeals of Burnside for more men, and more guns, to meet "the overpowering odds" against him, he had no reply to give. Contenting themselves with posting their beaten infantry, and their artillery so as to contest the passage of Hill, they awaited the night, which speedily came to their assistance. With this affair, the bloody day was closed. The two armies held the same positions which they occupied when it began, save that in the centre, the Confederate line was retracted about two hundred yards. In no battle of the war had the shock of arms been so violent as in this, or the cannonade so terrible. On both sides, portions of the forces engaged were almost totally disintegrated by the fury of the struggle. The whole organized remainder of brigades appeared in the form of a few companies, and divisions were reduced to the size of regiments.

The exhaustion of the Confederates forbade the thought of following up their successes. But had they been stronger, the adroit position of M'Clellan gave them little encouragement to attempt it. He was able to place the Antietam in his front, and to occupy upon the eastern side, ground of commanding height. Had he been forced back from this, he would have retired to ranges of hills still more elevated, whence his numerous and powerful artillery would have been employed with still more fatal effect; and had he been defeated, this would only have driven him to the mountain, where he would have been unassailable. But on the morning after the battle, General Lee firmly awaited another attack in his first position. His army had been recruited already, by the return of thousands of the foot-sore and the stragglers to their ranks, and he was nothing loth to try conclusions again, upon the same ground, with his gigantic adversary. M'Clellan had no stomach whatever for another wrestle of the sort he had just escaped; and thus, during the 18th, the two adversaries stood at bay, and busied themselves in burying their dead, and removing their wounded. In the afternoon, General Lee, learning that M'Clellan was about to receive large accessions of fresh troops, and having no corresponding increase of his own strength in prospect, determined to recross the Potomac at Shepherdstown. As soon as the darkness set in, this movement was commenced, and was continued all night. The trains, the artillery, the wounded, were passed safely over; while the troops forded the shallow stream in a continuous column.

Nothing was left to the enemy, except a few hundred wounded men, whose sufferings would have been aggravated by their removal, and a few disabled guns and caissons. The corps of General Jackson now brought up the rear; and its passage was not completed until 10 o'clock A. M. on the 19th. For hours, he was seen seated upon his horse in the middle of the river, as motionless as a statue, watching the passage of his faithful men; nor did he leave this station until the last man and the last carriage had touched the southern shore. He then retired with his troops; and having made suitable dispositions for guarding the fords, sought encampments for them, where they might find the much needed repose.

When M'Clellan perceived that the Confederates had retired he began to claim the battle of Sharpsburg as a glorious victory. He forgot that at Malvern Hill he had also claimed a splendid victory because he was permitted to do something similar to that which General Lee had now done, except that it was less successful. There he had stood on the defensive in the position of his choice; he had beaten off the assailants with a loss equal to his own; he had held his ground, in the main, until the close of the battle; and he had then stolen off in the darkness, leaving his enemy to bury his dead, and to care for many of his wounded. Here General Lee had received the attacks of his foe in his chosen position; had repelled them all with enormous slaughter; had slept upon his own ground; had sent his wounded to the rear; had buried his dead, save where the impetuosity of his victorious men had carried them into the enemy's line; had offered battle defiantly on the succeeding day; and, after this, had retired at his leisure, and unmolested. If Malvern Hill was a victory for M'Clellan, by parity of reasoning, Sharpsburg was more a victory for Lee. But the Confederates did not claim it as a decisive victory,

72

for it did not gain them the main object for which it was fought. It has been said that this object was gained, for it was the whole end of the battle to win a safe exit out of Maryland, after the brilliant capture of Harper's Ferry. This statement is incorrect. The evening of the day on which Harper's Ferry fell, more than half of the army was safely out of Maryland, the *corps* of Jackson, and the divisions of M'Laws, Anderson, and Walker; it was necessary for them to re-enter Maryland, in order to fight at Sharpsburg. Nor is it true that their return was necessary to extricate the remaining divisions of Longstreet, D. H. Hill, and Jones. These crossed the Antietam to Sharpsburg with impunity, in the face of M'Clellan's huge host, during the forenoon of September 15th, and the onset upon them did not begin in earnest until the dawn of the 17th. Surely the same skill and firmness might have conducted them in safety four miles farther, across the Potomac to Shepherdstown. The battle of Sharpsburg was fought by the Confederates, not to purchase a secure retreat, but to open their way for triumphant invasion; to redeem their offers of aid to oppressed Maryland; to conquer a peace by defeating their oppressors upon their own soil. This truth displays at once the daring and hardihood of General Lee's conceptions, and his confidence in the prowess of his army. He believed them capable of everything, and so was not afraid to require of them the greatest things.

In the daring policy of delivering this battle, General Jackson had emphatically concurred with him upon his arrival from Harper's Ferry in advance of his *corps*. When the Commander-in-Chief determined to withdraw across the Potomac again, he also approved this movement; but added that, in view of all the circumstances, it was better to have fought the battle in Maryland, than to have left it without a struggle. In the larger part of this admirable army, it may be truly said, his confidence was justly reposed; but in this instance, he exacted of them that of which human nature was scarcely capable. The marches and combats which introduced the great day of Sharpsburg, exhausted the strength of the men in advance. Many were absent because they were unable to march with deficient rations, and ill-shod; and many others, who had faithfully dragged their weary limbs to the field, had neither strength of muscle nor animal spirits for its duties. This army, jaded, foot-sore, and half famished, was sustained under the toils of the bloody day, only by its lofty principle, and its devotion to its leaders. To their adversaries, even, they appeared wan and haggard, albeit they were as terrible as hungry wolves. Men among them were seen, while advancing to the charge through orchards of the German farmers, under a hail of death, greedily devouring the apples from the trees.

Here, then, was one explanation of the imperfection of General Lee's victory. Another, more important, was in the miserable vice of straggling, which the mistaken good nature of officers had fostered. For in this army, so heroic as a body, there were two elements commingled, — the precious metal and the vile dross, — the true, patriot, citizen soldier, animated by a high principle, and the base skulker, who did nothing, save under compulsion. The great vice of the Southern armies was on this occasion prevalent: that the ignorance of the practical details of duty among officers, with the easy *bonhommie* of their character, remitted the bonds of discipline; so that the base were not compelled to act with the true, as one body. The losses of the army from straggling had begun upon the Rappahannock. When it moved thence against Pope, at Manassa's, the country behind it was left infested with thousands of laggards and deserters, who preyed upon the substance of the citizens, and wandered about, with arms in their hands, defying arrest. At every stage of the march this depletion increased, until, at the final struggle, there were fewer Confederate soldiers in line of battle, along the Antietam, than there were along the course of the Potomac, and the roads over which the army had marched. General Lee declares that the battle was fought with less than forty thousand men. The confusion reigning in many parts of the army make an accurate enumeration forever impossible. But the highest estimate made by well-informed actors in the scene gave him thirty-three thousand effective men. General M'Clellan declares officially, that Lee's line of battle was exeedingly short. All who fought in it testified that it was also exceedingly thin. In contrast with this sober revelation of facts, the confident estimates of the Federal General are set in a ridiculous light, when he formally announces, to a man, the exact number present in each of the Confederate *corps*, and makes up an aggregate of ninety-seven thousand four hundred and forty-five combatants, opposed to him on the Antietam. The fact that the Confederates defended themselves successfully against the ninety thousand men whom he hurled against them, supported by the most numerous and complete artillery ever arrayed on a field of battle, is a testimony to the heroism of the men and the skill of the officers, almost inexpressibly glorious. The commendation of Jackson is best written by his adversary, when he says, in his Report, " One division of Sumner's, and all of Hooker's *corps*, on the right, had, after fighting most valiantly for several hours, *been overpowered by numbers*, driven back in great disorder, and much scattered." Those numbers, so overpowering, were, as the reader has seen, less than seven thousand jaded men, supported by a few hundreds of reserves from M'Laws. That the Confederates accomplished so much with their fragment of an army, is the best apology for the daring policy of their commander. Had all his men been in their places, and had they fought as the thirty-three thousand fought, it is no idle vaticination to say, that the battle of Sharpsburg would have been a magnificent and decisive triumph. The apprehensions which M'Clellan confessed as possessing his breast after its close (September 18th), shall express its probable results. "At that moment, Virginia lost, Washington menaced, Maryland invaded, the national cause could afford no risks of defeat. One battle lost, and almost all would have been lost. Lee's army might then have marched, as it pleased, on, Washington, Baltimore, Philadelphia, or New York. It could have levied its supplies from a fertile and undevastated country, extorted tribute from wealthy and populous cities; and nowhere east of the Alleghanies was there another organized force able to arrest its march."

But it will be well to pause here, and answer a question which has doubtless been frequently raised in the reader's mind, by the astonishing discrepancies between the confident estimates made by M'Clellan of his adversary's numbers and the sober statements of the Confederate reports. The doubt has arisen, " Can it be, that a General of M'Clellan's acknowledged skill should be so incapable of measuring the size of the force acting before him, or that an official occupying so high a position among a civilized people can be so capable of deliberate lying concerning matters of fact?" The answer is to be found chiefly in the traits of his people. Their general vanity and falsehood prompted his officers and men, when beaten by the Confederates, to cover their own cowardice under wondrous tales of the overpowering numbers before which they gave way. Thus, M'Clellan, who, it was well known, was not accustomed to risk his person by too near an inspection of the incidents of battle, was perpetually made the victim of a system of lies and exaggerations, passed upon him by his subordinates, to cloak their own cowardice. It is to precisely this source that the most of his military blunders are traceable. And this is one among the manifold illustrations of the intrinsic weakness of sin. Virtue is always the stronger in the end.

To return. Another cause of imperfect success to the Confederate arms, was the too great dispersion of their forces before the battle. The fact that so much was effected with the portion present on the morning of the 17th, shows how complete the victory might have been, had all the divisions been on the ground, and suitably refreshed by rest and food. The prize at Harper's Ferry, left within General Lee's grasp, not by the forecast, but by the folly of the enemy, yet proved the occasion of their rescue from destruction. The splendid bait was seized; but it caused Jackson to arrive wearied and depleted by forced marches, and it detained the divisions of A. P. Hill, M'Laws, and Anderson, and then placed them at the scene of combat with exhausted strength, after it had been raging for hours. Had those forces been present at the beginning, which arrived during the day, a concerted onset would have converted the repulse of M'Clellan into a disastrous defeat.

The cause of the Confederates suffered also from indiscreet management of their artillery in some parts of the field. Inferior in number and range of guns, in the quantity and quality of ammunition, and in the experience of the gunners, it should not have attempted to cope with the distant Federal batteries. To them it should have made no reply: but, protecting itself from their fire until the auspicious moment, it should have confined itself to driving back their masses of infantry, when they ventured to expose themselves at close quarters.

The prime error of M'Clellan in this campaign was his mistake concerning the numbers of his opponent; for out of this his other errors grew. Of these, not the least was his timid delay in pressing General Lee at Sharpsburg, and M'Laws at Pleasant

Valley, on the 15th and 16th. He had then attained that opportunity to deal with the parts of the invading army separated, for which he represented himself as manœuvring: a great captain would have used the precious advantage while it lasted, by hurling his troops at once, with such imperfect preparation as they might have, against their foes. His handling of his forces on the 17th was also faulty in two important particulars. His attacks upon the Confederate left, centre, and right, were successive, instead of simultaneous. The one movement was decided adversely before the next was seriously begun, and the wings of his army consequently gave each other little mutual support. And second: it was an inexcusable error to permit the day to be decided against him, with fifteen thousand reserves of veteran troops lying passive behind the Antietam. For all useful purposes, the *corps* of Fitz-John Porter might as well have been in Washington City. It may be right for the General who is very distant from his supplies and reinforcements, to husband his reserves, even at the cost of surrendering a victory; but M'Clellan was very near to his, having two or three fresh divisions within a few hours' march. It appears, therefore, that the faults of his tactics here were again those of over-caution. His best apology is to be found in the indomitable quality of the troops opposed to him.

It remains to speak of the losses of the two parties to this sanguinary battle. General Jackson reported a total loss in his command, during the operations at Harper's Ferry and Sharpsburg, of three hundred and fifty-one officers and men killed, two thousand and thirty wounded, and fifty-seven missing. Nearly all of this loss was incurred at the latter place. The loss of the whole Confederate army, while in Maryland, was ten thousand three hundred, killed and wounded, of whom one thousand five hundred and sixty-seven were killed. The confusions of the campaign left no means to discriminate between those lost at Boonsborough and Crampton's Gaps, at Harper's Ferry, and in the final struggle. General M'Clellan asserts that the losses of the Confederates in killed and wounded, at the two places first named, were as great as two thousand five hundred. If this is true, then the casualties of the Confederates at Sharpsburg were under eight thousand. He sets down the aggregate of his own losses during the Maryland campaign at about fifteen thousand two hundred men, of whom two thousand were killed and wounded in the preliminary skirmishes and combats. He thus leaves thirteen thousand as his loss in the battle of Sharpsburg. His own blunders, in the indiscreet attempts he so often made to estimate the casualties of his adversary, are a lesson of caution against a too dogmatic attempt to correct this statement. It will therefore be left, with the accompanying fact, that the hospital returns of the medical authorities of his Government showed an increase of thirty thousand patients, from his command, as consequent upon the operations of this short campaign.

The close of this series of events was marked by one more combat, which shed a parting beam of glory upon the military genius of General Jackson, and the bravery of a part of his troops. After crossing the Potomac upon the 19th of September, he withdrew his *corps* four miles, upon the road toward Martinsburg, and caused them to encamp. Brigadier-General Pendleton, the chief of the reserved artillery of General Lee's army, was stationed with thirty guns upon the heights overlooking the river, supported by the shattered remnant of Lawton's brigade, to guard it against the passage of the enemy in pursuit. These arrangements had not long been made, when the Federalists began to establish heavy batteries of artillery upon the opposite heights, to protect the advance of their troops to the attack; and Fitz-John Porter's *corps*, which had been held in reserve at

Sharpsburg, appeared on the river-bank. This General,. after nightfall, sent a detachment across a point above the batteries of Pendleton; which, advancing unobserved, came so near the base of the heights upon which he was posted, as to be protected from an effectual cannonade; while the infantry, discouraged by their previous losses, and the absence of their accustomed commander, were seized with panic, and fled. The thirty guns of Pendleton were now exposed to capture, and four of them fell at once into the hands of the Federalists; while the captains of the other batteries withdrew the remainder, to rescue them from a similar fate. At midnight General Pendleton came to the camps of the army, to report these alarming facts; and added to them, what he then supposed to be true, that all his guns had met the fate of the four first taken.

"Lee had already made provision against a pursuit of M'Clellan, although deeming him probably too much crippled at Sharpsburg to venture immediately into Virginia, by entrusting the defence of his rear to General Jackson, and by sending General Stuart with his cavalry back across the river at Williamsport, to threaten the enemy's right flank and harass his movements. But now, concluding from the report of General Pendleton, that the Federal army might be attempting to follow him, he sent at once to General Jackson, directing him to prepare for assailing them, and informing him of his purpose to support the attack, if necessary, with his whole army. But General Jackson, to whom Pendleton had made the same report, as to the General commanding the approaches next the enemy, did not tarry for further prompting. He had already risen, and gone toward Boteler's Ford, a crossing a little below the position just lost by Pendleton, and had ordered the division of A. P. Hill, that of Early, (who was now the successor of Lawton,) and that of D. H. Hill, (which had the day before been perma-

73

nently assigned to his *corps*,) to follow him thither immediately. Meantime General Lee had sent orders to General Longstreet to countermarch his *corps* and rejoin him, that he might proceed with him to the support of Jackson. The messengers sent to place the latter in communication with the Commander-in-Chief, with difficulty found him, in advance of all his troops, without escort, examining the posture of the enemy's force, while the division of A. P. Hill was rapidly advancing to the front."

On the north bank of the Potomac were planted seventy pieces of heavy artillery, while under their protection, a considerable force of infantry had passed to the southern side, and were drawn up in line upon the high banks next the river. Under the direction of General Jackson, Hill formed his gallant division in two lines, and advanced to the attack, regardless of the terrific storm of projectiles from the batteries beyond the river. The enemy attempted for a time to resist him, by bearing heavily against his left; but his second line, marching by the left flank, disclosed itself from behind the first, and advanced to its support; when the two charging simultaneously, and converging toward the mass of the Federalists, swept them down the hill, and drove them into the river. Now occurred a scene of carnage, in which the bloodiest spirit of revenge might have sated itself for all the losses suffered at the hands of the enemy. The troops of Hill rushed down the declivity regardless of the plunging shot and shell of the opposing batteries, hurled their adversaries by hundreds into the water, and as they endeavored to struggle across, picked them off with unerring aim. The surface of the broad river was black with the corpses of the foe, and few of the luckless column ever reached the northern bank. This was one of those rare opportunities, which victory sometimes gives to her favorites, to repay themselves in one triumphant hour for all the sufferings and injuries of a campaign;

and well did the veterans of Hill employ the precious season. When the last of the intruders was destroyed or escaped, they withdrew a short distance, and guarded the ford for the remainder of the day; but M'Clellan had learned a lesson which inspired due regard for the Confederate rear, and henceforth kept a respectful distance. When a second messenger from General Lee arrived, to seek for General Jackson, he found him watching the repulse of the enemy. His only remark was: "With the blessing of Providence, they will soon be driven back." In this combat, General A. P. Hill did not employ a single piece of artillery, but relied upon the musket and bayonet alone. Early was at hand with his division to support him; but no occasion arose for his assistance. The whole loss of the Confederates was thirty killed, and two hundred and thirty-one wounded. The Federalists admitted a loss of three thousand killed and drowned, and two hundred prisoners; and one large brigade was nearly extinguished by the disaster.

General M'Clellan, in his narrative of his war, only notices the combat of Boteler's Ford as a *reconnoissance* of secondary importance, which he despatches in a few lines. But it does not admit of question, that it was the beginning of a General advance against General Lee. Commanders do not make mere *reconnoissances* with seventy pieces of heavy artillery, laboriously posted upon difficult heights. General M'Clellan declared himself under the most urgent pressure from Washington, not to allow the "Rebels," whom he had described to his masters as a herd of fugitives discomfited by his mighty arm, to escape without destruction. He was commanded to follow stroke with stroke, until they were consumed from off the face of the earth. He found it necessary to make a formal argument, to show that he was not blameworthy for postponing their destruction later than the morning of September 18th. He declared that all his dispositions were made to fight a general action on the 19th, and that nothing prevented it, save the retreat of General Lee during the night. The reader who duly weighs these things will hardly believe but that the advance of the 20th, at Boteler's Ford, was the commencement of that general assault, intended for the previous day.

This truth is necessary to enable him to apprehend the value of the service now rendered to his country by the military genius of Jackson. The Confederate army, wearied by almost superhuman exertions; reduced by battle and straggling; deprived of its known leaders, by the wounding or death of the larger number of the gallant field officers present; and disheartened by its terrible sufferings, — was in no condition to fight another pitched battle. General Jackson appreciated these facts, and hence felt the urgent necessity of avoiding a general action by a prompt resistance to the initial movements of the Federalists. When he had decided this, he showed equal judgment in selecting the division of A. P. Hill to lead the attack. This body of troops, arriving at Sharpsburg late in that dreadful day, had taken a short and comparatively bloodless, but glorious, share in its labors in repulsing the *corps* of the feeble Burnside. Their numbers were less diminished and their spirits less worn than those of any other troops in the army. To them, therefore, General Jackson entrusted the post of honor on this morning, — and well did they discharge the trust. Through them, General Jackson probably saved the army on that occasion from destruction.

It is always as unwise as it is evil, to misrepresent the truth. The Federalists, in their overweening vanity and arrogance, claimed a victory at Sharpsburg to which they knew they were not entitled; and filled the public ear with fictions of the discomfiture of the Confederates which they knew were exaggerated.

They thus created for themselves a moral necessity to press them with boldness, and the penalty was the slaughter of September 20th.   The three thousand corpses floating down the Potomac, or lining its banks, were the price paid by them for the vain boastings of September 17th.

CHAPTER XVIII.

FREDERICKSBURG.

A RESPITE now occurred in the storms of war, when it was permitted to contemplate General Jackson and his soldiers in a more peaceful and pleasing attitude. The army was withdrawn a few miles, to the banks of the Opequon, a tributary of the Potomac, which flows to the eastward of Winchester and Martinsburg, and empties into it a little above Harper's Ferry. Here they encamped for a number of weeks, in the bosom of the most charming regions of the lower Valley. The beauty of the season surpassed even the accustomed glories of the Virginian autumn; and amidst days of unclouded serenity, free alike from the ardors of summer, and the extremes of winter, the tired soldiers recruited their strength, reposing upon the rich meadows and pastures of the Opequon. Man and beast alike revelled in abundance; for the teeming productiveness of those Valley farms seemed to defy the exhaustion of war, and the sweet and luxuriant greensward made the war-horse forget the necessity of other provender. Here, a few days of repose restored the elastic spirits of the men; for the Southern soldier is quick to forget his toils, and resume his hopes. The *bivouacs* under the golden and crimson foliage of the trees, echoed with exuberant laughter and mirth; and the heroes of a score of deadly fields, with the light hearts of pleased children, made a jest of every trifle. Their passionate attachment to " Old Stonewall " was now at its height; and his appearance rarely failed to evoke a burst of enthusiasm. As the men heard the mighty cheer rolling toward them like a wave, from the distant camps, they sprung to their feet, saying, "There comes old Jack," and prepared to join in swelling the chorus. His heart also was soothed and gladdened with the rest, and the society of the people of his beloved District. He was now in the Valley, for which he had fought first and longest, the region of his chosen home, the scenery in which he most delighted, and amidst that sturdy population whose loyalty so cheered his heart. Winchester, that gallant and hospitable town, was near by; and he could once more mingle there with the friends of the first year of the war, and see them emancipated from the hated yoke of the Federals.

But General Jackson's rest was never idleness. He was diligently improving the interval of quiet, in refitting his men with shoes and clothing, in recalling the stragglers to the ranks, and composing the disorders of organization, produced by the arduous service of the summer. His regiments were again rapidly filled up by the return of the foot-sore, the wounded, and the sick, and the addition of new recruits; and his *corps* was enlarged to the proportions of a gallant army. On the 11th of October, the Government conferred on him the rank of Lieutenant-General, next to the highest military grade in its service. The army of General Lee was now divided into two great *corps*, or wings, of which the one was permanently assigned to Jackson, and the other to Longstreet. Henceforth these two great soldiers became as the two hands of their Commander, and served him with a generous emulation and mutual respect, as honorable to them as their well proved heroism. The organization of General Jackson's *corps*, was now confirmed. It consisted of four divisions, the original division commanded by him in the

Valley campaign, now led by Brigadier-General Wm. B. Taliaferro; the division of Ewell, commanded by Brigadier-General
Early, who was soon after rewarded for his eminent services by
the rank of Major-General; the division of Major-General A. P.
Hill; and that of Major-General D. H. Hill. To these were
attached numerous batteries, arranged into battalions of artillery
under the various division Generals, but all supervised by Colonel Crutchfield. A part of the spoils of Harper's Ferry was
now assigned to the most meritorious of these batteries; and
their equipment became more perfect than ever before. To the
famous company of Poague, of the Stonewall Brigade, especially,
were assigned four of the heavy rifled guns, upon the construction of which the Federals had exhausted all their resources of
skill and wealth; and this battery continued to hold its hardly
earned place as the *élite* body of the *corps*.

This pleasing leisure was also employed in a manner yet more
congenial to the heart of Jackson, in extraordinary labors for
the spiritual good of the men. Not only did the chaplains now
redouble their diligence in preaching, and instructing the soldiers
from tent to tent; but many eminent ministers availed themselves of the lull in the storm of war, and of the genial weather,
to visit the camps, and preach the gospel as missionaries. These
were received by General Jackson with affectionate hospitality;
and while no military duty was neglected for a moment, to make
way for their ministrations, his pious ingenuity found abundant
openings for them. It was now that the series of labors, and the
ingathering of precious souls began in the Confederate army,
which have continued ever since so extraordinary a feature of
its character. The most enlightened and apostolic clergymen
of the country, forgetting for the time the distinctions of sect,
joined in these meetings. Nightly, these novel and sacred scenes
might be witnessed, after the drill and the labors of the day

were over. From the bosom of some moon-lit grove a hymn was heard, raised by a few voices, the signal for the service; and, at this sound, the multitudinous noises of the camps died away, while the men were seen gathering from every side, until the group from which the hymn had arisen was swelled into a great crowd. The man of God then arose, and began his service by the light of a solitary candle, or a fire of resinous pine-wood, elevated on a rude platform. While his face and the pages of the holy Word were illuminated thus, all else was in solemn shadow; and his eye could distinguish nothing of his audience, save the dusky outline of the multitude seated all around, in a wide circle, upon the dry leaves, or the greensward. But though his eye could not mark the impress of the truth, it was drank in by eager ears; and many was the bearded cheek, which had not been blanched amidst the horrors of Sharpsburg, which was now wet with silent tears. At some of these meetings General Jackson was a constant worshipper, seated modestly in an unnoticed corner amidst the common soldiers, but setting the example of the most devout attention. In his letters to his friends, he related the success of the Word among his men, with ascriptions of warm and adoring gratitude to God. One of these, addressed to Mrs. Jackson, must suffice as an instance:—

"BUNKER HILL, October 13th.

"Mr. G—— invited me to be present at communion in his church yesterday, but I was prevented from enjoying the privilege. But I heard an excellent sermon from the Rev. Dr. S——. His text was I. Timothy, chap. ii: 5th and 6th verses." ("For there is one God, and one Mediator between God and men, the man Christ Jesus, who gave himself a ransom for all, to be testified in due time.") "It was a powerful exposition of the word of God. He is a great revival minister; and when he came to

74

the word '*himself*,' he placed an emphasis on it, and gave to it, through God's blessing, a power that I never before felt. . . . . And I felt, with an intensity that I never before recollect having realized, that truly the sinner who does not, under gospel privileges, turn to God, deserves the agonies of perdition. The Doctor several times in appealing to the sinner, repeated the sixth verse ' Who gave *himself* a ransom for all, to be testified in due time,' What more could God do than give *himself* a ransom ? . . . . He is laboring in a revival in General Ewell's division. Oh, it is a glorious privilege to be a minister of the gospel of the Prince of Peace ! There is no equal position in this world."

Such was the estimate of the worth of the minister's work, by one whose fame was then filling the civilized world. It may be added, once for all, that this religious reformation, which was destined to be spread so widely through the army by General Jackson's efforts, bore the fruits of a true work of God's grace. That there was more apparent bloom than fruit, as in every other ingathering which ever blessed the Church, from the Pentecostal down, is, of course, fully admitted. It is not to be supposed that there were no good people engaged in it, whose mistaken zeal led them to push it on by indiscreet means, and no converts whose temporary warmth was due rather to the gregarious sympathies of the camp, than to the truth and Spirit. But still, there was a glorious reformation in many souls to true holiness, diminishing permanently the wickedness of the camps, turning many finally away from their sins. It was the uniform testimony of even the ungodly, that the commands most largely blessed by this reform became the most efficient in the service of their country; with the best discipline, the fewest stragglers, and the steadiest behavior in battle. It was the general conclusion of the whole people, that the subsequent efficiency of the *corps* was promoted as much by this work of divine grace as by the professional ability of General Jackson.

It was a little after the date of the letter just quoted, that one of those instances arose in which he disclosed to others his spiritual emotions. The night was damp and rainy, when a brother officer whom he greatly valued visited him on business. After this was despatched, Jackson seemed to have a leisure unwonted for him, and urged his friend to remain, and spend a short time in relaxation. Although the latter did not yet call himself a Christian, indeed, he was one for whose spiritual good the General was greatly concerned. The conversation was soon insensibly turned on the things of Redemption. His friend related how Dr. S.,—the eminent minister mentioned in the last letter,— had been understood by him to declare, that the fear of wrath did not enter at all as an element of that godly sorrow for sin, which marks true repentance; but that it was prompted solely by love and gratitude. The General answered, that the doctrine intended by Dr. S. had probably been misapprehended by him. For his part, he supposed that, in the new-born believer, both fear and love actuated his repentance. But as his assurance became more clear of the Redeemer's mercy to his soul, his obedience became less servile, and more affectionate; until, in the most favored saints, perfect love cast out fear. He then declared that he had been, himself, for a long time, a stranger to fear of wrath; because *he knew and was assured* of the love of Christ to his soul; that he felt not the faintest dread that he should ever fall under the wrath of God, although a great sinner; because he knew that it was forever reconciled by the righteousness of Christ, and that love for God and Christ was now the practical spring of all his penitence. Speaking thus, Jackson arose from his seat, and, with an impressive union of humility and solemn elation, continued in substance thus: "Nothing earthly can mar my happiness. I know that heaven is in store for me; and I should rejoice in the prospect of going there to-morrow. Understand me: I am not sick; I am not sad; God has greatly blessed me; and I have as much to love here as any man, and life is very bright to me. But, still, I am ready to leave it any day, without trepidation or regret, for that heaven which I know awaits me, through the mercy of my Heavenly Father. And I would not agree to the slightest diminution of one shade of my glory there "——— [Here he paused, as though to consider what terrestrial measure he might best select to express the largeness of his joys]———" No: not for all the fame which I have acquired, or shall ever win in this world." With these words he sunk into his chair, and his friend retired—awe-struck, as though he had seen the face of an angel. But he did not fail to notice the revelation made of Jackson's master-passion by nature, in the object he had chosen to express the value of his heavenly inheritance. It was fame! Not wealth, nor domestic joys, nor literature — but well-earned fame. Let the young aspirant consider also, how even this passion, which the world calls the most honorable of all, was chastened and crucified in him by a nobler longing.

It was manifestly about the same time, that the following letter was written to Mrs. Jackson. Mentioning several presents, he says:

" Oct. 27.

" Our God makes me so many friends! I mention these things in order that you may see how much kindness has been shown me; and to express things for which I should be more grateful, and to give you renewed cause for gratitude." . . . .

" Don't trouble yourself about representations that are made of me. These things are earthly and transitory. There are real and glorious blessings, I trust, in reserve for us, beyond this life. It is best for us to keep our eyes fixed upon the throne of God, and the realities of a more glorious existence beyond the verge of time. It is gratifying to be beloved, and to have our conduct approved by our fellow men; but this is not worthy to be compared with the glory that is in reservation for us, in the presence of the glorified Redeemer. Let us endeavor to adorn the doctrine of Christ our Saviour, in all things; knowing that there awaits us 'a far more exceeding and eternal weight of glory.' I would not relinquish the slightest diminution of that glory, for all this world, and all that it can give. My prayer is, that such may ever be the feeling of my heart. It appears to me that it would be better for you not to have any thing written about me. Let us follow the teaching of inspiration: 'Let another praise thee, and not thyself.' I appreciate the loving interest that prompted the desire."

On the 18th of October, General Jackson removed his head-quarters from Bunker Hill to Martinsburg, to superintend the destruction of the Baltimore and Ohio Railroad, which was committed to his *corps*. The importance of this great thoroughfare between Washington and the West has been already described; and it was determined that the enemy should be as thoroughly deprived of its use as possible. General Jackson now applied a system of his own to dismantle it. Besides burning all bridges, and breaking up all culverts, he ripped the iron nails from the cross-ties, using the former as levers, collected the latter into heaps two or three feet high, and laying the bars of iron across the top, set fire to the whole. The heat of such log-heaps in full blaze rendered the iron red-hot, and the weight of the projecting ends warped and bent it into every imaginable shape. But as though this were not enough, the soldiers, seizing the great bars while heated in the middle, bent them around trees, and amused their ingenuity in reducing them to every fantastic use. From the hamlet of Hedgesville, west of Martinsburg, to a point near Harper's Ferry, the track was thus utterly destroyed, for a distance of thirty miles; and after the work was done, Jackson rode deliberately over the whole, to assure himself of its completeness.

At the end of the month, the *corps* moved toward the Shenandoah river and the Blue Ridge, and encamped upon the road from Charlestown to Berryville. The purpose of this change was to watch M'Clellan, who had now begun to cross the Potomac below Harper's Ferry. The Government at Washington had indicated their discontent with the sluggish movements of this General in many ways, and had urged him to advance into Virginia, and assail the Confederates again, before they could recruit their strength. But he had contented himself with a few *reconnoissances* of cavalry, and had refused to move until his vast army received large accessions, and a new outfit of clothing and equipments. At length all his requisitions were met: and with a thoroughly furnished army of one hundred and forty thousand men, he began to cross the Potomac from Berlin into the county of Loudoun, on the 23rd of October. But so vast was the *apparatus* of this huge host, six days were consumed in transferring it to the south bank of the river. The plan which its leader seemed to propose to himself was to occupy the passes of the Blue Ridge between himself and General Lee, as he proceeded Southward, so as to protect himself from an attack in flank; and by advancing toward the interior of the State, to compel him to leave Maryland free from invasion, in order to place himself between the Federalists and Richmond. In its first results, this strategy was successful; the Confederate army was promptly recalled from the neighborhood of the Potomac. As soon as the direction of M'Clellan's advance was disclosed, a part of General Longstreet's *corps* was thrown before him at Upperville, and the remainder speedily followed it, and took position in M'Clellan's front, on the east of Blue Ridge; while the *corps* of General Jackson was left to guard the Valley. M'Clellan, after his usual cautious fashion, advanced his outposts as far south as Warrenton, in Fauquier County, while his masses occupied the line of the Manassa's Gap road, and the country thereabouts. On the 5th of November one of his detachments, proceeding westward through Snicker's Gap, attempted to pass the Shenandoah at Castleman's Ferry, in the face of two brigades of A. P. Hill's division. They were chastised by him with a severe repulse, and the loss of two hundred men; and made no further attempts to penetrate the Valley.

General Lee, accompanying the *corps* of Longstreet and Stuart's cavalry, now took post at Culpepper Court House, and the two adversaries again confronted each other, with the Rappahannock, between them. M'Clellan was apparently pursuing the same line of operations which the unlucky Pope had found so difficult. If his purpose was to follow the Orange Railroad to Gordonsville, and thence turn eastward to Richmond, it was beset by the grave inconveniences, that in obliquely approaching the Rapid Ann by this line, he exposed his communications to a fatal side-thrust; and that, at Gordonsville, he must pass around an acute angle, which must present his flank most awkwardly to his adversary. If, forsaking the Orange Railroad, he marched directly southeast, the vast dimensions of his army, and the enormous consumption of supplies by it, would render it a difficult problem how it was to be provisioned without other transportation than wagon trains over the country roads of Virginia. If M'Clellan had expedients for overcoming these difficulties, they remained undisclosed; for about this time the political jealousies between him and his Government became so irrepressible, that he was suddenly relieved of his command, and ordered to retire into private life. His successor was Major-General Burnside, who seems to have been commended to the authorities chiefly by the fact, that the impatient public could say nothing against him, because nothing was known of him.

While the Federalists were advancing into Fauquier, and General Lee was confronting them in Culpepper, it was a subject of anxious discussion between him and General Jackson, what disposition should be now made of his *corps.* The latter desired to remain with it in the Valley, or at least, to continue to threaten the enemy's right wing by the passes of the Blue Ridge. Reasoning from the axiom, that one ought never to do the thing which his adversary desires him to do, he concluded that the manifest wish of M'Clellan to draw the Confederates away from the Valley, by his threatened advance into Eastern Virginia, should not be gratified. He believed that if one wing of the army held fast to that country and the Blue Ridge, his advance would be effectually checked; or if it were not, his communications would speedily be exposed to a side blow as disastrous as that which he had dealt to Pope at Manassa's. Moreover, his love for the country, and his knowledge of the inestimable value of its teeming resources, made him reluctant to see it vacated to the enemy. True, the disposition of forces which he advocated seemed to give the enemy the power to place himself between the two parts of the Confederate army. But Jackson's knowledge of the sluggish movements of that unwieldy force, and of its lack of enterprise, with his own vigilance and celerity, removed all fear of being beaten in detail. The Commander-in-Chief acquiesced, for a time, in his suggestions. An expedition to assail the Federal right and rear was proposed; but the lack of shoes and clothing in Jackson's *corps* prevented its execution. And new movements of Burnside, after a time, required the relinquishment of all the plans which have been detailed.

This General, after gathering the reins of authority into his hands, determined to direct his command to a new base, whence to attack the Confederate capital. The route by Fredericksburg, whence there ran a railroad of sixty miles' length, direct to Richmond, possessed at least the advantage that it had not yet been signalized by any Federal disaster. Burnside determined to adopt this line, making his base of supplies the landing of Acquia Creek, upon the Potomac, where the Fredericksburg Railroad terminated, thirteen miles north of that town. It was an important recommendation of this route to his jealous masters in Washington, that by pursuing it, he kept that city covered during his advance upon the rival metropolis, and composed the fears in the breast of the Government which had so retarded the operations of M'Clellan on the peninsula. In truth, the reasonings of the latter General in favor of the James river as the true line by which to take Richmond were just. But next to that line, the one selected by Burnside obviously offered the fewest difficulties. It gave him an unobstructed water-carriage for his supplies, more than one-third of the way. It was the most direct route between the two cities; and therefore he uncovered his own line of operations least, as he advanced. It gave him, from the Potomac to Richmond, a continuous line of railroad to transport the *apparatus* of his army. It was true, that this route brought him upon the Rappahannock where its current was enlarged by the accession of the Rapid Ann; but Burnside might have argued that military experience has proved a river is not usually an effectual obstacle to an attacking army, and that the vast resources of his Government would easily enable him to overcome it. The result, moreover, justified his action, so far as the river was concerned; for he did, in fact, experience little

75

difficulty in the actual passage of the stream. How much influence he may have allowed to the threatening attitude of General
Jackson upon the right of his position in Fauquier, cannot be
known; but his proposed change of base was manifestly the
most ready way to elude that danger. About the middle of
November, therefore, he began to transfer his army, by a side
march, down the north bank of the Rappahannock, to the heights
opposite Fredericksburg. He hoped to arrive there before his
designs were known to General Lee, to occupy the town and the
crossings of the river without resistance, and to commence the
race for Richmond in advance of the Confederates.

But the vigilance of his adversary, and the customary heavi-
ness of the movement of his plethoric army, disappointed his
hopes. On the 18th of November, General Stuart, crossing the
Rappahannock from Culpepper, made a thorough *reconnoissance*
as far as Warrenton, and learned with certainty that the whole
Federal army was moving upon Fredericksburg. When the
Federal General Sumner reached Falmouth, on the north side of
the Rappahannock, he found a force of Confederates guarding
the passage across it; and before he could overpower them, the
divisions of M‘Laws and Ransom appeared. The whole remainder of Longstreet's *corps* followed from Culpepper soon after,
and took up a strong position on the southern bank.

As soon as this movement of Burnside was unmasked, General Lee suggested to General Jackson the propriety of his
leaving the Valley of Virginia, to support Longstreet. He therefore complied at once, and beginning his march from Winchester,
November 22nd, in eight days transferred his *corps* with an interval of two days' rest, to the vicinity of Fredericksburg. His
journey was through the great Valley to New Market, and thence
by the Columbia Bridge, Fisher's Gap and Madison Court House,
to Guinea's Station upon the railroad, a few miles south of

Longstreet's position; where the troops arrived the 1st of December. But on the 21st of November, Sumner had summoned the town to surrender, under a threat of cannonading it the next day. The weather was rainy and tempestuous, and only a few hours of darkness were allowed the inhabitants to remove from their homes. General Lee assured the city authorities that he would pledge himself not to use the place for military purposes; but that he could not permit the enemy to occupy it. Although no garrison was within its precincts at that time, to justify the outrage of a bombardment, yet the Federal Commander refused to retract his threat, and only extended to the people the poor privilege of a prolongation of the time for removal to forty-eight hours. Nearly the whole population of the city now deserted their homes, at the beginning of winter, and with an unexampled patriotism, accepted all the horrors of exile, rather than submit to the yoke of the enemies of their country. The bombardment was, however, deferred.

When General Jackson arrived near Fredericksburg, several Federal gunboats had appeared at the village of Port Royal, upon the Rappahannock, twenty miles below. As the positions upon the southern bank were there less strong, it was surmised that the enemy might design a landing or a crossing. General Jackson was therefore directed to send the division of D. H. Hill to guard that place. When he gave him this order he said to him: "I am opposed to fighting here. We will whip the enemy but gain no fruits of victory. I have advised the line of the North Anna, but have been overruled." These words were prophetic. The objection which General Jackson stated had also been maturely weighed by the Commander-in-Chief; but it was counterpoised by other considerations, which he did not feel at liberty to disregard. To adopt the North Anna as his line of defence, would have been to surrender to the occupation of the enemy, a breadth of thirty-five miles of territory. The Confed erate Government was reluctant to submit to the political effect of such a retreat; and the waning resources of the Common- wealth warned them to relinquish no space to the enemy, which might yield important supplies for the sustenance of the army.

General D. H. Hill proceeded to Port Royal on the 3rd of December, constructed a slight entrenchment above that village during the night, and the next day, chose positions for his artil- lery. Carter's battery of Parrot guns was placed on a com- manding hill west of the place, and Hardaway's, with one English Whitworth gun of great power and range, was posted three miles below. On the 5th these two officers opened upon the Federal gunboats with such effect as to compel them promptly to change their position. By retiring behind the village they shielded themselves from the fire of Carter, but were still exposed to that of Hardaway. They now proceeded to vent their spleen in a dastardly outrage, which, were it not overshad- owed by so many others more enormous, would fix upon them the detestation of all men. Although the peaceful village was not occupied as a position by any Confederate battery or other force; the ships of war now opened a furious bombardment upon it, without a moment's notice. The little town was battered half into ruins; but although all the females, aged, sick, and children, were caught within it, in unsuspecting security, the superintend- ing mercy of Providence delivered them all from death. The only casualties were the killing of a dog, and the wounding of a poor African slave. But while this dastardly attack was proceed- ing, Hardaway continued pertinaciously to pound them with his Whitworth shot, until they gave up the contest, and retired with loss down the river, running the gantlet of the guns of Major Pelham's horse artillery, which lined the bank. A few days after, they returned toward Port Royal with five additional ships; but were again driven away by the artillery of Hill, reinforced by Colonel Brown from the reserves.

A few miles above Port Royal an insignificant stream, at a place known as the Hop Yard, enters the Rappahannock. The attention of General D. H. Hill was somehow called to it, as offering an eligible place for the passage of the enemy; and he resolved to examine it thoroughly. He found that the configuration of the country did, indeed, give special advantages to the force attempting to pass from the north side, and moreover, that there were marks not to be mistaken, of its occupation for that purpose by the enemy. When these facts were reported to General Jackson, he immediately appreciated their importance, and sent the division of Early to the place, which began diligently to fortify the southern bank. The reports of the Federal Generals subsequently disclosed the importance of these precautions. Halleck had himself selected the Hop Yard as the place for crossing, and Burnside had planned a surprise there, which was relinquished when they perceived that the ground was pre-occupied.

Meantime the Federal Government was urging that unhappy commander to force the line of the Rappahannock before further obstacles were accumulated in his front; and he was excusing himself by complaining that his pontoon trains had not been forwarded to him from the upper Potomac. Twenty days were spent in these mutual criminations. Of the merits of the quarrel, it is enough to say, that the delay of the bridge trains probably evinced the incompetency both of himself and Halleck. But the interval was diligently improved by him in perfecting his communications at Acquia Creek, fortifying the heights north of the Rappahannock, and arming them with the most potent equipment of heavy guns ever marshalled in the field by any general. The lavish preparations of his government supplied him with an

apparatus, compared with which the gigantic artillery of Napoleon was puny.   Besides innumerable field batteries of lighter
guns, which were intended to march and fight with his divisions
of infantry, one hundred and eighty heavy cannon, some of them
throwing shot of a hundred pounds' weight, frowned upon the
town and its approaches, from the opposing hills.   The "grand
army" was now arranged into three great *corps,* under Sumner,
Hooker, and Franklin, which made an aggregate of one hundred
and twenty-five thousand men, besides a *corps* of twenty-five
thousand more, under the German Sigel, which performed the
duties of a rear-guard.

Upon the 10th of December, Burnside at length received his
pontoon trains; and he determined at once to prepare for forcing
his way in the front of the Confederate army, and beginning
his onward march to Richmond.   He was confronted, upon the
heights before Fredericksburg, by the *corps* of Longstreet.   At
Port Royal was the division of D. H. Hill; between him and
Longstreet, was the division of Early; and the remainder of
Jackson's *corps* was held in reserve about Guinea's Station,
ready to support either point.   The cavalry division of Stuart
guarded the course of the Rappahannock for many miles above
and below; and prosecuted, with their usual audacity, their raids
within the enemy's lines.   The defensive force may be stated
with substantial, although not with exact correctness, at sixty-
five thousand men of all arms.   Of these, General Jackson's
corps included about twenty-five thousand effective men.

The impressive *drama* which was now about to occur upon the
plains of Fredericksburg, presents to the student of history one
of the most brilliant examples of defensive warfare.   To comprehend its true merits, he must acquire a distinct conception of
the topography of the *arena,* upon which it was enacted.   The
general course of the Rappahannock, though sinuous, may be

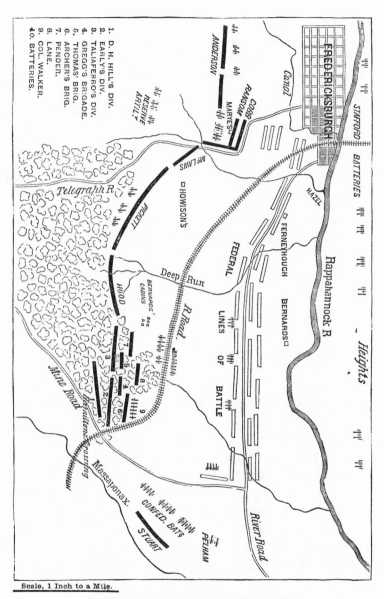

Scale, 1 Inch to a Mile.

BATTLE OF FREDERICKSBURG

said to be, here, from west to east; and it divides the county of Stafford on the north, from that of Spottsylvania on the south. The town of Fredericksburg is in the latter; and the village of Falmouth, a mile above, is in the former. The tides flow to the foot of the town; so that below, the stream is deep, though narrow; while immediately above, it is shallow and fordable during dry seasons. The country along its banks here has, in a marked degree, those features which characterize the tidal streams of Eastern Virginia. There are three stages, or grades, proceeding from the water, of which the second is more elevated than the first, and the third than the second. The first of these levels, next the water's edge, is the modern *alluvium*, or low ground proper, rarely marshy, yet subject to the inundations of the great freshets, with a horizontal surface, and a deep, black soil. It is of very variable width, spreading in some places to the extent of a beautiful meadow, and in others, contracted to a narrow strip of land. The traveller moving directly from the river, after passing over this low belt, ascends a short, steep hill, thirty or forty feet high, and then·finds himself upon a table land of greater extent, which is of an older alluvial deposit, but nearly horizontal likewise. It is this level, extending to the width of miles, in many places, which constitutes the great grain region of the Rappahannock. Its dry, kindly and fertile soil has long ago tempted the inhabitants to strip it of its forest; and the whole surface was divided into extensive fields, enclosed by wooden fences or hedge-rows, and dotted over with country mansions and the humbler homes of the servants. The streams making their way across the table land from the interior to the Rappahannock, as may easily be surmised, have excavated for themselves deep channels through its alluvial structure; along which they flow sluggishly upon the level of the first bottoms below. Finally, the river, like all other great streams, is inclined to throw the main bulk of its flats wholly on the one side or the other, by running at, or near, the base of the highlands; and at Fredericksburg, nearly all the level lands are on the south side. It is on this second stage or table land, that the town of Fredericksburg is seated; and it stretches along the river.for more than a mile, with a breadth of a half mile backward.

If the traveller would proceed farther from this table land toward the interior, he next ascends the highlands proper, which rise in swelling hills of the altitude of fifty or a hundred feet, nowhere rocky or craggy, but sometimes bold; and pierced here and there by the vales through which the inland rivulets descend to the lower stages. From the' top of this range of hills, the interior stretches away into a region of gentle hills and dales, of which the average altitude is far above the table lands. And as the soil of the highlands is thin and gravelly, the larger part of the bordering front of hills was left to the original forest, whence the fuel and timber for the vast farms of the table land were taken. It will now be easily understood how the town of Fredericksburg, with the narrow plain in which it is seated, is commanded both from the hills of Stafford, and from those of Spottsylvania, which are here separated by the distance of a mile. These heights are lofty, and perhaps of equal altitude near the town. Where the main country road going south, issues from the streets, it is overlooked near at hand by a noble hill, known, from the country seat upon its brow, as Marye's Hill. The highway, striking the base of this height, turns aside to the eastward, in order to avoid its acclivity, and thus skirts its base for a few hundred yards, until reaching the course of a sparkling rivulet called the Hazel, it again resumes its southern direction, and finds its way up the vale of that stream into the interior, by a gradual ascent. It will be perceived from this that the road has a tract of a few hundred yards, which runs

76

parallel with the edge of the town. This is bordered on the left, or town-ward side, by a massive stone fence, embanked with earth; and between it and the edge of the suburb, is a narrow and level field. After passing the Hazel, the highlands take a wide sweep to the southeastward (receding from the Rappahannock, until the ample table land acquires a breadth of nearly three miles); and continually declines in elevation and boldness, as it is followed in that direction. At the broadest place, the plain is watered by another rivulet, called Deep Run, whose springs, breaking from the base of the heights, collect into a stream, and make their way along a deep channel, to the Rappahannock, a half mile below the mouth of the Hazel, and a mile below the town. The rim of highland, after encircling the sources of Deep Run, again approaches the river somewhat, continually diminishing its altitude, until, at the distance of four and a half miles east of Fredericksburg, the height gently declines into a series of soft waves of land, which terminate at the valley of the Massaponax. This is a tributary of the Rappahannock, which taking its rise in the interior of Spottsylvania, flows northward with a current of greater pretensions than the Hazel and Deep Run, and enters the river five miles below Fredericksburg. It is itself bordered, for several miles upward, by an expansive valley of broad meadows and gentle slopes, which are, in fact, an extension of the greater table land of the Rappahannock. Immediately east of the Massaponax, the highlands approach the very margin of the river on both sides, and hug it closely for several miles.

A country road, known as the Port-Royal or River Road, issues from the town at its eastern corner, and proceeds down the middle of the great table land, at the distance of a mile from the river, and a mile and a half from the heights, until it crosses the Massaponax, and penetrates the eastern highlands. This road runs, the larger part of its course, between two fences, each of which is set upon an earthen bank of a yard's height, thickly grown with cedars and other hedge-row trees. It therefore offered to the occupants the advantages of a double line of low, but very substantial field-works; for the embankments, consolidated by time, and interlaced with the roots of trees, offered a perfect defence against rifle balls, and no mean protection against heavier projectiles. This whole lane of four and a half miles' length, was commanded by a multitude of Federal guns of long range, upon the Stafford heights. The railroad to Richmond, also emerging from the eastern end of the town, passed through the plain upon an embankment a couple of feet high, parallel to the river road, and between it and the hills, until approaching the Massaponax, it turned southward with a wide and sweeping curve, seeking to make its way, by the valley of that stream, to the interior. It is just where the heights finally sink into the wide valley of that creek, that the railroad crosses an old country thoroughfare, known as the mine road; and here was seated a little way-side station, called Hamilton's Crossing. The plain of Fredericksburg, which was destined to be the great battle-field, may be roughly compared to the half of a vast ellipsis, divided by its longer axis, with the west end containing the town, contracted to a narrow apex, and the eastern expanded into an ample section of a circle.

The reader is requested to master this somewhat particular description, because it is necessary to the correct understanding of transactions much misunderstood. The zeal of the Federals, of all mortals most passionately thirsting for that reputation for military prowess to which they are so little entitled, has led them with one voice to excuse their disaster, after it occurred, by attributing it to the excellence of the Confederate position, and the natural difficulties of the crossing. Justice both to the much-abused Burnside, and to the Confederate army, requires that the topography be correctly conceived. It will then be seen, that while the position of General Lee was good as a whole, and on his left strong, it gave him no advantage whatever upon his right (save a slight superiority of elevation for his batteries), which was not matched by at least equal advantages in the position of the enemy. The ground which Jackson so successfully held against the double numbers of Franklin and Hooker in the coming battle, was no stronger than that which he wrested from Shields at Port Republic, and not near so strong as that which he and Longstreet stormed at the Chickahominy, with inferior forces. When the battle of Fredericksburg was fought, General Jackson had not a yard of entrenchment in his front; indeed his *corps* only came upon their ground during the night, and the early morning preceding the struggle. The elaborate lines which the military tourist saw afterward, were all the work of subsequent weeks, provided by General Lee against the possibility of future attacks. On the left, the battle-line of Longstreet was strengthened, at several places, by light earthworks, or barricades of timber, and *abattis;* while the heavy field-guns upon Marye's Heights, and thence toward the west were protected by slight lunettes or *épaulements.* It should also be remembered, that the position of General Lee gave no effectual advantage toward the resistance of the passage of the river by Burnside, and his quiet establishment on the southern bank, in a situation perfectly tenable and secure. The configuration of the Stafford Heights and of the river flats and bluffs, the superiority of the Federal numbers, and the power of their countless batteries, made him master of those points. It was therefore with perfect truth that he claimed, in his despatches of the 12th of December, that the difficulties of the Rappahannock were surmounted, and that nothing remained between him and the march to Richmond except the equal grapple with the army of Lee upon a fair and open battle-field. It was only after that grapple had occurred, and the heroism of the Confederate soldiery, with the masterly skill of their leaders, had made it a frightful disaster, that these facts were diligently obscured. The river bank in the possession of the Federalists did not, indeed, present that concave curve which the military authorities recommend as favorable to the success of the assailants seeking to pass a stream in the face of an enemy. But it showed, in every other respect, all the requisites which they ask for a successful crossing; and the peculiar form of the opposite flats made the absence of this curvature wholly unimportant to Burnside. These truths will manifest themselves without discussion, as the narrative proceeds.

Before the break of day, on the 11th of December, the signal guns of the Confederates gave note that Burnside was moving, and the whole army stood to its weapons. The guardianship of the river bank had been committed to Barksdale's Mississippi brigade, from M'Laws's division. One regiment was at the mouth of Deep Run, and the remainder, assisted by the 8th Florida, was in the town; two of the regiments being posted in the cellars of houses overlooking the water, and in trenches and other hiding-places, to resist the construction of bridges. At Deep Run there was no protection from the overpowering fire of the numerous batteries on the Stafford Heights, and of the large bodies of infantry which lined the opposing bank. After a struggle, protracted, beyond all expectation, to the middle of the day, this detachment was compelled to retire; and about one o'clock, P. M., the Federalists completed a pontoon bridge, and immediately began the passage of a heavy column of infantry and artillery. Upon the low and narrow bench of the first bottom, and beneath the steep bluff which separates it from the second level, they found a secure place to land and extend their lines. Unless the Confederates could advance across the wide plain, to the very brink of that bluff, which was rendered impossible by the frowning batteries of the opposing heights, the enemy was as completely shielded from their fire as though behind the walls of a great castle. Having gained this lodgement, the Federalists busied themselves in laying down other bridges, and passing over additional troops. But at Fredericksburg they found sterner work. The riflemen of Barksdale, availing themselves of every covert, poured so deadly a fire upon the working parties and their guards, that they were again and again driven back with great slaughter, in their attempts to gain the southern bank. Nine times did the thronging multitudes encourage each other to return to the task. The floating bridge projected itself nine times from the northern shore, covered with a busy swarm of men bearing timbers; when the Mississippians, awaiting their approach within their deadly aim, opened upon them stinging volleys which strewed the bridge and the water with corpses. Until one o'clock, P. M., this contest continued, and no progress was made toward winning the southern bank. Burnside then opened upon the town every piece of artillery which could be brought to bear upon it. One hundred and eighty cannon began to belch their thunders upon the devoted city. To the spectators upon the opposing hill it seemed wrapped in a whirlwind of smoke and flame; while from the bosom of the gloom the crash of falling buildings, the explosion of shells, the hissing of the fires, and the yells of the combatants arose in frightful chorus, as from a *pandemonium*. Yet, amidst this terrific tempest, the little brigade of Barksdale clung to the bank with invincible tenacity; and it was only after three hours more that they stubbornly retired a couple of squares, before a heavy detachment of infantry landed from boats under the protection of the cannonade. But here they again resumed the contest, and, fighting from street to street, held the enemy at bay until far into the night. When they were told that they had now accomplished all that was desired, and commanded to withdraw, they said that their position was tenable enough still, and entreated to be allowed to remain and fight the enemy. He had now completed two or three bridges, by which heavy columns of infantry were pouring into the town. It was no part of General Lee's plan to contest the occupation longer; for his position was chosen, not to prevent the crossing of the river, but the advance from it. He therefore withdrew the regiments of Barksdale, during the early part of the night, to his lines about Marye's Hill. The desired time for preparing a reception for the enemy had been gained.

During all the next day, the landscape was obscured by a dense fog, beneath which as a mask the Federalists carried on their preparations for attack. Whenever this curtain was lifted up momentarily, the ravines leading from the Stafford Heights to the river bank, were seen black with the vast masses of Federal infantry pressing toward the bridges, and their lines were perceived upon the plain advanced as far as the river road. The Confederate artillerists now and then seized these glimpses, to direct a cannon shot where the throngs were thickest, never failing to elicit an angry reply from the opposing heights. But otherwise, the whole day passed without hostile collision. The two divisions of General Jackson near Guinea's Station, were brought forward to strengthen the right; and as it was now beyond a doubt that Fredericksburg was to be the place of the great collision, messengers were sent to Port Royal for the other divisions. The summons reached General D. H. Hill a little before sunset on the 12th. His troops were then eighteen miles from the post they were designed to occupy upon the battle-field; but such was the promptitude of their action, by dawn on the next morning they were in their places, and ready to meet the enemy. The division of Early, which was somewhat nearer at hand, preceded them in their arrival upon the field.

The morning of Saturday, December 13th, now arose, like its predecessor, calm and foggy. The city and the extended plain were wrapped in the impenetrable mantle of mist, until ten o'clock A. M.; but on both sides, every sound which arose from the obscurity gave token of grim preparation. The line of General Lee was stretched for five and a half miles, from the heights overlooking Falmouth, along the edge of the highlands, to Hamilton's Crossing, near the Massaponax. Upon the crests of the hills were placed his numerous batteries; while Marye's Hill, as the post of honor, was assigned to the Louisiana battalion of Colonel Walton. The *corps* of Longstreet held the left, and that of Jackson the right. Next the river, upon the extreme left, was the division of Major-General Anderson, extending to the neighborhood of Marye's Hill. Then came that of M'Laws in the front line, supported by that of Ransom, in reserve. To the brigade of General T. R. Cobb, of Georgia, from M'Laws's division, was assigned the post of advanced guard, along the road and stone wall which has been described as skirting the base of that hill. Upon another, still more commanding height, in its rear, were planted other powerful batteries, designed to sweep the Federalists from its crest, should they succeed in gaining it. Next to M'Laws came the division of Pickett, occupying the edge of the highlands opposite to the widest part of the plain; and next to him the division of Hood. On the right the country was less elevated; it offered every way fewer difficulties to the enemy; and it was flanked by the wide and smooth valley of the Massaponax, which was so favorable to the operations of his · vast masses. Here, therefore, General Jackson strengthened himself with a triple line of battle, to compensate for the weakness of his ground. His front line was formed of two regiments of the brigade of Field, from the division of A. P. Hill, with the brigades of Archer, Lane and Pender. These stretched in the order named, from Hamilton's Crossing to the right of Hood. But they did not form a continuous line; for the brigade of Lane in the centre was advanced two hundred yards to the front, to occupy a tongue of woodland which here projected itself far into the plain. This patch of forest was low and marshy; and behind it, the ridge sunk almost into the same level; so that no position for artillery could be obtained upon Jackson's centre. Behind the interval thus left between the brigades of Archer and Lane, was placed that of Gregg; and behind the space which separated the brigades of Lane and Pender, was that of Thomas. Thus the whole front was composed of the division of A. P. Hill. A second line was composed of the two divisions of Taliaferro and Early, the former behind Pender and Thomas, and the latter behind Gregg and Archer. The division of D. H. Hill was held as a reserve in the third line. All these troops were posted in the woods, which covered the base and the gentle acclivities of the hills, so that they were not disclosed to the view of the enemy. They formed a line of battle a mile and a half long. On General Jackson's right was Stuart with two brigades of cavalry, and his famous horse artillery, under the boy hero, Pelham, thrown forward toward the enemy's left flank in the plain. In front of Archer, near Hamilton's Crossing, the range of hills which, behind Pender, had sunk almost into the plain, rises again to the altitude of forty feet; with the open field extending to its summit. Here General Jackson placed fourteen picked guns from the artillery of A. P. Hill, under the command of Colonel Lindsay Walker. On the left of his line were posted thirty-three guns, from the batteries of Early and Taliaferro, twelve of them advanced into the plain beyond the

77

railroad track, and all on level ground; for the place offered no superior position for them. On the right, twelve more guns were also advanced to assist the movements of Stuart, and to cross their fire with those of Colonel Walker. And Captain Hardaway from the division of D. H. Hill, was sent with his long Whitworth rifle, to the Highlands east of the Massaponax; whence he enfiladed the Federal line of battle as it advanced from the river road.

Having ordered these dispositions, General Jackson now rode along his whole front, to assure himself of their completeness, accompanied by several general officers and a brilliant Staff. As he appeared this morning upon his favorite battle steed, clad in a new and elegant suit of uniform, the gift of his friend, Stuart, and the old drab fatigue cap, which had so long been to his followers as glorious a guide to victory as the white plume of Harry of Navarre, replaced by the hat of a Lieutenant-General, resplendent with gold braid, he was scarcely recognized by his veterans. They saw not in this gallant cavalier, so instinct in his gait with martial elation, the sunburned "old Stonewall," to whom their eyes were accustomed upon the field of battle. As he passed along his lines, his suite* was made the target of the Federal sharp-shooters. When he reached the tongue of woodland occupied by the brigade of Lane, he said: "The enemy will attack here;" a prediction which a few hours fully verified. Thence he proceeded to the station of the Commander-in-Chief, upon a commanding hill near the Hazel overlooking the whole plain, to receive his last suggestions. It was now past nine o'clock, and the sun, mounting up the eastern sky with almost a summer power, was rapidly exhaling the mist. As the white folds dissolved and rolled away, disclosing the whole plain to view, such a spectacle met the eyes of the Generals as the pomps of earth can seldom rival. Marshalled upon the vast arena beneath them, stood the hundred and twenty-five thousand foes, with countless batteries of field guns blackening the ground. Long triple lines of infantry crossed the field from right to left, and hid their western extreme in the streets of the little city; while down the valleys descending from the Stafford heights to the bridges, were pouring, in vast avalanches of men, the huge reserves. For once, war unmasked its terrible proportions to the view, with a distinctness hitherto unknown in the forest-clad landscapes of America; and the plain of Fredericksburg presented a *panorama* that was dreadful in its grandeur. To the Confederate soldiers, the multitudinous hosts of their enemies appeared as though all the families of men had been assembled there, for the great assize of the Last Day; but confident in their leaders, they beheld their numbers with steady courage. Not a cheek was blanched, nor a heart appalled. Lee stood upon his chosen hill of observation, inspiring every spectator by his calm heroism, with his two great Lieutenants beside him, and reviewed every quarter of the field with his glass. It was then that Longstreet, to whose sturdy breast the approach of battle seemed to bring gaiety, said to Jackson: "General, do not all these multitudes of Federals frighten you?" He replied; "We shall see very soon, whether I shall not frighten them." Such was the jest in which the stern joy of battle in their spirits found utterance, while other hearts stood still with awe. They then separated to seek their several posts, and as the last remnants of the mist rolled away, the battle began, with a general cannonade. Three hundred guns now burst forth from the opposing heights; hill answered to hill with their thunders, while the battle smoke rolling sullenly down their sides, again enveloped the plain in a more dreadful pall than the morning fogs; and through the gloom, the fiery projectiles flew shrieking across in stunning confusion. Under the cover of this tempest,

Burnside advanced his columns to the attack, at once, upon the right and upon the left.

In the plain before him General Jackson saw the wing of Franklin, supported by a part of the grand division of Hooker, drawn out in three vast lines of battle, which he estimated at fifty-five thousand men. They were supported by numerous batteries, which advanced with them upon the plain. But as they passed the line of the river road, Pelham dashed forward into the open fields with two chosen guns of his horse-artillery, and unlimbering upon their left flank, began to rake their massive line with a rapid and damaging fire. At this audacious diversion the Federalists paused, threw a division of infantry into *crotchet* at right angles to their main line, so as to confront Pelham, and directed upon him the whole fire of four batteries, besides the distant heavy guns upon the Stafford Heights. But for a whole hour the two guns maintained the unequal duel, shifting their position upon the plain as fast as the enemy obtained their range accurately, disturbing the aim of their cannoneers by an occasional shot of deadly accuracy, and still pouring a rapid fire into the infantry. It was not until Pelham was recalled by positive orders, that he would surrender his hazardous position; and yet he brought off his command without serious loss. Such was the prelude to the tragedy upon Jackson's side; and this splendid example, doubtless, did much to inspire the rest of the artillery with high determination.

The Federalists, having been relieved of this antagonist, now advanced in earnest, feeling the whole forest, which enveloped Jackson's position, with a shower of cannon-shots. He commanded his batteries to make no response. Apparently satisfied that the woods were not occupied by any heavy force, they now moved forward with confidence, but still covering their front with a storm of projectiles. When their lines of infantry had approached within eight hundred yards of Jackson's position, they at last awoke the response. The guns of Colonel Walker, upon the front of Archer, were thrust forward, and opened furiously upon the Federal infantry, firing to their front and left, while Pelham, supported by the twelve guns of Jackson in front of his extreme right, again scourged them with a cross fire. The Federals paused, wavered, while visible gaps were made in their ranks by every discharge, and then broke and retreated to the river road. For two hours the struggle now degenerated into a desultory skirmish of sharpshooters. While this lull in the tempest continued, General Jackson rode toward his extreme right, and dismounting, advanced on foot far into the plain, followed by no escort save a single aid. This was Lieutenant James Power Smith, a young man of that class of which the Confederate army contained so many honorable members, who, though educated and well-connected, had served long and faithfully as a private in the Poague battery. Jackson having noted his devotion and intelligence, with his wonted sagacity, selected him from the ranks, and promoted him to be his *aide-de-camp*,—a favor which, as will appear in the sequel, was requited by young Smith with a fidelity which deserves to link his name in enduring bonds with the memory of his patron. The General, followed by this zealous attendant, now walked far out into the fields, to observe the dispositions of the enemy, when a sharp-shooter, suddenly arising out of the tall weeds, at two hundred yards' distance, levelled his rifle, and fired at him. The bullet hissed between the heads of the General and his aide, who were standing about two paces asunder. Thereupon he turned to him with a sunny smile upon his face, and said, "Mr Smith, had you not better go to the rear? they may shoot you!" The audacity of the sharp-shooter seemed to strike him as a pleasant jest; but, insensible to fear for himself, his caution only concerned itself for those committed to his care. After he had deliberately satisfied his curiosity, he returned to his lines, to await another attack, which he knew was at hand.

Having remained passive until past noon, the Federalists now moved their left again. Three lines of battle advanced to the charge, preceded by clouds of skirmishers, and strengthened by ten batteries of field-guns upon the flanks. Again they approached under a furious cannonade, to which the batteries of Jackson made no response until their infantry was within point-blank range, when they replied with equal violence. But the Federal lines now advanced with determination, and, as General Jackson foresaw, directed their attack to the projecting point of woods occupied by Lane's brigade. They hoped to find here a lodgement, and a protection from the Confederate artillery; for, when they came to close quarters, the oblique fire of the batteries on the right and left was necessarily suspended, to avoid overwhelming friend with foe, and the place occupied by Lane offered no position for cannon. Yet his sturdy infantry stood their ground for a time against triple odds, until the thronging multitudes of enemies insinuated themselves into the gap between his right and the left of Archer, deployed rapidly in the woods, and attacked his flank and rear. Some of his men wheeled, and made front against the new advance of the Federalists upon their side; a part of his line was broken and overwhelmed in the tangled woods, and the remainder retired upon its supports, fighting stubbornly; while the twelve guns which had been advanced upon his left, across the railroad track, were hurriedly withdrawn to avoid capture, suffering not a little from the Federal sharp-shooters. The left of Archer's brigade met a like fate with Lane's. Finding themselves taken in reverse, they broke and fled before overpowering numbers; thus widening the great breach in the front line, through which the Federal columns poured into the woods. But Archer still held fast to the right of his position with two or three regiments, with a stubborn tenacity which contributed much to save the day; and attempted, with another regiment, to form a new front against the enemy's flank.

But Jackson had provided many additional resources against this casualty. The triumphant irruption of the Federalists was first checked by the brigades of Thomas and Gregg, which covered the intervals of the front line. As the throng of enemies spread themselves from the breach in divergent columns, the one bearing most toward the Confederate right found itself suddenly confronted, at close quarters, by Gregg. His foremost regiment, mistaking them for friends, received a sudden volley, and was thrown into confusion. As their lion-hearted General, Gregg, rushed forward to reinstate his battle, he was shot down with a mortal wound. But Colonel Hamilton speedily rallied a part of his brigade, and made head against the enemy until other succors could arrive. Another torrent of Federalists, directing themselves along Lane's rear, and toward the Confederate left, was met by Thomas, and their efforts were partially contained. The battle had now passed within the range of the artillery, which suspended its fire; but the struggle raged in a confused manner within the woods, and the fragments of the line of Hill and of his enemies were mixed in inextricable confusion. It was at this critical moment that General Jackson ordered up his second line. But the Generals commanding it, anticipating his wishes with intelligent zeal, were about to rush into the wavering conflict, when they received his instructions. General Early, whose division covered all the right of A. P. Hill's broken line, threw the Georgia brigade of Lawton, commanded by Colonel Atkinson, directly forward; and then moved the brigade of Walker by its left flank, at a double-quick, until it covered the

yawning chasm upon Atkinson's left. The two now dashed for
ward upon the confused masses of the enemy, with such a yell as
only the Confederate soldiers know how to give. Walker connected his left with the right of Thomas, of Hill's division, who
was still showing an unbroken front; and the three brigades
swept the intruders in a moment from the woods, and pursued
them, with heavy carnage, across the railroad track, and far into
the fields beyond. Here, indeed, the enthusiasm of the Georgi-
ans led them too far; for, rushing several hundred yards in
advance of the railroad, they exposed their right to a whole
division of Federal infantry, which fired into their flank, and
forced them back to that embankment, capturing among their
wounded the commanding Colonel and his Adjutant.

But no sooner had General Early assisted in restoring the
wavering fortunes of the centre, than he was entreated for succors for the fragment of the line of Archer, which was staggering under the unequal pressure. He therefore advanced the
brigade of Trimble, under Colonel Hoke, supported by Hays,
upon the extreme right, relieved Archer, and driving the enemy
across the railroad here also, established his men along that line.
As soon as the enemy's infantry was sufficiently disengaged from
the woods on their retreat, the gallant Colonel Walker opened
his guns upon them again, and before they reached the shelter of
the river road, inflicted a severe punishment. While these
events occurred on Jackson's right, the division of Taliaferro
also advanced with the greatest enthusiasm, to support the front
line upon his left. But so speedily was the irruption of the
enemy repulsed, nothing remained for them to do, save that the
2nd Virginia regiment, of the Stonewall Brigade, assisted in
driving out the Federalists who had threatened the right of
Thomas.

The division of General Hood, also, upon General Jackson's

left, instructed by Longstreet to lend a generous aid to their neighbors, had assisted with two or three regiments, to repulse a threatening attack there. A large detachment of the enemy advancing up the channel of Deep Run, shielded from view, suddenly emerged in line of battle, and confronted the left of Pender's brigade, and the numerous batteries which he supported. One of his regiments, assisted by those of Hood, immediately attacked them, and drove them back with great spirit. Especially did the 57th and 54th North Carolina, two new regiments of conscripts, which had never been under fire before, cover themselves with glory. They pursued the broken enemy, the 57th in front, across the railroad, and for a mile into the plain, although scourged by a flank fire from the channel of the creek; and it was not until repeated messengers had been sent to repress their ardor, that they were recalled. The gallant Hood said, that he verily thought the mad fellows would go to the Rappahannock in spite of him and the enemy together. And as they returned, some were seen weeping with vexation, because they were dragged from the bleeding haunches of the foe, and exclaiming: "It is because he has not confidence in Carolinians. If we had been some of his Texans, he would have let us go on!" But the men of Pender displayed equal merit, in enduring an ordeal of a different nature. Their chief part was to sustain the numerous batteries with which General Jackson had guarded his left upon the open plain. Lying behind these guns, insulted by a cloud of skirmishers, and receiving a large part of the projectiles aimed at the artillery, they patiently held their ground, unrelieved by the solace of active resistance, until the day was won.

A new front line was now formed by the Confederates, composed of portions of the divisions of A. P. Hill and Early, with the Stonewall Brigade, under General Paxton, along the railroad

78

embankment in front of their former position. It began near Hamilton's Crossing on the extreme right, and extending along the wide curve with which that thoroughfare sweeps into the plain, confronted the enemy all the way to the position of General Hood. The division of D. H. Hill, whose services had not been needed to complete the enemy's repulse, was now advanced to the second line; while the shattered portions of A. P. Hill's division were drawn to the third. The Federalists did not seriously renew their attack upon General Jackson during the day; but kept a spiteful cannonade, under which he suffered some loss. In this battle, Franklin had almost equal advantages of ground, and double numbers. But such was the skill of Jackson and his assistants, and the superior prowess of the Confederate soldiery, he was beaten, and driven hopelessly back to his starting place, before more than half of his antagonist's force had been displayed. He left about five hundred prisoners, besides many wounded men, and five thousand muskets in Jackson's grasp, as trophies of his victory.

While this battle was raging with General Jackson's *corps,* events of equal magnitude were occurring upon the left, in front of Fredericksburg, which are detailed with less fulness, only because the immediate subject of this narrative was unconnected with them. Here Burnside, with an almost insane policy, selected Marye's Hill as the point of pertinacious attack; a position which, in the hands of Confederate soldiers, was impregnable; and which, if captured, would have been found commanded in turn by other positions of greater strength. But, endeavoring to silence the batteries of Colonel Walton upon its crest, by the tremendous fire of his heavy guns upon the Stafford Heights, he hurled brigade after brigade of Sumner's wing against it, throughout the day, with no other result than the pitiable slaughter of his men. Six times his fresh reserves were

advanced to the attack. But Walton, disregarding the hurricane
of shells from the opposing hills, reserved his fire for the dense
lines of infantry; and as soon as they emerged from the town,
and formed for the charge, shattered them with well directed,
plunging volleys. The advanced line of Cobb, behind the stone
fence at the base of the hill, supported by Ransom upon the face
of the declivity, awaited the Federals whenever they advanced,
with withering discharges of musketry. The narrow field before
them was literally encumbered with corpses; the gallant Cobb,
statesman and orator, as well as soldier, was borne from his
post, mortally wounded, assigning it to Kershaw; but still the
night closed upon the carnage, and the Confederates had not
been dislodged from a single foot of the outworks of their position. The depressions of ground along the Hazel, in which the
routed columns of the Federalists sought refuge from the scathing
fires of Marye's Hill, were raked by the more distant batteries
near General Lee's position upon the centre; and the frightened
wretches found no refuge, save behind the dwellings of the town.
There, also, they were only secure, because the Commander-in-
Chief spared the city from bombardment, in mercy to a few
hundred of the inhabitants, who, he knew, had clung to their
homes throughout these horrors. In a word, the Confederates
at length had here, a position which was really strong, and
which they had adequate forces to defend. It was such a position as they had been accustomed to wrest from Federalists in
previous battles. The consequence was, that the attempt to
wrest it from them never approximated the first appearance of
success, and resulted only in a frightful loss.

On the right, the afternoon was wearing away without event,
save that the contest of artillery was still actively sustained
between Stuart and Colonel Walker, supported by some of the
guns of Colonel Brown, and the Federalists. General Jackson

desired them to attack him again in his position; but when he perceived that they had learned too much wisdom by their chastisement, he was desirous that the important juncture should not pass, without at least an attempt to turn their repulse into a defeat. He longed to try, whether by one grand advance, disregarding the fire from the Stafford Hills, their shattered masses might not be routed from their hold along the river road, forced back upon the deep river, mowed down at the narrow approaches to their bridges, and hurled into the water. He thirsted for at least one victory, where the blood of his faithful men, and his own cares and toils, should be rewarded by grand results, like those of an Austerlitz or a Waterloo. But he knew something of the double embankments of the river road, before him, and of the double numbers of the enemy's men and guns. He knew that while the Federal was no match in prowess for the Confederate soldier, yet he never permitted any advantage to fail him, which could be gained by adroit cunning or mechanical industry. He was well aware that it was no easy task for the inferior force to inflict an utter over-throw upon the superior, sustained by such resources, however the latter might be repelled, by a higher courage. As the sun declined toward the west, he was seen sitting upon his horse a long time, with his watch in his hand, considering the effect of the cannonade with which Stuart was still plying the enemy's left, and counting the minutes until the sun should touch the horizon. After anxious hesitation, his resolve was formed; he determined to make the essay, postponing it until the approach of night, in order that, if it were successful, the death grapple with the Federal infantry might be shielded from the fire of their protecting artillery by the darkness, and might be enhanced in its confusion and horrors; or, if it were unsuccessful, the same friendly veil might assist him in drawing off his forces without serious disaster. He therefore issued orders, that every gun, of whatever calibre or range, which was not disabled, should be advanced to the front; that, at sunset, they should move across the plain together, and open upon the enemy; that all the infantry should follow, in lines of battle, and that as soon as the Federal front showed signs of wavering under the cannonade, the whole should charge with fixed bayonets, and sweep the invaders into the river. The attempt was hurriedly made to effect these dispositions; a number of fresh batteries were advanced and opened upon the enemy; and the first line, which the General had committed to the charge of Early, was just springing to its work, when he recalled his orders. He perceived that the concert between his different batteries of artillery was too imperfect to promise him success; that his subordinates proceeded to the enterprise with doubtful determination; and that the enemy covered his whole front with so terrible a fire from his countless artillery, that it threatened too great a loss of patriot blood. He therefore, unwillingly relinquished the endeavor, and made his dispositions for the night, assigning the front to Early, and ordering all the troops to be relieved for a short time, by detachments, that they might replenish their ammunition for the morrow. With this exception the whole army lay upon their weapons during the night, in the positions they had held during the day.

The unfulfilled plan of General Jackson has not been related in order to impress the imagination of the reader with a picture which was, perhaps, impossible to be realized, of the horrors of Boteler's Ford, re-enacted on a grander scale, amidst the accessories of darkness and a stupendous confusion; of murderous lines of Confederate bayonets rushing through the gloom, revealed to the affrighted invaders by the angry glare of the cannon alone; of huddled masses of fugitives, mowed down by shot and thrust of invisible hands, and engulphed in the black waters; while Jackson and his fierce subordinates urged on the carnival of death. The purpose is to prove, by a great and notable instance, that General Jackson's determination had none of that headstrong imprudence which has sometimes been imputed to him. He was capable of grand resolves; no commander ever engaged his adversary with more of "the unconquerable will, and purpose never to submit or yield" than he; but none was ever more careful of the blood of his men, or tempered his daring with greater wisdom.

Thus ended the great battle of Fredericksburg, in which the Federalists confessed a loss of twelve thousand men killed and wounded, nine thousand small arms, and about a thousand prisoners. In repelling the attacks of their vast army, General Lee had employed less than twenty-five thousand men, and had experienced a loss of four thousand two hundred. Of these nearly twenty-nine hundred were killed and wounded in the *corps* of General Jackson; and there were, in addition, five hundred and twenty-six officers and men captured, chiefly from the division of A. P. Hill. That division also bore the heavier part of the loss in killed and wounded: a price which the brave are accustomed to pay for the post of honor. The batteries which were long engaged suffered much in this action, and especially those of Colonel Lindsay Walker. Placed in a prominent position, from which there was no retreat, and made the target for a continual fire for many hours, they were often struck, and lost many men and horses.

After all the necessary dispositions had been made for the night, General Jackson retired to his tent to seek a few hours' repose. There his friend, Colonel Boteler, awaited him, to whom he offered a share of his pallet; but long after the other had lain down, he continued to write and send despatches. At length, near midnight, he lay down beside him, without removing any of his clothing, and slept for two or three hours; when he again arose, lighted his candle, and resumed his writing. But, observing that the rays fell full in the face of his friend, whom he supposed to be still asleep, he immediately procured a book, which he so adjusted upon his table as to screen him from the light, that he might not disturb his slumbers. About four o'clock in the morning, he called to his faithful Jim for his horse; and, after a friendly altercation with him, concerning his desire to ride the same one which had borne him through the battle of the previous day, in which Jim came off victorious, he rode away with a single aide. He had mounted thus early in order to redeem an hour before the day dawned, to pay a visit to the dying soldier, General Maxey Gregg. This heroic man had fallen the day before, shot through the body in the irruption of the enemy through the line of A. P. Hill, and now lay in a neighboring dwelling, drawing near to his last hour; but still as calm as upon the field of battle, and as ready to render up his life a sacrifice for his country. General Jackson spent a few solemn moments by his couch, and bade adieu to him with tender sympathy. He then returned to the front, to meet the first dawn of day among his men, and to assure himself that they were prepared for the expected renewal of the assault.

General Lee, on his part, had spent the night in diligent preparations for such an event. The enemy had been so easily repulsed by a fraction of the Confederate army, and still possessed so enormous a superiority of numbers, that he could not believe Burnside would accept a final defeat on those terms. He therefore supposed that the attempt of Saturday was but the prelude to a more strenuous attack to be made on the Sabbath. He earnestly desired that the assault should be renewed; because the strength of his position assured him that it would only result in the further destruction of the enemy. His troops were therefore all prepared with supplies of ammunition for another day of yet more tremendous battle; and the weaker points of his line were strengthened with works hastily thrown up during the night. The morning disclosed the Federalists still drawn up upon the plain, in full array, and showing a steady front; but the day wore away without any demonstration, save a continual skirmish of the sharp-shooters and artillery. In truth, Burnside purposed a renewal of the attack; but his three Lieutenants, who seem to have assumed a practical independence of his will, remonstrated so boldly, and gave such representations of the demoralization of their troops, that he was compelled to relinquish his design. The next subject for his consideration therefore was, in what way he might best extricate himself from his perilous position. This was a problem which was not easy of solution; for, to retreat across his narrow floating bridges, in the face of a watchful and victorious foe, was to invite destruction. He therefore spent the day strengthening his position, especially before the front of the town, with hastily-dug trenches, and. kept his outposts pressed close up to those of General Lee, as though preparing for further aggressive movements.

During the night of the 14th of December, General Jackson held his troops in the same lines, except that the division of D. H. Hill was placed in the front, and that of Early was relieved by retiring to a less exposed place. During Monday, the 15th, a flag of truce was sent, requesting a few hours' truce between the Confederate right wing and the Federal left, in order that the latter might relieve their wounded, many of whom had now been lying upon the freezing ground two days and two nights. The note containing this request was signed by a General of subordinate rank. At Sharpsburg, some of the Confederate Generals had granted a temporary truce upon a similar application, which had been afterwards disclaimed by M'Clellan. General Jackson therefore replied to this, that when authenticated by the General commanding the Federal army, the application would receive an answer. After a time, it was returned with the authority of Burnside, when the truce was promptly granted. In his front, grim-visaged war now smoothed its horrors for a few hours; and while the hospital attendants were busy in removing the dead and wounded, officers and men from the adverse ranks mingled together in familiar intercourse.

The second day after the battle was now ended. The Confederates were eager in their hopes that the enemy would attack again on the morrow, when an opportunity would be again found to avenge, upon the invaders of their homes, the barbarities which had marked the war. Such was the enthusiasm which reigned among them, the division of D. H. Hill, which should, in turn, have been relieved from the front on the 15th, sent a written request to General Jackson, to be allowed to remain there another night, in the hope that they might have the honor of receiving the enemy's first attack the next morning. Their request was granted; but with the morning came a grievous disappointment. The whole opposing army was gone, with all its appurtenances, and had removed its bridges, and resumed its post upon the Stafford heights. The weather had come to their assistance, in the shape of a storm of rain, accompanied with a tempestuous wind from the south, which, driving from the Confederates toward the enemy, had effectually stifled the sound of every note of preparation for the march. Under cover of this wind and the Egyptian darkness, they had been busy all night, withdrawing their army and artillery over a number of bridges, while the numerous sentries close to the Confederate front kept up a bold show to the last. After all the rest had retired, these out-posts also were called in, their officers passing from man to

man, and giving the order to fall back in a whisper. With such
industry and adroitness was the retreat conducted, all the vast
multitude, with its countless carriages, was withdrawn in one
night, in the midst of intense darkness, and without the aid of
even a lamp; for they feared to draw on themselves the fire
of the Confederate cannon. When some of the citizens, who
had remained shut up in their houses during the whole struggle,
came with candles to their doors, to learn the cause of the
strange, dull buzz which filled the air, they were startled to find
the streets packed with dense columns of men, whose faces were
all turned toward the river, and who instantly greeted their
appearance with the stern whisper, "Put out that light! Put
out that light!" Some of the officers also sprung from the ranks,
snatched the lights from their hands, extinguished them, and thrust
the bearers back within doors. The movement was all accomplished before the Confederate pickets learned anything. When
the dull and dreary dawn began to steal over the ground, they
perceived that the sentries who had confronted them were either
gone or were motionless; and upon approaching the latter, they
found that they were dead corpses, stiff and stark, which the
Federals had propped up against stones or posts, placing
muskets in their hands!

On re-entering the afflicted city, the Confederates discovered
also, that the enemy had employed the leisure of the two days
after the battle, in sacking its dwellings from one end to the
other. The only houses which escaped were those which, being
occupied by wounded men, or by the quarters of general officers,
were guarded by their sentries. Not only was every species of
food and other portable property, which a soldier could desire,
carried away, but the most ingenious and laborious destruction
was wrought upon that which they did not need. Costly furniture and pianos were hewn to pieces with axes, the wardrobes

of ladies torn into shreds, mirrors precipitated upon the pavements, and the morocco-bound books of gentlemen's libraries carried in hampers to the river, and tumbled into the slime of the tides. But otherwise, the general aspect of the buildings gave singular proof of the difficulty of actually destroying a city by a bombardment. After all the tempest of projectiles by which it seemed the doomed city must be levelled with the ground, only a few houses were burned, and a few seriously broken down. In the others, the only signs of bombardment were a few small holes perforated in the walls and roofs by the shot, and a number of places, where glass and plastering had been broken by the explosions; while many buildings had almost miraculously escaped.

In this retreat, the Federalists had every circumstance to favor the secrecy of their movements; yet their success casts a reflection upon the watchfulness of the Confederates. It was true that the darkness, the rain, and the tempestuous wind, were sufficient to hide all the movements of the fugitives from the sentries; but surely, on all that extended front, there ought to have been some scouts adventurous and shrewd enough to penetrate the enemy's lines, by some mode, and gather some *data* which would be decisive of their purpose to fight or flee. The Confederate commander was much disappointed by the result. Another imperfect victory had been added to the list of his exploits, in which the glory of a masterly strategy and heroic courage at the beginning, was overclouded by a partial forfeiture of the anticipated fruits of victory. His beaten enemy had again extricated himself from a situation, which promised a complete triumph and a speedy peace to the Confederacy. Doubtless General Lee admitted in his own breast, that had he foreseen this escape of Burnside, he ought to have taken the aggressive against him during the two days of inaction, in some way. But what that way should have been, it was still not so easy to determine. His advantage over Burnside in position and facility of attack, was after all more seeming than real. In front of the Confederate right, the Federalists held fast to the two embankments of the river road, which they made almost impregnable with countless batteries, and double lines of infantry; and where they were protected by the fire of their guns of long range from the north bank. If General Jackson would reach these lines, he must leave his position in the wooded hills, and advance into the plain, where every advantage passed from his side to that of his enemy. At Fredericksburg, the more contracted space brought either party which took the aggressive immediately under a murderous fire from the opposing heights. If the Confederates advanced, they seemed to incur the same disadvantages which the Federalists had found so disastrous at Marye's Hill.

But in one particular, General Jackson differed from his associates, in his estimate of the situation. He did not consider the battle of the 13th of December as a mere prelude to a greater struggle. He appreciated the full influence of the events of that day upon the army of Burnside, and was convinced that it was at the end of that day a beaten army, and would attempt nothing more on that ground. He did not expect a renewal of their assaults the next morning, although his vigilance prompted to take every precaution against it. He saw clearly that it was for the Confederates to take the initiative next, or else the affair would continue incomplete. In this, he showed his customary sagacity, and that almost infallible insight into his adversary's condition and temper, which had guided him in previous campaigns. But his habitual modesty prevented his obtruding his opinions; and there is no certain evidence what plan of action he would have recommended.

The handling of Captain Hardaway's Whitworth rifle during the 14th, upon the highlands east of the Massaponax, gave one indication, which deserved to be followed up. Mounting a straw-rick which stood upon a bold hill there, in range with the distant line of the river road, he stationed his gun beside it; and glass in hand, directed a slow and accurate fire upon the enemy's position. They could make no effective reply; and with his one piece, he so enfiladed and raked that road as to compel them to remove their batteries to other ground. One of his shells was supposed to have slain the Federal General Bayard, near the centre of the Federal army, and three miles distant. Now, had a strong detachment of Jackson's guns of longest range been likewise posted in the Highlands, during the 14th, their fire might so far have counterbalanced that of the Federal artillery, as to enable him, with the remainder of his *corps*, to overwhelm their left, without ruinous loss to himself, by a front and flank attack combined. But the most obvious expedient for completing the discomfiture of Burnside's army, was to concentrate powerful masses of artillery on all the hills commanding the city itself, and disregarding the reply from the Stafford Heights, to overwhelm the whole locality with a sustained cannonade. The drift of the Federal troops was continually toward the streets of the town, after the battle of Saturday; there were their most numerous bridges; and thither the stragglers rushed for spoils. The streets and open spaces were doubtless so crowded with men during the whole occupation, that such a bombardment must have inflicted a bloody loss; and the approaches to all the bridges near the town being thus made impracticable, the sense of its insecurity might have plunged the whole army into panic. Two motives held back the hands of the Confederates from this obvious experiment; the expectation of having a more urgent use for the ammunition,

to fight another general action in their chosen position; and
compassion for two or three hundred citizens of the gallant
town, who were supposed to be still clinging to their ruined
homes.

The failure of this grand attempt of Burnside plunged the
Federal Government and people into mortification and rage.
For once, the disappointment was too bitter to be concealed;
and their anguish rendered them temporarily honest enough to
forego their customary boastings.   The butchery of their men,
and the profound discouragement of the survivors, were fully
avowed.   The Federal ministry compelled poor Burnside to
make himself the scape-goat for the fault, by assuming, in a published order, the whole responsibility of the movement.   The
blatant press now denounced their late favorite with an injustice
equal to their former senseless adulation.   And a Congressional
Committee of inquiry visited the army, and gathered the evidence
for completing his disgrace.   He was, after a little, removed
from his command, and succeeded by his insubordinate and boastful Lieutenant, Hooker.   His army was quietly withdrawn a
few miles from the river, and cantoned in winter-quarters in the
counties of Stafford and King George.

It is believed that the reader, in reviewing the affair of Fredericksburg, will concur in the assertion with which the narrative
began: that Burnside's plan was not ill-conceived.   With the
means which his Government placed at his disposal, the attempt
to cross the Rappahannock at Fredericksburg, in the face of
Lee's army, was feasible; and since Burnside's masters dictated
to him the necessity of marching on Richmond by some route, the
essay which he chose, was proper for him to make.   The only
real obstacle was the Confederate army; but that must be met
somewhere; and his Government and people were unanimous in
asserting that he both could and must overthrow it in some way.

The conception of Burnside, then, was good. His first fault was, that he did not estimate with practical wisdom the uncertainties and bureau impotency of the administration; so as to make sure of all the *apparatus* necessary for a prompt movement, such as pontoon trains, by his own personal superintendence. He began to move from Warrenton to his new base on the 13th of November. Two marches should have brought him to Fredericksburg. The last of Longstreet's *corps* did not arrive until the 21st. With all his preparations duly anticipated, and with reasonably prompt movements, he should have crossed the river in force, and been master of the southern bank, before the Confederates were in a condition to meet him. But the very odds which they found themselves compelled to bring against the Confederates, in order to cope with them, always rendered their army an unwieldy monster, too cumbrous for any one mind to comprehend or handle with precision.

After the opportunity for a sudden surprise was thus lost, Burnside proceeded with skill and judgment in the disposition which he made of his superior artillery, and in the measures by which he forced the passage of the river. But then his blunders began again. Of these the greatest was the direct attempt to storm Marye's Hill, which was the very last point to which his efforts should have been directed. An attack upon the extreme of the Confederate left, or upon their centre, — anything would have been less reprehensible. But his opportunity was, in fact, only upon the right; and all his real weight should have been thrown against Jackson. If he had moved promptly under the dense fog of the 12th of December, while as yet neither Early nor D. H. Hill were in position, he might have carried, by his infantry, positions which would have transferred the decisive battle to the interior of Spottsylvania, or to the North Anna. Or else, if he had employed that day in bridging the Massaponax near its mouth, and in opening ways for his vast artillery force near the eastern highlands; if he had made all his operations nearer Fredericksburg, on the 13th, a feint, and instead of allowing a large part of Hooker's grand division to hang as a useless reserve about the Stafford heights until the day was practically lost, had pressed forward the whole of it to support Franklin, and had thus moved in force upon both sides of the Massaponax, he might have reasonably promised himself a successful issue. It was manifest that the railroad from Fredericksburg to Richmond must be the essential part of General Lee's line of operations. But the direction of that thoroughfare down the valley of the Rappahannock, indicated that Burnside should advance only by his left; besides that, the country on his left flank was every way the more favorable to him. There is no boast in saying, that if it had been Jackson, with the Confederate army, who had seized the northern edge of the plateau of Fredericksburg, and Burnside who stood on the defensive upon the Spottsylvania hills, the former would have been as sure of occupying enough of the hills of the Massaponax to turn the position of the latter successfully, as the sun of the 13th rose upon the two armies.

It was manifest that the retreat of Burnside was the end of the campaign for the winter. The army of General Lee therefore proceeded to construct its winter-quarters in the wooded country behind the Rappahannock, the *corps* of General Jackson stretching from the neighborhood of Guinea's Station toward Port Royal. Very soon the men were comfortably housed in huts of their own construction, and settled down into the monotonous routine of the cantonment. General Jackson, after a few days' hesitation, established his head-quarters at Moss Neck, the hospitable mansion of Mr. Corbin, midway between Fredericksburg and Port Royal, and near the centre of his troops. Declining the offer of rooms in the commodious dwelling, lest he should unavoidably trespass upon the convenience of its inmates, he accepted the use of a sporting-lodge at the edge of the lawn for his lodgings. In the upper room of this cottage his pallet was spread; and the lower, still ornamented with the prints and trophies of the chase appropriate to its former uses, was occupied as his office. A large tent, erected near by, supplied the place of a dining-room for his mess. With these humble arrangements he addressed himself diligently to the improvement of his command, and the preparation of his official reports, to which the bustle of the extraordinary campaign just closed had forbidden his giving attention before. While the troops were steadily engaged in the construction of their winter-quarters, of roads to the stations whence they drew their supplies through the railroad, and of an elaborate line of entrenchments, which covered the whole country from Fredericksburg to Port Royal, he set himself busily to bring up this arrear of office-work. In the composition of the reports of his battles his reverence for truth and justice was conspicuous. The facts were laboriously examined by him; and then every sentence of his narrative was reviewed and scanned with most anxious care, that all might be true to the reality. The language of exaggeration was jealously avoided, nor did he descend to rhetorical portraiture: all was the severe simplicity of history. Yet these reports are models of perspicuity, of transparent plainness, and of true graphic power; and the literary man of true taste will esteem them as excellent specimens of narrative. This labor was continued, at intervals, throughout the winter; and was just completed when the advance of Hooker, in the following spring, summoned him to that crowning exploit, of which his death left the narration in other hands.

His attention was now addressed to an evil which had always been grievous in the Confederate armies,—absence from the

80

ranks without leave. Employing his friend, the Hon. Mr. Boteler, as his advocate in Congress, he urgently called the attention
of the Committee on Military Affairs to this abuse. He declared
that if it could be corrected even approximately, and the larger
part of the absentees could be recalled to the ranks, the army
would be so increased that, with the Divine blessing, one more
campaign would sweep the enemy from the soil of the Confederate States. One of his brigades reported twelve hundred
absentees! He proposed a novel plan, in which he expressed
great confidence, for abating the nuisance. This was, to offer a
pecuniary reward for the apprehension and delivery of all men
reported as absent without leave, to be paid at first by the Government, but afterwards re-imbursed from the pay of the delinquent. To carry out this conception, he proposed that it should
be embodied substantially in the following form: —

"Suppose, for instance, that a brigade-commander makes an
arrangement with persons not liable to military duty, to arrest
and deliver his absentees; and that he requires each company-
commander, as soon as he knows that one of his men is absent
without leave, to send up to brigade-headquarters a certificate of
the fact; and the brigade-commander sends the certificate to one
of the persons with whom he has previously agreed to arrest and
bring back his absentees; and that *whenever the delinquent and
certificate shall be delivered to the commanding officer of a military
post or camp, such commanding officer gives a receipt for the same;
and upon the presentation of such receipt to the Quartermaster of
the post or camp, he pays the reward, — say, fifteen dollars.* In
order to indemnify the Government, let the commanding officer
of the post or camp not only send to the company-commander
the man, but also a notification that a receipt has been given for
his delivery, in order that the company-commander may enter

the reward opposite the man's name on the muster and pay-roll, so as to have it stopped from his pay."

This proposal was never submitted to the test of experiment. General Jackson at least endeavored to set a wholesome example of the duty of adherence to the service. He had never had a day of furlough. When invited by a friend to allow himself a little respite for a visit at his house, where he might meet his wife and the infant daughter which he had never seen, he replied expressing the delight which such a vacation would give him; but firmly declining the proposal. A characteristic letter to Mrs. Jackson may be introduced here, illustrating this matter.

"CHRISTMAS, 1862.

"I do earnestly pray for peace. Oh that our country was such a Christian, God-fearing people as it should be! Then might we very speedily look for peace.

"It appears to me, that it is better for me to remain with my command so long as the war continues, if our ever gracious Heavenly Father permits. The army suffers immensely by absentees. If all our troops, officers and men, were at their posts, we might, through God's blessing, expect a more speedy termination of the war. The temporal affairs of some are so deranged as to make a strong plea for their returning home for a short time; but *our God* has greatly blessed me and mine during my absence; and whilst it would be a great comfort to see you, and our darling little daughter, and others in whom I take special interest, yet duty appears to require me to remain with my command. It is important that those at head-quarters set an example by remaining at the post of duty.

"Dr. —— writes, 'our little prayer meeting is still meeting daily, to pray for our army and leaders.' This prayer meeting may be the means of accomplishing more than an army. I wish that such existed everywhere. How it does cheer my heart, to hear of God's people praying for our cause, and for me! I greatly prize the prayers of the pious."

The new year brought him the sad news of the re-occupation of Winchester by the Federal army. His friends there were now subjected to the tyranny and outrages of the Federal General Milroy. Under his rule, the most vexatious and cruel restrictions were placed upon the people; and the plunder of their dwellings was shamelessly transferred to the private baggage of the Commander. Nothing which could. characterize the baseness of a petty despot, was lacking to the history of this man; and when, after the fall of General Jackson, Winchester was recaptured by his *corps* under General Ewell, Milroy crowned his infamy by running away from his command through by-roads, leaving them without a leader in the clutches of the avenging patriots. The story of the wrongs of the people now stirred the depths of Jackson's heart. His estimate of the value of the district to the Confederacy was revived by his grief and indignation, and he exerted all his influence with the Commander-in-Chief, to have an army sent for its deliverance. His constant judgment was still, that a force stationed in the lower Valley, and subsisted from the resources of the country, would render a service more efficient than the same numbers could render elsewhere, by preserving the riches of the country to the Confederacy, and by making a threatening diversion, which would embarrass any invasion of northern Virginia. He declared that the country would still sustain twenty thousand men, who should be sent there under an energetic leader, and he proposed General Early for the post. But General Lee did not deem that he had men to spare for the detachment; although the difficulty of provisioning his army in Spottsylvania did induce him, later in the season, to send General Longstreet, with a part of his *corps*, to southeastern Virginia; where they were detained until after the battle of Chancellorsville, without other result than some successful foraging.

While General Jackson was himself the commander in the Valley District, his modesty and disinterestedness had prevented his asking for larger powers, although he had felt, in the campaign of 1862, the cruel inconvenience of his subordination to a distant commander, who was necessarily ignorant of much which should guide his action there. But now, in asking that another should command there, he urged that the country should be elevated to an independent Military Department, with its own General, who should receive his orders directly from the supreme power. He strenuously declared that he did not desire to be again detached for that service, but every way preferred a subordinate command, near General Lee's person.

Indeed, it was manifest that his happiness was greatly increased by the removal of the load of separate responsibility, and administrative cares, which his present position gained for him. His companions in arms noted in him a considerable and pleasing change. The brow of care was more frequently relaxed; his warm social impulses were more freely indulged; and his meals, which had been usually despatched in haste and silence, became now seasons of cheerful relaxation, in which he was a quiet and unobtrusive, but joyous participant. Especially did he unbend, when visited after the hours of business, by his valued comrade in arms, General Stuart. In patriotism, in zeal for duty, in daring courage, and in military enterprise, these two men were kindred and sympathetic spirits; but in temperament, Stuart's exuberant cheerfulness and humor seemed to be the happy relief, as they were the opposites to Jackson's serious and diffident temper. To Jackson himself, it was a pleasure to have his· sobriety thawed by the gay laugh and jest of the great cavalier; while his occasional visits to the mess were the signals of high fun to the young men of the Staff. While Stuart poured out his " quips and cranks," not seldom at Jackson's expense, the latter sat by, sometimes unprepared with any repartee, sometimes blushing, but always enjoying the jest with a quiet and sunny laugh. The ornaments which the former proprietor of Moss Neck had left upon the walls of the General's quarters, gave Stuart many a topic for badinage. Affecting to believe that they were of General Jackson's selection, he pointed now to the portrait of some famous racer, and now to the print of some dog, celebrated for his hunting feats, as queer revelations of the private tastes of the great Presbyterian. He, with a quiet smile, only replied, that perhaps he had, in his youth, had more to do with race-horses than his friends suspected. He referred to his school-boy days at the forest home of his uncle, Cummings Jackson. It was in the midst of such a scene as this, one day, that dinner was announced; and the two Generals passed to the mess-table. It so happened that Jackson had just received, as a present from a patriotic lady, some butter, upon the adornment of which the fair donor had exhausted her housewife's skill, and that the print impressed upon its surface was a gallant cock. The servants, in honor of General Stuart's presence, had chosen this to grace the centre of the board. As his eye fell upon it, he paused, and with mock gravity, pointed to it, saying: "See there, gentlemen! If there is not the crowning evidence of our host's sporting tastes. He even puts his favorite game-cock upon his butter!" The dinner of course began with inextinguishable laughter, in which General Jackson joined with as much enjoyment as any.

His fame had now become world-wide; and while he attracted the enthusiastic admiration of his countrymen, strangers from

Europe made pilgrimages to the army to gain a view of the great soldier. They found him, not the *bizarre* and austere hero he had been described by popular fancy, but the modest, courteous gentleman, who offered the scanty hospitality of his quarters, and cared for their comfort with an almost feminine tenderness. His domestic tastes soon began to seek their solace among the children of the family near by; and he selected one, a sweet girl of six years, Jane Corbin, as his especial favorite. He requested of her mother that she should visit him every afternoon, after the labors of the day were finished; and he always provided himself with some present, suitable for her child's taste, which he laid away in his drawer: an apple, an orange, a bundle of candy, or a gay print. Sometimes the interview was passed with his little friend sitting upon his knee, engaged in eager converse; while at others, the noises which proceeded from the office showed that they were indulging in a good, hearty romp together. One evening, when she came, he had no gift for her. At the close of their play, his eye fell upon a new cap, which Mrs. Jackson had lately sent him, which was far plainer than that appropriate to a Lieutenant-General: but which still was encircled with one band of broad gold braid. Taking his penknife, he ripped this off, and saying to the child, "This shall be your coronet," fastened it with his own hand around her fair locks; and then stood contemplating her with delight. A letter to his wife contains the following reference to it:

"I became so much ashamed of the broad gold lace that was on the cap you sent me, as to induce me to take it off. I like simplicity." This gift, the reader will say, Jane Corbin doubtless preserved with jealous care, to be the most cherished ornament of her womanhood. Alas! no. The sweet child was destined to precede her hero-friend to that world where they both wear a purer crown; and the sad mother, now also a soldier's widow, guards it as the memorial of her bereavement. The very day General Jackson left Moss Neck to prepare for the spring campaign, little Jane was seized with that fearful scourge of the innocents, scarlet fever, and expired after a sickness of a day. The General felt her loss with a pungent grief; but the sterner cares of the army forbade his expending time in the indulgence of sorrow. He left his quarters for the last time, cumbered with the thousand wants of his great command, while the child lay dying. His sympathy with the bereaved parents was also quickened by his own parental anxieties. It was about this time that his letters brought him news that his own infant daughter, whose face he had never seen, was ill with a threatening disease. He stated the accounts of its symptoms to his friend, Dr. M'Guire, in whose medical wisdom he so confided, and asked his advice, that he might write it to his wife. As he closed his inquiries, he said, with a voice quivering with emotion, "I do wish that dear child, if it is God's will, to be spared to us." This prayer was answered; and the witnessing of its smiles was the last earthly joy which was assigned to him, as he finished his course.

The winter at Moss Neck was also marked by a farther increase of General Jackson's spirituality and Christian activity. Like the planet approaching its central sun, his soul moved with accelerated speed toward the Sun of righteousness. As he drew nearer to the centre of his divine attraction, his spiritual joy became yet more abundant. While his modesty was undiminished, his plans of exertion for the Church of God became more bold and comprehensive. His enjoyment of the Sabbath Day became higher than ever; and every source of happiness was traced up more gratefully to the heavenly Giver. A few extracts from his letters to his wife are introduced here, evincing the glowing piety of his affections: —

" Our ever gracious heavenly Father is exceedingly kind to me, and strikingly manifests it by the kindness with which He disposes people to treat me." (Then mentioning a number of presents.) "And so God, my exceeding great Joy, is continually showering His blessings upon me, an unworthy creature.

" I hope to have the privilege of joining in prayer for peace at the time you name, and hope that all our Christian people will; but peace should not be the chief object of prayer in our country. It should aim more specially at imploring God's forgiveness of our sins, and praying that He will make our people a holy people. If we are but his, all things shall work together for the good of our country, and no good thing will He withhold from it." . . . . " If I know my unworthy self, my desire is to live *entirely and unreservedly to God's glory.* Pray that I may so live."

January 17th, 1863. "I derive an additional pleasure in reading a letter, resulting from a conviction that it has not been travelling on the Sabbath. How delightful will be our heavenly home, where everything is sanctified!"

January 22nd. "I regret to see our Winchester friends again in the hands of the enemy. I trust that, in answer to prayer, our country will soon be blessed with peace. If we were only that obedient people that we should be, I should, with increased confidence, look for a speedy termination of hostilities. Let us pray more, and live more to the glory of God."

" Our heavenly Father is continually blessing me with presents. He withholds no good thing from me. I desire to be more thankful, and trust that through His blessing I shall grow in grace."

February 3d. "I trust, that in answer to the prayers of *God's people,* He will soon give us peace. I haven't seen my wife for nearly a year, and my home for nearly two years; and I never have seen my sweet little daughter." . . . . "My old brigade has built a log church; as yet I have not been in it. I

81

am much interested in reading Hunter's 'Life of Moses.' It is a delightful book, and I feel more improved in reading it than by an ordinary sermon. I am thankful to say that my Sabbaths are passed more in meditation than formerly. Time thus spent is genuine enjoyment."

Writing of some presents from *London*, he says: "Our ever kind heavenly Father gives me friends among strangers. He is the source of every blessing, and I desire to be more grateful to Him."

"To-morrow is the Sabbath. My Sabbaths are looked forward to with pleasure. I don't know that I ever enjoyed Sabbaths as I do this winter. I do hope, trust, and pray, that our people will religiously observe the 27th day of next month as a day of humiliation, prayer, and fasting, as the President has designated in his proclamation."

General Jackson, hoping, in common with many of his fellow-citizens, that the victories which God had vouchsafed to the Confederate arms in the year 1862, would convince the Federal people of the wickedness and unreasonable nature of their war, indulged some expectation that peace was not far off. It was his earnest desire, that when the people of the Confederate States then proceeded to adjust the working of their institutions, they should recognize the rights of God more distinctly, and that the Christian Church should put forth more saving power in society. One subject of his pious solicitude was, the laws of Congress which required the carrying and opening of the mails on the Sabbath; thus, not only permitting, but exacting, of a class of the citizens, the profaning of the day by secular labor. He had ever been accustomed to cherish a peculiar reverence for the Sabbath Day; and hearing that the propriety of this anti-Christian legislation was discussed in Congress, he exerted every lawful influence to bring about its repeal. To his friend, Hon. Mr. Boteler, he wrote as follows:—

"DECEMBER 10, 1862.

"MY DEAR COLONEL:

"I have read with great interest the Congressional Report of the Committee, recommending the repeal of the law requiring the mails to be carried on the Sabbath; and I hope that you will feel it a duty, as well as a pleasure, to urge its repeal. I do not see how a nation that thus arrays itself, by such a law, against God's holy day, can expect to escape His wrath. The punishment of national sins must be confined to this world, as there are no nationalities beyond the grave. For fifteen years I have refused to mail letters on Sunday, or to take them out of the office on that day, except since I came into the field; and, so far from having to regret my course, it has been a source of true enjoyment. I have never sustained loss in observing what God enjoins; and I am well satisfied that the law should be repealed at the earliest practicable moment. My rule is, to let the Sabbath mails remain unopened, unless they contain a despatch; but despatches are generally sent by couriers or telegraph, or some special messenger. I do not recollect a single instance of any special despatch having reached me, since the commencement of the war, by the mails.

"If you desire the repeal of the law, I trust you will bring all your influence to bear in its accomplishment. Now is the time, it appears to me, to effect so desirable an object. I understand that not only our President, but also most of his Cabinet, and a majority of our Congressmen, are professing Christians. God has greatly blessed us, and I trust He will make us that people whose God is the Lord. Let us look to God for an illustration in our history, that 'righteousness exalteth a nation, but sin is a reproach to any people.' . . . .

"Very truly, your friend,

"T. J. JACKSON."

Similar letters were also written to others, engaging their assistance to further the repeal of the law. To his friend, Colonel Preston, of Lexington, an elder of his church, he wrote to the same effect, seeking to enlist his pen; and afterward to secure, through him, the weight of the General Assemby of the Presbyterian Church, at its approaching meeting. To Colonel Preston he wrote thus: —

"I greatly desire to see peace, — *blessed peace.* And I am persuaded, that if God's people throughout our Confederacy will earnestly and perseveringly unite in imploring His interposition for peace, we may expect it. Let our Government acknowledge the God of the Bible as its God, and we may expect soon to be a happy and independent people. It appears to me that extremes are to be avoided; and it also appears to me that the old United States occupied an extreme position in the means it took to prevent the union of Church and State. We call ourselves a Christian people; and it seems to me that our Government may be of the same character, without connecting itself with an established Church. It does appear to me that as our President, our Congress, and our people have thanked God for victories, and prayed to Him for additional ones, and He has answered such prayers, and gives us a Government, it is gross ingratitude not to acknowledge Him in the gift. Let the framework of our Government show that we are not ungrateful to Him."

But the great work which most engrossed his heart was the spiritual improvement of the army, and especially of his *corps.* His soul had rejoiced, with unspeakable gladness, at the incipient showers of Divine grace which began to descend during the autumn. He had from the first lamented the destitutions of the army, where more than half the regiments were without chaplains, and the inefficiency of those who were present. He saw them laboring without plan and concert, and therefore without efficiency. He saw them leaving their charges in the midst of hardships and dangers, upon unnecessary grounds; thus unconsciously fostering the feeling of the unbelieving many, that the spiritual officer was less essential to the regiment than the secular; and so, inviting indifference to their labors when they were present. He was accustomed to say, that if an ecclesiastical organization and control for clergymen had been found necessary in civil life, they should equally be applied to these military pastors; and, again, that it was as reasonable that they should be held to their duties by a due subordination, as surgeons or captains. It had long been his desire to have some impulse communicated to their labors; and he now made the following suggestions to the Rev. Dr. White:—

"CAROLINE COUNTY, VIRGINIA, March 9th, 1863.
"MY DEAR PASTOR:

"Your letter of the 5th inst., was handed me yesterday. I am much obliged to you for it, and thankful to God and yourself for the deep interest you take in the army. I feel that, if you were a young man, you would delight to labor in the army Though your health will not admit of such constant labor, yet I trust that you will find it convenient to come and preach a few sermons. I do not feel that I can adequately express by letter, the inducements that exist for Christian labor among our troops. If you could come and spend a few days, and see for yourself, I believe that good would be accomplished, not only by your labors here, but by the impressions which you would carry away.

"When I wrote the letter to Colonel Preston, which he showed you, I had given up the idea that the Rev. B. T. Lacy would return." (The letter here referred to had authorized and requested Colonel Preston to invite the Rev. Dr. Palmer, an eminent minister recently driven from his pulpit in New Orleans, by the enemy, to come to his head-quarters, and labor as a missionary in his *corps;* promising to make a contribution of five hundred dollars per year to his support out of his private purse.)　" He had visited me soon after my arrival here; and I desired him to labor in my army *corps,* and expected him to return in about a week : though not necessarily to accept a proposition which I had made him : For he told me that, as he was in charge of a congregation, he could not decide what his course would be, until he should see more respecting his charge. Shortly after my writing to Colonel Preston, Mr. Lacy returned ; and I hope that through God's blessing, his labors will be with the army until the war terminates. . . . .

" Whilst I hope to have Mr. L. in my *corps,* yet if you think that our church, in making a proper distribution of her ministerial talent and piety, can send to my *corps* another of her gifted sons, I will be greatly gratified, and will contribute to his support as promised in my letter to Colonel Preston.　And I should like very much to have Dr. Palmer, judging from what I have heard of him.　But I do not wish to make invidious distinctions. My desire is to see just such a distribution of labors as will most promote the glory of God. . . . .

" You suggest that I give my views and wishes in such form and extent as I am willing should be made public.　This I shrink from doing, because it looks like presumption in me, to come before the public and even intimate what course I think should be pursued by the people of God.　I have had so little experience in church matters, as to make it very proper, it appears to me, to keep quite beyond the expression of my views to friends. Whilst I feel that this is the proper course for me to pursue, and the one which is congenial to my feelings, yet if you and Colonel Preston, after prayerful consultation, are of opinion that my name, in connexion with my wishes, will be the means of doing good, I do not desire any sensibility that I may have to be a draw-back in the way of doing good. I desire myself and all that I have to be dedicated to the service of God. So averse am I to appearing as though I would like to attempt in any way publicly to suggest what, in my opinion, the church should do, that I do not feel justified in consenting to my name being used as you have suggested, except after prayerful consultation between yourself and Colonel Preston. I take the liberty of writing to you and him my views: both of you have had large experience in the church, — you have both been known to the church for years, and after maturely considering what I write, *you* can with propriety publish, should you think best, any thing that I may have said *without saying that such was my view.*

"My views are summed up in a few words, which are these: Each Christian branch of the church should send into the army some of its most prominent ministers, who are distinguished for their piety, talents, and zeal; and such ministers should labor to produce concert of action among chaplains and Christians in the army. These ministers should give special attention to preaching to regiments which are without chaplains, and induce them to take steps to get chaplains, to let the regiments name the denomination from which they desire chaplains selected; and then to see that suitable chaplains are secured. A bad selection of a chaplain may prove a curse instead of a blessing. If the few prominent ministers thus connected with each army would cordially co-operate, I believe that glorious fruits would be the result. Denominational distinctions should be kept out of view, and not touched upon; and as a general rule, I do not think that a chaplain who would preach denominational sermons, should be in the army. His congregation is his regiment, and it is composed of persons of various denominations. I would like to see no question asked in the army, as to what denomination a chaplain belongs; but let the question be, does he preach the Gospel? The neglect of spiritual interests in the army may be partially seen in the fact that not half of my regiments have chaplains."

On the first of March, Rev. Mr. Lacy, a minister of the Presbyterian church, came, on General Jackson's invitation, to his head-quarters, to begin the species of labors described in the above letter. The Government, after a time, commissioned him as an army chaplain, without assigning him to a particular regiment; an exceptional act of courtesy accorded to General Jackson's high character and express request. In his letter to his other friends, he had modestly expressed his inexperience of ecclesiastical affairs, and his intention to commit the details of the plan of evangelical labors in the army to the advice of the clergyman, after Mr. Lacy had examined his ground. But the scheme adopted was that which the General had entertained in his own mind in the beginning of the campaign of 1862, and which, indeed, he had then attempted to effect. The exacting nature of the campaign, and the failure to enjoy at that time the assistance upon which he relied for its execution, had caused its postponement. But it was his design, which was now in substance resumed. His objects were three: to supply regiments destitute of chaplains with a partial substitute in the shape of the itinerant labors of efficient ministers; to supply a channel of intercourse between the army and the bodies of clergy of different denominations, through which the latter might learn the wants of the former, and to give to the labors of the chaplains and other ministers in the army, the unity and impulse of an ecclesiastical organization within their own peculiar field. His chaplain was intended by him to be an exemplar, who, he hoped, would be followed by many others from among the most efficient preachers of all churches, until they should be brought into vital sympathy with the army.

One of the measures adopted was the preaching of the gospel at the head-quarters of General Jackson, and under his immediate countenance, every Sabbath, while the troops were in their camps. For this end, a place in the open field was prepared, near Hamilton's crossing, (to which General Jackson removed his quarters soon after,) with rude seats and a temporary pulpit, where public worship was held in the open air. The example of so famous a warrior, always potent among soldiers when sustained by official rank, the curiosity to see him and the galaxy of celebrities who came to worship with him, the eloquence of the preachers, and the purer motives which the great religious awakening now began to propagate far and wide, soon drew a vast congregation to this spot on the Sabbath days. From hundreds it grew to thousands, until the assemblage surrounded the preacher in a compact mass, as far as his voice could be distinctly heard. Here, on a bright Sabbath in the spring, might be seen the stately head of the Commander-in-Chief, with a crowd of Generals, whose names had been borne by fame across the ocean, and of legislators and statesmen, bowed along with the multitude of private soldiers, in divine worship; while the solemn and tender wave of sacred emotion subdued the great and the unknown alike before it. At these scenes, which were so directly produced by his instrumentality, General Jackson was the most unobtrusive assistant. Seated in some retired spot amidst the private soldiers, he listened to the worship and the preaching with an edifying attention, and watched the power of the truth upon the great congregation, with a glow of elevated and tender delight. Never, since the days when Whitefield preached to the mingled crowd of peers and beggars in Moorfields, has the sky looked down upon a more imposing worship.

Another enterprise which marked the evangelical labors of

this winter, was the building of temporary chapels by the men for their own worship. Two or three contiguous regiments usually concurred in the work. Tall trees were cut down, and brought to the spot by the teams of the Quartermasters, and built into walls of logs. Chimneys were built of the same rude material, and plastered with clay, whence the huge fires, and the torches of resinous pine, diffused a ruddy glow of warmth and light. The structure was roofed with clapboards, and seated with rude benches formed from the split bodies of trees. The Stonewall Brigade was the first to begin this work, to General Jackson's great delight. No sooner had they completed their own huts, than they set to work, and by a multitude of willing hands, completed their church in a few days. The next Sabbath it was formally dedicated to the worship of God; and during the winter, was constantly occupied in turn by the chaplains of the several regiments. During the week, frequent meetings for prayer, and bible classes, were held here by torch-light, and the men were encouraged to expend their leisure in the study of the scriptures, and in sacred music, instead of the degrading amusements of the card-table. As this chapel was near the quarters of General Jackson, he often came to worship in it with his favorite brigade. Instead of affecting the chief seat in the synagogue, he delighted to sit among the rough, weather-beaten privates, and lay aside all official dignity to accompany them to the throne of grace on the common footing of worshippers. Their reverence for his person some-times led them to leave a respectful distance between themselves and the seat he occupied; but he would never consent that any space should be thus lost, where so many were crowding to hear the word. As he saw them seeking seats elsewhere, he was accustomed to rise, and invite them by gesture to the vacancies near him; and was never so well satisfied as when he had an unkempt soldier touching his elbow on either hard, and all the room about him compactly filled. Then he was ready to address himself with his usual fixed attention to the services. The most important measure which he introduced was the weekly chaplains' meeting. This was a temporary association of all the chaplains and evangelists of his *corps*, who, on meeting, appointed one of their own number to preside as a chairman or moderator, and another as their secretary, and after joining in public worship, proceeded to consult upon the spiritual interests of their charges, to arrange and concert their labors, and to devise means for supplying the destitutions of the army. These counsels were a true evangelical union. By a common and silent consent, which bears high testimony to the cultivation and honor of these laborious men, all subjects of sectarian debate, were effectually excluded, and their delibera- tions were confined to the interests of our common Christianity. But it was also a high evidence of the general soundness of religious opinion in the Confederate States, that there was not a single regiment in the army, which showed a disposition to introduce a minister who did not belong to an evangelical and orthodox communion, as their chaplain, except one or two priests of the Romish Church. On the other hand, the office in the Federal army was as frequently filled by Universalists, and other erratic heretics, or by laymen who never preached, as by regular ministers of the gospel.

General Jackson displayed his delicate sense of propriety by not attending these weekly synods of his chaplains statedly himself. But he watched them with lively interest. As soon as his own chaplain returned from them, he was accustomed to call him, and say: "Now come and report." He inquired into all that was said and done, and all the measures proposed, for evangelizing his command. When he was told of the fraternal love which reigned among the chaplains, of the devout spirit manifested in their worship, and of the news of the ingathering of souls which they brought from their several charges, his eyes were often filled with happy tears, and he blessed God for the grace. The stated meetings of the chaplains were the means of awakening them to a greatly increased zeal and fidelity, as well as for adding system and concert to their labors. So that this service, which, while adorned by the fidelity of a number of truly apostolic men, had yet fallen, in general, into no little disfavor, was now thoroughly renovated. Thus the energy of General Jackson's will, though so modestly exerted, made itself felt among his chaplains, just as among his staff and field officers, in communicating efficiency and vigor to all their performance of duty. It was remarked of him, that while no General officer had so unpretending a Staff, none other was so efficient as his. This was due not so much to the character of the men who constituted it, as to the force of his own example and energy, in inspiring the spirit of endeavor, among all who were subject to his authority.

The weekly meetings of the chaplains effected more good than he had hoped from them; for he had warned others not to anticipate too much. Hence, when he found that his plans were bearing so much fruit, he was filled with delight. One of the benefits of the movement was the bringing of the ministers in the army into closer connexion with his person. His own chaplain was a bond of union also between himself and the others, through which they were encouraged to visit his quarters more unreservedly, and to know and love him, not as a commander only, but also as a Christian. To every worthy preacher of the gospel his manner was full of warmth and tenderness, showing that he esteemed them very highly in love for their work's sake. Everything was done with a thoughtful affection, to facilitate their labors, and provide for their comforts. His contributions from his private purse were also large, to provide them with means for supplying their charges with Bibles and religious reading. The Government had never made any provision for the support of the chaplains in their work, other than a very inadequate salary. The General now applied to the Military Committee of Congress, to bring in a law enabling Quartermasters to provide chaplains, like other officers, with tents, fuel, and forage for horses. This just measure was indeed neglected amidst the hurry of the closing session, but was finally adopted by a subsequent Congress.

General Jackson, in his intercourse with his chaplains, often inculcated their obligation " to endure hardness, as good soldiers of Jesus Christ," to live with their regiments, and acquire their confidence by sharing their exposures, and to cleave to their work amidst all the pains and crosses which the common soldiers were compelled by the law of their country to endure. He said that a chaplain should not think of resigning his post for any less cause than would justify a field-officer in laying down his commission; and that they should no more think than he, of leaving his regiment without a regular furlough, founded upon just cause. To do so, he argued, taught the men by a practical lesson, that the soul was less important than the body, and that secular duties were more urgent than the business of redemption.

When with chaplains whom he esteemed like-minded, General Jackson was very sure to turn all conversation speedily into a spiritual channel. With intimate Christian friends, the things of God were almost his exclusive topics in private. His favorite subjects now were, the importance of an unshaken faith; of casting all our care upon God in the diligent performance of duty; and of the evidences of the Divine faithfulness in the course of Providence and redemption. He spoke emphatically of the duty of conforming our wills to God's, and of a thoroughly cheerful acquiescence whenever His will was manifested. He was often delighted to speculate upon the modes in which the Divine will might be safely ascertained. His favorite maxim was: " Duty is ours: consequences are God's." He spoke much also of the blessedness of a full and hearty obedience, in its effects upon the Christian's own happiness. He often declared that it was his first desire to command a "converted army." This, he believed, enjoying the spiritual favor of God upon their individual souls, engaged in a just cause, and undertaking every enterprise with prayer, must meet with success; and prove, in the end, invincible. He spoke frequently also of the connexion between national obedience and public prosperity; declaring that it is holiness which exalteth a people; and showing the supreme importance of the Government's at least refraining from placing itself, in any way, in opposition to God's laws and institutions. Hence his zeal for the outward and spiritual observance of the Sabbath, which has been noted.

One more favorite project remains to be mentioned, in which about this time, he sought to interest those who met him. This was the establishment of a Christian Daily Newspaper, which should honor God by refraining from all Sabbath work. He argued that their issue of Monday should contain nothing printed after Saturday evening; and that Christians should be willing to receive their news later by one day, once during the week, in order to honor God's law. If this delay should diminish the circulation of such a journal, and make it less remunerative than others; he declared that he was willing to repay a part of this loss out of his own means.

As soon as his quarters were established at Hamilton's Crossing, he began the custom of regular domestic worship in his mess, each morning. These services were willingly attended by all his staff, out of respect for his Christian character, or from their own interest in them. He, who was of all men least obtrusive in his religion, carefully forbore from commanding their attendance, although his beaming face indicated plainly enough the pleasure he felt in seeing them present. Whenever his chaplain was not there, he always conducted these services himself, with his customary unction and humility. On Wednesday and Sunday nights, there was also a prayer meeting observed at his quarters, where he was always a worshipper, and led the devotions of his brethren, when desired to do so by a minister. A few of the young men upon his Staff had cultivated the delightful art of sacred music. On the afternoon of the Sabbaths, when the necessary business, which he always reduced within the narrowest limits, was despatched, it was his favorite occupation to have singing; and frequently, as the little choir was concluding, he said; "Now let us have the hymn;"

> "How happy are they
> Who their Saviour obey."

On every intelligent Christian who approached him at this time, he made the impression of the most eminent sanctity. They all left him with this testimony: that he was the holiest man they had ever seen.

The following extracts from letters to Mrs. Jackson may be introduced here.

"MARCH 14th, 1863.

" On next Monday there is to be a meeting of the chaplains of my *corps*, and I pray that good may result from the meeting.

" The time has about come for campaigning, and I hope early next week to leave my room and go into a tent near Hamilton's crossing, which is on the railroad, about five miles from Fredericksburg. It is rather a relief to get where there will be less comfort than in a room; as I hope thereby persons will be prevented from encroaching so much on my time. I am greatly behind with my reports, and am very desirous of getting through with them before another campaign commences."

"APRIL 10th.

"I trust that God is going to bless us with great success, and in such a manner as to show that it is all His gift; and I trust and pray that it will lead our country to acknowledge Him, and to live in accordance with His will as revealed in the Bible. There appears to be an increased religious interest among our troops here. Our chaplains have weekly meetings on Tuesdays: and the one of this week was more charming than the preceding one," &c.

The effort thus begun in General Jackson's *corps*, was imitated in the others. The movement was not limited to the army of Virginia: but was also propagated in the South and West. Soon the General Assembly of the Presbyterian Church, and the other ecclesiastical authorities, encouraged by the advice which the friends of General Jackson were permitted to quote from him, began to take action on behalf of the army; and a number of the most distinguished ministers were sent to the different *corps* to labor with the chaplains as itinerants, and to communicate the wants of the army to the churches. The speedy fall of the originator of the work rather gave new *impetus* to it, than retarded it; and the result was, that general revival of religion in the Confederate armies, which has been even more astonishing to the world, than the herculean exertions of the Confederate States. A wide-spread reform of morals was wrought, which was obvious to every spectator, in the repression of profanity and drunkenness, the increase of order and discipline, and the good conduct of the troops in battle. It was just those commands in which this work of grace was most powerful, that became the most trustworthy in the post of danger. The brigade of Barksdale, for instance, which had held its ground in Fredericksburg with almost incredible resolution under the great bombardment, was equally noted for its religious zeal. Returning to their post of honor in the city, they occupied one of the deserted churches as their chapel, and maintained a constant series of nightly meetings, attended by numerous conversions, for many weeks. In short, the conversions in the various Confederate armies within the ensuing year, were counted, by the most sober estimate, at twelve thousand men. The strange spectacle was now presented, of a people among whom the active religious life seemed to be transferred from the churches at home — the customary seats of piety — to the army; which, among other nations, has always been dreaded as the school of vice and infidelity. Thus, the grief and fears of the good, lest this gigantic war should arrest the religious training of the whole youth of the land, cut off the supply of young preachers for its pulpits, and rear up for the country a generation of men profane and unchristian, were happily consoled; they accepted this new marvel, of an army made the home and source of the religious life of a nation, with grateful joy, as another evidence of the favor of God to the afflicted people.

The reader has seen an allusion of General Jackson's letter, to the bright hopes which he entertained of a prosperous campaign. By his diligence during the winter, his *corps* had been brought to such numbers and efficiency as it had never reached before. It now contained more than thirty thousand fighting men; and it was animated by a towering spirit of determination and confidence. It was soon after his removal to Hamilton's Crossing, that a member of his Staff, alluding to the

83

reported vast preparations of the enemy, described to him the
temper of his own men, and their eagerness for the coming
collision. As he listened, the fire of battle kindled more and
more in his face, until he sprung from his seat, and exclaimed:
" I wish the enemy would come on !" Then raising his eyes reverently, he added: "My trust is in God." Thus his spirit was
girding itself for the coming struggle, with faith and prayer.
The collision which was approaching promised indeed to be one
which might well have made the heart stand still with awe.
Hooker was again recruiting his monstrous army to its former
numbers, and was preparing every means for a new advance on
Richmond. The precursor of the new campaign was an irruption of three thousand Federal cavalry across Kelly's Ford into
the county of Culpepper. The design of their General, Averill,
was to reach the Central Railroad, ascertain something of the
positions and numbers of the Confederates, and break up their
line of supplies toward Gordonsville. But General Stuart met
him near Kelly's Ford with eight hundred men of the brigade of
FitzHugh Lee, and after a stubbornly-contested combat drove
him back across the Rappahannock.

The season of quiet was happily closed for General Jackson
by a visit from his wife and daughter. Having secured lodgings
for them at the neighboring country-seat of a gentleman, near
Hamilton's Crossing, he yielded at length to Mrs. Jackson's
solicitations, and to his own affection, and about the middle of
April met them at the railroad station. The arrival of the mail-
train from Richmond was the signal, every day, for the assemblage of a great crowd of officers and soldiers off duty, around
the place. In the midst of these the General came forward
to the doors of the cars, to receive his expected treasures.

" The infant, refreshed by long slumber, had just awakened,
and looked up at him with a countenance very fresh and bright.

His first care, after the accustomed salutation, was to get the mother and child safely through the crowd and rain into the carriage which was to convey them to their temporary home. Arrived there, he divested himself of his wet overcoat, and taking his baby into his arms, caressed it with tender delight, exclaiming upon its beauty and size. Henceforth, his chief pleasure was in caressing her, and he was several times seen, while she was sleeping, kneeling long over her cradle, watching her with a face beaming with admiration and happiness."

This visit was a source of unalloyed delight to him. His first care was to make arrangements for the baptism of the child; for the uncertainties of the day warned him that both the parents might not speedily meet again to concur in the sacred rite. He therefore caused his chaplain to administer baptism to it at the quarters of Mrs. Jackson, among a small circle of their personal friends. Such was his devotion to duty, that the attractions of his family made slight change in his busy habits; and his time was employed as strictly as ever, in the care of his command. After the labors of the day were completed, he was accustomed to leave his tent, and dine, with one or two comrades, with Mrs. Jackson, spending his evenings with her, chiefly in joyous romps with little Julia. She, on her part, immediately formed the closest intimacy with her new admirer, and learned to prefer his caresses to all others.

CHAPTER XIX.

CHANCELLORSVILLE.

As the time drew near for that resumption of active hostil·
ities, which General Jackson knew to be inevitable, his temper
began to rise in its animation and resolve, to meet the crisis.
He now spoke with less reserve than before, to the members of
his military family, concerning the general principles which should
govern the war, upon the Confederate side.   Speaking of the
coming campaign, he said with an intense concentration of fire
and will: "We must make it an exceedingly active one.   Only
thus can a weaker country cope with a stronger; it must make
up in activity what it lacks in strength.   A defensive campaign
can only be made successful by taking the aggressive at the
proper time.   Napoleon never waited for his adversary to
become fully prepared; but struck him the first blow, by virtue
of his superior activity."

Early upon the 29th of April, he was aroused by a message,
which said that an officer was below with something important
to communicate immediately.   As he arose he remarked: "That
sounds as if something stirring were afoot."   After a few
moments, he returned and informed Mrs. Jackson, that General
Early, to whom he had committed the guardianship of the river
bank, had sent his adjutant to report that Hooker was crossing
in force.   He said that great events were probably at hand, and
that he must go immediately to verify the news he had received;

that if it were as he supposed, and the hostilities were about to be resumed on a great scale, Mr. Yerby's would be no place for a lady and infant; and she would be compelled to retire to Richmond. He therefore, requested Mrs. Jackson to make immediate preparations for her journey, so that, if his surmises proved true, she might leave at a moment's warning, in the forenoon. He promised, if it were practicable, to return in person and assist her departure, but added that, as his duties might deprive him of the power to do so, he would say good-by now. Thus, after an affectionate leave-taking, he hurried away, without breakfast, and she saw him no more until she returned to the side of his dying bed. Her heart was oppressed with gloomy forebodings for his safety, arising from her anticipation of the desperate struggle into which she well knew, it was his purpose to plunge, rather than yield ground to his gigantic adversary; his animated eagerness seemed to leave him no time for such thoughts for self.

Hurrying to his troops, he now made it his first business to communicate the movements of the enemy to the Commander-in-Chief. The Aide whom he sent, found him still in his tent; and in reply to the message, he said, "Well, I heard firing; and I was beginning to think it was time some of you lazy young fellows were coming, to tell me what it was all about. Say to General Jackson, that he knows just as well what to do with the enemy, as I do." This answer indicated his high confidence in his great Lieutenant; and the strain of kindly pleasantry, habitual with Lee, had a happy influence in infusing into all who came near him, his own composure and serene courage in great emergencies. When General Jackson joined his troops, he found so much demanding his oversight, that he did not return to the assistance of his wife; but sent her brother, his Aide, Lieutenant Joseph Morrison, to provide her with an ambulance, and escort

her to Guinea's Station; whence she was to proceed by railroad
to Richmond. This young officer, eager to be in the post of
danger with his chief, transferred his task to his chaplain; who
convoyed her to Guinea's, and then also hurried back to his
duties with the army.

When General Jackson got his *corps* under arms, he saw that
the Federalists were crossing in great force below Deep Run,
and entrenching themselves at the edge of the *plateau*; on the
same ground occupied by Franklin and Hooker at the battle of
Fredericksburg. He estimated their numbers at thirty-five
thousand men. But he saw at a glance, that there was, as yet,
no sufficient evidence that Hooker was about to provoke a serious collision on the ground which had been so disastrous to
Burnside. That ground had now been strengthened by a con-
tinous line of field-works, along the edge of the *plateau* near
the Spottsylvania hills, and by a second partial line within the
verge of the forest. He suspected that this crossing was the
feint, while the real movement was made upon one or the other
flank; and he therefore awaited the reports of the vigilant Stuart,
whose cavalry pickets were stretched from Port Royal to the
higher course of the Rappahannock. It has already been explained, that the character of the ground, rendered an assault
upon the enemy near the northern edge of the plain inexpedient,
because of their commanding artillery upon the Stafford Heights.

The Confederate Generals were not left long in doubt. Stuart
soon reported appearances which indicated a passage of the
Rappahannock by Hooker west of Fredericksburg. He had now
restored the Federal army to the same vast numbers which had
accompanied Burnside; and discarding the three grand divisions
with their commanders, which had afforded to him, when one of
the three, so good a pretext for insubordination, had thrown his
forces into nine *corps d' armée* commanded by as many generals,

besides the cavalry division under Stoneman. The plan of campaign which he now adopted, was a complicated one. He proposed with three *corps* under General Sedgwick, to cross the Rappahannock below Fredericksburg, and make a demonstration sufficiently formidable in appearance, to occupy General Lee there. Meantime, the remainder of his great army was to proceed by forced marches up the northern bank of the Rappahannock, screened from observation by the forest country, and an intervening line of pickets, to Kelly's ford. There he proposed to force a passage into Culpepper, and marching rapidly to Germanna and Ely's fords, upon the Rapid Ann, in a southeasterly direction, to cross them while the Confederates were amused at Fredericksburg, establish himself in the Wilderness of Spottsylvania and fortify on General Lee's flank. If he remained at Fredericksburg, Hooker persuaded himself that he would be able, from this new temporary base, to command his communications with Richmond. If he left Fredericksburg, to make head against this formidable threat upon his left and rear, Hooker proposed to withdraw the larger part of his troops employed in the feint there, to bring them over by the United States' ford, which his movement into the Wilderness would uncover to him, and receive the attack of General Lee in his entrenched position. While his infantry was thus employed, nearly all his cavalry, under Stoneman, was to cross the Rapid Ann above the army, upon a grand raid, to penetrate the country across the Central Railroad, destroy it, pass down toward the junction of the Central and Fredericksburg roads, cut the latter, and thus break up all communication between the Confederates and their Capital. The Federal Commander had persuaded himself that General Lee was laid aside by sickness, that all his force, except Jackson's *corps*, was either absent with Longstreet, or disaffected and scattered, and that with his vast numbers he would easily surround and crush the remainder, leaving no organized foe between him and Richmond. In his usual boastful spirit, he exalted the invincibility of his host declaring it to be "the finest army upon the planet."

To meet this tremendous force, General Lee had the *corps* of General Jackson, and two divisions of the *corps* of General Longstreet, those of Anderson and McLaws. The other three, with Longstreet, under Hood, Pickett, Ransom, were absent in Southeastern Virginia, making a demonstration against Suffolk, whither they had been directed by the scarcity of forage and food in Spottsylvania. The *corps* of General Jackson now consisted of four divisions, — those of A. P. Hill; D. H. Hill, commanded by Brigadier General Rhodes; Trimble, commanded by Brigadier General Colston; and Early. General D. H. Hill had been detached to another and more important command, and Major-General Trimble was detained by infirmity at his home. The four divisions now contained about twenty-eight thousand muskets, and an aggregate of more than thirty thousand men and officers. They were supported by twenty-eight field batteries, containing one hundred and fifteen guns; but of these many were deficient in horses to move them with promptitude. The scarcity of forage had reduced the larger part of the artillery horses, and had destroyed not a few. Besides these batteries, the army was still accompanied by a reserved *corps* of artillery, commanded by Brigadier General Pendleton. Stuart's division of cavalry was also acting upon the left. So that General Lee had, in all, an aggregate of about forty-five thousand men, with which to meet one hundred and twenty-five thousand.

The enemy no sooner appeared upon the Rapid Ann, than General Anderson's division was marched westward to meet them, supported by a part of M'Laws's. On Thursday, the remainder of M'Laws's brigades, except one left upon Marye's Hill.

was sent to the support of Anderson. Meantime, General Jackson lay in the lines occupied by the Confederate army on the 13th of December, watching the proceedings of Sedgwick before him, who was ostentatiously parading his force, and seeking to magnify the impression of his numbers. The attitude of Hooker was now most threatening to the Confederates; but he had committed the capital error of dividing his army, and operating with the parts upon two lines, which, although convergent, were exterior lines to General Lee. The latter had his option to attack the one or the other part with the weight of his main force, and thus to deal with the two fragments in detail. No doubt could be entertained by the true strategist as to this leading principle. When some person about the Staff, after the development of Hooker's plan, expressed his anxiety and his fear lest the army should be compelled to retreat before him, General Jackson replied sharply, "Who said that? No, sir, we shall not fall back; we shall attack them." But the question to be decided was, which part should be attacked first? In favor of assailing Sedgwick were some plausible reasons. Time was an important element in the movements of the inferior army, possessing the interior lines; and if it were not improved, the loss of its own line of communications, or the approximation of the two separated parts of its enemy would speedily transfer the advantage of concentration to him again. But Jackson was already in front of Sedgwick, and no march was necessary to bring him into collision with him; whereas a day must be consumed in going to the Wilderness, to seek Hooker. Sedgwick's was also the smaller force; but still, its overthrow would probably decide the failure of Hooker's grand combination. These considerations were counterbalanced by the facts, that Sedgwick had now entrenched himself, and that the assault upon him must be made under the fire of the Stafford batteries. After animated discussion between

Generals Lee and Jackson, the former decided to meet Sedg-wick's feint by a feint; to leave Early's division, of about seven thousand men, in the entrenchments with Barksdale's brigade, upon Marye's Hill, to confront his thirty-five thousand, while the whole remainder of the army stole away to reinforce Generals Anderson and M'Laws, and to take the aggressive against Hooker. In this plan General Jackson cheerfully acquiesced.

Thursday, the 30th of April, had now arrived, and he prepared to break up his quarters. The opening of the campaign had metamorphosed the whole man. Those who had seen him in his winter-quarters, toiling with a patient smile over his heaps of official papers, who had received his gentle and almost feminine kindnesses there, who had only beheld him among his chaplains, or at public worship, the deferential and tender Christian, had been tempted to wonder whether this were indeed the thunderbolt of war, he was described by fame; and whether so meek a spirit as his would be capable of directing its terrors. But when they met him on this morning, all such doubts fled before his first glance. His step was quick and firm, his whole stature unconsciously erected and elate with genius and majesty, while all comprehending thought, decision, and unconquerable will, burned in his eye. His mind seemed, with equal rapidity and clearness, to remember everything, and to judge everything. In a firm and decisive tone, he issued his rapid orders to every branch of his service, overlooking nothing which could possibly affect the efficiency of his *corps*. The tents which for a month and a half had formed his quarters, were now about to be struck and removed, when he rode up to them for the last time; a mob of officers, aids, soldiers, and teamsters, was bustling around, in all the confusion of a hurried removal, when he dismounted and threw the rein of his horse to his servant Jim, and retired within his tent. A moment after, he raised his hand to the people

around, with a warning gesture, and whispered: "Hush. . . . .
The General is praying!" An instant silence fell on every person. After a full quarter of an hour he raised the curtain and
came out, with an elevated and serene countenance, and mounting his horse, after some final directions, rode away. That tent
had doubtless been pitched with prayer; and now the last act of
its occupant was prayer. With this final preparation he turned
to meet the enemies of his country.

General Lee had now proceeded in person to examine the
formidable demonstration of Hooker above, and had written
back to General Jackson, informing him of the situation of
affairs, and instructing him to move to his support. The enemy,
in great force, had crossed the Rapid Ann at Germanna and
Ely's fords, driving back the guards placed there by General
Stuart, had advanced into the country a number of miles, uncov-
ering for themselves the United States ford, which crosses the
Rappahannock a mile below the junction of the two rivers, and
had established themselves at the *villa* of Chancellorsville, fifteen
miles west of Fredericksburg. The reader's attention must now
be claimed for a description of the place. Two main roads
lead from Fredericksburg, westward to Orange; the one called
the old turnpike, because first made, the other, called the plank-
road; because once paved with wooden boards. The plank-
road is south of the old turnpike, and separated from it during
the most of its course, by a space of a few miles. But the traveller who proceeds along it from Fredericksburg, westward, at
the distance of fifteen miles from the town, finds the two
thoroughfares merge themselves into one, and continue to pursue the same track for three miles; when they again diverge,
even more widely than before; the plank-road, as before, bearing
toward the left or south. At the spot where the two highways
unite, stood the ample *villa* of Chancellor, in the midst of a

farm of a mile in extent, which, like an island amidst the waters, was surrounded on every side by forests. From the same spot, two other roads diverged, the one leading toward the northeast and Banks' ford, the other toward the northwest. This last, after proceeding two miles, divided into two, of which the right or northern branch led to the United States ford, and the left or western, to the ford of Ely, over the Rapid Ann. The surface of the country around Chancellorsville is undulating, but presents no hills of great altitude. Immediately west of that farm, begins the country known as the Wilderness of Spottsylvania; a region interspersed with a few small and inferior farms, but whose poor and gravelly soil is otherwise covered, for a few miles, with a tangled forest of oak and shrubbery. It was in this region, that the fuel had been cut, ever since the days when Governor Spottiswoode of the colony, first wrought the iron mines of the neighborhood, to supply the furnaces. Hence arose the dense coppices which covered the larger part of the surface of the country; in which every stump had sent up two or three minor stems in place of the parent trunk removed by the axe of the woodsman, and the undergrowth had availed itself of the temporary flood of sunlight let in upon the soil, to occupy it with an almost impenetrable thicket of dwarf oak, chinquepin, and whortleberry. But six or seven miles west of Chancellorsville, the Wilderness Run, a pellucid stream flowing northward to the Rapid Ann presents a zone of better soil, which is covered with handsome farms and country seats.

Hooker had concentrated, his forces at Chancellorsville by the 30th of April, and was now busy in protecting himself by barricades and earthworks fronting toward the east, south, and southwest; which, with an irregular circuit conformed to the gentle declivities of the surface, embraced, not only the whole farm of Chancellor, but an annular belt of the forest in which it was embosomed also. By this arrangement, Hooker's whole circuit of defences was masked in the woods; and, as the thickets in front were infested with his sharp-shooters, an exact discovery of the position and nature of his works could only be made by an attack in force. The difficulties of the assault were thus vastly increased; and it was with some show of reason that the braggart general declared on Thursday that he now had a position from which nothing could dislodge him. The longer axis of the partially entrenched camp thus formed, extending from east to west, was about two miles. But other works were stretched two or three miles farther westward, fronting toward the south and southwest, and designed to cover the turnpike and the two farms of Melzi Chancellor and Talley, which were also occupied with Federal camps, from an attack coming from the south.

Having thus established himself, Hooker began on Thursday to push forward his skirmishing parties to the east, in order to feel his way toward General Lee's supposed rear, and to reach his hand toward Sedgwick. Proceeding three miles toward Fredericksburg, he was estopped by the division of General Anderson, at Tabernacle Church, which was drawn up on a strong north and south line, and defended on its flanks by artillery and cavalry. To his assistance M'Laws also came speedily; and it was expected that General Stuart, who had retired out of Culpepper before the Federalists, and had placed himself upon their south front, would connect himself with General Anderson's left before dawn on Friday morning. Meantime Hooker was endeavoring to watch every Confederate movement, by means of sundry balloons raised to the sky from the north side of the Rappahannock; from which his scouts maintained a constant intercourse with the earth and with his headquarters by telegraph wires. Such was the position of affairs at nightfall on the last day of April.

General Jackson now debated with himself the question of moving to the support of General Anderson at once by a night march, or of awaiting the dawn of Friday, the 1st of May. He was reluctant to adopt the former determination, because the troops would be unfitted for the arduous work before them by occupying in the toil of a march the hours which should be devoted to sleep. But, on the other hand, he was powerfully persuaded to it by the facts that Anderson and M'Laws might be assailed with overwhelming numbers at the dawn of the next morning, and that a night march would conceal his withdrawal much more effectually from Sedgwick. Having obtained trusty guides, he therefore determined to draw his whole *corps*, except the division of Early, out of the trenches silently, beginning at midnight, to retire a few miles southward, as though proceeding toward Spottsylvania Court House, and then make his way by the country roads of the interior across to the Orange plank-road, and thus proceed westward. Orders were accordingly issued to all the staff departments and commanders of divisions, and the movement was begun at the appointed time by the light of a brilliant moon. The column was led by the division of General D. H. Hill, under Brigadier-General Rhodes. Before the mists of the morning had cleared away, the whole *corps* was far on its way, and securely out of view amidst the woods of the interior, beyond the most piercing espionage of Hooker's balloonists. General Jackson reached the position of Anderson about eleven o'clock A. M., and found him still confronting the detachments of Hooker, which were of unknown strength. The Confederate line now reached from the plank road northward to the old turnpike, and thence toward the Rappahannock through a region chiefly covered with dense woods and thickets.

General Jackson, as the superior officer under the Commander-in-Chief, was now entrusted with the direction of the field, and was ordered to take the aggressive and press back the Federal out-posts, until Hooker's real strength and position were disclosed. This he proceeded to do, with all his accustomed vigor. Some of the best regiments of Anderson's and his own divisions were deployed as skirmishers, and steadily advanced through the woods, hunting out the concealed enemy, and driving them in with continual slaughter. The rattle of the rifles was heard creeping along, upon a front of several miles' extent, like the crackling of some vast forest conflagration, while a few light field-pieces, advanced along the several roads, abreast of the riflemen, cleared the way as often as the enemy attempted to gather a force in any open space. General Jackson himself rode with the line of skirmishers, and often before them, urging them on whenever they paused, and assuring them of his powerful support. There are few services which put the nerve of the brave soldier to a more trying test, than such an advance upon a concealed enemy in a tangled wood. He knows not what danger is near him in front, or at what moment the stealthy shot may burst upon him from an unseen foe. He cannot practise the same concealment with the enemy who lies in ambush for him, because he is continually in motion. But the Confederate line, urged on by General Jackson and his Staff, kept up a slow but steady advance throughout the afternoon, until the Federal pickets were, at nightfall, driven in upon their main line. Hooker, on his part, endeavored to retard their advance by detachments of riflemen, and by batteries, which, masked behind the dense woods, dropped their shells over in every direction toward the roads which were occupied by the Confederates. But all this proved rather an annoyance than a resistance, and the successes of the day were won with slight loss.

When Friday night arrived, Generals Lee and Jackson met, at a spot where the road to the Catharine Iron Furnace turned southwestward from the plank-road, which was barely a mile in front of Hooker's works. Here, upon the brow of a gentle hill, grew a cluster of pine-trees, while the gound was carpeted with the clean, dry sedge and fallen leaves. They selected this spot, with their respective Staffs, to bivouac, while the army lay upon their weapons, a few yards before them, and prepared to sleep upon the ground, like their men. General Stuart had now joined them, and reported the results of his *reconnoissances* upon the south and west of Hooker's position. He had ascertained that the Federal commander had left a whole *corps*, under General Reynolds, at Ely's Ford, to guard his communications there, and that he had massed ninety thousand men around Chancellorsville, under his own eye, fortifying them upon the east, south and, southwest, as has been described. But upon the west and northwest his encampments were open, and their movements were watched by Stuart's pickets, who were secreted in the wilderness there. He had also ascertained, that almost all their cavalry had broken through the line of the Rapid Ann in one body, and had invaded the south, followed and watched by the brigade of W. H. Lee, evidently bent upon a grand raid against the Confederate communications.

Generals Lee and Jackson now withdrew, and held an anxious consultation. That Hooker must be attacked, and that speedily, was clear to the judgments of both. It was not to be hoped that the absence of Jackson's *corps* from the front of Sedgwick could remain very long unknown to that General; or that Early's seven thousand could permanently restrain his *corps*, with such additions as it might receive from Hooker. To hold the stationary defensive in front of Chancellorsville would, therefore, be equivalent to the loss of the whole line of the Rappahannock, with a hazardous retreat along a new and crooked line of operations; for the success of Sedgwick would deprive them of the direct one, and place him in alarming proximity to any other which they might adopt. Hooker, then, must be at once fought and beaten, or the initial act of the campaign would close in disaster.

" General Lee had promptly concluded, that while, on the one hand, immediate attack was proper, some more favorable place for assault must be sought, by moving farther toward Hooker's right. The attempt to rout ninety thousand well armed troops, entrenched at their leisure, by a front attack, with thirty-five thousand, would be too prodigal of patriot blood, and would offer too great a risk of ·repulse. He had accordingly already commanded his troops to commence a movement toward their left, and communicated his views to General Jackson, who warmly concurred in their wisdom. A report was about this time received from General FitzHugh Lee, of Stuart's command, describing the position of the Federal army, and the roads which he held with his cavalry leading to its rear. General Jackson now proposed to throw his command entirely into Hooker's rear, availing himself of the absence of the Federal cavalry, and the presence of the Confederate horse, and to assail him from the West, in concert with Anderson and M'Laws.

Stuart was there with his active horsemen to cover this movement; and he believed that it could be made with comparatively little risk, and, when accomplished, would enable him to crush the surprised enemy. He well knew that he was apparently proposing a " grand detachment "; a measure pronounced by military science so reprehensible, in the presence of an active adversary. It might seem that, in venturing one instance of this hazardous measure, — the detaching of Early to remain at

85

Fredericksburg, — they had tempted fortune sufficiently far, with-out again repeating it by a further division of forces before Hooker. But the maxims of the military art should be our servants, and not our masters; and the part of good sense is to modify their application to actual instances, according to circumstances. In this case, the only choice was between his proposed expedient, which he well knew was unusual and hazardous, and another measure still more hazardous. The unwieldy and sluggish strategy of the huge Federal armies was to be considered; and, along with that, the unsuspecting, boastful, and overweening temper of their chief, who was precisely the man to be thus dealt with. He was known to be a man who would make a stubborn fight against a plain, front attack; but whose lack of vigilance would make surprise practicable, and whose small resources of mind in the moment of confusion would probably offer him little aid in extricating himself from that surprise. It must be remem-bered also, that if General Jackson's proposal were adopted, it would be the body moving with him which would really be the main army, and the divisions of Anderson and M'Laws which would be the detachment. But if the issue of affairs at Chan-cellorsville were adverse, whatever were the plan of assault adopted, the retreat which must follow must be by a new line at any rate; so that the separation of his *corps* from its original line of operations was not, in this case, a valid objection. It would still have its chance of retreat upon the Central Railroad. in Louisa county; and in whatever shape a repulse came at Chancellorsville, if it should perchance come, the army there would have no other resort. But if the assault were a victory, then the question of lines of retreat lost all its importance. Last, the two parts of the army would be in supporting dis-tance during the whole movement.

After profound reflection, General Lee gave the sanction of

his judgment to this plan, and committed its execution to General Jackson. He proposed to remain with Anderson and M'Laws, and superintend their efforts to "contain "the vast army of Hooker until the hour for the critical attack should arrive. They then lay down upon the ground to seek a few hours of repose, which they so much needed. General Jackson, with his usual self-forgetfulness, had left his quarters, his mind absorbed in the care of the army, without any of those provisions of overcoat or blanket, which the professional soldier is usually so careful to attach to his saddle. He now lay down at the foot of a pine-tree, without covering. One of his adjutants, Colonel Alex. S. Pendleton, urged upon him his overcoat; but he, with persistent politeness, declined it. He then detached the large cape, and spread it over the General, retaining the body of the garment for himself. The General remained quiet until Pendleton fell asleep, when he arose and spread the cape upon him, and resumed his place without covering. In the morning he awoke chilled, and found that he had contracted a cold, but made no remark about it.

When his chaplain awoke in the morning, before the dawn of day, he perceived a little fire kindled under the trees, and General Jackson sitting by it upon a box, such as was used to contain biscuit for the soldiers. The General knew that his former pastoral labors had led him to this region, and desired to learn something from him about its by-roads. He therefore requested him to sit beside him on the box; and when the other declined to incommode him by doing so, made room for him and repeated: "Come, sit down: I wish to talk with you." As he took his seat, he perceived that Jackson was shuddering with cold, and was embracing the little blaze with expressions of great enjoyment. He then proceeded to state that the enemy were in great force at Chancellorsville, in a fortified position, and that to dislodge them by a front attack, would cost a fearful loss of life. He wished to know whether he was acquainted with any way, by which their flank might be turned, either on the right or the left. He was informed in reply, that after proceeding southward along the furnace road for a space, a blind road would present itself, leading westward and nearly parallel to the Orange plank-road, which, in its turn, would conduct into a plainer route, that fell into the great road four miles above Chancellorsville. The General, quickly drawing from his pocket an outline map, prepared for him by one of his engineers, and a pencil, said: "Take this map, and mark it down for me." When he saw it, he said: "That is too near: it goes within the line of the enemy's pickets. I wish to get around *well* to his rear, without being observed: Do you know no other road?" He replied that he had no perfect knowledge of any other, but presumed that the road which he had described as entering the Orange plank-road, four miles above Chancellorsville, must intersect the furnace road somewhere in the interior, because their directions were convergent. "Then," said Jackson: "Where can you find this out certainly?" He was told that everything could doubtless be learned at the house of the proprietor of the furnace, a mile and a half distant, whose son, a patriotic and gallant man, would be an excellent guide. He then said: "Go with Mr. Hotchkiss (his topographical engineer) to the furnace, ascertain whether those roads meet, at what distance, and whether they are practicable for artillery — send Mr. Hotchkiss back with the information, and do you procure me a guide."

The desired information was speedily obtained; and it was discovered that the two roads crossed each other at the distance of a few miles; so that, by a circuit of fifteen miles, a point would be reached near Wilderness Run, several miles above the

farthest outposts of Hooker. The intersecting road, by which
the Orange plank-road was to be regained, was known as the
Brock road. Leading from Culpepper southeastward, it crosses
the old turnpike near the Wilderness tavern, and the plank-
road two or three miles south of it; so that by this route General Jackson's purposes were perfectly. met. As soon as he
received the necessary assurance of this, he gave orders for his
corps to begin their march, and a little after sunrise appeared at
the furnace at the head of the column. He declined the urgent
request of the family there to partake of the breakfast which
they were preparing for him, and without any refreshment busied
himself in pushing on his troops. Forgetful of no prudent precaution, he directed that a regiment of General M'Laws should
be sent to guard the entrance of the blind road near the Furnace, lest the Federalists should attack the side of his passing
column by that outlet. He then caused the regiments of Stuart,
which were present, to patrol the country between his line of
march and their outposts, that they might learn nothing of his
journey.

But, before the whole column had passed the Furnace, some
of Hooker's scouts, mounted in the tops of the highest trees
southeast of Chancellor's house, perceived it, and reported its
movement to him. That sagacious commander was now perfectly certain that the disheartened "Rebels" were in full
retreat upon Richmond. Their early march to the southward
could bear, in his judgment, no other explanation. He therefore
prepared to harass the rear of their flight; and to this end
posted some artillery upon the declivities facing the Furnace
Road, which cannonaded the ammunition train of General Jackson; and sent down a few regiments, after a time, to ascertain
the direction of his retreat. These came into collision with the
regiment of M'Laws, captured a part of them, and were, in turn

driven off by a demonstration of other Confederate troops from the plank-road. Hooker now found the same firm resistance upon his eastern front which he had met the day before, and, after some feeble skirmishing of artillery and riflemen, became quiescent, awaiting further developments. It was here that he committed his fatal blunder, — a blunder inexcusable even when judged, in the absence of the light cast upon his situation by subsequent events, by his own professed conclusions. If he believed that the Confederate army was indeed retreating into the interior of Spottsylvania, and thence toward Richmond, it is strange that the bold front still maintained against him on the east by General Lee did not suggest an anxious doubt. Was not this a new manner for the rear-guard of a baffled and fleeing army to behave? Did it not point, too strongly for a moment's hesitation, to the propriety of his at once attacking them in such force as to learn what they truly meant? And if he found them obstinate and immovable upon his east front, would not that result dictate still more clearly that he should move upon their south or left flank, if necessary, with his whole force, until they were forced back, and the mystery of Jackson's disappearance on that side, and of the unaccountable gap which he was placing between himself and his friends, was cleared up? The history of war contains no stronger instance of the danger of the policy of "the stationary defensive," when adhered to in disregard of new circumstances. It was very properly a part of Hooker's *programme*, after gaining his strong position at Chancellorsville, to await the attack of the Confederates. But the prudence of this plan depended wholly upon their making that attack in that mode in which he had prepared himself to receive it. Just as soon as it became doubtful whether they purposed to do this, the defensive policy became of doubtful propriety; and sound judgment dictated that Hooker should modify his purposes also, and should immediately assume the aggressive, sufficiently, at least, to determine their true project. By sitting still now, he forfeited all the strength of his defensive position. The best justification of General Jackson's strategy is found in the fact that he so correctly estimated the temper of his adversary, and anticipated the blunder which he would commit.

The narrative returns now to his march. The troops, comprehending instantly that he was engaged in one of his famous assaults upon his enemy's flanks, responded to his eager spirit zealously, and pressed forward along the narrow country road at a rapid gait. Often the men were compelled to advance at a double-quick, in order to close up the column. After proceeding southwest, a few miles beyond the Catharine furnace, they came to the intersection of the Brock road, and turning to the right at a sharp angle, assumed a northwestern direction. When General Jackson reached the plank-road again, he quietly advanced the Stonewall Brigade down it, under General Paxton, with instructions to form across it at the junction of the road which led thence toward Germanna ford, so as to prevent egress at that place. He then continued his march, with the remainder of the *corps,* until he found himself in the old turnpike near Wilderness Run. He had marched fifteen miles, and three o'clock in the afternoon had arrived. He was six miles west of Chancellorsville, and upon precisely the opposite side of the enemy to that occupied by General Lee. He now addressed to him the following, which is the last of his official notes:

"NEAR 3, P. M., MAY 2nd, 1863.

"GENERAL : —

"The enemy has made a stand at Chancellor's, which is about two miles from Chancellorsville. I hope, so soon as practicable, to attack.

"I trust that an ever kind Providence will bless us with suc·
cess.
                    "Respectfully,
                              "T. J. JACKSON, *Lieutenant-General.*
"GENERAL ROBERT E. LEE.

"P. S.   The leading division is up, and the next two appear
to be well closed.   T. J. J."

The place here mentioned as Chancellor's, two miles west of
Chancellorsville, was the farm of Melzi Chancellor, which was
embraced within the western wing of Hooker's defences, and
occupied by the *corps* of Sigel, now commanded by General
Howard.   General Jackson found both the plank-road, and the
old turnpike guarded on the west by the vigilant pickets of
Stuart.   Advancing to these outposts, he gained a glimpse of the
position of the enemy, which convinced him that he had obtained
the desired vantage ground from which to attack them.   He
therefore directed his column to advance across the old turnpike,
and then to wheel to the eastward, so as to present a line toward
the foe.   The open fields near the old Wilderness Tavern
afforded him space in which to complete his array.   He now
formed his army in three parallel lines : the division of Rhodes
in front, that of Colston next, and that of A. P. Hill in the rear.
He detailed one or two picked batteries to advance along the
turnpike, which marked the centre of his lines; and such was
the extent of the thickets into which he was about to plunge, that
no position could be gained for his other artillery.   Two hours
were consumed by the issuing of orders, and the galloping of
aides and orderlies, when, between five and six o'clock, everything
was ready for the advance.   The three lines swept grandly forward, at the word, in battle array, and speedily buried themselves in the tangled forests.   So dense were the thickets, that the

soldiers had their clothing almost torn from their bodies, and could only advance by creeping through the thickest spots; but still the lines swept forward, in tolerable order, and with high enthusiasm. General A. P. Hill, finding this toilsome march unnecessary to support Rhodes, whose division had Colston just in their rear, was allowed to withdraw his men from line into column again, and thus advanced along the turnpike, leaving a part of its breadth open for the passage of artillery and ambulances, but ready to reinforce any part of the line which might waver.

As the Confederates approached the little farms of Talley and Melzi Chancellor, after a march of two miles through the woods, they came upon the right wing of Hooker's army, in all the security of unsuspicious indolence. Their little earthworks, which fronted the south, were taken in reverse, and the men were scattered about the fields and woods, preparing for their evening meal. With a wild hurra, the line of Rhodes burst upon them from the woods, and the first volley decided their utter rout. The second line, commanded by Colston, unable to restrain their impetuosity, rushed forward at the shout, pressed upon the first, filling up their gaps, and firing over their heads, so that thenceforward the two were almost merged into one, and advanced together, a dense and impetuous mass. For three miles the Federalists were now swept back by a resistless charge. Even the works which confronted the west afforded them no protection; no sooner were they manned by the enemy, than the Confederates dashed upon them with the bayonet, and the defenders were either captured or again put to flight. The battle was but a continued onward march, with no other pause than that required for the rectification of the line, disordered by the density of the woods. The eleven thousand German mercenaries of Howard fled almost without resistance, carrying away with them the troops sent to their support; they did not pause

86

in Hooker's entrenched camp, but dashing through his whole army in frantic terror, without muskets, without hats, they rushed toward the fords of the Rappahannock. Fugitives, armed men, ambulances, artillery, were mixed together in vast masses, all struggling madly to flee as rapidly as possible from the deadly volleys which were scourging their rear, and those terrible war-cries of the vengeful patriots. While these confused herds offered an unfailing mark for the bullets of the Confederates, they were able to make no effective reply. Hence the slaughter of the Federalists was heavy, and the loss of the assailants trifling. The ground moreover was left strewed with incalculable amounts of spoils. The lavish equipments with which the Federal Government fitted out its armies, now fell a prey, in a moment, to the victors. Blankets, clothing, arms, ammunition, cooking utensils, food, almost covered the surface of the highway, and were thickly scattered though the fields and coppices for three miles.

In this fashion General Jackson urged forward the attack until after nightfall. After the dispositions for the first attack were made, the only order given by him had been his favorite battle-cry: "Press forward." This was his message to every General, and his answer to every inquiry. As he uttered it, he leaned forward upon his horse, and waved his hand as though endeavoring, by its single strength, to urge forward his whole line. Never before had his pre-occupation of mind, and his insensibility to danger been so great. At every cheer from the front, which announced some new success, the smile of triumph flashed over his face, followed and banished immediately by the reverential gratitude, with which he raised his face and his right hand to the heavens in prayer and thanksgiving. It was evident that he regarded this as his greatest victory, and never before was he seen so frequently engaged in worship upon the field. Eight o'clock arrived, and the moon was shedding a doubtful light through the openings of the forest, but the darkness was sufficient to arrest the pursuit of the fugitives. The line of Rhodes was now within a mile of Chancellorsville, but still enveloped within the bushy woods which surrounded the entrenchments there; and they had no means of knowing what was the character of the ground, or of the defences before them. Their array had been much disordered by their rapid advance; and now, by a species of common impulse, the whole line, finding no visible enemy, and no firing in their front, paused to rest. The men, leaving their places in the ranks, were clustering in groups, to discuss the triumphs of the evening, and many were reclining at the roots of the trees. They had now marched more than twenty miles since the morning, had fought over three miles of difficult ground, and their weariness demanded repose. General Jackson perceiving this, determined to relieve his front line, by replacing them with the fresh troops of A. P. Hill, who had closely followed up his advance, keeping the head of his columns a little behind the line of battle, upon both margins of the turnpike. He therefore directed that General to file a part of his brigade to the right, and a part to the left of the highway, to replace those of Rhodes and Colston, which were to be withdrawn to the second line, as fast as the others were ready to take their places. But his vigilance was dissatisfied with the disorder to which the men in front had yielded; he knew that the present quiet was but a lull in the storm of war; and that the completion of his own movement would be so ruinous to Hooker, it was impossible that General could fail to make another attempt to arrest it. He therefore expected another collision, with fresh troops, and knew not when it might begin.

It was just at this moment that the gallant Colonel Cobb, of

the 44th Virginia regiment, in Colston's division, came to report
to him, that advancing through the woods on the right of the
turnpike, a little space beyond the line where the Confederates
had paused in their career, he had captured a number of prisoners, and had also ascertained the existence of a strong barricade of timber, fronted by an *abattis* which, beginning at the
right margin of the road, seemed to run down a gentle, sinuous
vale of the forest, an indefinite distance, toward the south and
east, and was now deserted by the Federalists. (This defence
was, in fact, a part of the main circuit by which Hooker had enclosed his entrenched camp at Chancellorsville, and was now
surrendered into General Jackson's hands, almost without a
struggle. So complete were the results of his attack, the very
citadel of Hooker was now in his grasp.) He found General
Jackson near the road, busily engaged in correcting the partial
disorder into which the men had fallen. Riding along the lines, he
was saying, " Men, get into line ! get i..to line ! Whose regiment is
this ? Colonel, get your men instantly into line." He was almost
unattended, and had obviously sent away his Staff to aid in correcting the confusion, or to direct the advance of A. P. Hill's division
to the front. Upon receiving the report of Cobb, he said to him,
" Find General Rhodes, and tell him to occupy that barricade at
once, with his troops." He added, " I need your help for a time;
this disorder must be corrected. As you go along the right, tell
the troops, from me, to get into line, and preserve their order."
He then busily resumed his efforts for the same object, and a
moment after rode along the turnpike toward Chancellorsville,
endeavoring to discover the intentions of the enemy.

His anticipations were, indeed, verified at once. Hooker was
just then advancing a powerful body of fresh troops, to endeavor
to break the fatal *cordon* which General Jackson was drawing
around his rear, and to escape from General Lee, who was

pressing his front. He was pushing a strong battery along the highway, preceded by infantry skirmishers, and in front of General Jackson's right, was sending a heavy line of infantry through the woods, to retake the all-important barricade. The latter, according to the usual perfidy of the enemy's tactics, was preceded by a flag of truce, which attempted to amuse General Rhodes with some trumpery fable, until the enemy could creep upon him unprepared. Rhodes, instantly perceiving the cheat, directed him to be taken to General Jackson with his message; and resumed the effort to man the barricade in accordance with his order. But the trick was partially successful. The men had not yet resumed their ranks, nor was the work fully occupied, before the Federal line of battle appeared upon the brow of the little hill within it, and poured a heavy volley upon the Confederates, at point blank distance. They replied, firing wildly, and made efforts to sustain the strife, but in a feeble and irrregular fashion. This combat upon the right was the signal for the resumption of the battle along the whole line; and in its opening upon the turnpike, General Jackson received a mortal wound.

He had now advanced a hundred yards beyond his line of battle, evidently supposing that, in accordance with his constant orders, a line of skirmishers had been sent to the front, immediately upon the recent cessation of the advance. He probably intended to proceed to the place where he supposed this line crossed the turnpike, to ascertain from them what they could learn concerning the enemy. He was attended only by a half dozen mounted orderlies, his signal officer, Captain Wilbourne, with one of his men, and his aide, Lieutenant Morrison, who had just returned to him. General A. P. Hill, with his staff also proceeded immediately after him, to the front of the line, accompanied by Captain Boswell of the Engineers, whom General

Jackson had just detached to assist him. After the General and his escort had proceeded down the road a hundred yards, they were surprised by a volley of musketry from the right, which spread toward their front, until the bullets began to whistle among them, and struck several horses. This was, in fact, the advance of the Federal line assailing the barricade, which they were attempting to regain. General Jackson was now aware of their proximity, and perceived that there was no picket or skirmisher between him and his enemies. He therefore, turned to ride hurriedly back to his own troops; and, to avoid the fire, which was, thus far, limited to the south side of the road, he turned into the woods upon the north side. It so happened that General Hill, with his escort, had been directed by the same motive almost to the same spot. As the party approached within twenty paces of the Confederate troops, these, evidently mistaking them for cavalry, stooped, and delivered a deadly fire. So sudden and stunning was this volley, and so near at hand, that every horse which was not shot down, recoiled from it in panic, and turned to rush back, bearing their riders toward the approaching enemy. Several fell dead upon the spot, among them the amiable and courageous Boswell; and more were wounded. Among the latter was General Jackson. His right hand was penetrated by a ball, his left fore arm lacerated by another, and the same limb broken a little below the shoulder by a third, which not only crushed the bone, but severed the main artery. His horse also dashed, panic-stricken, toward the enemy, carrying him beneath the boughs of a tree which inflicted severe blows, lacerated his face, and almost dragged him from the saddle. His bridle hand was now powerless, but seizing the reins with the right hand, notwithstanding its wound, he arrested his career, and brought the animal back toward his own lines. He was followed by his faithful attendant, Captain Wilbourne, and his assistant, Wynn, who overtook him as he paused again in the turnpike, near the spot where he had received the fatal shots. The firing of the Confederates had now been arrested by the officers: but the wounded and frantic horses were rushing, without riders, through the woods, and the ground was strewn with the dead and dying. Here General Jackson drew up his horse, and sat for an instant gazing toward his own men, as if in astonishment at their cruel mistake, and in doubt whether he should again venture to approach them. To the anxious inquiries of Captain Wilbourne, he replied that he believed his arm was broken; and requested him to assist him from his horse, and examine whether the wounds were bleeding dangerously. But before he could dismount he sunk fainting into their arms, so completely prostrate, that they were compelled to disengage his feet from the stirrups. They now bore him aside a few yards into the woods north of the turnpike, to shield him from the expected advance of the Federalists; and while Wynn was sent for an ambulance and surgeon, Wilbourne proceeded, supporting his head upon his bosom, to strip his mangled arm, and bind up his wound. The warm blood was flowing in a stream down his wrist; his clothing impeded all access to its source, and nothing was at hand more efficient than a penknife, to remove the obstructions. But at this terrible moment, he saw General Hill, with the remnant of his staff, approaching; and called to him for assistance. He, with his volunteer aide, Major Leigh, dismounted, and taking the body of the General into his arms, succeeded in reaching the wound, and stanching the blood with a handkerchief. The swelling of the lacerated flesh had already performed this office in part. His two aides, Lieutenants Smith and Morrison, arrived at this moment, the former having been left at the rear to execute some orders, and the latter having just saved himself, at the expense of a stunning fall, by leaping from his horse, as he was carrying him, in uncontrolable fright, into the enemy's ranks. Morrison, the General's brother by marriage, was agitated by grief; but Smith was full at once of tenderness, and of that clear self-possession, which is so valuable in the hour of danger. With the skilful direction of General Hill, they now effectually arrested the hemorrhage, and adjusted a sling to support the mangled arm.

It was at this moment that two Federal skirmishers approached within a few feet of the spot where he lay, with their muskets cocked. They little knew what a prize was in their grasp; and when, at the command of General Hill, two orderlies arose from the kneeling group, and demanded their surrender, they seemed amazed at their nearness to their enemies, and yielded their arms without resistance. Lieutenant Morrison, suspecting from their approach that the Federalists must be near at hand, stepped out into the road to examine; and by the light of the moon saw a field-piece pointed toward him, apparently not more than a hundred yards distant. Indeed it was so near that the orders given by the officers to the cannoneers could be distinctly heard. Returning hurriedly, he announced that the enemy were planting artillery in the road, and that the General must be immediately removed. General Hill now remounted, and hurried back to make his dispositions to meet this attack. In the combat which ensued he was himself wounded a few moments after, and compelled to leave the field. No ambulance or litter was yet at hand, although Captain Wilbourne had also been sent to seek them; and the necessity of an immediate removal suggested that they should bear the General away in their arms. To this he replied, that if they would assist him to rise, he could walk to the rear; and he was accordingly raised to his feet, and leaning upon the shoulders of Major Leigh and Lieutenant Smith, went slowly out into the highway, and toward his troops. The party was now met by a litter, which some one had sent from the rear; and the General was placed upon it, and borne along by two soldiers, and Lieutenants Smith and Morrison. As they were placing him upon it, the enemy fired a volley of canister-shot up the road, which passed over their heads. But they had proceeded only a few steps before the discharge was repeated, with a more accurate aim. One of the soldiers bearing the litter was struck down, severely wounded; and had not Major Leigh, who was walking beside it, broken his fall, the General would have been precipitated to the ground. He was placed again upon the earth; and the causeway was now swept by a hurricane of projectiles of every species, before which it seemed that no living thing could survive. The bearers of the litter, and all the attendants, excepting Major Leigh and the General's two aides, left him, and fled into the woods on either hand, to escape the fatal tempest; while the sufferer lay along the road, with his feet toward the foe, exposed to all its fury. It was now that his three faithful attendants displayed a heroic fidelity, which deserves to go down with the immortal name of Jackson to future ages. Disdaining to save their lives by deserting their chief, they lay down beside him in the causeway, and sought to protect him as far as possible with their bodies. On one side was Major Leigh, and on the other Lieutenant Smith. Again and again was the earth around them torn with volleys of canister, while shells and minie balls flew hissing over them, and the stroke of the iron hail raised sparkling flashes from the flinty gravel of the roadway. General Jackson struggled violently to rise, as though to endeavor to leave the road; but Smith threw his arm over him, and with friendly force held him to the earth, saying: "Sir, you must lie still; it will cost you your life if you rise." He speedily acquiesced, and lay quiet; but none of the four hoped to escape alive. Yet, almost by miracle, they were

87

unharmed; and, after a few moments, the Federalists, having·
cleared the road of all except this little party, ceased to fire along
it, and directed their aim to another quarter.

They now arose, and resumed their retreat, the General leaning upon his friends, and proceeding along the gutter at the
margin of the highway, in order to avoid the troops who were
again hurrying to the front. Perceiving that he was recognized
by some of them, they diverged still farther into the edge of the
thicket. It was here that General Pender of North Carolina,
who had succeeded to the command of Hill's division upon the
wounding of that officer, recognized General Jackson, and, after
expressing his hearty sympathy for his sufferings, added, "My
men are thrown into such confusion by this fire, that I fear I
shall not be able to hold my ground." Almost fainting with
anguish and loss of blood, he still replied, in a voice feeble but
full of his old determination and authority, "General Pender,
you *must* keep your men together, and hold your ground." This
was the last military order ever given by Jackson! How fit
was the termination for such a career as his, and how expressive
of the resolute purpose of his soul! His bleeding country could
do nothing better than to adopt this as her *motto* in her hour of
trial, inscribe it on all her banners, and make it the rallying cry
of all her armies.

General Jackson now complained of faintness, and was again
placed upon the litter; and, after some difficulty, men were obtained to bear him. To avoid the enemy's fire, which was again
sweeping the road, they made their way through the tangled
brushwood, almost tearing his clothing from him, and lacerating
his face, in their hurried progress. The foot of one of the men
bearing his head was here entangled in a vine, and he fell prostrate. The General was thus thrown heavily to the ground
upon his wounded side, inflicting painful bruises on his body

and intolerable agony on his mangled arm, and renewing the flow of blood from it. As they lifted him up, he uttered one piteous groan, — the only complaint which escaped his lips during the whole scene. Lieutenant Smith raised his head upon his bosom, almost fearing to see him expiring in his arms, and asked, " General, are you much hurt ? " He replied, " No, Mr. Smith; don't trouble yourself about me." He was then replaced a second time upon the litter, and, under a continuous shower of shells and cannon-balls, borne a half mile farther to the rear, when an ambulance was found, containing his chief of artillery, Colonel Crutchfield, who was also wounded. In this he was placed, and hurried towards the field hospital near Wilderness Run. As the vehicle passed the house of Melzi Chancellor, Dr. M'Guire met the party. Colonel Pendleton, the faithful adjutant of General Jackson, upon ascertaining the misfortune of his chief, had taken upon himself the task of seeking him, and bringing him to the General's aid. Indeed, one of the first requests made by the latter was to ask for this well-tried friend; and he was, therefore, summoned from the rear, where he was busily engaged organizing the relief for the numerous wounded from the battle. Upon meeting the sad cavalcade, Dr. M'Guire obtained a candle, and sprung into the ambulance to examine the wound. He found the General almost pulseless, but the hemorrhage had again ceased. Some alcoholic stimulant had been anxiously sought for him, but hitherto only a few drops could be obtained. Now through the activity of the Rev. Mr. Vass, a chaplain in the Stonewall Brigade, a sufficient quantity of spirits was found, and the patient was freely stimulated. They then resumed their way to the field hospital near Wilderness Run, Dr. M'Guire supporting the General as he sat beside him in the carriage. To his anxious inquiries he replied that he was now somewhat revived, but that several times he had felt as though he were about to

die. This he said in a tone of perfect calmness. It was, doubtless, the literal truth, and during the removal he was indeed
vibrating upon the very turn between life and death. The
artery of his left arm was severed; and, in consequence of the
inexperience and distress of his affectionate assistants, and yet
more of the horrible confusion of the battle, he had nearly bled
to death before his wound was stanched. Arriving at the hospital, he was tenderly removed to a tent which had been erected
for him; where he was laid in a camp bed, and covered with
blankets, in an atmosphere carefully warmed. Here he speedily
sank into a deep sleep, which showed the thorough prostration
of his energies.

The melancholy scene which has now been simply and exactly
described, occupied but a few minutes; for the events followed
each other with stunning rapidity. The report of the discovery
of the deserted barricade by Colonel Cobb, the order to General
Rhodes to occupy it, the attempt to restore the order to his line
of battle, the advance of the General and his escort down the
road, his collision with the advancing enemy, his hurried retreat,
and the fatal fire of his own men, all followed each other almost
as rapidly as they are here recited. While he lay upon the
ground, assisted at first only by Captain Wilbourne and his
man, and afterwards by General A. P. Hill and the officers of
the two escorts, the battle was again joined between Hooker and
the Confederates; and it was just as the difficult removal of the
General was made, that it raged through its short but furious
course. General Hill had scarcely flown to assume the command of his line, in order to resist the onset, and protect General Jackson from capture, when he was himself struck down
with a violent contusion, and compelled to leave the field, surrendering the direction of affairs to Brigadier-Generals Rhodes
and Pender. Colonel Crutchfield, chief-of-artillery, and his

assistant, Major Rogers, attempting to make an effective reply to the cannonade which swept the great road, were both severely wounded. In the darkness and confusion, the Federalists regained their barricade, and pushed back the right of the Confederates a short distance; but here their successes ended; and the brigades of Hill stubbornly held their ground in the thickets near the turnpike. The fire now gradually died away into a fitful skirmish, which was continued at intervals all night, without result on either side.

While General Jackson lay bleeding upon the ground, he displayed several traits very characteristic of his nature. Amidst all his sufferings, he was absolutely uncomplaining; save when his agonizing fall wrung a groan from his breast. It was only in answer to the questions of his friends, that he said, "I believe my arm is broken," and, "It gives me severe pain;" but this was uttered in a tone perfectly calm and self-possessed. When he was asked whether he was hurt elsewhere, he replied: "Yes, in the right hand." (He seemed to be unconscious that the other fore-arm was shattered by a third ball: nor did the surgeons themselves advert to it, until they examined it in preparing for the amputation.) When he was asked whether his right hand should not also be bound up, he replied: "No, never mind; it is a trifle." Yet two of the bones were broken, and the palm was almost perforated by the bullet! To the many exclamations touching the source of his misfortune, he answered decisively, but without a shade of passion: "All my wounds were undoubtedly from my own men;" and added that they were exactly simultaneous. When he was informed, in answer to his first demand for the assistance of Dr. M'Guire, that that officer must be now engaged in his onerous duties far to the rear, and could not be immediately brought to him, he said to Captain Wilbourne, "Then I wish you to get me a skilful surgeon." On the arrival of General Hill, the anxious inquiry was made of him, where a surgeon could be most quickly found. He stated that Dr. Barr, an assistant surgeon in one of the regiments of Pender, which had just come to the front, was near at hand; and this gentleman being called, promptly answered. General Jackson now repeated in a whisper, to General Hill, the question: "Is he a skilful surgeon?" He answered in substance, that he stood high in his brigade; and that at most, he did not propose to have him do anything until Dr. McGuire arrived, save the necessary precautionary acts. To this General Jackson replied: "Very good;" and Dr. Barr speedily procured a *tourniquet* to apply above the wound: but finding the blood no longer flowing, postponed its application. When General Jackson's field-glass and haversack were removed, they were preserved by Captain Wilbourne. The latter was found to contain no refreshments: its only contents were a few official papers, and two Gospel-tracts. No sooner had friends began to gather around him, than numerous suggestions were made, concerning the importance of concealing his fall from his troops. While he was lying upon General Hill's breast, that officer commanded that no one should tell the men he was wounded. General Jackson opened his eyes, and looking fixedly upon his Aides Smith and Morrison, said: "Tell them simply that you have a wounded Confederate officer." He recognized, on the one hand, the importance of concealment; but on the other hand, he was anxious that the truth should not be violated in any degree, upon his account. With these exceptions, he lay silent and passive in the arms of his friends; his soul doubtless occupied with silent prayer. As he was led past the column of Pender, the unusual attention paid him excited the lively curiosity of the men. Many asked: "Whom have you there?" and some made vigorous exertions to gain a view of his face. Notwithstanding the efforts of Captain Wilbourne to shield him from their view, one or two recognized him; and exclaimed, their faces blanched with horror and grief: "Great God! it is General Jackson." Thus the news of the catastrophe rapidly spread along the lines; but the men believed that his wounds were slight: and their sorrow only made them more determined.

About midnight, Dr. M'Guire summoned as assistants, Drs. Coleman, Black and Walls, and watched the pulse of the General for such evidences of the re-action of his exhausted powers, as would permit a more thorough dealing with his wound. Perceiving that the animal heat had returned, and the pulsations had resumed their volume, they aroused him; and on examining the whole extent of his injuries, were convinced beyond all doubt, that his left arm should be immediately removed. Dr. M'Guire now explained to him that it seemed necessary to amputate his arm; and inquired whether he was willing that it should be done immediately. He replied, without tremor: "Dr. M'Guire; do for me what you think best; I am resigned to whatever is necessary." Preparations were then made for the work. Chloroform was administered by Dr. Coleman; Dr. M'Guire, with a steady and deliberate hand, severed the mangled limb from the shoulder; Dr. Walls secured the arteries, and Dr. Black watched the pulse; while Lieutenant Smith stood by, holding the lights. The General seemed insensible to pain, although he spoke once or twice, as though conscious, saying with a placid and dreamy voice: "Dr. M'Guire; I am lying very comfortably." The ball was also extracted from his right hand, and the wound was dressed. The surgeons then directed Smith to watch beside him the remainder of the night; and after an interval of half an hour, to arouse him, in order that he might drink a cup of coffee. During this interval, he lay perfectly quiet, as though sleeping: but when he was called, awoke promptly and in full possession of his faculties. He received the coffee, drank it with appetite, and remarked that it was very good and refreshing. This was, indeed, the first nourishment which he had taken since Friday evening. He now looked at the stump of his arm; and comprehending its loss fully, asked Mr. Smith: "Were you here?" (meaning when the operation was performed.) He then, after a moment's silence, inquired whether he had said anything when under the power of the chloroform; and continued, after being satisfied on this point, in substance thus: "I have always thought it wrong to administer chloroform, in cases where there is a probability of immediate death. But it was, I think, the most delightful physical sensation I ever enjoyed. I had enough consciousness to know what was doing; and at one time thought I heard the most delightful music that ever greeted my ears. I believe it was the sawing of the bone. But I should dislike above all things, to enter eternity in such a condition." His meaning evidently was, that he would not wish to be ushered into that spiritual existence, from the midst of sensations so thoroughly physical and illusory. He afterwards exclaimed to other friends; "What an inestimable blessing is chloroform to the sufferer!" His condition now appeared to be every way hopeful; and Mr. Smith exhorted him to postpone conversation, and to resign himself to sleep. He acquiesced in this, and being well wrapped up, soon fell into a quiet slumber, which continued until nine o'clock in the Sabbath morning.

Leaving him to his much needed sleep, the narrative will now return to the history of the great battle which he had so gloriously begun; that the interest of the reader in it may be briefly satisfied. About dark on Saturday evening, General Jackson had directed Brigadier-General Pender, to send him a regiment for a special service. The 16th North Carolina, Colonel M'Elroy, was sent. Jackson commanded him to accompany a squadron of cavalry detached by General Stuart, to Ely's Ford, where they would find a *corps* of Federal troops encamped; to approach them as nearly as possible, and at a preconcerted signal, to fire 'three volleys into them, with loud cheers, and then make their way back to their Brigade. Colonel ,M'Elroy reached the enemy's encampment about midnight, and carried out his instructions to the letter. He returned to the field of battle at three o'clock in the morning; and remained for a time ignorant alike of the reasons and results of this strange proceeding. The Federal officers of Reynolds' *corps* at last revealed it. They, stated that while resting for the night at Ely's Ford, on their way to Chancellors-ville, they were so furiously attacked by the "Rebels" in the darkness, that their leader arrested his march, and commenced fortifying his position; and in this work the Sabbath was consumed. Had this large *corps* arrived at the main scene of battle that morning, the odds already so fearful against the Confederates, might have become overpowering. But by this adroit manœuvre they were detained where they were wholly useless. Such was the last of the strokes, by which the ubi-quitous Jackson was accustomed to astonish and baffle his foes.

Upon the retirement of General Hill from the field, a hurried consultation was held between Colonel Pendleton, the acting adjutant of the *corps*, and the remaining Generals, touching the command of the troops. The night was passing away, and they well knew that the morning must bring a fierce renewal of the struggle; or all that had been won would be lost. Brigadier General Rhodes, commanding the former division of D. H. Hill, was found to be the senior officer upon the field; and his modesty, with the lack of acquaintanceship between him and the army, made him concur in the suggestion, that Major-Gen-eral Stuart should be sent for, and requested to assume the

88

direction of affairs until the pleasure of the Commander-in-Chief
should be known. This measure was therefore adopted. It
has been said that he was selected by General Jackson, to complete the battle after he was himself disabled. This is an error.
He was too strict in his obedience to the rules and proprieties
of the service, to transcend under any circumstances, his powers
as the commander of a *corps*; and he knew that all his authority
could do, was to transmit his functions to the General next in
rank in his own command. If any other disposition was to be
made of them, he knew that it must be done by an authority
higher than his own. But when Colonel Pendleton, the next
morning, reported to him the assumption of temporary command
by General Stuart he cheerfully acquiesced. In reply to the
request of Stuart that he would communicate, through Pendleton,
his plans for the second day, he answered, that he preferred to
leave everything to his own judgment. This reply was an
eminent instance of his wisdom. He knew, on the one hand,
that as all the *reconnoissances* on which he himself had acted,
had been made by General Stuart, that officer was fully possessed
of the enemy's attitude. But on the other hand, he was not now
informed what changes in the posture of affairs might have
occurred, which, if he were on the field, might modify his plans.
To seem to enjoin upon General Stuart the execution of all his
purposes of yesterday, might therefore impose on him mischievous trammels. He well knew, moreover, that the wisdom of the
methods adopted by himself, depended in part on his own *prestige*,
his moral power over his men, his celerity in action, the *momentum*
of his tremendous will; properties in which no other leader
might be able to imitate him. He therefore left General Stuart
to adopt his own plan of battle, believing, what was doubtless
true, that an inferior conception of that commander's mind,
applied by him, would be more successful than the impracticable

effort to unite the plan of one, with the execution of another.

But both General Stuart and General Rhodes proved themselves worthy of the command: and both of them followed their great exemplar to a soldier's grave, in the subsequent campaigns of 1864. The brilliant execution of General Jackson's orders by Rhodes at Chancellorsville, won his warm applause; and he declared that his commission as Major-General should date from the 2nd of May: when, with one division, he drove before him the whole right wing of Hooker for three hours. This purpose of General Jackson the Government fulfilled immediately after his death; and General Rhodes was promoted and placed in permanent command of the division. He continued to lead this with consummate gallantry and skill, until the disastrous battle of Winchester, in the autumn of 1864; when he fell at its head, in the execution of an attack against the enemy as splendid and as successful as that of Chancellorsville. And with his fall victory departed from the Confederate banners, to perch upon those of the oppressors.

But we are not left in doubt concerning General Jackson's own designs. Speaking afterward to his friends, he said that if he had had an hour more of daylight, or had not been wounded, he should have occupied the outlets toward Ely's and United States fords, as well as those on the west. (It has been already explained that of the four roads diverging from Chancellorsville, the one which leads north, after proceeding for a mile and a half in that direction, turns northwestward, and divides into two, the left hand leading to Ely's, and the right to United States ford. And the point of their junction, afterwards so carefully fortified by Hooker, was on Saturday night entirely open.) General Jackson proposed, therefore, to move still farther to his left, during the night, and occupy that point. He declared that if he had been able to do so, the dispersion or capture of Hooker's army would have been certain. "For," said he, "my men sometimes fail to drive the enemy from their position; but the enemy are never able to drive my men from theirs." It has already been seen, that in the confusion of his fall, an important vantage-ground, won by him almost without loss, was forfeited; and it was necessary to fight over this ground again on the morrow. General Stuart now departed from the plans of General Jackson, by extending his right rather than his left, so as to approximate the Confederate troops on the southeast of Chancellorsville, under the immediate command of General Lee. Thus, the weight of his attack was thrown against the southwest side of Hooker's position. General Jackson would rather have thrown it against the northwest. But the true design of the latter was to assume the defensive for a few hours, on Sabbath morning, after occupying both the Orange turnpike, and the road to Ely's ford. He purposed to stand at bay there, and receive, amidst the dense thickets, the attack, which he knew this occupation of his line of retreat would force upon Hooker; while General Lee thundered upon his other side. Then, after permitting him to break his strength in these vain assaults, he would have advanced upon his disheartened masses, over ground defended by no works; and Hooker would have been crushed between the upper and the nether mill-stones. To comprehend the plausibility of this design, it must be remembered that Chancellorsville, with its few adjoining farms, was an island, completely environed by a sea of forests, through whose tangled depths infantry could scarcely march in line; and the passage of carriages was impossible. Of the four roads which centred at the Villa, General Lee held two, the old turnpike, and the plank-road, leading toward Fredericksburg. General Jackson proposed to occupy the other two. Had this been done, the strong defence of the surrounding woods, in which Hooker trusted, would have been his ruin; he would have found his imaginary castle his prison. The necessity which compelled him again to take the aggressive in the leafy woods, would have thrown the advantage vastly to General Jackson; by rendering the powerful Federal artillery, in which they so much trusted, a cypher, and by requiring the Federals to come to close quarters with the terrible Confederate infantry. And this was a work always more dreaded by them, than the meeting of a "bear bereaved of her whelps." But on the southwest side of his position, within the open farm of Chancellor, Hooker had constructed a second and interior line of works, upon the brow of a long declivity, consisting of a row of lunettes pierced for artillery, and of rifle-pits. General Stuart's line of battle, after running the barricade, once before won by General Jackson, and emerging from the belt of woods which enveloped it, found themselves confronted by these works, manned by numerous batteries; and hence the cruel loss at which the splendid victory of Sunday was won.

The Brigadiers of General Jackson's *corps*, after determining to offer the temporary command to General Stuart, sent Captain Wilbourne to General Lee, to announce what had been done, and to request that he would himself come to that side and assume the direction of affairs. That officer, accompanied by Captain Hotchkiss, reached the cluster of pines east of Chancellorsville, where he lay, before the break of day, and they announced themselves to his Chief-of-Staff. They found the General lying upon the ground, beneath a thick pine-tree; and he at once requested them to come to him and tell the news. They related the incidents of the battle, and described the glorious victory; but when they told the wounding of their General, he said, after a pause, in which he was struggling to suppress his emotion, "Ah! any victory is dearly bought which deprives us of the services of Jackson, even for a short time. When reminded that General Rhodes was now the senior officer in the *corps*, he said he was a gallant, efficient, and energetic officer. But he acquiesced in the selection of General Stuart to lead the troops on that day, and, after a multitude of inquiries, called his adjutant to write instructions for him. He also dictated that generous note to General Jackson, which has conferred equal honor on its author and its recipient, and which deserves to be immortalized along with the fame of the two noble men. It was in these words: —

" GENERAL : I have just received your note, informing me that you were wounded. I cannot express my regret at the occurrence. Could I have directed events, I should have chosen, for the good of the country, to have been disabled in your stead.

" I congratulate you upon the victory which is due to your skill and energy.

" Most truly yours,

(Signed)   " R. E. LEE,   *General.*"

One of the messengers then informed him that General Jackson, after his wounding, had only expressed this thought concerning the future management of the campaign : that " the enemy should be pressed in the morning." General Lee replied, " Those people shall be pressed immediately "; arose, and in a few moments was in the saddle, and busy with his dispositions for attack. Meanwhile, General Stuart, on his side, brought forward the Stonewall Brigade from the junction of the Orange and Culpepper plank-roads, and joined it to his line of battle. The remainder of the night was spent in busy preparation. When the light appeared, both wings of the Confederate army assumed the aggressive, and advanced against the Federal lines. General Lee thundered from the east and south, and General Stuart from the west. The latter, especially, hurled his infantry impetuously against their enemies, and a furious and bloody struggle ensued. Twenty-one thousand men now composed the whole of Jackson's *corps* present upon the field; and these, assisted by the two divisions of M'Laws and Anderson, now assailed eighty thousand. In three hours, seven thousand men, one-third of the whole number, were killed and wounded from the *corps*. But the enemy were steadily driven from every work, with frightful losses in killed, wounded, and prisoners, until they took refuge in a new line of entrenchments, covering the United States ford. Seven thousand captives, forty thousand muskets, and a quantity of spoil almost incredible fell into the hands of the conquerors. When the general onset was ordered by Stuart, the Stonewall Brigade advanced with the cry, " Charge ; and remember Jackson ! " Even as they moved from their position, their General, Paxton, his friend and former adjutant, was struck dead where he stood ! His men rushed forward, unconscious of his absence, and, without other leader than the NAME which formed their battle-cry, swept everything before them.

The sequel of the campaign of Chancellorsville may now be related in a few words. While this great struggle was raging there, General Sedgwick retired to the north bank of the Rappahannock, and laying down his bridges again opposite to Fredericksburg, on Sunday morning crossed into the town, and with one *corps* captured Marye's Hill by a surprise. His other *corps* were despatched, through Stafford, to the support of Hooker, while he retained about eighteen thousand men. General Early now confronted Marye's Hill on another line, while Sedgwick, leaving a detachment to hold him in check, marched westward to open his way to Hooker, at Chancellorsville. But the fate of that General had been already sealed. General Lee was now at liberty to send a part of his force to meet Sedgwick; so that on Monday, he found himself confronted and arrested in his march by his troops, while General Early re-captured Marye's Hill, and cut off his retreat toward Fredericksburg. Nothing now remained for him save a retreat across the river at Banks's Ford, — a point between that town and Hooker's position, — which, by the aid of his artillery upon the northern bank, he effected, though not without heavy loss. The next day, his chief also made preparation to retire; and during the night of Tuesday, withdrew the remainder of his army. Thus ended the invasion, and the short career of Hooker as a commander. His cavalry, which had met with slight resistance, had penetrated as far south as the River James, which they reached fifty miles above Richmond. Thence they spread themselves downward through the country, and some detachments had the audacity to venture within ten miles of the city. They caused temporary interruptions in the Central and Fredericksburg Railroads, and the James River Canal; and then, upon hearing of Hooker's disasters, retired precipitately, having effected no other result than a villanous plundering of the peaceful inhabitants.

The short campaign of Chancellorsville was the most brilliant of all which General Lee had hitherto conducted, and stamped his fame as that of a commander of transcendent courage and ability. With forty-five thousand men, he had met and defeated one hundred and twenty-five thousand, who were equipped for their onset with everything which lavish wealth, careful discipline, and deliberate preparation, could provide. He had inflicted on them a total loss nearly equal to his whole army, had captured enough small arms and camp equipage to furnish forth every man in his command, and, in precisely a week, had hurled back the fragments of this multitudinous host to its starting point, baffled and broken. His line of defence was successfully turned on his right and left, by an adroit movement; his communications severed; and his little army seemingly placed within the jaws of destruction. But with an impregnable equanimity, he had awaited the full development of his adversary's designs; and then, disregarding for the time those parts of his assault which his wisdom showed him were not vital, had concentrated his chief strength upon the important point, and with a towering courage which no odds could appal, had assailed his gigantic adversary on his vulnerable side with resistless fury. How much of the credit of this unexampled success is due to the assistance of General Jackson, has already been indicated. But the history would be incomplete if it failed to refute the statement, which has been made by some of the pretended assertors of Jackson's fame; that the victories of Lee were due wholly to his military genius, and ceased when he fell. The reputation of Jackson does not need to be supported by these invidious follies. The Commander-in-Chief was the first to recognize, with unrivalled grace and magnanimity, his obligations to Jackson's valued assistance. But he fell in the midst of the struggle, and Lee conducted it to its close with the same skill, genius, and happy audacity, with which it was commenced. It was the glory of Virginia that, superior to the lioness, which rears but one young lion, her fruitful breasts could nourish at once the greatness of more than one heroic son.

89

CHAPTER XX.

DEATH AND BURIAL.

THE history of Jackson now turns finally from the camp and the battle-field, to the sacred quiet of the sick room, and the dying bed. The far different scenes which are to be unfolded, may be appropriately introduced by a reference to the calm and thorough acquiescence of General Jackson in his sudden helplessness. So eager and determined a spirit as his might have been expected to chafe at his enforced inactivity at such a time. It might be expected that he would now be seen, like an eagle with broken pinion, beating against the bars of his cage, with a tumultuous struggle to soar again into the storm-cloud which was his native air. Such anticipations did injustice to the Christian temper which he constantly cultivated. To the amazement of his own nearest friends, from the moment he felt the hand of Providence laid upon his efforts, in the shape of those wounds, he dismissed all the cares of command, and the heat of his soul sank into a sweet and placid calm. He who, just before, seemed to be pursuing victory with a devouring hunger, was now all acquiescence. He cast upon God every anxiety for his country, and seemed unconscious of the grand designs which, the day before, were burning in his heart. When he awoke from his long and quiet slumber on the Sabbath morning, the distant sounds of a furious cannonade told his experienced ear, that a great battle was again raging. But the thought did not quicken his pulse, nor draw from him a single expression of restlessness. He waited for news of the result with full faith in God, and in the valor of his army, only expressing such anxieties as an affectionate female might feel, for the safety of his comrades in arms.

His first act, after receiving refreshments, was to request Lieut. Morrison to go to Richmond, and bring Mrs. Jackson to his bedside. He then admitted his chaplain, Rev. Mr. Lacy, who had just arrived, and learned his misfortune, to his tent. As he entered, and saw the stump where the left arm had lately been, he exclaimed in distress, "Oh, General ! what a calamity !" Jackson first thanked him, with his usual courtesy, for his sympathy, and then proceeded, with marked deliberation and emphasis, as though delivering his Christian testimony touching God's dealing with him, to speak in substance thus; and at a length which was unusual with his taciturn habits. "You see me severely wounded, but not depressed; not unhappy. I believe that it has been done according to God's holy will, and I acquiesce entirely in it. You may think it strange; but you never saw me more perfectly contented than I am to-day; for I am sure that my Heavenly Father designs this affliction for my good. I am perfectly satisfied, that either in this life, or in that which is to come, I shall discover that what is now regarded as a calamity, is a blessing. And if it appears a great calamity, (as it surely will be a great inconvenience, to be deprived of my arm,) it will result in a great blessing. I can wait, until God, in his own time, shall make known to me the object he has in thus afflicting me. But why should I not rather rejoice in it as a blessing, and not look on it as a calamity at all ? If it were in my power to replace my arm, I would not dare to do it, unless I could know it was the will of my Heavenly Father."

He then spoke, in answer to inquiries, of all the incidents of his fall, with entire freedom and quiet. After a little he added, that he thought when he fell from the litter, that he should die upon the field, and gave himself up into the hands of his Heavenly Father without a fear. He declared that he was in possession of perfect peace, while thus expecting immediate death. "It has been," he said, "a precious experience to me, that I was brought face to face with death, and found all was well. I then learned an important lesson, that one who has been the subject of converting grace, and is the child of God, can, in the midst of the severest sufferings, fix the thoughts upon God and heavenly things, and derive great comfort and peace: but, that one who had never made his peace with God would be unable to control his mind, under such sufferings, so as to understand properly the way of salvation, and repent and believe on Christ. I felt that if I had neglected the salvation of my soul before, it would have been too late then."

These are nearly the exact words, in which this valuable witness was borne by General Jackson; for the minister, impressed with their solemn weight, charged his memory with them, and speedily committed them to writing. It is needless to moralize upon them, in order that their lesson may be felt by every reader. The General was disposed to speak yet more upon these themes; but acquiesced in the friendly caution of his nurse and physician, and remained for a long time in perfect quiet.

About eleven o'clock, A. M., Captain Douglass, his Assistant Inspector, arrived from the field with definite news of the victory, and taking his faithful nurse, Lieutenant Smith aside, detailed such things as he thought would most interest the General. The latter went into the tent, and recited them to him, relating, among other things the magnificent onset of the Stonewall Brigade. General Stuart had gone to them at the crisis of the battle, and pointing out to them the work which he wished them to do, had commanded them to "charge and remember Jackson!" Whereupon they had sprung forward, and driving before them three-fold numbers with irresistible enthusiasm, had decided the great day. The General listened with glistening eyes, and after a strong effort to repress his tears said; "It was just like them to do so; just like them. They are a noble body of men." Smith replied; "They have indeed behaved splendidly; but you can easily suppose, General, that it was not without a loss of many valuable men." His anxiety was immediately aroused; and he asked quickly: "Have you heard of any one that is killed?" Said Smith, "Yes sir; I am sorry to say, they have lost their commander." He exclaimed: "Paxton? Paxton?" Smith.—"Yes sir, he has fallen." Thereupon he turned his face to the wall, closed his eyes, and remained a long time quiet, laboring to suppress his emotion. He then, without any other expression of his own sense of bereavement, began to speak in a serious and tender strain of the genius and virtues of that officer. Smith said that Mr. Lacy had talked confidentially with General Paxton about his spiritual interests, had found him by no means the stranger, that some supposed him, to the religion of the heart, and believed him a regenerate man. Jackson replied, in a tone of high satisfaction: "That's good; that's good!" It may be added in confirmation of this judgment, that the last occupation of General Paxton on the battle-field, after he had placed his regiments in position, was to employ the interval of leisure in reading his New Testament; and that as he received the order to carry them into action, he replaced the book in his pocket, and accompanied his command to move, with a brief exhortation to those around him, to entrust their safety into the hand of the Almighty, in the faithful performance of their duty. It was by this Christian courage, that the victories of the Confederacy were won.

General Jackson now directed Lieutenant Smith to obtain materials for writing, and dictated to him a note to General Lee. In the most unpretending words, he stated that he had been disabled by his wounds, and had accordingly demitted his command to the General next him in rank, A. P. Hill. He then congratulated the Commander-in-Chief upon the great vic· tory which God had that day vouchsafed to his arms. He received soon after the note of General Lee, which was given above. When this was read to him, he was evidently much gratified; and after a little pause, said: "General Lee is very kind: but he should give the glory to God." At a later hour he remarked: "Our movement yesterday was a great success: I think, the most successful military movement of my life. But I expect to receive far more credit for it than I deserve. Most men will think that I had planned it all from the first; but it was not so — I simply took advantage of circumstances as they were presented to me in the providence of God. I feel that His hand led me: Let us give Him all the glory." These words undoubtedly give the most exact representation of the character of his strategy. While no commander was ever more painstaking in his forecast, none was ever fuller of ready resource, or more prompt to modify his plans according to the new circumstances which emerged. And when he was once possessed of the posture of affairs, his decision was as swift as it was correct. The plan of attacking Hooker from the west was conceived and matured on the evening of Friday, almost in a moment. At that time he met General Stuart at the old furnace in front of Chancellorsville; he gained a view thence of the comparative altitude of that place; he saw the position of the Federal batteries which Stuart was then engaging; and, at a glance, divined thence the disposition of Hooker's forces; he learned the absence of the hostile cavalry; and the friendly screen of forests which surrounded Chancellorsville was described to him. It was then that his decision was made; and after a few moments anxious conference with General Stuart, he rode rapidly back to seek General Lee, and to communicate his conclusion to him.

During the Sabbath, General Lee sent word to him that he regarded the Wilderness as so exposed to the insults of the Federal cavalry, that it would be prudent to remove to Guinea's Station as soon as possible. Dr. M'Guire therefore determined to attempt the journey on the morrow. The General hoped, after resting there for a day or two, to proceed to Ashland, a rural village on the same railroad, twelve miles from Richmond, and thence to his beloved Lexington. He dreaded the bustle of the capital, and sighed for the quiet of his home; where, he said, the pure mountain air would soon heal his wounds, and invigorate his exhausted body. On Monday morning he appeared so exceedingly well, that it was determined to attempt the journey. A mattress was placed in an ambulance, and he was laid upon it, with every appliance for his comfort which could be devised. Dr. M'Guire took his place within, by his side, while Lieutenant Smith rode near, and Mr. Hotchkiss, with a party of pioneers, preceded the vehicle, removing everything from the road, which might cause a jostle to the sufferer. He seemed bright and cheerful during the journey, and conversed with spirit concerning military affairs and religion. The route taken led southward, by Spottsylvania Court House, and the distance to Guinea's was thus made twenty-five miles. The road was encumbered by the army teamsters, usually a rude and uncouth race, conveying supplies to the army at Chancellorsville. But when they were told that the ambulance contained the wounded General, they made way for it with tender respect; and their frequent reply to the escort was: "I wish it was I, who was wounded." At nightfall, the party reached the house of Mr. Chandler, near the railroad

station, whose hospitality General Jackson had shared the previous winter, when he first came from the Valley.   Here he was
gladly received, and everything possible was done for his comfort; for it was a notable trait of his character, that he inspired
in all the people, and especially in the purest and most Christian,
that unbounded devotion, which counted every exertion made
for him a precious privilege.   The house of Mr. Chandler was
already full of wounded officers, to whom he sent, by his attendants, most courteous and sympathizing messages.   He arrived
at this resting place wearied and painful, complaining of some
nausea, and pain in his bruised side; but still declared that he
had made the journey with unexpected comfort, for which he
should be very grateful to God.   Referring to his previous
advantage in the use of the remedies of *Preissnitz*, he earnestly
entreated that wet towels should now be placed on his stomach
and side.   Dr. M'Guire consenting to this, the ambulance was
arrested, fresh water was obtained from a spring on the road-
side, and the application was made, as he declared, to his great
relief.   When he was removed to his bed at Mr. Chandler's, he
took some supper with relish, and then spent the night in quiet
sleep.

During this journey, it has been remarked, General Jackson
appeared full of vivacity and hope, conversing with his physician, his chaplain, and Mr. Smith, on every topic of common
interest.   He referred again to the Stonewall Brigade, and to
the proposal which was mooted among them, to ask formal
authority from the Government to assume that name as their
own, on their rolls and colors.   He said with enthusiasm:
" They are a noble body of patriots; when this war is ended,
the survivors will be proud to say: 'I was a member of the old
Stonewall Brigade.'   The Government ought certainly to accede
to their request, and authorize them to assume this title; for it

was fairly earned." He then, with characteristic modesty, added, that "the name, Stonewall, ought to be attached wholly to the men of the Brigade, and not to him; for it was their steadfast heroism which had earned it at First Manassa's." Some one asked him of the plan of campaign which Hooker had just attempted to execute. He said: "It was, in the main, a good conception, sir; an excellent plan. But he should not have sent away his cavalry; that was his great blunder. It was that which enabled me to turn him, without his being aware of it, and to take him by his rear. Had he kept his cavalry with him, his plan would have been a very good one." It may be added, in accordance with this verdict of the highest authority, that the strategy of the Federal Generals, from that of M'Dowell on the first field of Manassa's, onward, was usually good enough, had it been seconded by the courage of their troops. The Federal is rarely found deficient in anything which cunning or diligence can supply; his defect is in the manhood of the soldiery.

On Monday morning, General Jackson awoke refreshed, and his wounds were pronounced to be in an admirable condition. He now began to look forward to his restoration to his command, and inquired of Dr. M'Guire, how many weeks would probably elapse before he would be fit for the field. He also requested his chaplain to visit him at ten o'clock each morning, for reading the Scriptures and prayer. These seasons were the occasions of much religious conversation, in which he unbosomed himself with unusual freedom and candor. He declared that his faith and hope in his Redeemer were clear. He said he was perfectly willing to die at that time; but believed that his time was not yet come, that his Heavenly Father still had a work for him to do in defence of his beloved country, and that until that was completed, he should be spared. During these morning hours, he delighted to enlarge on his favorite topics of practical religion; which were such as these: The Christian should carry his religion into everything. Christianity makes man better in any lawful calling; it equally makes the general a better commander, and the shoemaker a better mechanic. In the case of the cobbler, or the tailor, for instance, religion will produce more care in promising work, more punctuality, and more fidelity in executing it, from conscientious motives; and these homely examples were fair illustrations of its value in more exalted functions. So, prayer aids any man, in any lawful business, not only by bringing down the divine blessing, which is its direct and prime object, but by harmonizing his own mind and heart. In the commander of an army at the critical hour, it calmed his perplexities, moderated his anxieties, steadied the scales of judgment, and thus preserved him from exaggerated and rash conclusions. Again he urged, that every act of man's life should be a religious act. He recited with much pleasure, the ideas of Doddridge, where he pictured himself as spiritualizing every act of his daily life; as thinking when he washed himself, of the cleansing blood of Calvary; as praying while he put on his garments, that he might be clothed with the righteousness of the saints; as endeavoring, while he was eating, to feed upon the Bread of Heaven. General Jackson now also enforced his favorite dogma, that the Bible furnished men with rules for every thing. If they would search, he said, they would find a precept, an example, or a general principle, applicable to every possible emergency of duty, no matter what was a man's calling. There the military man might find guidance for every exigency. Then, turning to Lieutenant Smith, he asked him, smiling: " Can you tell me where the Bible gives generals a model for their official reports of battles ? " He answered, laughing, that it never entered his mind to think of looking for such a thing in the Scriptures. "Nevertheless," said the General, "there are such: and excellent models, too. Look, for instance, at the narrative of Joshua's battle with the Amalekites; there you have one. It has clearness, brevity, fairness, modesty; and it traces the victory to its right source, the blessing of God."

After Monday, the bright promise of his recovery began to be overcast; pain and restlessness gradually increased, and he was necessarily limited in conversation. It became necessary again to resort to his favorite remedy, the wet napkins, and to employ anodynes to soothe his nerves. Under the influence of the opiates, his sleep now became disturbed and full of dreams. He several times inquired anxiously about the issue of the battles. On Tuesday he was told that Hooker was entrenched north of Chancellorsville; when he said: "That is bad; very bad." Falling asleep afterwards, he aroused himself exclaiming: "Major Pendleton; send in and see if there is higher ground back of Chancellorsville." His soul was again struggling, in his dreams, for his invaded country; and he thought of his artillery crowning some eminence, and thence pelting the intruder from his stronghold. It was also on this day that the whole line of the railroad was agitated with rumors of the approach of Stoneman's vagrant cavalry; which had attacked Ashland, and was expected to advance thence toward Fredericksburg, ravaging all the stations. General Jackson expressed the most perfect calmness, in view of this danger, and said, that he doubted not if they captured him, God would cause them to treat him with kindness. The confusion prevalent along the railroad had retarded Mr. Morrison in his journey to Richmond; and now made it dangerous for Mrs. Jackson to travel by that route. On Thursday, however, she determined to delay no longer, and setting out by railroad, reached Mr. Chandler's in the forenoon.

But meantime, the symptoms of General Jackson's case had

become still more ominous. Wednesday brought a cold, drenching rain, with a chilling atmosphere, unhealthy for his enfeebled
system. Wednesday evening, Dr. M'Guire, who had scarcely
permitted himself to sleep for three or four nights, overpowered
by fatigue, retired to rest. But during the night, the General
began to complain of an intense pain in his side, and urged his
servant Jim, who was watching with him, to apply wet towels.
He complied; but the remedy failed to bring relief; and as morning approached, he summoned the Doctor again. The General
was found with a quickened pulse, laboring respiration, and severe
pain. Pneumonia was clearly developed, but not with alarming
intensity; the pain and difficult breathing being more accounted
for by a neuralgic *Pleurodinia*, constricting the muscles of the
chest, than by actual inflammation of the lungs. The physician
therefore resorted to the more vigorous remedies of sinapisms
and cupping; but with only partial effect. The chaplain was
now despatched to the army, which had returned to its old
quarters near Fredericksburg, to bring the General's family
physician, Dr. Morrison, now chief surgeon of Early's Division.
Mr. Lacy, while seeking him, called on General Lee, and told him
that the General's condition was more threatening. He replied
that he was confident God would not take Jackson away from
him at such a time, when his country needed him so much.
" Give him," he added, " my affectionate regards, and tell him to
make haste and get well, and come back to me as soon as he
can. He has lost his left arm; but I have lost my right arm."

Meantime, Mrs. Jackson had arrived with her infant. The
duties of the sick room delayed her introduction for an hour, and
they sought to prepare her feelings for the change which she
must see in her husband. He had asked for a glass of lemon-
ade, and some one proposed, as a kindly relief to her anxiety,
that she should busy herself in preparing it. When Mr. Smith

took it to him, he tasted, and looking up, said quickly; "You did not mix this, it is too sweet; take it back." Disease had produced a surprising change in his temper in one respect, that he who, in health, was almost indifferent to the quality of his food and drink, and satisfied with the simplest, had become critical and exacting in those particulars. He was now informed that Mrs. Jackson had arrived, and expressed great delight. When she entered his room, she saw him sadly changed; his features were sunken by the prostration of his energies; and were marked by two or three angry scars, where they had been torn by his horse, as he rushed through the brushwood. His cheeks burned with a swarthy, and almost livid flush. Yet his face beamed with joy, when, awaking from his disturbed slumber, he saw her near him. When he noted the shade of woful apprehension which passed over her face, he said tenderly, "Now Anna, cheer up, and don't wear a long face; you know I love a bright face in a sick room." And nobly did she obey. With a spirit as truly courageous as that of her warrior husband, she commanded her grief, and addressed herself cheerfully to the ministry of love. Many a tear was poured out over her unconscious suckling, yet she returned to his sick room always with a serene countenance; and continued to be, until the clouds of death descended upon his vision, what he had delighted to call her in the hours of prosperity, his "Sunshine." He now added, with reference to his impaired hearing, that he wished her to speak distinctly while in his room, because he wanted to hear every word she said.

At two o'clock, P. M., Dr. Morrison arrived. When he spoke to him, the General looked up, and said affectionately: "That's an old, familiar face." His condition was now examined thoroughly, and was found so critical that it was determined to send Mr. Smith to Richmond, to bring some female friend to Mrs.

Jackson's assistance, and to call in the aid of Dr. Tucker, of that city, whose skill in pulmonary diseases was greatly valued. But the best treatment which medical science could suggest was immediately commenced; and the symptoms of *Pneumonia* were partially subdued. Nature, however, did not rally as this enemy receded; the vital forces were too much exhausted to be effectually revived. There remained no organic disease of sufficient force to destroy the lungs of an infant; but still his "constitutional symptoms" grew steadily more discouraging. The causes of this decline were several; the cold which he had contracted Friday night; the fatigue and exhaustion of his long continued abstinence, labor and intense excitement during the march and battle; the cruel fall from the litter; and above all, the fatal hemorrhage. It was during the horrid confusion of that night combat in the thicket, that his strength was drained away; the deceitful appearance of the succeeding days was but a partial flowing again of the tides of life, which were proved too weak to fill their accustomed channel, and so ebbed forever. During his remaining hours, he was at times oppressed by something, which was not *delirium*, but the burthen of a profound prostration, combined with the slumberous drugs which were given to command his pain. Whenever he was addressed by any one whom he knew, he roused himself; and memory, reason and consciousness were found in full exercise; but at other times he lay with closed eyes, seemingly engaged in silent prayer, or overcome by sleep which was visited with disturbed visions; and at others again, he entered into the conversation around his bed, with so much intelligence and animation, that his physicians checked his exertions of his failing strength. During Thursday night, Dr. Morrison had occasion to arouse him from sleep, to take some draught, saying: "Will you take this, General?" He looked steadily into his face and said: "Do your duty."

Then, as though to signify that he intended what he said, and wished the physician to do for him precisely what his judgment dictated, he repeated, "Do your duty." His vagrant thoughts in sleep were obviously wandering back to the field of strife; at one time he was heard to say quickly: "A. P. Hill, prepare for action;" and several times: "Tell Major Hawks to send forward provisions for the troops."

On Friday morning Dr. Morrison suggested his fear of a fatal termination of his disease. He dissented from this expectation positively, and said, precisely in these words, "I am not afraid to die; I am willing to abide by the will of my Heavenly Father. But I do not believe that I shall die at this time; I am persuaded the Almighty has yet a work for me to perform." It was not at random that he then employed two different terms to denote God; but their use was intentional, and was a remarkable manifestation of his religion. The favorite term by which he was accustomed to speak of God in the relations of redemption to his own soul, as the attentive reader will have noticed already, was, "My Heavenly Father." It was this dear name which he now used, when he would express his acquiescence in the Divine will concerning himself. But when, in the next breath, he spoke of the work which he expected God, as the Ruler of nations, to assign to him, he called Him "The Almighty." He also insisted that Dr. M'Guire should be called in, and the appeal be made to him. When he entered, he candidly admitted that he shared his fears; but General Jackson, while perfectly willing to die, was still as sturdy as ever in declaring his expectation of life. It may be added, that even so late as Saturday night, when Dr. Morrison renewed the expression of his fears, he still dissented, saying: "I don't think so: 1 think I shall be better by morning."

On Friday morning Mr. Smith returned from Richmond with

the additional assistance which he had gone to seek. But medical skill could suggest no means to replace the vital forces
which were surely failing, at the fountain of life. It was on the
afternoon of this day that he asked Dr. M'Guire whether he
supposed the diseased persons healed by the miraculous touch
of the Saviour ever suffered again from the same malady. He
continued to say, that he did not believe they did; that the healing virtue of the Redeemer was too potent, and that the poor
paralytic to whom He had once said, "I will: be thou healed,"
never shook again with palsy. He then, as though invoking the
same aid, exclaimed: "Oh for infinite power!" After a season
of quiet reflection, he said to Mr. Smith, (who, being designed
for the pulpit, had received a thorough theological training,)
"what were the Head-quarters of Christianity after the cruci-
fixion?" He replied that Jerusalem was at first the chief seat;
but after the dispersion of the disciples thence by persecution,
there was none for a time, until Antioch, Iconium, Rome, and
Alexandria, were finally established as centres of influence. The
General interrupted him: "Why do you say 'centres of influence'! is not *Head-quarters* a better term?" He then requested
him to go on, and Smith, encouraged by Dr. M'Guire, proceeded
to explain how the Apostles were directed by Divine Providence, seemingly, to plant their most flourishing churches, at an
early period, in these great cities, which were rendered by their
political, commercial, and ethnical relations, "head-quarters" of
influence for the whole civilized world. Jackson was much
interested in the explanation, and at its end, said: "Mr. Smith,
I wish you would get the map, and show me precisely where
Iconium was." He replied that he thought there was no map at
hand, where that ancient city would be found. Said the General, "Yes, Sir: you will find it in the Atlas which is in my old
trunk." This trunk was searched, but the Atlas was not found

there, and Mr. Smith suggested that it was probably left in his portable desk. He said: "Yes, you are right, I left it in my desk," (mentioning the shelf.) Then, after musing for a moment, he added, "Mr. Smith, I wish you would examine into that matter, *and report to me*." His meaning was, that he should refresh his knowledge of this interesting feature of the history of the infant 'Church, by reference to books, and thus prepare himself to unfold it more fully to him.

On Saturday morning, while he was suffering cruelly from fever and restlessness, and tossing about upon' his bed, Mrs. Jackson proposed to read him some Psalms from the Old Testament, hoping their sublime consolations would soothe his pains. He at first replied that he was suffering too much to attend, but soon after added, "Yes, we must never refuse that; get the Bible, and read them." In the afternoon he requested that he might see his chaplain. He was then so ill, and his respiration so difficult, that it was thought all conversation would be injurious, and they attempted to dissuade him. But he continued to ask so repeatedly and eagerly, that it was judged better to yield. When Mr. Lacy entered, he inquired whether he was endeavoring to further those views of Sabbath observance of which he had spoken to him. On his assuring him that he was, he entered at some length into conversation with him upon that subject. Thus, his last care and labor for the Church of God was an effort to secure the sanctification of His holy day. As the evening wore away, his sufferings increased, and he requested Mrs. Jackson to sing some psalms, with the assistance of all his friends around his bed, selecting the most spiritual pieces they could. She, with her brother, then sung several of his favorite pieces, concluding, at his request, with the 51st Psalm,

"Show pity, Lord, O Lord forgive."

sung to the "Old Hundredth." The night was spent by him in feverish tossings, and without quiet sleep. During all its weary hours, the attendants sat by his side, sponging his brow with cool water, the only palliative of his pain which seemed to avail. Whenever they paused, he looked up, and by some gesture or sign, begged them to continue.

Thus the morning of Sabbath, the 10th of May, was ushered in, a holy day which he was destined to begin on earth, and to end in heaven. He had often said that he desired to die upon the Sabbath; and this wish was now about to be fulfilled. His end was evidently so near that Dr. Morrison felt it was due to Mrs. Jackson to inform her plainly of his condition. She remembered that he had often said, when speaking of death, that although he was willing to die at any time, if it was the will of God, he should greatly desire to have a few hours' notice of the approach of his last struggle. She therefore declared that he must be distinctly informed of his nearness to death; and agonizing as was the task, she would herself assume the duty of breaking the solemn news to him. He was now lying quiet, and apparently oppressed by the *incubus* of his deep prostration. She went to his bedside and aroused him, when he immediately recognized her, although he did not appear at first to apprehend distinctly the tenor of her announcement. The progress of the disease had now nearly robbed him of the power of speech. She repeated several times: "Do you know the Doctors say, you must very soon be in heaven? Do you not feel willing to acquiesce in God's allotment, if He wills you to go to-day?" He looked her full in the face, and said, with difficulty: "I prefer it." Then, as though fearing that the intelligence of his answer might not be fully appreciated, he said again: "I *prefer it.*" She said: "Well, before this day closes, you will be with the blessed Saviour in His glory." He replied with great distinctness and deliberation: "I will be an infinite gainer to be translated."

He had before requested that the chaplain should preach, as usual, at his head-quarters, but he now seemed to be oblivious of the fact. When Colonel Pendleton, his Adjutant, entered the room, he greeted him with his unfailing courtesy; and then asked, who was preaching at head-quarters. When he was told that the chaplain was gone to do it, he expressed much satisfaction. Mrs. Jackson now determined to employ the fleeting moments, to learn his last wishes; first asking for one final assurance more, that his Saviour was present with him in his extremity. To this he only answered with a distinct "Yes." His wife asked him whether it was his will that she and his daughter should reside with her father, Dr. Morrison. He answered: "Yes, you have a kind and good father; but no one is so kind and good as your Heavenly Father." She then inquired where he preferred that his body should be buried. To this he made no reply. When she suggested Lexington, he assented, saying: "Yes, in Lexington;" but his tone expressed rather acquiescence than lively interest. His infant was now brought to receive his last embrace; and as soon as she appeared in the doorway, which he was watching with his eyes, his face was lit up with a beaming smile, and he motioned her toward him, saying fondly: "Little darling!" She was seated on the bed by his side, and he embraced her, and endeavored to caress her with his poor, lacerated hand — while she smiled upon him with infantile delight. Thus he continued to toy with her, until the near approach of death unnerved his arm, and unconsciousness settled down upon him.

In his restless sleep, he seemed attempting to speak; and at length said audibly: "Let us pass over the river, and rest under the shade of the trees." These were the last words he uttered. Was his soul wandering back in dreams to the river of his beloved valley, the Shenandoah, (the "river of sparkling waters,") whose verdant meads and groves he had redeemed from the invader, and across whose floods he had so often won his passage through the toils of battle? Or was he reaching forward across the River of Death, to the golden streets of the Celestial City, and the trees whose leaves are for the healing of the nations? It was to these that God was bringing him, through his last battle and victory; and under their shade he walks, with the blessed company of the redeemed.

His attendants, now believing that consciousness had finally departed, ceased to restrain his wife; and she was permitted to abandon herself to all the desolation of her grief. But they were mistaken. Bowing down over him, her eyes raining tears upon his dying face, and covering it with kisses, she cried: "Oh, doctor; cannot you do something more?" That voice had power to recall him once more, for a moment, from the very threshold of heaven's gate; he opened his eyes fully, and gazing upward at her face, with a long look of full intelligence and love, closed them again forever. His breath then, after a few more inspirations, ceased; and his laboring breast was stilled. And thus died the hero of so many battles, who had so often confronted death when clothed with his gloomiest terrors; with his last earthly look fixed upon the face which was dearer to him than all else, except that Saviour, whom he was next to behold in glory.

While he was thus passing down beneath the shadow of the portals of death, two different scenes were enacting, connected with his fate, contrasted in their actors and accessories as widely as the extremes of earth well admit. But it is not easy to decide which paid the most touching tribute to the dying warrior. Mrs. Chandler, the hostess to whose affectionate hospitality the

General was now indebted for a shelter, had a daughter of five years old, whose heart he had won, as he stole the hearts of all the ingenuous, during his short visit of the previous winter. This winning child had noticed the tears which moistened her mother's cheeks, as she was engaged about her household duties; and for a long time, had followed her about the house with a restless and wistful countenance. At length she ventured to ask: "Mamma, will General Jackson die?" She was told that the Doctors said they could not save him, and he was going to die. Fixing her large, solemn eyes upon her mother's face with a look of intense earnestness, she replied: "Oh, I wish God would let me die for him, for if I did, you would cry for me; but if he dies, all the people in the country will cry."

The cotemporaneous scene was at the quarters of the Staff of General Jackson's *corps*, where a vast congregation of nearly two thousand men, with the Commander-in-Chief, and a brilliant assemblage of Generals, was collected for public worship. When General Lee saw the chaplain approaching, he met him, and anxiously inquired after the sufferer's condition. He was told that it was nearly, or quite hopeless; when with great feeling he said: "Surely General Jackson must recover. God will not take him from us, now that we need him so much. Surely he will be spared to us, in answer to the many prayers which are offered for him." He afterwards added: "When you return, I trust you will find him better. When a suitable occasion offers, give him my love, and tell him that I wrestled in prayer for him last night, as I never prayed, I believe, for myself." With these words, he hastily turned away, to hide his uncontrollable emotion. This message has not yet been delivered. After public worship, in which the whole multitude was melted into grief while joining in the prayers for his recovery, Mr. Lacy returned, only to find him gone. He had expired about three o'clock in the afternoon.

The dying scene has now been exactly related, without attempt at any dramatic embellishment; for it is believed that this faithful and homely narrative will be more impressive to every rightly constituted mind, than any effort of literary art. Nor will any reflections be added, upon the lessons of such a death to the hearts of the readers; but each one will be left, in the silence of his own soul, to draw them for himself. They are too plain and solemn to need repetition.

Colonel Pendleton immediately informed General Lee, and the Governor of the Commonwealth, of the departure of Jackson's soul; and by the latter, it was communicated to the Confederate Government. In a few hours the electric telegraph had conveyed the news to all the Confederate States; and to every heart it came as a chilling shock. All over the land, hundreds of miles away from the regions which he had illustrated by his prowess, the people who had never seen his face, grieved for him as men grieve for their nearest kindred. Other countries and ages may have witnessed such a national sorrow; but the men of this generation never saw so profound and universal grief, as that which throbbed in the heart of the Confederate people at the death of Jackson. Women, who had never known him save by the fame of his virtues and exploits, wept for him as passionately as for a brother. The faces of the men were black with dismay, as they heard that the tower of their strength was fallen. All felt what many mouths expressed, that no language could declare their sense of bereavement so well as the requiem of David for his princely friend, Jonathan. "How are the mighty fallen in the midst of the battle! O Jonathan, thou wast slain in thy high places. I am distressed for thee, my brother Jonathan; very pleasant hast thou been unto me; thy love was wonderful, passing the love of women. How are the mighty fallen, and the weapons of war perished!" Men said that they had never admitted among their fears of possible calamity, the apprehension that Jackson could fall in battle; for he had passed unscathed through so many perils, that he seemed to them to wear a charmed life. He was to his fellow-citizens the man of destiny, the anointed of God to bring in deliverance for his oppressed Church and Country. They had seen his form leading the van of victory, with such trust as the ancient Hebrews reposed in their kings and judges, when they went forth to turn to flight the armies of the aliens, anointed with holy oil, and guided to sure triumph by the oracles of Urim and Thummim and inspired seers. Even those who did not pray themselves, believed with a perfect assurance, that his prayers found certain access to the heavens, and that the cause for which he interceded was secure under the shield of omnipotence. The people of God, with a more intelligent and scriptural trust, gloried in his sanctity and Christian zeal, as a signal proof that the cause of their country was the cause of righteousness, in his pious example as a precious influence for good upon their sons who followed his banners, and in the homage done to Christ and His Gospel by his devotion. His soldiers trusted in his *prestige* with a perfect faith; for they had seen Fortune perch so regularly upon his flag, that the fickleness of her nature seemed to be changed, for him, into constancy. Jackson's *corps*, when fighting under his eye, always assailed the enemy with the certain expectation that victory, and nothing but victory, was to be the issue. His Commander-in-Chief, who best knew the value of his sleepless vigilance, his industry, his wisdom in council, and his vigor in action, appreciated his loss most fully of all. Men were everywhere speculating with solemn anxiety upon the meaning of his death. They asked themselves: Has God "taken the good man away from the evil to come?" Has he adjudged us as unworthy, because of our ingratitude and disobedience, of such a deliverer;

and after proving us for a time by lending a Jackson to our cause, has He now withdrawn the gift, in judicial displeasure? Or does He only mean to render the example of his military and Christian virtues more shining and instructive by his translation, and thus, while He teaches us to trust more exclusively in Himself, raise up, after this model, a company of Jacksons, to defend their country? While some answered these questions in both ways, according to their temperaments, the greater number wisely left them to be solved by God Himself, in the evolution of His providence. In one conclusion all agreed, that the imitation of Jackson's example by his countrymen would make his people invincible, and their final triumph absolutely certain, and that this was the practical lesson set forth by God in his life and death.

Gen. Jackson's remains were shrouded by his Staff, Sunday evening, in his military garments, and deposited in an open coffin of wood, which was procured near by. His coat had been almost torn to pieces by his friends, in their eagerness to reach and bind up his wounds, the night he fell; and it was now replaced by the civilian's coat which he sometimes wore in his hours of relaxation. But his military overcoat covered and concealed this exception. The Congress of the Confederate States had a short time before adopted a design for their flag, and a large and elegant model had just been completed, the first ever made, which was intended to be unfurled from the roof of the Capitol. This flag the President now sent, as the gift of the country, to be the winding sheet of the corpse. The Governor of Virginia, assuming the care of the funeral, sent up a metallic coffin, with a company of embalmers, on Sunday night, together with a deputation of eminent civilians and military men, to escort the remains to Richmond. During that night they were finally prepared for the tomb, and on Monday morning, May

11th, were conveyed to the Capital by a special train, attended by the General's Staff, his widow and her female friends, and the Governor's Committee. When they approached the suburb through which the Fredericksburg Railroad enters the city, the gathering throng warned them to pause and seek a more quiet approach for the afflicted ladies. The train was therefore arrested, and the wife of the Governor, receiving Mrs. Jackson and her attendants into her carriages, drove rapidly and by circuitous and less frequented streets, to his Mansion on the Capitol Square. The cars then slowly advanced into the city, through an avenue which, for two miles, was thronged with myriads of men and women. Business had been suspended, and the whole city, as one man, was come forth to meet the mighty dead: Amidst a solemn silence, only broken by the boom of the minute guns and the wails of a military dirge, the coffin was borne into the Governor's gates, and hidden for the time, from the eyes of the multitude, of which the major part were wet with tears.

For the next day, a great civic and military pomp was devised, which was thus described in a cotemporary publication. "At the hour appointed, the coffin was borne to the hearse, a signal gun was fired from near the Washington monument, and the procession began to move to the solemn strains of the Dead March in Saul. The hearse was preceded by two regiments of Gen. Pickett's division, with arms reversed, that General and his Staff, the Fayette artillery, and Wren's company of cavalry. Behind came the horse of the dead soldier, caparisoned for battle, and led by a groom; his Staff officers, members of the Stonewall Brigade, invalids and wounded; and then a vast array of officials, headed by the President of the Confederate States, and members of his Cabinet, followed by all the general officers in Richmond; after whom came a mighty throng of civic dignitaries, and citizens. The procession moved through the main

92

streets of the city, and then returned to the Capitol. Every place of business was closed, and every avenue thronged with solemn and tearful spectators, while a silence more impressive than that of the Sabbath, brooded over the whole town. When the hearse reached the steps of the Capitol, the pall bearers, headed by Gen. Longstreet, the great comrade of the departed, bore the corpse into the hall of the lower house of the Congress, where it was placed upon a species of altar, draped with snowy white, before the Speaker's chair. The coffin was still enfolded with the white, blue, and red, of the Confederate flag."

There the head was uncovered, and the people were permitted, during the remainder of the day, to enter and view the features of the dead for the last time. The face was found to be in perfect repose; the livid flush of fever had passed away; the broad and lofty forehead was now smooth and snow white, the cheeks thin, and bronzed by sun and breeze, the expressive mouth firmly closed; while an expression of shining calm shed a species of ghostly radiance over the countenance. During the whole afternoon the people streamed through the room, ladies, legislators, old men, children, rugged soldiers, in a mingled, silent throng, looked a moment on the dead face, and passed out another way; until twenty thousand persons had paid this last tribute of affection. The women brought some exotic or sweet flower to lay upon the coffin; and these offerings became so numerous, that they loaded the whole bier, and the table on which it rested, and rose to a great heap. Before the pious interest of the people could be satisfied, the hour had arrived for closing the doors, and the officials warned the throng of people to retire. Just then, a mutilated veteran from Jackson's old division, was seen anxiously pressing through the crowd, to take his last look at the face of his beloved leader. They told him that he was too late, that they were already closing up the coffin for the last time, and that the order had been given to clear the hall. He still struggled forward, refusing to take a denial, until one of the Marshals of the day was about to exercise his authority to force him back. Upon, this, the old soldier lifted the stump of his right arm toward the heavens, and with tears running down his bearded face, exclaimed: "By this arm, which I lost for my country, I demand the privilege of seeing my General once more." Such an appeal as this was irresistible; and at the instance of the Governor of the Commonwealth, the pomp was arrested until this humble comrade had also dropped his tear upon the face of his dead leader. And this was the last, and surely, not the least glorious tribute which was offered to him, before his remains were finally sealed up for the tomb. The Government shrouded Jackson in their battle-flag; but the people shrouded him in Mayflowers. The former contributed to the funereal pomp the outward circumstances of grandeur, the procession, the drooping banners, the dirge, and the gloomy thunders of the burial-salute; but the true tribute paid to the memory of Jackson was that given by the unprompted homage of the people. No ceremonial could be so honorable to him as the tears which were dropped around his corpse by almost every eye, and the order, and solemn quiet, in which the vast crowds assembled and dispersed. No such homage was ever paid to an American.

On Wednesday, the coffin, followed now by the widow and the General's Staff, was carried by way of Gordonsville to Lynchburg. At every station the people with a similar spirit, were assembled in crowds, with offerings of flowers. At Lynchburg the scenes of Richmond were repeated; and the remains were placed upon a barge in the Canal, to be conveyed in that way to Lexington. They reached the village Thursday evening, and were borne by the Cadets to the Military Institute, where they were laid in the Lecture Room, which Jackson had occupied as professor, and guarded during the night by his former pupils. Friday, the 15th of May, they were finally brought forth to the church where he had so much delighted to worship, and committed to his venerable and weeping pastor, Dr. White. This good man then celebrated the last rites before a great multitude of weeping worshipers, with an unpretending simplicity and tenderness, far more appropriate to the memory of Jackson than the pomp of rhetoric. Thence they bore the coffin, followed by the whole population of the vicinage, to the village burying-ground, and committed it to the earth. His grave was marked by nothing but a green mound, and the fresh garlands which the love of the people, unbidden, had never forgotten to renew. The cemetery covers the smooth crest of a hill, which swells up at the western entrance of the village, and commands a full view of all the smiling landscape, and of the grand ramparts of mountains in which it is encircled. It is a fit resting place for the body of the modest hero; amidst the village fathers, whose virtues had blessed their happy, Christian homes, with the peaceful sounds of domestic life and of the Sabbath worship near by, whose sanctities Jackson died to protect from the polluting invader. At the distance of a few steps rest the remains of his lamented comrade, General Paxton, and of his cousin, Alfred Jackson, who gave his life for the liberties of his native soil, which had exiled him for his patriotism. There is no mark to distinguish the grave of Jackson, the humblest in all that simple resting place; but the stranger needs none to guide him to it. Multitudes of feet, in their pilgrimage to it, have worn a path which cannot be mistaken; and no Confederate ever passes the spot without turning aside, to seek a new lesson of patriotism and fortitude from the suggestions of the scene.

The Stonewall Brigade, while expressing their sense of their bereavement, asked permission to assume the task of building his tomb. An association of gentlemen also began to raise funds to erect, at the Capitol, a grand monument to his memory. The continuance of the war has prevented the completion of both these designs, for the present. It would be tedious to recite all the formal expressions of sorrow made by the military, legislative, and judicial bodies of the country. Only the General Order of Lee, announcing his death to the army, will be appended, as giving utterance in the most happy and dignified terms, to the universal grief.

HEADQUARTERS ARMY OF NORTHERN VIRGINIA, }
May 11th, 1863. }

General Orders No. 61.

With deep grief, the commanding General announces to the army, the death of Lieutenant-General T. J. Jackson, who expired on the 10th inst., at quarter past three, P. M. The daring, skill, and energy of this great and good soldier, by the decree of an All-Wise Providence, are now lost to us. But while we mourn his death, we feel that his spirit still lives, and will inspire the whole army with his indomitable courage, and unshaken confidence in God, as our hope and strength. Let his name be a watchword to his corps, who have followed him to victory on so many fields. Let his officers and soldiers emulate his invincible determination to do everything in the defence of our beloved country.

R. E. LEE, *General.*

The narrative of Gen. Jackson's career is now closed. The full description given of his person, character and capacity at a former part of this work, makes it unnecessary to enter at length into a discussion of his merits as a commander here. Every reader will draw his own conclusions for himself, from the facts which have been faithfully related above. But, a few observations remain to be made, without which the historical portraiture of Jackson would be incorrect. It is to be remarked that, while he rose very rapidly, in the first two years of this war, to the foremost place as a great soldier, none of his comrades have yet displaced him from his eminence. His reputation is manifestly no "nine days' wonder," but one which is destined to endure, and to leave his name among the great of all ages. Few or none of those who inhabit with him the temple of Fame, won their way to it by a career so short. All of the events by which his glory was earned, are comprised within two years' time. As a strategist, the first Napoleon was undoubtedly his model. He had studied his campaigns diligently, and he was accustomed to remark with enthusiasm upon the evidences of his genius. He said that he was the first to show what an army could be made to accomplish, and to replace the old technical art of war with the conceptions of true science. Napoleon had shown what was the value of time as an element of strategic combinations, and had evinced that good troops could be made, if well cared for, to march twenty-five miles daily, and win battles besides. And this war should show that Confederate soldiers could do as much.

Few generals have waged war with such unvarying success as Gen. Jackson. It has been truly remarked of him, that he was never routed in battle; that he was never successfully surprised by his enemies; that he never had a train, or any organized portion of his army, captured by them; and that he never made entrenchments. His success did not come by chance. While no commander recognized so devoutly and habitually the direction of Divine Providence, none was ever more unwearied in providing the conditions of success. It was his rule that his chief Quartermaster and chief Commissary should see him every day at 10 o'clock, A.M., unless sent for at other hours, and report fully the condition of their departments. Twenty-four hours never passed without interviews with both of them; and he knew the exact state of all his supplies and trains, at all times. He was exceedingly jealous for the comfort of his men, so far as this was compatible with celerity of movement. Many instances might be cited of his care about their rations. When preparing for his march to Romney in the winter of 1862, he directed the chief Commissary to carry along rations of rice for the army, in addition to the other supplies. That officer remarked that rice was not much favored by the men as an article of food, and that they seldom drew it when in quarters. The General replied that nevertheless, they might desire it when on the march, and he did not wish them to be deprived of any part of their appointed supplies. Several hogsheads of rice were accordingly carried along, and brought back untouched. So, his care of his wounded was great, and no commander kept his medical department more efficiently organized than he.

Gen. Jackson's personal demeanor toward his soldiers was reserved, but courteous. It was impossible for any to assume an improper familiarity towards him; and no one could be farther than he from all the arts of the demagogue. He never did anything for dramatic effect or for popularity, and never practised any of those means for inspiring enthusiasm, in which Napoleon was such an adept. The only manifestation which he ever made of himself to his command was in the simple, single-minded performance of his duty. He never was known to show himself, of set purpose, to his troops, never made them speeches, and whenever they cheered him, escaped as quickly as possible. But his politeness to the men was unfailing, and carried its own evidence of sincerity. For instance, he was one day riding where scores of soldiers off duty were passing, and whenever one of these touched his hat to him he did not fail to return the same salutation. After thus noticing perhaps a hundred of them, one more deferential than the rest, lifted his hat from his head, when the General also, instead of touching his hat again, removed his wholly, and returned the soldier's bow.

His ideas of discipline and subordination were strict, and he was exacting of his subordinates, in proportion as their rank approximated his own. It was his maxim that he who would govern others, must himself set the example of punctilious obedience. Hence, to his Colonels he was a stricter master than to his private soldiers; and to his Generals, more exacting than to his Colonels. If he found in an officer a hearty and zealous purpose to do all his duty, with a willing and self-sacrificing courage and devotion, he was, to him, the most tolerant and gracious of superiors, overlooking blunders and mistakes with unbounded patience, and repairing them by his own exertions, without even a sign of vexation. But, if he believed that his subordinates were self-indulgent or contumacious, he became a stern and exacting master, seeming even to watch for an opportunity to visit their shortcomings upon them. It must, in candor, be added, that by this temper he was sometimes misled into prejudice; and during his career, a causeless friction was produced in the working of his government over several gallant and meritorious officers who served under him. This was almost the sole fault of his military character; that by this jealousy of intentional inefficiency, he diminished the sympathy between himself and the general officers next his person, by whom his orders were to be executed. Had he been able to exercise the same energetic authority, through the medium of a zealous personal affection, he would have been a more perfect leader of armies. But where he had committed unconscious injustice, he was ever ready to amend it, and to correct his estimate of his officers' merits: and nothing was so sure to melt away the last particle of his prejudice, as an act of courage and vigor upon the field of battle. The utter absence of the Puritanical turn of mind in him, was strongly displayed in the liberal spirit with which he disregarded his own personal tastes, and even his own moral and religious appetencies, in promoting every man who displayed the elements of efficiency, notwithstanding his private repugnance to his personal character. The man's manners, tastes, religious condition, might all be utterly repulsive to General Jackson's private preferences, but if he saw in him ability to serve the cause, he employed him. Yet all appearance of indifference to error or vice, or of a Sadducean temper, was removed effectually by the care with which he rebuked and suppressed every impropriety in his own presence.

That devotion to duty which he exacted of others, he practised with most exemplary fidelity himself. Never was there a man who lived more "as ever in his great Taskmaster's eye," consecrating every hour and every energy to his country, with an utter disdain of ease and self. From the day he left his home, in April, 1861, to that when he was brought back to it amidst the tears and benedictions of his people, he never had a furlough; was never off duty for a day, whether sick or well; never visited his family; and never even slept one night outside the lines of his own command.

His personal courage was of the truest temper. When the history of his early infirmities is recalled, it will appear very unlikely that he was by nature endowed with that hardihood of animal nerve, which makes the courage of the pugilist and gladiator. This surmise will appear more probable, when the strange confession is related, which he made to his medical director, Dr. M'Guire. His care for his wounded and sick has been stated; yet he rarely visited the hospital in person. He excused himself by saying that he would often do so, but that when he was in cold blood, the sight of wounds and all their disgusting accessaries was insupportable to his nerves! It was not unusual to see him pale and tremulous with excitement at the firing of the first gun of an opening battle. But the only true courage is

93

moral courage; and this was so perfect in him, that it had absolutely changed his corporeal nature. No man could exhibit a
more calm indifference to personal danger, and more perfect self-
possession and equanimity in the greatest perils. The determination of his spirit so controlled his body, that his very flesh
became impassive; the nearest hissing of bullets seemed to
produce no quiver of the nerves; and when cannon balls hurtled
across his path, there was no involuntary shrinking of the bridle
hand. The power of concentration was of unrivalled force in
his mind, and when occupied in profound thought, or inspired with
some great purpose, he seemed to become almost unconscious of
external things. This was the true explanation of that seeming
recklessness, with which he sometimes exposed himself on the
field of battle. The populace, who love exaggerations, called
him fatalist, and imagined that, like a Mohammedan, he thought
natural precautions inconsistent with his firm belief in an overruling Providence. But nothing could be more untrue. He
always recognized the obligations of prudence, and declared that
it was not his purpose to expose himself without necessity.

But this perfect courage does not wholly explain the position
which he held in the hearts of his people. In this land of heroic
memories and brave men, others besides Jackson have displayed
true courage. He was not endowed with several of those native
gifts which are supposed to allure the idolatry of mankind
towards their heroes. He affected no kingly mien, nor martial
pomp; but always bore himself with the modest propriety of the
Christian. His port on the battle-field was usually rather sug-
gestive of the zeal and industry of the faithful servant, than of
the contagious exaltation of the master-spirit. His was a master-
spirit; but it was too simply grand to study dramatic sensations.
It impressed its might upon the souls of his countrymen, not
through deportment, but through deeds. Its discourses were

toilsome marches and stubborn battles; its perorations were the thunder-claps of defeat hurled upon the enemies of his country. It revealed itself only through the purity and force of his action; and thence, in part, the intensity of the impression.

This aids to explain the enigma of his reputation. How is it that this man, of all others least accustomed to exercise his own fancy, or address that of others, has stimulated the imagination, not only of his own countrymen, but of the civilized world, above all the sons of genius among us? How has he, the most unromantic of great men, become the hero of a living romance, the ideal of an inflamed fancy, even before his life has been invested with the mystery of distance? How did that calm eye kindle the fire of so passionate a love and admiration in the heart of his people? He was brave; but not the only brave. He revealed transcendent military talent; but the diadem of his country glowed with a galaxy of such talent. He was successful; but it had more than one captain, whose banner never stooped before an enemy. The solution is chiefly to be found in the singleness, purity, and elevation of his aims. Every one who observed him was as thoroughly convinced of his unselfish devotion to duty, as of his courage, it was no more evident that his was a soul of perfect courage, than that no thought of personal advancement, of ambition or applause, ever for one instant divided the homage of his heart with his great cause, and that " all the ends he aimed at were his country's, his God's and truth's." The corrupt men, whose own patriotism was merely the mask of ambition or greedy avarice, and who had been accustomed to mock at disinterested virtue in their secret hearts, as an empty dream, when they saw the life of Jackson, had as heartfelt a conviction of his ingenuous devotion, as the noblest spirits who delighted to form their souls by the mirror of his example. In the presence of his sincerity, the basest were as thoroughly

silenced and convinced as the good. The confidence of his countrymen was, therefore, the testimony of the common conscience
to the beauty of holiness. It recognized the truth, that the
strength of Jackson was in his exalted integrity of soul. It was
the confession of our natures, that the virtue of the Sacred
Scriptures, is true greatness; grander than knowledge, talent,
courage, philosophy or success.

May it not be concluded then, that this was God's chief lesson
in this life and death! He would teach the beauty and power
of true Christianity as an element of national life. Therefore He
took an exemplar of Christian sincerity, as near perfection as the
infirmities of nature would permit, and formed and trained it in
an honorable retirement. He set it in the furnace of trial at an
hour when great events and dangers had awakened the popular
heart to most intense action; He illustrated it with that species of
distinction which, above all others, fires the popular enthusiasm,
military glory; and held it up to the admiring inspection of a
country grateful for the deliverances it had wrought. Thus God
teaches how good, how strong a thing, His fear is. He makes all
men see and acknowledge, that in this man Christianity was the
source of those virtues which they so rapturously applauded; that
it was the fear of God which made him so fearless of all else;
that it was the love of God which animated his energies; that it
was the singleness of his aims which caused his whole body to be
full of light, so that the unerring decisions of his judgment suggested to the unthinking the belief of his actual inspiration; that
the lofty chivalry of his nature was but the reflex of the spirit of
Christ. Even the profane admit, in their hearts, this explanation of his power, and are prompt to declare that it was Jackson's religion which made him what he was. His life is God's
lesson, teaching that "it is righteousness that exalteth a nation."

His fall in the midst of the great struggle for the existence of his country, and in the morning of his usefulness and fame, has appeared to his people a fearful mystery. But if his own interests be regarded, it will appear a time well chosen for God to call him to his rest; when his powers were in their undimmed prime, and his glory at its zenith; when his greatest victory had just been won; and the last sounds which reached him from the outer world were the thanksgivings and blessings of a nation in raptures with his achievements, in tears for his fall.

This tribute to his memory will now be closed with a record of the names of the zealous and faithful men, who at the time of his death, composed his Staff. In their selection, he had displayed a certain independence, or what many deemed a singularity of judgment. Not many of them were men of military education; for he was of all men least restricted by professional trammels. But their efficiency was the best justification of his judgment. His Adjutant and Chief of Staff, at the time of his fall, was the Hon. Charles James Faulkner, lately minister of the United States to France: who succeeded General Paxton in this office, when the latter took command of the Stonewall Brigade. At the battle of Chancellorsville Colonel Faulkner was absent on sick leave. The Assistant Adjutant was Lieutenant Colonel Alex. S. Pendleton, a zealous and spirited officer, who, after rising to the highest distinction, gave his life to his country in the disastrous campaign of September, 1864, in the Valley. The Chief Quartermaster was Major John Harman, and the Chief Commissary, Major Wm. Hawks. The Medical Director was Dr. Hunter M'Guire. These four served under Jackson during his whole career. The Chief of Artillery was Colonel S. Crutchfield, who was wounded at Chancellorsville a few moments after his General. The Chief of Engineers was Captain Boswell, who fell by the same fatal volley which cost Jackson his life. He was assisted by Mr. J. Hotchkiss, as Topographical

Engineer; an accomplished draughtsman, whose useful labors are still continued. Captain Wilbourne conducted the signal service. Colonel Allen managed, with unrivalled efficiency, the ordnance of the *corps*. Lieutenants Smith and Morrison were *Aides-de-Camp* and personal attendants to the General. The Inspectors of the *corps* were Colonel A. Smead, and Captain H. Douglass. These gentlemen formed a military family of the happiest character, and all, excepting those of the supply departments, messed together. While their mess table was simple as that of the privates of the army; and the General forbade that any luxuries should be habitually introduced, which were excluded from the soldiers' rations; refinement, courtesy, and purity presided over all their intercourse. Nothing was ever heard in that circle, which could raise a blush on the cheek of woman, or provoke a frown from the sacred ministers of religion. It is no detraction from the merit of the gallant men who composed it, to say that this propriety was, in part, the result of the elevated example of the General.